In Se

In Search of First Contact

*The Vikings of Vinland,
the Peoples of the Dawnland, and
the Anglo-American Anxiety
of Discovery*

ANNETTE KOLODNY

DUKE UNIVERSITY PRESS   DURHAM AND LONDON   2012

© 2012 Duke University Press
All rights reserved
Printed in the United States of America on acid-free paper ∞
Designed by C. H. Westmoreland
Typeset in Chaparral Pro by Tseng Information Systems, Inc.
Library of Congress Cataloging-in-Publication
Data appear on the last printed page of this book.

WITH DEEP LOVE AND ENDLESS GRATITUDE,
THIS BOOK IS DEDICATED TO MY TRUEST TEACHERS,
PAST AND PRESENT:

Sarah Katz Rivkind and David Rivkind,
doting grandparents who believed I could do no wrong

Esther Rivkind Kolodny, my loving mother who did her best

Blanche Gladstone, P.S. 139, Brooklyn, New York

Harriet Knight Felder, Erasmus Hall High School, Brooklyn, New York

Lillian Fischer Schlissel, Brooklyn College, New York

Odd Nordland, University of Oslo, Norway

Odd-Erik Bjarre, Oslo, Norway

Stanley E. Fish, University of California, Berkeley

Norman S. Grabo, University of California, Berkeley

Mark Schorer, University of California, Berkeley

Henry Nash Smith, University of California, Berkeley

Dorothee Finkelstein, Yale University, New Haven, Connecticut

C. Hugh Holman, University of North Carolina, Chapel Hill

Per Seyersted and Brita Lindberg Seyersted, University of Oslo, Norway

Gary Lindberg, University of New Hampshire, Durham

Patricia Clark Smith, Mi'kmaq, University of New Mexico

Arnie Neptune, Penobscot Nation elder and leader of ceremonies

Wayne Newell, Passamaquoddy elder and educator

James G. Sappier, Penobscot Nation elder and former elected chief

Charles Norman Shay, decorated World War Two hero,
Penobscot Nation elder, and grandson of Joseph Nicolar

Daniel James Peters, novelist, friend, and patient loving
husband since 1970

Contents

List of Figures ix
Acknowledgments xi
*Note on the Problematics of Word
Choice and Usage* xv

Prologue
The Autobiography of a Book 1

1. The Politics of American Prehistory
Isolation versus Contact 19

2. Contact and Conflict
What the Vinland Sagas Tell Us 44

3. Anglo-America's Viking Heritage
A Nineteenth-Century Romance 103

4. The New England Poets of Viking America and
the Emergence of the Plastic Viking 151

5. The Challenge to Columbus and
the Romance Undone 213

6. "We could not discerne any token or
signe, that ever any Christian had been before"
The Phantom of First Contact 256

7. Contact and Conflict Again
What Native Stories Tell Us 280

Epilogue
History Lessons 327

Notes 335
Works Consulted 379
Index 407

Figures

1. Spirit Pond runestone   15

2. Emanuel Gottlieb Leutze's painting
   The Landing of the Norsemen   118

3. Illustration of Dighton Rock   124

4. Drawing of the "skeleton in armor"   152

5. Tiffany and Company Viking Revival silver and narwhal tusk
   lady's dressing table and chair   211

6. Tiffany and Company Viking Punch Bowl and base   211

7. *New York Times* illustration of the replica Viking ship   221

8. Boston statue of Leif Eiriksson sculpted by Anne Whitney   232

9. Detail from Embden Petroglyphs in Maine   267

10. Penobscot Village at the World's Columbian Exposition
    in Chicago, 1893   312

Acknowledgments

For the past fifteen years, a series of outstanding graduate student assistants helped keep this project on track: Chadwick Allen, James D. Lilley, Melissa Ryan, Tom Hillard, Randi Tanglen, Cara Blue, Jay E. Caldwell, Mary Ellen Bell, and Jessica B. Burstrem. My deepest gratitude to all. You were a joy to work with.

In Denmark in May 1999, I benefited enormously from conversation with Max Vinner of the Roskilde Ship Museum. A few weeks later, in Oslo, Norway, my husband and I were warmly hosted by Anne and Odd-Erik Bjarre and by Brita Lindberg Seyersted and Per Seyersted. At the University of Oslo, Magnus Rindal generously shared his considerable knowledge of the Icelandic saga tradition, and Christian Keller shared firsthand information about recent archaeological excavations of the two medieval Norse settlements on Greenland. A long and wonderful afternoon in the company of Helge Ingstad, the discoverer of the only authenticated Viking-era site in North America, capped off this stage of my research. I am indebted to each of them for their generosity and expertise.

In May 2000, my Canadian colleague, Wendy Robbins, of the University of New Brunswick, and her brother, Neal Robbins, accompanied my husband and me on a research trip to L'Anse aux Meadows, the excavated and reconstructed Norse site located at the northern tip of Newfoundland. Later that month, in Halifax, Nova Scotia, Birgitta Linderoth Wallace, her husband, Rob Ferguson, and Ruth Holmes Whitehead each gave unstintingly of their time and expertise. Their help added immeasurably to the success of my research in the Canadian Maritimes, and their work is quoted throughout these pages.

From Canada, I traveled to Maine in June 2000, the first of many such trips. I owe a particular debt of gratitude to James G. Sappier, former chief of the Penobscot Nation, and I thank him for his kind permission to publish a story told by his mother, Madeline Polchies Sappier (Penobscot). For all of their help and many kindnesses, I am also grateful to Moses Lewey, Wayne Newell, and Rocky Keezer of the Passamaquoddy communities, and to the Penobscot Nation members Charles Norman Shay, Arnie Neptune, James Neptune, and James Eric Francis. Other Penobscot Nation members who shared indigenous

xii Acknowledgments

knowledge include Carol Dana, Gabe Paul, Michael Sockalexis, Maria Girouard, and Bonnie Newsom.

Also crucial to this project were discussions with Joseph Bruchac (Western Abenaki) and Patricia Clark Smith, of Euro-American and Mi´kmaq descent.

In September 2000, as the Smithsonian Institution launched its Viking Millennium Project with the touring exhibit titled *Vikings: The North Atlantic Saga*, and as both Canada and the U.S. geared up to recognize the thousandth anniversary of Leif Eiriksson's voyage to North America, my long-simmering project—which now seemed so timely—had to be put on hold when I was diagnosed with early-stage ovarian and endometrial cancer. Dealing with the cancer was complicated by the fact that I was also battling increasingly crippling rheumatoid arthritis. Three gifts helped me get through the surgery and months of grueling chemotherapy. My dear friend, the internationally known American studies scholar Cathy N. Davidson, alerted colleagues across the country so that every day brought new communications of good wishes and healing vibes from almost everywhere. My graduate students rallied round, staying with me when my husband needed to leave the house, driving me to various appointments, running errands, and on occasion even cooking for us. The third gift was the integration of conventional Western medicine and complementary alternative modalities designed for me by Dr. Andy Weil. The team of medical, dental, and alternative practitioners on whom I have relied—and, in some cases, still rely—include Christy Allen, Joseph Buscema, the late Joel Childers, Linda Karl, Evan Kligman, Randall Knuth, Jennifer Schneider, and Daniel E. Shapiro. For all these gifts of caring, "thank you" does not seem enough.

Upon returning to the project in late 2001, I continued to receive help and guidance from scholars and researchers in a variety of fields and disciplines. Whether we met in person, spoke by telephone, exchanged email and snail mail, or some combination of all of these, I am indebted to Ruth Holmes Whitehead, Harold W. Borns Jr., Bruce Bourque, Sivert Fløttum, Barbara S. Groseclose, William A. Haviland, Mark Hedden, Harald E. L. Prins, Conor McDonough Quinn, Dean R. Snow, Kerry Hardy, and Timothy Swindle. Substantial portions of William A. Haviland's essay "Who Was Here First?," Copyright © R. Nathaniel W. Barrows, Penobscot Bay Press, Inc., are reprinted by permission of the publisher and editor, R. Nathaniel W. Barrows.

For their help in putting together illustrative materials for this volume, I am indebted to Bettina Baumgärtel, head of the Department of

Painting, Museum Kunst Palast Düsseldorf; Horst Volmer, Wuppertal, Germany; Deanna S. Bonner-Ganter, curator of photography, art, and archives, Maine State Museum; James Eric Francis, tribal historian, Penobscot Nation; Kathy Garrett, manager of historical collections, Maymont Mansion; Tessa Clark Green and Josh Green; Mark Hedden, archaeologist; Rikke Johansen, Picture Library, Viking Ship Museum, Roskilde, Denmark; Eileen Sullivan, Image Library, Metropolitan Museum of Art; and Paula Work, registrar and curator of zoology, Maine State Museum.

From its inception to its completion, this book enjoyed the support of two wonderful editors at Duke University Press, Reynolds Smith and Ken Wissoker, and was much improved by the candid feedback from the Press's anonymous external readers. I am also grateful to the assistant managing editor Mark A. Mastromarino for his care in shepherding the manuscript through the production process.

Sadly, before the manuscript was finished, two extraordinary friends and colleagues who had read an early draft passed away: Paula Gunn Allen (Laguna Pueblo) and Patricia Clark Smith (Euro-American and Mi'kmaq). My former University of Arizona colleague, the late Vine Deloria Jr. (Standing Rock Sioux), also read that draft. Each one gave me just the encouragement I needed and pointed me in important research directions. I join both academic colleagues and nonacademic admirers of their work from around the world in missing them sorely.

When I thought the manuscript was finished, three outstanding scholars agreed to read it as a personal favor to me and helped me understand that I still had more work to do. I am deeply grateful to William A. Haviland, Amanda R. Ritchie, and Birgitta Linderoth Wallace for allowing me to impose upon them in this way.

I also want to thank a lifetime of students, both undergraduates and graduate students, for keeping alive my faith that ideas have power, that words matter, and that intellectual curiosity opens new worlds for each of us. I loved learning with you all.

Finally, my largest debt of gratitude is owed to my husband of over forty years, the novelist Daniel Peters. This book could not have been researched or written without his unfailing love and his willingness to accommodate the needs of a partner whose body, over the years, became increasingly enfeebled and crippled. His constant caretaking of me in recent years has placed a terrible burden on him, but he has more than once saved my dignity, my sanity, and my life. I could not have survived without his wicked sense of humor. In our next life together, it will be my turn to do the heavy lifting.

Note on the Problematics of Word Choice and Usage

When applied to the Americas, the term "prehistory" has generally been used to designate that grand span of time before the Americas and their indigenous peoples entered into the writings and, hence, the mental world of Europe. Concomitantly, the term "the historic period" has referred to the period commencing with the appearance of the Americas and their peoples in European documents. Of course, the histories of the peoples of the Americas did not begin with Christopher Columbus's voyage in 1492 or with those peoples' earliest appearances in European texts and on European maps. These terms thus distort and truncate the long continuum of Native American presence in the Americas. But because several of my sources have used these terms, and because these terms continue to be operative across several disciplines, both locutions necessarily find their way into some of my chapters.

"Precontact" is another problematic term because it seems to imply the period preceding some certifiable *first* moment of contact between Europe (or elsewhere) and the Americas. Also, the word seems to attribute significance to that initial contact moment. My own research suggests that the concept of a first contact is a convenient European construction and may not reflect Native American understandings. The notion of *pre*contact is thus slippery at best and, at worst, inherently imprecise. But, again, because the term is so prevalent in the historical and archaeological literature, I have been unable to avoid it in these pages.

Nineteenth-century references to the Scandinavian countries are often confused and confusing because, at the time, those countries were not the clearly separate independent nations they once had been and are today. Until 1814, Norway was a part of Denmark. Then, as an outcome of the Napoleonic Wars, Norway entered into a union with Sweden. After a peaceful secession from Sweden in 1905, Norway finally achieved its modern independence. As a result, some nineteenth-century writers described journeys to Denmark or to Sweden and incorporated time spent in Norway without naming it as such.

Some wrote about aspects of life and culture in Denmark or Sweden when they were really describing aspects of Norway. Similarly, Finland, which had long been a quasi-autonomous grand duchy under the control of Sweden, during the Napoleonic Wars was invaded by Russia and annexed in 1809. Finland's national identity was thus also sometimes blurred (or entirely lost) in some nineteenth-century texts.

Leif Eiriksson's name is differently spelled throughout these pages, depending on the source cited or quoted. All the variants are easily recognizable and often derive from attempts to replicate or transliterate Norwegian, Icelandic, Danish, or Swedish renderings of the name. My own choice for spelling his name follows the spelling used in the particular translation of the two Vinland sagas quoted in this book.

As used in these pages, "runes" and "runic writing" refer to ancient characters used in Teutonic, Anglo-Saxon, and Scandinavian inscriptions, probably beginning as early as ca. A.D. 300. Runes were used extensively in northern Europe, Iceland, and the British Isles through the Middle Ages and appear to have persisted in parts of Scandinavia until the nineteenth century. Adapted to carving and later to vellum and paper, runic characters consisted of perpendicular, oblique, and a few curved lines. Ancient runic inscriptions have been found all across Scandinavia.

The term "Native American" is now commonly used in the U.S. to refer to the indigenous peoples of North America. In Canada, the terms "Aboriginal," "First Nations," or "First Peoples" are commonly used and have sometimes been adopted by both Native and non-Native writers in the U.S. Also used in both countries is the phrase "Native peoples." While most Native peoples of my acquaintance identify themselves by the name of their pueblo, tribe, or ethnic community, they also write and speak of themselves as "Indians." Because it is not my place to privilege any one of these locutions over the others, I have employed almost all of them in these pages.

One important aspect of the decolonizing project of Native peoples has been the reappropriation of the right to name themselves. While, in some instances, this entailed a dramatic throwing-over of names imposed by European writers and administrators, in other cases this meant little more than a change of spelling to correct a linguistic error. The relatively recent preference for Mi′kmaq over the older "Micmac" is one such example; the preference for Maliseet over "Malecite" is another. Wherever possible, I have endeavored to use the name currently preferred, although older forms repeatedly appear in some of my quoted sources. Where the currently preferred name has not yet been widely adopted or would not be recognizable to most readers, I have retained the older name to avoid confusion and indicated the current preferred name in parenthesis. In this way, for example, I hope to make clear that the people once called the Montagnais now call themselves the Innu.

Although the term "tribe" is used within quoted materials in this book, wherever possible I have tried to avoid using it in relation to the particular Eastern Algonquian-speaking peoples who are the main actors in some of these chapters. Europeans originally coined the term as a way of designating groups whom they considered inferior as compared to the supposedly superior established nations or organized states of the "civilized" world. Later, the U.S. imposed the term on Native peoples as a means of defining them as legal entities and simultaneously also imposed a centralized political organization on Indian communities, many of whom traditionally had functioned in a variety of ways, including through villages, bands, and chiefdoms with shifting and often temporary alliances. While the Maliseet, Penobscot, Passamaquoddy, and Mi´kmaq who make up the Wabanaki Confederacy each today have centralized governments with elected chiefs (or governors) and elected councils, throughout most of their history and into the early decades of the nineteenth century, these groups were constituted by shifting alliances between various bands and villages, each with their own unique structures of organization and authority. In the twenty-first century, many ethnologists and anthropologists (including Native anthropologists) prefer to speak of Eastern Algonquian-speaking peoples in terms of ethnicities, linguistic groups, and dialect differences. Among these groups, only the Penobscot Nation officially calls itself a "nation" (even though the official title of their historian is "Penobscot Nation *tribal* historian"). Where appropriate to some particular Indian group, the term "tribe" *is* used in these pages.

As much as possible, I have tried to avoid using totalizing racially inflected constructs such as "white man," "red man," and "black man." Nonetheless, where this terminology actively informs the texts or particular situations that I am examining, in order not to distort the text being discussed, I am sometimes unable to avoid these usages.

Prologue

THE AUTOBIOGRAPHY OF A BOOK

> The Great Spirit said unto me, "There shall be other people live on the land as well as your people."
> —KLOSE-KUR-BEH'S PROPHECY TO THE INDIANS,
> Joseph Nicolar, *The Life and Traditions of the Red Man* (1893)

> *Wodin'it atog'agan.*
> Mi´kmaq: "This is a story..."

This book has had a very long genesis, a genesis that, in retrospect, seems to have stretched across most of my adult life. Although I did not realize it at the time, the project began when, as an undergraduate at Brooklyn College in New York, I elected to use a study abroad scholarship to enroll in the Literature Program at the University of Oslo in the summer of 1961. There, struggling through texts in Old Norse as well as modern Norwegian (with few reliable English translations available to help me), I had the good fortune to study Old Norse mythology, Norwegian folklore traditions, and, most important for this present study, the sagas of medieval Iceland. My teachers included Drs. Bjarne Berulfsen, Reidar Th. Christiansen, and Odd Nordland, all scholars whose work is still honored by today's literary critics and literary historians in Norway.

Upon my return to Brooklyn College for my senior year, I again picked up my major in English with a concentration in American literature. While I remained fascinated by the medieval sagas I had studied in Norway, I couldn't connect them to anything else I was studying at the time.

Eventually I pursued graduate studies in early American literature at the University of California at Berkeley. My Ph.D. dissertation examined the literary language and symbolic systems that had facilitated one environmental devastation after another as a colonial enterprise became a new nation and as that nation spread itself across the continent. Out of this work came an ongoing commitment to the newly developing field of ecocriticism and my first two books, *The Lay of the Land: Metaphor as Experience and History in American Life and Letters* (1975) and *The Land before Her: Fantasy and Experience of the American Frontiers, 1630–1860* (1984). In time, I also came to identify my work as American frontier studies. Based on this research, I developed both undergraduate and graduate courses that combined analysis of the literatures of the seriatim American frontiers with gender studies and environmental concerns.

Meanwhile, my husband, the novelist Daniel Peters, was researching and publishing a trilogy of historical novels about the great pre-Columbian civilizations of Mesoamerica and South America: the Aztec, the Maya, and the Inca.[1] Because I read Spanish easily and spoke it serviceably, I accompanied Dan on all his research travels to archaeological sites from Mexico to Bolivia and Peru. For his part, my husband studied the languages of the peoples he was attempting to re-create. Together, we read and spent countless hours discussing all the available historical, anthropological, and archaeological data. In the process, my courses on the American frontiers took on a new shape. Where my husband *ended* each of his novels with the arrival of the Spanish, I now *began* my courses with the journals of Christopher Columbus and the extant writings of the Spanish explorers, conquistadores, and priests. Instead of identifying the beginning of an American frontier with the arrival of the Pilgrims at Plymouth in 1620, I relocated the first frontier to the explorations of the Hispanic Southwest in the sixteenth century. The frontier hadn't moved from east to west, I argued, but rather, at first, from west to east and from the south to *el norte*. Increasingly, I pushed back the meaning of "frontier" to its origins in the earliest European texts of exploration and contact, beginning with Columbus. And I asked my students to consider the possibility that American literature really began in these early "contact" narratives that constructed a so-called New World and its peoples through and for the contemporary cultural understandings of the European imagination. Many of those constructions were still with us, I pointed out, even if in repressed or disguised formulations.

At the same time, I also introduced in my courses the extant stories and recorded legends of the Native peoples who had been encountered at each frontier site. I tried to emphasize to my students that, even before the contact period, Native peoples had migrated from one location to another and confronted their own new frontiers. When I could find them, I especially enjoyed teaching Native American versions of what had transpired in the collisions of cultures, whether with other

Native peoples or with Europeans. My understanding of "frontier," in other words, had gradually shifted back to include what was then generally called the *pre*contact period.

Then I thought again about *Eirik's Saga* and *The Greenlanders' Saga*, both of which I had studied in Norway all those years ago, and both of which told stories about the Norse explorations and attempted colonization of North America somewhere around the year A.D. 1000. After years of letting them gather dust, I finally unpacked the boxes of notebooks from my summer at the University of Oslo. As I read through old handwritten notes, I remembered how the two sagas recorded delight with the mild climate and fertility of the place the Norse named Vinland the Good, and I remembered that the sagas recorded encounters with Native peoples (whom the Norse dubbed, pejoratively, *Skraelings*, meaning "wretches" or "people who screech"). These, I realized, were the earliest known European narratives of contact with North America. With no little excitement, I started to rethink everything I thought I already knew. First, I composed a kind of position paper for reconceptualizing the literary history of the American frontiers, a literary history that would necessarily include, among scores of other texts, Native American materials and the two Vinland sagas. My position paper appeared as an article in the journal *American Literature* in 1992, under the title "Letting Go Our Grand Obsessions: Notes toward a New Literary History of the American Frontiers." Then, in the fall of 1994, after stepping down as dean of the College of Humanities at the University of Arizona and taking up full-time teaching duties again, I tried an experiment: I assigned English translations of the two Vinland sagas as required reading in my undergraduate survey of American literature and, as well, in my yearlong graduate seminar on the theory and literature of the American frontiers. By then, a great deal of excellent interpretive criticism and historical scholarship on the entire saga tradition was available in English, so I felt I could prepare to teach the two sagas in a reasonably up-to-date manner.

To my surprise, student responses in the two courses were markedly different. Despite my attentiveness to the literary conventions informing the sagas, the undergraduates wanted to read them as history and were thrilled to encounter what were to them rather exotic "discovery" narratives that most of them had never heard of before. In contrast, the graduate students protested that the sagas weren't written in English; they weren't composed for an "American" audience; and they had had no known influence on *real* American literature. So why had I assigned them in an *American* literature course? For those students who had read "Letting Go Our Grand Obsessions," the inclusion of the sagas in our seminar on frontier literature was less problematic. But these same students posed yet another set of important questions: Where was Vinland located, and what had *really* happened there? And were there any Native American stories about this early contact?

In the summer of 1995, I began searching for answers to all those questions and objections. This book is the product of that search.

I began by trying to identify the Native peoples with whom the Norse might have come in contact. Based on what we know about Norse explorations to the west and north of Greenland—in addition to their contacts with Inuit (an Eskimoan people) in the Arctic—the Norse could also have encountered the Beothuk, who once inhabited Newfoundland, as well as the caribou-hunting Naskapi and Innu (formerly known as the Montagnais) of Quebec and Labrador. But if reports of wild grapevines in the sagas were accurate, then the Skraelings encountered in Vinland were located farther to the south, from the Canadian Maritime Provinces to New England and beyond. In that case, the Norse probably met the ancestors of one or more of the peoples who today comprise the Wabanaki Confederacy (also called the Wabanaki Alliance). These include the Mi´kmaq, the Maliseet, the Penobscot, the Passamaquoddy, and several closely related groups who identify as Western Abenaki or, simply, as Abenaki. The terms "Wabanaki" and "Abenaki," sometimes used interchangeably, are, respectively, the English and French approximations of the Eastern Algonquian word *Wôbanakikiiak*, meaning Peoples of the Dawnland, that is, the peoples living farthest to the east, where the sun first rises. All are Algonquian peoples who speak related dialects of Eastern Algonquian. Through a variety of complicated and changing historical circumstances, these peoples at times made war upon one another, but they also joined as allies, intermarried, took in one another's refugees from European diseases and raids, and shared stories and traditions. According to reports from the Smithsonian Institution's Bureau of Ethnology, as late as the 1880s there was evidence of the continuity of traditional practices among these peoples, including storytelling, pictographic writing on birch bark scrolls, and the pecking of petroglyphs on rock faces. Despite the crushing population losses and European cultural impositions that began at the end of the fifteenth century, I wondered, might *any* trace memories of the Norse contact have managed to survive?

But all this was only conjecture because what is known as the Historic Period doesn't really begin until the sixteenth century and early seventeenth, when most historians say that Europeans first began to record in writing their encounters with Native peoples. Unfortunately, even at this early period, Native peoples were already experiencing significant population declines and geographic relocations due to imported diseases, and the European records are not always trustworthy about which Native group lived where. Moreover, the French and English often had different names for the same Native group or territory. So any estimation of specific Native territorial distributions around the year 1000 must necessarily rest on a sometimes shaky foundation of incomplete archaeological evidence, ongoing indigenous memory, and often conflicting observations in documents from European explorers, missionaries, merchants, and would-be colonists.

Even so, one fact seemed certain: the Norse *had* been in North America, around the year 1000. The stories in the sagas had been given a physical reality in 1960, when the Norwegian adventurer Helge Ingstad discovered the remains of a Viking-era site at Épaves Bay, near the fishing village of L'Anse aux Meadows, at the northeast tip of Newfoundland. Excavated in subsequent years by Ingstad and his archaeologist wife, Anne Stine Ingstad, the site showed evidence of having been used for Norse ship repair as well as evidence of the presence of women. A comprehensive report of the excavations from 1961 through 1968 was produced in 1977 by Anne Stine Ingstad, with additional contributions from several of her coworkers. In that volume, titled *The Discovery of a Norse Settlement in America*, Anne Stine Ingstad detailed the unearthing of the remains of eight house sites, four boat sheds, a charcoal kiln, evidence of domestic animals, a woman's spindle whorl, a smithy for forging iron, iron nails and nail fragments, and a "ring-headed pin, which is a Viking Age form of jewelry" used for fastening a cloak (239). Carbon-dating of these finds, combined with the specific architectural features of the tiny settlement, led Anne Stine Ingstad to conclude that it "suggest[ed] Iceland as its cultural source," but that it ultimately "derive[d] from Norse Greenlanders and is of an early date, probably of the first half of the eleventh century" (238).[2] As her husband argued in 1969 in *Westward to Vinland*, his account of the discovery and excavations written for a popular audience, all this coincided perfectly with the descriptions of the Vinland venture found in the two sagas. Indeed, as Helge Ingstad made clear, the sagas had provided important and "reliable information" that guided him to this northern outpost (33). And, as he strongly hinted, for him, the L'Anse aux Meadows site *was* Vinland.

Helge Ingstad's theories aside, there was still no conclusive evidence that L'Anse aux Meadows was the Vinland of the sagas, and some of the details from the sagas seemed to suggest otherwise. Most notable is the absence of any sign of wild grapes ever having grown at L'Anse aux Meadows. The scientific analysis of ancient soil cores demonstrates no evidence of wild grapes growing north of the Penobscot River. During periods of climatic warming—as when the Norse ventured to North America—wild grapes could be found on the East Coast only as far north as Passamaquoddy Bay. The attempted Vinland colony, therefore, had to have been south of L'Anse aux Meadows, possibly in southern Maine or southern New Brunswick, or even farther south. Again, this pointed to the territories once occupied by the ancestors of today's Wabanaki and Abenaki peoples.

As I continued to read all the available archaeological, ethnographic, and historical studies of the northeastern Indians, I received a serendipitous telephone call from my friend and colleague, the late Patricia Clark Smith, then a professor in the Department of English at the University of New Mexico in Albuquerque. Pat was calling about other matters, but I insisted on telling her about my current project. With her Ph.D. in American literature from Yale, Pat had shared my longtime frustration that almost none in our generation of scholars had been taught anything about Native American literatures and oral traditions in our graduate school training as Americanists. Pat had been one of the first to introduce such material into her own courses and to write about it. Her motivation was both scholarly and personal: she was herself part Native American.

On the phone that evening, I confided that, because the sagas described Skraelings in "skin-boats" (or hide canoes), I was leaning toward identifying the Mi'kmaq (who had used moose-hide canoes in earlier periods) as one possible candidate for the Skraelings encountered by the Norse in Vinland.[3] This was not a detail the Norse would have gotten wrong, I explained to Pat, because their own ancestors had also once used boats constructed of hides stretched over some kind of ribbed framework, and Norse mythology was full of references to skin-boats (see Gardiner 72; also Brøgger and Shetelig 12–17).[4] Moreover, the Mi'kmaq had once lived in territories that *could* have been Vinland. Up until the contact period, the Mi'kmaqs' principal territories are believed to have included Nova Scotia, Prince Edward Island, and most of New Brunswick north and east of the St. John River. During the sixteenth century, they occupied the territory south and west of the Gulf of Saint Lawrence: the Maritime Provinces and the Gaspé Peninsula, as well as a small piece of northern Maine. At that, Pat stopped me abruptly. "My skin is rising," she said with excitement. "My grandmother was Mi´kmaq." Until she said it, I hadn't made the connection.

Pat said that everything she knew about her Mi´kmaq ancestry—especially their expertise as mariners and the alacrity with which they mastered European sailing vessels in the sixteenth century—seemed to confirm my hunch. She pointed me toward a number of French sources for descriptions of the Mi´kmaq written by early explorers and missionaries. And through her, both directly and indirectly, I came to meet not only other Mi´kmaqs but also members of the two Passamaquoddy communities in Maine and members of the Penobscot Nation.

Over several years, my husband and I made trips to Nova Scotia and New Brunswick and, still today, almost annual trips to Maine. As friendships developed and trust gradually grew, many of my Indian friends took a genuine interest in this project and tried to help me. They taught me about their language and their history, and, in some instances, they shared what they believed were very old stories still told within their family. In every case, I promised that I would publish nothing of what they told me without their prior permission, and I would write about nothing that was considered sacred or privileged knowledge. Additionally, I sent drafts of everything I was writing to my various helpers and assured them that I would make whatever changes they required (or, if needed, drop the material altogether). Never once did I receive anything other than helpful suggestions or friendly corrections to something I had gotten wrong. I then rewrote and sent back the corrected draft for a final approval. Inevitably, this slowed the process of composition, but since I was not a member of any of the communities I was writing about, I felt—and still feel—that it was the only ethical way to proceed. As many of my Native friends and teachers had explained to me in great detail, they had already suffered a long history of finding themselves and their cultures misrepresented and distorted in the writings of generations of "outsider" researchers and scholars. *They* now wanted to control how they were represented.

Research for this book brought me to the Archives of the Indies at the University of Seville in Spain and also took me three times to Norway and once to Denmark. In Norway and Denmark, I visited medieval archaeological sites and again talked with scholars at the University of Oslo about the sagas, Vinland, and the excavations on Greenland. At least some of these meetings were arranged by my dear friends, Professors Brita Lindberg Seyersted and Per Seyersted, internationally known American literature scholars who taught at the University of

Oslo. In fact, in 1993, when I made the decision to teach the Vinland sagas, I had written to Per and asked him to recommend a good English translation. Per replied that he'd gone "just up the road" from his home in the wooded area outside of Oslo to consult with "a very knowledgeable neighbor" to get me an answer. That neighbor was Helge Ingstad. As a result, through Per's good offices, on an overcast afternoon in June 1999, my husband and I spent four hours with Helge Ingstad in his home in the woods outside of Oslo. Trained originally as a lawyer, Ingstad served for a time as the governor of Spitsbergen, a large island belonging to Norway, located in the Arctic Ocean, but he eventually gave up the law and became a self-taught ethnographer, historian, and explorer. His many early adventures included four years in Canada, where he lived as a trapper with the Chippewa (who now refer to themselves as Anishnabek), a sojourn with the Apache near their White Mountain Reservation in Arizona, and a journey to the Sierra Madres in the 1930s in search of a fabled "lost tribe" of Apache. After first ushering us into his study, with its maps and site plans of L'Anse aux Meadows spread on large tables, Ingstad took us into a living room filled with the souvenirs of his adventurous life. The head of a musk ox was mounted on one wall, a polar bear rug lay across the polished wood floor, and Indian blankets served as throws on several chairs. There were also photos of him and Anne Stine Ingstad (who had died in 1997) at L'Anse aux Meadows.

Ingstad was then ninety-nine (he died the next year, at one hundred) and in particularly good spirits that day because he'd just learned that *Time* magazine was about to name L'Anse aux Meadows one of the hundred most important discoveries of the twentieth century. Although frail in body, he was mentally as alert and as argumentative as ever, and his excellent English-language skills more than compensated for my rusty Norwegian. For him, L'Anse aux Meadows *was* still Vinland. And even though, as a young man, he had lived for years among aboriginal peoples in the Arctic and in the American Southwest—and despite the fact that he himself had sought out stories and legends among the Naskapi of Labrador in 1961, hoping to find additional Norse sites—he dismissed as "inventions" and "fantasies" any stories by Algonquian speakers that claimed to relate Viking contacts south of L'Anse aux Meadows. Ingstad didn't believe that Native peoples had been able to hold on to ancient traditions or to cultural memories in the face of European colonization and radical population declines. But above all else, it was clear he feared that if L'Anse aux Meadows proved *not* to be Vinland, that fact might diminish the significance of his discovery. Our conversation, therefore, meandered into other subject areas.

Ingstad began by recounting how the Norse ventured south from Greenland, passed the bleak, stormy coastlines of Baffin Island and northern Labrador, then sailed south along the wooded coasts of central Labrador and across the strait of Belle Isle to make a first landfall and set up a base camp at L'Anse aux Meadows. We discussed the findings at L'Anse aux Meadows and what they revealed about the lives of the men and women who had lived there a thousand years ago. We discussed the impact of a roughly three-hundred-year period of climatic warming, known as the Medieval Warming, during which air and sea temperatures were warmer, storms in the north Atlantic were both less severe and less frequent, and the pack ice was significantly lessened. This had certainly facilitated the Norse voyages to North America, said Ingstad, while the later return of colder climates forced Columbus to take a southern route rather than retrace the Vinlanders' northern route. Ingstad was also willing to speculate that at least some knowledge of the sagas and the Norse voyages to Vinland had circulated in the ports of Europe before Columbus. And he said he found it curious that the documents authorizing Columbus's first voyage were vague about the admiral's ultimate destination. Even allowing for the probability that the Spanish crown was intent on thwarting Portuguese spies in the court, Ingstad said he was still puzzled by the fact that Columbus was commissioned not to seek a water route to the Indies or to the kingdom of the Great Khan but, rather, more ambiguously, to seek "certain islands and mainlands in the Ocean Sea" (qtd. in Zamora 28). This language seemed to Ingstad to open all sorts of possibilities. When Dan and I finally took our leave of this determined and brilliant man, I found myself replaying all his reasons for designating L'Anse aux Meadows as Vinland.

Yet when my husband and I finally visited L'Anse aux Meadows in May 2000, it seemed to us that it resembled every early medieval ship-repair station we'd seen excavated on the Danish and Norwegian coasts. And a thousand years of climate change notwithstanding, this landscape didn't resemble the Vinland of the sagas. When, that same spring, we met in Halifax with the archaeologist Birgitta Linderoth Wallace, who had followed the Ingstads and completed the L'Anse aux Meadows excavations for the Canadian Park Service, she offered additional evidence for why that site probably wasn't Vinland. Over dinner, she detailed the evidence found at the site for Norse explorations southward and confided where she thought a colony might have been located. On another afternoon in Halifax, Ruth Holmes Whitehead, a historian, museum curator, and recognized expert on Mi´kmaq history and material culture, listened patiently as I asked endless questions and speculated wildly. She thereby helped me prepare more questions for those I would meet a few weeks later, when I visited reservations in Maine.

During the early years of pursuing this project, I used to tell people that I intended to read the sagas through whatever Native traditions might survive, and that, conversely, I was going to read the Native traditions though the images in the sagas. This, I hoped, would be my way of answering graduate students' questions about what *really* happened in Vinland and justify assigning medieval Icelandic texts in an *American* literature course. If I could find even traces of memory of that contact in Native sources, then I could legitimately claim an (indigenous) "American" contact narrative continuity. I even dared hope that if I could find any evidence that Columbus was aware of the sagas and the Norse expeditions to North America, then I could also claim the sagas as *the* precursor contact narratives that had enabled all the European contacts and narratives to follow.

But as I proceeded, reliable facts and conclusive evidence were hard to come by, while *stories* were everywhere. Eighteenth- and nineteenth-century Euro-Americans enunciated all sorts of theories about the origins of the Indians and invented fantastical stories about the continent's prior settlement by non-Indian "superior races," including the Norse. Popular nineteenth-century American literature was filled with tales of Viking adventurers in a New England Vinland. For their part, some of the Algonquian-speaking communities of the Canadian Maritime Provinces, maritime Quebec, and northern New England have traditions about the *many* comings of "the white man" and at least one recorded story about a *first* arrival. Stories of Viking forebears are still sometimes heard along the Miramichi Bay in Canada to explain early explorers' statements about encountering Natives with light skin and blue eyes. And despite deep roots in oral tradition, when finally written down sometime in the thirteenth century, both *Eirik's Saga* and *The Greenlanders' Saga* were composed not solely as history but also as *literature*, that is, as good stories to be recited at public entertainments.

Not surprisingly, then, although it takes full advantage of much recent scholarship in archaeology, anthropology, ethnology, and American history, this book is overwhelmingly about stories: about who told them, when, and where. It is a book that seeks to understand why stories of this particular contact endure, and what functions those stories perform in the communities that so assiduously preserve and retell them. In ways we in the United States do not always recognize, how we shape and reshape our stories about discovery and first contact reveal how we are simultaneously shaping and reshaping our understanding of who we think we are as Americans.

Most Native Americans of my acquaintance say that if anyone discovered America, it was they and their ancestors. Whether their peoples' lore speaks of ancestral journeys from other places, describes an emergence from within the earth, or claims the traditional homeland as itself the place of origin, for them the very language of "the Columbian discovery" is both ahistorical and demeaning. For several years now—and especially since the 1992 Quincentenary—in many cities, the annual Columbus Day festivities have become sites of protest and conflict. Ironically, in 1992, the planned parade in Denver had to be canceled due to threats of violence, even though Colorado had been the first state to declare Columbus Day a holiday in 1905. The American Indian Movement (AIM), as well as many other Native groups and individuals, have asked to have Columbus Day removed as a national holiday.

It is an issue around which, understandably, passions run deep. In the view of the nation's Italian American communities, Columbus Day does not just celebrate the man they believe first connected Europe to the Americas, but it also honors their own ethnic tie to their adopted country. Indeed, amid the overheated anti-immigrant rhetoric of the nineteenth century, claiming Columbus as their precursor provided these newcomers with a sense of legitimacy as Americans. Their forebear, too, had played a vital role in the nation's history. By contrast, in the view of many Native Americans, what happened to Native peoples in the wake of Columbus's so-called discovery was nothing short of a catastrophe. And for them, in the words of an AIM statement prepared in 1991, Columbus Day represents only "a perpetuation of racist assumptions that the Western Hemisphere was a wasteland cluttered with savages awaiting the blessings of Western 'civilization'" (qtd. in Grinde, iv).[5]

What most Americans may not realize, however, is that Columbus was a relatively inconsequential figure up until the Revolutionary War, and his primacy as "discoverer" had been challenged long before Native peoples raised the issue in the twentieth century. In fact, Columbus's name is almost entirely absent in the writings of colonial America, and he only became a figure of consequence during the Revolutionary

War period when rebellious partisans sought to construct a national history that diminished the significance of England. "Columbia" was even briefly put forward as a possible name for the new nation. Thus a largely invented and heroicized Columbus first began to appear in schoolbooks and enter the national imagination only toward the end of the eighteenth century. For example, in Joel Barlow's sprawling epic poem, *The Columbiad*, published in 1807 (a revision of his earlier poem, "The Vision of Columbus," published in 1787), Columbus is an old man dying in prison, all his sufferings vindicated by a vision of the future glories of the America that he has discovered.

Images like these, linking Columbus to discovery and to the nation's future promise, went largely uncontested until the late 1830s, when English-language translations of the two Vinland sagas began to circulate in both scholarly venues and the popular press. Subsequently, as this book demonstrates, Anglo-Americans, especially, eagerly embraced the romantic notion of a Viking heritage and a Vinland colony located in New England. As these ideas gradually fed into national anxieties over changing patterns of immigration, the figure of the bold, enterprising Northman, Leif Eiriksson, increasingly challenged the Italian Catholic Columbus for the title of "discoverer." Just as during the Revolutionary War, the nation's origin story again required adjustment. And while this book follows the development of America's romance with a Viking past only through the nineteenth century and up until its demise in the early decades of the twentieth century, for good and for ill, its echoes and reverberations are still very much with us.

Consider, for example, an embarrassing episode at Yale University in 1966. A year earlier, with great fanfare in October 1965, Yale University Press had published *The Vinland Map and the Tartar Relation*, and the library announced the acquisition of the originals through a gift from a then-anonymous donor. *The Tartar Relation*, which gives an account of a thirteenth-century papal mission from France to the Mongols, was of interest mainly because, at some point in its history, the Vinland map was bound into it. This map created a worldwide sensation. Originally dated by researchers to about 1440, a good fifty years before Columbus's initial voyage in 1492, in its extreme northwest the map depicts a large island with two deep inlets, identified as "Vinilanda Insula." A Latin legend next to that landmass describes its discovery in about the year 1000 by Leif Eiriksson and Bjarni Herjolfsson. Almost immediately, the authenticity of the map was called into question, and it remains even today a subject of controversy. Over the years, several different scientific tests of the map have produced widely variant conclusions as to its date. When I personally examined the map, in Yale's climate-controlled Beinecke Rare Books Library in May 2000, I queried the librarian's view of the map's authenticity. He declined to reply. But while the possibility that the Yale Library had accepted the gift of a fraud was certainly embarrassing, even more so were the antics in one of the freshmen dormitories on Old Campus a year after the map's much-heralded publication.

On Columbus Day 1966, students strung together several bed sheets and inked on them, in large black letters, "Erikson Sí, Columbus No." They then proceeded to hang the bed sheet banner out of a window facing Chapel Street, just as New Haven's annual Columbus Day parade went marching by. The insult to the city's large Italian American population was palpable. And it repeated, even if unwittingly, the racist slights and ethnic slurs that had once marked the discovery debates of the nineteenth century.

When I arrived in New Haven three years later as a new-minted Ph.D. from Berkeley, taking up my first full-time teaching post in the English Department at Yale, all of these young men were now seniors, and some of them became my students. To this day, I have no idea what they were thinking when they hung out their bed sheet banner, although a few said it was only intended as a joke to display their support for the authenticity of their school's controversial map. Whatever their conscious or unconscious motives, however, a nation self-consciously made up of the descendants of immigrants is necessarily always nervous about national origin stories. That is why successive waves of newcomers always try to find ways to claim their right to be here. Thus, despite what politicians like to proclaim, the U.S. has never been *simply* a nation of immigrants.

Almost from the beginning of colonization, Euro-American immigrants and their progeny facilitated brutal abductions from Africa and prospered from three hundred years of unpaid slave labor. And even when slavery was finally abolished, those same immigrants, and their sons and daughters, refused to share the bounty of the continent with the now freed slaves and their sister and fellow citizens, instead opting for a hundred years of discrimination, segregation, and Jim Crow laws. Pertinent to this study is also the fact that the immigrant newcomers from Europe invaded, dispossessed, and almost annihilated a long-settled and thriving indigenous population. By what right did those seeking new homelands for themselves take over the homelands of those already here? The inability to offer a satisfying answer to that uncomfortable question has left this so-called nation of immigrants with an ongoing anxiety of legitimacy, though it is rarely named as such. Even so, the nineteenth-century belief in a "superior race" predating the Indians and the debates over who first discovered America were, at least in part, an expression of that anxiety. The question of discovery thus became intimately intertwined with the question of who *really* belongs here.

There are still many Euro-Americans unwilling to abandon the idea that the Vikings were *here*. Even proven frauds and fakes do not deter them. To cite just one instance, in 1971, a part-time carpenter and jack-of-all-trades from Maine named Walter Elliott claimed to have found three engraved stones on the banks of the Morse River near where it widens into what is called Spirit Pond in the area of Popham Beach and the township of Phippsburg. Two of the stones were covered with incised symbols, while the third appeared to show a map of Popham Beach. The find generated a great stir of publicity when Elliott identified the strange markings as medieval Norse runes. Based on his discovery, Elliott declared himself "convinced that Maine is Vinland," and many of his fellow enthusiasts began looking forward to the prestige and tourism dollars that would surely now flow into Maine (qtd. in Trillin, "U.S. Journal," 70). "As all of the people involved acknowledged" to Calvin Trillin when he covered the story for the *New Yorker*, "They *want* to believe the stones are real—to believe that Viking ships once sailed through the islands that lie off Popham Beach and up the Morse River and into the shelter of Spirit Pond" (72). But the stones *weren't* real. Like a number of other imputed artifacts that Elliott claimed to discover in subsequent years, the Spirit Pond stones, too, proved to have been etched with an electric steel engraving tool (though Elliott denied this to his death).[6] Elliott's attempts to sell the stones for money were thwarted by the fact that they had been found on state land and were thereby legally state property. In the end, Elliott was "encouraged" to turn them over to the state by a $4,500 gift from a private donor. At that point, performing its due diligence, the state had the stones examined by several expert runologists, and all concluded that they were fakes. (See figure 1.) In 1977, the eagerness of so many local citizens and dignitaries to accept the stones as genuine became the subject of Trillin's gentle satire in his novel *Runestruck*, set in a fictional Maine town.

Today the Spirit Pond stones are housed in the Maine State Museum in Augusta and, when exhibited, are clearly labeled as fakes. None-

1. One of the three Spirit Pond runestones supposedly "discovered" in Maine in 1971 and subsequently identified as faked Viking artifacts made in the twentieth century with an electric drilling tool. Courtesy of the Maine State Museum.

theless, as late as the 1990s, at least one self-taught runologist and modern-day antiquarian was publishing articles claiming to have deciphered "the Spirit Pond inscription" by identifying its medieval Norwegian origins in "an obscure poetic meter which has evaded [previous] investigators" (Carlson, "The Spirit Pond Inscription Stone," part 1, 1). For this writer, the stones are authentic, and the "inscription takes us back a thousand years" (1). From the point of view of devoted amateurs like this, the so-called experts trained by the universities are too often doctrinaire and unwilling to contemplate what another such writer called "alternative scenarios" (Friedrich 12). Certainly, it is true that dedicated amateurs in a number of fields have always made lasting and significant contributions, often by challenging the accepted orthodoxies espoused by established experts. But, as seems to have been the case here, amateurs can also allow their theories to get ahead of the evidence, and they can become enthralled by the allure of some romanticized past that never was.

A small group of us saw the power of that allure firsthand in Maine in June 2000. I traveled there with my husband, Dan, and my former research assistant, Chadwick Allen, a scholar of comparative indigenous literatures. In advance of our arrival, I had arranged for Moses Lewey (Passamaquoddy) to help with our research as our local guide and assistant. I had told Moses about my project and asked him to introduce me to people who might be helpful. In addition to introducing me to individuals within the Passamaquoddy communities, Moses had also taken the initiative to call all the local historical societies in the area and inquire about their holdings. A member of one of these societies told Moses that his group's small museum possessed what he and his fellow members believed to be a Viking-era carved stone. So Moses made an appointment for all of us to visit the museum.

When we arrived at the small building, we were greeted by an older retired gentleman who volunteered as the museum's part-time director and caretaker. He began by showing us drawer after drawer of glass display cases filled with (mostly unidentified) Indian arrowheads. In response to our questions, he admitted that no one in the society had attempted to contact any of the local Indian communities in order to share their holdings or to inquire about the possible uses, age, or tribal affiliation of any of the arrowheads. "We just store whatever anybody brings in or donates," he told us. Clearly, Indian history and Indian artifacts were not this group's keen interest. Instead, as he gradually revealed to us, most of the members of this local historical society were convinced that ancient visitors from Europe and even Africa had once plied the Maine coast and perhaps established a settlement for a time. And then he offered to show us the society's most prized possession.

Unlocking a large wooden wall case, he brought out a locked glass box that housed a gray stone about six inches in diameter and eighteen inches long. One side of the stone was relatively flat, and on this side was a crude graven image of some sort of male warrior figure holding in front of him a round shield. This was the Viking artifact about which Moses had been told. It had been found locally years before and donated to the museum, though no record of the place and date of the find seemed to be available, not even the name of the person who first uncovered it. When I explained to the museum's caretaker-director that my husband and I had studied Viking-era artifacts on our trips to

Norway and Denmark, and we now wished to examine the stone more closely, he unlocked the glass box, removed the stone, and gingerly placed it in my hands. Dan and I turned the stone over and over, looking at it in full daylight as well as under the incandescent and fluorescent lamps of the museum. We also peered at it through a magnifying glass. "I don't think this is Norse," I told the gentleman. "It doesn't resemble anything I've ever seen in the museums and archives of Scandinavia." "Then it must be Phoenician," he replied. "They were here too, you know." Finally, I asked if Moses could examine the stone, and the gentleman agreed. "No, it's definitely not Indian," Moses declared with conviction. "It looks to me like it was done with a Dremel tool," he added.

The museum's caretaker-director had clearly hoped that, as a university-affiliated researcher, I might validate and add authority to his and others' belief that the carved stone was an authentic Viking artifact. When I didn't, he immediately switched to his alternate theory that the stone was Phoenician, and he completely ignored Moses's quite accurate observation that the engraving on the stone was a modern fake. As we drove Moses back to his home in Pleasant Point that evening, he kept asking over and over again, "Why would anybody make these fakes?" and "Why do they want to do that?" Unfortunately, the many and complex motivations behind the forging of ancient artifacts—fame, money, the desire to "fool the experts," a commitment to some particular view of history for which no other evidence is available, or some combination of these—were beyond any of our abilities to explain. One impression emerged clearly, however. Many non-Native people are fascinated by the mysteries of the remote past, and some of them will hold on to an improbable theory rather than approach their Native American neighbors in order to ascertain whatever insights into a knowable past might be gained by sharing collections of Indian arrowheads.

With Moses's questions still unanswered, the conversation turned to the stories that Native peoples tell about ancient contacts. These are rarely "discovery" stories in the way that term is commonly understood. Instead, the Native stories are largely *fulfillment stories* in the sense that the events they unfold represent the fulfillment of what has already been prophesied or foreseen. As the Great Spirit prophesied to the Penobscot culture hero, Klose-kur-beh, in Joseph Nicolar's masterpiece, *The Life and Traditions of the Red Man* (1893), "The white man will feel it as a duty to his children to seek new lands for them, and . . . he will not rest until he finds the land the Great Spirit gave unto you. . . .

Therefore look for him always" (115). Within Nicolar's narrative construction, it is the Indian who discovers the white man, for whom he has all along been prepared.

To end where I began, my graduate students were certainly correct when they said that the Vinland sagas were never intended for an American audience or composed as American literature. Nonetheless, the many nineteenth-century English-language translations and redactions of those sagas entered the national imaginary and had a profound impact on major American writers. As a direct consequence of the sagas' popular circulation, moreover, Euro-Americans were forced to rethink the previously orthodox Columbian discovery story and, however briefly, reconceive the accepted origin myth. Equally important, at least some residual trace memories of first contact—or just first sightings—remain inscribed in the stories told by Native peoples. In other words, Native peoples have preserved their own traditions about first contacts and what Euro-Americans still too often call "discovery." And these stories, too, are part of the rich tapestry of our shared American literary inheritance.

As for the two remaining questions—Where was Vinland located? and What *really* happened there?—I have no conclusive answers. Regarding Vinland's geographical location, these pages offer the most authoritative speculations now available from historians and archaeologists. Clearly, L'Anse aux Meadows was a landing site and a place for repairing ships, but it was not the Vinland where grapes grew wild. Perhaps it is best, therefore, to think of Vinland as what it became for Euro-Americans in the nineteenth century, that is, a geographical site that was transfigured into an imagined landscape for the projection of dreams. As for what really happened there, the evidence is both incomplete and inconclusive. The stories told in the sagas only imperfectly coincide with the stories Native peoples tell. But where we have clues in the archaeological record, it is reasonably clear that conflict was at least one outcome of the encounter. Unlike the encounters of later centuries, however, in Vinland the Native peoples prevailed, and it was the Europeans who were driven out.

1

The Politics of American Prehistory

ISOLATION VERSUS CONTACT

> We are permitted to go behind the Indians in looking for the earliest inhabitants of North America, wherever they may have come from or whenever they may have lived.
> —WILLIAM CULLEN BRYANT AND SYDNEY HOWARD GAY,
> *A Popular History of the United States* (1876)

Challenging Orthodoxy

In the midst of the national debate in 1992 about the meaning and impact of Christopher Columbus's so-called discovery of America, Vine Deloria Jr. attempted to alter the context of the debate by insisting that "we need to know the truth about North American prehistory." By using the term "prehistory," Deloria followed common practice among archaeologists and anthropologists when referring to events in the Americas that predate Columbus and (European) written accounts, also known as the "precontact" period. "I am still uncomfortable with the idea that NO contacts were made between Europe and North America before Columbus," stated Deloria. His address to the Society for American Archaeology posed the proposition, "Unless and until we [Indians] are in some way connected with world history as early peoples, . . . we will never be accorded full humanity. We cannot be primitive peoples who were suddenly discovered half a millennium ago." A member of the Standing Rock Sioux and a longtime analyst of Indian-white relations, Deloria wanted his audience of professional archaeologists and anthropologists to understand how the various Quincentenary observances (including their own) of Columbus's "discovery" inevitably ended up "regard[ing Indians] as freaks outside historical time" (Deloria, "Indians, Archaeologists" 597).

As was so often the response to Deloria's work, this address stirred up a bit of a hornet's nest. From his point of view, Deloria was simply urging that the history and origins of America's indigenous populations be examined within a more complex tapestry of transcontinental human contacts than the standard theories of relative isolation before Columbus would allow. But in so doing, he seemed to be unraveling the heroic efforts of recent generations of archaeologists who had labored mightily to dispel earlier notions of a superior non-Indian people who had established themselves on the continent *before* the arrival of the Indians and built the great mounds and fortifications that once dotted western New York State and the Ohio and Mississippi valleys. As the celebrated Maya scholar Arthur Demarest of Vanderbilt University explained to a writer for the *Atlantic Monthly* in 2000, the mid-nineteenth century "was the period of the frontier wars with the Native-Americans—a period especially after Custer, when there was a lot of enmity and hatred toward Native Americans. So that fed into the idea that these earlier societies, not only the Maya, Aztecs, and Inca but even the ones up here—the Moundbuilders, for example—were somehow the product of some other white race that came in, was less savage, and was able to achieve these monuments and other things" (qtd. in Stengel 44). Demarest's point was that, as a corrective to this outdated and inherently racist and imperialist narrative, modern archaeology had been demonstrating the very real cultural achievements of the ancestors of today's Native peoples. Yet challenges like those posed by Deloria *could* potentially invite renewed theories about allegedly "superior races" predating the arrival of the Indians. After all, as Deloria made clear in his address, he was willing to contemplate the possibility that "early peoples" had arrived on this continent "perhaps even as refugees from Old World turmoils and persecutions" ("Indians, Archaeologists" 597).

That said, Deloria was not unaware of the controversial implications of his position. As he acknowledged in his remarks, "Many people feel they cannot advocate Precolumbian contact for to do so would mean demeaning the Indians and suggesting that they could not have made discoveries [or cultural advances] on their own. Strangely this debate also rages in Indian circles, and a few of my best friends are adamant about maintaining the theory of isolation in order to enhance the achievements of our ancestors" ("Indians, Archaeologists" 597).[1] Still, he declared, "Here I part company with other Indians," and he again urged his audience to "take a good look at all possible theories of Precolumbian contacts" (597).

With the passage of time, Deloria's comments in 1992 have come to seem far less controversial. Twenty-first-century archaeologists and anthropologists increasingly uncover evidence for multiple ancient migrations to the Americas, by both land and sea, emanating from Europe as well as Asia. As one of the most prominent of these archaeologists, Thomas D. Dillehay, wrote in 2000, "The diversity of the early archaeological, genetic, linguistic, and skeletal record suggests a shared American identity rooted in multiple migrations and, to state it in contemporary terms, no true categories of race or ethnicity" (293). Additionally, the date for the first arrivals of permanent human populations in the Americas is every day being pushed back in time, with some researchers citing signs of human habitation as early as 40,000 years ago. No longer are the possibilities of chance (or even intentional) pre-Columbian arrivals of voyagers from Japan, China, Polynesia, Africa, Europe, or elsewhere wholly discounted. Even Demarest told the *Atlantic Monthly* writer that he put himself "in that group who don't doubt there's been contact": "I don't think that the transport problems are such that they prevented people from moving between continents. What we doubt is the transformative impact of ephemeral contact. These visitors, whoever and whatever they were, simply didn't transform the societies they found here" (qtd. in Stengel 47). Of course, not everyone agrees on that point, and a lively debate over the possible impacts of pre-Columbian contacts continues still. In short, much that was once considered settled *fact* about American prehistory is now open to question.

This includes even the formerly orthodox view that groups of nomadic human hunters first arrived in the Americas at the end of the Ice Age, about 14,000 years ago as the glaciers retreated, pursuing the large Ice Age animals southward into more temperate latitudes, and thereafter becoming relatively isolated from the rest of the world. The story of crossings *only* and exclusively across the Bering land bridge, followed by isolation, just doesn't seem plausible anymore. In Dillehay's view, the crossing of the Bering land bridge was only one of "the many dispersal patterns taken by our early ancestors": "We now know that the first Americans were far more culturally complex and sophisticated than just simple big-game hunters" (292). To make matters even more complicated, a few scholars have recently adduced evidence suggesting that different groups of ancient indigenous Americans put "out in boats into the waters of the Caribbean, off the mouth of the Amazon, in the Florida Straits, or in the Gulf Stream farther north," and journeyed across the Atlantic to Europe (and elsewhere) long before Columbus's arrival (Forbes 105). However controversial their thesis, these scholars locate first contacts between Europeans and the indigenous peoples of the Americas not in the Americas but in Europe, the result of "Ancient Americans as seafarers, mariners, and navigators" having set out purposefully or perhaps having been blown off course by errant storms (1).

But the image of Native peoples as *primitives* "outside historical time" (to use Deloria's wording) has a long and authoritative lineage ("Indians, Archaeologists" 597). It began with Columbus, of course, but gained even wider currency in the sixteenth century, when Bartolomé de las Casas chronicled his personal observations of the Spanish conquest of Mexico and South America. In a series of works that were subsequently translated into most of the languages of Europe, las Casas "describ[ed] the [Native peoples] as having lived since the Flood behind the 'locked doors of the Ocean Sea,' doors which Columbus had been the first to unlock" (Pagden 7).[2] The Spanish priest's firsthand accounts of what he witnessed enjoyed not only credibility but three centuries of wide circulation. In the early nineteenth century, Alexander von Humboldt, a German naturalist and the father of modern physical geography, visited the Americas and gave the imprimatur of science to this old and popular notion. His comment in 1810 that "the peoples of America" had been "separated, perhaps since the beginning, from the rest of the human race" was, like las Casas's work, repeatedly translated and reprinted (qtd. in Pagden 8).[3]

So pervasive were these views that, in 1838, as the Cherokee were being forced to leave their lands in Georgia and walk the fatal Trail of Tears to Indian Territory west of the Mississippi, the influential *North American Review* could declare without equivocation, "The moment the new world was discovered, the doom of the savage races who inhabited it was sealed; they must either conform to the institutions of the Europeans or disappear from the face of the earth" (qtd. in Maddox 26). The obvious intent of the statement was to articulate, yet again, what Lucy Maddox has called "the almost universally shared assumption that there were only two options for the Indians: to become *civilized*, or to become *extinct*" (24). But behind that assumption, lending it authority, stood the old belief that the Native peoples of North America were isolates, long cut off from contact with other peoples and other cultures, and thereby also cut off from the progress of history itself.

The imputed "science" of that belief had always implicitly been called upon to support public policy toward the Indian. But in 1850, the veneer of scientific justification and public policy were inextricably intertwined when the early ethnologist Henry Rowe Schoolcraft prepared a five-volume report commissioned by Congress. The Indian "probably broke off from one of the primary stocks of the human race, before history had dipped her pen in ink, or lifted her graver on stone," suggested the first volume (*Historical and Statistical Information* 1:17). Having served as an Indian agent, living among and studying various Native groups for thirty years, Schoolcraft carried considerable weight—and affirmed long-held Euro-American suppositions—when he concluded that "the Indian race appears to be of an old—a very old stock," but in comparison with other peoples, a stock that had "changed the least" over time (1:17, 15). Their isolation, in other words, had permitted the Indians to "preserve their physical and mental type, with the fewest alterations" (1:15).

As Maddox and others have demonstrated, for some time this construction of the Indian past proved politically useful. Innocent of history and thus without advanced culture, it was claimed, Native peoples stood helpless and vulnerable before the onslaught of more "civilized" whites. Early nineteenth-century proponents of removing the Indians to lands west of the Mississippi could thus argue that theirs "was actually the most humane and beneficent policy the government could adopt, since the only way to accomplish the civilizing of the Indians, and thus assure that they did not become extinct, was to move them beyond the reach of unscrupulous whites who wished to do them harm.... Left on their own to compete with superior whites for territory in the East, the argument went, they were certain to be decimated" (Maddox 25). In his *Historical and Statistical Information Respecting the History, Condition and Prospects of the Indian Tribes of the United States*, "published by the authority of Congress," Schoolcraft reinforced these arguments. It was inconceivable, he wrote to the commissioner of Indian affairs, "that erratic and predatory hordes of hunters, without agriculture, arts, or letters, and with absolutely nothing in their civil polity that merits the name of government, should have been able to ... cope with the European stocks who landed here with the highest type of industrial civilization" (1:v).[4]

Yet in that same volume, Schoolcraft also revealed that, as he understood the matter, long before Columbus, the Indians had already coped with "European stocks." In other words, Schoolcraft contradicted himself. Elsewhere in his first volume, he put forth an alternative and competing version of pre-Columbian American history—a version with its own long and authoritative lineage. Citing as his authority Carl Christian Rafn's *Antiquitates Americanæ* (condensed and published in English in 1838), Schoolcraft confidently asserted "that America was visited early in the tenth century by the adventurous Northmen from Greenland, and that its geography and people continued to be known to them so late as the twelfth century" (*Historical and Statistical Information* 1:106). Rafn's edition of two medieval Icelandic sagas depicting voyages and colonizing efforts in a place called Vinland, as well as other documents collected by Rafn, persuaded Schoolcraft (and many other Americans, too) that the Norse had visited "Newfoundland and Nova Scotia," attempted a colony somewhere near "the present area of Massachusetts and Rhode Island," and explored the Atlantic coast as far south as Florida (1:106). But for Schoolcraft, there were also other candidates for pre-Columbian "discovery." "Not Scandinavia only," he averred, "but Phoenicia, Gaul, and old Britain, may be considered as claimants" (1:118).

To his credit, Schoolcraft expressed a healthy skepticism about easy interpretations of rock drawings as evidence of Phoenician scripts, or misreadings of Indian petroglyphs as Viking runestones. Nonetheless, as the young nation eagerly sought to establish a coherent identity, in part by uncovering the continent's unique ancient history, such errors were wholly understandable to Schoolcraft. "As Americans, we are particularly susceptible to this species of newly awakened interest," he explained. "Every thing in our own history and institutions is so new and so well known that . . . it appears refreshing to light on any class of facts which promises to lend a ray of antiquity to our history" (*Historical and Statistical Information* 1:109). Schoolcraft himself was hardly immune to that same "refreshing" temptation, even contemplating in his fourth volume the possible ancient arrival of a "people of higher civilization than the ancestors of the existing aboriginal race" (4:132).[5]

The problem, as Schoolcraft well understood, was that most "facts which promise[d] to lend a ray of antiquity" to America were interpreted as evidence that Native peoples and their forebears were not the builders of the mounds and ceremonial centers that dotted southern Ohio, nor the artisans who created the effigy pipes inlaid with bone and pearl, nor the makers of the copper jewelry found at ancient burial sites. In 1820, the antiquarian and amateur archaeologist Caleb Atwater studied the mounds of Ohio and linked them with peoples from "Hindoostan" (Atwater 105–267). More popularly, the mounds were either attributed to ancient European visitors or were viewed as natural features, since, as one newspaper account in 1842 of the leveling of a mound outside of Gallipolis, Ohio, phrased it, "It is hardly probable that such elevations were made by savages." The reasons attested were that the Indians "were ignorant of the use of iron" and could not command "the amount of labor . . . require[d] to construct them." Thus, in total ignorance of what is now called the Hopewellian civilization that once flourished in that area, the reporter for the *Louisville Advertiser* confidently concluded that thoughtful observers would "not be very likely to ascribe their origin to the Indians" ("An Indian Mound Opened" n.p.).[6]

More informed observers attempted to counter such assertions—but they still had to contend with them. The artist George Catlin, who lived among and painted the Plains tribes for eight years, described in some detail Sioux, Pawnee, and Crow "*picture writings* on the rocks, and on their robes." It wasn't "anything like a *system* of hieroglyphic writing," Catlin reasoned, but an "approach somewhat towards it." Variously interpreting the rock drawings as totemic figures and the pictorial buffalo robes as "represent[ing] the exploits of their military lives," Catlin recognized all these as the "state of the fine arts" among an "ingenious and talented" people (2:246). But to do so, he challenged the increasingly popular notion that pre-Columbian visitations—and most especially, visitations from the Norse—accounted for any and all sophisticated artifacts:

> Many of these have recently been ascribed to the North-men, who probably discovered this country at an early period. . . . I might have subscribed to such a theory, had I not at the Red Pipe Stone Quarry, where there are a vast number of these inscriptions cut in the solid rock, and at other places also, seen the Indian at work, recording his totem amongst those of more ancient dates; which convinced me that they had been progressively made, at different ages. (2:246)

Passages like these from Catlin's *Letters and Notes on the Manners, Customs, and Conditions of the North American Indians* (1841) had two potentially salient effects. First, he offered authoritative testimony that the Indians were capable of creating art and artifacts on their own. And, second, although he didn't identify either the rock carvings or the illustrations on the robes as a *system* of writing, he nonetheless recognized their formalized communicative and representational import. In this, he provided a somewhat different viewpoint from that of Indian agents who were everywhere arguing, "As fast as possible, let Indians forget their own languages, in which nothing is written, and nothing of course can be preserved" (qtd. in Maddox 24).[7] But Catlin's efforts had only limited impact.

With assimilation and acculturation as the goals, official government policy was bent on eradicating Indian languages and cultures as part of the so-called civilizing process. And no amount of contrary evidence could weaken the belief that America had been visited by

Phoenicians, Carthaginians, Celts, Hebrews, Norse, and others—and that these visitors, rather than Native ancestors, had left behind evidence of their presence. The reason for the tenacity of that belief was not simply the inherently racist contemporary attitude toward Native peoples nor even the unquestioned respectability of those who had for so long promulgated such theories. All that was important, of course. The real appeal, however, was political and derived from a young nation's determination to construct (as Schoolcraft later intuited) a self-serving "antiquity to our history."

Inventing Providential History

In 1773, a Boston minister, the last of the Puritan Mather dynasty, Samuel Mather, cited biblical, classical, and medieval sources in *An Attempt to Shew, That America Must Be Known to the Ancients*. As Mather explained in a prefatory letter to his little pamphlet, he had employed himself "in collecting, and putting together, such Testimonies, both sacred and profane, as will render it most highly probable, if not certain, that *America* must be known before the modern Discoveries of it, and even in very ancient times" (3). Mather was hardly the first cleric to put forward such a view. Catholic missionaries in Canada had long held that the various cross symbols employed by the Indians were evidence of some prior contact with Christian disciples or apostles. And Mather's father, the Boston minister Cotton Mather, had been convinced that the carvings on Dighton Rock on the Taunton River in Berkley, Massachusetts, were ancient Hebrew letters. But while most of his predecessors had contented themselves with tales of a single ancient visitation, Samuel Mather described an entire series of visitations and possible settlements.

Without ever identifying which group made up the ancestors of the Indians, Mather nonetheless offered a sequential history of the peopling of America:

> Thus it appears with sufficient Probability, that *America* not very long after the Flood was settled; and that, after the first Settlement of it, there were successive Removals to it, especially from the *Northern Parts of Europe and Asia*: And then, after some Ages had revolved, the *Phoenicians* might arrive and trade and settle here. And, by these various Ways, *America* became very well settled; and vast Numbers of People were found in this *Western World*, when *Columbus, Americus* [Vespucci] *and* succeeding Voyagers came to it: And perhaps the Inhabitants here might, for their Numbers, vie with those of the other Continent. (18–19)[8]

Mather sent his pamphlet to, among others, Benjamin Franklin, then in London.

Franklin, himself a student of natural history and a founder of the American Philosophical Society—established, in part, to pursue such scientific inquiries—was not entirely convinced by Mather's proofs. While Franklin did not dismiss the possibility of "Ancient" contacts, he nonetheless observed that "the Intercourse could never have been very considerable" because the Native "Inhabitants" were "totally ignorant of the use of Iron" (20:287). In a letter to Mather written in July 1773, Franklin added that "about 25 Years since," he had been persuaded by "a learned Swede . . . that America was discovered by their Northern People long before the Time of Columbus" (20:287).[9]

The exchange between Mather and Franklin is instructive. It establishes the seriousness with which learned Euro-Americans early on contemplated the possibility of pre-Columbian contacts. And it offers evidence that, by the formative years of nationhood, Americans had developed a powerful competing set of images that pictured the continent and its people, not as isolated but, instead, as densely settled and thickly embedded in transcontinental history, long before Columbus. Indeed, in 1821, just as the Indian removal debates were beginning in earnest, a book of travels written by a former president of Yale College and published posthumously simply assumed this more complicated history as fact.[10] In his *Travels in New England and New York*, Timothy Dwight outlined the case for multiple waves of immigration to North America, including "origin[s] from the north of Europe," and added, "Nor is there a single known fact which forbids us to believe that the Phoenicians and the Carthaginians in their voyages to different countries on the Atlantic . . . wandered . . . to the western continent" (1:91). But to understand the vitality of this competing historical frame, we need to understand the circumstances in which it was being articulated.

Dwight's *Travels* is more than a detailed account of the scenery, local history, and social conditions that he encountered while hiking and taking horseback trips through New England and upstate New York in the years just after the Revolution. In reworking his experiences for publication, Dwight offered the small, self-governing, agrarian townships he had visited earlier as a model of democracy for the new nation. And in offering local history, he sought also to weave a larger fabric of national history. Within this schema, a pattern of multiple immigrations to North America and significant pre-Columbian contacts served the purpose of anchoring the fledgling nation within events that long predated its British colonial beginnings. In other words, Dwight was trying to create a historical narrative in which British origins were only one among many other origins. The creation of the new nation, after all, required creating its history (and thus its meaning) anew.

Similarly, the exchange between Mather and Franklin had deep political roots. Franklin was in London in 1773 in what was virtually an ambassadorial role, protesting the incremental abrogation of colonial rights and arguing against the duties imposed on imported goods under the notorious Townshend Acts of 1767 and the Tea Act of 1773.[11] Mather's pamphlet on the *ancients'* knowledge of America included an appendix that protested those same Acts. In Mather's view, the British Parliament had exceeded its legitimate authority when it asserted its right "to tax [the colonists] when, and how, and as often and as much as they please" (30). To Mather, these policies constituted "so much *Malevolence and Enmity* manifested towards the *natural and constitutional Rights and Liberties* of the *Americans*, as cannot well admit of any just Apology, or fair Excuse" (29). He even went so far as to hint at the possibility of outright rebellion if the Acts were not rescinded. "The generous and brave *Americans* will be *disposed and resolved to defend* themselves and their Rights, and *prepare* in the best Manner they can for doing so," wrote Mather (34). And, lest any reader miss his intention, he prefaced those words with some lines of martial poetry from George Lillo's verse drama, written in 1735, "The Christian Hero"—lines that called for the need to "rebel" when "Tyranny prevails" (Mather 33).

Because Mather feared that, in "An Appendix; Concerning the American Colonies, and the Late Managements Against Them," he had overstepped the bounds of ministerial decorum, Franklin reassured him. "The Remarks you have added, on the late Proceedings against America," responded Franklin, "are very just and judicious; and I cannot at all see any Impropriety in your making them tho' a Minister of the Gospel" (20:288).

Clearly, by 1773, both men foresaw the almost certain inevitability of revolution, and both were poised for nation building. "But all these Oppressions evidently work for our Good," hinted Franklin in his letter to Mather. "Providence seems by every Means intent on making us a great People" (20:289). What Franklin did not say explicitly was that Mather had already outlined a justifying providential history for the new nation in his little pamphlet and its appendix. In fact, when read together, *An Attempt to Shew, that America Must Be Known to the Ancients* and the appendix "Concerning the American Colonies," create a single, unified narrative.

Mather's interest in pre-Columbian contacts, it turns out, derived not from scientific curiosity but from a commitment to situate America in a biblical past and a redeemed future. "The *primary Inhabitants of America,*" according to Mather, arrived "after the Flood" (14). "But, after *this first dispersion* to the *Western World,*" he continued, "we readily grant, that there might be *various Removals* to it from various Nations: For after the *Scythians* or *Tartars,* were settled here; the *Norwegians* and *Icelanders* might come; and so might some of the *Sinensians* [Chinese] from the East" (15). Only after cataloguing other possible early arrivals, however, did Mather get to the heart of his central argument: although he did "not presume to declare, that there is a *clear, full and express Discovery of this Western Continent* in the holy Writings," nonetheless he "affirm[ed], there are various Passages ... from which attentive and considerate Minds might form [such] a Judgment" (19). To prove his point, Mather painstakingly reinterpreted selected Bible passages in order to demonstrate that "*the Gospel of* CHRIST ... *was brought here by* one or more of the Apostles and Disciples and many Brethren, *and produced Fruit*" (24–25).

With that assertion, Mather not only diminished British claims to priority—as Dwight, too, would do—but, even more important, he effectively erased the symbolic significance of putative "discovery" by an evangelizing *Catholic* Columbus. To put it another way, Mather's construction of American prehistory essentially *saved* the continent from false religious affiliations and associated it with an earlier authentic (that is, Protestant) "*Gospel of* CHRIST." A gospel, he believed, that did once produce fruit.

Mather never stated what happened in the ensuing centuries. But he acknowledged that the Indians appeared to have had no concept of Christianity prior to the most recent arrivals of the Europeans, and he suggested, without explanation, "that this *Western World* sinned away the Gospel" (25). That loss then became for him a promise of and a justification for the restoration of the gospel in the future. "We have good Grounds for hoping," he insisted, "that *the Gospel and Religion of Jesus* will recover their lost Possession." In that event, according to the closing paragraph of *An Attempt to Shew, that America Must Be Known to the Ancients,* "*this whole Continent,* as well as the *Old World,* may find the fullest and most perfect Accomplishment" (25). But before what was lost could be redeemed, certain impediments had to be removed. Those impediments—the abrogation of colonial liberties and the imposition of onerous taxes—were then the subject of Mather's appendix.

The appendix opened with a reference to an earlier Puritan divine who had determined "that this Part of the World *seemed to him to be reserved in Providence for the* great Seat of Empire and Religion and the Theatre of considerable Events before the End of the World" (27). England, however, had interrupted this providential progress by "*abridg-[ing] the Freedoms*, and cramp[ing] the Improvements of these Colonies" through its taxation policy (28). This left the American colonist with no choice other than "an honest and manly Resolution not to abide by it," observed Mather (33). Then, deftly mixing political appeals with Christian rhetoric, he converted the probability that "the generous and brave *Americans* will be *disposed and resolved to defend* themselves and their Rights" into a kind of divinely sanctioned crusade. "They will *hope and trust in HIM*," Mather says of his imagined rebels, "*as their Cause is just and right . . . For JUST & RIGHT is HE*" (34).

In other words, read as a whole from cover to cover, Mather's 1773 pamphlet outlined a history in which America was once part of the larger world, had even received the gospel from some of Christ's followers, but then had somehow "sinned away the Gospel." Providentially destined for both material and spiritual greatness, America must now be redeemed—so that what was once lost might be restored. And the path to that redemption was a righteous rebellion (a rebellion which latter-day Puritan ministers like Mather welcomed as a rejection of English Anglican Protestantism that was, for them, still too close to Catholicism). Thus Mather concluded what was purportedly an argument against unjust taxation with an appeal to the "*Avenger of Wrongs.*" "*Shine forth, and arise, and stir up thy Strength, and come & save us*," Mather implored his god. "*Maintain our Cause against them, that would strive with us: Take hold of Shield and Buckler, and stand up for our Help*" (35). Few readers would have missed the implication that revolution wore the vestments of a holy war, redeeming a continent that had once already enjoyed the promise of salvation and needed now to be saved again.

Curiously, Mather never once mentioned Indians by name nor explicitly articulated a place for them in his redemptive schema. Are we to assume that they were those "*primary Inhabitants of America*" who arrived "after the Flood"? Mather doesn't say. And nowhere does Mather suggest interactions between Indians and "Apostles and Disciples" or between Indians and any of the other ancient civilizations that may once have peopled the continent. Racial mixing was not part of Mather's narrative.[12] All he will say is that, by the time of Columbus and Vespucci, "*America* became very well settled; and vast Numbers of People were found in this *Western World.*"

But those "vast Numbers of People" were, of course, the Native peoples. Thus, at least by implication, they too must become part of the redemption of the continent. After all, with America now enfolded into biblical beginnings in which "the Apostles, *went forth and preached* every where," the sacred responsibility of modern Christians in America must be to "recover their lost Possession" (Mather 23, 25). For true believers like Mather, there could be only one ending to this particular story: even if armed revolution were required, *"the Gospel and Religion of Jesus* will . . . gain a more wide and extensive Spreading, than has yet been known" (25). And this "Spreading" would embrace the Indians, too. For the sake of redeeming the continent, Native peoples would have to be included within Christian religious institutions and practices.

To be sure, with notable exceptions like the early ministers John Eliot and Roger Williams, the Puritans were, at best, erratic and often perfunctory in their efforts to convert the Indians.[13] Other Christian sects, however, proved more zealous. With both governmental sanction and support, missionaries were dispatched to proselytize and civilize, the two often indistinguishable in intent. As a consequence, not only would Indians be forced onto reservations to save them from "superior whites," but they would also be stripped of traditional beliefs and religious practices in order to save their souls and advance a national destiny which Mather had declared "reserved in Providence." Finally, intended or not, Mather's little pamphlet provided yet another rationale for removing Indians from their traditional lands. In the face of multiple pre-Columbian contacts and arrivals, the continent had never *solely* belonged to the Indians in the first place.

Whether or not attached to religious beliefs like Mather's, this view was pervasive throughout the early decades of the new republic. On 23 November 1816, the popular *New-York Weekly Museum*, for example, printed a lecture recently delivered "by Dr. MITCHILL, in the College of Physicians at New-York, which relates to the migration of Malays, Tartars, and Scandinavians, to America" (53). This was probably the Columbia University professor of natural history Samuel Latham Mitchill (1764–1831). Based on the work of many writers, his lecture advanced the theory that "the North American natives of the high [or colder] latitudes" were "of the same race with the Samoieds [i.e., Siberian Mongols] and Tartars of Asia," while "the North American tribes of the middle and low latitudes" were "akin to the Malay race of Australasia and Polynesia" (54). "But," continued Mitchill, "there is another part of the American population which deserves to be particularly considered. I mean the emigrants from Lapland, Norway, and Finland who, before the tenth century . . . settled themselves in a country which they called Vinland" (54). In the course of developing this theory of Scandinavian immigration, Mitchill explained that by "Finns," he also meant "Danes," and he added "Welshmen" to his list of migrants (54). What followed these various migrations were successive contests "for primacy and rule," that is, epic battles for control of the continent (54).

According to this version of American prehistory, the "Asian colonists probably exterminated the Malays," but "had probably a much harder task to perform" in "subdu[ing] the more ferocious and warlike European colonists who had already been entrenched and fortified in the country before them" (54). Mitchill cited the opinion of New York's governor DeWitt Clinton that "a part of the old forts and other antiquities" of western New York "were of *Danish* character" (54). And around such places, "long and bloody wars were waged" (54). In the end, however, "the Scandinavians . . . seem to have been overpowered," their survivors retreating to Labrador (54–55). The vanquishing forces were "of the Tartar stock," which Mitchill's lecture identified with the Iroquois. He then described the ultimate outcome: "The Iroquois . . . converted the country of the exterminated [Europeans], into a range for bears, beavers, bisons, and deer" (55). In other words, original and superior European settlers, capable of constructing "old forts and other antiquities," had been overcome by later-arriving peoples of Asian (or Tartar) stock—the ancestors of the Iroquois—who returned the country to its *uncivilized* beginnings. This was a scenario that, in one version or another, would be repeated by poorly informed antiquarians until almost the end of the nineteenth century.

Given the fascination with Vikings that seized Americans little more than two decades later, what is noteworthy in this lecture is its evidence that European scholarship about medieval Norse voyages to North America was neither discounted nor wholly unknown even at this early date. Franklin was not alone in believing that, long before Columbus, "America was discovered by [the] Northern People." In fact, as this lecture reprinted in the *New-York Weekly Museum* made clear, its author was persuaded that Scandinavians were both the continent's discoverers and its first settlers. "The antiquarian of America will probably find," stated Mitchill's closing paragraph, "that the Scandinavians emigrated about the tenth century of the Christian era, if not earlier. They may be considered, not merely as having discovered this continent, but to have explored its northern climes to great extent, and to have peopled them, three or four hundred years at least, before Christopher Columbus was born" (55).

Exterminated Nations

If the continent truly had lain undiscovered by the rest of the world before the coming of Columbus, its inhabitants "a branch of the human race whose history is lost in the early and wild mutations of men," then removing Indians to remote territories where they would not have "to compete with superior whites" could be justified as reasonable, even humane (Schoolcraft, *Historical and Statistical Information* 1:ix; Maddox 25). If, on the other hand, the continent and its people had not been isolated, but had experienced multiple visitations and settlements—from the Phoenicians and Carthaginians to the Celts and Norse—then claims to Indian civilization and artisanship could be undermined by assertions that any and all sophisticated artifacts from the past really belonged to the more advanced ancient arrivals. When petroglyphs were "ascribed to the North-men," for example, Indian agents plausibly argued that the Indians had never developed symbolic forms of communication or writing systems. And this provided even stronger justification for removal and reeducation west of the Mississippi. Either way, the Indians lost out.

But no version of American prehistory proved as lethal to Native peoples as the version that converted the burial and ceremonial mounds of the Southeast, the Ohio Valley, and the Midwest into the products of a prior, more advanced civilization. A civilization, moreover, that not only predated the Indian, but was somehow displaced by the Indian newcomer. Whatever their origins—Egyptians, a lost Tribe of Israel, early Christians, Asians, Europeans, or ancient Norse (and all were put forward by someone)—one fact was considered indisputable. As Governor DeWitt Clinton put it in his 1811 address to the New-York Historical Society, "without the aid of agriculture ... without the use of iron or copper; and without a perseverance, labor, and design which demonstrate considerable progress in the arts of civilized life," neither the Indians nor their ancestors were capable of constructing any of "these antient fortresses" found in western New York State (60). Therefore, he concluded, long before the arrival of the Indians, "a great part of North America was then inhabited by populous nations, who had made considerable advances in civilization" (60). What had eventually routed these earliest settlers was "the irruption of a horde of barbarians, who rushed like an overwhelming flood from the North of Asia"—in other words, the ancestors of the present-day Indians (61). In the wake of that barbaric "horde," the mounds and raised earthworks that were the subject of Clinton's address constituted "the only remaining monuments of these antient and exterminated nations" (61).

Given what was happening to the Indians of his own day, Clinton's word choice—"exterminated"—was both pointed and deliberate. The instrumentality of the term was not lost on succeeding politicians. Already committed to a policy of forced removals, when President Andrew Jackson addressed Congress in 1830, he followed Clinton's lead: "In the monuments and fortresses of an unknown people, spread over the extensive regions of the west, we behold the memorials of a once powerful race, which was exterminated, or has disappeared, to make room for the existing savage tribes" (qtd. in David Hurst Thomas 128).[14] This particular construction of American prehistory provided Jackson yet another pretext for the removals of the Creek and Cherokee. As Robert Silverberg, the most thorough historian of the growing myth that the mound builders were non-Indians, comments, "Conscience might ache a bit over the uprooting of the Indians, but not if it could be shown that the Indians, far from being long-established settlers in the land, were themselves mere intruders who had wantonly shattered the glorious Mound Builder civilization of old. What had been a simple war of conquest against the Indians now could be construed as a war of vengeance on behalf of that great and martyred ancient culture" (58).[15] The very real genocidal policies then in progress could thus be rhetorically subsumed (and tacitly justified) within this larger mythic narrative of prior displacement and "extermination."

Despite the transparency of political motives and a wealth of archaeological evidence that clearly linked the mounds and their contents with Native manufacture, the notion of a superior pre-Indian civilization tenaciously held on as both scientific fact and established history. In 1851, the *Proceedings of the American Ethnological Society* published a paper by Dr. C. A. A. Zestermann of Leipzig entitled "A Memoir of the European Colonization of America in Ante-historic Times." For Zestermann, the mound builders of Ohio were early peoples from northwestern Europe, most probably "bearded men from Ireland," who had arrived in America during pre-Christian times (see Silverberg 98). Even the well-regarded and usually careful historian of the West, Herbert Bancroft, could write as late as 1875 that "most and the best authorities deem it impossible that the moundbuilders were ever the remote ancestors of the Indian tribes" (qtd. in David Hurst Thomas 127).

In 1879, responding to the continuing "interest . . . in American archaeology, especially in that branch relating to the Mound Builders," a self-taught antiquarian and amateur archaeologist, John Patterson MacLean, published a study of "the ancient earth-works" of his native Ohio (*The Mound Builders* 3). Again, like so many others before him, he offered as established fact that "an ancient race, entirely distinct from the Indian, possessing a certain degree of civilization, once inhabited the central portion of the United States" (13). The origin of that race, he averred, remained "enveloped in impenetrable mystery" (138). But while MacLean, unlike many of his contemporaries, was reluctant to speculate about origins, he was wholly in agreement with those same contemporaries in imagining "what became of this people" (144). "They were expelled from this territory by force," wrote MacLean, "harassed by the inroads of the warlike bands of a foreign race" (144). As MacLean described it, the contest gave to American prehistory an almost epic scope. The Mound Builders (as MacLean called them) "offer[ed] the most stubborn resistance. Those mounds were covered with multitudes of brave and self-sacrificing men, who shed their blood in defense of their home and religion." Eventually overcome, "at last this peaceable and quiet people were expelled from the Ohio, and never after returned" (95).[16] According to the literary scholar Gordon Sayre, in the many retellings of scenes like this, over time "the Mound Builders became like the Romans, a great civilization pillaged by vulgar hordes of invading barbarians" (229). Thus, at least by association, such stories gave to America what Sayre terms "an imperial historiography" and thereby provided an antecedent for the nation's belief in its own, even greater imperial future (229).

A Myth Dies Hard

Although best known for leading a team of nine other men in the first attempt to map the Green and Colorado Rivers and their surrounding canyons in 1869, John Wesley Powell later became the director of several federal agencies that oversaw the exploration of the West. As director of the U.S. Geological Survey and subsequently founder of the Smithsonian Institution's Bureau of Ethnology (later the Bureau of American Ethnology), Powell believed that science should guide public policy. In his role as director of the Bureau of Ethnology, he sponsored rigorous and extensive fieldwork, and he demanded that his researchers supplement their field materials "by a study of all the connected literature and by a subsequent comparison of all ascertained facts" (Powell, "Report of the Director," *Twelfth Annual Report* xxi). The outcome was a series of compendious reports which, in the words of one of Powell's researchers, would help Americans to "generally discard . . . the fanciful hypotheses which have been formed without corroboration" by facts or evidence (Mallery, "Picture-Writing of the American Indians" 35). Among the most important of these was the eight-hundred-page report "Picture-Writing of the American Indians," compiled in 1888–89 by Garrick Mallery (and published, with illustrations, in 1893).[17]

Three emphases marked Mallery's report. To begin with, he employed a comparativist approach, examining various forms of Indian "picture-writings"—whether petroglyphs pecked on stone or the pictographic script written on birch bark by the Mi´kmaq and Passamaquoddy peoples—in relation to forms of picture-writings in other civilizations and other historical periods. To be sure, Mallery was not untouched by late nineteenth-century social Darwinist theories about classifications of cultures and races. In several places he suggested a taxonomy that progressed from mere "picturing" to "ideography" to "picture-writing" to the most advanced form of writing, alphabetic "phonetic writing." To his credit, he acknowledged that this taxonomy "is not in all respects approved," but he generally accepted it as a "chronologic if not evolutionary arrangement" ("Picture-Writing" 204). Still, even if he saw "the invention of alphabetic writing [as] . . . the great step marking the change from barbarism to civilization," at least he respected picture-writing as "one distinctive form of thought-writing" (26, 25). Above all else, however, Mallery's comparativist approach returned Native peoples to prehistory in a new way. Picture-writing may have been for him "a phase in the evolution of human culture," but it was a phase that the Indians shared with "the graphic systems of Egypt, Assyria, and China," and other great early empires (26).

The second significant aspect of Mallery's report was that it linked an indigenous past with a Native present (and presence). Just as Catlin had earlier challenged the notion that rock inscriptions were the product of "the North-men," asserting that he had himself "seen the Indian at work, recording his totem . . . in the solid rock," so too Mallery affirmed that picture-writing "is in actual daily use." He had himself "obtained a valuable collection of birch-bark pictographs . . . still made by the Passamaquoddy and Penobscot tribes . . . in Maine" ("Picture-Writing" 201). Indeed, he continued, Algonquian-speaking peoples of the Northeast "still use marks and devices on birch bark in the ordinary affairs of life," such as leaving messages for one another (201). And, again like Catlin, Mallery also affirmed that the petroglyphs were of Indian origin. The important point to be made, according to Mallery, was that Indian cultures were not homogeneous but, rather, various and distinct. "American pictographs, whether ancient on stone or modern on bark, skins, linens, or paper," he wrote, employed "symbolism . . . of individual origin" and "require separate study in every region" (35). Thus, not only were contemporary Indians reconnected to their past, but they were reconnected to a past in which cultural differences were scientifically established.

Mallery's third major emphasis was the debunking of prior "fanciful hypotheses." For example, early missionaries had misunderstood the many and age-old uses of cross figures among the Indians and so had erroneously explained their "presence . . . by a miraculous visit of an apostle" ("Picture-Writing" 773). Mallery also reproduced and then debunked Cotton Mather's distorted rendering in 1712 of the carvings on Dighton Rock as Hebrew letters, and he criticized Schoolcraft for reproducing illustrations of authentic rock inscriptions but then offering interpretations "nearly all colored according to his fancy" (82–83, 758). As Mallery explained in the concluding pages of his volume, he had undertaken the study of "petroglyphs, because it has been supposed that if interpreted they would furnish records of vanished peoples or races," particularly "peoples so far advanced in culture as to use alphabets" (772–73). Clearly, that had not been the case. Petroglyphs were a form of picture-writing, but they were not alphabetic in structure, and Mallery demonstrated that they continued to be produced by existing Native peoples and had been produced by their direct ancestors. Similarly, with regard to "pictographs on other substances," these objects too "are in hand and their current use as well as their significance is understood" (773). In Mallery's opinion, theories about lost superior races represented only "dazing infusions of perverted fancy" and were "repulsive to the sober student" (773). Mallery asserted that his meticulous research had once and for all put an end to "the theory about the mythical mound builders or some other suppostitious race. All suggestions of this nature should at once be abandoned," he pronounced (773).[18]

Just a year after Mallery's work appeared, the Bureau of Ethnology published its *Twelfth Annual Report* in 1894, and this volume included the 730-page "Report of the Mound Explorations" by Cyrus Thomas. Sharing Mallery's impatience with unsubstantiated fancies, Thomas detailed the results of his own field researches and those of others, concluding that "all the leading archaeologists of the present day" concurred in the view that the massive mounds and ceremonial centers were the work of the Native peoples who had inhabited the region at the time of contact (or their direct ancestors), "especially as they are the only pre-Columbian inhabitants of that region of which we have any knowledge" (730). In his director's report, which opened the volume, Powell stressed the thoroughness of the field research ("more than 2,000 mounds have been explored") and the extensiveness of those explorations "conducted in Alabama, Arkansas, Florida, Georgia, Illinois, Iowa, Kentucky, Louisiana, Michigan, Minnesota, Mississippi, Missouri, New York, North Dakota, North Carolina, Ohio, Pennsylvania, South Carolina, South Dakota, Tennessee, Wisconsin, and West Virginia" ("Report of the Director," *Twelfth Annual Report* xlv). Powell also underscored Thomas's conclusions, stating, "The spade and pick, in the hands of patient and sagacious investigators, have every year brought to light facts tending more and more strongly to prove that the mounds, defensive, mortuary and domiciliary, which have excited so much curiosity and become the subject of so many hypotheses, were constructed by the historic Indians of our land and their lineal ancestors" (xliii–xliv).[19]

Without question, as a man of science, Powell certainly believed that the mounds had been constructed by "the historic Indians of our land" and their ancestors. Yet at the heart of Powell's otherwise sober report lies another story entirely. "In 1858, 1859, and 1860," Powell had himself examined "prehistoric mounds in Ohio, Indiana, Illinois, and Missouri," and, for a time at least, he had come to share "the prevailing opinion" that these were "vestiges of a people more ancient and more advanced in culture than the tribes of Indians that occupied the continent at the time of the discovery by Columbus" ("Report of the Director," *Twelfth Annual Report* xxxix). His present purpose, he asserted, was to eradicate that erroneous notion by presenting the latest authoritative research on the subject. Thomas's "treatise . . . will be of interest," Powell continued, because "it seems to disprove the attractive theory that the ancient tumuli of the eastern half of the United States are the remains of a people more highly cultured than the tribes of who were Indians found by the white man, and who had vanished from the country anterior to the Columbian discovery" (xli). But consider his choice of language: "*seems* to disprove" rather than the simple declarative *disproves*; a theory so "attractive" that, in claiming to dismiss it, he repeated it yet again; and, rare in Powell's writings, he composed the awkwardly phrased "tribes of who were Indians," suggesting Powell's continuing resistance to the conclusion that the tribes who built the mounds *were* Indians after all. Despite all the evidence amassed by Mallery, Thomas, and other researchers, Powell revealed that he was himself still in thrall to the outdated "prevailing opinion."

As he put together this particular annual report, therefore, Powell (perhaps unconsciously) composed a kind of elegy to that outdated view:

> It is difficult to exaggerate the prevalence of this romantic fallacy, or the force with which the hypothetic "lost races" had taken possession of the imaginations of men. For more than a century the ghosts of a vanished nation have ambuscaded in the vast solitudes of the continent, and the forest-covered mounds have been usually regarded as the mysterious sepulchers of its kings and nobles. It was an alluring conjecture that a powerful people, superior to the Indians, once occupied the valley of the Ohio and the Appalachian ranges, their empire stretching from Hudson Bay to the Gulf, with its flanks on the western prairies and the eastern ocean; a people with a confederated government, a chief ruler, a great central capital, a highly developed religion, with homes and husbandry and advanced textile, fictile, and ductile arts, with language, perhaps with letters, all swept away before an invasion of copper-hued Huns from some unknown region of the earth, prior to the landing of Columbus. ("Report of the Director," *Twelfth Annual Report* xli–xlii)

The grandiose language reveals that it was not only the generalized "imaginations of men" which had been possessed, but also Powell's own imagination.

Instead of simply dismissing the fallacy *as* fallacy, Powell resurrected its romance and offered a lamentation that appears to commemorate a people who never were. He mentions the Indians, the people who *did* exist, only briefly in an appositive phrase. But then, in highly charged language, tinged by the influence of Sir Walter Scott's historical romances (which remained enormously popular in the U.S. throughout the nineteenth century), he devoted the bulk of the paragraph to retelling the story of a great empire and its heroic defeat. "For more than a century," wrote Powell, "the ghosts of a vanished nation have ambuscaded" not in the *perverted fancies* of deluded believers, as Mallery had demonstrated, but in "the vast solitudes of the continent." The very structure of the sentence thus establishes a momentary reality for those ghosts. They have "ambuscaded" in the sense of having been concealed (as ghosts are wont to be), but in the more generalized sense of the word, they have also been lying in wait to ambush the enemies who will nonetheless vanquish them. By situating his ghosts "in the vast *solitudes* of the continent," moreover, Powell willfully ignored all the available archaeological evidence of densely populated precontact Native sites across the continent and further erased Indian presence in favor of the "vanished nation." Perhaps inadvertently catering to popular nineteenth-century notions of the Indians as wandering nomadic bands without governance or political structures, Powell further supplanted Native prehistory by offering in its place the romantically appealing notion of a confederated empire with "kings and nobles" and "a great central capital." And then, even as he claimed to be dismissing it all as merely "an alluring conjecture," he nonetheless proceeded to people the continent with this once "powerful people," leaving virtually no segment of the continent untouched as far west as the prairies and no civilized art (textiles to metallurgy) unnamed.

Finally, apparently unmindful of the way he was racializing the myth, Powell pictured the "vanished nation," the "powerful" and "superior" people, as "swept away before an invasion of copper-hued Huns." Here the Indians return, imaginatively associated both by skin color ("copper-hued") and by place of origin (Asia) with the Huns, a nomadic people who, as every nineteenth-century schoolboy was taught, had swarmed out of Asia in ravaging military hordes to invade China and, later, most of western Europe.[20] In other words, intended or not, Powell portrayed a "copper-hued" people overcoming a "superior" and, given the social Darwinist theories then in ascendancy, by implication a white (or Caucasian) "vanished nation." It is Governor DeWitt Clinton's scenario of 1811 all over again, couched in even more compelling language, albeit in the guise of now debunking "this romantic fallacy."

Strongly resembling the classical elegy in its commemoration of those "vanished" peoples, the paragraph lacks what the more popular nineteenth-century form of the elegy—that is, the pastoral elegy (modeled on Milton's "Lycidas")—always offered: consolation. Nothing here consoles readers for the loss of the "vanished nation," unless, of course, readers can find consolation in the fact that it was all only "hypothetic." Yet it is precisely that fact that the paragraph finally laments. For Powell, as for so many of his readers, there could be no consolation in the knowledge that it was, after all, *only* a myth.

Consequences and Implications

There is a peculiar irony in the fact that the decimation of one orthodoxy succeeded only in reinforcing another. Having proved the indigenous origins of the mounds and thus undermined theories about lost races, Cyrus Thomas reverted to the other competing paradigm of continental prehistory: "the long continued isolation." Summarizing his own and others' views, Thomas sounded much like las Casas, von Humboldt, and Schoolcraft when he agreed that the Indians' "long and isolated residence in this continent has molded them all into a singularly homogenous race, which . . . has maintained its type unimpaired for countless generations." Approvingly paraphrasing the work of another anthropologist, Thomas wrote, "Never at any time before Columbus was it [that is, the Indian race] influenced in blood, language, or culture by any other race" (726–27).

But there is another, perhaps even deadlier irony that emerges from the research of Mallery and Thomas. Together they had effectively demolished the idea that the cultural difference of the Indian was a difference that was both hereditary and unalterable. Mallery had understood the various forms of picture-writing as "a phase in the evolution" of more advanced writing systems, and he noted that the "transition" to more sophisticated forms—at least among the Aztec and Maya—had been "arrested by foreign conquest" ("Picture-Writing" 26). Similarly, Thomas had described flourishing and sophisticated mound-builder cultures, some of them also known to have been arrested and destroyed by contact and conquest during the historic period. In other words, even if the Indians *as a race* appeared relatively homogeneous to some, they had never been *culturally* static or incapable of progressive cultural development.

Powell reinforced these findings in his director's report for the Thomas volume, noting that Native cultures were in transition or "in the stage commonly traversed toward higher culture" ("Report of the Director," *Twelfth Annual Report* xxiii). Yet in making that statement, Powell actually helped justify governmental policies intended to "civilize" Native peoples by forcing them to "become farmers and adopt 'American' economic and cultural values" (Greenwald 1). However inadvertently, Powell (and his Bureau's annual reports) fueled increased support for the General Allotment Act of 1887, also known as the Dawes Act.

Those who considered themselves friends of the Indian utilized the new scientific studies to prove that the Indian not only was capable of change, but *deserved* the opportunity for further cultural development through enlightened government intervention. The view that "separate property in land is the basis of civilized society" had been argued by commissioners of Indian affairs since the 1830s (qtd. in Rogin 116).[21] Armed with the Bureau of Ethnology reports of the 1880s, those determined to save Indians from extinction by integrating them into the dominant culture could now argue for helping them traverse the next transitional stage "toward higher culture": the private ownership of land. As the historian Emily Greenwald explains, the Dawes Act of 1887 "sought to assimilate Indians into the American mainstream by dividing collectively controlled reservations into individually owned allotments of land" (1). In this way, Greenwald continues, "traits that Euroamericans associated with savagery—such as nomadism, collective economic strategies, and tribalism—would be replaced by traits associated with civilization—sedentary agriculture, private property, and individualism" (2).

Not surprisingly, western land developers had their own motives for supporting the Dawes Act. It permitted Indians to sell their "allotments" to non-Indians. Thus, as Greenwald so aptly puts it, the "attempt by humanitarians to assimilate Indians through the institution of private property" neatly "harmonized the interests of policy reformers with those of Western developers" (5). The end result, of course—both through government mismanagement of the Act and unscrupulous dealings by white land speculators—was that, by the early decades of the twentieth century, "Indians had lost more than half of their lands" (5).[22] Clearly, the Bureau of Ethnology's careful reconstructions of Native American history and prehistory were either ignored or exploited in ways that Powell and his staff could never have predicted and did not approve.

When Schoolcraft composed his volumes for Congress, he understood perfectly that notions about the prehistory of the American continent inevitably became implicated in the construction of *national* origin stories as a new nation tried to assert a unique (and, as with Mather, even a *providential*) destiny for itself. Vine Deloria Jr. added to that insight the notion that, in the process, stories about the accessibility or the isolation of the continent ineluctably also became stories about the history and identity of its Native peoples. In addressing the Society for American Archaeology in 1992, Deloria expressly intended to dislodge what he called "the baggage of former days" ("Indians, Archaeologists" 596). For Deloria, "the efforts of the previous century" had left the field of archaeology "stuck" with a body of data that too often proved "derogatory and demeaning to American Indians" (598). To correct this, he called for a renewed study of American prehistory and for a permanent rejection of "a fictional doctrine that places American Indians outside the realm of planetary human experiences" (597).

Then, in 2000, Deloria shot yet another salvo across the contested bow of American prehistory. This time, his remarks focused on the most popular and most persistent of the early contact stories and coincided with the millennial celebration of the Viking landing in North America, sometime around the year 1000. Authenticated by the excavations at L'Anse aux Meadows, a small isolated site at the northernmost tip of Newfoundland, by 2000 the Norse presence in North America was no longer a matter of myth and conjecture. Benjamin Franklin's speculation in 1781 that there "arriv'd in America . . . Danes . . . some Ages before Columbus" had been confirmed (35:35–36). The only difference was that the "Danes" were actually mostly Norwegians from Iceland and Greenland. What had not yet been definitively determined, as Deloria realized, was how far south the Norse explored, how long they stayed, and the location of their fabled Vinland colony. We also do not know with absolute certainty the identity of the Native peoples they encountered. For all these reasons, Deloria tacitly challenged the view that L'Anse aux Meadows represented the beginning and end of the Norse explorations in North America. As Deloria put it in 2000, "Can we pretend that the Vikings, the premier sailors and explorers of the Christian era, were content to set up a small winter village on the continent and explore no further?" (foreword xvii).

2

Contact and Conflict

WHAT THE VINLAND SAGAS TELL US

> The archaeological and historical records can do no more than hint at the nature of relationships between the Norse and the aboriginal peoples of northeastern North America. Yet these hints point in a consistent direction: toward a suggestion that over a period of several centuries these peoples knew one another and knew of both the dangers and the benefits of meeting with strangers whose cultures had developed on opposite sides of the world.
>
> —PATRICIA SUTHERLAND,
> "The Norse and Native North Americans" (2000)

Iceland and the Saga Tradition

According to the archaeologist William W. Fitzhugh, the term "Viking" probably derives from a place in southern Norway called Vik, "an early center of Viking raiding fleets" (14). But *viks* also meant a bay or harbor in Old Norse. And it was certainly bays and harbors in which medieval Norsemen landed their ships and then sallied forth to raid and pillage, "seeking adventure and profit" (14). As Fitzhugh further notes, "Those 'bay men' who went off raiding were said to go 'a-viking' or were simply called 'vikings,'" a term often used in fear by the British, who were repeatedly the victims of Viking raids (14).[1] Yet the early Icelanders used the term *víkingar* to refer to men who grouped together in bands to raid from ships, and in that usage, the term could connote both pirates and marauders as well as men of honor and courage.

What is popularly known as the Viking Age lasted roughly 250 years, from the infamous attack on the defenseless monastery on Lindisfarne Island off the northeast coast of England in A.D. 793 through 1066, when the Normans (a contraction of the North-men), French-speaking descendants of former Viking raiders, crossed the channel from France to invade and conquer England. During this period of significant territorial expansion, Norwegian Vikings sailed west across the North Atlantic to invade the Shetland Islands and the Orkneys.

They then used these as bases for raiding northern Scotland, Ireland, and the west coast of England. Danish Vikings raided along England's eastern coast and along the northwestern shores of the English mainland. Over time, however, what began as marauding raids—what the English called "the curse of the north"—turned into trade and settlement (see Fitzhugh 14–15). To be sure, as Fitzhugh writes, "the raids continued sporadically throughout the British Isles and western Europe for the next two centuries," and even extended to Spain, the Mediterranean, and North Africa (15). But many of those who went raiding also "returned to regions they had first visited as marauders and took wives and land and settled there permanently" (15). Eventually, between the Norwegian and the Danish Vikings, whole swaths of England and places like Dublin in Ireland, York in England, and Normandy in France became Nordic territories, home to burgeoning populations of mixed local and Scandinavian origins. Those who had once gone a-viking now became landowners and farmers, like their forebears in Denmark and Norway.

For the most part, economic pressures originally sent young men a-viking, and the dearth of available arable land in Norway continued to do so. By the closing decades of the ninth century, unoccupied land suitable for farming and the grazing of sheep and cattle had become scarce in Norway, especially along its western coast. As a result, a different pattern of territorial expansion was established by those seeking *un*peopled lands where they might settle and farm. Except in the imaginations of later generations of Europeans and Euro-Americans, these men and women were never known as Vikings, even though some of the men might once have gone a-viking in their youth. But as colonizers and settlers, these people were simply known as the Northmen, or the Norse.

About 870, would-be farmers from western Norway first began new settlements in Iceland. Except for a few Irish monks (who were either driven out or left of their own accord), Iceland was uninhabited at that time. The settlers from Norway were soon joined by other Scandinavians who had been living in the Nordic colonies of the British Isles, and some Celtic cultural influences thereby came with them. Once again, the motive behind immigration was primarily economic, although attempts to consolidate greater power in a kingship system in Norway also drove out some local chieftains and their retinues. Because the distinctive form of society that developed in Iceland emerged out of a period when Scandinavian kings were attempting to enlarge their authority at the expense of the traditional rights of the freemen, many nineteenth-century Americans later tended to glamorize the medieval Icelanders as freedom-fighters and founders of an American-style republic. But, in fact, medieval Iceland was a hierarchical and highly stratified society, with slaves (or bondsmen and bondswomen) at the base and, at the top of the social pyramid, chieftains (or *jarls*, earls) who wielded a great deal of political and religious power and controlled vast landholdings. In between were gradations of freemen who might work as tenant farmers or be small landholders in their own right. It was hardly an egalitarian system, even though bondsmen and bondswomen did sometimes become freemen and landholders.

What attracted the notice of nineteenth-century Americans, however, was the Icelanders' increasing dependence on local *things*, or public assemblies, "which had been the major forum for meetings of freemen in the Old Scandinavian (and Germanic) social order" (Byock, *Medieval Iceland* 4). But as the saga scholar and historian Jesse L. Byock points out in *Medieval Iceland*, "The tenth-century Icelanders, by extending the mandate of such assemblies, transformed them into a self-contained governmental system without overlords. At its core was the Althing, a national assembly of freemen, established around 930" (4). In this way, like the Americans of a much later century, the Icelanders appeared to have organized a quasi-republican system and established a unique social order different from the one they had left behind. Together, local things plus the national Althing "regulated disputes and fostered a political stability that lasted from soon after the end of the settlement period until the thirteenth century" (3). Even so, without a centralized state administration, it was difficult to enforce the laws, and Iceland was repeatedly beset by strife between chieftains feuding for power. Although, for their own purposes, many nineteenth-century Americans grossly exaggerated both the democratic and republican features of this system, it *did* function, and what became known as the Old Icelandic Free State "lasted until 1262–64 when, after more than 300 years of independence, the Icelanders agreed to pay tribute to the Norwegian Crown" (8).

Its three hundred years of relative political independence and stability notwithstanding, Iceland could not accommodate its burgeoning population. Despite its size (a fifth larger than Ireland), only the coastal regions could support settlement, while the interior was largely uninhabitable. Thus, as Iceland became more populous, its land-hungry farmers in turn began settling Greenland in the closing decades of the tenth century. Along with settlement, Iceland and Greenland carried on an active merchant trade with one another and with Norway and

England (through the port at Bristol). Given the remarkable seaworthiness of the Norse cargo ships, it was only a matter of time before these hardy sailors and eager colonizers would encounter still other new lands even farther to the west: the northeastern coast of North America and the place the Norse called Vinland, or Wine Land.

Much of what we know about the expeditions to Vinland derives from two texts which are part of an extraordinary body of oral literature that first began to be written down in Iceland sometime in the second half of the twelfth century. In written form, these are the *Islendinga sögur*, the Sagas of the Icelanders, vernacular prose narratives often considered "the crowning achievement of medieval narrative art in Scandinavia" (Kellogg xviii). The word *sögur* (or sagas) is related to our English word "say" and originally meant "what is said." The sagas began as oral tellings of real events, passed on to memorialize exceptional deeds and persons as well as to honor the histories and genealogies of prominent families. It was not unusual, therefore, for different sagas to contain overlapping (or even somewhat divergent) versions of the same events and to depict the same characters. The sagas moved from oral to written texts with the introduction of Christianity and Christian institutions into a previously polytheistic belief system and a pagan world inhabited not just by humans but by other supernatural beings, too. But as Scandinavians sought greater integration into a larger European fold, the adoption of Catholicism became both culturally and politically attractive. The kings' conversions were especially important. King Harald Bluetooth took credit for bringing Christianity to the Danes around 960. King Olaf Tryggvason is credited with converting Norway during his short reign, 995–1000. Iceland, then functioning as a wholly independent country, officially adopted Christianity at its annual Althing in 1000. Greenland followed soon thereafter. Excavations in Greenland have unearthed the remains of a large stone cathedral, several parish churches, and a small wood and turf chapel on the property of Eirik the Red. Since Eirik the Red never converted to Catholicism, the chapel is thought to have been built at the behest of his wife, Thjodhild, who was a convert. This fact further underscores evidence in the sagas that, for some time, Christianity and the Old Norse religion and religious practices intermixed and overlapped, sometimes living side by side. The sagas emerge from this period of syncretic blending.

Following Iceland's adoption of Christianity, many of the wealthier and important chieftains sent their sons to England or to the Continent to be educated in clerical institutions. After the first Icelandic bishop was appointed in 1056, the Church organized its own institutions of learning in Iceland and trained clerics locally. Most Icelanders in religious orders came from chieftains' families. What must be understood about the sagas, therefore, is that those who committed them to writing lived in a far more Christianized world than did the subjects of the sagas. These (often anonymous) writers were generally Latin-trained clerics or men with ecclesiastical training who had a vested interest in accommodating the original oral material both to Christian belief patterns and also to the conventions of the emerging vernacular literatures and historical chronicles of greater Europe. Some sagas also show the influence of these churchmen's knowledge of the writings of classical antiquity. In short, the sagas probably went through several hands, repeatedly adapted and adjusted so as to become part of European literature and the classical learning that reached an increasingly literate and wealthy Iceland through its foreign trade and through the Church and its clergy. Yet because the sagas, even in written form, were still considered *popular* entertainments, they moved from orality to writing not in Latin but in the vernacular. This was the language of medieval Norway and Iceland before it diverged into Norwegian and Icelandic, and it is variously referred to as Old Norse, Old West Norse, or Old Icelandic.

The two extant sagas that tell of the Norse discovery, exploration, and attempted colonization of North America are *The Greenlanders' Saga* and *Eirik the Red's Saga*, commonly referred to together as the Vinland sagas. Although neither is considered by literary scholars "among the best sagas," they are nonetheless typical (Kellogg xxxii). In each there is a straightforward, sometimes blunt telling of events, a relative absence of narrative attempts to explain the characters' motivations or analyze the meaning of their actions, and, without comment, a mixing of both pre-Christian and Christian practices.[2] Moreover, since neither saga survives in one piece in anything close to its original oral or written form, the two Vinland sagas as we know them today are really compilations from different extant sources. Over the years, various editors and translators have sometimes made different decisions about which surviving manuscript sources to follow and which to disregard or use only piecemeal. As Magnus Magnusson and Hermann Pálsson comment in the introduction to their own English-language translation of the Vinland sagas, every scholar who studies or attempts to offer a translation of any of the Icelandic sagas must grapple with the fact that these "sagas were never museum pieces embalming for all time a literary act; they were living things, and later generations thought nothing of adapting and rewriting them to suit changing tastes" (31). With regard to the two Vinland sagas in particular, like many saga scholars, Magnusson and Pálsson argue that *The Greenlanders' Saga* came first and that "*Eirik's Saga*, which was written somewhere around or after the middle of the thirteenth century" was "a deliberate revision of *Grœnlendinga Saga*," possibly based on the later writer's access to "better information about the major characters involved" (34; see also Kunz 631). Other scholars have argued that the Vinland sagas "were written down independently of each other, drawing on the same or similar traditional material, which was circulating in oral tradition" (see Sigurðsson, "The Quest for Vinland" 233). Either way, while *The Greenlanders' Saga* and *Eirik the Red's Saga* retell many of the same events, they tell them differently and with different emphases. All these differences notwithstanding, what makes these sagas compelling for American readers is that they are the first written narratives about Europe's encounter with the North American landscape and with its Native peoples.

The Greenlanders' Saga

The oldest surviving text of *The Greenlanders' Saga* is inconspicuously included in *Flateyjarbók*, a mid-fourteenth-century vellum compendium of longer sagas mostly about the Norwegian kings.[3] The saga's opening line is demarcated only by the decorated letter Þ (or *thorn*). But even this source is incomplete. Depending on which additional medieval manuscript sources the translator used in order to reconstruct the entire text, *The Greenlanders' Saga*, the shorter of the two sagas, is divided into either eight or nine sections or chapters. Positing "a lost *Eirik's Saga* which told the story of Eirik's life ... fully," Magnusson and Pálsson interpolated material "borrowed from" Ari Thorgilsson's twelfth-century compilation, *Landnámabók* (*The Book of Settlements*), which, they believe, contains "a condensed summary" of the biographical information that had been provided in the lost *Eirik's Saga* (49, n. 4; also 31–32). (Ari Thorgilsson, also known as Ari the Learned, born in 1067 in Iceland, was Iceland's first historian in the vernacular.) Because of this opening interpolated section from *Landnámabók*, the Magnusson and Pálsson translation of *The Greenlanders' Saga* runs to nine chapters. Unless otherwise noted, all quotations from the following summary of *The Greenlanders' Saga* are from their translation.[4]

Chapter 1 opens with the information that "a man called Thorvald" and his son "Eirik the Red ... left their home in ... Norway, because of some killings and went to Iceland, which had been extensively settled by then" (49). This relocation is usually dated at about 960. What follows is the genealogy of Eirik the Red (so-called because of his red hair) and that of his wife, Thjodhild. These genealogies indicate Eirik's social status and (to a knowledgeable medieval Icelander) reveal that he has married into an important and relatively powerful family on Iceland. We also learn that he and his wife "had a son called Leif," their first child (49). Further, we learn that Eirik was banished from Iceland after another killing and went to live on a small island. Upon his return, he quarreled with a neighbor, "was sentenced to outlawry," and condemned this time to a three-year period of banishment (49). He is no longer welcome within civilized bounds. Consequently, he prepares "for a sea voyage." With some of those who had taken his side in the quarrel, Eirik sets out to explore lands to the west, which were first sighted (but never explored) years earlier by another Icelander when he and his crew had been blown off course and "driven westward" (49–50).[5] Sometime in 981 or 982, Eirik finds the new land he is seeking, explores it for three years, chooses a prime location where he himself will make a new home, and "gave names to many landmarks there" (50).

Having decided to establish a settlement, Eirik "named the country he had discovered *Greenland*, for he said that people would be much more tempted to go there if it had an attractive name" (50). Upon his return to Iceland, Eirik persuades others to join him in removing to Greenland. This interpolated section from *Landnámabók* then tells us that "in the summer in which Eirik the Red set off to colonize Greenland, twenty-five ships sailed" with him, "but only fourteen reached there; some were driven back [to Iceland], and some were lost at sea" (51). While the text gives no further details, medieval Icelanders would have recognized in these lines a reference to the sometimes high winds and brutal storms at sea, as well as the dangers of drifting polar ice. During a period between the ninth century and about 1350, known as the Medieval Warming, however, these dangers were substantially mitigated, if not entirely eliminated, by rising temperatures in the Northern Hemisphere. This period of climatic warming made the crossing to Greenland (and, subsequently, to North America) relatively safe in most seasons, even if not entirely danger-free, and also accounts for the somewhat more hospitable appearance of parts of Greenland at the time.

The chapter ends by dating these events "fifteen years before Christianity was adopted by law in Iceland" (51). This sets the year as 985, well within the Medieval Warming period. The list of men (most accompanied by their families) "who went abroad with Eirik [and] took possession of land in Greenland" is linked to the names of their homesteads (51). This device functioned to establish family and individual land claims as well as to honor those enterprising enough to settle new lands.

Altogether, though, and even without editorial comment, this opening chapter tells us a great deal about the patriarch whose children will push even farther west to North America. Eirik the Red is short-tempered, quarrelsome, even a killer, but he is also able to marry advantageously and garner the loyalty of those willing to follow him into unknown territories. Unlike the earlier Icelander who had spotted Greenland but never explored it, Eirik is curious, brave, risk-taking, and enterprising—yet also a bit of a charlatan in his exaggerated naming of the largely cold, glaciated, and barren Greenland. Still, to be fair, during the Medieval Warming, Greenland offered coastal areas with conditions not unlike those in Iceland—areas that could support substantial farms and animal husbandry—as well as fjords and rivers teeming with fish. For those seeking to leave an overpopulated Norway and an Iceland on the verge of overpopulation, *any* promise of newly discovered habitable lands was more than welcome.

What appears as the second chapter of Magnusson and Pálsson's translation of *The Greenlanders' Saga* functions in many other translations as the opening. Were the saga simply, or even mainly, about the discovery and exploration of new lands to the west—that is, North America—this would make good chronological sense because this chapter first reveals that there *are* unknown, "well wooded" lands yet to be explored (53). But *The Greenlanders' Saga* is what is known as a "family saga," and the purpose of these family sagas was the tracing of multigenerational family histories and the deeds of family members. In *The Greenlanders' Saga*, the main emphasis is on the family of Eirik the Red. And that emphasis, presumably, would have been established by what Magnusson and Pálsson postulate is a lost opening chapter for which they substituted passages borrowed from *Landnámabók*, as discussed earlier.

Thus their second chapter opens with the genealogy of Herjolf Bardarsson and the fact that he had sold his farm in Iceland "and emigrated to Greenland with Eirik the Red" (51). We also learn that Herjolf has a very successful son named Bjarni who "sail[ed] to foreign lands," "earned himself both wealth and a good reputation," and now owns "a merchant ship of his own" (51). The focus then shifts back to Eirik the Red and his family. Clearly, Eirik has become the de facto leader, or chieftain, of his settlement. We are told where Eirik located his farm and that "he commanded great respect, and all the people in Greenland recognized his authority. He had three sons—Leif, Thorvald, and Thorstein. He also had a daughter called Freydis, who was married to a man named Thorvard. . . . Freydis was an arrogant, overbearing woman, but her husband was rather feeble; she had been married off to him mainly for his money" (52). In keeping with most extant sagas' characteristic imperative to date and historicize events, we are then informed that "Greenland was still a heathen country at this time" (52). This places subsequent events in the chapter prior to the year 1000, when Greenland followed Iceland in officially adopting Christianity.

The main actor in this second chapter is not any member of the Eiriksson family but, rather, the son of Herjolf Bardarsson, Bjarni Herjolfsson. Sailing from Norway on his merchant ship, Bjarni is headed for his first visit to his father's new home on Greenland—probably in 986—and acknowledges to his crew "This voyage of ours will be considered foolhardy, for not one of us has ever sailed the Greenland Sea" (52). En route to Greenland, Bjarni and his crew are blown off course and get lost in a dense fog. "For many days they had no idea what their course was" (53).[6] When the sun finally reappears, they sight land, but Bjarni realizes "it could not be Greenland" because it is not mountainous and there are no "huge glaciers" (53). Instead, this land is "well wooded and with low hills." The second land they sight is "flat and wooded" (53). For the medieval Norse living on Greenland, where forests were sparse and timber for home-building and shipbuilding was scarce, as for those in Iceland, where limited forest areas were fast disappearing under the pressures of settlement, "well wooded" lands would have seemed very attractive. Yet despite his crew's repeated entreaties to land and explore, "Bjarni refused. . . . He was criticized for this by his men" (53). Stubbornly, Bjarni orders his men "to hoist sail" and resume their journey to Greenland (53). After three days at sea, "they sighted a third land" which was "high and mountainous, and topped by a glacier" (53). Bjarni declares this country "worthless" and again rejects his men's suggestions "to land there" (53). Finally, after struggling through "a gale," followed by four more days at sea, Bjarni's ship "made land . . . where Bjarni's father, Herjolf, lived," in Greenland (54). The chapter ends with the information that "Bjarni now gave up trading and stayed with his father" to farm (54).

In chapter 3, the criticism of Bjarni implied in chapter 2 is made explicit: "some time later, Bjarni Herjolfsson sailed from Greenland to Norway," visited the royal court, and told "about his voyage and the lands he had sighted. People thought he showed a great lack of curiosity, since he could tell them nothing about these countries, and he was criticized for this" (54). After a brief time as "a retainer at . . . court," Bjarni returned to Greenland "and carried on farming there after his father's death" (54). Here Bjarni and his family disappear from the story. The narrative then tells us, "There was now great talk of discovering new countries," and returns to its main focus, the exploits of the Eiriksson family (54).

Unlike the stubborn and incurious Bjarni, "Leif, the son of Eirik the Red," is eager to seek out new lands. In this, he is like his father. So Leif "went to see Bjarni Herjolfsson and bought his ship from him, and engaged a crew of thirty-five" (54). "Leif asked his father Eirik to lead this expedition," but soon afterward Eirik is injured in a fall from a horse—a very bad omen for the journey—and declares, "I am not meant to discover more countries than this one we now live in" (55). Without his father, Leif and his crew "put out to sea" (55). Although the saga does not say so, sea-hardy medieval Icelanders would have taken for granted that Leif obtained sailing directions when he visited Bjarni and probably employed members of Bjarni's original crew among his own "crew of thirty-five." What the saga does say is that Leif's first landfall "was the country that Bjarni had sighted last." Leif and some of his crew go ashore, find the place bare of grass, its "hinterland . . . covered with great glaciers, and between glaciers and shore the land was like one great slab of rock" (55). But even though "it seemed to them a worthless country"—just as Bjarni had declared it—nonetheless Leif is proud of his accomplishment: "Now we have done better than Bjarni . . . we have at least set foot [on this new land]" (55). Consistent with the Norse habit of naming places not for their location but for their physical characteristics (or resources), because of its expanse of rock, Leif names the place *Helluland*, which translates literally as Stone Slab-Land. This is generally considered by most modern archaeologists to have been Baffin Island or northernmost Labrador (55).

"They returned to their ship and put out to sea, and sighted a second land" (55). Upon going ashore, Leif and his crew discover that "this country was flat and wooded, with white sandy beaches . . . and the land sloped gently down to the sea" (55). Once again, in the quintessential European act of taking possession, Leif names the place: "This country shall be named after its natural resources: it shall be called *Markland*" (55). This name translates as Forest Land and is generally thought to have been Labrador.

54 Chapter Two

After two more days at sea, "they sighted land again" and go ashore on "an island which lay to the north of it" (55). Everything is promising. "The weather was fine. There was dew on the grass, and the first thing they did was to get some of it on their hands and put it to their lips, and to them it seemed the sweetest thing they had ever tasted" (55). They then returned to their ship and "sailed into the sound that lay between the island and the headland jutting out to the north" (56). They round the headland and enter "extensive shallows . . . at low tide," which leaves their ship "high and dry" (56). "But they were so impatient to land that they could not bear to wait for the rising tide to float the ship; they ran ashore to a place where a river flowed out of a lake. As soon as the tide had refloated the ship they took a boat and rowed out to it and brought it up the river into the lake, where they anchored it" (56). They carry their gear ashore and begin building stone and turf *buðir*, or "booths," enclosures which could be roofed and used for temporary living quarters. "Then they decided to winter there and built some large houses" (56). The following paragraphs fully explain the decision to winter over, presenting us with the earliest known written description of Europeans' first encounter with the attractions of North America:

> There was no lack of salmon in the river or the lake, bigger salmon than they had ever seen. The country seemed to them so kind that no winter fodder would be needed for livestock; there was never any frost all winter and the grass hardly withered at all.
>
> In this country, night and day were of more even length than in either Greenland or Iceland: on the shortest day of the year, the sun was already up by 9 a.m., and did not set until after 3 p.m. (56)

These passages and those preceding have been the subject of much speculation and many competing interpretations. Saga scholars, archaeologists, and amateur history buffs have long disputed just which part of the North American coast is being described here. For nineteenth-century Americans especially, it was a matter of national pride to prove that this landscape was located within the territorial U.S., probably in New England but also possibly as far south as Florida. For its part, however, the saga is silent on this question, concerning itself with describing the new land and, even more important, the quality of Leif's leadership in exploring it.

As the third chapter nears its close, Leif divides his crew into "two parties" (56). He says that "half of the company are to remain here at the houses while the other half go exploring," but he cautions that those who go exploring "must not go so far that they cannot return the same evening, and they are not to become separated" (56). Also, as a good leader, "Leif himself took turns at going out with the exploring party and staying behind at the base" (56). Having now established Leif as a fair and wise leader, careful for the safety of his men, the chapter closes with its final appraisal: "Leif was tall and strong and very impressive in appearance. He was a shrewd man and always moderate in his behavior" (56). The implicit comparison with the "foolhardy" Bjarni Herjolfsson, who got lost on his way to Greenland because neither he nor his crew had "ever [before] sailed the Greenland Sea," is now complete (52). Bjarni may, by accident, have spotted this new and inviting land, but the shrewd Leif Eiriksson is its true discoverer.

In the fourth chapter of Magnusson and Pálsson's translation of *The Greenlanders' Saga*, we learn about the discovery of wild grapevines. When one of his company fails to return one evening, "Leif was very displeased ... rebuked his men severely, and got ready to make a search with twelve men" (57). The missing man is named Tyrkir, a German who "had been with the [Eiriksson] family for a long time, and when Leif was a child had been devoted to him" (57).[7] "Only a short distance from the houses," the search party sees Tyrkir "walking towards them" (57). He is clearly very excited and finally declares, "I have some news. I found vines and grapes" (57). Initially, Leif is skeptical. "'Is that true foster-father?' asked Leif" (57). The answer is unequivocal, and Tyrkir reminds Leif that he comes from a country well known to the Norse for its wine production. "'Of course it is true,' [Tyrkir] replied. 'Where I was born there were plenty of vines and grapes'" (57).

The alcoholic drinks usually made at home by the medieval Norse were mead, whose basic ingredient is honey, "and beer, made from malted barley and hops" (Kaland and Martens 45). But the wealthier families also prized wine, which they "imported from the Rhine" in jugs of German stoneware (45). Thus the resources of this new land provided both utility and luxury: trees for shipbuilding and grapes for winemaking. Leif is quick to exploit both, telling his men, "Now we have two tasks on our hands. On alternate days we must gather grapes and cut vines, and then fell trees, to make a cargo for my ship" (57). The "tow-boat," a boat towed behind the large merchant ship, "was filled with grapes," while the large merchant ship purchased from Bjarni Herjolfsson "took on a full cargo of timber" (57). Once again "Leif named the country after its natural qualities and called it *Vinland*," or Wine-Land (58). Then in the spring of what was probably the year 1001, with the ship and the tow-boat fully loaded, Leif and his men "put out to sea," headed back to Greenland with their valuable cargo (58).

Just as their ship came in sight of Greenland, however, the keen-eyed Leif spotted a group of people stranded on a reef (their ship presumably having broken up on the rocks). Leif is characteristically cautious in his approach to the reef (or skerry) in case the people there "are hostile." "[But] if they need our help," says Leif, "it is our duty to give it" (58). As it turns out, the group's leader is a merchant named Thorir, "a Norwegian by birth" who is acquainted with Leif's father, Eirik the Red. Leif takes Thorir, his wife, Gudrid, and Thorir's entire crew aboard his own ship, bringing them safely to Greenland. Thus "Leif rescued fifteen people in all from the reef" and "from then on was called Leif the Lucky. He gained greatly in wealth and reputation" (59). In this way, the saga continues to flesh out Leif's qualities: his heroism in rescuing the stranded company and his generosity in finding lodgings in Greenland for everyone, including his own crew. In medieval Icelandic, the sobriquet translated here as "lucky" denoted an inherent attribute of character, not merely chance or happenstance. In other words, because his "luck" is both the cause and the expression of his success, Leif almost inevitably earns "wealth and reputation."

As the chapter moves toward its conclusion, we learn that "a serious disease broke out amongst Thorir's crew that winter," and among the dead are Thorir himself and Eirik the Red (59). Then we read, "Now there was much talk about Leif's Vinland voyage, and his brother Thorvald thought that the country had not been explored extensively enough" (59). Leif agrees to lend his ship to his younger brother—"to go to Vinland, if you like,"—and chapter 5 depicts Thorvald's exploration of Vinland and the first known recorded encounter between the Norse and the Native peoples.

As this chapter opens, "with his brother Leif's guidance," Thorvald prepares his own expedition to Vinland "and engaged a crew of thirty" (59). The saga tells us "there are no reports of their voyage until they reached Leif's houses in Vinland. There they laid up the ship [on dry land] and settled down for the winter, catching fish for their food. In the spring Thorvald said they should get the ship ready, and that meanwhile a small party of men should take the ship's boat and sail west along the coast and explore that region during the summer" (59). We are not told for how long or how far the boat explored, but, consistent with Leif's earlier reports, "they found the country there very attractive, with woods stretching almost down to the shore and white sandy beaches. There were numerous islands there, and extensive shallows" (60). On "one westerly island," they find what appears to be a wooden container for storing grain but otherwise, "no traces of human habitation" nor any other "man-made thing" (60). This last statement is worthy of notice because it underscores that the Norse, having previously settled an uninhabited Iceland and an uninhabited Greenland, were now again seeking uninhabited lands to colonize. And because, in the absence of any other signs of "human habitation," the single grain container did not suggest to them that this was a populous country, Thorvald's men continued to explore. Then, in the autumn, "they returned to Leif's Houses" and again spent the winter there (60).

The next summer, his second year in Vinland, "Thorvald sailed east with his ship and then north along the coast" (60). En route, they run into "a fierce gale off a headland and were driven ashore" (60). Having shattered their keel, "they had to stay there for a long time while they repaired the ship" (60). Thorvald decides "to erect the old keel here on the headland," thus establishing a kind of signpost for future explorations, and calls the place *Kjalarness*, or Keel Point (60). They then continued their explorations, sailing "away eastward along the coast" (60).

"Soon they found themselves at the mouth of two fjords [long narrow arms of the sea located between high cliffs], and sailed up to the promontory that jutted out between them; it was heavily wooded. They moored the ship alongside [the wooded promontory] and put out the gangway, and Thorvald went ashore with his men. 'It is beautiful here,' he said. 'Here I should like to make my home'" (60). The unspoken suggestion, of course, is that Thorvald has found a country that reminds him of Norway, complete with fjords and thick forests like the ones that supported Norway's shipbuilding and merchant economy. But instead of becoming his home, this land is shortly to become his grave, as the Norse first come upon the Native inhabitants called "Skraelings" in the sagas:

> On their way back to the ship they noticed three humps on the sandy beach just in from the headland. When they went closer they found that these were three skin-boats [probably moose-hide canoes], with three men under each of them. Thorvald and his men divided forces and captured all of them except one, who escaped in his boat. They killed the other eight and returned to the headland, from which they scanned the surrounding country. They could make out a number of humps farther up the fjord and concluded that these were settlements.
>
> Then they were overwhelmed by such a heavy drowsiness that they could not stay awake, and they all fell asleep—until they were awakened by a voice that shouted, "Wake up, Thorvald, and all your men, if you

want to stay alive! Get to your ship with all your company and get away as fast as you can!"

A great swarm of skin-boats was then heading toward them down the fjord.

Thorvald said, "We shall set up breastworks [i.e., shields] on the gunwales and defend ourselves as best we can, but fight back as little as possible."

They did this. The Skrælings shot at them for a while, and then turned and fled as fast as they could. (60–61)

Without some knowledge of pre-Christian Norse religion and belief patterns, these passages are difficult to comprehend, especially the apparently unmotivated and unprovoked violence by the Norse against the men under the skin-boats.

"Skraelings," a term first used in the 1120s by Ari "the Learned" Thorgilsson to designate "both Amerindians and Eskimo peoples," is a nasty and contemptuous term, meaning something like "little wretches" or "wretches who screech" (Seaver, *The Last Vikings* 62). And even though many nineteenth- and twentieth-century readers of the sagas assumed that the skin-boats referred to the sealskin *umiaks* of the Eskimo and that the Skraelings were an Eskimo group migrating south, it is far more probable that the nine men encountered on the beach were an Algonquian hunting party. Before they developed their lighter and more maneuverable bark canoes, the ancestors of the Eastern Algonquian-speaking peoples of the Canadian Maritime Provinces and New England are known to have constructed canoes of animal skins—usually moose hides—sewn together and stretched over a frame of bent saplings. (Indeed, animal skin canoes for temporary use were still being made by Mi´kmaqs, Maliseets, Passamaquoddies, and Penobscots well into the twentieth century.)[8] "When making long canoe trips," it was a "widespread practice" to turn the canoe upside down and use it "as a shelter at night" (Adney and Chapelle 71). Yet this encounter takes place while there is still light enough for the Norse to scan the surrounding country and see settlements—probably the rounded or conical bark wigwams (the "humps") typical of the Algonquians—"farther up the fjord." It is therefore more likely that the Indians were using the overturned canoes not to sleep under but to conceal themselves, as in a modern-day duck blind.[9] In other words, the Indians were awaiting the approach of game on an exposed sandy beach which offered no other cover.

But while this may explain what the Indians were doing on the beach, it only adds to the puzzle of the Norse response. Since Thorvald, like his brother Leif, appears to have been in the habit of dividing his men into separate exploratory parties (one group using the ship, the other the boat), it isn't clear how many men were with him. Still, the saga gives no hint that the nine Indians posed any obvious or immediate threat. Even so, the Norse may well have feared discovery. After all, they were a relatively small party, they knew little about this new country and nothing of its inhabitants, and they were certainly vulnerable if attacked by larger forces. In trying to kill all the Skraelings, the Norse may have been attempting to prevent news of their presence from getting abroad.

That said, another explanation also presents itself. The pre-Christian Norse inhabited a world of many different creatures who, like trolls and dwarves, could appear to be almost human. One way to distinguish the human from the nonhuman was by the use of an iron (or steel) weapon: A spirit or supernatural being could not be killed by an iron blade, while a human could. So unfamiliar may the Indians have seemed to Thorvald and his crew that the anxious explorers felt the need to test the others' humanity with their swords and knives. Whatever the motivation behind the carnage—and the saga offers none—the killings are followed by more elements that seem at heart folkloric and decidedly pre-Christian. First there is the mysterious sleep that overwhelms Thorvald and his men, and then there is the mysterious voice that warns them of danger.

Scandinavian folklore, legends, and fairy tales are filled with mysterious slumbers that overcome the protagonist. More often than not, these provide occasions for some kind of guardian, as in a dream, to prophesy the future, communicate messages, or warn of impending danger. The pre-Christian Norse believed in a pantheon of gods and goddesses (and other mythic beings) who would sometimes induce such a slumber specifically in order to transmit a warning and protect a favored human. Thus dreams and premonitions in the sagas often set the stage for the scene to follow. Here, as the passages quoted above indicate, one of the Skraelings did escape and has now brought "a great swarm of skin-boats" to destroy or drive off the aggressive newcomers. But because of the mysterious voice that breaks their slumber, Thorvald and his men are awakened in time to defend themselves, with Thorvald attempting to limit the bloodshed ("fight back as little as possible") in order not to make their precarious situation even worse. This ploy apparently works because, after a while, the Skraelings finally withdraw—although for what reason the saga does not comment. (Did they simply exhaust their supply of spears and arrows? Or did their efforts seem futile to them because none of their arrows appeared to have pierced the Norsemen's metal shields?)

At this point, Thorvald inquires if any of his men have been wounded and learns that all are "unhurt" (61). He then reveals that he himself has been mortally wounded. "An arrow flew up between the gunwale and my shield, under my arm.... This will lead to my death" (61). Concerned for his men's safety, he advises them to return to their base camp, Leif's houses, "as soon as possible," but asks first that he be buried at "the headland [he] thought so suitable for a home": "I seem to have hit on the truth when I said that I would settle there for a while. Bury me there and put crosses at my head and feet, and let the place be called *Krossaness* [i.e., Cross Place] for ever afterwards" (61). The body of a high-status individual like Thorvald Eiriksson would not have been left behind under ordinary circumstances. But these are not ordinary circumstances, and Thorvald wants his men to remove themselves from the area as quickly as possible. Yet he could certainly have anticipated that his body might one day be retrieved and taken back to Greenland for proper burial at the Eiriksson farmstead. The crosses would have served as markers in such an eventuality.

Here the saga writer's voice interjects the information that "Greenland had been converted to Christianity by this time, but Eirik the Red had died before the conversion" (61). While this sentence awkwardly interrupts the flow of the narrative, it reasserts the growing hegemony of Christianity in the Nordic world (despite the pagan and pre-Christian elements earlier in the chapter) and both underscores and explains in religious terms Thorvald's burial request. The sentence also dates Thorvald's expedition to well after the year 1000 and relegates the patriarch, Eirik the Red, to a disappearing pagan world.

When Thorvald dies, "his men did exactly as he asked of them," and then they sailed back to their base "and joined the rest of the expedition and exchanged all the news they had to tell" (61). For the third time, Thorvald's crew wintered over in Vinland, gathered "grapes and vines as cargo for the ship," and in the spring returned to Greenland, where they "had plenty of news to tell Leif" (61). Like his brother Leif before him, Thorvald has been shown to be both prudent in judgment and careful for his men's safety. Chapter 5 thus ends, having established Thorvald, like Leif, as brave, curious, enterprising, and a wise leader of men.

Unfortunately, the youngest brother has only a limited opportunity to demonstrate these same traits. In chapter 6, Thorstein Eiriksson—the youngest of Eirik the Red's three sons—attempts his own journey to Vinland, but he is thwarted before he ever gets there. Unlike his older brothers, Thorstein's express purpose for going to Vinland is not exploration but the honorable desire "to fetch back the body of his brother Thorvald" (62). For this purpose, Thorstein readies the same ship used previously by Leif and Thorvald and engages a crew of twenty-five, "the biggest and strongest men available" (62). He brings "his wife Gudrid as well" (62).

In fact, the chapter opens with the information that while Thorvald had been in Vinland, "in Greenland, Thorstein Eiriksson . . . had married Gudrid Thorbjornsdottir, the widow of Thorir," the Norwegian whom Leif had rescued from the reef (along with Thorir's crew and wife, Gudrid) in chapter 4 (61). Upon returning safely to Greenland, Leif had "invited Thorir and his wife Gudrid . . . to stay with him" (59). But "a serious disease broke out among Thorir's crew that winter and Thorir himself . . . died of it" (59). The widowed Gudrid had stayed on at Leif's farm and has now become a member of the Eiriksson family by marrying Thorstein.

Their journey to Vinland is repeatedly thrown off course, however, by bad weather. "Eventually, a week before winter," facing the prospect of even more dangerous winter storms at sea, "they made land . . . in the Western Settlement of Greenland" (62). This was the second major Norse settlement on Greenland, located on the west coast significantly north of the Eastern Settlement where the Eiriksson family held its lands. There, in the Western Settlement, Thorstein "found lodgings for all his crew," while he and Gudrid were invited to spend the winter at the farmstead of Thorstein the Black and his wife, Grimhild.[10] Just before this invitation is proffered, however, the saga again interrupts the narrative flow to note, "At this time, Christianity was still in its infancy in Greenland" (62). That fact is borne out when Thorstein the Black acknowledges, "I am . . . of a different faith from yours, although I consider yours to be better than mine" (62). Even so, Thorstein the Black assures Thorstein Eiriksson, "There is no lack of means to provide for you" (62). The differences in religion notwithstanding, Thorstein Eiriksson and Gudrid decide to accept Thorstein the Black's invitation. "They moved over to his house to stay and were well looked after there" (62).

"Early that winter," though, "disease broke out amongst Thorstein Eiriksson's crew and many of them died. Thorstein ordered coffins to be made for the dead and had the bodies laid out in the ship: 'For I want to have all their bodies brought to Eiriksfjord [part of the Eiriksson family landholdings] in the summer,' he said" (62). Thus, like his older brothers before him, Thorstein Eiriksson also demonstrates caring and a sense of responsibility for his men.

But "not long afterwards the disease spread to Thorstein the Black's house and the first to fall ill was his wife, Grimhild.... Soon Thorstein Eiriksson caught the disease, and for a time the two of them were in bed ill, until Grimhild died" (63). Subsequently, "Thorstein Eiriksson's illness grew worse," and he too died (63). Thorstein the Black tries to comfort and console the grieving Gudrid "and promised that he would take her to Eiriksfjord with her husband's body and the bodies of his crew" (63). And since the two are now the only inhabitants of the house, out of both courtesy and propriety, Thorstein the Black also promises to "bring some more servants here ... for [her] comfort and pleasure" (63).

As happens so often in sagas, scenes of death and dying evoke pre-Christian folkloric elements. In this chapter of *The Greenlanders' Saga*, even after her death, Grimhild appears to be "raising herself on her elbow ... and groping for her shoes" (63). And after his death, "the corpse of Thorstein Eiriksson suddenly sat up and said, 'Where is Gudrid?'" (63). Good Christian that she is, Gudrid is hesitant to respond, but Thorstein the Black has no such reticence and asks, "What is it you want, namesake?" (63). Consistent with old Norse religious beliefs that the spirits of the deceased may animate their dead bodies and prophesy to the living, Thorstein Eiriksson's corpse replies, "I am anxious to tell Gudrid her destiny, so that she may resign herself better to my death, for I have now come to a happy place of repose" (63–64).

The saga has already established Gudrid as a loyal and courageous woman, accompanying her husbands—first Thorir and now Thorstein Eiriksson—on potentially dangerous sea voyages, and chapter 6 further adds to her qualities. After Thorstein Eiriksson and Gudrid accept Thorstein the Black's invitation to winter over with him and his wife, we read, "Gudrid was a woman of striking appearance; she was very intelligent and knew well how to conduct herself amongst strangers" (62). But it is in the dead Thorstein Eiriksson's prophetic foretelling of Gudrid's future destiny that her signal importance and a motivating subtext of *The Greenlanders' Saga* emerges clearly:

> "I have this to say to you, Gudrid: you will marry an Icelander and you will have a long life together and your progeny will be great and vigorous, bright and excellent, sweet and fragrant. You and your husband will go from Greenland to Norway and from there to Iceland, where you will make your home and live for a long time. You will survive your husband and go on a pilgrimage to Rome, then return to your farm in Iceland; a

church will be built there and you will be ordained a nun and stay there until you die." (64)

Having relegated the original patriarch, Eirik the Red, to a dying pagan world in chapter 5 ("Eirik the Red had died before the conversion"), here the saga makes Gudrid the matriarch of the newly emerging Christian world. For, as every Icelander hearing this saga was aware, the "great and vigorous" progeny to whom Gudrid (and her next husband) would give life included three of Iceland's most prominent twelfth-century Catholic bishops. In fact, it is with this genealogy that chapter 9, the last chapter of *The Greenlanders' Saga*, will close. But for now, chapter 6 simply ends by tying up the loose ends of the narrative.

"Thorstein the Black fulfilled all the promises he had made to Gudrid. In the spring, he sold up his farm and livestock, took Gudrid and all her possessions to the ship, made the ship ready, engaged a crew, and then sailed" to the Eiriksson family seat in the Eastern Settlement (64). "Gudrid went to stay with her brother-in-law Leif Eiriksson," while Thorstein the Black made his home nearby "and lived there for the rest of his life" (64).

Despite Thorstein Eiriksson's aborted venture and subsequent death, interest in Vinland continued. Leif's and Thorvald's expeditions had been undertaken for the purposes of exploration and the gathering of valuable commodities like lumber and grapevines. In chapter 7, however, we read about the first known attempt by Europeans to establish a permanent colony in North America. This comes about when a wealthy merchant from Iceland named Thorfinn Karlsefni sails his ship from Norway to Greenland, spends "the winter with Leif Eiriksson," and "quickly fell in love with Gudrid and proposed to her" (64). Following their wedding, the saga tell us, "there was still the same talk about Vinland voyages as before, and everyone, including Gudrid, kept urging Karlsefni to make the voyage. In the end, he decided to sail and gathered a company of sixty men and five women. He made an agreement with his crew that everyone should share equally in whatever profits the expedition might yield. They took livestock of all kinds, for they intended to make a permanent settlement there if possible" (64–65). Leif again agreed to lend "the houses in Vinland," and after a voyage which is not described, we read that Thorfinn Karlsefni's expedition "arrived safe and sound at Leif's Houses" (65).

The expedition was well provisioned, and, soon after their arrival, Karlsefni's company also found "a fine big rorqual," a kind of whale, stranded on the beach, which they cut up, "so there was no shortage of food" (65). They put their livestock "out to grass," which apparently made them unusually "frisky and difficult to manage," including a bull "they had brought . . . with them" (65). "They made use of all the natural resources of the country that were available, grapes and game of all kinds and other produce" (65). And consistent with Karlsefni's plans to establish the economic viability of a permanent settlement, "Karlsefni ordered timber to be felled and cut into lengths for a cargo for the ship, and it was left out on a rock to season" (65). Thus, initially, everything looked promising.

But as "the first winter passed into summer, . . . they had their first encounter with Skrælings" (65). Because the word "Skraeling" served the Norse as a generic term for all the indigenous peoples of North America, including the Eskimoan peoples of the Arctic, there is no way to determine whether these are the same peoples encountered earlier by Thorvald and his crew. The Norse themselves probably didn't know, and the clerics and scribes who wrote down or copied the sagas probably didn't care. All we learn, therefore, is that "a great number of them came out of the wood one day," near where "the cattle were grazing" (65). At this, "the bull began to bellow and roar," which "terrified the Skrælings" (65). The Skraelings flee, "carrying their packs which contained furs and sables and pelts of all kinds. They made for Karlsefni's houses and tried to get inside, but Karlsefni had the doors barred against them" (65). Then, in what is perhaps the saddest line in the entire narrative, the saga states simply, "Neither side could understand the other's language" (65).

Despite the inability of the Norse and the Natives to communicate in words, the purpose of the Skraelings' visit is immediately apparent: they have come to trade. "The Skrælings put down their packs and opened them up and offered their contents, preferably in exchange for weapons; but Karlsefni forbade his men to sell arms. Then he hit on the idea of telling the women to carry milk out to the Skrælings, and when the Skrælings saw the milk they wanted to buy nothing else. And so the outcome of their trading expedition was that the Skrælings carried their purchases away in their bellies, and left their packs and furs with Karlsefni and his men" (65).

For the modern reader, these sentences reveal information of which the medieval Norse could never have been aware. To begin with, the Natives must have been observing the Norse—albeit without alerting the strangers to their presence—so that, by the time the Natives came out of the woods, they had observed enough about the newcomers to know that the Norse would value "furs and sables and pelts of all kinds." The Natives also knew precisely what they hoped to gain in the trade: metal goods and weapons. Sadly, unknown to the Norse, among trade items, "weapons had great symbolic value." For many Algonquian peoples, "the exchange of real or symbolic weapons was an important means of disarming suspicion of evil design or unfriendly intent" (Haviland and Power 214). The refusal of the Norse to trade these items surely raised at least some concerns among the Natives. That said, the Skraelings appear to have happily accepted instead the milk and cheese products offered them by the Norse women. Most likely, the Indians mistook these fatty products for something akin to the fat of game animals so prized in the otherwise low-fat diet of the ancient Indians. What neither the Norse nor the Natives could have known, however, is that these milk-based (rather than animal fat–based) delicacies would soon cause painful cramps and other digestive system discomforts in the lactose-intolerant Indians. Of course, *The Greenlanders' Saga* never hints at any of this.

Karlsefni, though, recognized that the Skraelings represented a potential threat to his little settlement. After the Skraelings depart, he "ordered a strong wooden palisade to be erected round the houses, and they settled in" (66). Then we read about the first European known to have been born in North America: "About this time Karlsefni's wife, Gudrid, gave birth to a son, and he was named Snorri" (66).

Early the next winter—the colony's second winter in Vinland—"the Skrælings returned, in much greater numbers this time, bringing with them the same kind of wares as before" (66). Karlsefni tells the women to "carry out to them the same produce [that is, milk and cheese] that was most in demand last time, and nothing else" (66). When the Skraelings saw this, "they threw their packs in over the palisade" (66).

The passage that follows takes us back to Gudrid. It is a passage that continues to stir scholarly debate about its many possible meanings.

> Gudrid was sitting in the doorway beside the cradle of her son Snorri when a shadow fell across the door and a woman entered wearing a black, close-fitting tunic; she was rather short and had a band round her chestnut-coloured hair. She was pale, and had the largest eyes that have ever been seen in any human head. She walked up to Gudrid and said, "What is your name?"
>
> "My name is Gudrid. What is yours?"
>
> "My name is Gudrid," the woman replied.
>
> Then Gudrid, Karlsefni's wife, motioned to the woman to come and sit beside her; but at that very moment she heard a great crash and the woman vanished, and in the same instant a Skræling was killed by one

of Karlsefni's men for trying to steal some weapons. The Skrælings fled as fast as they could, leaving their clothing and wares behind. No one had seen the woman except Gudrid. (66)

Is the woman with "chestnut-coloured hair" an apparition? That is, is she a kind of doppelgänger from the Scandinavian folklore tradition, whose visitation is interrupted by "a great crash" and the simultaneous killing of a Skraeling "by one of Karlsefni's men"? The woman's statement that her name, too, is Gudrid, combined with her silent entrance and her equally mysterious sudden disappearance, suggest a doppelgänger apparition or some sort of protective spirit who arrives at a moment of crisis. On the other hand, might this be a Native woman? Given the rest of the little colony's fixed attentiveness to the Skraelings attempting to trade their pelts, a single Native woman might well have entered the palisaded compound unseen and, amid all the noise, silently slipped away. Unable to understand the Norse language, her response, "My name is Gudrid," might simply record the not-uncommon act of repeating what she has just heard as a gesture of communication. Linguists know that in situations where there is no common language, the repetition of one party's speech by the other usually signifies a kind of mimicry intended to convey the desire to communicate. The lines here have some of that same quality.

The details of the woman's appearance do not definitively identify her. Her hair color could be either Native or Norse, and women from both cultures wore garments that resembled tunics. The "band round her chestnut-coloured hair" is similarly ambiguous. Norse and Native women alike wore various kinds of bands around their hair, and the word in the original sources for this saga can also correctly be translated as "shawl" (see Kunz 647). At first reading, the strange woman's pale skin and unusually large eyes seem to tilt toward her identity as a spirit being. But if such a moment as depicted in this scene ever really occurred, then it is wholly possible that some original oral source was awkwardly trying to convey Europeans' first impressions of a people never before encountered. In the view of the Norse, these people may well have seemed to have unusually large dark eyes, while their skin—unlike that of the North African peoples earlier encountered by the Vikings—appeared no differently hued than their own. Since some medieval Norse geographers believed Vinland to be connected to Africa, the light skin color of its Natives would have been both noteworthy and a surprise. And, in fact, many of the Europeans who later explored the northeast coasts of North America frequently described the Indians' skin color as pale or like their own.[11]

Clearly, though, whatever the identity of the strange woman, Gudrid appears not to have felt threatened, showed no fear either for herself or for her son, and invited the woman "to come and sit beside her." And this may be precisely the point of the passage. The excellent Gudrid, mother of Snorri and, through him, the progenitor of some of Iceland's most important future bishops, is a kind of serene ideal, fearless and always composed and gracious even in the midst of chaos and altercations going on around her. If, in fact, it is this thematic element that the saga writer (or some later redactor) hoped to emphasize in the scene, then the particular identity of the strange woman was irrelevant. Only her strangeness was of interest. In that case, there exists at least one tantalizing possible explanation for why the scene reads so ambiguously: it is really a hybrid. In other words, we may have in this scene a faint trace of a brief first encounter between a Norse woman and a Native woman, but an encounter so incomprehensible to those who later told or wrote down the story that they turned it into something with which they *were* familiar: the folklore of apparitions and doppelgängers rather than the fledgling attempt of two women from different cultures to communicate.

In stark contrast to this brief interlude—and, ironically, underscoring the lack of communication between the two peoples—the Skraelings and the Norse come to blows. Again, there is no way to know if these Skraelings are members of the same group as those who had visited the colony the previous summer. News of the colony and its interest in trading for pelts would certainly have been circulated widely through Native trade networks and seasonal gatherings. And what appeared to the Norse as an attempt "to steal some weapons" may really have been, on the part of the Indians, only an attempt to examine some potential trade items with great symbolic meaning. We cannot know. All we know is that, again, "a Skræling was killed" by a Norseman. The Skraelings flee, and based on what he knows of Thorvald's earlier experience, Karlsefni correctly anticipates that the Skraelings "will pay us a third visit, and this time with hostility and in greater numbers" (66). He therefore devises a plan to lure the Skraelings into a clearing "when the Skrælings come out of the forest" and ambush them there. He also hopes to intimidate the Natives by keeping the colony's bellowing bull "to the fore" (66).

Karlsefni's plan works, "and the Skrælings came right to the place that Karlsefni had chosen for the battle. The fighting began, and many of the Skrælings were killed" (67). Then one intriguing moment from the battle is recounted in some detail:

68 Chapter Two

> There was one tall and handsome man among the Skrælings and Karlsefni reckoned that he must be their leader. One of the Skrælings had picked up an axe, and after examining it for a moment he swung it at a man standing beside him, who fell dead at once. The tall man then took hold of the axe, looked at it for a moment, and then threw it as far as he could out into the water. Then the Skrælings fled into the forest as fast as they could, and that was the end of the encounter. (67)

This brief narrative glimpse suggests several things at once. First, despite the pejorative and demeaning implications of the term "Skraeling," the Norse did not necessarily perceive the Natives as physically unattractive. As would later European explorers, Karlsefni characterizes one man as "tall and handsome." Second, Karlsefni may have been in error when he suspected the Skraelings of coveting Norse weapons for evil purposes. The Native who kills his fellow tribesman with the axe seems not to have recognized the axe *as* a weapon, that is, as something that *could* kill. At this point, the Natives may have observed the Norse using axes only for felling trees, not as weapons. Conceivably, what fascinated and attracted the Natives was the hardness of the metal—aside from copper, a material unknown to them—rather than the potentially lethal use of these implements. If that is plausible, then this entire battle is laced with a tragic irony because it was precipitated by the killing of a Skraeling who was thought to be "trying to steal some weapons." Given the absence of any kind of cross-cultural understanding or communication between the two groups, it is entirely possible that the Native was examining what he viewed as a potential new trade item, and the Norse wholly misinterpreted what they thought they were seeing. Third and last, the scene suggests that the "tall and handsome man," whom Karlsefni judges to be a leader of sorts, decides that the strange object is more dangerous to his people than valuable. And so he throws what was probably an iron- or steel-bladed axe "as far as he could out into the water."[12] He may even have feared that, in its strangeness, the unfamiliar hard metal carried some kind of threatening power or malicious spirit.

Finally, the Skraelings flee the battleground, and the Norse colony spends its third and last winter in Vinland. Presumably because Karlsefni has recognized the colony's vulnerability in the face of a potentially large and hostile Native population (though the saga does not explicitly state his motivation), "in the spring he announced that he had no wish to stay there any longer and wanted to return to Greenland" (67). The cargo with which Karlsefni returned included timber and grapevines, the same kind of cargo as had been gathered previously by Leif's and Thorvald's expeditions. But Karlsefni's ship also carried the fruits of their trade with the Natives of Vinland. As the saga makes clear, they "took with them much valuable produce, vines and grapes and pelts" (67).

Chapter 8 opens with the statement, "Now there was renewed talk of voyaging to Vinland, for these expeditions were considered a good source of fame and fortune" (67). Obviously, the potential threat posed by the Native population has not dissuaded some individuals from further expeditions, although there is no longer any suggestion of attempting a permanent colony. In this, the penultimate chapter, the individual who initiates the last of the Vinland voyages described in *The Greenlanders' Saga* is Freydis, daughter of Eirik the Red. She proposes to partner with "two brothers called Helgi and Finnbogi . . . Icelanders by birth," whose large merchant ship "arrived in Greenland from Norway" the same summer "that Karlsefni returned from Vinland" (67). Freydis asks Helgi and Finnbogi to "join her with their ship on an expedition to Vinland, sharing equally with her all the profits that might be made. . . . They agreed to this" (67). Freydis then approached "her brother Leif and asked him to give her the houses he had built in Vinland; but Leif gave the same answer as before—that he was willing to lend them but not to give them away" (67).

The saga next makes clear that, unlike her brothers, Freydis is not a person of her word. "The two brothers and Freydis had an agreement that each party should have thirty able-bodied men on board, besides women. But Freydis broke the agreement at once by taking five more men, whom she concealed; and the brothers were unaware of this until they reached Vinland" (67–68). Once arrived in Vinland, Freydis continued to break the terms of her agreement with the two brothers, including barring them and their crew from sharing Leif's houses as their quarters. "We brothers could never be a match for you in wickedness," responds Helgi (68). The two brothers move "their possessions out and built themselves a house farther inland on the bank of a lake, and made themselves comfortable there. Meanwhile Freydis was having timber felled for her cargo" (68).

"When winter set in" and many of the expedition's exploratory and gathering activities slowed down for a time, "the brothers suggested that they should start holding games and other entertainments" (68). But after a while "trouble broke out and ill-feeling arose between the two parties. The games were abandoned and all visiting between the houses ceased" (68). Freydis's wicked machinations did not cease, however. "Early one morning," fully dressed but without her shoes on,

Freydis walks through the "heavy dew outside," makes her way to the two brothers' dwelling, and has a conversation with Finnbogi. Freydis explains the reason for her visit: "I want to exchange ships with you and your brother, for your ship is larger than mine and I want to go away from here" (69). To this, Finnbogi agrees, saying, "'If that will make you happy.' With that they parted" (69).

But as it turns out, Freydis had another motive altogether for her shoeless walk in the early morning dew. "When she climbed into bed her feet were cold and her husband Thorvard woke up and asked why she was so cold and wet. She answered with great indignation, 'I went over to see the brothers to offer to buy their ship, because I want a larger one; and this made them so angry that they struck me and handled me very roughly'" (69). This statement initiates a goading speech not uncommon in Norse sagas, except for the fact that in most goading scenes where a woman is the speaker, her goal is to incite friends or kin to carry out blood vengeance or otherwise seek recompense for an insult to her own or her family's honor.[13] Here, by contrast, Freydis dishonors herself by lying in order to goad her husband into what turns out to be nothing short of the slaughter of innocents: "You, you wretch, would never avenge either my humiliation or your own. I realize now how far I am away from my home in Greenland! And unless you avenge this, I am going to divorce you" (69).

In those few sentences, Freydis is essentially accusing her husband of cowardice and reminding him that he has married into the powerful Eiriksson family, a chieftain's family, and a family that certainly would avenge an assault on the honor of any of its members. And her threat of divorce, which would prove a further humiliation to Thorvard, is no idle threat. At this period, Icelandic law decreed that a woman had equal rights in marriage and could obtain a divorce simply by declaration.[14] Thorvard neither challenges nor questions Freydis about her accusations, thus confirming the earlier statement in chapter 2 that he "was rather feeble" (52).

Unable to "bear her taunts" any longer, Thorvard orders "his men to get up at once and take their weapons" (69). They break into Helgi and Finnbogi's longhouse "while all the men were asleep, seized them, and tied them up, and dragged them outside, one by one. Freydis had each of them put to death as soon as he came out" (69). This dispatches the two brothers and their crew of "thirty able-bodied men," but the women servants who have been brought along to attend to domestic chores yet remain. "Soon only the women were left; but no one was willing to kill them" (69). Then, in an act of unbridled cruelty rarely enacted by women in Norse sagas, "Freydis said, 'Give me an axe.' This was done, and she herself killed the women, all five of them" (69). The saga's narrative voice, usually reticent about expressing judgment, characterizes Freydis's actions as "this monstrous deed" (69). In a sense, one thematic trajectory of *The Greenlanders' Saga* has now come full circle. Freydis's "monstrous deed" repeats the earlier murders by her father, Eirik the Red, for which Eirik was sentenced to outlawry and banished from Iceland (that is, banished from civilized society). Such banishments forced the outlaw into remote areas, sometimes called "the wild places" by the Norse. Freydis has now turned the promising Vinland itself into another "wild place," and with that act, the Eiriksson family's contacts with Vinland cease entirely. For the Church-trained clerics who committed the saga to writing, there must surely have been in all this an echo of the biblical garden also desecrated and abandoned through the deeds of a woman.

For her part, however, "Freydis thought she had been very clever" and simply wants to silence any word of the massacre (69). "She said to her companions, 'If we ever manage to get back to Greenland I shall have anyone killed who breathes a word about what has just happened. Our story will be that these people stayed on here when we left'" (70). In the early spring, Freydis and her crew prepare "the ship that had belonged to the brothers"—presumably using her five extra crew members to sail her own, smaller ship—"and loaded it with all the produce they could get and the ship could carry" (70). After "a good voyage," they reach Greenland "early in the summer" (70). "Karlsefni was still there when they arrived . . . waiting for a favourable wind" (70). The closing sentence of chapter 8 underscores again the riches of Vinland that has now been abandoned. "It is said that no ship has ever sailed from Greenland more richly laden than the one Karlsefni commanded" (70).

Chapter 9, the final chapter of *The Greenlanders' Saga*, metes out the saga's version of justice. Karlsefni, Gudrid, and their progeny prosper, while Freydis's progeny do not. First, the narrative deals with Freydis's punishment. She returns to her farm in Greenland and "loaded all her companions with money, for she wanted them to keep her crimes secret" (70). "But her companions were not all discreet enough to say nothing about these evil crimes and . . . eventually word reached the ears of her brother Leif, who thought it a hideous story" (70). Leif declares that he doesn't have the heart "to punish [his] sister Freydis as she deserves," but he predicts "'that her descendants will never prosper.' And after that no one thought anything but ill of her and her

72 Chapter Two

family" (70). Thus condemned both by her own brother and by the details of her crimes "becoming known," Freydis and her family lose both reputation and status.

The chapter then turns to its main subjects, Thorfinn Karlsefni, his wife, Gudrid, and their progeny. After Karlsefni left Greenland, he sailed his ship to Norway, where he sold the valuable cargo brought from Vinland. He and Gudrid spend the winter in Norway, where they "were made much of by the noblest in the country. Next spring he prepared his ship for the voyage to Iceland" (70). The narrative then digresses briefly and, whether intentionally or otherwise, hints at the distribution of Vinland artifacts beyond Scandinavia. Just before his ship is ready to leave Norway for Iceland, Karlsefni is approached by a German—"a man from Bremen, in Saxony"—who offers him a handsome sum of gold to purchase a decoratively carved gable-head (70). These were used on the gables of Norse houses and sometimes also on the prows of ships. Although Karlsefni is not particularly eager to sell the carving, he "thought this a good offer," and "the bargain was struck" (71). The saga never makes clear whether the man from Bremen values the piece for the excellence of its carving or for its unusual (and perhaps unfamiliar) wood. The saga only states that "Karlsefni did not know what kind of wood it was made from," but adds, "It was maple, and had come from Vinland" (71).[15]

The rest of this closing chapter plays out in greater detail the destiny previously prophesied for Gudrid in chapter 6 by the spirit of her deceased former husband, Thorstein Eiriksson. Karlsefni settled permanently in Iceland, purchased land, "farmed there for the rest of his life, and was considered a man of great stature. Many people of high standing are descended from him and his wife Gudrid" (71). "After Karlsefni's death Gudrid and her son Snorri, who had been born in Vinland, took over the farm. When Snorri married, Gudrid went abroad on a pilgrimage to Rome; when she returned to her son's farm he had built a church [there]. . . . After that Gudrid became a nun and stayed there as an anchoress for the rest of her life" (71).

What follows is a genealogy of the descendants of Karlsefni and Gudrid. The saga scholar and historian Byock points out that rather than serving as merely "antiquarian flourishes," these genealogies were a standard and functional feature of almost all the sagas, "contributing to the social configuration of specific acts of advocacy and obligation" that governed medieval Icelandic society (*Feud in the Icelandic Saga* 69). Genealogies were thus essential "components of a traditional store of information" that covered everything from establishing ancestry to providing evidence in "famous court cases" to "the passing of land from one family to another" (*Feud in the Icelandic Saga* 60). In this particular genealogy, we learn that, in addition to their "son Snorri, who had been born in Vinland, . . . Karlsefni and Gudrid had another son, who was called Bjorn" (71–72). The main point, however, is that Snorri and Bjorn both beget lines that, between them, produce three prominent twelfth-century Icelandic bishops, each of whom is named in the text. As if this weren't impressive enough, the text adds, "A great many people are descended from Karlsefni; he has become the ancestor of a prolific line" (72).

It is thus Karlsefni rather than Leif who—at least symbolically—inherits the patrimony from Eirik through his marriage to Gudrid. In other words, Karlsefni and Gudrid—daughter-in-law to Eirik the Red through her earlier marriage to Thorstein Eiriksson—in effect regenerate Eirik's line. Together, Karlsefni and Gudrid produce the future generations of those who will be both "people of high standing" and also pillars of the Catholic Church in Iceland. As a result, *The Greenlanders' Saga* turns out not to pay homage only to Eirik the Red and his descendants on Greenland, but also to those who succeeded them and returned to Iceland. The last sentence in the saga perhaps explains why: "It was Karlsefni himself who told more fully than anyone else the story of all these voyages, which has been to some extent recorded here" (72). Karlsefni is the authority who establishes the saga's veracity, but he—and presumably at least some of his descendants—are also the interested parties who surely influenced the particular shape and emphasis of the saga when it was finally committed to writing.

Whether read aloud or recited from memory, oral storytelling was a favorite pastime both on Icelandic farmsteads and at the Norwegian court. The recitation of sagas was also a staple of the gatherings for both local things and the national Althing. Encouraged by the Church as a wholesome form of entertainment, intended to replace dancing (of which the Church disapproved), the sagas thus easily entered the realm of serious secular literature. Although *The Greenlanders' Saga*, as a work of literature, is "fairly unsophisticated," it was nonetheless "entertaining, in that it was a good yarn about people of heroic stature and spectacular achievement. It was educational, in that it was a form of popular history and geography. It was also edifying, in that it told the story of the ancestor (Thorfinn Karlsefni) of three of the bishops of the twelfth century. . . . And at the same time it retained much of the vigorous coarse-grained pagan nature of popular folk tale—the ghostly voice that warns the sleeping explorers of imminent attack" by Skraelings in chapter 5, for example, or "the blood-thirsty atrocities committed by Freydis" in chapter 8 (Magnusson and Pálsson 37–38).

Eirik the Red's Saga, the more self-consciously artful of the two Vinland sagas, is also an entertainingly "good yarn." But it diverges from *The Greenlanders' Saga* in some significant ways. As the archaeologist Birgitta Linderoth Wallace has noted, "The major difference between the *Greenlanders' Saga* and *Erik the Red's Saga* is that the four successful expeditions described in the *Greenlanders' Saga* . . . have been combined into one in *Erik the Red's Saga*. . . . Thorfinn Karlsefni has assumed Leif Eriksson's role as the actual explorer, the major expedition leader, and the person who names Helluland and Markland. Leif has been reduced to the accidental discoverer and does not figure in the expeditions at all" ("An Archaeologist's Interpretation" 225). There are other differences as well. For example, the emphasis on the importance of Thorfinn Karlsefni and his wife, Gudrid, in *Eirik the Red's Saga* is even more pronounced than it is in *The Greenlanders' Saga*. Indeed, in some editions, the saga was actually called *The Saga of Thorfinn Karlsefni*. Also, in *Eirik the Red's Saga*, Gudrid is given a role unusual for women in the sagas generally. Her life story virtually structures the saga. Additionally, the struggle between Christianity and the Old Norse belief system is more obvious than in *The Greenlanders' Saga*, and Thorvald Eiriksson dies not from an arrow shot by a Skraeling but from an arrow shot by a Uniped (a one-legged being). What has not changed is the depiction of Vinland as "the good land."

This saga survives in two versions in two different vellum manuscripts, both based on the same original, now lost. The older of these vellum manuscripts is *Hauksbók*, "a large codex of sagas and learned writings which was compiled in Iceland early in the fourteenth century by Hauk Erlendsson the Lawman, who shared the work of transcription with his two secretaries" (Magnusson and Pálsson 30). As Magnusson and Pálsson note in their introduction, Hauk Erlendsson "had a special interest in *Eirik's Saga*, for he himself was descended from [Gudrid and] Thorfinn Karlsefni" (31). For that reason, Magnusson and Pálsson continue, "he inserted additional genealogical material . . . and made several slight alterations designed to add further lustre to his ancestor's fame" (31). More faithful to the lost original *Eirik the Red's Saga*, however, is the version found in *Skálholtsbók*, "a codex dating from the late fifteenth century"; it is therefore on this *Skálholtsbók* text that Magnusson and Pálsson have based their translation (see 30–31). In the summary that follows, all quotations are again from the translation by Magnusson and Pálsson.

Eirik the Red's Saga

Scholars who study the full corpus of the medieval Icelandic sagas repeatedly observe that "it is rare to find a saga that is wholly devoted to women," and then add that *Eirik the Red's Saga* is "unusual in this respect" (Tómasson 135).[16] Such comments derive from the fact that, despite its title, *Eirik the Red's Saga* puts Gudrid on center stage from the outset. This is not immediately apparent, however, because the saga's opening chapter focuses on a Viking queen named Aud the Deep-Minded and, secondarily, on her bondsman named Vifil. Vifil is a man "of noble descent" from the British Isles who, like many other "well-born men, . . . had been taken captive in the British Isles by Vikings and were" made slaves or bondsmen by their Viking captors (75–76). Vifil is one of several male slaves owned by Aud the Deep-Minded.

Aud is the wife of the "warrior king called Olaf the White, who . . . went on a Viking expedition to the British Isles, where he conquered Dublin and the adjoining territory and made himself king over them" (75). But "Olaf was killed in battle in Ireland," and, not long after, Olaf and Aud's son, who had conquered and ruled over much of Scotland, was himself "betrayed by the Scots and killed in battle." At this turn of events, Aud the Deep-Minded made her escape from Britain. She sailed first to Orkney and then "set out for Iceland," where her brother lived (75). Soon enough, "she took possession" of considerable landholdings in Iceland "and made her home at Hvamm" (75). As one of the earliest settlers in Iceland, Aud the Deep-Minded arrived well before Iceland officially adopted Christianity. Yet the saga tells us, "She used to say prayers at Kross Hills; she had crosses erected there, for she had been baptized [presumably by priests in Dublin] and was a devout Christian" (75). The clear implication is that Aud the Deep-Minded, like many other Vikings, had been converted while in the British Isles and brought the new religion with her to Iceland.

We then learn that, upon arriving in Iceland, Aud the Deep-Minded "granted [Vifil] his freedom," told him "that he would be considered a man of quality wherever he was," and gave him land (76). Vifil, now a freed man, settles on his land (called Vifilsdale), marries, and has two sons, "both promising men" (76). Subsequently, the lineage that is outlined in some detail in chapter 3 is Vifil's and reveals that Gudrid is the daughter of Thorbjorn Vifilsson, one of Vifil's "promising" sons.

In between is chapter 2, which finally introduces Eirik the Red. In large measure, chapter 2 covers much of the same material that appears in the first chapter of *The Greenlanders' Saga*: Eirik's lineage, his removal from Norway to Iceland, and, in greater detail, the several feuds and killings that finally precipitated his banishment. The chapter also describes Eirik's discovery of, exploration of, and decision to settle in Greenland. But it adds the information that a man named Thorbjorn Vifilsson was one of Eirik's strongest supporters in the feud that finally led to Eirik's banishment. The two "parted in great friendship; Eirik said he would return [Thorbjorn Vifilsson's] help as far as it lay within his power, if ever [Thorbjorn] had need of it" (77). Then Eirik tells Thorbjorn (and other supporters) that he now intends "to search for the land" that another Icelander had sighted earlier "when he was driven westwards off course" (77). Eirik "added that he would come back to visit his friends if he found this country" (77). Of course, as in *The Greenlanders' Saga*, Eirik does find the new land to the west, determines "to colonize the country he had discovered," and decides to name it "*Greenland*, for he said that people would be much more tempted to go there if it had an attractive name" (78).

With chapter 3, though, Eirik is mentioned only in passing, while Gudrid's life story continues. We learn that Gudrid's father, Thorbjorn Vifilsson, is "a man of considerable stature; he was a chieftain and ran a large farm" (78). Gudrid's mother's lineage is also given, and it is clear that she is the daughter of a prominent family and brought considerable land with her to the marriage (see Kunz 655). Gudrid herself is described as "very beautiful and a most exceptional woman in every respect" (78). The narrative then tells us that Gudrid is "rather particular about her husbands, and so is her father," which is why she has not yet married, despite many suitors (79). Most important in chapter 3, we learn the circumstances that bring Gudrid from Iceland to Greenland. These circumstances differ radically from those in *The Greenlanders' Saga*. In *Eirik the Red's Saga*, there is no mention of a first marriage to the Norwegian merchant Thorir and no rescue by Leif Eiriksson from a reef off Greenland. Instead, in *Eirik the Red's Saga*, Gudrid's father finds himself "in financial difficulties." As a consequence, he explains, "I have decided to take up the offer that my friend Eirik the Red made to me when we took leave of one another.... I intend to go to Greenland this summer" (80). Thorbjorn Vifilsson then "sold up his lands and bought a ship.... Thirty people decided to go with him to Greenland; among them were ... Thorbjorn's friends who did not want to part from him" (80). They have a difficult voyage, beset by bad weather and disease, and finally "made land" in Greenland "right at the beginning of winter" (81). "A capable and worthy" farmer "invited Thorbjorn and all his crew to stay for the whole winter, and treated them with great hospitality. Thorbjorn and all his crew liked it there" (81). In retrospect, the previous chapter, chapter 2, now seems really to have been less about Eirik the Red than about establishing the connection between Eirik and Gudrid's father, a connection that eventually introduces Gudrid into the Eiriksson family.

Given how most sagas are organized, there are two glaring oddities in this structure. First, the saga begins with the ancestry of a woman, Gudrid, rather than its eponymous hero, Eirik the Red. Eirik's family history does not appear until chapter 2, where it is rather unceremoniously sandwiched between the continuing history of Gudrid and her family in chapters 1 and 3. Second, the saga opens with the Viking warrior-king Olaf the White and his wife, Aud the Deep-Minded, neither of whom has any blood or family relationship either to Gudrid or to Eirik. But Aud the Deep-Minded *is* responsible for recognizing the superior qualities of her slave, Vifil, Gudrid's grandfather, freeing him, giving him land in Iceland, and thus making possible the line that he will father. In a sense, then, Aud the Deep-Minded is also responsible for Gudrid's very existence. She is a kind of symbolic foremother whose attributes—especially her courage and her devotion to her faith—foreshadow those of the "exceptional" Gudrid.[17] Thus the saga's structure, from the very beginning, foreshadows whose life story really organizes the whole.

Chapter 4 continues the story of Gudrid's life in Greenland. Gudrid, her father, and those who came with them have arrived during a period of "severe famine in Greenland" (81). In an effort "to find out when the current hardships would come to an end," the wealthy farmer who had invited Thorbjorn Vifilsson and his company to spend the winter asks a local sybil, or prophetess, "to his house" (81). The details of the preparations to receive the prophetess, her dress, demeanor, and the divining ritual itself, have all been of enormous interest to scholars. This is one of the few extant descriptions of a pre-Christian Scandinavian spiritual ritual performed by a recognized seeress. For the purposes of this study, however, what is significant in these scenes is Gudrid's reluctant participation in the ritual and the sybil's foretelling of Gudrid's destiny.

With the preparations for beginning the ritual complete, the sybil "asked for the assistance of women who knew the spells needed for performing" it (82). No one comes forward. "Then Gudrid said, 'I am neither a sorceress nor a witch, but when I was in Iceland my foster-mother [i.e., an affectionate neighbor and her husband, with whom Gudrid sometimes lived] . . . taught me spells'" (82). But Gudrid also

78   Chapter Two

protests, "This is the sort of knowledge and ceremony that I want nothing to do with ... for I am a Christian" (82). The sybil replies that Gudrid "could be of help to others" by participating "and not be any worse a woman for that" (83). The farmer who is hosting the sybil also "now brought pressure on Gudrid, and she consented to do as he wished" (83). The other women in the room "formed a circle round the ritual platform" on which the sybil was seated. "Then Gudrid sang the songs so well and beautifully that those present were sure they had never heard lovelier singing. The prophetess thanked her for the song" (83). Gudrid's singing has "charmed" the spirits which are now "present," says the sybil: "Now many things stand revealed to me" (83). The sybil assures everyone that "this famine will not last much longer, and that conditions will improve with the spring; and the epidemic which has persisted for so long will abate sooner than expected" (83). The sybil then turns to Gudrid, saying, "I shall reward you at once for the help you have given us, for I can see your whole destiny with great clarity now. You will make a most distinguished marriage here in Greenland, but it will not last for long, for your paths all lead to Iceland; there you will start a great and eminent family line, and over your progeny there shall shine a bright light" (83). The text then tells us "there were few things that did not turn out as she prophesied" (83).

True to the sybil's words, "the weather quickly improved as spring approached," thereby allowing Thorbjorn Vifilsson to make "his ship ready" and sail to the Greenland settlement where Eirik the Red resided (83). Eirik "welcomed him with open arms" and invited Thorbjorn and his family to stay with him "the following winter" (83–84). The next spring, "Eirik gave Thorbjorn land ... ; Thorbjorn built a good house there, and lived there from then on" (84). In sum, then, chapter 4 allows us to see Gudrid's devotion to her faith, a devotion tempered by the Christian ideal of helping others, even if this entails a pagan prophecy ritual. The chapter also makes clear how Gudrid came to be known by Eirik the Red and his family, a connection that will culminate in her "distinguished marriage" to Eirik's son Thorstein in chapter 6.

We first meet Thorstein in chapter 5, the same chapter in which Leif discovers Vinland, though this fact is given scant attention by the text. Clearly, the author of *Eirik the Red's Saga* wanted to emphasize other things in the chapter. Thus, the two central subjects of chapter 5 are the conversion of Greenland to Catholicism, here attributed to Leif Eiriksson, and the many superior qualities of Leif's brother Thorstein Eiriksson, the man who will marry Gudrid. Chapter 5 opens with the information that "Eirik was married to a woman named Thjodhild, and had two sons," Thorstein and Leif, "both promising young men" (84). There is no mention of a younger son named Thorvald or a daughter named Freydis, even though both appear in subsequent chapters related to the Vinland colony. Some scholars have interpreted the omission of their names in chapter 5 as a signal that both were illegitimate; in one of the extant sources for *Eirik the Red's Saga*, there is persuasive textual evidence for this interpretation (see *Eirik the Red's Saga* 84, n. 1 and 93, n. 5). In terms of the chapter's real interests, however, more to the point is the fact that the opening describes Thorstein as follows: "No one in Greenland at that time was considered so promising" (84). The chapter thus begins the process of establishing Thorstein as an appropriate marriage partner for a woman "rather particular about her husbands."

First, however, the chapter turns to the adventures of Leif Eiriksson. We learn that "Leif had sailed to Norway, where he stayed with King Olaf Tryggvason" (84). But before reaching Norway, Leif's ship had been "driven off course to the Hebrides," where he and his men remained "most of the summer . . . waiting for favourable winds" (84). While in the Hebrides, "Leif fell in love with a woman called Thorgunna . . . of noble birth . . . [and] a woman of unusual knowledge" (84). As Leif is about to depart the Hebrides and resume his journey to Norway, Thorgunna reveals that she is pregnant with Leif's child and has "a premonition that [she] shall give birth to a son" (84). She says, "I intend to bring the boy up and send him to you in Greenland as soon as he can travel with others" (84). Leif departs the Hebrides after giving Thorgunna valuable gifts, including a gold ring, and the saga notes that when Thorgunna's son "later arrived in Greenland, . . . Leif acknowledged him as his son" (85). Most medieval Icelanders would have recognized in this episode a reference to the full story of Thorgunna and her son as elaborated in another saga, *Eyrbyggia Saga*.[18] *Eirik the Red's Saga* does not retell that story, however, instead returning to the story of Leif at "the court of King Olaf Tryggvason," who entrusts Leif "with a mission . . . to preach Christianity in Greenland" (85).

Leif accepted what the king commanded, "but added that in his opinion this mission would be difficult to accomplish in Greenland. The King replied that he could think of no one better fitted for it than him—'and your good luck will see you through'" (85). In *Eirik the Red's Saga*, it is during Leif's return to Greenland on this Christianizing mission that he discovers and explores "lands whose existence he had never suspected" (85–86). Unlike *The Greenlanders' Saga*, there is no suggestion here of any previous discovery by Bjarni Herjolfsson, nor is there any extended description of the land itself. All the saga tells us is "There were fields of wild wheat growing there, and vines, and among the trees there were maples. They took some samples of all these things" (86). The narrative juxtaposition of King Olaf's commission to Leif and Leif's subsequent discovery of new lands effectively links Vinland to an enlarging Christian world, a linkage that did not go unnoticed by nineteenth-century Americans seeking evidence of a Christianized Viking heritage.

That the historical record does not clearly substantiate the saga's assertion that Leif brought Christianity to Greenland is beside the point (see Magnusson and Pálsson 32–33). Within the context of the saga, *this* act—rather than his discovery and exploration of Vinland—constitutes Leif's heroism. Indeed, as the saga tries to suggest in the next sentences, Leif's heroism is expressed in and through his Christian "magnanimity and goodness" (86). Continuing his journey back to Greenland, "Leif came across some shipwrecked seamen and brought them home with him and gave them all hospitality throughout the winter. He showed great magnanimity and goodness by bringing Christianity to the country and by rescuing these men; he was known as Leif the Lucky" (86). The saga's religious subtext then continues as we read that, upon returning to Greenland, Leif "at once began preaching Christianity and the Catholic faith throughout the country . . . telling [people] what excellence and what glory there was in this faith" (86).

Leif's father, Eirik the Red, "was reluctant to abandon his old religion; but his wife, Thjodhild, was converted at once, and she had a church built not too close to the farmstead" (86). She also now refuses to sleep with the unconverted Eirik, "and this angered him greatly" (86). Like Thjodhild, however, "many others . . . accepted Christianity" (86).

"There was now much talk of going to search for this country that Leif had discovered." The leader in this is Leif's "brother, Thorstein Eiriksson, a well-informed and popular man" (87). Eirik the Red is approached to join the expedition, but again, as in *The Greenlanders' Saga*, a fall from his horse (which Eirik now interprets as punishment for his having tried to conceal some "gold and silver") dissuades him. Under Thorstein Eiriksson's leadership, then, a crew of twenty sets out in "the ship that Thorbjorn Vifilsson had brought to Iceland" (87). "But they ran into prolonged difficulties and were unable to reach the seas they wanted" (87). Finally, storm-tossed and "worn out by exposure and toil," Thorstein and his men "turned back towards Greenland" (87). In keeping with the chapter's aim of presenting Thorstein well, we then read Thorstein's appeal to his father, Eirik the Red, that "it would be a noble gesture to provide for all those [crew members] who are now without resources, and find them lodgings for the winter" (89). Eirik agrees, and "all those who had nowhere to stay went ashore and went home with Eirik and his son" (88). So ends chapter 5.

Having now established Thorstein Eiriksson as a good and worthy man, in chapter 6 the saga announces his marriage to Gudrid. "The wedding-feast was well attended and was a great success" (88). The newly married couple move to a farm that Thorstein co-owns with another man, also named Thorstein, and his wife Sigrid. "Early in the winter," however, "disease broke out at the farm," and with the ensuing deaths, folkloric elements again enter the narrative. Many in the area begin to die from the unnamed disease and, in time, both "Thorstein Eiriksson and Sigrid, the wife of his namesake, fell ill" (88). Sigrid has a vision in which she sees all those who have already died and, with them, she tells Gudrid, "your husband Thorstein . . . and I can also see myself" (89). True to her vision, Sigrid dies the next morning, and "Thorstein Eiriksson died at nightfall" (89). But his corpse does not rest easy.

As in *The Greenlanders' Saga*, Thorstein Eiriksson's corpse demands to speak to Gudrid. The farmer Thorstein awakens Gudrid, who is willing to speak with her husband's corpse: "I have faith that God will protect me. With God's mercy I shall take the risk of talking to him" (89). When she approached the corpse, "it seemed to her that he was shedding tears" (90). The religious subtext of the saga again becomes prominent as Thorstein Eiriksson tells Gudrid "that blessed were they who were true to their faith, for that way came help and mercy; but, he said, there were many who did not observe the faith properly" (90). As Thorstein's corpse goes on to explain, he is concerned that Greenlanders are developing "a bad custom" of "bury[ing] people in unconsecrated ground with scarcely any funeral rites" (90). He does not want this for himself and tells Gudrid, "I want to be taken to church, along with the other people who have died here" (90).[19]

Having made his plea for proper Christian burial practices, Thorstein then tells Gudrid "about her future, and said that she would have a great destiny; but he warned her against marrying a Greenlander. He also urged her to give their money to the church, or to the poor; and then he fell back for a second time" (90). As Thorstein had requested, his and the others' bodies were taken to a church, "and funeral rites were performed over them by priests" (90). Chapter 6 ends with the information that Gudrid's father, Thorbjorn Vifilsson, died "some time later" and "Gudrid inherited everything." Now both widowed and fatherless, she is welcomed into the household of Eirik the Red, who "looked after her affairs well" (90).

Chapter 7 introduces the husband who is truly Gudrid's destiny, as predicted both by the sybil and by the corpse of Gudrid's late husband. As in *The Greenlanders' Saga*, this husband is Thorfinn Karlsefni, a wealthy "sea-going merchant" from Iceland and a man "of noble lineage" (91). Chapter 7 opens with his genealogy and the details of his preparations for this "voyage to Greenland" (91). He is joined by another Icelander, Snorri Thorbrandsson, "and they had forty men with them" as crew (91). That same summer, another two merchants from Iceland—Bjarni Grimolfsson and his partner, Thorhall Gamlason—prepared another ship for the trip to Greenland, also "with forty men on board" (91). Both ships reached Greenland "in the autumn," at which time "Eirik [the Red] and some other settlers rode down to the ships and the trading went well" (91). Because Eirik is the local chieftain at the settlement where the ships have docked, "the captains invited Eirik to have whatever he wished from their cargoes" (91). Not to be outdone in courtesy and generosity, Eirik "invited both crews to be his guests [at his farmstead] for the winter. The traders accepted the invitation and went home with Eirik," while the ships' cargoes were transported to and stored for the winter in Eirik's many barns and outbuildings (91).

It is during this stay at Eirik the Red's farmstead that Thorfinn Karlsefni meets Gudrid, whom he thought "good-looking and capable," and approaches Eirik to ask "for the hand of Gudrid" (92). Thorfinn approached Eirik first—rather than Gudrid herself—because "he regarded [her] as being under Eirik's care" (92). Eirik agrees to "fully support the proposal," adding, "It is likely that she is fulfilling her destiny if she marries you" (92). As most readers of the saga would have understood, of course, the decision was ultimately Gudrid's, since women in Iceland and Greenland at this period enjoyed a good deal of autonomy. When "the proposal was put to her," Gudrid "agreed to accept Eirik's advice," and "the marriage took place" (92). As a result, "the Christmas feast was extended into a wedding feast" (92). That winter, everyone at Eirik's farmstead—guests, servants, family, and neighbors—"all had a splendid time . . . ; there was much chess-playing and story-telling, and many other entertainments that enrich a household" (92–93).

In the next chapter, chapter 8, *Eirik the Red's Saga* begins the story of the extensive exploration and attempted colonization of Vinland. In fact, the opening sentence is the first place in this saga in which the name Vinland is used. "There were great discussions . . . that winter about going in search of Vinland where, it was said, there was excellent land to be had. The outcome was that Karlsefni and Snorri Thorbrandsson prepared their ship and made ready to search for Vinland that summer. Bjarni Grimolfsson and Thorhall Gamlason decided to join the expedition with their own ship and the crew they had brought from Iceland" (93). Using "the ship that Thorbjorn Vifilsson had brought from Iceland" and with "mostly Greenlanders on board," "a man named Thorvard"—the husband of Eirik's daughter Freydis—and Eirik's son Thorvald organize yet a third group to join the expedition (94, 93). "Altogether," states the saga, "there were 160 people taking part in this expedition" (94).

Among those on board the ship with Thorvard and Thorvald is "a man named Thorhall, who was known as Thorhall the Hunter; he had been in Eirik's service for a long time, acting as his huntsman in summer" (93). Thorhall the Hunter "went with Thorvald and the others because he had considerable experience of wild regions," presumably having explored widely in Greenland and perhaps up into the Arctic (94, 94 n. 1). But Thorhall the Hunter was "swarthy and uncouth; he was . . . bad-tempered and cunning, taciturn as a rule but abusive when he spoke, and always a trouble-maker" (93). Worst of all, like his friend Eirik the Red, "he had not much to do with Christianity since it had come to Greenland" (93). This fact will have consequences later in the chapter, contributing to the saga's ongoing effort to undermine the older Norse religious practices in favor of Christianity.

First, though, we follow the ships to Vinland. Where *The Greenlanders' Saga* had described Leif Eriksson's explorations and his naming of places in Vinland, here the credit is given to Karlsefni's expedition. From the west coast of Greenland "they sailed before a northerly wind and after two days at sea they sighted land and rode ashore in boats to explore it. They found there many slabs of [huge] stone" and called this country Helluland, or Stone Slab-Land (94). After two more days at sea, they again sighted land. "This was a heavily-wooded country abounding with animals," which they named Markland, or Forest-Land (94). Another two days at sea bring them to a land that "was open and harbourless, with long beaches and extensive sands" (94). Again they go ashore to explore and, without any explanation for how it got there, they find "a ship's keel on the headland, and so they called the place Kjalarness," or Keel Point (94). Because of the extensive sand beaches, "they called this stretch of coast Furdustrands," or Wonder Beaches (94). Once past the length of beaches, "the coastline became indented with bays and they steered into one of them" (95). Two swift runners are sent ashore to explore southward; after three days, the runners returned, "carrying some grapes, and . . . some wild wheat [probably a wild rye or wild rice]. They told Karlsefni that they thought they had found good land" (95).

In *Eirik the Red's Saga*, the naming of places is attributed to the Karlsefni expedition. Those place names—and their geography—are identical to the geography and place names associated with Leif Eiriksson's explorations in *The Greenlanders' Saga*. Now, however, *Eirik the Red's Saga* begins to introduce both new place names and somewhat more detailed descriptions of the land itself. After the two runners were taken back aboard Karlsefni's ship, "the expedition sailed on until they reached a fjord. They steered their ships into it. At its mouth lay an island around which there flowed very strong currents, and so they named it *Straum Island*," that is, Stream Island or Strong Current Island (95). "There were so many birds on it that one could scarcely set foot between their eggs" (95). The ships then "steered into the fjord, which they named *Straumfjord*," Stream Fjord or Strong Current Stream, and there they anchored, "unloaded their ships and settled down. They had brought with them livestock of all kinds and they looked around for natural produce. There were mountains there and the country was beautiful to look at, and they paid no attention to anything except exploring it. There was tall grass everywhere" (95).

Here they decided to spend the winter, "which turned out to be a very severe one" (95). As a result, "they ran short of food and the hunting failed. They moved out to the island in the hope of finding game, or stranded whales, but there was little food to be found there, although their livestock throve. Then they prayed to God to send them something to eat, but the response was not as prompt as they would have liked" (95–96). At this juncture, Thorhall the Hunter reenters the narrative.

Thorhall has disappeared, and, after four days of searching, Thorfinn Karlsefni and Bjarni Grimolfsson "found him on top of a cliff . . . staring up at the sky" and generally acting strangely (96). Thorhall refuses to explain what he is doing but agrees to return to the settlement with Karlsefni and Bjarni. Although not stated explicitly, the implication is that Thorhall has been performing a pagan rite in order to secure food. And, in fact, "a little later a whale was washed up," which the colonists immediately cut up, boiled, and ate. "But when it was eaten it made them all ill" (96). Then Thorhall the Hunter boasts that his namesake, the thunder god, Thor, "turned out to be more successful than your Christ": "[The whale] was my reward for the poem I composed in honour of my patron, Thor" (96). Once this is revealed, "the others... refused to use the whale-meat and threw it over a cliff, and committed themselves to God's mercy" (96). With this rejection of the fruit of pagan prayer and a renewal of Christian faith, the weather cleared, "allow[ing] them to go out fishing, and after that there was no scarcity of provisions" (96). Chapter 8 ends on that same note of abundance: "In the spring they went back to Straumfjord and gathered supplies, game on the mainland, eggs on the island, and fish from the sea" (96).

Chapter 9 is relatively brief, but it accomplishes two things. First, it disposes of Thorhall the Hunter. Since this expedition has not yet come upon Leif's houses, Thorhall decides "to go north beyond Furdustrands and Kjalarness to search for Vinland there" (96). But after Thorhall and the "nine others who joined him... sailed northward past Furdustrands and Kjalarness, and tried to beat westward from there," they were driven off course by "fierce headwinds" (97). According to the saga, their ship was blown "right across to Ireland," where "they were brutally beaten and enslaved; and there Thorhall died" (97). In this way, the colony's one recalcitrant pagan is removed and, by implication, punished for his rejection of Christianity.

Second, and more important, chapter 9 prepares the reader for the further exploration of this new country. Where Thorhall decided to go north to search for Vinland, "Karlsefni wanted to follow the coast farther south, for he believed that the country would improve the farther south they went" (97). This southward exploration and, with it, the expedition's first encounter with the indigenous inhabitants is the subject of chapter 10.

"Accompanied by Snorri and Bjarni and the rest of the expedition," Karlsefni sails "south along the coast... for a long time" (97–98). Eventually they "came to a river that flowed down into a lake and from the lake into the sea," a place of "extensive sand-bars outside the river mouth" (98). They "sailed into the estuary and named the place *Hope* (Tidal Lake)" (98). Here they remained "for a fortnight, enjoying themselves" (98). And once again, the saga emphasizes the bounty of the land: "Here they found wild wheat growing in fields on all the low ground and grape vines on all the higher ground. Every stream was teeming with fish. They dug trenches at the high-tide mark, and when the tide went out, there were halibut trapped in the trenches. In the woods there was a great number of animals of all kinds" (98). But this idyll is temporarily interrupted "early one morning as they . . . caught sight of nine skin-boats; the men in them were waving sticks which made a noise like flails, and the motion was sunwise" (98).

Uncertain of what those in the skin-boats are trying to communicate, Karlsefni and Snorri hope the moving sticks are "a token of peace" and "take a white shield and go to meet" the Indians (98). Those in the skin-boats "rowed towards them and stared at them in amazement as they came ashore. They were small and evil-looking and their hair was coarse; they had large eyes and broad cheekbones. They stayed there for a while, marveling, and then rowed away south round the headland" (98). Unlike the episode in *The Greenlanders' Saga* where Thorvald Eiriksson and his men murdered the first Natives they encountered, here that first encounter is one of mutual surprise. The two Norsemen took up a white shield as a gesture of peace, albeit a gesture the Natives would have had no way to interpret, just as the Norse really had no way properly to assess the meaning of the Natives' waving sticks. Both groups are stuck with their incomprehension of the other, but at least there is no overt threat by either side.

Again, there is no way to know just who these Natives were. The use of moose-hide canoes at this period was common among the many Algonquian groups along the eastern seaboard north of Boston. And the saga's physical description of the Natives is probably not entirely trustworthy. Given their relatively healthy high-protein diet, the Native peoples on the coast were then no shorter than the Norse (among whom the average male was only about five-foot-five).[20] Moreover, the statement in *Eirik the Red's Saga* that the Natives "were small" runs counter to Karlsefni's observation in *The Greenlanders' Saga* that at least one Skraeling was "tall and handsome." Additionally, a different (and later) manuscript source for this saga describes the Natives not as "small" but as "dark-coloured," consistent with the Norse belief that Vinland was attached to Africa (98 n. 3).

Whoever these Natives might have been, what is significant in this episode is that Karlsefni appears not to have anticipated any threat from them. There is no suggestion that he constructs a palisade or any other fortification. The colony "stayed there that winter," a winter with "no snow at all, and all the livestock were able to fend for themselves" (98). But however attractive, this settlement on the Tidal Lake, Hope (or, more properly, *Hóp*), does not become permanent.

In chapter 11, the Natives return, this time for trade. "Early one morning in spring, . . . a great horde of skin-boats approach[ed] from

Contact and Conflict   87

the south round the headland" (99). Once more, "sticks were being waved from every boat. Karlsefni's men raised their shields and the two parties began to trade" (99). The Natives trade animal pelts, but in this saga, rather than milk or cheese products, "what the Natives most wanted to buy was red cloth; they also wanted to buy swords and spears, but Karlsefni and Snorri forbade that" (99). As the Norse use up their supply of red cloth, however, that very scarcity makes it appear more valuable, and the Natives are effectively cheated. At the beginning, "the natives took a span [i.e., about nine inches] of red cloth for each pelt, and tied the cloth round their heads" (99). When "the cloth began to run short . . . Karlsefni and his men cut it up into pieces which were no more than a finger's breadth wide; but the Skrælings paid just as much or even more for it" (99). This trading, so advantageous to the Norse, is interrupted when "a bull belonging to Karlsefni and his men came running out of the woods, bellowing furiously" (99). The Natives, who have never seen such an animal and had no domesticated livestock of their own, "were terrified and ran to their skinboats" (99). Given what happens next, the saga suggests that this is the event that precipitated hostilities.

For three weeks there was no sign of the Natives, and "then Karlsefni's men saw a huge number of boats coming from the south. . . . This time all the sticks were being waved anti-clockwise and all the Skrælings were howling loudly. Karlsefni and his men now hoisted red shields and advanced towards them" (99). In the ensuing "fierce battle," the Indians employed a kind of catapult that showered the Norse with "a hail of missiles" (99). The workings of the catapult described in the saga are consistent with known and very old Algonquian war practices, as are the "howling" battle cries (see 99 n. 3). So frightened were Karlsefni and his men by the "ugly din" made by the catapult when its missiles flew over their heads and "struck the ground" that "they retreated farther up the river" to "some cliffs, where they prepared to make a resolute stand" (99–100).

At this point, Eirik the Red's (perhaps illegitimate) daughter makes her appearance. Seeing her countrymen in retreat, Freydis chastises them, asking, "Why do you flee from such pitiful wretches, brave men like you? You should be able to slaughter them like cattle. If I had weapons, I am sure I could fight better than any of you" (100). It is a far more conventional goading speech than the one she utters in *The Greenlanders' Saga*. Not content merely to goad, however, Freydis actually tries to join the retreating men, "but she could not keep up with them because she was pregnant. She was following them into the woods when the Skrælings closed in on her" (100). Now cornered, Freydis sees a dead Norseman nearby, snatches up his sword, "and prepared to defend herself" (100). Then, in a gesture the saga does not explain, as "the Skrælings came rushing towards her she pulled one of her breasts out of her bodice and slapped it with the sword. The Skrælings were terrified at the sight of this and fled back to their boats and hastened away" (100). No comparable act by a woman is depicted in any other saga.

To date, this scene has defied scholarly explanation. Did anything like this ever really take place? If so, did Freydis's gesture make her appear to the Indians as some kind of witch or demon, and so they ran off? Did an Icelandic scribe who never saw Vinland and knew nothing of American Indians so distort and garble some prior version of these events as to make them wholly unintelligible? Or was this the invented and interpolated psychosexual fantasy of some monkish cleric bent on representing Freydis—a woman with an already ambiguous reputation—as a kind of Amazonian harpy? And is it even really Freydis we are seeing here? After all, the only woman explicitly identified as pregnant in both Vinland sagas is Gudrid, who gives birth to her son Snorri while still in Vinland. Thus it may be that, in some other version, this scene was meant to valorize a heroic and courageous Gudrid, and some nodding scribe simply confused the two women and wrote down the wrong name.

Whatever the case, in this version, Freydis saves the day. Even so, when the Norse retreat upriver, they also experience an attack "from inland" (100). After the battle was over and Karlsefni and his men "pondered what force it was that attacked them from inland[,] they then realized that the only attackers had been those who had come in the boats, and that the other force had just been a delusion" (100). Unfamiliar with Native fighting tactics, the Norse simply had no way of detecting what were probably the feints and decoys to which they had been subjected. In other words, the Norse were made to *think* themselves attacked both from the water and on the land, although at least some of the boats and warriors may have been only decoys to lure them into ambush or to make the Native forces appear larger than they actually were. Given what we know of Algonquian fighting tactics during the colonial period, this is a wholly reasonable interpretation. Of course, it is also the case that confrontations with radical *otherness* commonly lead to the ascription of magical or supernatural powers in the *Other*. Thus, the Skraelings responded to Karlsefni's bellowing bull as some kind of malevolent demon, and here Karlsefni and his men responded to the Indians as conjurers capable of overcoming the Norse by "delusion" during warfare.

Following the conflict, "Karlsefni and his men" realize that "although the land was excellent they could never live there in safety or freedom from fear, because of the native inhabitants" (100). So they prepare "to leave the place and return home" (100). They sailed "north along the coast," toward their previous residence at Straumfjord, and en route "came upon five Skrælings clad in skins, asleep" (101). This was probably a hunting party because "beside them were containers full of deer-marrow mixed with blood," or *pemmican*, an excellent source of protein and iron, easily portable and used by the Indians for sustenance on long trips. Inexplicably, "Karlsefni's men reckoned that these five must be outlaws, and killed them" (101). No threat is hinted at and no further motivation offered. The scene is thus eerily akin to Thorvald and his men's killing of the eight Natives sleeping under the skin-boats in *The Greenlanders' Saga*.

Upon their arrival at Straumfjord, the Norse again "found plenty of everything," but the coherence of the saga begins to unravel. Clearly, the saga writer was trying to piece together several conflicting sources: "According to some people," reads the text, "Bjarni Grimolfsson and Freydis had stayed behind there with a hundred people . . . while Karlsefni and Snorri had sailed south with forty men and, after spending barely two months at Hope, had returned that same summer" (101). This sentence contradicts the earlier statements in chapter 10 that on the exploratory voyage to the south, Karlsefni was "accompanied by Snorri and Bjarni and the rest of the expedition" (97). The sentence also contradicts the prior information that Karlsefni's company had brought their livestock with them, "built their settlement on a slope by the lakeside," with other houses either "close to the lake" or "farther away," and "stayed there [at Hope] that winter" (98). This hardly constitutes only a two-month residence. Moreover, the battle with the Skraelings does not take place until the next spring. And how do we explain Freydis residing in two places at once, that is, at both Hope (where she bared her breast to the Natives) and also at Straumfjord? Again we must consider the possibility that a copyist scribe made an error and confused Freydis with the pregnant Gudrid. In another manuscript source for *Eirik the Red's Saga*, it is Gudrid, not Freydis, who "had stayed behind" at Straumfjord (see 101 n. 2). Even so, a copyist's error does not explain the two very different versions of Karlsefni's stay at Hope and the length of that stay. The only plausible explanation is that one or more of this saga's authors were attempting to reconcile disparate oral and written sources or perhaps introduce a version of events still in oral circulation, even if it didn't neatly fit into the rest of the narrative. After all, Iceland's rich oral culture had continued to flourish alongside the written culture introduced by the Church.

An analogous but rather different attempt to stitch together disparate materials appears in the next chapter, chapter 12. Here some author or redactor has introduced material derived from learned treatises on geography. Since several medieval Icelandic texts located Vinland as attached to Africa, and medieval European scholars generally believed that Unipeds (or one-legged people) lived in Africa, this writer depicted the Norse encountering a Uniped at Straumfjord (see 101, n. 3; also Magnusson and Pálsson 39). "One morning," says the saga, "Karlsefni and his men saw something glittering on the far side of the clearing," and when it moved, "it proved to be a Uniped" (101). The Uniped then "came bounding down towards where the ship lay. Thorvald, Eirik the Red's son, was sitting at the helm. The Uniped shot an arrow into his groin" (101–2). Soon afterward, Thorvald "died of the wound"; a Uniped thus displaces the Skraelings as the cause of his death (102).

In pursuit of Thorvald's killer, "Karlsefni and his men gave chase," but "the weird creature" was too swift, "and the pursuers turned back" (102). They then sail their ship north, in the direction the Uniped had fled, "and thought they could see Uniped-Land" (102). But again they turn back rather than "risk the lives of the crew any further" (102). Clearly, whether the threat comes from Skraelings or Unipeds, this may be "a rich country"—as the dying Thorvald attests—but it is also a dangerous country for the relatively small Norse colony.

Following their unsuccessful pursuit of the Uniped, Karlsefni and his men "returned to Straumfjord and spent the third winter there" (102). But it is an uneasy winter because, as the saga hints, the unmarried men are attempting to impose themselves on the wives of the married men. Then we learn that Gudrid and Karlsefni's son Snorri had been born "in the first autumn," and "he was three years old when they left" (102). And leave they do, the following spring, "sail[ing] before a southerly wind and reach[ing] Markland" first (102). As Vikings so often did in the foreign lands they invaded, on Markland Karlsefni and his men take captives.

When they "reached Markland, . . . they came upon five Skrælings—a bearded man, two women, and two children. Karlsefni and his men captured the two boys, but the others got away and sank down into the ground. They took the boys with them and taught them the language, and baptized them. The boys said that their mother was called Vætild and their father Ovægir. They said that the land of the Skrælings was ruled by two kings, one of whom was called Avaldamon and the other Valdidida. They said that there were no houses there and that people lived in caves or holes in the ground" (102–3). If, as most archaeologists now agree, Markland refers to the "timber-rich forests" of Labrador, then the Skraelings encountered in this episode were most likely the ancestors of the caribou-hunting Montagnais and Naskapi (or Innu, as they now prefer to be called) of Quebec and Labrador (Wallace, "An Archaeologist's Interpretation" 228). In that event, the boys' statement that their "people lived in caves or holes in the ground" may refer to what archaeologists call "pit houses" or "semi-subterranean dwellings," that is, structures dug into the ground. This kind of house has been found at the archaeological sites of the ancestors of the Naskapi (Innu) and Beothuk as well as at several other ancient coastal Algonquian sites (see Wallace, "L'Anse aux Meadows, Leif Eriksson's Home in Vinland" 115; Sanger 23). The boys' statement about being "ruled by two kings" undoubtedly reflects the habitual European inability to understand Native leadership patterns, resulting in a repeated confusion of band chiefs with local "kings." The names of these kings—Avaldamon and Valdidida—appear to have no relation to any sound patterns or naming practices in any of the known Eastern Algonquian dialects, and, again, probably reflect the repeated distortions imposed when Europeans attempted "to render Aboriginal names into their own sound system" (Wallace, "L'Anse aux Meadows, Leif Eriksson's Home in Vinland" 115).

If, in fact, the Norse took captives on Labrador and taught them their language, this indicates at least some intention to return to this land (if only for trade). The captives would then serve as invaluable interpreters and intermediaries. Recent genetic studies of the modern Scandinavian population of Iceland suggest that the two boys from Markland may not have been the only Native Americans abducted by the Norse. Although the research is still ongoing, one particular genetic lineage from Iceland "seems most likely" to have "a [female] Native American origin" and to derive from the era of Norse pre-Columbian contacts with "the Eastern coastline of the Americas . . . around the year 1000" (Ebeneserdóttir et al. 7). If this proves to be the case, it adds further credibility to the real-world basis of the episode in *Eirik the Red's Saga*, however garbled or laced with error-ridden medieval learning.

The interpolation of medieval learning then continues as the Markland Skraelings are said to tell the Norse that "there was a country across from their own land where the people went about in white clothing and uttered loud cries and carried poles with patches of cloth attached. This is thought to have been *Hvítramannaland*" (103). Because Hvítramannaland translates literally as "White Men's Land," this statement has provoked wild speculation as well as serious scholarly debate. Some nineteenth-century American readers interpreted it as evidence of a prior, pre-Norse colonization of North America by Europeans, perhaps Irish Christians. The *Hauksbók* version of the saga glosses Hvítramannaland as an Asian "Greater Ireland," which itself derives from Icelandic versions of various European works of learning that placed a country of white men somewhere in Asia (see 103, n. 1). (And Asia was believed to be across the Atlantic, directly west of Europe.)[21] In short, what we probably have here is a self-conscious attempt at erudition, introducing learned (if erroneous and confusing) notions of foreign lands into a story about other foreign lands to the west. But there is another possibility: however garbled, the text may actually be repeating real information. Wallace suggests that the Skraeling boys may have "referred to Dorset people [a Paleo-Eskimo people], who then inhabited most of northern Labrador" and may have worn clothing made of polar-bear skins "with the fur side in" ("An Archaeologist's Interpretation" 231). This could be "the people [who] went about in white clothing." All these speculations aside, with the closing sentence of chapter 12, the text returns to familiar territory, and the journey back from Vinland ends: "Finally they reached Greenland, and spent the winter with Eirik the Red" (103).

Chapter 13, another notably short chapter, details the death of Bjarni Grimolfsson, the captain of the second ship that accompanied Karlsefni to Vinland. In so doing, the chapter memorializes Bjarni as a man of honor and courage and also reminds readers of the dangers of these western voyages.[22]

Chapter 14, the closing chapter of *Eirik the Red's Saga*, initially returns to the life stories of its two central characters, Karlsefni and Gudrid. Surprisingly, however, unlike the closing chapter of *The Greenlanders' Saga*, here there is very little information offered about their later years. We learn of their return, along with their son Snorri, to Karlsefni's farm on Iceland. But there is no reference to Karlsefni's wealth and stature within the Iceland community, no mention of his and Gudrid's voyage to Norway, and no discussion of Gudrid's journey to Rome or her entry into religious orders after Karlsefni's death. The effect is to foreshorten abruptly what had earlier promised to be a saga organized around her life story. But in truth, in the *Skálholtsbók* version upon which Magnusson and Pálsson base their translation, Gudrid really disappeared from the story much earlier, in chapters 8 through 12, when Vinland and its Native inhabitants replaced her on center stage and became the text's main focus.

Now, at the end of *Eirik the Red's Saga*, after the opening sentences of chapter 14 return Karlsefni and Gudrid to Iceland, the saga writer's interest turns immediately to naming their progeny and, most important, to naming the three Icelandic bishops who are their descendants. While this genealogy is relatively succinct in the *Skálholtsbók* version, it is quite lengthy and far more extensive in *Hauksbók*, where the final editor (or redactor) was Hauk Erlendsson, a direct descendant of Karlsefni and Gudrid. Whichever variant one reads, though, whether *Skálholtsbók* or *Hauksbók*, it is clear that *Eirik the Red's Saga* intended to pay homage to the "exceptional" Gudrid and to valorize Thorfinn Karlsefni in place of Leif Eiriksson.

Because both *The Greenlanders' Saga* and *Eirik the Red's Saga* were understood to be amalgams of multiple sources of information, written and oral, always available for revision and adaptation to changing tastes, the many discrepancies between the two Vinland sagas and their several variants do not appear to have presented a problem for medieval Icelanders. Each saga, in its own way, was simply an entertainingly good yarn about real people and past events. For Helge Ingstad, who followed the information in the two Vinland sagas all the way to the tip of Newfoundland, the sagas were "based on accounts ... made by young seamen and were retold through the centuries from generation to generation, in houses made of turf and stone, to people sitting on an earthen floor by an open fire" (*Westward to Vinland* 34). And because they were retold through the generations, whether recited from memory or read from a book, the two sagas long kept alive in the memory of the Norse the persons, places, and events that were associated with a land to the west called Vinland.

Where Was Vinland, and Who Were the Skraelings?

Because an appreciable number of the settlers of Iceland "came from Ireland and the Western Isles of Scotland," medieval Norse culture in Iceland inevitably absorbed "certain Celtic features" (Pálsson 14). Among these were "Irish tales about Atlantic voyages and 'wine-lands' or 'wine islands' which were supposed to be somewhere far away in the ocean" (32). Such "legendary lore," suggests Hermann Pálsson, may well have been part of the "poetic imagination" of those who actually ventured to Vinland as well as those who later wrote down their stories. As a result, argues Pálsson, the Vinland sagas are laced with "echoes of Irish stories about a legendary land west beyond the sea" (30).[23] That said, the surviving written versions of the Vinland sagas—however embellished to make them more entertaining or embroidered to make them more literary—tell us two things that are beyond dispute. First, some five hundred years before Columbus, Europeans had explored and attempted to colonize a land to the west of Greenland that appeared to them abundant with natural resources. Second, long before the better known explorations of the sixteenth and seventeenth centuries, Europeans and Native peoples had met one another, briefly engaged in trade, and subsequently clashed. What the sagas do not tell us are the precise geographical locations of Straumfjord, Hope, or even Vinland itself. And the sagas allow us only to speculate about the identity of the Native groups encountered by the Norse.

In part, this is because the two sagas sometimes offer inconsistent sailing directions or do not provide sufficiently detailed sailing information, and they do not always indicate the number of days traveled between one landfall and another. Such information may well have been part of the earlier oral tradition when these details would still have been vital to any Icelanders considering their own voyage to Vinland. But by the time the sagas were being transmitted in written form—with all the changes by different scribes along the way—their primary purpose was clearly no longer the recording of detailed travel information. And without even a word for map or chart in their vocabulary, the Norse never made any graphic record of these western travels, either. So, even today, the precise location of Vinland remains a much-disputed mystery. Accordingly, without firmer knowledge of the particular areas where the Skraelings were encountered, and without further ethnographic information about them, it is also difficult to determine exactly which indigenous group—or groups—are being described. Moreover, because the contacts as portrayed in the sagas give no indication that there was much verbal communication between the two groups, we have no hint of what the Skraelings called themselves or how—or if—they even attempted to identify themselves to the Norse. And we never read anything more about the two Skraeling boys taken captive in Markland.

Despite these limitations, a wealth of recent archaeological finds in combination with the information that *can* be gleaned from the sagas has induced a number of modern researchers to offer often persuasive educated guesses and informed speculations. Probably the most authoritative voice in the ongoing debate over the location of Vinland and the identity of the Natives is that of Birgitta Linderoth Wallace, the archaeologist who worked with the Ingstads at L'Anse aux Meadows and later took over directing the excavations for Parks Canada from 1973 through 1976. A thorough analysis of these excavations has revealed that the L'Anse aux Meadows site at the northern tip of Newfoundland was not, as Helge Ingstad wanted to believe, the Vinland of the sagas but, rather, a Norse gateway to Vinland.

Built for year-round occupation, the sturdy buildings of sod over timber frames at L'Anse aux Meadows "had room for anywhere between 30 and 160 people," and there is clear evidence that both men and women had resided there (Wallace, "L'Anse aux Meadows, the Western Outpost" 41). But this was not a geographical location where the grapes and other commodities from Vinland could be found. And "at the time of the Norse, there were no native people at L'Anse aux Meadows" (40). Instead, as Wallace explains, the L'Anse aux Meadows site functioned as a place for ship repair and as "a basecamp for exploration for and exploitation of new resources for the new Greenland settlement, a gateway to Vinland where lumber, grapes, and other riches were collected" (41). That place of riches, Wallace concludes, "the area closest to L'Anse aux Meadows that meets all criteria . . . is northeastern New Brunswick, the Chaleur Bay and Miramichi area" ("An Archaeologist's Interpretation" 229).

In a careful but somewhat selective reading of the sagas that takes into account all the available archaeological data, Wallace notes that *Eirik the Red's Saga* "describes two settlements, Straumfjord in the north and Hóp in the south. Straumfjord is a year-round settlement from which expeditions were launched in the summer and to which everyone returned in the winter. No grapes grew there. Hóp is a camp used in the summer in southern Vinland where the Norse cut lumber and found *mosur* (burl) wood. It is a wonderful place where there is self-sown wheat, and grapes grow wild. Hóp was named for its tidal lagoons on river estuaries inside sand barriers, so shallow that a ship could enter only at high tide" ("An Archaeologist's Interpretation" 227). By contrast, she continues, *The Greenlanders' Saga* "describes only one settlement, Leifsbudir. Leifsbudir incorporates elements of both Straumfjord and Hóp. Its physical description is close to that of Hóp, but its function is that of Straumfjord. What is clear is that both Straumfjord and Leifsbudir are gateways to Vinland. Resources were sought from a vast hinterland and brought back to the base to be shipped to Greenland" (227). Wallace then avers, "There is no doubt in my mind that Hóp was in eastern New Brunswick" (230).

Based on this geographical identification and the ethnographic evidence supplied by the sagas, Wallace further concludes that the Skraelings encountered at Hope "were the ancestors of today's Micmac, who have inhabited the rivers and lagoons of New Brunswick ever since the lagoons were formed 2,500 to 3,000 years ago" ("An Archaeologist's Interpretation" 230). In a more recent article, Wallace added that the notation of skin-boats in the sagas was another clue to the identity of the Hope Skraelings because "the Mi´kmaq did use canoes made from moose or deer skin." And "in protohistorical times," such "canoes were rarely used south of central Maine, and not at all south of Boston" ("L'Anse aux Meadows, Leif Eriksson's Home in Vinland" 122). Because the Skraelings encountered by Karlsefni's expedition on their return to Greenland in *Eirik the Red's Saga* were encountered in Markland, Wallace identifies these as yet another Algonquian-speaking people: "In the eleventh century, the only natives present in central Labrador (Markland) would have been the Indian ancestors of the Innu (Montagnais and Naskapi)" ("An Archaeologist's Interpretation" 230). Yet while few scholars today question Wallace's view that the Norse encountered Algonquian-speaking Native peoples in Vinland and Markland, not everyone agrees that the fabled Vinland "was in eastern New Brunswick."

Gísli Sigurðsson of the Árni Magnusson Institute in Reykjavik, Iceland, for example, concurs with Wallace and states that he has "a strong feeling that Leif's Vinland was in the Gulf of Saint Lawrence and that Karlsefni and Gudrid ventured south along the eastern coast of Nova Scotia, possibly as far south as the Bay of Fundy and perhaps even farther" ("The Quest for Vinland" 236). He also notes that "the Miramichi Bay on the coast of New Brunswick" offers "all the Vinlandian delicacies . . . except for the mild winter referred to in [*The Greenlanders' Saga*], which would then be the only misfit in all these descriptions" (236). He is therefore reluctant to dismiss the work of the many other reputable scholars who locate Vinland farther to the south. "How far south from Straumfjord to Hóp Karlsefni may have gone," writes Sigurðsson, "is impossible to tell but reasonable suggestions have been made for anywhere along the coast of New England, even as far south as New York" (237).[24]

As a result of these uncertainties, the search for Vinland goes on still. Persuaded that "in those seafaring environments, the sailing directions would have the best chances to survive unabridged," a retired Norwegian farmer named Sivert Fløttum has devoted more than thirty years to a careful study of the sagas, this time with a mariner's eye for the ways the medieval Norse "express[ed] distances and directions at sea" (n.p.). Based on his research, which included sailing parts of the Atlantic coast in a replica Viking vessel in 1986–87, Fløttum proposes that "Leif's Vinland [in *the Greenlanders' Saga*] was in the Cape Cod/Massachusetts Bay" area, while Karlsefni's settlement was in the Penobscot Bay area in Maine (n.p.). Unfortunately, however, if there were Norse encampments anywhere in New England, we may never find their traces because the rising sea levels of the past century significantly eroded large tracts along New England's Atlantic coast. And since the Norse tended to set up their camps close to the shoreline, physical evidence of Norse structures in New England has probably long ago been swept out to sea. In short, theories like Fløttum's may never be proven (or disproven). That said, despite significant site loss, archaeologists have uncovered coastal Indian sites with remains that go back three and even four thousand years. So it is not absolutely impossible that more Norse sites may yet be discovered somewhere along the Atlantic seaboard.

Available archaeological evidence provides at least some certainty of contact between Norse and Natives. For example, two projectile points, "stylistically identical" to those made by the Indians of Newfoundland and Labrador at this period, "were recovered from Norse sites in western Greenland" (Odess, Loring, and Fitzhugh 203). One made from chert was found in the Sandnes cemetery on Greenland, while the other, made from quartz, "was recovered from rocks on the shore below the Norse ruins at Brattahlid, the very site from which Thorfinn Karlsefni left on a Vinland expedition" (203). The Indians known to have made these kinds of projectile points were the Algonquian-speaking people whom Wallace identified as the "ancestors of the Innu (Montagnais and Naskapi)" encountered by Karlsefni's expedition in Markland ("An Archaeologist's Interpretation" 230). But while the presence at Norse sites in Greenland of projectile points made by Native peoples on Labrador strongly suggests contact, it does not definitively tell us what kind of contact. As the archaeologists Daniel Odess, Stephen Loring, and William W. Fitzhugh pose the questions, "Were these projectile points from stray arrows lodged in the deck of a Viking boat or in one of the Vikings themselves? Were they trophies gathered from a raid on a *skraeling* camp or were they gifts cautiously exchanged?" (203). In this case, the evidence does not speak for itself.

In 1957, the purported discovery of an eleventh-century Norwegian coin at an age-old Native American trading site on the coast of Maine led to all sorts of excited speculations. There were theories about a possible Norse presence in the Penobscot Bay area or, at the very least, the possibility of direct trading relations between Norse and the Algonquian-speaking peoples of the Canadian Maritimes and Maine. But while the coin itself proved authentic, its "discovery" has been seriously questioned. Many archaeologists now believe that the coin may have been planted at the site by someone involved in the dig.[25]

What we do know is that the finds at L'Anse aux Meadows, including butternuts and "a butternut burl that had been cut with a metal tool," clearly "indicate that the people who lived at L'Anse aux Meadows made excursions to regions farther south.... Butternut trees are a North American walnut species, also called white walnut, which are not indigenous to Newfoundland and have never grown there" (Wallace, "The Viking Settlement" 213). Instead, "the area closest to Newfoundland where [grapes and] butternuts grow is the Saint Lawrence River valley," and especially eastern New Brunswick. There, writes Wallace, "the butternuts and grapes grow along the Miramichi River and Restigouche River in Chaleur Bay. This is a rich area, with large hardwood forests, inviting meadows, grapes, and walnuts" ("L'Anse aux Meadows, Leif Eriksson's Home in Vinland" 121). Yet as Wallace has also acknowledged, both butternut trees and wild grapes are often found together "farther to the south, in New England, and farther south yet" ("The Viking Settlement" 213). In that case, if the Norse traveled south through the Canadian Maritimes "and along the coast of Maine," they would have encountered "a succession of ... Indian groups, the ancestors of the Micmac, Maliseet, and Eastern Abenaki.... Had they traveled west toward the mouth of the Saint Lawrence River they would have encountered an even more formidable force—the Iroquois who were then aggressively expanding eastward into Algonquian territories" (Odess, Loring, and Fitzhugh 204). But, as yet, there is no hard archaeological evidence.

Similarly, there is no hard archaeological evidence of Norse contact with the Beothuk, another Algonquian people who, at the time of the Vinland voyages, occupied parts of Newfoundland (though not the area immediately around L'Anse aux Meadows). At some point around or just after the Vinland voyages, the Beothuk appear to have abandoned their coastal communities and moved inland. Members of related Algonquian groups in Maine have sometimes wondered whether this move was related to unwelcome or even violent encounters between Beothuk and Norse.[26] Certainly the Beothuk's habitations in

Newfoundland in the eleventh century make them prime candidates for the first indigenous peoples of North America to have met the Norse. But we will probably never know. The last surviving member of the Beothuk people died in 1829, and with her died her people's language and cultural memories.

What the archaeological evidence does make clear, however, is that the sagas do not tell the whole story of the Norse in North America. Indian groups were not the only indigenous peoples with whom the Norse made contact. Eskimoan archaeological sites in Arctic Canada provide evidence of the "transfer of metal and other European artifacts" in these regions, while several other finds suggest continued contacts, through about 1350, between Norse and Dorset and Thule peoples "over a wide area from Labrador to the High Arctic" (Sutherland 239, 241). But the Canadian Arctic is hardly the landscape described in the Vinland sagas, and there is nothing on the ground at these sites to suggest any attempted settlement. Perhaps that explains why these later voyages were not memorialized in sagas. And we know that there were later voyages. For example, the *Icelandic Annals* contain "an account of a small Greenlandic ship being storm-driven to Iceland . . . while on a voyage from Markland" in 1347 (Sutherland 240). The ship was probably carrying timber from Labrador intended for construction needs on relatively treeless Greenland. Yet this voyage, too, is never mentioned in any saga. Still, as the *Annals* entry and the Norse artifacts found at Arctic sites make clear, the Norse made many more journeys than those recorded in the Vinland sagas, and they entered the territories of several different North American indigenous peoples, both Eskimoan and Indian. Thus, as the archaeologist Patricia Sutherland comments, "We must assume that other unrecorded contacts did occur, and perhaps only encounters of a certain nature were thought worthy of record" (239). More recently, in 2010, the scholar Kirsten Seaver offered her own "perfectly good reason why there is no literary record of continued crossings" from Greenland to North America: "The reason is that the two Vinland sagas merely commemorated events that had involved a good many Icelanders, including some very prominent ones, and that what the Greenlanders did on their own later was of little concern to Icelandic writers intent on preserving historical details of interest to Icelanders" (*The Last Vikings* 58).

The account of the ship from Greenland blown off course on its return from Markland in 1347 is the last surviving written reference to voyages made by the Norse to the western lands. The last recorded voyage to the place named Vinland is dated even earlier: Bishop Eirik's voyage to Vinland in 1121. To be sure, well into the fifteenth century, the Greenland Norse continued to avail "themselves of North American lumber for their shipbuilding" and probably also gathered both lumber and high-grade bog iron from Labrador, where there were fewer Indians (Seaver, "Unanswered Questions" 273, 274). But statements about the bishop's journey are the last known historical references specifically naming Vinland.

Tentatively identified as Bishop Eirik Gnupsson, the bishop was an Icelander by birth and is generally thought to have served for some years as a bishop in Greenland before embarking on his journey to Vinland. The intent and outcome of his journey, however, are ambiguous at best. Recorded in several different compilations of *Icelandic Annals*, each with slight variations in wording and nuance, the brief sentences about Bishop Eirik's voyage in 1121 have long been subject to competing scholarly interpretations. "The Annales Reseniani, probably the oldest collection, perhaps compiled before 1319, have the entry: 'Bishop Eirik sought Vinland.' . . . The entry in the Annals included in the Flatey Book reads: 'Eirik, Bishop of Greenland, went in search of Vinland'" (Skelton 224). In summarizing the differing scholarly interpretations of these sentences, the late British cartographer R. A. Skelton asked whether the bishop's voyage was made "in search of a land whose very existence was doubtful, or . . . in search of one which was known to exist but the route to which, unfrequented for nearly a century, had been forgotten? Or did the bishop . . . sail by a familiar navigation route to a land where Norse settlers still maintained themselves and needed the ministrations of the Church?" Then, acknowledging the improbability of a Norse colony surviving in Vinland into the twelfth century, Skelton added yet another scholar's view that "the motive for the bishop's visit must have been evangelization of the heathen . . . a missionary expedition to the Skraelings" (225). But because there are no further references to Bishop Eirik in any Scandinavian source, all these questions go unanswered. We cannot even know if he ever reached Vinland. Thus, after 1121, it appears that the place called Vinland faded from the known written record as a site of continuing activity.

This may be because prominent Icelanders were no longer involved in journeys to Vinland. Or, as the would-be Vinland colonists of the eleventh century came to understand, Vinland was a land already densely settled. And the Norse population on Greenland, which at its peak numbered no more than 2,500, was never large enough to supply enough immigrants to Vinland to sustain and defend a viable colony. As a result, Karlsefni's recognition of these realities in *Erik the Red's Saga* may have proved prophetic: "Karlsefni and his men had realized by now that although the land was excellent they could never live there in safety or freedom from fear, because of the native inhabitants. So they made ready to leave the place and return home" (100).²⁷

By about the year 1500, Greenland—the jumping-off point for voyages to Vinland—was also abandoned by the Norse. Because documentary explanations for the final Norse depopulation of Greenland are scarce, scholars rely on evidence from the ongoing archaeological excavations there. "In the absence of incontrovertible datings, modern scholars assume that the Western Settlement ceased to exist before 1400 and that the Eastern Settlement cannot have been viable past 1500" (Seaver, "Unanswered Questions" 277–78). But scholars are divided over the ultimate causes of the collapse. Many theories have been put forward, including the impacts of a cooling climate; mismanagement of Greenland's fragile natural resources; the expansion of other European merchants and fishermen into Greenlandic waters, resulting in more severe competition for trade with Europe; pirate raids; internal political dissension; hostilities from invading Eskimoan peoples; or some combination of these. And no one is quite certain of just where the surviving Greenlanders may have gone. As Seaver put it, "The Norse Greenlanders disappeared, seemingly without a trace" (*The Last Vikings* 201). In other words, much still remains unknown about the longevity of the Vinland colony, the purpose of Bishop Eirik's journey there in 1121, and the causes and final destination(s) of the Greenland exodus.

Even so, both before and after the Civil War, many nineteenth-century Americans were sure they had answers to all these questions. The Greenlanders had migrated to the Vinland colony, and their refuge was the mysterious Norumbega that appeared on several early maps; the Vinland colony was both long-lived and Christian; and without doubt, Vinland was located within the borders of the U.S. Even the skeptical and always circumspect *North American Review* in 1838 repeated the "tradition" that the Vinland colony had persisted "for three centuries," that Bishop Eirik had journeyed there "for the purpose of converting the inhabitants to Christianity," and that "the colonial establishments [in Vinland] either became amalgamated with the native population, or from other causes disappeared, till the existence of Vinland was forgotten in Europe" (E. Everett, "The Discovery of America" 165). To put the matter succinctly, once the two Vinland sagas and the excerpts from many other related medieval documents became widely available in English translations in the early nineteenth century, Americans began the process of incorporating them into an *American* national narrative. And by the end of the nineteenth century, Leif Eiriksson and Christopher Columbus were in stiff competition for the title of *discoverer*.

3

Anglo-America's Viking Heritage

A NINETEENTH-CENTURY ROMANCE

> Consider what stuff history is made of,—that for the most part it is merely a story agreed on by posterity.
> —HENRY DAVID THOREAU, *Cape Cod* (1865)

> In the distinctions of the genius of the American race it is to be considered, that, it is not indiscriminate masses of Europe, that are shipped hitherward, but the Atlantic is a sieve through which only or chiefly the liberal adventurous sensitive *America-loving* part of each city, clan, family, are brought. It is the light complexion, the blue eyes of Europe that come: the black eyes, the black drop, the Europe of Europe is left.
> —RALPH WALDO EMERSON, entry in Journal CO (1851)

The Romance Begins:
The Impact of Carl Christian Rafn's *Antiquitates Americanæ*

Whether in music, painting, or literature, the Romantic movement in Europe was marked by a renewed (and sometimes politicized) re-engagement with the history, legends, and folklore of a national past. In the original languages and in translations, Europe's romantic literature made its way to American shores, where it was eagerly devoured. But as Americans read Sir Walter Scott's collection of ancient British poetry, *Minstrelsy of the Scottish Border* (1802), or his novel *Ivanhoe* (1820), set in medieval England; Jacob and Wilhelm Grimm's collections from old German folktales, *Grimm's Fairy Tales* (1812); or Alessandro Manzoni's novel, *The Betrothed* (1825), set in seventeenth-century Milan, they came to recognize the limitations of their own past, at least for the purposes of art. Proud of their hard-won political independence from England, and equally proud of their decided victory over the English in the War of 1812, Americans nonetheless missed having what the painter Thomas Cole called "the gigantic associations of the storied past" (qtd. in Noble 263). Thus, by the opening decades of the nineteenth century, Americans of European descent were hungry for a romantic history they could call their own.

To be sure, American writers celebrated the settling of western frontiers, the heroics of the Revolutionary War, and the symbolism of the first Thanksgiving. In New England, men delivered speeches and sermons about that small boulder called Plymouth Rock, the "noumenous signifier of arrival" (Seelye 640).[1] But while there was certainly both romance and history in all of this, there was not much antiquity. As the art critic James Jackson Jarves would observe a little later in the century, the full development of all the arts in America had been slowed because the country had "no legendary lore more dignified than forest or savage life, no history more poetical or fabulous than the deeds of men almost of our own generation, too like ourselves in virtues and vices to seem heroic" (151). And even though many Americans remained convinced that the burial and ceremonial mounds of the Southeast and the Ohio Valley represented remnants of some lost advanced ancient civilization that predated the Indians' arrival on the continent, it was difficult to compose historical romances around silent artifacts when the customs and identity of the ancient people remained solely a subject of antiquarian speculation. Therefore, American writers were encouraged to work with what was available.

In 1833, the politician and orator Rufus Choate delivered in Salem, Massachusetts, a lecture entitled "The Importance of Illustrating New-England History by a Series of Romances like the Waverley Novels." In that lecture, Choate urged American writers to give "to the natural scenery of the New World, and to the celebrated personages and grand incidents of its early annals, the same kind and degree of interest which Scott has given to the Highlands, to the Reformation, the Crusades, to Richard the Lion-hearted, and to Louis XI" (2). Choate's favored example of one of America's early "grand incidents" was the landing of the *Mayflower* and the arrival of the Pilgrims "on the bleak sea-shore and beneath the dark pine-forest of New England" (24).

In a sense, Choate was simply restating what many American writers were already doing. By 1833 Catharine Maria Sedgwick had published her first historical romance, *Hope Leslie* (1827), set in seventeenth-century Massachusetts, which she followed with *The Linwoods* (1835), another historical romance, this one set in New York during the Revolutionary War. Beginning in 1823 with *The Pioneers*, James Fenimore Cooper created his Leatherstocking character and in four subsequent novels combined both romance and adventure in the stories of a frontiersman "formed for the wilderness" (475). As a result, Cooper came to be known as the American Scott. Between 1835 and 1855, Cooper's contemporary, the southern novelist William Gilmore Simms, published six loosely connected romances, each centered around the Revolutionary War exploits of the guerrilla patriot Francis Marion, popularly known as "The Swamp Fox."[2] All of Cooper's Leatherstocking novels were bestsellers, while Simms fared almost as well with his Revolutionary War romances.[3] And when it first appeared in 1827, Sedgwick's *Hope Leslie* rivaled the sales of both Cooper and Scott. Alongside these works, however, Americans continued to demand the romantic novels and ballads of ancient times then being brought to the U.S. in sometimes pirated editions from England and further circulated by serialization in popular newspapers and magazines.[4] In short, while American readers eagerly purchased American novels about forested frontiers and romances that featured Revolutionary War guerrilla raids, they also sought ruined castles and lichen-covered towers. Little Plymouth Rock seemed insignificant next to the moldering abbey of a mysterious antique past. Clearly, as Choate's lecture indicated, because the Scottish poet and novelist dominated the bestseller lists in America between 1811 and 1821, Scott had helped influence the public taste for highly colored romances set amid picturesque surroundings.[5]

Echoing his compatriot Cole's earlier complaint that only in Europe could he paint pictures authentically "representing a ruined and solitary tower, standing on a craggy promontory," Nathaniel Hawthorne perfectly caught the temper of the times and the consequent dilemma of the American romancer in his preface to *The Marble Faun* of 1859 (qtd. in Noble 263). There, opening a novel set amid the shadows and mysteries of Catholic Italy, Hawthorne complained of "the difficulty of writing a romance about [the U.S.,] a country where there is no shadow, no antiquity, no mystery, no picturesque and gloomy wrong, nor anything but a commonplace prosperity, in broad and simple daylight" ("Preface to *The Marble Faun*," 590). Although Hawthorne's pretty picture of his "dear native land" was entirely exaggerated and probably intentionally ironic, nonetheless, he spoke for many other writers when he said that historical romances, like "ivy, lichens, and wall-flowers, need ruin[s] to make them grow" (590).

But even before Hawthorne issued his famous complaint, a Danish philologist named Carl Christian Rafn seemed to provide exactly what was needed, including the ruins. Under the imprimatur of the Royal Society of Northern Antiquaries, a society that he himself helped found in Copenhagen in 1825, in 1837 Rafn published a massive 479-page tome entitled *Antiquitates Americanæ, sive Scriptores Septentrio-*

106   Chapter Three

nales Rerum Ante-Columbianarum, in America (American antiquities, or the writings of the northern historians regarding pre-Columbian America). In that volume, Rafn assembled—whole or in part—eighteen documents, mostly written in medieval Iceland and all in their original languages. In his view, taken together, these documents confirmed "the truth of the historical fact, that during the tenth and eleventh centuries, the ancient Northmen discovered and visited a great extent of the eastern coasts of North America; and . . . that during the centuries immediately following, the intercourse never was entirely discontinued" (Rafn, *America Discovered in the Tenth Century* 31). Most important among the documents compiled by Rafn were the two Vinland sagas in their original Icelandic, each accompanied (as were all the Icelandic texts in the volume) by translations into both Danish and Latin.

For corroboratory ruins, or at least "traces of the residence and settlement of the ancient Northmen . . . still to be met with in Massachusetts and Rhode Island (the countries which formed the destination of their earliest American expeditions)," Rafn pointed to the carved inscriptions on Dighton Rock (*America Discovered in the Tenth Century* 31). In the inscriptions on that rock—the same rock on which, a century earlier, Cotton Mather had seen ancient Hebrew letters—Rafn claimed to discern a mix of runic markings and Latin letters, together forming a date and the name "Thorfins." These he interpreted as referring to Thorfinn Karlsefni's taking possession of the land there. In the pictographs on the rock, Rafn saw images of Karlsefni's wife, Gudrid, their son Snorri, and the famous bellowing bull.

Still more "traces . . . of the ancient Northmen" in New England were offered in 1841. That year, Rafn and the Royal Society of Northern Antiquaries published a twenty-seven page *Supplement to the Antiquitates Americanæ* containing two main items: a discussion of a drawing of a crumbling round stone tower in Newport, Rhode Island, the drawing having been supplied by the president of the Rhode Island Historical Society; and an analysis by several Danish scholars of some metal pieces found in conjunction with an apparently ancient skeleton dug up several years earlier near Fall River, Massachusetts. Although the skeleton itself had been destroyed in a museum fire in the 1830s, the Rhode Island Historical Society sent the remaining metal pieces to the Royal Society in Copenhagen for examination and identification. The ruined stone tower in Newport, claimed Rafn, was indubitably what remained of a baptistery built by the newly Christianized Norse. In the opinion of Rafn and his fellow scholars in the Royal Society, the metal pieces found with the skeleton could very well have been the armored breastplate or the remnants of chain mail from some ancient Northman buried long ago. But without the skeleton, and given the charred condition of the metal pieces, the Danish scholars admitted that their opinions on this matter could not be conclusive.

In order to secure American reviews and an American readership for the original volume of *Antiquitates Americanæ*, Rafn opened the volume with a summary of its contents in English. This summary began with a lengthy retelling of selected events from both *The Greenlanders' Saga* and *Eirik the Red's Saga*, the two combined into a single unified narrative. Leif Eiriksson retained his status as the true discoverer of Vinland and its first real explorer, while Thorfinn Karlsefni retained his status as the leader of the first colonizing venture. By conflating the two sagas into a single connected narrative, however, Rafn effectively presented them to American readers not as works of literature, or even as folklore, but as reliable evidentiary documents from which geographically specific locations and datable historical events could be extracted.

Significantly, Rafn himself never set foot in America nor personally viewed Massachusetts Bay and the Narragansett region of Rhode Island, the places he identified as sites of Norse landfalls. Instead, his theories were based on his reading of the sagas and on materials gathered from American correspondents. For some years before his work was published, Rafn had been advertising actively in the U.S., soliciting information and artifacts, and developing a wide correspondence with American antiquarians and historical societies. Rafn and his Danish colleagues also invited a number of prominent Americans to become members of the Royal Society of Northern Antiquaries, and several of these artistic, political, and cultural leaders later reviewed *Antiquitates Americanæ* quite favorably when it finally appeared.[6] It was from one of these American correspondents—the president of the Rhode Island Historical Society—that Rafn had received a somewhat inaccurate description of the Newport tower, along with an equally inaccurate drawing of its remains, and from other correspondents that he had received (again inaccurate) sketches of the markings on Dighton Rock. All of these he reproduced in *Antiquitates Americanæ* or its *Supplement* of 1841. And because Rafn had been advertising his project long before actual publication, as well as arousing interest in his theories through his many correspondents, by the time *Antiquitates Americanæ* appeared in 1837, many magazines and journals, like the *North American Review*, hailed it as "a work of great interest" that "has been long expected with impatience" (E. Everett, "The Discovery of America by the Northmen" 161).

Accompanying the massive volume was a five-page "Abstract" in English, distributed by the Royal Society of Northern Antiquaries to magazine and journal editors in order to further encourage reviews.[7] The "Abstract" summarized the contents of *Antiquitates Americanæ* and, perhaps most important, justified its existence. Calling upon the authority of no less an international eminence than the famous German naturalist and world traveler Alexander von Humboldt, the "Abstract" began by noting Humboldt's conclusion that "the Scandinavian Northmen were the true original discovers of the New World." The "Abstract" then noted that Humboldt regarded the available public information on this subject as "extremely scanty" and had called upon "the Northern Literati" to "collect and publish all the accounts relating to that subject. The Royal Society of Northern Antiquaries considers it a matter of duty to comply with this request," the "Abstract" explained. In so doing, the Society "embrac[ed] a threefold purpose: that of illustrating ancient geography and history; that of perpetuating the memory of our forefathers, and lastly that of everlastingly securing to them that honorable station in the history of the World, of Science, of Navigation, and of Commerce, to which they are justly entitled" (rpt. in Schoolcraft, "The Ante-Columbian History of America" 430).

Having thus laid out the project's seemingly unobjectionable motivating rationale, only then did the "Abstract" mention material that, in later decades, would become a subject of heated controversy: "The latest researches have rendered it in a high degree probable, that the knowledge of the previous Scandinavian discovery of America, preserved in Iceland, and communicated to Columbus when he visited that island in 1477, operated . . . as one of the most powerful of the causes which . . . enabled him to effect the new discovery of the New World." Anticipating Americans' resistance to this radically new twist on the accepted discovery story, the authors of the "Abstract" made clear that they had no wish to diminish Columbus's achievement, "whose glory cannot in any degree be impaired by the prior achievement." They only wished "not to forget his meritorious predecessors" (rpt. in Schoolcraft, "The Ante-Columbian History of America" 431). In 1837, these mollifying statements were taken at face value, although some reviewers of *Antiquitates Americanæ* did question the persuasiveness of the alleged evidence for Columbus's knowledge of the earlier voyages by the Norse. Others accepted the possibility but emphasized that only Columbus's voyages had had any lasting impact on history.

For the most part, however, the five-page "Abstract" functioned as a kind of narrative table of contents. It identified itself as "a brief sketch, mentioning only the principal sections of *Antiquitates Americanæ*" (rpt. in Schoolcraft, "The Ante-Columbian History of America" 432). These "principal sections," of course, included the two original Vinland sagas as well as "detailed *Geographical Inquiries* . . . whereby the sites of the regions and places named in the Sagas . . . are pointed out under the names by which they are now commonly known, viz. Newfoundland, Bay of St. Lawrence, Nova Scotia, and especially the States of Massachusetts and Rhode-Island, and even districts more to the South" (433–34). The "Abstract" listed all the main pieces of evidence for these designations that had been assembled in *Antiquitates Americanæ*, including facsimile reprints of medieval manuscripts and copies of old maps.

Just as its "Abstract" suggested, *Antiquitates Americanæ* was an expensive and ponderous book, with a mass of material in languages that most Americans could not read. In order to prevent misappropriations and misrepresentations of that work, in 1838 Rafn also published the shorter (and less expensive) *America Discovered in the Tenth Century*, a "concise and summary view" in English of the materials "now published in the 'Antiquitates Americanæ'" (iii–iv). Only forty pages long, this small booklet was intended both for sale and for selected complimentary distribution as a promotional device for the larger volume. The heading on page 1 even reads "An Abstract of the Historical Evidence Contained in the 'Antiquitates Americanæ.'" Like the summary with which *Antiquitates Americanæ* opened, this shorter work, too, began with a lengthy retelling of events from the Vinland sagas. Rafn starts with Eirik the Red's founding of the Greenland colony in A.D. 986 and Bjarni Herjolfsson's initial sighting of previously unknown lands that same year. He continues with Leif Eiriksson's exploratory voyage "in the year 1000," Thorvald Eiriksson's expedition "in the year 1002," Thorstein Eiriksson's aborted voyage, and, in some detail, the "settlement erected in Vineland, by Thorfinn" Karlsefni, commencing "in the spring of 1007" (*America Discovered in the Tenth Century* 6, 8, 10). Most of the folkloric and fabulistic elements in the sagas have been removed, as have all the narrative contradictions between the two. Instead, we get a rather flattened but coherent single narrative of multiple seriatim voyages from Greenland to Vinland, ending with the expedition of Freydis and the brothers Helgi and Finnbogi, an expedition that Rafn dates to the year 1012 through "the spring of 1013" (15). (Freydis's role in the "massacre [of] the brothers and their followers" is notably brief and understated.)

Following this highly selective recapitulation of the two sagas, Rafn then went on to analyze them as "evidence" for "fixing the position of the lands and places named" (*America Discovered in the Tenth Century* 17). Certain that the sagas accurately "preserved not only *geographical*, but also *nautical*, and *astronomical facts*," Rafn located Vineland (as he spelled it) on the coast of Massachusetts and followed his hardy Icelanders south from there (16). Based on the supposed *facts* in the sagas as well as "several other ancient Icelandic geographical works," Rafn identified Helluland (Stone Slab-Land) with Newfoundland; Markland (Forest Land) with "Nova Scotia, New Brunswick, and Lower Canada . . . [all] almost everywhere covered with immense forests"; and Vineland with Cape Cod (16–17). The Furdustrands (or Wonder Beaches) were "*Nauset Beach*, *Chatham Beach*, and *Monomoy Beach*," while Straumfjord (the Fast-Current Stream) was Buzzard's Bay and the nearby island of "Martha's Vineyard" (19). Hóp (or Hope), Rafn suggested, corresponded to "Mount Hope's Bay, or Mont Haup's Bay, as the Indians term it, . . . through which the Taunton River flows, and, by means of the very narrow, yet navigable, Pocasset River, meets the approaching water of the Ocean at its exit at Seaconnet. It was at this Hóp that Leifsbooths were situate; it was above it, and therefore most probably on the beautiful elevation called afterwards by the Indians, Mont Haup, that Thorfinn Karlsefni erected his dwelling-houses" (19–20). After reviewing the climate, the quality of the soil, and the natural abundance of the area, Rafn concluded, "A country of such a nature might well deserve the appellation of 'The Good' which was the epithet the ancient Northmen bestowed on it" (20).

According to Rafn, "the ancient Northmen" traveled farther south, as well. "The party sent by Thorvald Ericson [Leif's younger brother] . . . from Leifsbooths, to explore the southern coasts," claimed Rafn, "most likely examined the coasts of Connecticut and New York,—probably also those of New Jersey, Delaware, and Maryland" (*America Discovered in the Tenth Century* 23). Moreover, added Rafn, Hvítramannaland (White Men's Land) was "probably that part of the coast of North America which extends southwards from Chesapeake Bay, including North and South Carolina, Georgia, and Florida" (24). And even though the Norse of the sagas had not visited Hvítramannaland, but only heard about it from Natives, Rafn produced old Indian legends and other medieval sources to suggest that there had been European contact in these southern regions and that the white men referred to were other "ancient Northmen" and also "an Irish christian people who, previous to the year 1000, were settled in this region" (24).

Rafn devoted the closing pages of *America Discovered in the Tenth Cen-*

tury to a review of several other "authentic documents" that pointed to a continuing "intercourse between Greenland and America" at least until the year 1347, the year the *Icelandic Annals* reported a Greenland ship blown off course on its return from Markland (31). Finally, he urged readers to examine for themselves the wealth of documents compiled in the larger volume, *Antiquitates Americanæ*. As Rafn explained, "It seems of importance that the original sources of information should be published in the ancient language, so that every one may have it in his power to consult them, and to form his own judgment as to the accuracy of the interpretations given" (*America Discovered in the Tenth Century* 31).

Although much abbreviated, *America Discovered in the Tenth Century* offered a fairly accurate account of the overall argument presented in *Antiquitates Americanæ*. Missing, of course, were all the extracts from the original sources, the maps, and various line drawings intended to illustrate the evidence for Norse artifacts in America. Missing also — no doubt as a politic gesture — was the suggestion from *Antiquitates Americanæ* that Christopher Columbus had had knowledge of the Norse voyages and perhaps been influenced by them. Clearly, Rafn intended this smaller volume for popular sales, not controversy.

Not content with offering the larger compilation, *Antiquitates Americanæ*, as well as the shorter version, *America Discovered in the Tenth Century*, Rafn also contributed articles to a variety of magazines and journals, some written for general audiences and others for professional and more specialized readers. He continued this for several years, at once garnering new readers for his two books and also further fleshing out his theories as more so-called evidence became available.[8]

As might be expected, the appearance of *Antiquitates Americanæ* in 1837 made quite a splash. It was reviewed everywhere, often in lengthy articles with appended excerpts. The *North American Review* even enclosed the five-page "Abstract" of the work in a mailing of one of its regular issues (Falnes 226). The popular lecturers of the day, "who during that time enjoyed great favor with American audiences," now had exciting new subject matter for their "repertoires" (226). According to the New England historian Oscar J. Falnes, "Asahel Davis, a former chaplain of the senate of New York, called his discourse on the subject: *A Lecture on the Discovery of America by the Northmen, five hundred Years before Columbus, delivered in New York, New Haven, Philadelphia, Baltimore, Washington, and other Cities; also in some of the first literary Institutions of the Union*" (227).[9] Many popular magazines, like the *Family Magazine; or, Monthly Abstract of General Knowledge*, simply reprinted

112 Chapter Three

portions of Rafn's English-language summary of the sagas in monthly installments, at the end of each promising "To be continued in our next" ("Settlement Effected in Vineland, by Thorfinn" 328). And even if a reviewer found some small point for question or quibble in the massive volume, almost everyone concurred in the general consensus that *Antiquitates Americanæ* was "a learned, interesting, and important work" for which "the public" should be grateful (Folsom 352). Looking back on these events from the perspective of 1891, an anonymous reviewer for the *Nation* recalled that the book "created much sensation in the learned and curious world . . . [giving] rise to a multitudinous literature of books and booklets, articles in reviews and magazines, and papers in the proceedings of historical societies" ("The Icelandic Discovery of America" 54).

In fact, within two years of the appearance of *Antiquitates Americanæ*, several books that rehearsed its contents for a general audience began to appear. The first and most prominent of these was Joshua Toulmin Smith's *The Northmen in New England, or America in the Tenth Century* (1839). Written in "the form of a *dramatic dialogue*" between three fictional gentlemen, Smith's book was explicitly intended to remedy the fact that Rafn's *Antiquitates Americanæ* "must be inaccessible to the majority of readers" (ix, vii). "The object of this work," therefore, explained Smith, "is . . . to make the whole subject familiar to all" (vii). In pursuit of that goal, Smith revealed another underlying motive: the glorification of New England. "New England was . . . the portion of this continent which the Northmen especially explored; in New England for a time they dwelt; in New England one, at least, of their race was born,—the first of European blood that ever saw the light upon these shores; in New England the bones of more than one of these bold navigators and explorers were committed to the earth, where they even now lie mouldering" (vi–vii). As a result, "New England may be said to have become *classic ground*," meaning that it was both ancient and of the highest importance (Smith's emphasis vii).[10]

Following upon many more books like Smith's, after the Civil War the notion of a New England Vinland was almost a commonplace in some circles. When the beloved poet William Cullen Bryant partnered with his friend and fellow journalist Sydney Howard Gay to produce the illustrated *A Popular History of the United States* (1876), the assertion of Norse discovery was so noncontroversial as to become, without comment, part of the book's subtitle: *From the First Discovery of the Western Hemisphere by the Northmen to the End of the First Century of the Union of the States*.[11] The whole of chapter 3, titled "The Northmen in America," followed the Northmen from Iceland to "the coast of New England," although Bryant and Gay acknowledged that "precisely where is a disputed question" (40). Even so, all the illustrations for "The Northmen in America" depicted easily recognizable New England landscapes consistent with those identified by Rafn.

The possibility of a pre-Columbian discovery of America by the Norse was not wholly unknown, of course. Immigrants to the colony of New Sweden, established in 1638 on the Delaware River, surely brought with them at least some knowledge of the Vinland sagas.[12] And even before Rafn, European scholarship on the subject had also made its way into American libraries and periodicals. For example, in London in 1770, the antiquarian Thomas Percy published his English-language translation of a multivolume earlier work by Paul Henri Mallett, a Swiss historian of Scandinavia who taught at the University of Copenhagen.[13] Under the title *Northern Antiquities*, Percy's translation of Mallett began to be available in the U.S. sometime in the late 1780s. From 1789 through 1790, those portions of Percy's translation that pertained to "the discovery of Vinland, or America, by the Icelanders, in the eleventh century," were serialized in the *American Museum*, a monthly magazine. In a prefatory note to the first installment in August 1789, the editors of the *American Museum* assured readers, "The authorities from which Mons. Mallett, has compiled the following account, are of most unquestionable credibility" ("An Account of the Discovery of Vinland, or America, by the Icelanders" 159). That first installment loosely followed most of the events in *The Greenlanders' Saga*, beginning with the accidental sighting of new lands to the west by Bjarni Herjolfsson through Thorfinn Karlsefni's establishment of a colony and the colonists' first encounter with "Skrelingues." The final installment, printed in the June 1790 issue, summarized the colony's second encounter with the "Skrelingues," Thorfinn Karlsefni's decision to leave Vinland and eventually return to Iceland, and Freydis's "massacre of thirty people" ("An Account of the Discovery of Vinland, or America, by the Icelanders" 340). To this, Mallett added historical information not found in the sagas and married that to some of his own historical speculations.

Most notably, Mallett believed that at least a portion of the Vinland colony had remained behind after Thorfinn Karlsefni's departure and that "those who escaped" Freydis' massacre remained, too, and "settled in the country" ("An Account of the Discovery of Vinland, or America, by the Icelanders," June 1790, 340). Mallett then went on

114 Chapter Three

to explain how, over time, "all remembrance of the discovery was at length utterly obliterated: and the Norwegian Vinlanders themselves having no further connexion with Europe, were either incorporated into, or destroyed by their barbarian neighbours" (341). The rest of this final installment from Percy's translation of Mallet analyzed the information given in the sagas as well as in several other medieval documents and concluded that the Native peoples encountered in Vinland were "Eskimaux" and, further, "that there can be no doubt, but that the Norwegian Greenlanders discovered the American continent; that the place, where they settled, was either the country of Labrador, or Newfoundland: and that their colony subsisted there a good while" (343, 344).

The arrival of the sloop *Restauration* in New York Harbor in 1825, carrying the first boatload of Norwegian immigrants, only added to the numbers of people in the new nation who had heard of Leif Eiriksson and the discovery of Vinland.[14] Moreover, by 1825, Mallett's work had joined similar work by many other European scholars and antiquarians, all of it now circulating in the U.S. either in translation or in the original languages, and all of it using the Vinland sagas to substantiate a Scandinavian connection to the early history of North America. As a result, when Washington Irving published his extensively researched *Life and Voyages of Christopher Columbus* in 1828, he could hardly ignore these accumulating claims to a Scandinavian priority. Thus, in his opening pages, Irving acknowledged "the Scandinavian voyagers . . . and their mysterious Vinland" and added as an appendix to his biography of Columbus an article entitled "Scandinavian Discoveries" (9-10). Reluctantly, Irving accepted the possibility that Vinland may have been "the coast of Labrador or the shore of Newfoundland," but he insisted that any Norse presence there must have been "transient" and that the Icelandic sources might yet be proven only "legends" (9).[15] For Irving, as for most Americans, Columbus still held pride of place as "the mariner who first . . . brought the ends of the earth into communication with each other" (10).

The first American to write at length about the Northmen did not contest that view. In his *History of the Northmen*, published in 1831, Henry Wheaton (1785-1848) gave full credit to Columbus's accomplishment, affirming "there is not the slightest reason to believe that the illustrious Genoese was acquainted with the discovery of North America by the Normans five centuries before his time." But he added pointedly that "the Icelandic records . . . well authenticated [the] fact" of a prior Norse discovery (31). In other words, confident of "the authenticity of the main narratives"—including the two Vinland sagas and other Icelandic documents—Wheaton established that the Normans or Northmen (terms he used interchangeably) had been here first (28). And based on the passage in *The Greenlanders' Saga* describing the site where Leif and his crew first constructed their booths (stone and turf enclosures), Wheaton also established the location of Vinland. "The days were nearer of an equal length than in Greenland or Iceland," was Wheaton's translation of the passage, "and when they were at the shortest, the sun rose at half-past seven, and set at half-past four o'clock" (24). The footnote to this sentence, printed at the bottom of the page, read, "Supposing this computation to be correct, it must have been in the latitude of Boston, the present capital of New England" (24).

Born in Providence, Wheaton later gained prominence in the fields of international law and diplomacy. Sent as a chargé d'affaires to Denmark in 1827, he remained in Copenhagen until 1835. There he "found himself in the most lively centre of... Scandinavian studies" in Europe (Falnes 214). He learned Danish, "and eventually he taught himself to read all the modern Scandinavian languages" (214). Wheaton made the acquaintance of many Scandinavian scholars (including Rafn) and published articles on "Scandinavian mythology and literature" as well as "the maritime expeditions of the Normans... in the North-American and Philadelphia Quarterly Reviews" (Wheaton vi). When his *History of the Northmen* was published in London in 1831, it quickly made its way to the U.S. and won high regard on both sides of the Atlantic.[16] But because the historic sweep of Wheaton's survey was so large, with the Norse in Vinland comprising only a footnote and a relatively small part of the whole, and because Wheaton did not really challenge the Columbus discovery story, his book generally attracted learned readers while arousing no general stir. Thus, without either fanfare or controversy, Wheaton's work entered the contemporary admixture of sometimes contested discussions of Scandinavian voyages and relatively uncontested accolades for Columbus—precisely the context in which Rafn's work was received only six years later.

As a consequence, the more authoritative and scholarly reviewers of *Antiquitates Americanæ* all acknowledged the significance of Columbus but were also quick to list at length the many works that had already mentioned "a supposed discovery of some part of the eastern coast of our continent, by Northmen" (A. H. Everett, "The Discovery of America by the Northmen," article 1, 85). After providing his own list, which included Wheaton, the reviewer for the *United States Magazine and Democratic Review*, Alexander Hill Everett, explained, "We mention the names of these writers, in order to show that this supposed discovery of America by the Northmen is not, as some have imagined, a recent revelation of matters before unknown, but is founded in ancient authorities, which have always to a greater or less extent occupied the attention of the scientific geographer, and even of the general reading public" (86). Similarly, his younger brother, the reviewer for the highly influential *North American Review*, Edward Everett, began by assuring readers "of the title of Columbus to the glory of discovering our continent," but then he acknowledged "the tradition ... familiar to the reading world" regarding "a reputed prior discovery of the continent from the north of Europe" ("The Discovery of America by the Northmen" 165). Edward Everett's list of earlier books on the subject contained both European and American authors, including Irving and Wheaton, and was followed by this summary:

> The general purport of the tradition is, that about the beginning of the eleventh century of our era, some portion of the Atlantic coast of North America was discovered by Norwegian navigators sailing from Greenland; that they touched at various parts of the coast, and finally made a settlement upon it; that they called the portion, where this settlement was made, Vinland, or Wineland, from the abundance of wild grapes which it produced; that in the twelfth century, a missionary enterprise was undertaken from Greenland to America, for the purpose of converting the inhabitants to Christianity; and that after an intercourse kept up with the American continent for three centuries, the colonial establishments either became amalgamated with the native population, or from other causes disappeared, till the existence of Vinland was forgotten in Europe. Such in general is the tradition. (165)

This supposedly familiar tradition notwithstanding, Edward Everett left no doubt as to "the richness and importance" of Rafn's volume because it "has collected the original documents and thrown a new light" on the entire subject (162, 165).

That "new light" was the assertion of an unimpeachable scholarly foundation for removing the Vinland venture from some vague "portion of the Atlantic coast of North America" to specific sites within the United States. Just as Wheaton had done before him, Rafn claimed to adduce evidence locating the Vinland colony not simply within U.S. borders but in New England, the already iconic site of the Pilgrims' first arrival. In other words, by introducing American readers to the sagas and to related documents in far greater detail than had earlier writers, and because his interpretation of these works was quickly popularized, Rafn transformed what had previously been regarded as legend or tradition into what the *United States Magazine and Democratic Review* called "a portion of authentic history" (A. H. Everett, "The Discovery of America by the Northmen," article 2, 157). America had a long and storied past, after all. (See figure 2.)

Even the esteemed but highly skeptical George Bancroft took notice and amended his original edition of *History of the United States* (1834) to include, in later editions, citations to Rafn (and others) and a slightly expanded opening paragraph about "these early adventurers" from Greenland (3). Still, Bancroft was cautious. He acknowledged the claims by Rafn and others that "these early adventurers anchored near the harbour of Boston, or in the bays of New Jersey; and . . . entered the waters of Rhode Island." But he also noted that "the story of the colonization of America by Northmen, rests on narratives, mythological in form, and obscure in meaning." For Bancroft, these sources were "fictitious or exaggerated" (3).

Other historians followed Bancroft's lead and opened their own volumes with the story of the Norse in America, albeit most often without Bancroft's skepticism. Citing "the authority of Mr. Rafn," the well-regarded historian John S. C. Abbott opened his *The History of Maine* (1875) with a nine-page discussion of how "the Northmen discovered America more than six hundred years before Columbus" and how they sailed the coast of Maine and then proceeded south to explore and settle the new lands (13n, 14). As in Rafn, for Abbott too, Leif Eirikssson's Vinland was on Narragansett Bay, "probably not far from the present site of Newport in Rhode Island" (14). Thorvald was killed by a Native's arrow "near Boston Harbor" (15). And Thorfinn Karlsefni's expedition settled somewhere along "the beautiful sheet of water . . . the Narraganset Bay" (17). Abbott catalogued Vinland's many riches and attractions and, in his own voice, editorialized that nowhere could there be "a more genial climate than that of southern New England" (17). Additionally, along with many other historians, Abbott accepted as wholly plausible Rafn's and Mallett's rather thin evidence that, even after Thorfinn Karlsefni's departure, "a few men were left in the colony at the bay" (18). Then, based on the statement in the *Icelandic Annals* that "in the year 1121, a bishop by the name of Erik visited Vinland," Abbott further speculated, "It is probable that there was some colony on the coast, or perhaps scattered colonies, where Northmen were engaged in trading with the natives, fishing, and wood-cutting." After all,

2. *The Landing of the Norsemen* in Vinland, by the German American artist Emanuel Gottlieb Leutze (1816–68), was privately commissioned by a Philadelphia art patron and publicly exhibited in 1846 at the National Academy of Design in New York City and, in June 1864, at the Great Central Fair in Philadelphia. Unabashedly Romantic in its lushly detailed execution, the painting catered to the contemporary taste for images of a grand and heroic American Viking heritage. A suggestively pregnant Gudrid is carried ashore, flanked by two male figures wearing chain mail, Leutze's intentional visual allusion to Henry Wadsworth Longfellow's poem "The Skeleton in Armor" (1841). From the back of the boat, a young man reaches out for grapes from an overhanging vine. Reproduced by permission of Stiftung Sammlung Volmer, Wuppertal, Germany; on permanent loan to the Museum Kunst Palast, Düsseldorf.

Abbott explained, "the beauty, salubrity, and fertility of the country . . . must have presented strong inducements to visit the sunny realm, and to remain there" (19). Thus Abbott, too, subscribed to the notion of a thriving Norse presence somewhere in New England well into the twelfth century and beyond.

In a lengthy article in the *Round Table: A Saturday Review of Politics, Finance, Literature, Society*, composed upon the occasion of Rafn's death in 1866, Rafn was celebrated for his "connection with American history." According to this anonymous writer, Rafn had taken what once "appeared to be a misty bridge of romance, over which the legendary heroes of Norseland passed into the life of this continent," and proven it "as an historical fact of deep and suggestive interest" ("Carl Christian Rafn and the Ante-Columbian Era" 145). In so doing, Rafn's work provided a "glimpse of the marvelously grand and romantic era in the history of America" (146). As this writer put the matter, the entire story of the Norse in America, with its "weird, adventurous, solemn, and suggestive pageantry, the primitive heroism of the subject, the facts which make it history, and the close which shrouds it in mystery, are tempting incentives to the imagination, and should not be lost sight of by our poets and fictionists" (147).

"Poets and fictionists," however, were hardly the only writers who found in Rafn's work "tempting incentives to the imagination." In an era when the writing of the nation's history was meant to be both literary and celebratory, a bolstering of the national self-image in the face of Europe's greater power and ancient cultures, even historians found the romantic resonances of the Vinland story too compelling to ignore. In such instances, the historian's language moved almost seamlessly from the factual to the poetic. Abbott's *History of Maine* offers a characteristic example. Below a small engraving of the Newport tower on the same page, Abbott puzzled over the demise of the Vinland colony which, in his view, had been long-lived.

> One or two hundred years of silence pass away. The storms of winter wail through the forests of Vineland. The suns of summer clothe the extended landscape in verdure, opening the flowers, and ripening the grapes. Indian hunting-bands, of unknown name and language, wander through the solitudes. . . . But from these awful solitudes no voice reaches us. . . . The fact must forever remain inexplicable, why the Northmen, after having discovered and partially colonized the fair realms of Vineland, should have abandoned them entirely, while they continued their settlements in the dreary regions of Greenland and Iceland. They called the region "Vineland the Good." They extolled, in mer-

ited praise, the capacious harbors and the beautiful rivers with which this goodly land was blessed. Here the purple grapes hung in clusters; apples, pears, peaches, and an innumerable variety of plums, grew in orchards which Nature's hand had planted. Indian corn waved gracefully in spontaneous growth. They found pure water, fertile fields, and sunny skies. Wood was in abundance, for buildings, to cheer the winter fireside, and for the mechanic arts. Yet all this they abandoned for bleak and frigid realms. . . . And yet Vineland was left, for several hundred years, to the undisturbed possession of its savage inhabitants. (20–21)

Because it would have seriously undermined the story he was trying to tell, Abbott entirely omitted the fact that it was the "savage inhabitants" who, by careful management of certain nut- and fruit-bearing tree species, had created the orchards and cultivated the "fertile fields" with corn, squash, and beans. Instead, he described an idyllic *natural* landscape that the Norse alone appeared capable of appreciating and exploiting.

In no uncertain terms, Abbott celebrated America's abundant natural resources and the potential great wealth of "this goodly land." He even gestured toward the increasing industrial capacity of his own age when he mentioned the rivers and harbors that facilitated trade and shipping as well as the resources for "the mechanic arts" which were then producing manufactured goods. Yet while Abbott's paragraphs were at once retrospective and also suggestively prospective, above all else, they were elegiac. Where once the Norse had settled and thrived, in their absence the land became a place of "awful solitudes," where anonymous "Indian hunting-bands . . . wander through." No longer were the Norse present to witness and enjoy the grapes and other fruits "which Nature's hand had planted." And because Abbott refrained from suggesting the hostility of the Native peoples as an explanation for the Norse withdrawal from Vinland, "all this" abundance was simply and inexplicably "abandoned." Abbott's narrative thus left readers with only a romantic mystery in which a sense of unrealized possibilities predominated.

It is not enough to say that Rafn's work initiated an ongoing rewriting of North America's early history and a gradual popular revision of Euro-Americans' view of the continent's past. Nor is it enough to observe that Rafn's work supplied just what the artistic temper of the times demanded: an antique history shrouded in romantic mystery, with a ruin or two thrown in for good measure. All this was true, of course. But what proved even more consequential was that Rafn's work also opened to Americans new possibilities for retelling their stories of who they were as a people. Abbott's *The History of Maine* hinted at these possibilities but finally closed the section on the Northmen with only the fact of the Norse abandonment of Vinland and the attendant mystery of why so much promise went unfulfilled. Other writers, though, saw the story differently.

In language that rendered opaque the racial anxieties at its core, the popular New England poet, novelist, and short story writer Sarah Orne Jewett furnished an alternate ending to Abbott's narrative. What had not come to pass under the sway of the original Norse settlers had now been realized by their descendants. In *The Normans* (1886), Jewett declared that "Leif Ericson's lack of interest in [permanently settling] the fertile Vinland, New England now," had been a serious error. As a result, "Vinland waited hundreds of years after that for the hardy Icelander's kindred to come from old England to build their houses and spend the rest of their lives upon its good corn-land and among the shadows of its great pine-trees" (18). In other words, the land had all along been waiting for the sons and daughters of its first (European) discoverers to return. The English, "kindred" descendants of the Viking invaders of an earlier era, were the ones finally to colonize New England permanently. Contemporary New Englanders were their progeny. Behind them, in an unbroken chain of descent, loomed "Leif Ericson," the original discoverer and "kindred" ancestor.

It was a story that, in one version or another, echoed for decades after the publication of Rafn's *Antiquitates Americanæ*. As the Massachusetts clergyman and historical writer Benjamin Franklin DeCosta put it in the preface to *The Pre-Columbian Discovery of America by the Northmen* (1868), "We fable in great measure when we speak of our 'Saxon inheritance.' It is rather from the Northmen that we have derived our vital energy, our freedom of thought, and, in a measure that we do not yet suspect, our strength of speech" (v).

William Gilmore Simms and the Location of a Southern White Man's Land

Soon after the publication of *Antiquitates Americanæ* in 1837 and its *Supplement* in 1841, Rafn's two main pieces of physical evidence for a Norse landfall in the U.S. were called into question. In April 1839, the *American Biblical Repository* reprinted the entire five-page "Abstract" of *Antiquitates Americanæ* as a preface to an article by the highly regarded Indian expert Henry Rowe Schoolcraft.[17] Concerned that their readers might not yet be familiar with Rafn's volume, the editors of the journal included the "Abstract" in order to give them at least some acquaintance with the text to which Schoolcraft was responding. In his article, and in no uncertain terms, Schoolcraft dismissed Rafn's statements about runic inscriptions and Latin numbers and declared the markings on Dighton Rock to be of local Indian origin, with an overlay of more recent Euro-American graffiti. As an Indian agent in the Great Lakes area, Schoolcraft had pioneered in the ethnographic study of several Central Algonquian-speaking Native groups, and he thus carried considerable weight when he identified "the event recorded [on the rock] to be one of importance in Indian history; and the characters, hieroglyphics of the Algic [i.e., Algonquian] stamp" ("The Ante-Columbian History of America" 444).[18]

Then in 1858, John Gorham Palfrey, formerly a faculty member at Harvard and later Massachusetts's secretary of state, published the first volume of his meticulously researched three-volume *History of New England during the Stuart Dynasty*. In the second chapter, after acknowledging Schoolcraft's earlier work on the "origin and meaning" of the Dighton Rock inscriptions, Palfrey offered evidence that the Newport tower was a colonial-era artifact (56). It had been constructed as a windmill by the first governor of Rhode Island, Benedict Arnold, the great-grandfather of the Revolutionary War turncoat of the same name. He noted the improbability of there being no mention of "so singular an edifice" in any of the writings of the first New England settlers (56–57). According to Palfrey, it was inexplicably "strange that the first English settlers should not have mentioned the fact, if on their arrival they had found a vestige of a former civilization, so different from everything else within their view" (56–57). In fact, continued Palfrey, the first known reference to the Newport tower "is in the will of Governor Benedict Arnold, of Newport, dated December 20th, 1677." Arnold called it "my stone-built windmill" (57). Palfrey even tracked down the original model for Arnold's windmill: a similar windmill, designed by Inigo Jones, in Warwickshire, England, near where Arnold had lived until the age of twenty, when he left for the colonies. This structure, too, had been "known in the vicinity as 'the stone windmill'" (58).

Subsequent studies of Dighton Rock and several twentieth-century excavations of the Newport tower have only confirmed the original researches by Schoolcraft and Palfrey.[19] Today, most professional archaeologists and ethnologists concur in the view that the symbols and pictographs on Dighton Rock were incised by an Algonquian people and that the Newport tower is unquestionably a seventeenth-century construction. But this has hardly persuaded the few remaining Viking enthusiasts of our own day, and resistance to the conclusions of Schoolcraft and Palfrey was even more pronounced in the nineteenth century. For many, Rafn's massive scholarship was so overwhelming as to seem beyond question, while, for others, their investment in the idea of a Norse colony in the U.S. — and especially in New England — was just too powerful to let go.

Palfrey's work was either ignored or dismissed, and Schoolcraft was immediately challenged in the next issue of the *American Biblical Repository*. Interestingly, Schoolcraft nowhere disputed Rafn's main argument, instead stating that it seemed to him "beyond doubt that the Northmen made repeated voyages into the northern Atlantic, early in the 10th century, and visited and wintered at various points on the New England coast" ("The Ante-Columbian History of America" 435). Schoolcraft's only objections centered on Rafn's (mis)identification of the Skraelings as belonging to "the Esquimau race" and Rafn's (mis)-reading of the Native pictographs on Dighton Rock as "Runic characters" (437, 444). Familiar as he was with Central Algonquian-speaking peoples from his work in Michigan and Wisconsin, Schoolcraft was convinced that the Natives encountered by the Norse were a related Algonquian people and that the markings on Dighton Rock were "characteristic of . . . the Algic race" (446). Still, for those invested in Rafn's work being widely accepted, *any* challenge — even a relatively minor ethnographic correction like Schoolcraft's — was seen as threatening to the entire edifice.

Writing in the July 1839 issue of the *American Biblical Repository*, the Reverend Alonzo Bowen Chapin of New Haven argued that while the pictorial figures that Schoolcraft called "hieroglyphics" might well be "the work of Indians," "the letters and numerals" were not the "idle" graffiti of "the moderns," as Schoolcraft proposed (192). Laboriously examining every available extant drawing of Dighton Rock from 1680 onward, Chapin attempted to demonstrate that what appeared to be Latin letters and numerals engraved on the rock "were made *before* the English came to this country" (193, Chapin's emphasis). Then, after a tortuous interpretation of each supposed letter or number as either Latin or Icelandic script, "and in characters peculiar to the age of Thorfinn," Chapin concluded that the weight of the evidence leaned toward the "genuineness" of "the inscription in the Icelandic tongue." (See figure 3.) It read, Chapin continued, as a "commemoration" of Thorfinn Karlsefni's taking possession of "the place where the inscription is found" (195, 197). In this, he basically repeated Rafn's analysis and

Inscriptions on Dighton Rock.

3. Reduced-size copy of the interpretive illustration of the inscriptions on Dighton Rock, originally published by Carl Christian Rafn in *Antiquitates Americanæ*, 1837. Reproduced here from John Warner Barber's *The History and Antiquities of New England* (1842, 12).

conclusions. Finally, rather than trying to refute the well-established authority of Schoolcraft, Chapin acknowledged, "If the Northmen selected this rock, on which to record their possession of the country; what more natural, than that the natives should choose *the same* rock on which to record their expulsion from it?" (197, Chapin's emphasis). With this interpretation, Dighton Rock told a piece of New England's early history consistent with Rafn's basic narrative: an initial discovery and settlement inscribed on the rock by the Norse, followed by the expulsion of the Norse by the Native inhabitants who inscribed *that* event on the rock also. Schoolcraft's authority remained intact but, important to Chapin, the rock remained for Euro-Americans "an important relic of antiquity" related to them (197).

Like Schoolcraft, Palfrey also admitted the likely possibility "that eight or nine hundred years ago the Norwegian navigators extended their voyages as far as the American continent." After all, reasoned Palfrey, they "possess[ed] the best nautical skill of their age," and after a relatively easy voyage from Greenland to Labrador, a visit to "the coast of North America . . . would require only a coasting voyage" (51–52).

Palfrey's argument was only with the particular pieces of evidence—textual interpretations and physical artifacts alike—"used to identify these spots" where the Norse supposedly traveled or established homesites. In his view, the evidence for locating these specific geographical sites was simply "insufficient" (55). But for those who most strongly supported Rafn's conclusions, the specific geographical locations were precisely the point.

One example comes not from New England, as might be expected, but from the South. In September 1841, William Gilmore Simms—by then becoming known as "the southern Cooper" for his historical frontier and Revolutionary War romances set in the Carolinas—published an article titled "The Discoveries of the Northmen." The article was based on Rafn's *Antiquitates Americanæ* and the subsequent popular abridgement of that work in 1841 by a proud Irishman from Cork named North Ludlow Beamish. Beamish had his own agenda. As he explained in the preface to *The Discovery of America by the Northmen*, his book had two main goals. Speaking of himself in the third person, he said he first wanted "to put before the public in a cheap and compendious form, those parts of Professor Rafn's work, which he considered were likely to prove most interesting to British readers, the greater part of whom, from the expense and language of the original publication, must necessarily be debarred from its perusal" (n.p.). In addition to making Rafn's work both more affordable and accessible "to British readers," Beamish also had a political message for those same readers. Thus his second goal was to rehabilitate a "neglected portion of Irish history" and, with that, the reputation of Ireland itself (n.p.). As he noted in his preface, "It has been too much the practice to decry as fabulous, all statements claiming for the earlier inhabitants of Ireland, a comparatively high degree of advancement and civilization" (n.p.). Recent scholarship challenging this view had been ignored, Beamish complained, especially by "those who, with the anti-Irish feeling of the bigotted Cambrensis [i.e., the Welsh] would sink Ireland in the scale of national distinction, and deny her claims to that early eminence in religion, learning, and the arts" (n.p.).[20]

In order to amend such bigotry, Beamish ended his preface with a promise to readers:

> The following pages [will] clearly shew: that sixty-five years previous to the discovery of Iceland by the Northmen in the ninth century, Irish emigrants had visited and inhabited that island;—that about the year 725, Irish ecclesiastics had sought seclusion upon the Faroe islands;—that in the tenth century, voyages between Iceland and Ireland were of

ordinary occurrence; and that in the eleventh century, a country west from Ireland, and south of that part of the American continent, which was discovered by the adventurous Northmen in the preceding age, was known to them under the name of White Man's Land or GREAT IRELAND. (n.p.)

To this project, Beamish devoted all of part 3 of his book, a full sixty-two pages of analysis and selected extracts from narratives collected by Rafn in *Antiquitates Americanæ.*

Although Beamish thought he was designing *The Discovery of America by the Northmen* for a British audience, his book found eager readers and sold well across the Atlantic. Many Americans were happy to have a more accessible and affordable version of Rafn's tome, while others—like Simms—found Beamish's political motives consonant with their own. Expressly written for *Magnolia*, a monthly magazine that came out of Simms's beloved Charleston, Simms's article asserted that the evidence and "proofs" supplied by both Rafn and Beamish, including Dighton Rock, "are sufficiently strong and plausible" as to make all of Rafn's conclusions about the travels and settlements of the Norse in North America nothing short of a wholly believable "revelation of wonders." As a writer of historical romances, Simms eagerly embraced "the discoveries . . . of antiquities in our Western World, which prove it to be quite as old as the European" ("The Discoveries of the Northmen" 418). And he urged that one particular segment of Rafn's work "adds a new world to the resources of the American Romancer" (421). That segment was not about the various Norse voyages to and settlements in New England, however. These Simms summarized in a single page. Rather, what fascinated Simms were the discussions by Rafn and Beamish of Hvítramannaland, "'WHITE-MAN'S LAND, or GREAT IRELAND' . . . where white men and Irishmen dwelt at this period." *Magnolia* readers will "prick up their ears and open their eyes, with very great amaze," predicted Simms, to learn that, "according to the solemn opinion and serious researches of Professor Rafn," this ancient land of white men was "no other than our own dearly beloved region of SOUTH CAROLINA AND GEORGIA" (417).

At some length, Simms recapitulated both Rafn and Beamish, arguing that Northmen had traveled "to our twin States of Georgia and Carolina . . . in the years 999, and 1029—and that these Northmen discovered traces in this region of a white population so identical with that of Ireland, with which they were familiar—identical in look, language and costume—that they conferred upon it this name, by which the country was generally recognized and known among their voyagers and people." That name was "Hvitramanna land . . . i.e. Whiteman's land or Great Ireland." "There is nothing marvelous or strange," continued Simms, in the revelation "that the Western Hemisphere had been visited and settled by whites, . . . [and] that these whites should be Irish." Paraphrasing Beamish, he explained, "The Irish were among the earliest explorers of Europe—among the most learned—. . . [and] of a comparatively high degree of civilization." Moreover, Irish monks were believed to have inhabited Iceland some sixty-five years before the Norse first arrived there in the ninth century, and many antiquarians assumed that from Iceland the monks had probably gone on farther westward. From the artifacts left behind in Iceland—"Irish books, bells and croziers"—"it could be seen that they were Christian men," added Simms ("The Discoveries of the Northmen" 418).

Much of Simms's article was then taken up with a detailed retelling of the legendary adventures of the two Norse heroes who had supposedly visited Hvítramannaland and its Irish colonists. These stories did not appear in the two Vinland sagas but were teased out of other medieval sources, including the *Eyrbyggja Saga*, which Rafn had excerpted and commented upon in *Antiquitates Americanæ*. Beamish simply had restated and amplified that same material, and thus Rafn and Beamish were again Simms's sources. Simms was convinced that out of these stories of Norse and Irish in Hvítramannaland, "fifty spirited ballads might be manufactured with ease" or even a short "epic" like "the Border Tales of Scott" ("The Discoveries of the Northmen" 421).

Gradually, as his article moved toward a close, Simms began to reveal the epic narrative that now engaged his imagination. Making the most of Rafn's "opinion that the White Man's Land or great Ireland of the Northmen was the country lying south of the Chesapeake and extending to East Florida," and making use also of Rafn's wholly unreliable compilation of Indian lore, Simms asserted the following: "The tradition of our Indians . . . was, that they had come from the southwest, that they had destroyed a civilized and superior people—a white people who used iron instruments" ("The Discoveries of the Northmen" 420). In a subsequent statement, Simms repeated the popular antiquarian canard of his day, that the Indians and their ancestors were simply too lacking in civilization ever to have built "the Tumuli, the works of defence and worship" still in evidence from the great Mississippian and Hopewell cultures of the past (421). Then, by linking these fallacious notions of Indian history to the Norse materials disseminated by Rafn, and expanded upon by Beamish, Simms came up with the by now familiar outline of "a most romantic tale":

> A judicious artist would make a most romantic tale of that colony of Green Erin [on] the shores of Carolina and Georgia;—showing how, driven by stress of weather, and finding so lovely a land, greener than their own beloved Island, they pitched their tents for good:—how they built cities, how they flourished amid songs and dances; with now and then a faction fight by way of reminiscence:—how, suddenly, the fierce red men of the south-west came down upon them in howling thousands, captured their women, slaughtered their men, and drove them to their fortresses:—how they fought to the last, and perished to a man! And, in this history, you have the history of the Tumuli, the works of defence and worship—the thousand proofs with which our land is covered, of a genius and an industry immeasurably superior to any thing that the Indian inhabitants of this country ever attempted. (421)

For Simms, this was the perfect American historical romance: an antique tale of heroism and the picturesque and a tale perfectly attuned to the racial politics of the moment.

Neither Simms nor any other southern writer of the period took up the task of composing a romance about the "colony of Green Erin [on] the shores of Carolina and Georgia." Even so, the appeal of this story line for someone like Simms is hardly difficult to understand. Although born into a family of quite modest means, shopkeepers without wealth or large landholdings, Simms grew up to become both an apologist for slavery and an admirer of what he perceived to be the superior culture and genteel society of the plantation oligarchy.[21] Yet with a growing abolitionist movement both in the North and in some of the new western territories, this world that he celebrated in his fiction was increasingly coming under attack.

At the same time, the South had now become the major site of the nation's Indian removal policies. In 1834, under the terms of a fraudulent treaty signed two years earlier, the U.S. government began trying to force the Seminole Nation from its lands in Florida to territory west of the Mississippi. Seminole resistance began in earnest the next year and continued until 1842.[22] As unpopular as were the Seminole Wars in Florida, the removal of the Cherokee from Georgia elicited even greater public outrage. Both were among the so-called Five Civilized Tribes that had taken on many Euro-American social, educational, and economic practices. But when, in 1827, the Cherokee adopted a constitution modeled on that of the U.S. and asserted their land boundaries as a sovereign nation, they did so only a year before President Andrew Jackson pushed through Congress the first of the Indian Removal Acts. And after gold was discovered on Cherokee land in 1829, the state of Georgia renewed its efforts to remove the tribe and confiscate its lands. A court battle ensued that ended in 1831 with a decision by Supreme Court Justice John Marshall in favor of the Cherokee. In a widely circulated opinion, Marshall affirmed Cherokee sovereignty and added that "the acts of Georgia are repugnant to the constitution, laws, and treaties of the United States" (qtd. in Alexander 127). But President Jackson ignored the Marshall decision and allowed Georgia to proceed with its plans for removal. When Martin Van Buren succeeded to the presidency in 1836, he responded to the growing public outcry by trying to delay removal. Ominously presaging the South's later rationale for secession, the Georgia governor rejected Van Buren's plan. As the date for removal approached, even Ralph Waldo Emerson, who generally shied away from direct political engagement, felt compelled to compose an open letter to Van Buren, citing a great flaw "in the *moral* character of the government" ("Cherokee Letter" 104). "From Maine to Georgia," wrote Emerson, "the soul of man . . . does abhor this business" (103). In its treaty relations with Native peoples, he charged, once again the government appeared bent on "an act of fraud and robbery" (104).

As with many other statements of protest, Emerson's letter had no effect. In May 1838, federal troops and Georgia militia began rounding up the Cherokee for their removal from Georgia to Indian Territory in what is now eastern Oklahoma. On the infamous forced march known as the Trail of Tears, over four thousand Cherokee men, women, and children perished. And as these facts became known, there were again expressions of outrage from many quarters.

In short, whether on behalf of slaves or Native Americans, a growing chorus of opprobrium directed against the federal government in general and the southern states in particular marked the late 1830s and early 1840s. Against this background, it is hardly surprising that a writer with Simms's ardently pro-southern views sought some alternative narrative about "our own dearly beloved region." He thus gleaned from Rafn and Beamish a narrative that seemed tacitly to cancel out one wrong in the face of another. However disturbing the Trail of Tears and the ongoing Seminole Wars, Simms's article told of an earlier and even more horrific aggression: how a colony of white people, supposedly the original and rightful first settlers, once "fought to the last, and perished to a man" at the hands of "the fierce red men of the southwest [who] came down upon them in howling thousands." In other words, Simms's article did not need explicitly to justify the South's (or the nation's) racist policies. Instead, by echoing a narrative frame that had been in place since the years of the early republic, Simms subtly suggested a balance to the scales of justice. After all, he was claiming, the white man *had* been there first.

Although Simms never wrote a romance about the Norse and Irish in pre-Columbian America, in *The History of South Carolina*, written in 1844, he nonetheless enshrined *as fact* the original occupation of the southern region by white people. Designed both as a school textbook and as a history for general readers, Simms's *History* went through several updates and new editions through the 1860s. With each new and revised edition, Simms affirmed again and again that the South had originally been "occupied by . . . white men" (9). In every edition, the first chapter opened with a version of material condensed from his *Magnolia* article of 1841, albeit without the melodrama of bloodshed:

> The Carolinas, North and South, forming twin provinces under the British dominion in America, were anciently a part of that extensive territory, known to the European world under the several names of Virginia, Florida, and New France. Still more anciently, according to tradition and old chronicles of the Northmen, the region was occupied by a race, or races, of white men, to whom, if these traditions are well-founded, we are to ascribe the tumuli, earthworks, and numerous remains of fortified places in which the whole country abounds, rather than to the nomadic red men who occupied the territory at the time of the discovery, by Columbus and other voyagers, within the modern and historical period. (9)

Immediately following these sentences, Simms offered a short and fact-laden statement naming the northern and southern borders of "the two Carolinas": Virginia and "the bay of Mexico" (9). In this way, he positioned the lengthy sentence about ancient white races within a surrounding discourse of well-known and verifiable historical information, thereby making it appear equivalent in truth-value (or historicity) to the sentences preceding and following. As a result, the mild caveat — "*if* these traditions are well-founded" — loses much of its potential to arouse doubt or invite further inquiry (my emphasis).

Then, because *The History of South Carolina* functioned primarily as a textbook, Simms placed questions at the bottom of selected pages in order to prompt memorization of what he considered the most salient facts on the page. Following the passage just quoted, Simms offered four questions, two of which emphasized the racialized prehistory to which he was committed: "What was the tradition of the Northmen, as to the inhabitants of this region?" and "To what races are we to ascribe the ancient remains in the country?" (9). The other two questions pertained to the different early names for the Carolinas in "the European world" and to the geographical borders of "the territories of the Carolinas" (9). Again, Simms thus implied a factual equivalence to the pieces of information to be memorized. With that act, as in Abbott's *The History of Maine*—although with different motives—the romantic and the historic once more merged seamlessly, the former overwhelming the latter.

Racing the Norse

In the twenty-three years between the initial outpouring of reviews and articles that greeted the appearance of *Antiquitates Americanæ* in the U.S. in 1838 and the commencement of civil war with the attack on Fort Sumter in Charleston, South Carolina, in 1861, Rafn's work continued to reverberate widely across the country. From the beginning, articles and reviews appeared not only in magazines and newspapers published in all the major eastern urban centers but in the West as well. The *Western Messenger*, which came out of Cincinnati, published two related articles in 1838, the first a lengthy review and summary of *Antiquitates Americanæ* and the second a discussion of "inscription rocks" found in Massachusetts and Rhode Island.[23] That same year, the *Catholic Telegraph*, which also came out of Cincinnati, carried a one-page abstract of *Antiquitates Americanæ*.[24] In Chicago in 1852 the *Christian Advocate and Journal* published yet another article "communicated by Charles C. Rafn, and . . . founded on his work 'Antiquitates Americanæ.'" As this journal explained to its western readers, Rafn's "short sketch" gave "still further publicity to historical facts so important" to Americans ("Discovery of America by the Northmen" 208).

As a result of this continuous stream of books and articles, by the 1850s "the discovery of America by the Icelanders" was hardly "absolute *news*" to anyone. As a writer for *Graham's American Monthly Magazine* put it in 1853, "The subject [had], many years ago, been discussed freely by the press, and investigated by various historical societies of our country." Given the information to be gleaned from the sagas and "the monuments found in our country," this writer expressed no doubt about "the principal proof[s] of the early presence of the bold Northmen on our shores" (Grund 545). Another writer for *Graham's* that year, William Dowe, reminded any readers who might have "perhaps forgotten, that an Ericsson was the first discoverer of America." And he further pronounced "the authenticity of these Icelandic accounts . . .

beyond a doubt" (385, 387). Typical of articles in the popular press of the period, these pieces in *Graham's*, which came out of Philadelphia, simply reflected the relatively widespread acceptance of Rafn's main ideas and conclusions. And as the stories of the Norse as original discoverers and would-be New England settlers spread across the culture, gradually a new image of the Norse began to emerge. No longer were they only brutal Viking conquerors and piratical marauders. Instead, they began to be associated with more civilized qualities, a process of imaginative rehabilitation that began almost immediately in the initial reviews of *Antiquitates Americanæ*.

One way to rehabilitate the Norse was to appreciate their wealth of medieval literature, a literature that Rafn had culled exclusively for its historical data. But in 1838, George Folsom, the reviewer for the *New York Review*, praised "the general characteristics of the Icelandic tongue ... [as] consciousness, energy, and flexibility, to an extent which rivals every modern language, and which enables it to enter into successful competition with the Greek and Latin" (367). The people who spoke that tongue, Folsom averred, had been "accustomed from childhood to deeds of daring and of dauntless courage, ... unhesitatingly [steering] into the untraversed ocean without chart or compass" (364). And when these dauntless Northmen "conver[ted] to Christianity about A.D. 1000," they simultaneously adopted "Roman letters" and thereby initiated "the commencement of the Golden Age of Icelandic literature" (364).

Another way to rehabilitate popular conceptions of the Norse was to make them appear not only as "poetical" but also, and far more consequentially, as American antecedents. Consider again, for example, the two-part review in 1838 by a scion of an old and prominent Massachusetts family, Alexander Hill Everett, then serving as a diplomat in Washington and writing for the Washington-based *United States Magazine and Democratic Review*, an organ of the Democratic Party. As Everett well understood, any article in such a venue, whatever its subject, would certainly be read as having political and national implications, however understated.

In the second of his two articles, Everett made explicit what had only been implicit in the first. In the May 1838 issue, he expressed his "belief in the credibility of the main facts" of all the documents compiled by Rafn and declared it "impossible, in fact, to follow the Northmen in their course ... without perceiving that you are brought to the southeastern coast of New England" ("The Discovery of America by the Northmen," article 2, 147, 151). He therefore concluded, "The identity of Wineland with Massachusetts and Rhode Island . . . appears to be fully proved" (157). Aware that he was now promoting a new view of New England's—and the nation's—early history, Everett seems to have understood the need somehow to integrate that new view into a larger national narrative. He accomplished this in the earlier article, published in April 1838, by adjusting the accepted picture of the Northmen.

To be sure, in that April issue, Everett acknowledged that the "piratical squadrons [of the Northmen] showed themselves successively on the coast of almost every known region" from Europe to the Mediterranean and "for a time gave law from the thrones of Jerusalem and Constantinople" ("The Discovery of America by the Northmen," article 1, 87). Yet he attributed these imperial conquests not to violence or brutality but, rather, to the Northmen's "superior activity, energy and courage," and he emphasized not the conquests but the law-giving. Further, Everett explained, "at the time when the discovery [of America] is supposed to have been made," the Northmen "were just in their palmy [i.e., celebrated or honored] state of expansion and activity." There is little condemnation in this language and much quiet admiration. It is a response perhaps to be expected from a diplomat supportive of his party's and his nation's increasing eagerness for an analogous experience of "expansion and activity." After all, the icon of the Democratic Party was none other than the old Indian-fighter and two-term (1829–36) former president Andrew Jackson, whose Indian removal policies both facilitated and encouraged westward expansion. And it was a period when at least a few Americans openly began contemplating a nation that stretched westward to the Pacific and southward into Mexican territory. Thus it is hardly surprising that Everett led his readers to see in the Norse an anticipation of Americans' own developing self-image: "They displayed every where a hardihood and enterprise, in which they have never been surpassed" (87).

That said, what made an identification between Norse and Americans important to Everett was not solely the fact of the Northmen's pre-Columbian presence in New England. For Everett, whose family line went back to the seventeenth-century Puritans, the Norse were not simply discoverers. They were also ancestors and progenitors. Although Everett never argued that point directly, his brief summary of the Northmen "spread[ing] themselves over all the islands of the British Archipelago" made clear that Norse blood—not just Saxon blood—ran in the veins of most Anglo-Americans. It is *this* "stock," he was saying, that is also *our* heritage as Americans.

He then pressed the point further through an implicit analogy that played to a then-popular notion of the course of historical progress. Everett emphasized that "with all their wild habits of predatory violence, [the Northmen] were nevertheless a highly imaginative and poetical people; in their later period, they became a refined, accomplished and literary one." Influenced by Cooper's Leatherstocking novels, Americans could see a version of their own story in this scenario. In other words, those rude, untutored, and sometimes violent Natty Bumppo frontiersmen who first fought the Indians and conquered a wilderness, like the wild Northmen, eventually made it possible for those who followed them to embrace "the gentle graces of civilization" ("The Discovery of America by the Northmen," article 1, 87). This, promised historical precedent, would also be the nation's progress.

Finally, Everett too invoked the romantic in his portrayal of the Norse. "At the time when we meet them in America," he wrote, the Northmen "justified completely the beautiful description given of them by Scott, in the Lay of the Last Minstrel, in speaking of the Western Islands—

> Thither came in times afar,
> Stern Lochlin's sons [i.e., Scandinavians] of roving war,
> The Northmen, trained to fire and blood,
> Skilled to prepare the raven's food,
> Kings of the main, their leaders brave,—
> Their barks, the dragons of the wave."
> ("The Discovery of America by the Northmen," article 1, 87–88)

Wrapped in the appealing mantle of Scott's romantic and roving Northmen, for Everett the Norse who had come to America embodied not only the nation's antique romantic past but also its striving and energetic present. He constructed the Northmen as hardy, energetic, enterprising, courageous, and "the greatest navigators in Europe"— in short, as proto-Americans and precursors of the hardy Yankee seamen of his own day ("The Discovery of America by the Northmen," article 1, 87). And not insignificantly, he quietly suggested that the traits of these precursors were already, so to speak, *in the blood*.

Throughout the ensuing decades, this idea of a blood tie between Norse and Americans—especially New Englanders—gained greater and greater currency. By the 1840s it was not unusual for cultural commentators to declare, "The modern New England character has in it much more of the Norse than of the Saxon" ("Discovery of America by the Norsemen," *Massachusetts Quarterly*, 189). In an unsigned omnibus essay review in the *Massachusetts Quarterly Review* of March 1849, the writer discussed four books about the Norse in America—Rafn's *Antiquitates Americanæ*, Beamish's *The Discovery of America by the Northmen in the Tenth Century*, and two German books on the subject—and found himself drawn inevitably to a consideration of "the influence of blood" (189). While this writer insisted that he did not "hold to the doctrine that all traits and qualities are derived from one's ancestors, . . . nevertheless, in the *foundation* of the character, in the instinctive tendencies and predilections of a man or nation, the influence of blood is not to be denied" (189). By way of example, he offered "the restless activity, the impatience of control [i.e., the innate resistance to tyranny], and the practical faculty which distinguish the Yankee" as evidence that New England's Yankees were, indeed, "the genuine descendants of the [Viking] invaders of England" (189–90). And unlike those of solely German and Anglo-Saxon descent, he added, "one of the most prominent features of the New England character is a talent for maritime affairs. The New Englander," like his long-ago Viking ancestors, "is born with a love for the ocean and an intuitive skill in navigation" (190).

This purported genealogy appealed to many Americans—not just to New Englanders—because it brought together two emerging and increasingly accepted views of the world. First, supplanting the older idea of history as cyclical, a repeated pattern of the rise and fall of civilizations, was a more optimistic belief in history as ultimately progressive, despite temporary stumbles or backsliding along the way. Second, adumbrating older descriptions of racial hierarchy that relied mainly on skin color and other physical characteristics, there now developed a more "modern," supposedly more scientific understanding of racial *types* anchored in societal development and cultural difference. That is, there developed the view that race and culture were imbricated within each other.

According to the reigning racial theory of the day, one particular stock of the human family, commonly designated as Indo-European or Aryan, had produced a far-flung dispersal of peoples and languages, among whom the Germanic branches—the chief subdivision of the Aryan stock—enjoyed a special capacity for promoting culture and seeking liberty. One prominent nineteenth-century historian saw in these Germanic branches a "vast brood of children; Franks, Goths, Saxons, Lombards, Normans, Netherlanders, Americans—Germans all"

(Motley 106). The "Gothic branches" had toppled "the once-mighty Roman empire," while the "energetic Norman [i.e., Northmen] branch" had seated themselves "on every throne in Europe" from the British Isles to Russia (106). By the mid-nineteenth century, the potentialities of these Germanic peoples "seemed most vigorously manifest in the Anglo-Saxon and Germanic nations" and, of course, that included the U.S. (Falnes 212). In this way, what the twentieth century would come to identify as the contingencies of cultural, regional, and ethnic differences, the nineteenth century codified as racial and inherent. To some degree, all these strands of thought were originally imports from Germany, but American intellectuals quickly domesticated them, made them their own, and adjusted them to reinforce America's Viking connection.

One version of these ideas about race, culture, and history, intended specifically to appeal to his fellow New Englanders, was actively espoused throughout the 1840s and 1850s by George Perkins Marsh, later known as a skilled diplomat, foreign ambassador, and early student of the impact of human activity on the natural environment.[25] But before he turned to those vocations, Marsh first considered it his patriotic duty to extol the virtues of New England, "whose sons are most honourably distinguished by true nobility of origin" (6). In a series of articles and public addresses, Marsh attributed America's "national greatness" and adherence to the "principle of progressive development" to its Puritan origins, and he attributed the Puritans' capacity to develop democratic values and, later, religious tolerance to "that great race from which, with little intermixture, we are lineally descended" (8, 21). That "great race," claimed Marsh, was "the Goths, the common ancestors of the inhabitants of North Western Europe, . . . the noblest branch of the Caucasian race" (14). Conflating all the many ancient Germanic tribes under the umbrella term "Goths," Marsh declared of his fellow New Englanders, "We are their children. It was the spirit of the Goth, that guided the May-Flower across the trackless ocean; the blood of the Goth that flowed at Bunker's Hill" (14).[26]

In an address delivered at Middlebury College in Vermont in 1843 and published as a pamphlet with the title *The Goths in New-England*, Marsh fully elaborated his racialized version of English and American history. "England is Gothic by birth, Roman by adoption," he asserted (14). Thus he distinguished between the various Germanic peoples who had invaded and inhabited England over the centuries and the Roman conquest of A.D. 43 which initiated four centuries of Roman rule.

Each represented something very different. "Whatever [England] has of true moral grandeur, of higher intellectual power, she owes to the Gothic mother; while her grasping ambition, her material energies, her spirit of exclusive selfishness, are due to the Roman nurse" (14). As Marsh and his listeners tacitly understood, that nurse was replaced by the true mother when Germanic peoples—the Angles, Saxons, and Jutes—successfully initiated new waves of invasion and settlement at the time of the disintegration of the Roman Empire in the early fifth century. Subsequent invasions by other Germanic peoples, most notably Norwegian and Danish Vikings, began in the late eighth century. The Dane Canute ruled England by 1016, and the Normans (or Northmen) conquered England from France in 1066.[27]

Then, in a purposeful slippage of terminology that fused rule by the Roman Empire with Roman Catholicism, Marsh characterized the Reformation, "that grand era in British history," as "the English mind . . . striving to recover its Gothic tendencies, by the elimination of the Roman element" (11). That reassertion of the Gothic character, wrote Marsh, removed "the shackles and burdens, which the spiritual and intellectual tyranny of Rome had for centuries imposed" (10). In other words, Roman Catholicism had been as tyrannical in its own way as the political rule imposed by the Roman Empire. In Marsh's view, the purest avatar of the Reformation was found in "the intellectual character of our Puritan forefathers . . . derived by inheritance from our remote Gothic ancestry" (10). As a result, "the founders of the first New England colony . . . belonged to the class most deeply tinctured with the moral and intellectual traits of their Northern ancestry" (19). And once having "freed themselves from the last remnant and most offensive peculiarity of the Roman spirit, religious intolerance," and having fully embraced the "principle of the absolute legal equality of all men," the admirable progeny of these Puritan forebears laid "the foundation of a new republic, destined . . . long to remain as a model of a system of human government based on . . . doctrines of civil and religious liberty" (19, 13). Through the Puritans, American exceptionalism was thus ultimately rooted in a Germanic (or Northern) racial ancestry.

An even more influential proponent of these views was another New Englander, John Lothrop Motley (1814–77), best known in his own day as a historian and diplomat. Motley attended Harvard College from 1827 to 1831 and, like many other promising young men with literary interests, he was encouraged by his professors to go abroad and pursue further studies at German universities. There he studied German language and literature and witnessed firsthand the resurgence of a

German nationalism intimately tied to the new German romanticism that was sweeping the continent. Upon his return, Motley attempted a brief and unsuccessful career as a novelist but soon brought his literary skills to his true métier, the writing of history. Although his three major historical works on Holland and the Netherlands are little read today, at the time they significantly contributed to the dissemination in America of ideas Motley had encountered in Germany, ideas that he and others were also applying to their representations of the United States.[28]

First and foremost was an idea earlier espoused by Motley's friend and mentor, the historian George Bancroft. Although one nation might temporarily rise to power only to fall before another, thus seeming to suggest a continuing cycle, in fact, when seen over long periods of time, historical events actually revealed an underlying and inevitable law. "That law is progress," declared Motley, "—slow, confused, contradictory, but ceaseless development, intellectual and moral, of the human race." To this he added, "The law is Progress; the result Democracy" (87). Then, paraphrasing the German poet and philosopher Johann Gottfried von Herder (1744–1803), whom Motley called "one of the most thoughtful writers who ever dealt with human history," Motley stated that the progress of civilization required the right climate. "Nothing good or great could come out of the eternal spring or midsummer of the tropics, nor from the thick-ribbed winter of the poles. From the temperate zone, with its healthful and stimulating succession of seasons, have come civilization and progress" (89). In addition to the right climate, the progress of civilization also seemed to follow a particular direction. "The orbit of civilization," wrote Motley, "seems preordained from East to West. China, India, Palestine, Egypt, Greece, Rome," northern and western Europe, and, finally, America, "a virgin world" (95, 101). Altogether eradicating Native history and presence, Motley made "the discovery of this continent" the end to which human progress had been moving. "Here a vast empire had been waiting for its empty spaces to be peopled, three millions of miles with never a town on its surface. Clearly the phenomenon was a new one and culture here could only mean Democracy" (101).[29] In Motley's schema, America had everything going for it: a temperate climate, its location as the stopping place for the steady movement of civilization from east to west, the right racial ancestry, and many "physical advantages," or natural resources (101). As a result, America was fast developing all the institutions requisite for a true democracy, the ultimate end of the law of progress.

In "Historic Progress and American Democracy," a talk delivered before the New-York Historical Society in December 1868—a talk published as a pamphlet in New York and London the next year and the talk from which I have been quoting—Motley summarized the theories that had permeated his work since the antebellum decades. But in 1868 he could express those theories with a renewed optimism. "The inestimable blessing of the abolition of slavery," he asserted, had significantly advanced "the cause of progress." The nation's one "standing reproach to Democracy is removed at last," he declared (117–18). The country could now move forward on its steady progressive march, further strengthening those institutions that Motley considered crucial for "this Republic": political freedom and regular elections; "universal education, the only possible foundation of human freedom"; "the free school, and that immense instrument of civilization, the daily press" (101). Motley also praised the enterprising and inventive spirit that was "making democracy on an imperial scale possible" and named specifically the steam engine and the telegraph (101). Most important, though, after surveying the long sorry history of what he called Europe's "incestuous union" between the Catholic Church and the state, Motley particularly emphasized the separation of church and state in America, the nation's "freedom of religion," and its habits of "mutual toleration" (98). "Religion can be honestly and ardently cherished" in the U.S., he argued, "because priesthood is deprived of political power" (101).

While Motley acknowledged that "the inexorable law of Freedom and Progress" had not yet unfolded itself perfectly in the U.S., he nonetheless saw the nation, now unburdened of slavery, as a model of progress and an international beacon of hope. "This nation," he insisted, "stands on the point toward which other peoples are moving" (87). As a result, he concluded, "the toiling multitudes of the earth are interested in the fate of this great republic of refuge" (105).

Unsurprisingly, in "Historic Progress and American Democracy," Motley rearticulated ideas previously put forward by Bancroft, who, like Motley, had also followed a path from Harvard to Germany. The first edition of Bancroft's *History of the United States* contained an author's preface written in 1834 (and reprinted in subsequent editions), in which Bancroft, too, explained that his goal was to elucidate "the *progress* of American institutions" (iv, my emphasis). In a prefatory note affixed to the third edition of 1840, Bancroft added, "The American Revolution [had been] achieved by our fathers, not for themselves alone and their posterity only, but for the world" (iii–iv). Guided by what he called "a favouring Providence," and what Motley later referred to as both Providence and Destiny, the U.S. thus stood as an exemplar "for the world" and an emblem of the law of progress inevitably unfolding itself in liberty, freedom, and independence (Bancroft 2). Yet as both Bancroft and Motley—as well as most of their educated contemporaries—also believed, Providence alone had not "call[ed] our institutions into being, [nor] conducted the country to its present happiness and glory" (2). A racial ancestry from that "great German heart, yearning for . . . freedom," had also played a role (Motley 106).

With their sometimes contorted chronologies, confused and confusing racial nomenclature, and raw jingoism, these ideas must strike us today as preposterous. But in the mid-nineteenth century, they represented the lingua franca of historical discourse. As David Levin punningly pointed out in his classic study, *History as Romantic Art* (1959), in that period, "when a scholar went off in search of the germs of liberty, he could not return without a sample of Germanic blood" (78). According to Levin, Americans who dabbled in history in the antebellum decades believed in "a clear division between the traits of . . . the Northern and Southern 'races'" (75). Germanic tribes "were the ancestors of all the great peoples," while other groups "were naturally inferior" (75). Racial differences manifested themselves not only in physical characteristics—"fair against dark" peoples—but also in and through cultural expression. "The essential libertarian gene was Teutonic" (74). What Levin called "genealogical relationship" mattered profoundly (75). For, as these midcentury historians all agreed, "Americans were descendants of a 'race' that had long been fated to carry liberty across the earth" (75).

It was never only dabblers in history who employed these concepts, however. They were everywhere. For example, when Emerson visited England (first in 1833 and again in 1847–48), he claimed to recognize blood relatives everywhere. "The American has arrived at the old mansion-house, and finds himself among uncles, aunts, and grandsires" (*English Traits* 36). In a series of lectures delivered in 1848 and subsequently published in 1850 as *English Traits*, Emerson examined the racial components—and the associated "traits"—of Americans' English forebears. The English "stock," he wrote, was derived from "mainly three" groups: "the oldest blood . . . the Celtic"; "mainly from the Germans, whom the Romans found . . . impossible to conquer"; and the "Northmen" who invaded from the sea, conquered, and then applied "the same skill and courage . . . for the service of trade" (30–31). Having read almost all the Icelandic sagas in an English translation of 1844, Emerson was particularly taken by the Northmen, in whom he detected an incipient predilection for egalitarian and democratic values. The Northmen, he believed, gave "high worth to every man," with "the government disappear[ing] before the importance of citizens" (31). Albeit occasionally murderous and piratical, the Northmen of the sagas seemed to Emerson "excellent persons in the main, with good sense, steadiness, wise speech, and prompt action" (32). They were brave, courageous, and filled with "animal vigor"—in short, admirably *manly* (33). And then, by way of contrast, in what was clearly a swipe at nations whose populations were both Catholic and only marginally endowed with Norse ancestry, Emerson approvingly noted, "The heroes of the sagas are not the knights of South Europe. No vaporing [i.e., feminizing] of France and Spain has corrupted them" (31).

That the Celts and the earlier Germanic conquerors of England had "yielded to the Danes and Northmen in the tenth and eleventh centuries" proved a boon to England, according to Emerson, because that nation thereby became the fortunate "receptacle into which all the mettle of that strenuous population was poured" (*English Traits* 33). Indeed, because of its geographical location, as soon as England "got a hardy people into it, they could not help becoming the sailors and factors of the globe" (35). But what had really secured England's empire was the happy confluence, or amalgamation, of "the Saxon and the Northman . . . both Scandinavians" in Emerson's racial taxonomy. "From the residence of a portion of these people in France, and from some effect of that powerful soil on their blood and manners, the Norman has come popularly to represent in England the aristocratic,— and the Saxon the democratic principle" (41). Additionally, because race was believed to express itself not just in "traits" or "principle" but also in physical characteristics, the Saxon and Norman had together, as separate branches of the same racial group, produced in the English "a handsome race. . . . Both branches of the Scandinavian race are distinguished for beauty" (36). And then he made explicit his assumption that racial superiority both explained and justified empire: "When it is considered what humanity, what resources of mental and moral power, the traits of the blonde race betoken,—its accession to empire marks a new and finer epoch" (36).

Although ostensibly written to describe the English, in effect *English Traits* also applied to Americans, the progeny now embarking on their own empire, who found in "the old mansion-house . . . uncles, aunts, and grandsires" (36). However overlapping and confused Emerson's racial and national categories—Scandinavians, Danes, Northmen,

Normans, Saxons, Germans, Goths, and so on—his general argument both followed and bolstered contemporary assumptions. The northern peoples were racially superior to the southern peoples of Europe (like the Spanish); fair-skinned blond people were more beautiful than the darker complected; it was the superior "blonde race" that, by virtue "of mental and moral power," was destined for empire; and race and religion intersected. Emerson's many allusions to these ideas—dotted throughout his works—only point to how commonplace they were.

Commonplace and long-lasting. In 1886, for example, when Jewett published her history of "the Norman conquest of England" (her book's subtitle), she redeemed at least a portion of the otherwise "vaporous" French by reminding readers that in the ninth century, Northmen "began to settle down" in parts of France, "becom[ing] conquerors and colonists instead of mere plunderers" (*The Normans* 22). As the invading Northmen gradually became the Norman French, they nonetheless remained "different from other Frenchmen . . . in being more spirited, vigorous, and alert" (23). "As the Norman," added Jewett, the Northmen's "glorious energy . . . [brought] a new element into the progress of civilization" (24). This distinction between the Norman French and the indigenous French was crucial for Jewett because it was the Normans who invaded England in 1066, thereby adding another quantum of northern blood to the English Saxons. "It is the Norman graft upon the sturdy old Saxon tree that has borne best fruit among the nations," she insisted (365). And this had consequences not just for England but, more important, for the U.S., England's "kindred" offshoot. Thus, asserted Jewett, "much of what marked the Northman and the Norman marks us still" (360). *We* are "the Normans of modern times," she concluded (360).

Whether we point to Emerson's journal entry of 1851 celebrating the fact that it is only those with "the light complexion, the blue eyes of Europe" who immigrate to America or whether we analyze his barely concealed disdain for the "vaporous" French and Spanish, it is clear that just beneath the surface of the antebellum discourse of race and social progress was a palpable anti-Catholicism. According to the racial stereotypes of the period, "the blue eyes" of western and northern Europe were most likely to have freedom-loving Germanic (or Teutonic) blood in their veins and to practice some form of Protestantism. By contrast, the hot-blooded, dark-eyed southern Europeans—in Spain, Portugal, Italy, and even parts of France—were only marginally of Germanic descent and therefore had remained in thrall to what most Protestants perceived as "the evil organizational genius of the Roman church" (Franchot 363). Because of their Germanic blood, Protestants were thought to be, by lineal inheritance, freedom-loving, vigorous, enterprising, and manly. Less endowed with this superior bloodline, those who practiced Catholicism were indolent, "vaporous," and because still gripped by "the spiritual and intellectual tyranny of Rome," lagging behind in both social and political progress (Marsh 10).

In *Roads to Rome*, the literary historian Jenny Franchot cogently noted, "Antebellum America understood its privileged status as emerging from the doctrinal revolutions of the Reformation and from the ethnic superiority of those 'Teutonic' rebels against 'Latin' tyranny" (4). But as Franchot also acknowledged, midcentury antebellum America saw both poles of its "privileged status" as threatened. Protestantism appeared under assault from within and without. A few prominent liberal intellectuals were moving toward a kind of agnosticism, while, at the other end of the spectrum, passionate adherents were moving into several new evangelical and millennialist groups. At the same time, beginning in the 1840s, "large waves of immigrants from Ireland and Catholic Europe" were importing what was then labeled "the foreign religion" (xx).[30] With the Celtic Irish, moreover, came not only their Catholicism but also the threat of racial contagion. As the historian Matthew Frye Jacobson pointed out in *Whiteness of a Different Color*, the Irish soon became associated with a "fixed set" of supposedly inherited and observable racial traits (48). "The Irishman was 'low-browed,' 'brutish,' and even 'simian' in popular discourse; a *Harper's Weekly* piece in 1851 described the 'Celtic physiognomy' as 'distinctly marked' by, among others things, 'the small and somewhat upturned nose [and] the black tint of the skin'" (48). The Irish were also viewed as congenitally lazy, prone to drunkenness, and, in the terminology of most local health boards, *poor stock*.[31]

Arriving in ever-increasing numbers, all the new immigrant groups—Irish, Germans, Italians, Scandinavians, and somewhat later, Eastern Europeans—exerted downward wage pressures on the already impoverished Protestant working poor. Not even New England's rapid industrialization could absorb all the unskilled labor now available. In the years leading up to the Civil War, urban labor riots and workers' organizing efforts divided along both religious and "racial" lines. Nativist clubs turned into vicious street gangs. And the nativist anti-immigration Know-Nothing Party advocated electing only native-born Americans to public office and requiring a period of twenty-five consecutive years of residence before any newcomer could apply for citizenship. In 1854, the party "carried scores of local elections in the Northeastern and Mid-Atlantic states on an unlikely mix of xenophobia, opposition to slavery, and working-class rage" (Bell 135).

In the popular rhetoric of the day, fear of racial degeneracy was inextricably linked to paranoid fantasies of "Jesuitical plots" and "Popish" takeovers of democratic and Protestant America. Such anxieties had a long history, of course, dating back to the period when "the English colonies were wedged between two hostile Catholic empires, France and Spain" (Higham 6). But many Protestant Americans in the antebellum decades saw a *present* threat. "Despite continuing and widespread antagonism to their faith, Irish and [other] European Catholics continued to immigrate in such numbers that by 1860, with approximately 3.1 million adherents, their church represented the largest single religious body in America" (Franchot xx).

In response, antebellum attitudes toward the accepted stories of the nation's history and character began to shift and revolve around this perceived dual racial and religious challenge. The story of America as a refuge for the downtrodden and suffering masses of Europe was no longer entirely comfortable. Instead of welcoming the hard-working poor of Europe, some Americans now began to see themselves as besieged by hordes of arriving foreign "savages" ruled not by law and reason but by unbridled animal passions (see Jacobson 24–26).

Also beginning to become uncomfortable were some aspects of the schoolbook discovery story: an Italian Catholic Columbus sailing for the monarchs of Catholic Spain just as the Inquisition was starting up in earnest. As Franchot noted, in 1853 Edward Everett had argued in a public oration on the discovery of America that "Columbus's fateful landing had in fact enslaved the New World to the Spanish" (36). Addressing the New-York Historical Society, Everett asserted that when "the keel of [Columbus's] vessel grated upon the much longed for strand, it completed with more than electric speed, that terrible circuit which connected the islands and the continent to the footstool of the Spanish throne" (*The Discovery and Colonization of America* 8). Columbus himself, still for Everett "the great discoverer," received no censure, but Everett charged Ferdinand, Isabella, and the pope with the responsibility for destroying and then permanently enslaving the "remnant" indigenous populations of America (6, 8, 11). Like William Prescott's earlier three-volume *History of the Conquest of Mexico* (1843), such comments added at least a little tarnish to the Columbian discovery story.

There were, of course, endless inconsistencies and contradictions in all this. First, while a new anti-immigrant xenophobia was rampant, accompanied by calls to close the borders against certain racially and religiously undesirable groups, Americans simultaneously welcomed expanding the nation's borders into the territories of yet another suspect racial and religious Other: Mexicans. As the historian John Higham remarked in 1955, "Many an American, during the annexation of Texas and California, saw himself in the role of his conquering ancestors, executing a racial mandate to enlarge the area of freedom. The penny press roared that the Anglo-Saxon impulse would carry the American flag throughout the continent" (10).

No less a contradiction was the fact that, to quote Higham again, "the romantics sought in the mists of an early medieval (or 'Gothic') past the indestructible core not only of their political institutions but of their whole national character" (10). Ironically, then, American romanticism was steeped in a medieval—and hence Catholic—past, even as its practitioners hailed the Reformation as a signal event in the history of human progress.[32] Almost all the major American writers traveled to Europe and wrote about the beauty and mystery of ruined stone towers, lichen-covered abbey walls, the architecture of Gothic cathedrals, and the incense and candles of Catholic ritual. For many American readers, these represented the exotic side of European romanticism.

Perhaps the saddest irony of all, however, was this: that same romantic racial nationalism that had once identified itself with a relatively liberal and progressive Protestantism was now expressing itself in extremes of intolerance and a jingoistic xenophobia. In the introduction to the original 1834 edition of his *History of the United States*, Bancroft had written confidently of a nation "sustained by . . . the convictions of an enlightened faith" and a nation where "religion [is] neither persecuted nor paid by the state" (2). Without equivocation, he invoked the then-popular (if idealized) view of America as "an asylum": "An immense concourse of emigrants of the most various lineage is perpetually crowding to our shores; and the principles of liberty, uniting all interests by the operation of equal laws, blend the discordant elements into harmonious union" (2). But by the early 1850s, that vision was fast being displaced by a popular rhetoric which bespoke fear of racial contagion, anxiety over "the foreign religion," and distrust of the "influx of foreign pauperism" (E. Everett, *The Discovery and Colonization of America* 31).

Despite Edward Everett's discomfort with Columbus having "connected . . . the continent to the footstool of the Spanish throne," and similar sentiments expressed by others, no one seriously proposed replacing Columbus with Leif Eiriksson as the *true* discoverer of America until after the Civil War. Yet, even in the antebellum decades, a space began to open for shifting the discovery story from the Italian to the Viking. An 1854 article in *Putnam's Monthly Magazine*, published in New York, exemplified the changing pattern. Titled "The First Discoverers of America," this unsigned piece ran thirteen pages, paid due homage to Columbus, followed the history of the Norse from the eighth century to their discovery and colonization of New England in the tenth and eleventh centuries, and then evoked the by now familiar romantic image: "Rude men they doubtless were, living in an iron age, and little 'trained to deeds of tender courtesy,' yet abounding in valor and daring. Courting danger, braving hardships, overcoming obstacles, shrinking from no perils however great, and no consequences however fatal. With minds full of courage, and hearts full of faith, they boldly launched their barks upon an unknown, trackless sea, venturing upon its virgin waters without compass, or quadrant, or chart, their only guide the stars, by night; by day, the sun" (13). What annoyed this writer for *Putnam's* was that "the truth of Scandinavian discovery" was not more widely known (13).

Careful not to seem too radical on the subject, while still advocating change both in the nation's schoolbooks and in public attitudes, this writer ended his article with the following comment: "While we must ever consider Columbus as the true herald of western Civilization, the father of a new era in history,—the founder of our American Cycle, ... it is taking nothing from his real glory to say, that the bold Scandinavian sea-rovers preceded him in the discovery of America" ("The First Discoverers of America" 13). Ever since the Revolutionary War, Columbus had been embraced within Protestant America's providential history as the man ordained to discover a refuge for those earliest Pilgrims fleeing religious persecution in Europe. He was thus, as the *Putnam's* writer phrased it, "the founder of our American Cycle." But in 1854, many writers, like this one, were making a case for at least *adding* the heroic and romantic Norse to the discovery narrative.[33]

New England as America's Birthplace and Gateway

In October 1849, the writer and naturalist Henry David Thoreau took a walking tour of Cape Cod in the company of his friend, the poet William Ellery Channing. Thoreau walked the Cape again the following June, this time alone. He made a third visit, again with Channing, in July 1855, and a final visit to Cape Cod, by himself, in June 1857.

On 5 November 1849, shortly after returning from his first walking tour of the Cape, Thoreau borrowed from the Harvard College library Rafn's *Antiquitates Americanæ* and several other books about early explorations of North America. As is clear from the several articles he later wrote about walking Cape Cod, Thoreau tried to reconcile Rafn's assertions with what he himself observed. Finally, though, while the habitually skeptical Thoreau professed "great respect for [the Norse] as skilfull and adventurous navigators," he nonetheless concluded, "We must for the present remain in doubt as to what capes they did see. We think that they were considerably farther north" (*Cape Cod* 196). Even so, after sighting a mirage of what appeared to be standing water in the middle of the sand on a long Provincetown beach, Thoreau was not above a punningly playful claim to a Norse genealogy of his own: "But whether Thor-finn saw the mirage here or not, Thor-eau, one of the same family, did; and perchance it was because Leif the Lucky had, in a previous voyage, taken Thor-er and his people off the rock in the middle of the sea, that Thor-eau was born to see it" (151).

Thoreau's playfully dismissive skepticism notwithstanding, his walking companion, Channing, was eager to accept Norse connections with the Cape. In a long poem called "The Wanderer," composed over several years and finally published in 1871, Channing identified the nineteenth-century fishermen of Cape Cod with the ancient Norse who also once fished these same waters (*The Collected Poems of William Ellery Channing* 106):

> As old tradition lives
> Along this coast, like those who came of old
> (Danes or bold Norse), and named it Wonder Strand,
> The men are fishers.

Unlike Thoreau, Channing had no problem contemplating the possible validity of the legend "that gives the hardy Norse, seafaring men, / The true discovery of our rock-bound world" (102). He even suggested that attributing "the strange name of Vineyard to the sound" came originally "from Vinland and the Dane" (103).

Like Channing, many of Thoreau's fellow New Englanders were also eager to claim some kind of Norse connection, genealogical or otherwise. Crumbling stone walls were regularly assumed to be remnants of Norse habitation, scratches or odd markings on large rocks and boulders were interpreted as runic inscriptions, and any anomalies in the natural features of the landscape were happily pointed to as evidence of ancient Norse construction. Thus it is no accident that the vast majority of writers who accepted and propounded Rafn's theories about New England landfalls and the location of Vinland were themselves New Englanders by birth. But there was something else, too. New England was in decline.

Looking back from the perspective of the 1890s, the historian and scion of presidents, Henry Adams, located the beginning of that decline in the decades following the War of 1812. "Peace produced in the United States a social and economical revolution which greatly curtailed the influence of New England," wrote Adams in his multivolume *History of the United States* (3:221). Among the many forces at work, according to Adams, was "the invention of the steamboat [which] counterbalanced ocean commerce" and gradually refocused shipping from the transatlantic—the strength of the New England shipping industry—to internal trade using rivers and canals (3:221). But, he continued, "neither steamboats, canals, nor roads" could help his beloved Massachusetts because, with a "prostration of the manufacturing" sector in 1816, "thousands of its citizens migrated to [western] New York and Ohio" (3:160). Only the postwar increase in immigration from Europe would make up these population losses. To be sure, the change "from prosperity to adversity" had been suffered by "all the cities of the coast," but after the war "New York and Philadelphia began to recover their lost ground, [while] Boston was slow to feel the impulse" (3:97). In short, according to Adams's *History*, by "the close of the year 1815," the impact of the peace that followed the War of 1812 "was already well defined.... The new epoch of American history began by the sudden decline of Massachusetts to the lowest point of relative prosperity and influence she had ever known, and by an equally sudden stimulus to the South and West" (3:103).

From the 1830s through the 1850s, the nation as a whole, and New England in particular, were shaken by a series of financial panics and bank closings. The economy went through repeated boom-and-bust cycles. There was a rising incidence of poverty and pauperism in the cities, especially in New York, but Boston was not immune. The continuing rapid expansion westward, with its consequent pull on New England populations, both "diminished the region's representative power in Washington and drained the available labor pool" (Seelye 253). At a period when New England was a center of advocacy for social reform—from the antislavery movement to the movements for women's suffrage, banking reform, and prison reform—the loss of population that resulted in a shrinking of proportional representation in Congress was particularly galling. A national Protestant hegemony, expressed more as cultural than as religious orthodoxy and emanating from New England, now began to fall apart. Protestant sects continued to splinter and proliferate in number, while increased immigration from Ireland in the 1840s and 1850s brought significant numbers of practicing Catholics to American shores. No longer did New Englanders feel, as they once had, that *their* culture was the *national* culture. Boston declined into a comparatively provincial city as New York City began to overshadow it as a center of commerce, finance, political influence, and, yes, literature too. Even a beloved son of New England, the poet of nature and New England, William Cullen Bryant, was drawn to the vibrancy of New York, moving there from Massachusetts in 1825 to become coeditor of the *New York Review and Athenaeum Magazine* and subsequently serving as the editor and owner of the *New-York Evening Post*.

New England's most ardent sons and supporters well understood what was happening. Railing against "the money-changers of Wall Street," Marsh told his Middlebury College audience in 1843, "I do not expect for New-England a high degree of pecuniary prosperity, or political influence. . . . The population of our mountains and our valleys will increase in a ratio far short of the rapid multiplication of the inhabitants of the newer [western] states; and our proportional weight in the national legislature will diminish with every census" (35, 39). Marsh's solution to this apparently inevitable reality was twofold. First, he urged his college audience to study the nation's—and particularly New England's—history so that one day they could "expound from the pulpit, the chair, and the bench . . . the principles of your country's laws" as exemplified in "the lives of your Puritan ancestors" (39). In other words, he was urging his audience to follow the population westward, spreading New England values and culture so that "the mighty West will look back with filial reverence to the birth-place of the fathers of her people, and the schools of New-England will still be nursing mothers to the posterity of her widely scattered children" (39). It was an appeal to maintain at least some sort of cultural influence when real political clout was no longer available.

Symbolically related to this was Marsh's second solution. Ignoring the establishment in 1607 of the Jamestown colony in Virginia, he wanted to reassert New England's primacy as both the progenitor of the nation and the original gateway when many immigrants were now entering the country through New York, Baltimore, and Philadelphia, as well as Boston and Providence. Throughout his address, he called the Middlebury students "sons of the Pilgrims," and he presented "the emigration of the Puritans" as the familiar type of God leading the chosen out of Egypt (34). Thus, in the standard Puritan typology of an earlier era, America was the new Promised Land and New England the gateway to Canaan. "To the true American," declared Marsh, there were "no memories more venerable than the landing of the Pilgrims, no spot more sacred than the Plymouth Rock" (34).

Wholly unmindful of prior European arrivals by both the Spanish and the French, nineteenth-century writers repeatedly lauded the Pilgrims' first landing.[34] It was a characteristic feature of most historical writing of the period. In the face of New England's declining financial and political fortunes, this trope invested the region with its continuing status as, in Marsh's words, "birth-place" and "nursing mother" of the nation. And while the belief in a first arrival and brief colonization by the Norse never came close to supplanting the symbolic resonances of the Pilgrims' arrival, it did at least reinforce the notion of New England as *the* significant and original gateway. The Norse thus became kindred ancestors and historical precursors. With that, New England's most prominent poets now possessed another New England arrival moment through which to explore the meaning and fortunes of their region and the nation.

4

The New England Poets of Viking America and the Emergence of the Plastic Viking

> For how can one immediately experience the present without regard to the shaping presence of the past? Yet Americans have been, at least in the expressions of their artists and scholars, profoundly present-oriented and idea- or fantasy-centered. Their past has fascinated them, in a made-up form, but the real past is denied as though it is too painful—too opposed to the fantasy, the dream, to be spoken.
>
> —PAULA GUNN ALLEN (Laguna Pueblo),
> "The Savages in the Mirror" (1974)

Longfellow's "Skeleton in Armor"

In 1831, in the Massachusetts town of Fall River, while leveling what they thought was only an inconveniently located hill (but was more probably an Indian grave mound), local workmen uncovered "a body buried in a sitting posture" (Sparks 68). The body, which appeared quite ancient, along with several items with which it had been buried, were deposited in a small museum in Fall River. According to Jared Sparks, who examined the find and wrote about it for the *American Monthly Magazine* in 1836, the body had been enveloped in two coverings, the outer "of coarse bark" and the inner "of coarse cloth, made of fine bark" (69). On a few parts of the skeleton, wrote Sparks, "the skin and flesh are in good preservation." And because "the teeth are sound," Sparks determined the skeleton to be that "of a young man." He estimated the stature to be "about five and a half feet" (69). What truly intrigued Sparks, however, was not the corpse alone but also the implements with which it had been adorned. (See figure 4.) These included what appeared to be a brass breastplate and "below the breast-plate and entirely encircling the body, . . . a belt composed of brass tubes. . . . This belt was so placed as to protect the lower parts of the body below the

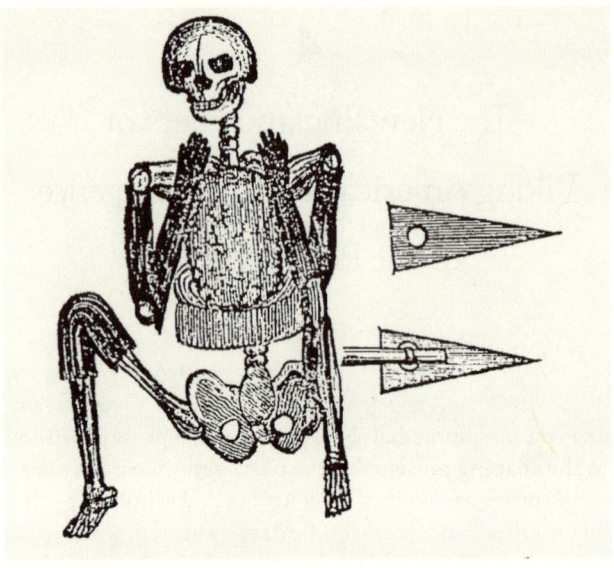

4. Drawing of the famous "skeleton in armor" unearthed in Fall River, Massachusetts, 1831. From Jared Sparks's "Antiquities of North America," *American Monthly Magazine*, ns 1 (Jan. 1836).

breast-plate" (69). There were also "arrows . . . of brass, thin, flat, and triangular in shape," designed to be fastened to a wooden shaft (69).

Like most of his contemporaries, Sparks was wholly ignorant of the fact that precontact northeastern Algonquian peoples had access to worked copper and often buried high-status individuals with breastplates and girdles of worked copper and copper beads. As far as Sparks was aware, "the Indians found here by the discoverers never used . . . metals in any way; but wood, stone, shells, &c. supplied them with weapons and ornaments" (68). Therefore, mistaking the tarnished and corroded copper for brass, and thinking the skeleton too tall for an Indian, Sparks concluded that "the body was not one of the Indians" (70).[1] Sparks, who was to become a professor of history at Harvard and, later, its president, "incline[d] to the belief that the remains found at Fall River belonged to one of the crew of a Phoenician vessel" (71). In 1836, when Sparks was writing his article, "Antiquities of North America," the Mediterranean maritime empire of Phoenicia was considered by most antiquarians the likeliest ancient civilization to have chanced upon New World shores before Columbus. Moreover, for Sparks, this "hypothesis" seemed to make sense of "'Dighton Rock,' famed for its hieroglyphic inscriptions, of which no sufficient explanation has yet been given" (71). After all, he reasoned, "the spot where [the remains] were found is on the sea-coast, and in the immediate neighborhood of 'Dighton Rock'" (71). It was thus entirely plausible to him "that these [Phoenician] mariners . . . lived some time after they landed; and after having written their names, perhaps their epitaphs, upon the rock at Dighton, died, and were buried by the natives" (71).

When Rafn's *Antiquitates Americanæ* appeared in 1837, however, there was a new option for identifying the Fall River skeleton. Could it be the body of some ancient Northman, and the metal breastplate his hauberk or chain mail, part of his protective armor? Unfortunately, before there could be any clear answer to that question, some time in 1838 or 1839, most of the skeleton was destroyed in a fire at the Fall River museum. What remained, including the metal pieces, was sent for analysis to the Royal Society of Northern Antiquaries in Copenhagen.

At this point, a poet's voice entered the discussion, linking the mysterious skeleton not with Dighton Rock but with the round tower in Newport. That voice belonged to Henry Wadsworth Longfellow, who first published his "Saga of the Skeleton in Armor" in 1841. The timing of the poem's appearance is itself of interest. Although there is nothing to suggest that Longfellow planned it this way, the poem's first publication in the January 1841 issue of the *Knickerbocker*, a monthly magazine published in New York, coincided with the publication of John Greenleaf Whittier's poem "The Norsemen" in that same issue. Both poems benefited from the publication that same year of two other related texts: Beamish's *The Discovery of America by the Northmen*, which renewed popular interest in pre-Columbian Norse visits to America, and Rafn's *Supplement to the "Antiquitates Americanæ."* The *Supplement* allowed for the possibility that the Fall River skeleton might in fact be the remains of a Norseman and, at the same time, contained Rafn's emphatic identification of the Newport tower as dating to the period of the Norse explorations in North America. No less noteworthy is that the publication of these two poems on Norse themes, both written by New Englanders, was neatly sandwiched between Cooper's *The Pathfinder* (1840) and *The Deerslayer* (1841). In effect, these two poems and Cooper's novels represented the two poles of the nation's romantic patriotism. Where the last two novels of Cooper's Leatherstocking series took readers to the colonial frontiers, Whittier (who will be discussed later) and Longfellow took readers to a far more shadowy pre-Columbian frontier. By association, Cooper's novels invited readers to look west. Whittier and Longfellow invited readers to look to New England.

For several years, Longfellow had been educating himself in Scandinavian materials. From 1826 to 1829, in preparation for taking up a professorship of modern languages at his alma mater, Bowdoin College in Maine, he traveled to France, Spain, Italy, and Germany, perfecting his knowledge of those countries' languages and literatures. Appointed to the Smith professorship of French and Spanish at Harvard in 1835, he again went abroad, both to improve upon and to add to his knowledge of European languages and literatures. This trip included two months, July and August, in Sweden (which then incorporated Norway and Denmark).[2] Clearly, his visit to Scandinavia made an impression. In Copenhagen, Longfellow met most of the major Danish scholars and literary eminences of the day, including Rafn. In a letter to his father written in September 1835, Longfellow described Rafn as "an Historian and publisher of old Icelandic books, . . . a very, friendly, pleasant man, and gives me lessons in Icelandic" (*Letters* 1:515). A postscript to the letter added, "In Copenhagen I was made a member of the Northern Antiquarian Society, whose object is the cultivation of the ancient Literature of the North" (1:516). A subsequent letter from Longfellow to Rafn, written from Heidelberg in December 1835, thanked Rafn for sending the formal certificate of Longfellow's membership in "the Royal Society of Antiquaries" and promised, "I shall do all in my power to make the Literature of the North better known to my countrymen, on the other side of the Atlantic" (1:531).[3]

True to his word, upon his return to the U.S., Longfellow began to publish articles on Swedish poetry, and on 1 February 1837 he wrote to a friend about preparing a new course of lectures for Harvard: "In this course something of the Danish and Swedish (the new feathers in my cap) is to be mingled" (*Letters* 2:13). It may not be entirely a coincidence that Longfellow decided to add the Scandinavian materials to his Harvard lectures in the same year that Rafn's long-awaited *Antiquitates Americanæ* first appeared in the United States. After all, Rafn's work promised definitively to link the ancient Norse with New England, particularly Massachusetts, and this surely piqued the interest of the students at Harvard as much as it was then arousing Longfellow's interest. As he noted in his journal on 3 May 1838, Longfellow had "been looking at the old Northern Sagas, and thinking of a series of ballads or a romantic poem on the deeds of the first bold viking who crossed to this western world."[4]

Possibly with this in mind, in 1838—and prior to the fire— Longfellow traveled with members of the Ward family to the museum in Fall River. The group included Julia Ward (later Julia Ward Howe), poet and social activist, perhaps best remembered as the author of the words to "The Battle Hymn of the Republic," and her brother Samuel Ward, a journalist and later a Washington lobbyist for New York financial interests. As Samuel Ward remembered the occasion, crossing "the Newport beaches" in the carriage back to Cambridge, Longfellow "challenged [his] sister . . . to make a poem out of the rusty hauberk and grim bones they had been inspecting" (460). Julia never took up the challenge, but as Longfellow later confided to Samuel Ward, "he had carried the scheme [for such a poem] in his head ever since . . . having visited . . . the skeleton in armor, dug up at Taunton" (460). In a prefatory headnote to the publication of "The Skeleton in Armour" in his *Ballads and Other Poems* (1842), Longfellow confirmed this, writing that only after seeing the skeleton in the Fall River museum did he get the idea "of connecting it with the Round Tower at Newport" (29).[5]

Just a year after his trip to the Fall River museum, in a journal entry dated 24 May 1839, Longfellow recorded a visit from a friend during which the poet "told him of [his] plan of a heroic poem on the Discovery of America by the Northmen, in which the Round Tower at Newport and the Skeleton in Armour have a part to play." There is another brief mention of the poem in a journal entry dated 17 December 1839, and Longfellow appears to have completed the poem in the following months. Ward provides no date, but in his brief memoir of Longfellow, written after the poet's death, he recalled, "[Longfellow] told me that he had recently written a poem which smiled to him, but which his habitual counselors and companions"—two Harvard colleagues—"frowned upon as beneath the plane of his previous lyrical performances. He then proceeded to read me the 'Skeleton in Armor'" (459). The poem "so stirred my blood," Ward remembered, that he "took the manuscript from his [i.e., Longfellow's] hands and read it to him, with more dramatic force than his modesty had permitted him to display." At that, Longfellow's doubts seemed to have been calmed and, says Ward, Longfellow "sprang to his feet and embraced me" (459). In Longfellow's mind, "the doubting Thomases" were now dispatched (459).

In a letter dated 13 December 1840, Longfellow wrote his father, "[I have] prepared for the press another original ballad, which has been lying by me for some time. It is called 'The Skeleton in Armour,' and is connected with the old Round Tower at Newport. The skeleton really exists. It was dug up near Fall River, where I saw it some two years ago. I suppose it to be the remains of one of the old Northern sea-rovers, who came to this country in the tenth century. Of course I make the tradition myself; and I think I have succeeded in giving the whole a

156   Chapter Four

Northern air" (*Letters* 2:269).[6] Then, as though nervously recalling his two Harvard friends who had "frowned upon" the poem, he added the following: "I hope it may be successful; though I fear, that those who only glance at it, will not fully comprehend me" (2:269).[7]

He need not have worried about the poem's success. When "Saga of the Skeleton in Armor" first appeared in the *Knickerbocker* in January 1841, it was an instantaneous hit. Readers loved it, and the poem was "extensively copied into the newspapers" ("Longfellow's Poems" 241). Pleased at the enthusiastic response, Longfellow shortened the title and positioned "The Skeleton in Armour" as the opening poem in his collection *Ballads and Other Poems*, which came out the next year and was itself a success.[8] Thereafter—with "Armor" spelled variously "Armor" and "Armour"—Longfellow included "The Skeleton in Armour" in most of his collected works. The poem also enjoyed independent publication well into the 1870s as both a gift book, with illustrations, and as a separate pamphlet. As a reviewer for an illustrated gift-book edition of 1876 observed of the poem, "It has never lost the hold which it [first] took upon the popular fancy" ("The Skeleton in Armor" 6).

In the *Knickerbocker*, "Saga of the Skeleton in Armor" was printed in the center of the page with a brief prose gloss for each of its twenty stanzas printed flush to the margin. These marginal glosses were printed in a reduced typeface. Longfellow did not use this device subsequently, omitting the marginalia in reprintings of the poem in books, including *Ballads and Other Poems*. The marginal glosses weren't really necessary, after all, since none of the poem's stanzas required this kind of summary, explanatory, or interpretive apparatus. Nor was the poem long enough to require the reader's memory to be prompted in this manner. But the marginalia served a purpose. It reminded readers of the glosses added to difficult archaic works whose meaning might otherwise be obscure, and it hinted that this poem, too, might carry meanings that were not immediately obvious. Most *Knickerbocker* readers, though, would simply have enjoyed the gloss as an additional evocation of authentic antiquity. Others might have chuckled at the way Longfellow had thus cast himself in the role of a pedantic antiquarian. Several early reviewers of *Ballads and Other Poems*, however, noted that the English romantic poet Samuel Taylor Coleridge had previously employed the identical device in later editions of his famous "Rime of the Ancient Mariner," and at least one complained, "The opening lines [of Longfellow's poem] bear a stronger resemblance than we could wish to the commencement of the 'Ancient Mariner'" ("Longfellow's Ballads and Poems," *United States Magazine and Democratic Review* 184).[9] Even so, the predominant critical view was that Longfellow had entirely succeeded in giving his poem the antique "Northern air" he mentioned in the letter to his father. As the critic for the *North American Review* commented, "'The Skeleton in Armour' reads like an old Scandinavian poem" ("Longfellow's Ballads and Other Poems" 115).

As printed in the *Knickerbocker*, with the marginal gloss, the three opening stanzas of "Saga of the Skeleton in Armor" read as follows:

I.

"Speak! speak! thou fearful guest
The Poet questions Who, with thy hollow breast
the Skeleton in Armor Still in rude armor drest,
at Fall River, and   Comest to daunt me!
asks why his imagination Wrapt not in Eastern balms,
should be haunted by so But with thy fleshless palms
fearful an apparition. Stretch'd, as if asking alms,
    Why dost thou haunt me?"

II.

Then, from those cavernous eyes
A spectral light Pale flashes seem'd to rise,
gleams in the hollow As when the Northern skies
eyes of the Skeleton,   Gleam in December;
and a low, mournful And, like the waters flow
voice issues from his Under December's snow,
chest. Came a dull voice of wo
    From the heart's chamber.

III.

"I was a Viking old!
The Skeleton speaks; he had been My deeds, though manifold,
a Northern Viking, or Pirate; but No Skald in song has told,
no song of the bard nor popular   No Saga taught thee!
tradition had preserved his heroic Take heed, that in thy verse
deeds from oblivion. Thou dost the tale rehearse,
Else dread a dead man's curse!
    For this I sought thee."[10]

As several reviewers had noted, resonances from Coleridge's "Rime" echo in the background of these lines. Both poems open with a ghostly apparition who accosts a stranger, and in both, urgent to tell his tale, the apparition holds the stranger bound to his will. That said, the

158   Chapter Four

skeleton of the "Viking old" has a story to tell which only tangentially coincides with the Ancient Mariner's, and a story, moreover, that connects him to New England. But it begins in Norway.

In stanzas 4 and 5, the skeleton recounts the adventures of his boyhood years "far in the Northern Land," where he "tamed the ger-falcon" and "track'd . . . the grisly bear." At once reckless and fearless, he skated "the half-frozen Sound, / That the poor whimpering hound / Trembled to walk on." "But when I older grew," he continues in stanza 6, he joined "a Corsair's crew," traveling "o'er the dark sea . . . / With the marauders." As the marginal gloss makes clear, he has become "a pirate." Theirs was a "wild" life, full of bloodshed and, as he boasts in stanza 7, a life also filled with all-night revels, telling tales of their adventures and drinking until dawn: "We the Berserk's tale / Measured in cups of ale, / Draining the oaken pail."

During one of these midnight revels, in the words of Longfellow's gloss for stanza 8, "as he tells a story of the sea, the eyes of a maiden gaze at [the young Viking], and he becomes enamored." In stanza 9, he describes how he successfully "woo'd the blue-eyed maid . . . / And in the forest's shade / Our vows were plighted." Their mutual love notwithstanding, the maiden's father, Old Hildebrand, will not consent to the marriage because "she was a Prince's child, / I but a Viking wild." Humiliated and angered that his suit was answered only by "the loud laugh of scorn" from Hildebrand and his retainers, the young man finds his beloved "unguarded" in the night and abducts her. With her, he puts out to sea. The two are pursued by Hildebrand and his retinue, but just when the couple seemed to be getting away, "the wind fail'd us" (stanza 14). Hailed by Hildebrand's crew with threats of "Death without quarter!," the young Viking turns his own ship around and rams Hildebrand's fast-approaching vessel. The maneuver works and, with all aboard, "down . . . / Through the black water" sinks Hildebrand's ship (stanza 15). The wild Viking has now killed the proud father of his beloved.

Stanzas 16 through 19 bring the fleeing couple to America. "Through the wild hurricane, / . . . Three weeks we westward bore, / And when the storm was o'er, / Cloud-like we saw the shore" (stanza 17). Unlike the Vinland sagas, there is no mention of exploring this new land nor any description of it. We learn in stanza 17 only

>   There for my lady's bower
>   Built I the lofty tower,
>   Which, to this very hour,
>   Is looking sea-ward.

This, of course, is the famous Newport tower.

In keeping with the relative brevity and rapid forward narrative flow of traditional Icelandic sagas, stanza 18 in quick succession tells us that the couple lived there "many years; / Time dried the maiden's tears," and she became "a mother." Whether childbirth was the cause or something else is never stated. The very next line says only "Death clos'd her mild blue eyes." There is no further mention of the child. Instead, in stanza 18, the skeleton informs the poet that he buried his dead wife "under that tower." Then, in utter despair at the loss of his beloved and with nothing left to live for—"Hateful to me were men, / The sun-light hateful!"—in stanza 19 the skeleton describes how he took his own life:

> In the vast forest here,
> Clad in my warlike gear,
> Fell I upon my spear,
>   O, death was grateful!

Upon his death, the skeleton tells the poet, he followed the final path of all the fabled Vikings of old. In Longfellow's words in the marginal gloss to stanza 20, the skeleton's "soul ascend[ed] to the Hall of Odin":

	XX.
His soul ascends to the Hall of Odin; and with the souls of warriors, drinks a *skoal* or health to the Northland. The Saga ends.	"Thus, seam'd with many scars Bursting these prison bars, Up to its native stars My soul ascended! There from the flowing bowl Deep drinks the warrior's soul, *Skoal!* to the Northland! *skoal!*" —Thus the tale ended.

Unlike Coleridge's Ancient Mariner, Longfellow's ghostly skeleton is not bound to walk the Earth, telling his story over and over again. The task of passing on his tale now falls to the poet.

If this is a love story, it is a decidedly disturbing one. Significantly, Longfellow reifies the unromanticized image of the Vikings as piratical marauders rather than employing the newly emergent rehabilitated image of romantic explorers and freedom-loving heroic warriors. He repeatedly characterizes his Viking protagonist and his exploits as "wild," identifies him with bloodshed and mayhem, and has him proudly reciting "the Berserk's tale," the old term for a wild Norse warrior who fights with a mad frenzy.[11]

To be sure, the Viking's love for the maiden—and her love for him—seem somewhat to soften these associations. The maiden's tender gaze has penetrated her lover's "dark heart." But Longfellow's choice of imagery points to something more complicated. In stanza 9, the Viking woos the maiden, who is described as "yielding, yet half afraid." Then he tells the poet that under her "loosen'd vest / Flutter'd her little breast, / Like birds within their nest / By the hawk frighted." The language here is suggestively erotic. It conjures up images of innocence and vulnerability (and possibly also arousal) on the part of the maiden. But the hawk is clearly predatory. And in fact, breaking all the rules of hospitality, the Viking enacts predation in stanza 12 when he abducts his host's daughter. Rather than a hawk, however, in this stanza Longfellow compares the Viking to "the sea-mew," a common gull, scavenger and predator both, snatching his "dove so white" from "her nest unguarded." Finally, however much he may love her, the Viking views his beloved as prey. This is made explicit in stanza 16. Having taken off with the maiden and put to sea, and after ramming and sinking her father's vessel, the Viking now compares himself to "the fierce cormorant."

Like a bird of prey,	XVI.
Bears off the maiden.	"As with his wings aslant,
	Sails the fierce cormorant,
	Seeking some rocky haunt,
	With his prey laden,
	So toward the open main,
	Beating to sea again
	Through the wild hurricane,
	Bore I the maiden."

Clearly, Longfellow did not want any reader to miss his meaning. The marginal gloss indentifies the cormorant—a sea bird that dives for fish—as "a bird of prey." And Longfellow constructs the rhyme scheme so as to pair the fourth and eighth lines, a pairing which emphasizes that the Viking bears away the maiden *as* his *prey*. There is not even anything appealing in their supposed immediate destination, "some rocky haunt." For the careful reader, the language here must seem at least a little unsettling.

The Viking's ship heads westward across the open ocean, beating its way through hurricane and storm. Unlike Coleridge's "Rime," there is no suggestion here that the storm represents any kind of punishment—either for the abduction or for the killing of Old Hildebrand and his crew. Rather, like the old sagas he hoped to emulate, and consistent with the ballad form, Longfellow offers neither overt judgment nor direct moralizing. Instead, he brings his fleeing couple to America. They "land near Newport," states the marginal gloss, and there the Viking "builds the Round Tower" (gloss to stanza 17). Adding yet another note of ambiguity to the tale, in stanza 18 the Viking skeleton recalls, "There lived we many years; / Time dried the maiden's tears; / She had forgot her fears, / She was a mother." We are never told the cause(s) of her weeping or what her fears were. Yet by leaving the answers to these inescapable questions to his readers' imaginations, Longfellow cleverly invited them to come up with myriad plausible answers, none of them easily consonant with a simple love story. Any lingering notion that this is some kind of straightforward heroic saga about true love triumphing over obstacles must surely by now be compromised.

Then, without learning anything more about the maiden, in quick succession in stanza 19, we are informed that she died and that the Viking buried her "under that tower." What follows is the outpouring of his anguish at losing her. His heart becomes "still as a stagnant fen," and all the world is now "hateful" to him, so in heroic Viking fashion, he falls on his spear. The stanza is at once angry and passionate in its expression of despair. And the final stanza, stanza 20, depicts the Viking's self-inflicted death as a kind of release—"Bursting these prison bars"—followed by his soul's ascent to the Hall of Odin, foremost of the Norse war gods. There, in Walhalla (Hall of the Fallen Warriors), he will join in the endless feast and rejoin the revels of his Viking past.

Based on Longfellow's letters and journal entries, we must conclude that his concept of what he would write changed over time. In his first journal entry on the subject, dated 3 May 1838, his proposed subject was "the deeds of the first bold viking who crossed to this Western world with storm-spirits and devil-machinery underwater."[12] But it was his visit to the skeleton in the Fall River museum in the summer of 1838 that gave Longfellow the idea of somehow connecting the skeleton with the nearby "Round Tower at Newport" and making these a part of his projected Viking poem (*The Complete Poetical Works* 651).

162   Chapter Four

Yet almost a year after his visit to Fall River, according to a journal entry of 24 May 1839, Longfellow still had no very clear idea about the specifics of the story his poem would unfold. All he could say was that he planned "a heroic poem on the Discovery of America by the Northmen, in which the Round Tower at Newport and the Skeleton in Armour have a part to play." What part wasn't yet clear. It would appear, therefore, that Longfellow struggled with this poem and eventually jettisoned the idea of making it focus on "the discovery of America by the Northmen." The stories of the Norse in Vinland then available in the works of Rafn and others obviously did not serve his purposes. So, as he wrote his father in December 1840, "I make [up] the tradition myself" (*Letters* 2:269). When his poetic intentions finally did become clear to him—probably some time in the winter and spring of 1840—the poem "flashed upon me," Longfellow told Samuel Ward ("Days with Longfellow" 460).

What flashed upon him was his own deep discomfort not with the relatively sober would-be colonists of Vinland who were more merchants than adventurers, but with their wild berserker forebears whom New Englanders were now also embracing as ancestors. Familiar as he was with brutal and out-of-control characters in some of the old sagas, Longfellow decided to explore the implications of *this* aspect of the Viking romance. As the Skeleton in Armor recounts his life story, he is by turns reckless, wild, cruel, ardent, rapacious, predatory, and, finally, so inconsolable that he takes his own life. The little boy who skated on thin ice, skimming "the half-frozen Sound," has grown into a similarly reckless and willful adult (stanza 4). And for all the apparent romance and adventure of this Viking's tale, nonetheless Longfellow cast an anxious and suspicious eye on a life lived so wholly without restraint. This refusal to ignore the mayhem and bloodshed caused by the "Corsair's crew" and the insistent images of birds of prey were intended to make clear that this poem was to be read as a kind of cautionary tale. The Romantic movement's glorification of the unfettered self might have its limits. The Viking who follows only his own passions could hardly be an ancestral role model for New England Brahmins who still cherished notions of civic virtue and the common good.

To put it another way, Longfellow was quietly espousing a message that was, at its heart, essentially political and conservative. He was asking his readers to recognize the potential excesses of the romantic nationalism that then seemed so appealing. The illustrious history that began with Goths and morphed into Vikings was not simply a glorious pageant of freedom-seeking heroics that led inexorably to the Reformation and then to Plymouth Rock. It was also a pageant of individuals seeking only the satisfaction of individual desires, whether for conquest, gold, land, love, or salvation. And the romantic aggrandizement of the self that issued from some versions of this history—of which Longfellow's "The Skeleton in Armour" was meant to be an example—could come at the expense of community. After all, once the Viking has achieved his end by stealing his bride and causing the death of her father, he is able to exist only in exile. He has broken all the rules and customs that tied Hildebrand's community together. His story thus portends a threat to the public sphere when only private passions and private interests govern the individual.[13]

That said, the usually reserved and emotionally reticent Longfellow knew all too well the temptation to give oneself over to private passions. Like the Skeleton in Armor, he too had lost a beloved wife. In September 1831, Longfellow had married Mary Storer Potter, a beauty five years his junior. Less than four years later, in April 1835, the happy couple sailed to Europe, where Longfellow was to spend a year preparing himself to take up the Smith professorship of languages at Harvard. After visiting England, Denmark, and Sweden, they journeyed to Holland, where, on 5 October in Amsterdam, Mary suffered a miscarriage. She seemed to rally, and the couple moved on, but she relapsed in Rotterdam and died there on 29 November.[14] At age twenty-nine, having been married barely four years, Longfellow now found himself a grieving widower far from home. According to the Longfellow scholar Edward Wagenknecht, Longfellow spent the winter of 1836 in Heidelberg "attempting to drown his grief in hard study and only succeeding in finding his dead wife in everything he tried to read" (*Henry Wadsworth Longfellow* 6). Upon returning to the U.S., Longfellow burned Mary's journals as well as the love letters they had exchanged, and in a sonnet written in 1842, he described his life during this period as one of "sorrow, and a care that almost killed" ("Mezzo Cammin" 40).[15]

But for Longfellow, who described himself as "oft depressed and lonely," there was no release from pain by falling on his sword and no escape for his anguished soul by ascending to Walhalla ("Footsteps of Angels" 4). He had duties to take up at Harvard. "His only comfort," according to Wagenknecht, "was that Mary had promised on her deathbed that she would not leave him," and he thereafter felt "'assured of her presence'" (*Henry Wadsworth Longfellow* 6). Even so, there was a long and painful period of grieving, a grieving that was still with Longfellow as he struggled to compose a poem about the Northmen. In fact, at some moments, the struggle with the poem's subject and his own grief must have merged because, in 1839, Longfellow composed a sonnet titled "Footsteps of Angels" in which he used imagery similar to that which would be employed a year later by the Viking skeleton in *his* evocation of his beloved. In the sonnet, Longfellow senses Mary's presence "gaz[ing] at me / With those deep and tender eyes, / Like the stars, . . . / Looking downward from the skies" ("Footsteps of Angels" 4). In stanza 8, the Skeleton in Armor responds to his loved one's "soft eyes . . . gaz[ing] on me, / Burning yet tender," and compares them to "the white stars [that] shine / On the dark Norway pine." Of course, the trope of the loved one's tender gaze and the comparison of the loved one's eyes to stars are both poetic commonplaces and hardly original with Longfellow. Yet the fact that Longfellow inserted such congruent language in two poems written within a year of one another strongly hints that he was not entirely unsympathetic to his ghostly invention. For all his suspicion of the Viking's unrestrained life, the grieving poet fully and passionately gave vent to his own pain through his protagonist's selfish and passionate temperament. "The Skeleton in Armor" thus offered a voice and an emotional register rarely available to Longfellow. For the usually reserved poet, this represented a kind of release.

In part because it was the poem that opened *Ballads and Other Poems*, "The Skeleton in Armour" received the lion's share of critical attention. The volume as a whole was greeted with enthusiastic praise, and "The Skeleton in Armour" was generally pronounced "a very beautiful ballad" ("Longfellow's Ballads and Poems," *United States Magazine and Democratic Review* 183). But despite the poem's immediate popularity, Longfellow's fear, as expressed in his letter of December 1840 to his father, "that those who only glance" at the poem "will not fully comprehend me," proved prescient (*Letters* 2:269). To be sure, the many laudatory and lengthy review articles hardly suggest that reviewers only *glanced* at "The Skeleton in Armour," but they do suggest that Longfellow's complex intentions were rarely comprehended.

The problem may derive from the fact that most reviewers characterized Longfellow's poetry as "bear[ing] the Romantic impress, as distinguished from the Classical" ("Longfellow's Ballads and Other Poems" 115). Within this frame, "The Skeleton in Armour" was easily seen as Longfellow's imaginative evocation of a medieval—and particularly Scandinavian—verse romance, calling up a remote and "legendary" past full of wonder and adventure, yet a past importantly infused with local associations (116). The writer for the *North American Review*, for example, praised Longfellow both for "skillfully avail[ing] himself of the circumstance that a skeleton was found buried, some years ago, near the famous Round Tower of Newport," and also for equally successfully exploiting the assertions of the "Danish antiquaries . . . that this structure was raised by the northern adventurers, who are supposed to have discovered this continent centuries before the birth of Columbus" ("Longfellow's Ballads and Other Poems" 115). The historical veracity of those assertions was not at issue because, for this reviewer, the poem was a romance and therefore not bound by the rules of absolute verisimilitude. In language that closely anticipated Hawthorne's later defense of the romance, this reviewer argued, "Whatever we may think of [the Danish scholars'] opinion as a matter of sober historical inquiry, we must admit that there is ground enough for a poet to stand upon, while constructing a romantic poem like this one now before us. There is both ingenuity in the narrative, and sufficient probability in the story for all poetical purposes" (115).[16] Thus, according to this reviewer, the poem succeeded not just because "it reads like an old Scandinavian poem" but also because it had just enough "probability" to invite tantalizing imaginative speculations about New England's connection to "the Vikings, the robbers of the sea" (115, 116).

The writer for the *United States Magazine and Democratic Review* was even more emphatic about his eagerness to be seduced by the poem's imaginative inventions. After briefly describing the discovery of the Fall River skeleton, this reviewer noted that Longfellow had "give[n] increased interest to his poem" by "connect[ing] the supposed story of a warrior of a by-gone age with . . . the well-known tower at Newport." "For our part," he continued, "we are so willing to be agreeably deceived in such matters, that, instead of admitting the more reasonable, but less poetical supposition, that the Newport structure was erected by the earlier settlers as a stronghold and place of refuge against Indian attack, we shall henceforth believe it to have been the bona fide property of a Northern Viking, who brought to the western world a practical knowledge of Saxon architecture, long before Columbus" ("Longfellow's Ballads and Poems" 183–84). The reviewer applauded Longfellow for restoring the spirit of "the old, manly Anglo-Saxon poetry" with this work and proceeded, like so many other reviewers, determinedly to read it as though it were a romantic medieval ballad that told a love story. The reviewer characterized the awakened skeleton as "the spectral representative of Scandinavian chivalry," even though Longfellow suggested nothing at all noble or chivalrous about his ghostly protagonist, and the reviewer made the maiden a full participant in her abduction, even though Longfellow nowhere described the maiden as a willing actor in these events (185).[17] Yet the very fact of this kind of overheated misreading underscores the eagerness of Longfellow's contemporaries to read the poem in a certain way.

More than thirty years later, that same pattern still obtained. In January 1877, the *Atlantic Monthly* hailed the new illustrated gift-book edition as "the only acceptable legend attached to its subject": "Whatever theory one may choose for explaining the origin of the Round Tower at Newport, no history of the building will ever seem so real as that which Mr. Longfellow has established for it in one of his noblest ballads" ("Recent Literature" 114). In its review of the same gift-book edition, the *New-York Tribune* for 3 November 1876 called the poem Longfellow's "finest ballad" and praised it for "making picturesque Norse associations to an American locality" ("The Skeleton in Armor" 6). Clearly, no reviewer—whether in the 1840s or the 1870s—accepted as uncontested historical fact that the Newport tower was of Norse construction or that the mysterious skeleton was somehow connected to it. Nonetheless, as these reviews make plain, readers were looking for both an antique romantic American past and for a romance that told the story. The theories about ancient Viking visitations to New England provided at least a *probability* of such a past, and Longfellow's ballad offered a story that was at once wholly imaginative yet also seductively plausible. In February 1842, the reviewer for *Arcturus* put it best. Pleased that the poem "relate[d] to original American themes," and describing it as "an attempt to plant a legend on the seashore of Newport," he then explained the real source of the poem's appeal: "Barren and unproductive as these modern times are of romance, this is a manufactured tradition that deserves to take root" ("Longfellow's Ballads and Poems" 215).[18] In short, these otherwise *un*romantic times are hungry for just such a legend.

But because it took root as both a romance, with all the romance's potent nostalgia for an adventurous and glorious past, *and also* an exemplar of the period's reigning Romantic impulse, with all of Romanticism's celebration of the individual and his personal fulfillment, "The Skeleton in Armour" could not be read as the cautionary tale Longfellow intended. Readers purposefully missed the darker cues embodied in and through the persona of Longfellow's rash and daring Viking. Romantic poetry was not expected to critique aspects of Romanticism itself. And the romance was not expected to undermine the very past it invoked. In other words, the limits of Romantic self-expression was not a theme anyone was prepared to discover in the work of a poet so generally considered to have been influenced by the lyricism of the German Romantic poets and whose own "genius," according to the *New York Review*, "bears more affinity to that of the romantic, than of the classical school" ("Longfellow's Poems" 240).[19]

In 1840, as Longfellow put the finishing touches on "Saga of the Skeleton in Armor," his great narrative poems on historical American subjects were still ahead of him: "Evangeline" (1847), "Hiawatha" (1855), and "The Courtship of Miles Standish" (1858). The composition of the "Saga of the Skeleton in Armor," however, helped solidify his confidence that he could tell a story in verse and, especially, a story about the past which commented on the present. Although he never gave up writing either lyrical or meditative poetry, Longfellow essentially became a public poet by using verse narrative to carry on a conversation with his contemporaries. The two Harvard colleagues who "had frowned upon ['The Skeleton in Armor'] as beneath the plane of his previous lyrical performances" clearly did not comprehend the new direction in which Longfellow was moving (S. Ward 459). They could not see that he was well on his way to embracing the notion that "writing poems would come to mean not Romantic self-expression but participation in a public conversation" (Irmscher 173). Or, as Samuel Ward put the matter somewhat inelegantly, Longfellow's real aim as a poet was not lyric flight but "efficient usefulness to his own country" (465).

Whittier's Viking Rovers, Norman Knight, and the Answer to the Indian Question

Like Longfellow, John Greenleaf Whittier (1807–92) also had his doubts about uncritically adopting the ancient Norse as ancestors and precursors. Farmer, poet, journalist, crusading newspaper editor, political activist, and ardent abolitionist, Whittier was also a lifelong Quaker with strong pacifist leanings. Both his temperament and his religion inclined him to disapprove of "the fire-eating Vikings and red-handed [i.e., bloody-handed], unwashed Berserkers" who "regarded as meritorious the unrestrained indulgence of the passions" ("The Poetry of the North," *Prose Works* 396). In a short essay titled "The Poetry of the North," written in 1847 to commend the recent publication of Bayard Taylor's poem "The Norseman's Ride," Whittier found an occasion both to reprint Taylor's poem—thereby bringing it to the attention of a wider audience—and also to praise the transformation of the Northmen by the gentling influence of Christianity.[20] In Whittier's view, the pre-Christian Northmen were "bold, defiant, and full of a rude, untamed energy," their gods "brutal giant forces, patrons of war, robbery, and drunken revelry" (396, 397). But after the introduction of Christianity, "the hard and cruel Norse heart [was] . . . softened and humanized" (397). As a result, over time, the "rude, savage" Icelanders "of the tenth century" became imbued with "peaceful and gentle virtues" (397). Both these images—that is, the rude pagan adventurers and the gentle peaceful Christians—are represented in Whittier's two very different poems about the medieval Norse.

Written in rhymed tetrameters, like a ballad, the earlier poem, "The Norsemen," appeared in the same January 1841 issue of the *Knickerbocker* as Longfellow's "Saga of the Skeleton in Armor." Despite its ballad meter, however, Whittier's poem did not tell a story but rather unfolded a reverie in which the poet first hears and then sees an ancient Norse vessel gliding "up the Merrimack" (16).[21] What precipitates the reverie is the poet's fascination with a "gift from the cold and silent Past! / A relic to the Present cast" (16). As Whittier explained in a headnote to the poem, "Some three or four years since, a fragment of a statue rudely chiseled from dark gray stone, was found in the town of Bradford, on the Merrimack. Its origin must be left entirely to conjecture. The fact that the ancient Northmen visited New-England, some centuries before the discoveries of Columbus, is now very generally admitted" (16). Just as Longfellow made no special claims for the Newport tower, so too Whittier acknowledged the uncertain provenance of the statue fragment and linked it to the Norse simply by implication. He even addressed to the statue fragment a series of questions in his opening stanza:

> Who from its bed of primal rock
> First wrenched thy dark, unshapely block?
> Whose hand, of curious skill untaught,
> Thy rude and savage outline wrought? (16)

Then, following the local habit of identifying *any* odd and seemingly old artifact as Norse, Whittier happily used the location of the stone's discovery to situate his poem in the Merrimac River Valley, a landscape he both knew and loved. He had grown up on a farm near Haverhill, in northeastern Massachusetts, a farm that had been in the Whittier family since the mid-seventeenth century. And in 1836, when failing health forced him to sell the farm, he established a new home for himself, his mother, and his sister in nearby Amesbury.

That familiar landscape begins to disappear, however, as the poet falls under the spell of the "old gray stone." The features of civilization vanish, replaced by dark and wild woods reclaiming their "primeval" possession of the land.

> A spell is in this old gray stone—
> My thoughts are with the Past alone!
>
> A change!—the steepled town no more
> Stretches along the sail-thronged shore;
> . . .
> Spectrally rising where they stood,
> I see the old, primeval wood. (16)

Only "the same bright river" flows on "unchanged." And to the poet's ear, from the river come the sounds of Norse vessels (16):

> But hark!—from wood and rock flung back,
> What sound comes up the Merrimack?
> What sea-worn barks are those which throw
> The light spray from each rushing prow?
> Have they not in the North Sea's blast
> Bowed to the waves the straining mast?
> Their frozen sails the wintry sun
> Of Thulé's [Iceland's] night has shown upon.

These are the Viking Icelanders of the tenth century who, as subsequent lines make clear, journey from cold to warmth, from "wintry sun" to "green earth and summer sky" (17):

> Onward they glide—and now I view
> Their iron-armed and stalwart crew;
> Joy glistens in each wild blue eye,
> Turned to green earth and summer sky:
> Each broad, seamed breast has cast aside
> Its cumbering vest of shaggy hide;
> Bared to the sun and soft warm air,
> Streams back the Norsemen's yellow hair.
> I see the gleam of axe and spear,
> The sound of smitten shields I hear,
> Keeping a harsh and fitting time
> To Saga's chaunt, and Runic rhyme.

In subsequent lines, these Norsemen will be identified with the worship of Odin and with the lands and "trembling" peoples once conquered by Vikings (17). Yet we do not actually see them acting rudely within the poem itself. Even their weapons—the axes, spears, and struck shields—are associated with keeping the rhythms of "Saga's chaunt, and Runic rhyme" rather than with deeds of bloodshed.

Clearly, Whittier had chosen momentarily to transform the "iron-armed" warriors, not by Christianity, but by the gentling effects of a New England summer. "Joy glistens in each wild blue eye" as it takes in the surrounding "green earth and summer sky." The Northmen cast aside their bearskin capes, and "each broad, seamed breast" is now bared "to the sun and soft warm air." The breeze "streams back the Norsemen's yellow hair."[22] For the few brief seconds it takes to read these lines, the Northmen are gloriously unencumbered and rendered almost innocent by the world that now surrounds them. But it doesn't last. The idyll evaporates as a dark and violent history is called up by those same saga chants and runic rhymes. For the Gaals (that is, the Gaels from Galicia, the last conquerors of Ireland prior to the Norse invasions), the Franks (that is, the French), and the Scots, that "Runic rhyme" heralded only oncoming attacks and celebrated brutal incursions (17).

> The Gaal has heard its [i.e., the runic rhyme's] stormy swell,
> The light Frank knows its summons well;
> Iona's [in the Hebrides] sable-stoled Culdee [i.e., priest][23]
> Has heard its sounding o'er the sea,
> And swept with hoary beard and hair
> His altar's foot in trembling prayer!

The bucolic image of men "bared to the sun" is effectively displaced, and with that, the vision itself disappears (17):

> 'Tis past—the 'wildering vision dies
> In darkness on my dreaming eyes!
> The forest vanishes in air—
> Hill-slope and vale lie starkly bare;
> I hear the common tread of men,
> And hum of work-day life again.

The rudely carved gray stone no longer casts a spell. Instead, "the mystic relic seems alone / A broken mass of common stone" (17):

> And if it be the chisseled limb
> Of Berserker or idol grim—
> A fragment of Valhalla's Thor,
> Or Tyr, the restless god of war,
>
> . . .
>
> I know not—for no graven line,
> Nor Druid mark, nor Runic sign,
> Is left me here, by which to trace
> Its name, or origin, or place.

None of the questions posed in the opening lines have been answered, and so the mystery of the origins of the carved stone is still unsolved.

But solving the mystery of the stone was never the poem's real purpose. Instead, Whittier was invoking an experience that was essentially religious. As he stated at the outset, the stone had been "left on the ever-changing strand / Of shifting and unstable sand, / Which wastes beneath the steady chime / And beating of the waves of Time!" (16). Yet, ancient as it was, the statue fragment remained. The very fact of the stone's survival impelled the poet to seek further assurance of that which is eternal and immutable, something that endures beyond the "beating of the waves of Time." For a Quaker like Whittier, influenced by the new ideas of the Transcendentalists, that something could only be an immanent and beneficent deity. What the poem's reverie unfolds, therefore, is Whittier's eagerness to reassure himself of the Quaker belief in the Inner Light, that is, the possibility of communion between the human spirit and the divine eternal spirit. The closing lines make clear that the stone itself, whatever its origin, is merely the means to initiate that experience of communion (17):

> Yet, for this vision of the Past,
> This glance upon its darkness cast,
> My spirit bows in gratitude
> Before the Giver of all good,
> Who fashioned so the human mind,
> That from the waste of Time behind,
> A simple stone, or mound of earth,
> Can summon the departed forth;
> Quicken the Past to life again—
> The Present lose in what hath been,
> And in their primal freshness show
> The buried forms of long ago.

> As if a portion of that Thought
> By which the Eternal will is wrought,
> Whose impulse fills anew with breath
> The frozen solitude of Death,
> To mortal mind were sometimes lent,
> To mortal musings sometimes sent,
> To whisper—even when it seems
> But Memory's phantasy of dreams—
> Through the mind's waste of wo and sin,
> Of an immortal origin!

The poet expresses his gratitude for this vision of Vikings on the Merrimac because it reassures him that god purposefully "fashioned . . . the human mind" so that it *could* transcend "the waste of Time" and apprehend "the buried forms of long ago." The reason it can do so is that the human mind is itself "a portion of that Thought / By which the Eternal will is wrought." In other words, the human mind is "a portion" of the mind of god, a portion of that which is immortal and beyond time. Thus, from that "immortal origin," the "mortal mind were sometimes lent" and "to mortal musings sometimes sent" the kind of reverie outside of time that Whittier has just experienced. And because of the mortal mind's participation in the "Thought" of "the Eternal will," the mortal mind can sometimes summon forth from even "[a] simple stone" glimpses and whispers "from the waste of Time behind." Such moments may seem only "Memory's phantasy of dreams," but in fact these are moments of communion that reveal the human mind's potent capacity—as part of the mind of god—to "summon the departed forth; / Quicken the Past to life again."

In effect, "The Norsemen" collapses time, losing the present in the "primal freshness" of "the buried forms of long ago." In an instant, the "sail-urged keel and flashing oar" of Whittier's day are replaced by the sails and masts of the Northmen's ships "com[ing] up the Merrimack" (16). And erasing the seeming enormity of the intervening centuries, a kind of intimacy is established between the poem's earlier picture of "cultured field and steepled town" on a sunny summer morning and the later picture of the blue-eyed Norsemen gazing upon "green earth and summer sky" (16, 17). Both in the Eternal Mind and in the poet's imagination, the town and the Norse—albeit ages apart—have all shared the same environs of what Whittier called early in the poem "The waters of my native stream / . . . glancing in the sun's warm beam" (16).

Although never reticent about pointing out the faults and foibles of New England—religious bigotry, witch trials, only lukewarm opposition to slavery, etc.—Whittier always pronounced himself "a son of New-England, and proud of my birth-place" (*Legends of New-England* 3–4). In the preface to his first book, *Legends of New-England* (1831), he had written, "New-England is rich in traditionary lore—a thousand associations of superstition and manly daring and romantic adventure, are connected with her green hills and her pleasant rivers" (3). In 1837, Rafn's *Antiquitates Americanæ* added to the store of "manly daring and romantic adventure" in New England, and Whittier's "The Norsemen" eagerly took advantage of that fact. And while, on the one hand, the visionary appearance of medieval Norse in contemporary New England provided a pretext for what was essentially a very personal spiritual and religious quest, on the other hand, the vision of the Norse also provided an opportunity for composing a paean to New England itself, and particularly to that part of New England that Whittier called home. As he had written to a friend just a year earlier, nothing pleased him more than "see[ing] the sunset light streaming through the valley of the Merrimack" (*Letters* 1:349). In his reverie, Whittier's imagined Norsemen also saw "the same bright river / Flow[ing] on" (16).

Approached by the author and editor Rufus Griswold, who, in 1841, began planning a series of anthologies of American writers, Whittier urged him to include "The Norsemen" in his first anthology volume.[24] Having appeared just a few months before in the *Knickerbocker*, the poem "has been well spoken of by those in whose taste and judgement I have a good deal of confidence," Whittier wrote Griswold (*Letters* 1:524). When Whittier himself reprinted "The Norsemen" in *Lays of My Home, and Other Poems* (1843), the poem received generally favorable notices. A review in the *North American Review* cited it as one of the three "most vigorous, finished, and the best conceived pieces in this volume" (Felton 510). The praise meant a great deal to Whittier because he—like the poem itself—was emerging from a period of severe crisis.

In *John Greenleaf Whittier*, John B. Pickard points to the decade of the 1830s as "the most physically trying of Whittier's life" (25). In addition to editing a series of antislavery periodicals, "he traveled all over the North, attending conventions, lobbying, cajoling votes, even publicly speaking in an effort to win support for the Abolitionist cause" (25). He stood for election and in 1835 was voted into the Massachusetts legislature on an antislavery platform. On some occasions during the 1830s, he encountered—or was even the target of—anti-Abolitionist mob violence.[25] Still, in the face of popular hostility to the cause and repeated political setbacks, Whittier soldiered on. In 1840 he helped organize the Liberty Party as a protest party and later assisted in its merger with the more powerful Free-Soil Party, "which in turn formed the nucleus for the [new] Republican party" (23).

Unfortunately, Whittier's always uncertain health could not long sustain this fever pitch of activity. As Pickard has written, "The strain of constant editorial duties, growing political activity, and finally mob violence brought on so serious a physical breakdown in 1840 that his doctors feared permanent injury. Whittier resigned as editor and returned to his new home in Amesbury" (25). A careful reading of Whittier's letters, however, reveals that the breakdown was not solely physical and not exclusively attributable to the crush of duties and activities. Exacerbating his frustration that the public at large had not more readily rallied to the antislavery banner was his growing disenchantment with a movement that was splintering over arguments about tactics and direction, and a movement whose factionalism was becoming increasingly personal and nasty. Even Whittier became a target. "For the sake of peace—for the slave's sake, while Editor of the Freeman, I forbore to reply to the attacks," he confided in a letter to a fellow abolitionist in July 1840. But now he found it more and more difficult to conceal "my sentiments in reference to the recent unhappy dissensions in our organizations" (*Letters* 1:421).

Something else also troubled Whittier. As a younger man, he had hoped to become a poet and a serious writer. Early on, that part of his life had been thwarted. His father's limited financial resources meant that the boy had to work on the farm and could not get much formal schooling or attend college. But after some of young Whittier's poems were published in local New England newspapers, including the *Newburyport Free Press*, edited by William Lloyd Garrison, several people—most notably Garrison—importuned the practical-minded farmer to allow his son at least some formal schooling. "Penniless and proud, the father could only respond to Garrison's heated argument with the dry observation that poetry would not buy bread" (Pickard 11). In the end, though, Garrison prevailed, insisting that the young man's "poetry bears the stamp of true poetic genius" (qtd. in Pickard 11). Reluctantly, in 1827, Whittier's father consented to allow his son "to earn his own way through the first term of the newly opened Haverhill Academy" (11). Whittier was then twenty years old.

In the six years following what became his two terms at the Haverhill Academy, Whittier wrote nearly two hundred poems, edited several books, and, to earn a reliable income, edited three New England newspapers. In 1831, he made an unsuccessful bid for a congressional seat. Until his health collapsed in 1840, he increasingly allied his writings—including his poetry—to social justice causes and became a leader in the Abolitionist movement. Looking back at this part of his career from the perspective of the post–Civil War years, Whittier (*The Complete Poetical Works* 243) described himself as someone

> Who, with a mission to fulfill,
> Had left the Muse's haunts to turn
> The crank of an opinion-mill,
> Making his rustic reed of song
> A weapon in the war with wrong.

In other words, as he himself so often acknowledged, the youthful would-be poet had become the eloquent propagandist for a cause in which he passionately believed. And for this he had paid dearly.

Now back in Amesbury, with most responsibilities lifted from his shoulders and the opportunity to write what he wished, Whittier found it was not easy to return to "the Muse's haunts." In a letter written in July 1840, he ruefully reflected, "I have . . . written nothing of consequence for the last six months" (*Letters* 1:427). Less than a month later, in August, he elaborated in still another letter to another friend: "My relish for poetry is as strong as ever—but the pleasure of composition has in great degree ceased. It has become all taskwork. The last eight years of my life have been devoted to the cause of the slave—and I have found little leisure for literary pursuits" (1:433).

But that was not all. Whittier was also undergoing a crisis of religious faith. In 1839 he could still write about Jesus, the mortal carpenter, as representing "the beautiful and affecting union of the humblest form of our common humanity with the holy attributes of a Redeemer—this light of heaven shining through the depths of earthly humility" (*Letters* 1:377). Sadly, his work in the Abolitionist movement was making it difficult for Whittier to sustain that faith. When good churchgoing Christians could ignore (or even profit from) the evils of slavery and stone those who spoke against it, and when even professed antislavery advocates could threaten the larger cause by attacking one another, it was hard to believe in the power of Quaker brotherly love or the truth of the "light of heaven shining through" to "our common humanity." Yet it had been for this movement and for the tenets of this belief system that Whittier had put aside personal and lyric poetry and dedicated a decade of his life. Even his confidence in his relationship to god was slipping away.

By the summer of 1840, at least one close friend sensed Whittier's inner turmoil. This friend privately confided to Whittier "that he had been sensible of a deep trial and exercise in [Whittier's] own mind." The friend counseled Whittier "to put aside every weight that encumbers, and to look unto Him who was able to deliver from every trial." In the letter in which Whittier reported this conversation, he asked its recipient, "Pray for me that I may not suffer this most evident day of the Lord's visitation to pass over and leave me as before" (*Letters* 1:425). Clearly, Whittier saw his friend's intervention as "the Lord's visitation," and just as clearly, he admitted that he did not want to return to the state he had been in "before."

Yet only a few weeks later, Whittier wrote another friend, "I feel daily, that my heart is not *fixed*—that my Faith is weak—that in me, of myself, is no good thing. I am at best, a sinful and unworthy servant" (*Letters* 1:434). The language here expressed not only a faltering religious faith but, in its self-accusations, an accompanying deep depression. To be sure, Whittier endured almost chronic physical pain. He was often plagued by headaches, and on some days he could not write for more than a half hour at a time due to aches in his hands and arms. Repeatedly in his letters, he complained of "suffering under a good deal of weakness and pain of body" (1:467). Without question, this level of constant physical distress, by itself, can precipitate clinical depression. But Whittier's letters indicate that he understood his physical pain as separate and apart from a far less bearable spiritual pain. In a letter written in November 1840, Whittier "lament[ed] over [his] protracted seasons of doubt and darkness" and admitted "shrink[ing] back from the discovery of some latent unfaithfulness and insincerity" in himself (1:466).[26] He castigated himself for "selfishness and pride and vanity, which at times manifest themselves—in short, to find the law of sin and death still binding me" (1:467).

Part of the problem was that, confined by fragile health to rural Amesbury, with only occasional trips to New York, Philadelphia, Boston, Maine, and elsewhere, Whittier felt alone and isolated. In that same letter of November 1840, written to a fellow Quaker, Whittier admitted, "I think often of our [Quaker] meeting at Rhode Island, and at times something of a feeling of regret comes over me that I am so situated as not to be permitted to enjoy the company and the care and the watchful ministrations of those, whose labors [were also devoted to the cause of abolition]" (*Letters* 1:467). Things were very different in Amesbury. "Sitting down in our small meeting," Whittier told his friend, "[I felt] in myself, and in the meeting generally a want of life, and of the renewing baptism of that Spirit, which can alone soften the hardness and warm the coldness of the heart" (1:467). Thus, without the strong activist Quaker community that had embraced and looked out for him in previous years, he found insufficient spiritual sustenance in the small Amesbury Quaker meetinghouse. He felt himself alone, cut off from god, and beset by "the shadows of thick-coming doubts" (1:467).

Also in that letter of November 1840, almost as an aside, Whittier wrote this: "I mourn for the neglected opportunities of my past life" (*Letters* 1:467). He did not explain to what he was referring—whether to neglected political opportunities, to lost personal relationships, or, as previous letters had hinted, to his unfulfilled youthful dreams of pursuing a career as a serious poet. What is clear from the letters, though, is that in 1840, at age thirty-three, with his circumstances radically altered by poor health, Whittier was adrift and his future uncertain. And he was no longer at the center of a national movement. Impatient and still ambitious to somehow make his mark, he found himself "illy adapted to that quiet, submissive introverted state, of patient and passive waiting for a direction and support" (1:467). Even standard Quaker meditative practice was failing him.

Because "The Norsemen" first appeared in the *Knickerbocker* in January 1841, we may reasonably assume that it was composed in 1840, sometime during what Whittier called "protracted seasons of doubt and darkness" (*Letters* 1:466). The act of writing the poem, followed by praise for it from "those in whose taste and judgement I have a good deal of confidence," responded to two of his urgent needs (1:524). First and foremost, the vision that precipitated the poem allowed Whittier to experience yet another "evident day of the Lord's visitation" (1:425). Whatever Whittier saw and heard—or imagined he saw and heard— that day on the Merrimac, he understood it as emanating from "an immortal origin!" If only for a moment, despite "the [mortal] mind's waste of wo and sin," his mind had entered "that Thought / By which the Eternal will is wrought" and overcome both death and time. The "sun's warm beam" glancing on the river had been metaphorically transmuted into the Inner Light of Quaker belief. In sum, the poem brought Whittier to an act of communion that vindicated his belief, however faltering, in "man's relationship, even in his lowest estate, to his Creator and Preserver" (1:377). The poem thus captured at least one reassuring episode in Whittier's ongoing struggle against "the shadows of thick-coming doubts."

Secondarily, while the writing of "The Norsemen" responded to

Whittier's need for spiritual reassurance, the critical praise accorded the poem allayed his fear that he had forever "left the Muse's haunts." As the *North American Review* declared, he could still write poetry that was vigorous, finished, musical, and "spirit-stirring" (Felton 510). With the publication in 1843 of *Lays of My Home*, which included "The Norsemen," Whittier took the first crucial step in establishing himself as a serious poet, rather than merely an abolitionist versifier or editor and reformer. As Pickard commented in his edition of Whittier's collected letters, "*Lays of My Home* . . . heralded the birth of a mature poet" (1:479).[27]

After the Civil War—a conflict he dreaded yet saw as inevitable—Whittier continued to write and publish voluminously. In addition to his continuing concern for the situation of those now freed from slavery, he also now composed pro-labor poetry. He finally gained real financial security in 1866 with the publication of his best-known work, *Snow-Bound*. The next year he achieved bestseller status with *The Tent on the Beach*. In 1868, he showed an increasing interest in religious themes and devotional writing, and in 1869 he published "Norembega," a poem that returned to a religious theme he had first enunciated in his essay of 1844, "The Better Land."[28] In that essay, Whittier had observed that, because the scriptures provide too few solid clues about the afterlife, and because the mortal mind is thereby limited in its ability to call up authoritative images of the world to come, the human "imagination has a wide field for its speculations" (280). In pursuit of those speculations, he added, more often than not, we humans "transfer to our idea of heaven whatever we love and reverence on earth" (280). Christian tradition, of course, had long promulgated the idea of a heavenly city imagined as golden, bejeweled, and without pain or want. The discovery of the New World, with all its riches, had revivified that image, promising the real-world discovery of cities of gold whose wonders approximated those of the heavenly city. Thus, during the first century of European exploration and discovery, explorers and adventurers alike set out in search of Cibola, El Dorado, and, less well known, Norumbega.

As with Whittier's earlier poem, "The Norsemen," "Norembega" too rested on a kernel of plausibility. Unlike the "rudely chiseled" gray stone fragment found "in the town of Bradford, on the Merrimack," the foundation for "Norembega" was more probably a scholarly publication of 1869. As William Willis of the Maine Historical Society explained in his preface to that scholarly work, some years earlier, the

Society had contacted the German geographer and historian Johann Georg Kohl, who had spent four years traveling across North America from 1854 to 1858 and was an expert on the earliest charts and maps of America made by Europeans.[29] What the Society wanted, according to Willis, was a comprehensive study "of authentic information . . . brought together [from all sources] on the discovery and early voyages to America," especially along the coast of Maine (iii). Among the several subjects of particular interest noted by Willis was "ancient *Norumbega*," prominent on several old maps, "embracing sometimes the whole of New England . . . [and sometimes] a narrower region" (iii–iv). Also to be examined from "the penumbra of our history," wrote Willis, "were the voyages of the Northmen to the Gulf of Maine" (viii). With both private funding and an initial grant from the State of Maine, the project was undertaken, and in 1869 the Maine Historical Society published Kohl's *A History of the Discovery of the East Coast of North America, Particularly the Coast of Maine; from the Northmen in 990, to the Charter of Gilbert in 1578 . . . Illustrated by Copies of the Earliest Maps and Charts*.

Consistent with this title, Kohl's survey of all the early European voyages began with the Northmen, who "stand forth in the middle ages foremost and alone, without allies or rivals," as both "discoverers and colonizers of North America" (19). Kohl followed Rafn in also tracing their later "influence on the subsequent undertakings of Columbus and the Cabots" (19). Indeed, as Kohl acknowledged in a footnote, almost his entire discussion of the Norse was "taken—sometimes literally—from that excellent work, 'Antiquitates Americanæ,' . . . written and collected by C. C. Rafn" (57n). The only exceptions were "some general remarks, and the observations on the old history of the coast of Maine, which are my own" (57n). These included the suggestion that the place where Thorfinn Karlsefni sighted the Uniped "might have been somewhere in the inner parts of the Gulf of Maine," and the observation that, because of the "early exploring, searching, and trading voyages of Thorfinn and Gudrida, . . . the coast of Maine, in the year 1008, was, for the first time, coasted along by European ships from north to south" (76, 79).

From the point of view of the Maine Historical Society, which had commissioned his study, among Kohl's most important "observations on the old history of . . . Maine" were those pertaining to a mysterious realm called Norumbega. With different spellings, the name had continued to appear on maps through the eighteenth century, and stories persisted that it had once been a thriving and wondrous place.

180 Chapter Four

Although the origin of the name remains obscure, it was generally attached to the area between Cape Cod and Cape Breton.[30] One reason for the Maine Historical Society's particular interest in Norumbega may have derived from the claim, dating back to the end of the sixteenth century, that the name "was a variant of 'Norway' and indicated that this was where one should look for descendants of the Norse [from] Greenland" (Seaver, *The Last Vikings* 215–16). For some, this explained why early explorers had reported encountering "tall and fair-skinned natives" (217). Of course, Samuel de Champlain had effectively deflated the myth with his explorations up the Penobscot River and "his 1612–13 map of the St. Lawrence region show[ing] norembegue as just a minor [Native] settlement on the outer Penobscot shore" (217).

Ignoring entirely Norumbega's fabulous (and fabulistic) associations, Kohl's research led him to conclude that the word had originally been an Indian place name, picked up and first used by the French in the sixteenth century. His examination of all the extant sixteenth-, seventeenth-, and eighteenth-century maps and charts revealed that the name was attached to slightly different areas on different maps and charts, and that sometimes it appeared as a name for a river and at other times for the land surrounding the river. Kohl summarized, "The French . . . gave the Indian name, 'Norumbega,' to a portion of New France; and we find it applied on some old maps to the country of the Bretons [i.e., Cape Breton] and Nova Scotia. . . . The centre of the region covered by this aboriginal name, however, appears always to have been the Penobscot River, 'the great river of Norumbega'" (489).

What Whittier took from Kohl's study was confirmation that there really had once been some place called Norumbega and that its center was the Penobscot River. What he also gleaned from Kohl was the scholar's certainty—even more so than in Rafn—that the ancient Norse had been familiar with the coast of Maine, and especially the Penobscot Bay area. Moreover, because he had friends in Maine, Whittier was surely also aware of contemporary reports that runic inscriptions and the remains of ancient Norse habitations had supposedly been discovered in Maine.[31] All of this, along with some well-known statements by Samuel de Champlain, was just what Whittier needed in order to ground his second poem about Northmen in at least a quasi-historical context. And he established that context at the outset, in his headnote to "Norembega" (Whittier's choice for spelling the word):

> Norembega, or Norimbegue, is the name given by early French fishermen and explorers to a fabulous country south of Cape Breton, first discovered by Verrazzani in 1524. It was supposed to have a magnifi-

cent city of the same name on a great river, probably the Penobscot. The site of this barbaric city is laid down on a map published at Antwerp in 1570. In 1604 Champlain sailed in search of the Northern Eldorado, twenty-two leagues up the Penobscot from the Isle Haute. He supposed the river to be that of Norembega, but wisely came to the conclusion that those travellers who told of the great city had never seen it. He saw no evidence of anything like civilization, but mentions the finding of a cross, very old and mossy, in the woods. (*The Complete Poetical Works* 92)

The detail about the cross is probably what prompted Whittier to see in the Norumbega legend the potential for yet another religiously themed poem.

The poem centers on a quest for Norumbega undertaken by an aged and dying Norman knight. Normandy, in northwest France, bordering the English Channel, was repeatedly raided in the ninth century by the Norsemen, for whom the region is named. In 991 the territory was ceded to Rollo, a Norse chieftain, who then became the first duke of Normandy. Thereafter, the region became a Norse territory, its population an amalgam of Norse immigrants and the prior inhabitants. From Normandy, in 1066, under Duke William (or William the Conqueror), French-speaking Normans crossed the Channel and invaded England. By this time, the Norse in Normandy were converted to Catholicism and became only more so with their conquest of England. In Whittier's day, a resurgent medievalism that followed the Civil War was marked, in part, by the reading public's renewed interest in tales of gallant knights and beautiful ladies, courtly love, and heroic religious quests, like the quest for the Holy Grail. Norman knights were a staple of the genre.

Whittier exploited that fact in "Norembega" by casting his protagonist as a pious "Christian knight" from "Normandie" (*The Complete Poetical Works* 92, 93). In so doing, he was able to portray his alternative image of the Northmen—that is, what became of "the hard and cruel Norse heart" once it had been "softened and humanized" by Christianity ("The Poetry of the North," *The Complete Poetical Works* 397). However improbable the premise, Whittier's Norman knight, enfeebled by age, is in North America, embarked on what is presumably his final quest, this time for the fabled Norumbega. As the knight explains, "The baffling marvel calls" ("Norembega," *The Complete Poetical Works* 92).

The first four stanzas of "Norembega" display some of Whittier's most successful nature poetry as he describes a winding river making its way through the enclosing "forest wall" (*The Complete Poetical Works*

92). In the fifth stanza, we meet the knight, leaning on his "henchman" (92). For some time, the two have been following the path of the river. Immediately, the major pattern of the poem is revealed: in the "embers of the sunset's fires" glowing over river and forest, the knight believes he sees "the domes and spires / Of Norembega town." But his henchman is quick to correct him (92):

> "Alack! the domes, O master mine,
> Are golden clouds on high;
> Yon spire is but the branchless pine
> That cuts the evening sky."

Again and again the pattern is repeated. When the knight thinks he hears "chants and holy hymns" coming from the fabled city, his henchman explains that this is merely "the breeze that stirs the trees / Through all their leafy limbs" (92). When the knight thinks they are approaching "a blessed cross" set there for him by Christ, his henchman explains that it is only a "blasted tree / With two gaunt arms outright" (92). In short, despite his companion's repeatedly corrective explanations, the knight persists in transforming his surroundings into signs of the city he so ardently seeks. As he tells his companion, "I fain would look before I die / On Norembega's walls" (93).

Unwilling to give up his quest, but exhausted by the long trek, the knight asks for "an hour of rest" and bids his henchman scale a nearby hill in hopes of his seeing "the valley even now / . . . starred with city lights" (93). The faithful servant does so, but of course "saw nor tower nor town, / But, through the drear woods, lone and still, / The river rolling down" (93). He reports this to his dying master, declaring "We are but men misled; / And thou hast sought a city here / To find a grave instead" (93). The knight accepts his fate, reasoning that it doesn't matter where "a true man's [grave] cross may stand" since it will still be under heaven "here as there / In pleasant Norman land" (93). In subsequent stanzas, he recognizes that Norembega was but "a dream / Whose waking is in Heaven," and he realizes, "A city never made with hands / Alone awaiteth me" (93). In other words, he understands that he has confused a nonexistent earthly city with his true destination, the heavenly city. And he exclaims, "Let me be, / Dear Lord, a dweller *there*" (93, my emphasis). Upon the knight's death, his "henchman dug at dawn a grave," committing his master's "keeping" to the land along the river (93).

"Years after," continues the poem, "when the Sieur Champlain / Sailed up the unknown stream, / And Norembega proved again / A shadow and a dream," the French explorer "found the Norman's nameless grave" (93). It is marked by the same "cross-boughed tree" that, earlier in the poem, the knight had taken for "a blessed cross" set there for him by Christ (93, 92). That cross, says the poem, now "marked the spot / And made it holy ground" (93). The pious knight's supposed error has, after all, proved prescient. And with that, in the last two lines, the poem enunciates its motivating message: "He needs the earthly city not / Who hath the heavenly found" (93).

It is a conclusion not far removed from what Whittier had written in his essay, "The Better Land" (1844). There he had argued, "We should not forget that 'the kingdom of heaven is within'; . . . that it is the state and affections of the soul, . . . the sense of harmony with God" (283). Throughout "Norembega," we never doubt that the "Christian knight" already possesses "the kingdom of heaven" within himself. He has only to give up his deluded quest for discovering the marvels of heaven in *this* world. When he understands this, he is ready to enter the heavenly city. It is all a familiar and unexceptional Christian theme. Thus, the questing of a Catholic knight has led to an acceptably Protestant conclusion.

That said, when "Norembega" first appeared in the *Atlantic Monthly* in June 1869, its appeal rested on more than its obvious religious theme. At a far more subtle level, the poem responded to the changing national mood that followed the Civil War, implicitly substituting the pious questing Norman knight for the popular iterations of his warrior-pirate-Viking forebears that had gained prominence in the antebellum decades. A nation wearied of bloodletting and eager for reconciliation was no longer enthusiastic about representations of bloodthirsty warriors and cruel conquerors. Moreover, as the historian Jackson Lears pointed out in *No Place of Grace*, "In the excitement of postwar economic expansion, it seemed to many that commercial necessity had rendered the martial virtues obsolete" (100). Given this historical context, "Norembega" reveals yet another aspect of its contemporary resonance. The poem ends with the knight's gravesite being discovered by Champlain, the explorer who founded New France and established French commercial interests in the New World.[32]

In Whittier's view, Christianity had transformed violent Vikings into pious Norman knights. As he wrote in 1846 in "The Poetry of the North," "the hard and cruel Norse heart . . . of the sea-kings and robbers of the middle centuries" had "been so softened and humanized" by the influence of the Gospels that, in Whittier's day, their descendants in Iceland displayed only "the peaceful and gentle virtues" (*The Prose Works* 397). Those who had once been "unwashed Berserkers" were now a people of "peaceful disposition, social equality, hospitality, industry, intellectual cultivation, morality, and habitual piety" (396, 397–98). In short, he concluded, "In Iceland Christianity has performed its work of civilization" (398). Might it not then have the same beneficial effect on "the nomadic habits and warlike propensities of the native tribes" of America ("Indian Civilization," *The Prose Works* 233)? After all, racial differences notwithstanding, according to one popular trope of the period, the wild Vikings and the wild Indians were really not all that different.

Thus, in 1877, in the midst of what became known as the Nez Percé War and just a year after the rout of George Armstrong Custer's troops at the Battle of Little Bighorn, as the U.S. Army continued to round up the scattered remnants of the Plains tribes and confine them on reservations, Whittier wrote the following: "The wildest of [the Indian tribes] may compare not unfavorably with those Northern barbarian hordes that swooped down upon Christian Europe, and who were so soon the docile pupils and proselytes of the peoples they had conquered. The Arapahoes and Camanches of our day are no further removed from the sweetness and light of Christian culture than were the Scandinavian Sea Kings of the middle centuries" ("Indian Civilization," *The Prose Works* 233). Therefore, as Whittier put it, "the Indian is not inferior to the Norse ancestors of the Danes and Norwegians of our day in capability of improvement" (235).

That "improvement," of course, could best be accomplished through "the progress of education, civilization, and conversion to Christianity" promulgated by the various Christian missionary societies, including the Quakers, who brought textbooks, Bibles, and seed corn to the reservations ("Indian Civilization," *The Prose Works* 233). All this Whittier encouraged. But when he composed his essay "Indian Civilization" as an introduction to a book by an English Quaker critical of U.S. Indian policy, Whittier did so with a larger purpose in mind.[33] He wanted both to plead the Indians' cause and to "awaken" a heightened sense of "the responsibility which rests upon us as a people to rectify, as far as possible, past abuses, and in our future relations to the native owners of the soil to 'deal justly and love mercy'" (235). In other words, given the record of wrongs and abuses to which they had been subjected, Whittier saw "nothing exceptional in the Indians' ferocity and vindictiveness." Their responses were not unlike those of "the whole family of man" throughout history (235). "It is scarcely necessary to say," urged Whittier, "that the wars waged by the Indians against the whites have, in nearly every instance, been provoked by violations of solemn treaties and systematic disregard of their rights of persons, property, and life" (234).

By 1883, when Whittier again addressed the Indian question, the situation of Native peoples had only grown more desperate. The earlier policy of isolating the tribes west of the Mississippi and supposedly protecting them on remote reservations no longer seemed feasible. As Whittier acknowledged in a talk written for a meeting in Boston that year, "The westward setting tide of immigration is everywhere sweeping over the lines of the reservations. There would seem to be no power in the government to prevent the practical abrogation of its solemn treaties and the crowding out of the Indians from their guaranteed hunting grounds. Outbreaks of Indian ferocity and revenge, incited by wrong and robbery on the part of the whites, will increasingly be made the pretext of indiscriminate massacres" ("The Indian Question" 238).[34] As a consequence, Whittier saw only two possible outcomes: "education and civilization," that is, assimilation "or extermination" (238).

Preferring the former, Whittier lauded the work of the Indian residential schools, insisting that the "experiments at Hampton, Carlisle, and Forest Grove in Oregon have proved... that the roving Indian can be enlightened and civilized" ("The Indian Question" 238). The purpose of Whittier's talk, therefore, was to plead for money "not only [that] these schools should be more liberally supported, but that new ones should be opened without delay" (239). In his view, "the laudable example set by the Friends and the American Missionary Association should be followed by other sects and philanthropic societies" (239). Under their paternalistic wing and in these residential schools, he believed, the "enlightened and civilized" Indian could be "taught to work and take interest and delight in the product of his industry, and settle down on his farm or in his workshop, as an American citizen, protected by and subject to the laws of the republic" (238–39). Without any hint that he recognized the underlying irony, Whittier was, in effect—like most of his contemporaries—proposing to turn America's first nations into *real Americans* by changing them into the assimilated citizens of the invading settler nation.

And that is where all the popular analogies between Indians and Norse should have broken down. As Whittier knew well, the invading pagan Scandinavians had adapted to and absorbed the indigenous cultures, and willingly, for their own purposes, they had also adopted the languages and religion of the conquered. In other words, it was the invading settler Scandinavians who assimilated into the world of the indigenous peoples, and not the reverse. Now, in an effort meant to "save" the Indian, Whittier and most of his like-minded contemporaries invoked the "Northern barbarian hordes" only to ignore this inconvenient aspect of their historical counterexample. Amid all the enthusiasm for invoking the Northmen wherever possible, here was a glaring contradiction collectively ignored.

Lowell's Conflicting Visions of Vinland

Both before and after the Civil War, the poet, satirist, political essayist, antislavery advocate, literary critic, Harvard professor, magazine editor, and diplomat James Russell Lowell (1819–91) was one of the best at exposing the nation's contradictions and skewering the hypocrisies of national policy. His most famous contributions to this kind of truth-telling were his two series of *Biglow Papers*. Full of gentle humor, sharp satire, and pointed parody, these were letters supposedly written by a young New England farmer named Hosea Biglow and then edited and collected by a scrupulously pedantic clergyman named Homer Wilbur. Several other New England characters contribute their own letters, speeches, poems, and ruminations which both Biglow and Wilbur dutifully quote, edit, versify, and include in the whole. Written in a variety of New England dialects, *The Biglow Papers* included everything from parodies of the pomposities of recent U.S. Senate debates to a character invented specifically to represent the "incarnation . . . of national recklessness as to right and wrong" (appendix, *Complete Poetical Works* 442). The humor embedded both in Lowell's assemblage of Yankee characters and in his portrayal of their often colorful speech aside, *The Biglow Papers* were intended as serious political discourse. Both series were motivated by Lowell's opposition to slavery.

The first series, consisting of nine letters or "papers," first appeared individually from June 1846 to September 1848 in the *Boston Courier* and the *National Anti-Slavery Standard*. They were collected and first published together as a book in 1848. Their target was the array of sham excuses used to justify the Mexican War (1846–48). Lowell indicted the U.S. invasion of Mexico as merely a stratagem to extend the south's slaveholding territory and political power. As Hosea Biglow puts it in one of his poems, "They jest want this Californy / So's to lug new slave-states in" (*The Biglow Papers* 51–52). The second series of *Biglow Papers* was published in eleven installments in the *Atlantic*

Monthly during the years of the Civil War and the early Reconstruction period. They were collected in book form in 1866. Again, as with the first series, Yankee dialect, humor, and satire predominate, but Lowell's targets were serious: the self-serving arguments of those who supported the southern cause, the immorality of the opposition to President Lincoln's Emancipation Proclamation of 1862, the carnage and loss of life in wartime, and, in the last "paper," the problems with Reconstruction and the resistance to the Civil Rights Act of March 1866 (finally passed by both houses of Congress over the veto of President Andrew Johnson). Taken together, said a reviewer in the *Nation* in November 1866, *The Biglow Papers* in both their incarnations "gave their author the highest place among living satirical and humorous writers" ("The New Biglow Papers" 387).

Anchored as they were in New England lore and lifeways, it was almost unthinkable that *The Biglow Papers* would not carry allusions to the region's outsized pride in its past. Thus, in addition to more serious considerations, Vikings and alleged Viking artifacts were repeatedly invoked to make a point. These were, after all, part of the common parlance of the day. In number 7 of the first series, written during the war with Mexico, the pedantic pastor Homer Wilbur advises potential presidential candidates on how to compose written responses to questions about their position on the war. Understanding that most politicians prefer not to be pinned down to a single position on any topic because they are always looking ahead to how they may be judged by posterity, the good reverend recommends Dighton Rock as a template. He advises, "If letters must be written, profitable use might be made of the Dighton rock hieroglyphics, . . . every fresh decipherer of which is enabled to educe a different meaning" (*The Writings* 8:115).

Continuing with that same satiric take on the antiquarians who claimed to interpret authentic historical inscriptions from what looked like "bird tracks" on stone, Lowell turned Wilbur into just such a fellow. In a letter to the *Atlantic Monthly* dated 12 April 1862, written from Jaalam, Wilbur's (wholly invented) hometown, the good reverend asks the editors of that magazine "to withdraw our minds a moment from the confusing din of battle to objects of peaceful and permanent interest" (*The Writings* 8:312). In this, the fifth installment in the second series of *Biglow Papers*, the pedantic Reverend Wilbur would have the *Atlantic Monthly* readers turn away from the sometimes heart-stopping ups and downs of the Union Army's performance on the battlefield and attend instead to his recent discovery of a stone with a "Runick inscription" (8:312).

Replete with often error-ridden or misused Latin phrases, a vocabulary laced with malapropisms, and all the exaggerated knowledge of a truly pretentious gentleman, the letter is hilarious both in its style and in its send-up of antiquarians' certainties about "the ante-Columbian discovery of this continent by the Northmen" (*The Writings* 8:312). "Touching Runick inscriptions," says Wilbur, "they may be classed under three general heads": those understood by the Danish Royal Society and Professor Rafn; those understood *only* by Professor Rafn; and those which nobody can decipher or understand. Wilbur's find falls into the third category. His method for unlocking its message is ingenious (and not far off the mark of some contemporary practice): "I would write down a hypothetical inscription based upon antecedent probabilities, and then proceed to extract from the characters engraven on the stone a meaning as nearly as possible conformed to this *a priori* product of my own ingenuity" (8:314). The end result is (8:315)

> Here
> Bjarna Grimolfsson
> First drank Cloud-Brother
> Through Child-of-Land-and-Water.

Wilbur interprets this gibberish as recording the first smoking of tobacco "by an European on this continent," in this instance "Bjarna Grimolfsson" from *Eirik the Red's Saga* (8:315). And now, because Jaalam will henceforth forever be linked "with one of the most momentous occurrences of modern times," Wilbur's "native town" can take its place "on the historick roll" (8:316–17). Like other New England towns with claims to evidence of ancient Viking presence, Jaalam too would be known as a "theatre of remarkable historical incidents" (8:316).

In other works, however, Lowell expressed a more complicated engagement with what Wilbur called "the ante-Columbian discovery of this continent by the Northmen" (*The Writings* 8:312). That engagement began rather modestly with two poems first published in 1848 in *Poems, Second Series*. Left undated by the poet, the shorter and more perplexing of the two, "The Growth of the Legend," was subtitled by Lowell "A Fragment." The poem projects a dark and foreboding mood as it traces the growth of some unspecified legend from "the vast / Norwegian forests of the past" and follows its transit to a lumbermen's "pine-shadowed" campfire in Maine (7:198, 201). As Lowell repeatedly revealed in "A Moosehead Journal," the record of his camping and hiking trip to Maine in August 1853, unlike Thoreau (whose love of raw nature Lowell never entirely understood), Lowell was not a man easily at home in the woods.[35] He could appreciate the beauties of Maine, but he preferred the signs of civilization to "the immemorial pines" (1:11). For Lowell, "The forest primeval is best seen from the top of a mountain," that is, from a distance and not from within (1:40). Yet this apparent personal unease with densely forested landscapes only partially accounts for the mystery at the heart of the poem.

The central subject of the poem, the legend itself, we are told, first "grew in the forest's hush" of Norway "ages ago," initiated by "a word some poet chanced to say" ("The Growth of the Legend" 7:198). The legend then "grew and grew, / . . . like a true Northern pine" and, taking more than his fair share of poetic license, Lowell made the boughs of that tree themselves the singers of the legend (7:198):

> Its cloudy boughs singing, as suiteth the pine,
> To snow-bearded sea-kings old songs of the brine,
> Til they straightened and let their staves fall to the floor,
> Hearing waves moan again on the perilous shore
> Of Vinland, perhaps, while their prow groped its way
> 'Twixt the frothed gnashing tusks of some ship-crunching bay.

This is the first hint in the poem that the legend may have something to do with Vinland and that, in the legend, Vinland is remembered as a "perilous shore" with dangerous currents and "ship-crunching" bays. Upon hearing Vinland's "waves moan again" in the singing of the pine boughs, even the old "snow-bearded sea-kings" (i.e., Vikings) straightened to attention "and let . . . fall to the floor" their wooden staffs (used both as weapons and as walking sticks). Clearly, they have been reminded of something that, even in retrospect, still frightens.

As the poem continues, so too "pine-like the legend grew" until, finally, it crosses the Atlantic. Then, in a kind of interlude, the poem asserts that "wherever the pine-wood has never let in, / . . . the light and the din" of the modern world, there the "primeval . . . shade" has sheltered in safety "the weird Past with its child-faith alive" (7:200). As Lowell and his contemporaries well knew, "weird" did not simply connote the supernatural or uncanny. More important here, it derived from the Scandinavian and Old English *wyrd*, a word associated with the Fates and with destiny. The line suggests that within the dark primeval pine forests, an ancient past governed by the Fates and by some pre-Christian "child-faith" is still "alive." Even "mid the hum and the stir of To-day's busy hive," another time and another reality lives still in the woods. And it is "there the legend takes root in the age-gathered gloom, / And its murmurous boughs for their sagas find room" (7:200). Thus, having crossed the ocean, the legend again takes root in ancient forests. But this time the forests are in Maine.

The last long section of "The Growth of the Legend" opens with a reference to the Aroostook River, which runs near the border between northern Maine and New Brunswick, Canada. The area is heavily wooded and, in the nineteenth century, provided prime lumber for New England's shipbuilding industry. The scene set by the poem is a lumbermen's camp in the dead of winter "where the lumberers sit by the log-fires that throw / Their own threatening shadows far round o'er the snow" (7:200). Finally, the fragment ends with the following four lines (7:201):

> There the old shapes crowd thick round the pine-shadowed camp,
> Which shun the keen gleam of the scholarly lamp,
> And the seed of the legend finds true Norland ground,
> While the border-tale's told and the canteen flits round.

Immediately, the scene begs comparison with popular images of medieval Scandinavians sitting around their own hearths or campfires, passing the drinking horn, and reciting the sagas and retelling their stories of gods and heroes. In the lumbermen's penchant for swapping stories around a fire on a cold winter's night, the legend has indeed found "true Norland [i.e., Northland] ground." But we still do not know what the legend is about, nor can we identify "the old shapes" crowding round the camp. All we have are unsatisfying clues. The legend hails from the Norwegian past and the words of some poet; it is somehow connected to memories of and sagas about Vinland; there appears to be something dark or menacing in the legend; and it can take root only in the gloom of ancient forests, away from the light of the modern world. Moreover, whatever its subject, the legend has made its way from the Old World to the New.

Because many nineteenth-century poets used the word "saga" as a generic for "story," there is no way to know whether Lowell had in mind a specific tale from a particular Icelandic saga or intended to invent his own story or utilize some other medieval Scandinavian source available in English. The poem breaks off before the legend is revealed. Even so, the fragment lays bare a deep and disturbing ambivalence about this mysterious legend, a legend that, finally, Lowell could not bring himself to write down. While *The Biglow Papers* expressed an amused skepticism about all the recent revelations of Norse activity in New

England, "The Growth of the Legend" expressed a radically different form of ambivalence, one emanating from the contemplation of something altogether alien, dark, and primeval from out of New England's "weird Past." Lowell never returned to the poem.[36]

In a very different mood, Lowell again alluded to the Norse while retelling a piece of the familiar Columbus discovery story. Titled "Columbus" and probably written between 1844 and 1845, this poem was structured around a theme popular in the nineteenth century: the nobility of striving, against all odds, for some worthy goal or ideal. Written as a soliloquy in blank verse, spoken by Columbus, the poem has him upbraiding those "earthen souls" whose limited vision had so long made him a "prisoner to beat my wings / Against the cold bars of their unbelief" (7:148). Still he persevered, clinging to his commitment to this "highest endeavor" (7:149). Now, near the end of his first voyage, Columbus contrasts "the old world" that he has left behind with the "unknown shore" that he is sure lies ahead (7:149, 148). Clearly, this is not the Columbus who accidentally stumbled on a new continent while seeking a water route to the fabled riches of the Indies. Rather, this is an Americanized Columbus, a man with a mission, who all along sought to "break a pathway to . . . unknown realms" (7:154, 155). His certainty that such realms really exist, he says, began when he was a boy, listening to the "hoary legends of the sea," and solidified when, as a man, he read the great literatures of times past (7:153). "Entertain[ing] the poet's song," he "brooded on the wise Athenian's tale / Of happy Atlantis, and heard Björne's keel / Crunch the grey pebbles of the Vinland shore" (7:154). "I believed the poets," declares Columbus; "it is they / Who utter wisdom" (7:154).

In addition to making a case for the inspirational importance of his own vocation, Lowell also revealed in this line that he was well aware of — and perhaps even accepted — then-popular theories put forward by Rafn and others that Columbus had at least heard of the sagas and did, in fact, know of the prior discovery by the Norse of a new land to the west of Greenland. Lowell's own familiarity with the original sources is questionable, however, because both in *The Greenlanders' Saga* and in Rafn's retelling, Bjarni Herjolfsson and his crew only *sighted* the new land, around 985 or 986, but never went ashore. Not until the year 1000 did Leif Eiriksson and his crew first explore and name Vinland.

But historical accuracy was hardly Lowell's main concern. Instead, he used Columbus as a vehicle to encourage readers to explore the *outcome* of the discovery. To do this, Lowell had Columbus first characterize the world he has left behind. "The old world is effete," states Columbus, an emasculated realm of struggling humanity where "Life is trod underfoot" (7:149–50). "Yes, Europe's world / Reels on to judgment," he declares (7:150). Then Lowell has Columbus pose two key questions: "What gift bring I to this untried world?" and "Shall the same tragedy be played anew?" (7:150). Will the very fact of discovery—Columbus's "gift"—ensure that "Ignorance and Sin and Hunger" once again lead to "one dread desolation" (7:151)? Or, on a more optimistic note, could a "commonwealth" erected in this new land make humankind "whole... once more" (7:151)? In other words, will this new land and, by implication, this new nation, live up to their initial promise and potential? The questions are left unanswered, purposefully intended for readers' contemplation.

We may speculate, however, that, given Lowell's abhorrence of slavery and his disgust at the invasion of Mexico for the purpose of extending slaveholding territory, he viewed the U.S. at this time as insufficiently unlike Columbus's fifteenth-century Europe. That is, as a nation, the U.S. was yet sadly lacking in any "large Humanity" (7:150). Indeed, the very purpose of the poem was to caution the nation against squandering that potential "commonwealth" of which Columbus dreamed. After all, Lowell emphasized, the discovery of America was no accidental happenstance. Even had he wanted, Columbus could never "turn back to other destinies" (7:151). As Lowell portrays Columbus, "there is work that he must do for God" (7:155). The voyage was thus providential *and* ordained.

Only near the end of the poem does Lowell reveal that Columbus has delivered his soliloquy in the early dawn hours of the last day that his crew will "leave the helm to me" (7:156). Lowell was here referring to the story—probably apocryphal but repeated in Irving's enormously popular *History of the Life and Voyages of Christopher Columbus* (1828)—that, on the first voyage, never before having sailed so far west, Columbus's frightened crew threatened to mutiny if they did not soon reach land. In order to avert mutiny, Columbus calculated a date and promised to turn over to the crew the helm of his lead ship if they did not sight land on or before that designated date. "One poor day!" he muses and then remembers, "It is God's day, it is Columbus's" (7:157). With his faith and courage renewed, in the closing lines Columbus declares, "One day, with life and heart, / Is more than time enough to find a world" (7:157).

Both the fragment, "The Growth of the Legend," and "Columbus" concerned themselves with a moment of European discovery, albeit in very different ways. The differences between the two poems notwithstanding, they contained material that Lowell would take up again in future years. The questions posed by Columbus *would* be answered— but this time by the prophesying Gudrid en route to Vinland. Lowell was not yet done with discovery or with Norse legends.

The year 1848, which saw the publication of both "The Growth of the Legend" and "Columbus" in *Poems, Second Series*, has been labeled by most modern critics as Lowell's *annus mirabilis*. As one critic noted, "No year in Lowell's long and fruitful life was to prove more richly productive" (McGlinchee 35). In addition to his responsibilities as corresponding editor for the *National Anti-Slavery Standard*, Lowell published some forty articles and poems in magazines and newspapers as well as four volumes of poetry.[37] At this point, Lowell was only ten years out of Harvard College and not yet thirty years old.

But despite a booming career, domestic tragedies hounded him. In 1847, his first-born, a daughter named Blanche whom he adored, died at fifteen months. Lowell's wife, the poet Maria White Lowell (1821–53), was already pregnant with their second child at the time of Blanche's death, and in September of that same year, gave birth to a second daughter, christened Mabel. Still, more tragedies lay ahead. A third daughter, Rose, died in infancy in 1850. Walter, Lowell's only son, died in Naples in June 1852 during the family's first trip abroad; he was just two years old. Then in October 1853, Lowell's beloved wife, always frail and fragile, died of tuberculosis. It had been Maria's radical antislavery views that, years before, had won Lowell to the cause.[38]

Broken as he was by Maria's death, Lowell continued to write and publish actively. Work provided both income and an escape from grief. He traveled again to Europe in 1855 to improve his knowledge of European languages and literatures, and in 1856 he succeeded his friend and neighbor Longfellow as the Smith professor of modern languages at Harvard. He became the first editor of the *Atlantic Monthly* in 1857, a post he held until 1861. Also in 1857, he married Frances Dunlap, who proved an ideal and loving companion for both Lowell and his only remaining child, Mabel.

Before the end of the Civil War, in 1864 he began editing the *North American Review*. Poems, essays, and reviews continued to flow from his pen, slowing only during his years in diplomatic service. In 1877, President Rutherford B. Hayes, a great fan of *The Biglow Papers*, appointed Lowell to the U.S. legation in Madrid. In 1880 he was appointed minister to the Court of St. James (England) and continued in that position until 1885, when recalled by the newly elected president Grover Cleveland. About a month before his resignation was accepted, Lowell's second wife died, probably of a brain lesion. Grief-stricken yet again, Lowell returned to the United States. Remarkably, until his death from cancer in 1891, Lowell remained active. In 1889 he delivered several major public addresses, including "The Study of Modern Languages," read before the Modern Language Association of America, and in 1890 he helped oversee preparations for the completion of the ten-volume Riverside edition of his collected works.

Random allusions to the Vikings and to Vinland are scattered throughout this huge corpus of writings, even when Lowell's subject was something entirely different. For example, in 1854 in a retrospective essay titled "Cambridge Thirty Years Ago," Lowell recalled how Harvard College's sloop (also named *Harvard*) once "made annual voyages" to Maine for the purpose of "bringing back the wood that, in those days, gave to winter life at Harvard a crackle and a cheerfulness" that the more recent coal-burning stoves could not. And, he added, "those periodic ventures of the sloop Harvard made the old Viking fibre vibrate in the hearts of all the [Cambridge] boys" (1:68–69).

The "old Viking fibre" was also the subject of a poem that Lowell had been thinking about at least since the end of 1849. In a letter dated 23 January 1850, Lowell informed his good friend, the editor and novelist Charles F. Briggs, that he was planning a poem to be titled "the 'Voyage of Leif' to Vinland, in which I mean to bring my hero straight into Boston Bay, as befits a Bay-state poet" (*Letters* 1:171).[39] Despite this sentence's apparently joking tone, Lowell assured Briggs that he intended the poem to be both serious and "far better" than his previous efforts: "I intend to confute my critics, not with another satire, but by writing better" (1:171). In fact, Lowell never published a poem titled "The Voyage of Leif to Vinland." Instead, in *Graham's American Monthly Magazine* in January 1855, he published "Hakon's Lay," a poem clearly composed as the opening section for some larger (as yet unwritten) work about Leif Eiriksson's Vinland explorations.

Written in blank verse like "Columbus," "Hakon's Lay" opens in the great hall of the home of Thorstein Eiriksson, Eirik the Red's second son and the younger brother of Leif. As entertainment for his guests, Thorstein asks the old bard (or "skald"), Hakon, to "sing now an olden song, / Such as our fathers heard who led great lives" (72).[40] Hakon obliges, singing of those whom Fate chooses for great deeds: "Souls straight and clear, of toughest fibre." The skald goes on to confirm that "Good were the days of yore," but adds, emphatically, "While the gods are left, and hearts of men, / And the free ocean, still the days are good." His point is that "opportunity [yet roams] through the broad Earth . . . / And knocks at every door of hut or hall, / Until she finds the brave soul that she wants." Sitting apart from the company and listening intently, a "musing" Leif is inspired to his own "resolve" to venture "across the unventured seas." The poem ends with a projection of the future, when "the brave prow . . . cut[s] on Vinland sands / The first rune in the Saga of the West." Thus, with "Hakon's Lay," Lowell again returned to the theme of discovery, albeit in a wholly truncated form. This may be because, in the 1850s, as the idea for a poem about Leif Eiriksson and the Vinland voyage percolated in Lowell's imagination, American beginnings could only have seemed to presage equivocal outcomes.

The bitter debates in Congress over what became the Compromise of 1850 revealed the strength of the pro-slavery forces, while the new, stronger Fugitive Slave Act required citizens even in the free states to turn in runaway slaves.[41] The Gadsden Purchase of 1853, the last acquisition of contiguous territory by the U.S., also threatened to provide additional areas for the extension of slavery as what is now southern New Mexico and Arizona moved from Mexican to American control. In 1854, the Kansas-Nebraska Act, roundly condemned by abolitionists, led to what became known as "bleeding Kansas," with both pro- and antislavery settlers pouring into the territory and confronting one another in almost open warfare.[42] Meanwhile, Native Americans continued to be forcibly removed from their traditional lands, labor unrest and growing poverty continued to roil the cities, and a series of cholera and yellow fever epidemics swept through various areas, both urban and rural. Furthermore, following the two women's rights conventions of 1850—the first in Worcester, Massachusetts, and the second in Seneca Falls, New York—activism on behalf of women's suffrage gained momentum. It became increasingly clear that the promises of American democracy had been withheld not just from Native peoples and African Americans, but from the working poor and women, as well. Given these ugly realities, Lowell was not yet prepared to answer the questions earlier posed by his soliloquizing Columbus. Not until after the Civil War, in his long poem, "The Voyage to Vinland," would Lowell attempt an answer and complete what he began in "Hakon's Lay."

On 13 April 1865, just days after Robert E. Lee's surrender to Union forces under General Ulysses S. Grant at Appomattox Court House, and just a day before the assassination of President Lincoln, Lowell wrote to his close friend Charles Eliot Norton that news of the fighting's end had left him "feeling devoutly thankful. There is something magnificent in having a country to love." "I worry a little about reconstruction," he added, "but am inclined to think that matters will very much settle themselves" (*Letters* 1:344). Of course, matters did not settle themselves.

The assassination of Lincoln at Ford's Theater the very next day rocked the nation, both north and south, and, in the words of Lowell's biographer, Martin Duberman, "Lowell, like many others, shed tears for a man he had never seen" (223). As Andrew Johnson succeeded to the presidency, Lowell became increasingly concerned with Johnson's willingness "to have the Southern states come back into the Union with no provision for securing political and civil rights for the Negro and no guarantee that the ex-slave would be protected from mistreatment by his former master" (Duberman 226). Lowell's own program for Reconstruction was rather different. He wanted to see former slaves awarded reparations in the form of both land and money, and he wanted not just emancipation but also full voting rights for the former (male) slaves.[43]

Lowell had long hoped that a civil war might be avoided. But in its aftermath, he discovered in himself a new love of country and marveled at "the amazing strength and no less amazing steadiness of democratic institutions" (*The Writings* 5:210). Not even his disappointment with President Johnson's policies and the obvious inadequacies of efforts at Reconstruction could shake his faith that, in the end, the nation would come out all right. As Lowell wrote to a friend in England in April 1866, a year after the war's ending and Lincoln's assassination, "I had an *instinct* that the American people would come out of the war stronger than ever" (*Letters* 1:359). Lowell's friend and coeditor at the *North American Review*, Norton, perfectly captured the optimism of the two men when he wrote, in 1867, that America had "something not only finer in promise but in reality than is to be found in Europe ... more simplicity ... more humanity ... more truthfulness, than has ever before found expression in the world" (qtd. in Duberman 233). And when the former Civil War *general* was elected *President* Grant in 1868, Lowell—and most of his circle—had high hopes for the success of his tenure. This, then, was Lowell's mood as he returned to "Hakon's Lay" and rewrote it as "The Voyage to Vinland."

Years earlier, when Lowell replaced Longfellow at Harvard, Longfellow had suggested that Lowell acquaint himself with the great body of Scandinavian literature. Lowell followed that good advice and, in

1861, wrote to Norton that he had been reading an "excellent" translation of the medieval Icelandic masterpiece "Njal's Saga." "It has revived my old desire to write the story of Leif's Voyage to Vinland," he told Norton, "and I shouldn't wonder if something came of it" (*Letters* 1:312). Something did come of it, although not until a few years later. As he explained in a letter to Norton dated October 1868, while putting together his "new volume of old poems," "[I] was suddenly moved to finish my 'Voyage to Vinland,' part of which, you remember, was written eighteen years ago" (2:1, 2). When he had first contemplated writing "Voyage to Vinland," Lowell told Norton, he had expected the poem to be "much longer, but maybe it is better as it is": "I clapt a beginning upon it, patched it in the middle, and then got to what had always been my favorite part of the plan. This was to be a prophecy by Gudrida [the Latinate form of Gudrid, used in early Latin translations of the sagas], a woman who went with them, of the future America" (2:2). Thus, the recasting of "Hakon's Lay," and especially the composition of Gudrida's prophecy, transpired during the period of Lowell's revived affection for his country and his renewed confidence in its future prospects.[44]

When the final version of "The Voyage to Vinland" appeared in *Under the Willows, and Other Poems* (1868), a collection of previously published (and, in some cases, newly revised) works, it received generally favorable critical notice. A reviewer for the *Atlantic Monthly*, which Lowell had edited until 1861, approvingly commented on the poet's "fancy . . . that the grand and mysterious past foreboded the present, and clothed us in the poetry of its prophetic desire and wonder." This same critic particularly praised Gudrida's prophecy as "mighty lyrics that close the poem" ("*Under the Willows*" 262). What critics did not remark upon was that Lowell had taken substantial liberties with then-generally accepted historical accounts of the Vinland explorations, a fact which suggests that the poem was immediately understood by Lowell's contemporaries to be something other than poeticized history.

Part 1, called "Biörn's Beckoners," introduces "Biörn, the son of Heriulf" (that is, Bjarni Herjolfsson), who subsequently displaces Leif Eiriksson as the first adventurer to Vinland. In part 1, we see him as restless and ambitious. In dreams at night and in daydreams, he searches for "some purpose of his soul, / Or will to find a purpose" ("The Voyage to Vinland" 9:220). His sleep is "haunted" by those who beckon to him, "mighty men of old," whose deeds he seeks to emulate so that he, too, may "survive in song for yet a little while" (9:221). He does not want his name merely to sink into "oblivion" (9:221).

198   Chapter Four

Part 2, titled "Thorwald's Lay," provides the occasion for Biörn to resolve his "comfortless" unease. Clearly a reworking of "Hakon's Lay," here the ancient skald is named Thorwald, and the event is a "Yuletide feast" at the home of one Eric Thurlson (9:222). Again, the host asks the skald to "sing now an olden song, / Such as our fathers heard who led great lives" (9:222). And again, the skald sings of the qualities of those from the past whom Fate had chosen for greatness: "Souls straight and clear, of toughest fibre." Then, as in "Hakon's Lay," with only a slight change in wording, the skald insists (9:223)

> "But while the gods are left, and hearts of men,
> And wide-doored ocean, still the days are good.
> Still o'er the earth hastes Opportunity,
> Seeking the hearty soul that seeks for her."

This time it is Biörn, not Leif, who "sat apart / Musing" and hears in old Thorwald's words the purpose he has been seeking (9:224). The "wide-doored ocean" will be *his* door to "Opportunity," and *he* will be "the hearty soul that seeks for her" (9:224).

As part 2 closes, Biörn's "resolve" is firm, and that resolve imaginatively projects "across the unpathwayed seas / ... the brave prow that cut on Vinland sands / The first rune in the Saga of the West" (9:224).

Continuing the blank verse of the first two sections, part 3 opens with a description of the voyage: "Four weeks they sailed, ... / Alone as men were never in the world" (9:224). They pass icebergs, other "ominous" features of the ocean, and finally, "on the thirtieth day / Low in the west were wooded shores like cloud" (9:225). At this point, the poem takes a seemingly odd turn. With the sight of land, Biörn's crew "shouted as men shout with sudden hope; / But Biörn was silent, such strange loss there is / Between the dream's fulfillment and the dream" (9:225). In other words, unlike his crew, Biörn does not rejoice, apparently let down by the very accomplishment of his dream. For him, it is almost an anticlimax, the "sad abatement in the goal attained" (9:225). Now he no longer has a purpose to pursue.

Like the historical Bjarni Herjolfsson of *The Greenlanders' Saga*, who was never even curious enough to make landfall, Lowell's Biörn, too, is a man of limited vision. He sought to emulate the "mighty men of old" only in order to become, like them, "safe as stars in all men's memories" (9:221). In short, what he really sought was not so much achievement for the thing itself, but for renown. Ironically unable to see the newly encountered land as itself the Opportunity he pursued, Biörn does not understand what he has really accomplished, nor can he conceive that the world in which he so ardently sought renown is one day to be eclipsed by the one he has just discovered. That revelation comes from Gudrida, whom Lowell casts as "a prophetess," channeling a "vision" that is not hers, but "the dreaming shore's" (9:225). As "the New Land" begins to manifest itself through her prophetic voice, so too the blank verse disappears and, in the final and longest portion, the poem itself changes form.

In Lowell's letter to Norton of October 1868 in which he described his rewriting of "The Voyage to Vinland," he told Norton that, in his "favorite part" of the poem—"a prophecy by Gudrida, ... of the future America"—he had done something very different. Influenced by the medieval Scandinavian literature with which he was acquainted, Lowell composed Gudrida's prophecy "in an unrhymed alliterated measure, in very short verse and stanzas of five lines each. It does not aim at following the law of the Icelandic alliterated stave, but hints at it" (*Letters* 2:2). That dramatic shift in prosody subtly signals the poem's similarly dramatic shift in direction. In contrast to Biörn, to whom beckoned the "mighty men" of the past, Gudrida sings of the future, Lowell's true subject in writing the poem.

"Looms there the New Land," intones Gudrida, a land long "locked in the shadow" by ancient gods "o'er old" (that is, overly old) and gods resistant to "newness." Although the land now "sleeps ... silent," one day "great ships shall seek it, / Swarming" across "two seas," that is, the Atlantic and the Pacific (9:225–26). All sorts will arrive—"Men from the Northland, / Men from the Southland, ... Dark hair and fair hair, / Red blood and blue blood," rich and poor. In this New Land, all these "shall be mingled," and the "force of the ferment / Makes the New Man" (9:226). It is the old image of America as the place of rebirth and regeneration, an asylum forging a new humanity out of all the shards of difference. "Here men shall grow up / Strong from self-helping," and become "builders of empire" (9:226–27). Lowell even honors his own dour Puritan forebears whose unceasing labors "shall subdue" the land. Their work ethic leaves "their son's sons / Space for the body, / Space for the soul." But, at the same time, they leave "their son's sons / All things save song-craft." Poetry and the arts require "long-growing" and will have to come later (9:226).

What distinguishes these new men of the future is their lack of abject reverence for tradition ("Eyes for the present / ... Blind to the Past"). They are unafraid to "make over / Creed, law, and custom" (9:227). As a result, "these the old gods hate," foreseeing in the willingness to jettison the past and create something new their own "gods' Twilight" (9:227). And so "the old gods / Shut it [i.e., the New Land] in

200   Chapter Four

shadow" (9:228). But the old gods are doomed. Appropriating details from the foretelling of the fate of the world in an Icelandic text called the *Voluspá*, Lowell has Gudrida refer to the final conflagration when "the Old World" and its gods will "Flare up in fire" (9:228). Even so, Gudrida reassures her "Northmen" that this will not be the final "doomsday." Following the great conflagration, a new Earth is to arise from the sea. Combining elements from the *Voluspá* with Gudrida's vision of the New Land, Lowell has her explain (9:228)

> Over the ruin
> See I the promise;
> Crisp waves the cornfield,
> Peace-walled, the homestead
> Waits open-doored.

While some of this is obviously derived from the *Voluspá*, several critics have also detected in these stanzas allusions to the upheavals of the Civil War, the destruction of the old outdated slaveholding oligarchy, and the hoped-for prosperous peace that was to follow the war's ending.[45] Those connections are certainly and purposefully present in the poem. But they are embedded within a larger whole. Important to Lowell was the moral foundation of the idealized republic that was, he hoped, now emerging in the postwar New Land.

With the death of the old gods, a new god walks "the New Earth" (9:229):

> Lo, a divine One
> Greets all men godlike,
> Calls them his kindred,
> He, the Divine.

This is Christ, who, even though "weaponless," is still "Stronger than Thor" (son of Odin and the strongest of the Nordic gods). Under Christ's beneficent influence, "here [in the New Land] shall a realm rise / Mighty in manhood," governed by "Justice and Mercy" (9:229-30). In an allusion both to ongoing immigration and to the Civil War, Lowell has Gudrida address the New Land directly and predict (9:230):

> Lowly shall love thee,
> Thee, open-handed!
> Stalwart shall shield thee,

Thee, worth their best blood,
Waif of the West!

For all the New Land's "Beauty of promise," however, warns Gudrida, "Silent it sleeps now" (9:230, 225). As she explains to her Northmen (9:228):

There lies the New Land;
Yours to behold it,
Not to possess it.

Yet in the future, "from your strong loins / Seed shall be scattered," and that seed will one day become part of the mix of those who settle the New Land. They will be "Wilderness tamers" and seamen ("Walkers of waves") and all "Men to the marrow" (9:228). Finally, as the poem closes, Gudrida predicts that in the fullness of time shall come poets heralding the birth of the new kind of man made possible by the New Land (9:230):

Then shall come singers,
Singing no swan-song,
Birth-carols, rather,
Meet [i.e., fit] for the man child
Mighty of bone.

In a sense, this is Lowell describing his own poem: a birth carol or, rather, given its historical moment, a rebirth carol following the fratricide of civil war. It is also the voice of Lowell as a national poet, declaring the time now ripe for "song-craft." The season of "long-growing" is at last over. The nation has matured.[46]

Both in "Columbus" and in "The Voyage to Vinland," the importance of the historical event at the heart of each poem—the European discovery of America—resided not in the event itself but in its meaning for the future. For Lowell in the 1840s, that meaning seemed as yet uncertain, and so he left the darkly ominous "The Growth of the Legend" unfinished, and he left Columbus's questions unanswered. By 1868, buoyed by the outcome of the Civil War, the apparent stability of the Union, and the ascendant postwar national rhetoric of rebirth, renewal, and regeneration, Lowell responded with optimism. The ancient Scandinavian mythology of a world conflagration followed by the emergence of new gods and a new Earth served as a convenient symbolic precursor for what he hoped was now happening—or was about to happen—in America. Urging the nation to live up to its professed Christian principles, he had Gudrida describe a land that "shall fold peoples / Even as a shepherd / Foldeth his flock" ("The Voyage to Vinland" 9:225). And he embedded in her prophecy, as the moral foundation for the nation, a future that was welcoming to all sorts, treating all with "Justice and Mercy" (9:230). Thus Columbus's dreamt-of "commonwealth" became Gudrida's prophesied "New Land."

Still optimistic about the nation's future, but personally tiring of his teaching duties and eager to rejuvenate his poetic impulses, Lowell took a two-year break from Harvard and in July 1872 sailed with his wife to Europe. Upon his return in July 1874, the country seemed much changed—but not for the better. Lowell thought that the nation had become overwhelmingly crass and materialistic in the immediate postwar economic boom years. Corruption was everywhere. Robber barons, railroad tycoons, and political bosses—"swindlers," Lowell called them—were robbing the public coffers.[47] The immigrant populations of "new Americans" were easily manipulated by demagogues and party hacks who bought votes with money or patronage. Grant's second term in office was embroiled in multiple scandals; many of the president's appointees were accused of fraud. The Republican Party was in disarray, and the party's program of Radical Reconstruction in the South had proven a dismal failure. Not only had the nation's reunion been bungled, but, in Lowell's view, those who had formerly been enslaved still had neither all their rights as citizens nor secure protection. Where once this would have occupied his full attention, he now also saw the urgency of other reforms—in the patronage-ridden civil service system, in protectionist tariff policies, and in the stabilizing of the currency. Uncharacteristically, he became personally active in politics; his "activities centered on the Presidential election of 1876" (Duberman 277). A year later, his work on behalf of Republican candidates indirectly led to President Hayes appointing him to the U.S. legation in Madrid, the beginning of Lowell's diplomatic career abroad.

But once the Lowells were settled in Spain, the news from the States continued to be distressing. Hayes's election had been secured by a compromise between congressional Republicans and Democrats that ended Reconstruction. Federal troops were withdrawn from the South, leaving freed slaves in a more precarious situation than before, while large sums of federal monies were appropriated for railroads and other internal improvements to rehabilitate the ravaged former Confederacy. As a consequence, capitalists and bankers from the Northeast were now helping to restore the old southern oligarchy. As Duberman sums it up, "Oliver Wendell Holmes wrote [to Lowell] that the present 'ignoble aspect of the great republic' was enough 'to sicken any people of self-government,' and Norton flatly asserted that the Hayes Administration had been a failure and politics never in worse condition" (289). Strikes, labor riots, demonstrations against the banks and for currency reforms "all seemed dire symptoms of the country's decay. Norton reported to Lowell that President [Charles W.] Eliot of Harvard had been promoting rifle clubs and drilling among the students, feeling the time might soon come when they would be needed for service in the streets" (290).

Behind all this bad news was the fact that, from 1873 through the 1890s, seriatim periods of economic depression followed the Civil War. With the exponential growth of industrial capitalism in those same decades, a small percentage of the population amassed enormous wealth. At the same time, the working poor, many of whom were immigrants or "new Americans," became even poorer, and class divisions were stark. As many historians have long documented, the unremitting exploitation of labor and the economic injustice of the period led many of the working poor and the unemployed into "class-oriented social movements like populism, trade unionism, [and] socialism" (Lears, *No Place of Grace* 29). All these "presented frightening spectacles to the middle and upper classes," especially in the face of protest marches, torch-lit mass meetings, and labor strikes that sometimes turned violent—most often provoked by the police or by private security guards employed by railroad and factory owners; (29). So, as Norton wrote to Lowell, even the president of Harvard had begun student rifle drills in 1877 in case rioting workers threatened propertied New Englanders.

A son of patrician and Brahmin New England, Lowell had sympathy for neither the grasping bankers and industrialists nor the organized grassroots populism that had begun in the West in the 1870s and then spread eastward. In response, Lowell turned increasingly conservative.[48] I am "by temperament and education of a conservative turn," he announced to an audience in England in 1884 ("Democracy" 6:7). But in that same address, titled "Democracy," despite all the problems at home, Lowell was still reluctant to abandon his faith in either democracy or "universal suffrage" (6:11). And in 1888, in an address delivered in New York City called "The Place of the Independent in Politics," he acknowledged that he could no longer maintain allegiance to any one political party, but he would not foreswear allegiance to his country. Patriotism, he insisted, gave "men an ideal outside themselves, which would awaken in them capacities for devotion and heroism that are deaf even to the penetrating cry of self" (6:219). In "The Voyage to Vinland," Gudrida had enunciated Lowell's idealistic patriotism and, with that, given voice to what the critic John Seelye called "a fierce nationalism, always a conservative impulse" (235).

The Plastic Viking

There is a peculiar irony in the observation that those who were once considered the wild berserkers of medieval Scandinavia could become, in the poetry of nineteenth-century America, conduits for what were essentially conservative impulses. But consider the works we have just examined. Longfellow's "Skeleton in Armor" was intended to warn against the excesses of unconstrained selfhood and unrestrained romantic self-expression. Whittier's "The Norsemen" and "Norembega" both worked toward a restatement of conventional Protestant religious faith and a reassurance of Christian immortality. Lowell used "The Voyage to Vinland" to proclaim an idealized national destiny dressed in all the early trappings of American exceptionalism. And Whittier, like so many others, employed the image of Christianized and newly "gentled" Vikings as an emblem of the future civilizing and assimilation of the allegedly "wild Indians."[49]

What was happening is clear: following the publication of Rafn's *Antiquitates Americanæ* in 1837, decade by decade, subsequent books and articles constructed a pre-Columbian discovery story that emphasized the plasticity of the images of the Norse. The process had begun well before the Civil War, of course, but it accelerated in the postwar decades. Depending on the purpose at hand and the sources cited, the Norse could be depicted variously as heroic warriors and empire builders, barbarous berserker invaders, fighters for freedom, courageous explorers, would-be colonists, seamen and merchants, poets and saga men, glorious ancestors, bloodthirsty pagan pirates, and civilized Christian converts. This plasticity rendered the Northmen perfect progenitors for a nation whose own postwar identity was then in flux.

As a fallen South symbolically resurrected itself through romantic images of the gallant Confederate cavalier and the sentimentalizing of the Lost Cause, all harking back to some imagined medieval code of chivalry and honor, New Englanders could identify instead with the heritage of supposedly freedom-loving Northmen and the enterprising spirit of a merchant like Thorfinn Karlsefni. At the same time, "while many white Southerners strained to contain and thwart the aspirations of freed blacks, [and] old-stock Northeasterners recoiled from hordes of [ethnically diverse] would-be 'new Americans,'" what the two groups shared was a sense of both racial and cultural superiority derived from their common Anglo-Saxon heritage (Lears, *Rebirth of a Nation* 98). Thus postwar reconciliation narratives often took on the language of racial parables. For example, "A War Debt," a short story by Jewett first published in January 1895 in *Harper's New Monthly Magazine*, reads as a love story between the wealthy Boston grandson of a former Union officer and the granddaughter of a former Confederate colonel who now typifies the impoverished yet genteel plantation aristocracy of old. But the incipient romance across regional lines is rendered plausible because the two share what Jewett called the "advantage of race" (231). The young man's pedigree is established in the first two paragraphs. He is the fourth generation of his family to live in the "fine old-fashioned house" on Boston's Beacon Street, lined with "English elms" (227). Like all the men in his line, he attended Harvard and identifies with his family's original English roots. When he travels to Virginia for some autumn hunting, the young woman whom he sees on the train, and who is to become the object of his affections, is described as "high-bred and elegant in her bearing" (231). And Jewett makes clear that her pedigree is identical to his. Her family, too, has English roots, and her grandfather was a classmate of the young man's grandfather at Harvard. Also, Jewett tells us, this young woman "was the new and finer Norman among Saxons . . . the highest type of English civilization" (231). The story's prediction of their eventual union thereby effectively symbolizes the national *re*-union and its unifying racial underpinnings.

If this strikes us today as a shaky foundation for national reconciliation, we need only recall that the postwar years were a period when, according to the historian Jackson Lears, "origins were becoming a crucial source of social identity" (*Rebirth of a Nation* 98). "For many citizens of the republic during the decades following the Civil War," their identity as Americans "increasingly came to mean being a Caucasian," and Caucasian mainly meant being a descendant, through England, of ancient northern (Germanic and Scandinavian) peoples (94). Consequently, as in Jewett's story, it was not difficult for national reconciliation based on theories of race to trump almost all consideration of the justice still owed to the racial Other, those freed slaves whom Jewett characterized as "lawless, and unequal to holding their liberty with steady hands" ("A War Debt" 230).

Assertions of Nordic or Viking heritage responded to other current concerns, too. Not only did postwar America need to overcome the divisions of regional conflict, but now, given what Lincoln had called "a new birth of freedom," the reborn and healing nation needed once again to distinguish itself from Europe.[50] Fears that European nations, especially England, might have actively backed the South in the Civil War now abated, but European aristocracies were still ridiculed onstage and in the popular press as pretentious, effeminate, and foppish. "The old world is effete," Lowell's Columbus had declared, echoing the common wisdom. But Lowell's Gudrida prophesied an America "mighty in manhood," where "men shall grow up / Strong from self-helping." The nation of self-made men, in other words, was thereby inherently unpretentious, virile, and manly. And in "The Voyage to Vinland," Lowell left no doubt that at least some of the seeds of that manliness had come, as Gudrida told her Northmen, "from your strong loins." Thus Viking genealogies served as biological warrants of inherited national manhood.

Yet self-made or not, for relatively privileged white males, manhood and manliness—which Americans had always identified with both moral worth and physical vigor—were getting harder to define, let alone to exhibit. In a period when men of the middle and upper classes found themselves increasingly sedentary, tethered to often routinized desk jobs, and hemmed in by Victorian proprieties imported from England, true manliness seemed at best elusive. The heroic and strenuous life belonged to the pioneers moving ever westward and, in the nation's mythology, to the soldiers and Indian-fighters charged to protect them. For the bankers, capitalists, and growing numbers of office workers in the cities, by contrast, modern life was becoming "dry and passionless," devoid of both "physical and emotional vitality" (Lears, *No Place of Grace* 142). Office work had made men soft, and the nation's much-vaunted material progress threatened to reproduce European luxury and effeminacy. As the century drew toward its close, observers like George M. Beard, the author of the widely read *American Nervousness* (1881), worried that the educated upper classes were suffering from "neurasthenia," or what others called "the contagion of nervous diseases" brought on by what Beard identified as "*modern civilization*" itself (see Bederman 84–88; Appleton 232).

In response, the training grounds for upper-class American manhood, schools like Harvard and Yale, encouraged a variety of vigorous team sports. For the men who could afford them, organizations like the Boone and Crockett Clubs arranged regular campouts and hunting expeditions to wilderness areas. For men of more modest means, Young Men's Christian Associations (the YMCA movement) provided gyms and swimming pools alongside prayer meetings and Bible study (see Lears, *Rebirth of a Nation* 102). For those who simply sought escape, a vast literature of popular historical romances set in medieval castles and on medieval battlefields emerged again. Boys' adventure books offered tales of heroic Vikings on the high seas and tales of pioneer Vikings garbed in "deer-skin," colonizing a frontier Vinland (Liljencrantz, *Randvar the Songsmith* 5).[51]

The ultimate proof of American manliness, of course, was victory on the battlefield, especially the battlefield of overseas imperial expansion. In the nineteenth century, most of those who wrote about the ancient Scandinavians commented repeatedly on their expansionist impulse, settling colonies all over Europe, "from the North Sea to the Mediterranean" (Bryant and Gay 36). While this once might have been characterized as brutal conquest, by the decades following the Civil War, the Northmen were more often represented not as invaders but as liberators. "Planting wherever they trod, the germs of a glorious freedom," wrote the poet Julia Clinton Jones in 1878, "they were the revolutionists of that age, and all succeeding ages owe them a lasting debt of gratitude for the ... liberty and truth by them sown" (11). Thus the image of the Norse in the postwar decades helped provide Americans with both historical precedent and a racially inherited legitimacy for their latest dreams of empire.

Claiming economic and geopolitical motives, and under the pretext of supporting Cuban independence from Spain, in 1898 the U.S. declared war on Spain. In what Secretary of State John Hay called a "splendid little war," the Spanish forces were defeated in three months (qtd. in Zinn 309). Out of the conflict came the indelible image of Teddy Roosevelt leading the charge on San Juan Hill, the avatar of manly patrician Anglo-Saxon racial superiority. As one prominent political scientist from Columbia University phrased it at the time, "The Teutonic and Anglo-Saxon races were 'particularly endowed with ... the mission of conducting the political civilization of the modern world'" (qtd. in Zinn 299). By the end of the century, the U.S. had successfully defeated Spain in the Spanish-American War of 1898, secured its interests in Cuba, and taken possession of Puerto Rico, Guam, and the Philippines. In 1899, the U.S. annexed Wake Island in the central Pacific, and in 1900 a previously independent Hawaii was declared a U.S. territory. Like their Viking ancestors, the Americans brought both martial prowess and law-giving.

What remained constant in all this was that the popular and often contradictory images of the Vikings continued to respond to nineteenth-century America's many needs and anxieties. Despite

Longfellow's intended anti-Romanticism, for example, to the Victorian ethic of emotional self-control, his "Skeleton in Armour" opposed passion. It was ardor that drove the "wild" Viking to America. In the face of regulated and routinized office work that was nothing short of enervating, Whittier's "stalwart" Norsemen, their broad chests "seamed" with battle scars, embarked on their mission of exploration with manly vigor and "joy glisten[ing] in each wild blue eye." If contemporary Protestantism seemed dry and lifeless, Whittier's Norman knight in America suggested that the search for salvation could also be a heroic quest. Norumbega may have been only a dream, but it was a dream that inspired. And, finally, in response to merely escapist historical literature, Lowell's Gudrida reminded Americans that this was the time for "birth-carols, rather." America was now its own proper literary subject.[52]

For many observers, Emerson and Lowell among them, even the achievements of American literature ultimately had Scandinavian roots. If American literature developed out of English antecedents, so too English literature, wrote Emerson in *English Traits*, owed a debt to "the *Heimskringla*, or Sagas of the Kings of Norway . . . the Iliad and the Odyssey of English history" (31). In an essay on Chaucer first published in 1870, Lowell made basically the same point. "The Anglo-Saxons never had any real literature of their own," he wrote. "They produced monkish chronicles in bad Latin, and legends of saints in worse metre." The true poetry of the English, the "imported . . . divine power of imagination" that led to Chaucer and finally to "the miracle of Stratford" (i.e., Shakespeare) "is essentially Scandinavian," he asserted (*The Writings* 3:320). "It was . . . this adventurous race, which found America before Columbus, which . . . typif[ied] the very action of the imaginative faculty itself" (3:320). Thus, while American literature was now singing its own "birth-carols," American writers were acknowledging literary forebears who, through the English, originated in Scandinavia. And with that crucial connection in place, American manliness could now also embrace physical vigor *and* cultural refinement, adventurousness *and* "the imaginative faculty" both. It was all in the blood.

Taking the Vikings Home

Having been removed over the decades from the exclusive possession of the learned and entered popular history, by the postwar era, the Vikings and medieval Scandinavia in general became subjects of common discourse. Taking advantage of that fact, some in the activist women's rights movement thought they found in Norse forebears models of enlightened policy. The most intellectually gifted leader of the movement was Matilda Joslyn Gage (1826–98), best remembered today as a coauthor, with Elizabeth Cady Stanton and Susan B. Anthony, of the six-volume *The History of Woman Suffrage* (1881–89).[53] But Gage wrote much more, including her most important work, *Woman, Church and State: A Historical Account of the Status of Woman* (1893). In it, Gage argued that "the entire civilization of christian centuries has tended to the debasement of woman." The patriarchal bias of Christianity, she continued, had resulted in "a non-recognition through the ages of the sanctity of womanhood, and a disbelief in her rights of person within the marriage relation, or without." She added that "this lesson has been [taught], by the church, and emphasized by the laws of the state" (358). She therefore looked to pre-Christian history and to non-Christian cultures for counterexamples, and she found many in pagan Scandinavia. "The women of ancient Scandinavia," wrote Gage, "were treated with infinite respect; breach of marriage promise was classed with perjury; its penalty was outlawry [i.e., banishment], marriage was regarded as sacred and in many instances the husband was obliged to submit to the wife" (42). Gage also approved the fact that rape was "a capital crime" (367). Moreover, in medieval Denmark, "the king decreed that . . . daughters should inherit one-third of their father's property." Although the situation of women in pagan Scandinavia was actually far more varied and complex than Gage portrayed it, according to Gage, unlike the contemporary U.S., "Old Scandinavia possessed many laws for the protection of woman" (371).[54]

For the privileged wives and daughters of Gilded Age America, however, "Old Scandinavia" could also mean something entirely different. What was known as the "Viking Revival" in crafts and design produced a wealth of expensive wares, from ladies' jewelry to home furnishings. In many ways, Tiffany and Company of New York took the lead and set the standards. Their "Viking style" silver jewelry boxes, vases, and bejeweled silver coffee service sets were in high demand. When the wealthy sugar merchant and investor Henry Osborne Havemeyer (1847–1907) commissioned Lewis Comfort Tiffany (the son of the company's founder) to decorate his new mansion at Fifth Avenue and Sixty-sixth Street, Havemeyer's "fortune was such that" Tiffany "was given carte blanche" (Purtell 128). To the delight of his socially active wife, the end result was a home stocked with treasures and design influences from all over the world, including a grand library with furniture and woodwork based on Viking designs and the curvilinear Celtic motifs adopted by the medieval Scandinavians.

Sometime just after the turn of the century, Tiffany and Company produced two of its most unusual Viking-style pieces: a ladies' dressing table and matching chair "fashioned from sterling silver and four long, twisting narwhal tusks" (Wheary, "Tiffany and Company Tour de Force" 18). Silver dragon-head finials, reminiscent of the curved prows on Viking longships, capped the narwhal support tusks on both the chair and the mirrored table. The single tusk of the narwhal (an arctic whale) had long been prized by medieval Scandinavians as a substitute for elephant ivory from Africa and as a material for making everything from sword hilts to royal thrones. As Herman Melville had reminded his readers in *Moby-Dick* (1851), "In old Norse times, the thrones of the sea-loving Danish kings were fabricated, saith tradition, of the tusks of the narwhale" (113). Thus, as one knowledgeable curator of historical objects observed in 2004, "The use of entire narwhal tusks [as supports of the table and chair] was a particularly brilliant stroke that further heightens the overall Nordic character of the set" (Wheary, "Tiffany and Company Tour de Force" 20).[55] Probably designed for exhibition at the Louisiana Purchase Exposition in St. Louis in 1904, the chair and dressing table were then returned to Tiffany's New York store and there purchased by Sallie and James Henry Dooley of Richmond, Virginia.[56] (See figure 5.) James Dooley, formerly an officer in the Confederate Army, was now one of the major railroad financiers in the post–Civil War South.

Without question, extravagant pieces like Sallie Dooley's dressing table and chair came out of the era's "prevailing affinity for design derived from historical sources, and the 'conspicuous consumption' of rich and exotic materials that appealed to the growing class of multimillionaires" (Wheary, "Tiffany and Company Tour de Force" 18). But this affinity for home furnishings designed to replicate historical sources, and especially the emphasis on all things Viking, suggests something else, too. In the absence of inherited family heirlooms and long-established family status, some of the newly self-made Gilded Age multimillionaires could purchase at least the simulacrum of pedigree and old wealth by surrounding themselves and their families with its representations. The purchase of history and the historical thereby became a valuable palliative for the class-conscious and anxious nouveau riche. Moreover, the purchase of Viking Revival pieces, in particular, brought to the home associations with ancient Nordic bloodlines, manly vigor, heroic deeds, and, on a patriotic note, first discovery.

While the taste for Viking Revival design crossed from the nineteenth into the early twentieth century, interest in producing such pieces had initially accelerated as the nation approached the four-

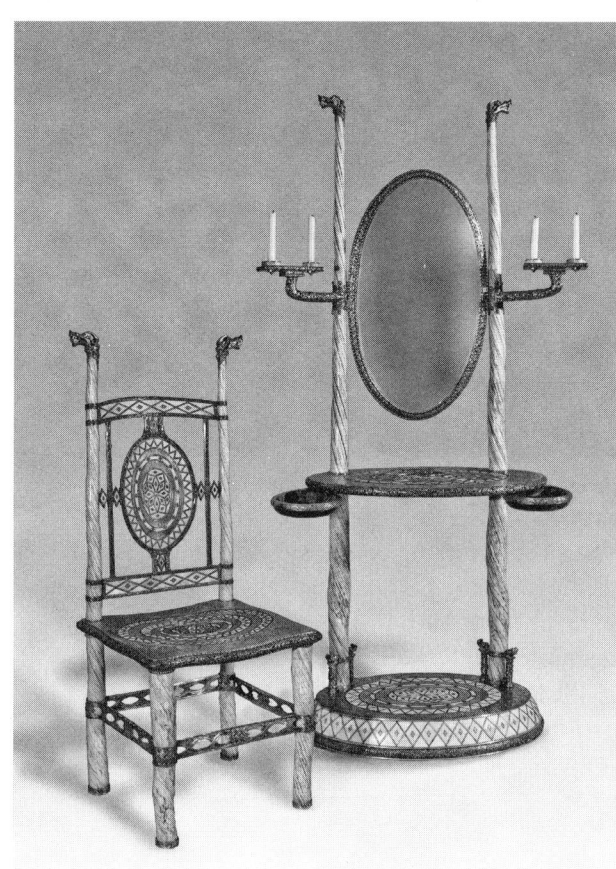

5. Tiffany and Company Viking Revival lady's dressing table and chair, constructed of silver and narwhal tusk, probably designed for exhibition at the Louisiana Purchase Exposition in St. Louis in 1904. Published by permission of Maymont Mansion, Richmond, Virginia.

(below) 6. The Tiffany and Company Viking Punch Bowl and base, an example of late nineteenth-century Viking Revival motifs, was designed by Paulding Farnham and exhibited at the Chicago World's Columbian Exposition of 1893. Image Copyright © The Metropolitan Museum of Art / Art Resource, New York.

hundredth anniversary of Columbus's first landing and the World's Columbian Exposition in 1893 (also known as the Chicago World's Fair). Tiffany and Company created several major pieces for exhibit at the fair. Among these was the much-admired and much-talked-about Viking Punch Bowl, designed specifically to commemorate *pre*-Columbian explorations of North America. (See figure 6 on p. 211.) Twenty and a half inches in diameter, with a plain silver interior, the Viking Punch Bowl was made of "'decarbonized iron,' meaning iron that has been heated to a very high temperature to eliminate virtually all carbon content in order to make it malleable" (Loring 203). With this nod to the advanced iron technology of medieval Scandinavia, the Tiffany designer Paulding Farnham (1859–1927) then proceeded to *work* the now-malleable iron. It was hammered, etched, and inlaid with complex patterns in gold and silver. "Its eight handles [with Norse mythological creatures etched into them] pass through the lip to terminate in shapes like the prows of Viking ships" (Loring 203). The punch bowl was so successful that Farnham designed more Viking Revival pieces for subsequent fairs, both in Europe and the U.S. But the Viking Punch Bowl exhibited at the World's Columbian Exposition had a special resonance. Whether intended or not, it seemed to take sides in the swelling national debate that led up to the fair: Should the nation be celebrating Columbus as its discoverer or Leif Eiriksson?

5

The Challenge to Columbus and the Romance Undone

> It may be said that a number of circumstances indicate that it was at L'Anse aux Meadows that Leif Eiriksson built his "large houses" and that northern Newfoundland is the Vinland of the sagas. But whether they were actually Leif's houses is not the important thing. What is of importance is the fact that, given the archaeological assessment and carbon datings, the house-sites at L'Anse aux Meadows are Norse, pre-Columbian, and date from about A.D. 1000.... No other indisputable traces of Norsemen have been discovered in North America.
>
> —HELGE INGSTAD, *Westward to Vinland* (1969)

Looking toward the Fair: The Contested Quadricentennial

In an article published in February 1888 in the *Independent*, a journal published in New York City, a virulently anti-Catholic writer named Marie Adelaide Brown discussed a "Viking Exhibition, which [she] proposed should be held in Washington in 1889, in conjunction with the celebration of the forming of our Constitution" ("The Viking Exhibition" 5). By honoring "the discovery of America" by pagan Icelanders who had established their own early republic, argued Brown, Americans would add further luster to the festivities planned for honoring one hundred years of republican governance under a ratified U.S. Constitution. To make the occasion even more memorable, she further proposed including in the exhibition "a full-sized model of the famous Viking ship exhumed at Gokstod [sic], in Norway, in the year 1880" (5). In this way, Brown hoped to fit the Norse into the nation's master narrative not simply as first discoverers but also as pre-Christian freedom-seeking republican precursors.

Not to be outdone, albeit with very different motives, Catholic writers too joined the chorus of prominent voices advocating "a public and national recognition" of Leif Eiriksson during "the approaching celebration of the centenary of the Constitution" ("America Discovered and Christianized in the Tenth and Eleventh Centuries" 211). A densely argued twenty-six-page article in the *American Catholic Quarterly Review* of April 1888, for example, credited the Northmen—and Leif Eiriksson in particular—with "the discovery and colonization of the western continents, and parts of our own country, and the introduction of Christianity therein, five hundred years before . . . Columbus" (211).

In this version of America's early history, the Norse were again figured as seekers of freedom. "The despotism of the Kings of Norway drove from the country many of the bravest, boldest and most independent of the leaders and their families" ("America Discovered and Christianized in the Tenth and Eleventh Centuries" 213). Iceland "became a favorite asylum of most of these bold and unconquered refugees," and there a republic was established (213). "The community of Icelanders in Greenland modelled their political institutions after those of Iceland," and "a new and independent state sprang up, . . . the first republic established in the western hemisphere" (215). Although this story has a kernel of historical validity, medieval Iceland was hardly a *democratic* republic in the way we understand those terms today, and both Iceland and Greenland were under the sometimes contested control of powerful local chieftains.

The article then went on to repeat the probably spurious story from the *Saga of Olaf Tryggvason*, part of which was interpolated by medieval Christian clerics into *Eirik the Red's Saga*. In this story, the king of Norway, himself a Christian convert and, later, *Saint* Olaf, charged a Christianized Leif Eiriksson with "the glorious mission of introducing Christianity into Greenland" ("America Discovered and Christianized in the Tenth and Eleventh Centuries" 220). Not satisfied with this bare-bones version of events, the writer for the *American Catholic Quarterly Review* further embroidered the story with the equally spurious notion that, to help with this mission, the king "appointed a priest and several other holy men" to return to Greenland with Leif (220). Thus Leif's return journey, with "the Christian missionaries" aboard his ship, became simultaneously "a veritable voyage of discovery" *and* "a mission of Christianity" (220). In other words, instead of setting out from Greenland to explore the lands previously sighted by Bjarni Herjolfsson, as described in *The Greenlanders' Saga*, in this version, following *Eirik the Red's Saga*, Leif discovers and explores "Vinland the Good" on his way back from Norway and *before* first returning to Greenland (221). As a result, "the ecclesiastics who accompanied the expedition were the first Christian priests in that early age that visited America"

(222). And only subsequently did Leif and the missionaries "introduce Christianity into Greenland" (222).

The purpose of insisting upon this version of events, of course, was to make the discovery of America part of a larger evangelizing mission which planted Catholic priests in New England long before the arrival of seventeenth-century dissenting Protestant ministers. For, in describing the lands explored by Leif, this writer followed Rafn exactly and left no doubt that Leif and his missionaries traveled through various parts of Massachusetts and Rhode Island. Consequently, the article implied, Catholics in the U.S. could no longer hold only to the Columbus discovery story. As the article itself acknowledged, "the claim of Norse discoveries on this continent has entered into the living and current national traditions and life of our people" ("America Discovered and Christianized in the Tenth and Eleventh Centuries" 212). Catholics were therefore to embrace two discovery stories, five hundred years apart, but both inflected by Catholic associations. The difference was that the first discovery, by the Norse, had no lasting impact since the Vinland colony was eventually abandoned. But due to "the philosophical and religious mind of Columbus," the second discovery resulted in a new "continent given to civilization, a new world to Christendom" (218).

However compelling all the newspaper and magazine articles, and despite the various petitions and campaigns to honor Leif Eiriksson, in the end, there were no ceremonies celebrating "the successful completion of a hundred years of Constitutional Government" in Washington in 1889 ("The National Centennial" 4). The entire event was canceled when Congress failed to appropriate the required funding. As the *New York Times* explained, and the *Washington Post* quoted at length, "the centenary of the 'adoption of the Constitution' ha[d] already been celebrated . . . in Philadelphia," and any additional spending to mark the occasion would simply be "wasteful and ridiculous excess" (4). As a consequence, competing claims for the Northmen and for Columbus as first discoverers got refocused on the upcoming World's Fair in Chicago. And if the author of the article in the *American Catholic Quarterly Review* thought he had put an end to the debate by embracing both Columbus and the Norse, he was sadly mistaken. Many writers, Catholic and non-Catholic alike, continued to question the evidence behind the Norse claims to discovery, while others argued that Columbus's achievement was based on his knowledge of the earlier Norse voyages. Still others argued adamantly that Columbus had been an authentic original hero.

An anonymous review essay in the *Nation* on 15 January 1891 revealed some of the rancor in the ongoing debate. The fact that the *Nation* had been founded in 1865 by its continuing editor, Edwin Lawrence Godkin (1831–1902), who had come to America from Ireland at the age of twenty-five, may have influenced the sometimes snappish tone of the piece. It is certainly also possible that Godkin himself was its author. Titled "The Icelandic Discovery of America," the article praised the wealth of learning in Arthur Middleton Reeves's book, *The Finding of Wineland the Good* (1890), unquestionably the most scholarly and trustworthy translation and discussion of the medieval Norse materials produced by an American in the nineteenth century. As the reviewer noted approvingly, Reeves casts no aspersions on Columbus and "draws no conclusions as to the precise site of Wineland" (55). But before getting to Reeves, this reviewer first cast his own aspersions on Rafn and the many credulous New England writers who had accepted his theories. In place of Rafn, he recommended not only Reeves but also the work of the Norwegian scholar Gustav Storm, whose *Studies on the Vinland Voyages* had now been translated into English. Accepting Storm's arguments, this reviewer concluded "that no part of New England can be regarded as the site of the Icelanders' Wineland," which was more probably "Nova Scotia and the island of Cape Breton" ("The Icelandic Discovery of America" 55).[1] New England, this writer opined, had endorsed Rafn and his followers because the region wanted to find "itself discovered six centuries before the landing of the Pilgrims, and able to dispense altogether with the services of Columbus" (55). But with this new Norwegian scholarship now available, the reviewer continued in the same tone, "Rhode Island loses its age of fable, and can participate, without any scruples of conscience, in the celebration at Chicago of the fourth centenary of Christopher Columbus" (55). Prejudice, not history, he suggested, was motivating the "devotees of Rafn." They "have even manifested an iconoclastic willingness to trample on the memory of Columbus, because he had the hardihood to rediscover America after his Northern predecessors had abandoned it," and because "the Genoese sprang from the Latin race, . . . [and] he believed in [the] teachings" of the Catholic Church (55).

Somewhat more temperate in tone, though no less dismissive of New England credulity, was a series of four articles that appeared in the *American Antiquarian and Oriental Journal* throughout 1892. The articles were written by John Patterson MacLean, a native Ohioan who was the son of Scots immigrants.[2] A much-published amateur archaeologist and antiquarian, MacLean had previously written books about the Scots Highlanders in America, about his own MacLean clan, and about the vanished race of mound builders who had once inhabited the Ohio and Mississippi Valleys. MacLean's articles of 1892 challenged the evidentiary value of the sagas, asserted that Leif Eiriksson had discovered western Greenland, not America, and debunked all of the physical evidence on which claims to Norse presence in New England had been based. The general title for all the articles was "Pre-Columbian Discovery of America," with each successive article bearing a different subtitle.

The third in the series, subtitled "The Sagas and America," was published in May 1892 and emphasized the "indefiniteness" of the geographical information in the sagas. According to MacLean, all the sentences about the coasts and lands "might apply almost as well to one country as another" (149). MacLean did not question the probable historical existence of "a Leif Erikson" or that "he came upon a land which he gave various names to." But then, in a somewhat skewed representation of the sagas, he argued the following: "That the land he [i.e., Leif Eiriksson] discovered was not so well situated or attractive as the home of Erik is proved from the fact that he abandoned his houses in Vinland and returned to his former home [in Greenland]." And, concluded MacLean, "All the facts in the case would point to Western Greenland as the scene of the achievement of Leif Erikson" (153). In sum, insisted MacLean, the sagas were a kind of proto-fiction, their authors, "although supposed to be Christians, were swayed by the superstitions of their age," and their writings were therefore wholly untrustworthy as history (154).

In the fourth article in the series, subtitled "Norse Remains in America," MacLean demolished "these purported evidences" for Norse presence in New England, pointing to "the Dighton Rock Inscription, the Old Stone Mill at Newport and the Skeleton in Armor" (189). For the most part, his arguments followed those already discussed in these pages, adding only that because they had "been put on the trail" by communications from "the Copenhagen antiquarians," the antiquarians in New England had "been quick to respond," and "the evidence was forthcoming" (189). The implication was that the New Englanders found what they *wanted* to find. What most irked MacLean, however, was that the "unhappy theory" of Norse settlement in New England was now becoming part of the nation's accepted official history. "The idea has found its way into our school books," he complained, "and a picture of [the Newport Tower] is given, in attestation of the early visit of the Icelanders" (197).

In the book in which he expanded upon these articles, *A Critical Examination of the Evidences Adduced to Establish the Theory of the Norse Discovery of America* (1892), MacLean's tone was far less temperate. He mercilessly attacked most of the prominent Norse discovery proponents. He promoted "the genius of Columbus" and asserted that the anti-Columbus party was "governed by race prejudice and religious rancor" (1). In the place of that party, he cited with approval the Orkney scholar Samuel Laing, whose work "confin[ed] the [Norse] discoveries to the coast of Labrador, 'or some places north of the Gulf of St. Lawrence'" (preface n.p.).[3] Those who persisted in finding Norse presence in New England, insisted MacLean, were "unscrupulous," mainly because "their zeal has outstripped their judgement" (55).

Those determined to recognize Leif Eiriksson, those convinced that Vinland and New England were one and the same, and especially those with ties to New England had had long practice in countering such objections. Many spoke with voices of respected authority. In 1890, for example, when Benjamin Franklin DeCosta issued a new edition of *The Pre-Columbian Discovery of America, by the Northmen*, originally published in 1868, he made clear in his preface that his views generally remained "the same as . . . in the original work" (6). Indeed, he continued, speaking of himself in the third person, "time has only served to strengthen his belief in the historical character of the sagas, while all his geographical studies point now as formerly to New England as the scene of the Northmen's exploits" (6). As DeCosta remarked with some pride, the earlier edition, "owing to an unexpected demand, soon went out of print," and he had decided to issue this second edition both because of the ongoing public "discussion" of the topic and because of "the nearness of the proposed Columbian Celebration" (5).

In a period when the study of history was only beginning to become a formal academic discipline, and when those who wrote about more remote historical eras were often poorly trained self-styled *antiquarians*, DeCosta stood apart. From 1864 on, he had been publishing actively, mainly on the early explorations of America, traveling often to Europe to collect or examine original documents, and for a time (1882–83) he served as editor of the *Magazine of American History*. The son of an old Massachusetts family, DeCosta had served as an Episcopal minister in various New England townships before turning to his favored avocation, historian.[4] Until the appearance of Reeves's *The Finding of Wineland the Good* in 1890, DeCosta's work of 1868 offered the most reliable retelling of events from the two Vinland sagas and brought together a wealth of related Icelandic documents not otherwise available in English.

DeCosta concurred in the view of many other scholars that "Columbus had . . . ample opportunities for learning of the voyages of the Northmen," but this did not, for him, "detract from the glory of the achievements of Columbus" (*The Pre-Columbian Discovery of America* 55, 56). Nor did DeCosta—who would convert to Roman Catholicism in 1899—participate in any bashing of the Church. "The author does not find evidence of any plan or even any desire on the part of the authorities of the Roman church to suppress knowledge of the Icelandic voyages, in order to exalt Columbus." On the contrary, he averred, "the establishment of the Icelanders in New England" was being used by American Catholics as "a ground of their own ecclesiastical priority" (56 n2). Then, in a fascinating section titled "The Present State of the Discussion," written expressly for the new edition, DeCosta actually thanked those who had opposed the general proposition that the Icelanders had visited New England long before Columbus; he also thanked, in particular, those who had opposed the "erection of a statue to Leif Ericson in the City of Boston" in 1887 (58). These opponents, although "small in numbers," nonetheless merited "respectful consideration," said DeCosta, because of their "general attainments and devotion to the study of historical subjects." But, at the same time, their objections represented "a conservative element" that "often, however, misses its aim." In this case, DeCosta continued, "that opposition has stimulated investigation and advanced the influence of the Sagas as historical documents" (58). The end result had been an outpouring of continuing studies and a generally accepted current belief that the case had been proved. The sagas and several related medieval Icelandic documents were considered to have established "convincing and unanswerable proof of the fact that Leif Ericson and other adventurers found America and visited New England . . . in Pre-Columbian times" (59). Unlike MacLean, DeCosta observed with approval that "a large proportion of the American school histories give the voyages of the Northmen to America, and there is now being raised up a generation that will be free from that old bias, which formerly gave Columbus the field, to the exclusion . . . of the Northmen" (58).[5]

Speaking in a voice no less authoritative than DeCosta's was Charles Sprague Smith, an instructor at Columbia, where he taught the first course in Icelandic ever offered at an American university.[6] Like DeCosta, Smith hailed from Massachusetts, and also like DeCosta—but based on his scholarly firsthand knowledge of the original texts—Smith, too, "affirm[ed] unhesitatingly that, about the year 1000, some portions of the eastern American coast were discovered by Norsemen and an attempt was made to colonize them" (535). Smith's careful examination of all the known Icelandic documents, coupled with an equally careful discussion of what was then known about medieval Icelandic history and culture, led him to the conclusion that "the record is genuine and Helluland, Markland and Vinland [are] not myths, but parts of a discovered Western Continent" (535).

What he did not say was *where* those "parts" were located. Essentially a philologist rather than a geographer or antiquarian, Smith refrained from speculation about that particular aspect of the debate. Even so, in "The Vinland Voyages," a lengthy article that appeared on 1 January 1892 in the *Journal of the American Geographical Society of New York*, he offered an explanation of why, "as is claimed, no authentic traces of the Norsemen's visit have as yet been discovered" (533). Since the Vinland colony lasted for "only . . . three winters, divided between two places, Stream-firth and Hop," it was only to be expected "that all traces of such a settlement should disappear in nine centuries" (533). It was unjust, therefore, to "demand of the short-lived Vinland settlement runic inscriptions, or any other archaeological remains, as indispensible vouchers of the truthfulness of the old Norse records" (533). The written record was itself sufficient.

Obviously, Smith was responding to all the many doubters who continued to question the authority of the written materials and who still insisted on physical, tangible proofs of Norse visits to America. For them, the upcoming World's Fair was intended to offer precisely the kind of proof that was required. Americans were to have supposedly irrefutable evidence that the tenth- and eleventh-century Norse could and did cross the ocean to New England.

The Viking Ship Comes In

On 2 May 1893, in a modest notice on page 11, the *New York Times* announced that two days before, "The Viking ship, to be exhibited at the Chicago World's Fair . . . sailed . . . for New York" ("The Viking Ship Sails"). The ship was a replica of a medieval vessel excavated in Norway in 1880. On 14 June, a headline on page 1 of the *New York Times* blared "The Viking Ship Is Here"; a subhead read "Anchored Safe and Sound in New-London Harbor." After "a voyage of forty-four days from Bergen, Norway," the article reported, the ship had anchored at New London, Connecticut, "the first American port she has entered. All are well on board and the ship is in excellent condition." (See figure 7.) Four days later, on 18 June, the first page of the *New York Times* again carried the headline "The Viking Ship Is Here," but this time the subhead read

The Challenge to Columbus 221

The Viking Ship.

7. Illustration of the Viking ship from the first page of the *New York Times*, 14 June 1893.

"New-York's Hearty Welcome to the Bold Voyager." The lengthy article that followed described in some detail the "royal reception" accorded the ship as it made its way through New York Harbor to "her anchorage in the North River" (i.e., the Hudson). The article then noted, "Her decks swarmed with bearded, sunbrowned men, with fierce moustaches and fair hair" (1). Not only had a replica Viking ship arrived, this language suggested, but, with her, also came her manly replica Viking crew.

After a little over a week of celebrations and festivities in New York—all of it widely covered by the newspapers—the page 1 headline of the *New York Times* of 27 June announced "Viking Starts to Chicago." The *Viking*, the name of the ship as well as its descriptor, was to "proceed to Chicago by way of the lakes and canals." En route, in order to give some respite to the original Norwegian crew, "college men who . . . are students of Yale, Harvard, and the Massachusetts Institute of Technology" were brought aboard to help sail her (1). Thus the perceived U.S. inheritors of a Viking lineage returned, as it were, to their roots. And with their help, on 12 July 1893, the *Viking* completed the last leg of its journey across Lake Michigan from Racine, Wisconsin, to Chicago, Illinois.

Under the headline "The Viking Ship at Chicago," the *New York Times* reported, "Even more hearty than the greeting accorded a week ago to the caravels was the welcome that went out . . . to Capt. Magnus Andersen and his crew of the Viking ship" (8). The three caravels that had arrived previously, of course, represented replicas of Columbus's three ships, the *Nina*, the *Pinta*, and the *Santa Maria*. The arrival of the *Viking*, however, with its "golden dragon's head at the prow," transformed the exposition intended originally to commemorate only the Quadricentennial of Columbus's first voyage to the Americas into what was now a simultaneous celebration of another and much earlier discovery voyage (8). As the *New York Times* described the scene, to greet the *Viking*, "a great throng of people . . . was packed along the lake front," and "the trip from Racine was one great ovation to the sturdy Norsemen and their historic craft" (8).

In truth, the *Viking* was not precisely the "historic craft" the article intended. It was not, as the notice on 2 May had stated, "a model of the ships in which the Norsemen are supposed to have discovered America" ("The Viking Ship Sails" 11). Instead, the *Viking* replicated a late ninth-century Viking-era vessel discovered in 1880 that probably had once served as the personal traveling ship of wealthy or even royal owners, and its shape was closer to that of the sleek longships than to the bulkier merchant ships, called *knarrs*, used by most of those who traveled to North America.[7] Still, when it was excavated in 1880 from a burial mound along the outer Oslo Fjord area near Gokstad, Norway, there was worldwide fanfare about the recovery of a relatively intact Viking-era ship. Indeed, so much publicity had attended the discovery of the Gokstad ship that, in September 1892, "the Government of the United States . . . ask[ed] the loan of the old Viking ship found at Gogstad [sic] for the Chicago Columbian Exhibition. The United States Government offers to send a war ship to convey the Viking ship to America" ("Not to See the Viking Ship" 6). But as the *New York Times* reported on 25 September, the Norwegian archaeologists "who have charge of this relic of a by-gone age" considered it too fragile for such a journey and, "fearing that it might be damaged in transit," turned down the request (6). The very fact that the U.S. government had made the request, however, and even offered "a war ship" as conveyance, testifies to the strength of the contemporary belief in the pre-Columbian Norse discovery story.

When efforts to bring over the original Gokstad ship fell through, those who favored recognizing Leif Eiriksson as the first European to discover America seized upon another opportunity to prove their case: a replica of the Gokstad ship could be built in Norway and sailed across the Atlantic to New England. This would then prove conclusively that the medieval Norse really had possessed the requisite ship technology for their transatlantic voyages of discovery. Private funds were solicited and generously donated both in the U.S. and in Norway, and the project was quickly under way. The next year, members of the Norwegian World's Fair Committee were pleased to report back home that the *Viking* had become one of the fair's most popular attractions. And as the World's Fair shut down at the end of October 1893, those same officials could also report that the *Viking* was now headed for a lengthy tour around the U.S., with multiple stops "at Illinois, Wisconsin, and Minnesota ports, where the fellow-countrymen of the Captain and his crew have extended invitations for receptions and other entertainments" ("The Viking Ships Sails Away" 8). As the *New York Times* further explained on 1 November 1893, "From the Twin Cities the ship will be rowed down the Mississippi to New-Orleans, stopping at St. Louis. Then the ship will be sailed around the Atlantic coast to Washington, New-York, and Boston. In March [1894] the Norseman boat will leave the New World at Boston on its return voyage to Norway" (8).[8] During its time in the U.S., therefore, the *Viking* managed to visit all the main pockets of Scandinavian American immigration as well as those places in the Northeast believed to be associated with the Vinland colonists. Upon the *Viking*'s first arrival, this had included a stopover at Newport, Rhode Island, and a champagne toast on board when the ship first sighted Cape Cod (see "The Viking Ship is Here," 14 June 1893, 1).

"Even more hearty than the greeting accorded a week ago to the caravels was the welcome that went out" to the *Viking*, the *New York Times* had reported ("The Viking Ship at Chicago" 8). On the one hand, this triumphal reception during the year that was supposed to celebrate Columbus reflected a growing postwar nativist hostility toward Italian immigration and the concomitant nativist resistance to honoring the Genoese navigator by making Columbus Day a legal holiday. On the other hand, these events also reflected the current growing unease with the accepted discovery story, an unease that had been simmering since well before the Civil War.

When Edward Everett, then serving as a U.S. senator from Massachusetts, published *The Discovery and Colonization of America* in 1853, for example, he had studiously ignored Columbus's Catholic religion and, instead, in what might be read as a subtle poke at the Catholic Church's supposedly superstitious resistance to scientific inquiry, portrayed "the illustrious adventurer" as a man of science. "The discovery of America," wrote Everett, "is owing to the distinct conception in the mind of Columbus of this single scientific proposition,—the terraqueous earth is a sphere" (5). Two years later, in 1855, almost as a rejoinder to Everett, Thomas D'Arcy McGee published *The Catholic History of North America*, the first history of its kind intended for a popular audience. McGee depicted Columbus as the great Catholic explorer who had discovered America under the special patronage of the Virgin Mary. Appealing particularly to the upwardly mobile sons and daughters of Irish immigrants, McGee made abundantly clear throughout his text that his purpose was to challenge "our boastful Anglo-Saxon theorists" and in his "work of historical retribution" to reinstall Catholics and Catholicism in the history and fabric of the nation from its earliest beginnings (121).[9] "I might almost assert," wrote McGee, "that every Catholic order is represented in the history of this continent. Why be at war with history?" (66).

Of course, history itself wasn't the question but, rather, which *version* of history would come to dominate the nation's stories about itself. Works like McGee's threatened the earlier hegemonic narrative of a Protestant republic first conceived in the landing at Plymouth with a quest for religious freedom, later fully birthed during the Revolutionary War, fought for political freedom, and then renewed in "a new birth of freedom" with the Union's victory over the Confederacy in the Civil War. That this narrative neglected or suppressed much of the historical record and was grossly oversimplified is beside the point. For Anglo-Saxon Protestant Americans, it gave Protestants and Protestantism a special role in the formation and meaning of the nation. And to this master narrative, the stories of the supposedly freedom-loving and enterprising Northmen in New England added a racially related and thematically consistent preface. Therefore, ever since Rafn's *Antiquitates Americanæ* appeared in 1837, old stock New Englanders had been happily identifying New England with Vinland and emphasizing their own Viking or Nordic roots.

At the same time, however, as DeCosta noted in *The Pre-Columbian*

Discovery of America by the Northmen, "in this country writers of the Roman church incessantly use the establishment of the Icelanders in New England as a ground of their own ecclesiastical priority" (56 n2). In other words, for U.S. Catholics, tenth-century converted Northmen predated the pious seventeenth-century Pilgrim Congregationalists. Thus, just as different figurations of Vikings and Northmen—the two terms often used interchangeably—could be employed both in Catholic-inflected and in Protestant-inflected versions of American history, so too images of Columbus as a secular man of science and images of Columbus as an emissary of the Virgin Mary could be invoked by Protestants and Catholics, respectively. In short, Columbus could be as plastic as the Vikings.

The Passionate Partisan from Wisconsin: Rasmus B. Anderson

The newfound plasticity of Columbus derived not only from his ability to be represented as both a man of science and a devout Catholic but also from his ability to represent, in his own person, the patriotic ethnic Other. According to an article in the *Christian Union* for 22 October 1892, the grand five-day Columbus Day celebration in New York City that year provided a perfect example. "A journey on the elevated trains around the city," stated the unsigned article, "revealed every fire-escape, window, door, and store-front of even the poorest tenements giving evidence of the interest of the poorest citizens in the Columbus celebration. Pictures of Columbus that represented him as a type of every known race except the African were to be seen on every side. One was forced to conclude that when the artist was an Italian he produced an Italian Columbus, when the artist was an American he produced an American Columbus, when he was a German he gave us a German Columbus, and when he was an Englishman Columbus became a veritable beef-eater" ("The Columbus Celebration in New York" 726). Thus, precisely because of his foreignness, Columbus had become the American Everyman. In urban centers swelling with new and diverse immigrant populations, evidence like this was greeted as yet another hopeful sign of a successfully simmering melting pot.

Challenging both the power of this new plasticity as well as Columbus's long-established iconic status were three particularly partisan proponents of the Norse discovery story. First among them was Rasmus Bjorn Anderson (1846–1936), a professor at the University of Wisconsin and the son of Norwegian immigrants. In 1874, Anderson published *America Not Discovered by Columbus*.[10] The book, like its title, was an unequivocal salvo in the discovery debate. Anderson's aim, as enunciated in his first chapter, was to vindicate the claims of "the intrepid Norsemen" to first discovery "and to prove that Columbus must have had knowledge of this discovery by the Norsemen before he started to find America" (37, 35). A professor of Scandinavian languages and the founding head of the Department of Scandinavian Studies at the University of Wisconsin, Anderson had previously published one book on Scandinavian languages and would go on to write about Norse mythology and Viking tales, as well as produce English translations of Norse sagas and, in Norwegian, *Den Norske Maalsag* (The Norwegian language question). Despite this firsthand familiarity with Scandinavian languages and texts, in *America Not Discovered by Columbus*, Anderson appears to have based his arguments on the prior work of Rafn, DeCosta, and others (most of whom are cited in his relatively sparse notes) rather than on any new or original research of his own. Indeed, many of Anderson's paragraphs are merely paraphrases or even direct quotes from the works of predecessors, too often without quotation marks or attribution.

Anderson followed Rafn in identifying Helluland with Newfoundland, Markland with Nova Scotia, and Leif's Vinland with the area around Mount Hope Bay, and he located "Leif's booths . . . at or near Fall River, Massachusetts" (71–73). He speculated that "a *skeleton in armor* . . . found in the vicinity of Fall River" may have been the body of "Thorvald Erikson [who]. . . . was buried in Vinland" after having been killed by a Native's arrow (75). And he repeated Rafn's interpretation of "the Dighton Writing Rock" as evidence of "the presence of Thorfinn Karlsefne and the Norsemen at Taunton River" (83). His larger story, however, was far more elaborate. According to Anderson:

> The antiquities of the North furnish a series of incontestable evidence that the coast of North America was discovered in the latter part of the tenth century; . . . furthermore, that this same coast was visited repeatedly by the Norsemen in the eleventh century; furthermore, that it was visited by them in the twelfth century; nay, also, that it was found again by them in the thirteenth century, and revisited in the fourteenth century. But even this is not all. These Northern antiquities also show that Christianity had been introduced in America, not only among the Norsemen, who formed a settlement here, but also among the aborigines, or native population, that the Norsemen found here. (42–43)

This last, of course, was based both on the questionable tradition that Leif Eiriksson had brought priests with him from Norway to Vinland before returning to Greenland, and also on the assumption that Bishop Eirik Gnupsson's voyage to Vinland in 1121 had resulted in a ministry to the Indians.

Proceeding then to summarize the various recorded voyages to America, Anderson first told the story of the freedom-seeking Icelanders, thereby linking the Norse with a similarly freedom-seeking American nation. In language that would be many times quoted by others, Anderson explained that "political circumstances in Norway urged many of the boldest and most independent people" to emigrate. "Some went to the Hebrides, others to the Orkney Isles; some to the Shetland and Faroe Isles; many went as Vikings to England, Scotland, and France; but by far the greater number went to . . . Iceland," a country they came to love, despite its harsh climate, "because they were *free*" (Anderson's emphasis, 53–54). "It was . . . the constant voyages between this island and Norway, that led to the discovery, first of Greenland and then of America," added Anderson (54). A few pages later, after discussing the great literary heritage of Iceland and the seaworthiness of Norse ships, he articulated one of his main themes: "Yes, the Norsemen were truly a great people! Their spirit found its way into the Magna Charta of England and into the Declaration of Independence in America" (63).

In order even more persuasively to valorize the Norse and their claim to discovery, Anderson also felt he had to deconstruct the Columbus discovery story. With that as his goal, he offered "*five* reasons why Columbus must have known the existence of the American continent before he started on his voyage of discovery" (Anderson's emphasis, 88). The first was a letter supposedly written by Columbus—quoted in his son's biography of him and popularized in Irving's biography of Columbus—which stated that Columbus had visited Iceland in 1477.[11] Anderson followed Rafn's suggestion that in Columbus's "conversation with the Bishop and other learned men of Iceland, he must have been informed . . . that their countrymen had discovered a great country beyond the western ocean" (85). In fact, there was never any evidence that such conversations ever took place (and none are mentioned in the supposed letter).

Anderson's second reason was based on the information in *The Greenlanders' Saga* that "Gudrid . . . made a pilgrimage to Rome after the death of her husband." Anderson assumed that "she certainly must have talked there of her ever memorable trans-oceanic voyage to Vinland, and her three years' residence there." Playing to Protestant America's anxious suspicion of a Catholic Church thought to be seeking worldwide political and religious domination, Anderson further asserted that "Rome paid much attention to geographical discoveries" and would have taken careful note of Gudrid's information about Vinland. "Every new discovery was an aggrandizement of the papal dominion, a new field for the preaching of the Gospel," Anderson continued. So while "the Romans might have heard of Vinland before, . . . she brought personal evidence" (86).[12]

As his third reason, Anderson again asserted that "Vinland was known at the Vatican," this time citing as his evidence a version of the brief statement in the *Icelandic Annals* that in the year 1121, "Erik Upsi [Erik Gnupsson], Bishop of Iceland, Greenland and VINLAND, . . . went personally to Vinland" (86–87).[13] Continuing his focus on Rome, Anderson put forward as his fourth reason his belief that "Columbus . . . had opportunity to see a map of Vinland, procured from the Vatican" (87). Anderson seems to have suspected that the existence of such a map was at best speculative (and none has ever been authenticated), and so he bolstered his fourth reason with the relatively accurate observation that "Columbus lived in an age of discovery," when all the great European powers "were vying with each other in discovering new lands and extending their territories" (87). Therefore, Anderson concluded, Columbus, "with his nautical knowledge," *must* have "hear[d] of America" (87).

Anderson's fifth and last reason for this belief was that "ADAM OF BREMEN, a canon and historian of high authority," had described Vinland in a work written about 1075, versions of which were available in the twelfth or thirteenth century, based on the Hamburg original (87). In that work, titled *Gesta Hammaburgensis Ecclesiae Pontificum*, Adam had constructed a history of the archbishopric of Hamburg until the death of Archbishop Adalbert in 1072 and, in part, had tried to justify the late archbishop's claim to the Hamburg-Bremen see's ecclesiastical authority over the Church in all of Scandinavia. When discussing affairs in Denmark, Adam, a German cleric, repeated a conversation he had had with the king of Denmark in which he was told about a place named Vinland. Anderson quoted this passage from a nineteenth-century translation: *"there is still another region, which has been visited by many, lying in that Ocean (the Atlantic), which is called* VINLAND, *because vines grow there spontaneously, producing very good wine; corn likewise springs up there without being sown"* (88). Aware that there existed no evidence that Columbus knew this work, still Anderson insisted that it had been "read by intelligent men throughout Europe" and so asked, "Could he be ignorant of so important a work?" (88).

Confident that he had now proven his case, Anderson cagily claimed "to be vindicating the great name of Columbus, by showing that he must have based his *certainty*" upon study and real facts, particularly the fact of the earlier "discovery of America by the *Norsemen*" (Anderson's emphasis, 90). Anderson then went on to specify "the fault that we find with Columbus": "He was not honest and frank enough to tell where and how he had obtained his previous information about the lands which he pretended to discover; . . . he talked of himself as chosen by Heaven to make this discovery; and . . . he made the fruits of his labors subservient to the dominion of the inquisition" (90–91). Having now poked again at the scab of Protestant America's unease with many aspects of Catholic practice and belief, Anderson implied that, by any measure, Columbus did not deserve his current heroic status, especially not in "honest and frank" America.

Finally, in the last chapter of *America Not Discovered by Columbus*, Anderson arrived at his informing motive. "Let us remember LEIF ERIKSON," he wrote, "the first white man who turned the bow of his ship to the west for the purpose of finding America." And then Anderson revealed the project he hoped to initiate: "Let us erect a monument to Leif Erikson worthy of the man and the cause" (93).

While his book was widely reviewed, Anderson did not garner universal praise. An unsigned review in the *Literary World* on 1 November 1874 faulted him for "his unwarranted assumptions and his gigantic leaps over missing evidence," at the same time characterizing him personally as "proud of his [Norwegian] descent, and not disinclined to arrogate for his race a very large share of credit for whatever mankind has accomplished" ("America Not Discovered by Columbus" 86). Even more harsh was another unsigned review, probably written by the historian and Brahmin senator from Massachusetts Henry Cabot Lodge, that appeared in January 1875 in the *North American Review*. Here Anderson was faulted for his "utter contempt of all historical method . . . stat[ing] facts as a basis of argument, without the slightest proof of their truth" ("A Historical Sketch of the Discovery of America" 196). But what most irritated this reviewer was Anderson's adoption of the increasingly common habit of turning the medieval Norse into modern-day proto-Americans. Any *real* Norseman reading this book, declared the reviewer, would be "thoroughly astounded . . . if he were told that he was a highly cultivated gentleman of great astronomical acquirements, with a love of free institutions based on profound constitutional study, and with a civilizing mission in the world" (195). Instead, offered the reviewer, "let us admire the Norsemen for what they really were, brave savage men passionately fond of liberty, great fighters, and the greatest robbers and pirates the world has ever seen. No useful purpose is served, and history is terribly distorted, by depicting the emigrants to Iceland and Greenland as American citizens, and members of the Young Men's Christian Association, with the dress and manners of the tenth century" (195).[14]

Such criticism notwithstanding, Anderson's book clearly was riding a rising tide of like-minded studies and certainly had an impact. When Anderson issued a second edition three years later, in 1877, his "Preface to the New Edition" opened with the observation, "Since the first edition of this little book was published, the discovery of America has received much attention" (7). Anderson then devoted several pages to listing "what has been put in book form . . . since the publication of our volume" (7). Among other things, Anderson noted his "great pleasure" that all "the recent histories of the United States have . . . call[ed] attention to the pre-Columbian discoverers" (10). But he remained impatient with those writers who "freely admit the fact that the Norsemen . . . discovered and explored parts of America long before Columbus," yet remained "unwilling to believe that there is any historical connection between [the two] . . . or . . . that Columbus profited in any way by the Norsemen's knowledge of America" (11–12). So he rehearsed his arguments yet again in the preface.

A few pages later in his "Preface to the New Edition," Anderson discussed "the plans of the distinguished [Norwegian] violinist Ole Bull . . . [for] a monument in honor of the Norse discoverers of America" to be located in Boston (29). While the idea seems to have originated with Anderson, it was the much-lauded violinist who launched it publicly at a concert and reception in his honor in Boston in December 1876. At this reception, the Unitarian minister and author of, among other works, *The Man without a Country* (1865), Edward Everett Hale, took the floor to say that "New Englanders had never forgotten . . . their Norse ancestors." Then Hale formally proposed "a physical memorial of Thorvald, Leif and Thorfinn" (31). The same eminent gentlemen who had arranged the reception, Hale suggested, should now constitute a committee "to take this matter in special charge" (31). The upshot, according to Anderson, was "the committee of the Norsemen Memorial," also known as the Scandinavian Memorial Association, a committee of "men renowned throughout the world in science, in letters, and in art" (31). They included, among many others, Ole Bull himself, the governor of Massachusetts, Alexander H. Rice, Henry Wadsworth Longfellow, John Greenleaf Whittier, Eben Norton Horsford, Oliver Wendell Holmes, James Russell Lowell, and the Reverend Hale. In addition to planning some sort of monument "in honor of the Norsemen," the committee was also tasked "to obtain the title to [the Dighton Rock], ... in order to protect and remove it to Boston" (32–33).

Plans for the removal and preservation of Dighton Rock eventually came to nothing. Many of those most interested in this part of the committee's charge died before anything could be accomplished, and most of the committee's fundraising efforts were directed toward the monument or statue.[15] Thus, in the end, only the dreams of Anderson and Ole Bull were realized. On 29 October 1887, a statue of Leif Eiriksson, modeled by the sculptor Anne Whitney, was unveiled at the intersection of Commonwealth Avenue and Charlesgate East in Boston, where it still stands today. (See figure 8.) Eben Horsford, one of the major financial backers of the project, was the orator for the occasion. Again thanks to the efforts of Anderson, an almost identical Leif Eiriksson statue, also by Anne Whitney, was erected that same year in Juneau Park in Milwaukee.

But Anderson wasn't through yet. Continuing his campaign for greater acknowledgment of the Norse discovery story, he now pressed for an official day of recognition. He found eager supporters throughout the upper Midwest, where large numbers of Scandinavian immigrants (including his own parents) had first settled. In 1930, Wisconsin became the first state officially to adopt an annual Leif Erikson Day, followed a year later by Minnesota. The date chosen for the holiday was 9 October, a date with no known significance for Leif Eiriksson, but a date that commemorated the arrival of the sloop *Restauration* in New York Harbor, on 9 October 1825, marking the start of the first organized immigration from Norway to the United States. Anderson's parents had been aboard that ship. In 1964, Congress authorized the president to create a national observance of Leif Erikson Day by annual proclamation, a practice initiated by Lyndon Baines Johnson and followed by every president since. In his proclamation of 7 October 2009, the first Leif Erikson Day proclamation of his presidency, President Barack Obama proclaimed 9 October a day "to honor Leif Erikson and celebrate our Nordic-American heritage" within "the diversity of our country."

The Passionate Partisan from Cambridge: Eben Horsford

"More enthusiastic than critical" is how a select group within the Massachusetts Historical Society, the oldest historical society in the U.S., characterized the promoters of the Leif Eiriksson statue (qtd. in Falnes 239). These Historical Society members were the same men whom De-

8. Bronze statue of Leif Eiriksson dressed in chain mail with protective metal breastplates, designed by the American sculptor Anne Whitney, unveiled on 29 October 1887 in Boston and subsequently criticized for its historical inaccuracies. Leif's left hand is raised to shield his eyes as he looks into the distance, while his right hand holds a telescope against his hip. Photograph by Joshua Green, 2009.

The Challenge to Columbus 233

Costa described as "small in numbers but entitled to respect." From their point of view, those who held to the thesis that the Norse had made landfalls in and attempted to colonize New England were a kind of "cult . . . striving by every means, legitimate or otherwise, to impose [their ideas] upon the minds of the rising generation" (qtd. in Falnes 239). Shortly after the Eiriksson statue was unveiled, therefore, this group urged the Massachusetts Historical Society to appoint a committee to review all the available evidence regarding Norse discoveries. The committee concluded that the Norse probably had made landfalls in North America but "found the details cited in support of the discoveries, *as applied to any one locality*, too weak to be accepted as historical evidence" (my emphasis, Falnes 240).[16] Committee members did not want the already iconic history of their region clouded by unproven or potentially fraudulent claims.

Such caution held no sway with an enthusiast like Eben Norton Horsford (1818–93), however, who was certain he knew just where the Norse had landed and colonized. Not long after delivering the oration at the unveiling of the Leif Eiriksson statue, Horsford defied the worthies of the Historical Society and had a plaque mounted on Memorial Drive at Gerry's Landing Road (along the Charles River) in Cambridge, reading, "On this spot in the year 1000 Leif Erikson built his home in Vine Land." Two years later, in 1889, Horsford hired an architect and saw to the construction of a vaguely Norman-looking thirty-foot stone tower, ten feet in diameter, "set up . . . in Weston, at the mouth of Stony Brook" (Horsford, *The Discovery of the Ancient City of Norumbega* 41). The inscription on a tablet set in the wall of the tower identified it as a memorial to the ancient city of Norumbega, the main seat of a once-thriving Vinland colony.

The plaque and the tower were only two of several historical markers related to the Norsemen that Horsford left to posterity at different sites along the Charles River. For, while claims had been put forward for Norse presence at many sites in Maine, Rhode Island, Connecticut, and Massachusetts, Horsford was the first to assert, "Here, at the modern Watertown, was the ancient CITY OF NORUMBEGA," which once functioned as "the ancient seaport of Vinland, for the colony that came after Thorfinn left." Mistaking crumbling colonial-era structures and natural features of the landscape for remnants of Norse activity, Horsford argued that "the basin, wharves, docks, canals of this ancient seaport underlie the city of Watertown to-day. . . . Here came and went the commerce of the Northmen," with the Charles as their connecting conduit (*The Discovery of the Ancient City of Norumbega* 40). In fact, on the up-river side of the bridge over the Charles at Watertown, Horsford had yet another plaque installed, this one reading, "Outlook upon the stone dam and stone-walled docks and wharves of Norumbega, the seaport of the Northmen in Vineland." As the prominent installation of permanent plaques and the erection of an architect-designed stone tower indicate, unlike most of his fellow enthusiasts, Horsford enjoyed the financial means to enshrine his theories in conspicuous physical emblems.

Horsford was born in western upstate New York (near present-day Livonia) to native New Englanders who had removed there so that his father, Jedidiah Horsford, could act as a missionary to the Indians. After graduating from Rensselaer Polytechnic Institute in Troy, New York, in 1838, with a degree in civil engineering, Horsford worked for a time on a geological survey of New York State and then, for four years, taught chemistry and the natural sciences at the Albany Female Academy. In 1844 he went to Germany for two years to study analytical chemistry. Soon after his return to the U.S., in 1847 he was appointed Rumford professor and lecturer on the application of science to the useful arts at Harvard. He was then transferred to Harvard's newly established Lawrence Scientific School, where, for sixteen years, he taught analytical chemistry. Particularly interested in the chemistry of food and food preparation, Horsford founded the Rumford Chemical Company in 1856. Under its auspices, he invented processes for manufacturing baking powder and condensed milk and thereby made his fortune. During the Civil War, his company produced rations made of grain and meat for the Union army. In 1863, in order to engage in industrial chemistry full time, he resigned from Harvard but continued to live for the rest of his life in Cambridge.

In his later years, Horsford became an armchair antiquarian, collecting rare books, manuscripts, and old maps relating to the early explorations of North America. His particular interest in the Northmen may have been piqued by his great admiration for Ole Bull. The only explanation ever offered by Horsford himself appeared in 1891, when he wrote that he hoped "to widen the base of the glory of the State of [his] adoption" (*Defences of Norumbega* 3). He had hinted at that theme earlier, in 1889, in *The Discovery of the Ancient City of Norumbega*, the book in which he first fully laid out his theories and "discoveries." There, reiterated in several different places, Horsford expressed his desire to "allay the blind scepticism . . . that would deprive Massachusetts of the glory of holding the Landfall of Leif Erikson, and at the same time the seat of the earliest colony of Europeans in America"

(41). Over time, this became almost an obsession. Instead of highly regarded articles in major scientific journals on such topics as phosphates, condensed milk, fermentation, and emergency rations, he now published—often at his own expense—articles and books about his supposed archaeological discoveries. He even set aside monies so that, after his death, his daughter Cornelia could continue some of his excavations and also fund certain archaeological investigations in Iceland. The Iceland digs sought evidence of "similarities in burial practices and structural ground plans" between the Norse and "various Indian tribes, among them the Shawnees and Iroquois," to prove that these Native peoples "had in them traces of Norse blood" (Falnes 237–38).

Needless to say, Horsford's theories derived from layer upon layer of misinterpretations, misunderstandings, and unfounded assumptions. Because the *Icelandic Annals* record that Bishop Eirik Gnupsson set out for Vinland in 1121, some years after Thorfinn Karlsefni's expedition returned to Greenland, Horsford concluded that the cleric must have intended to "hold up the symbols of the Faith" for "the colony that came after Thorfinn left" (*The Discovery of the Ancient City of Norumbega* 40). Because those *Annals* also record the arrival in Iceland in 1347 of a ship laden with wood from Markland, Horsford appears to have melded the harvesting of timber in Markland with activities in Vinland and concluded that the Vinland colony lasted at least until the mid-fourteenth century. But perhaps his most unexpected assertion was that colonizing "Norsemen were here earlier" than Thorfinn's supposed arrival in 1010 (42).

As proof, Horsford pointed to that odd passage in *The Greenlanders' Saga* where Gudrid is approached by the strange woman who appears to be mimicking her by stating that her name, too, is Gudrid. The woman subsequently vanishes as mysteriously and as silently as she had entered. In *The Greenlanders' Saga*, this woman is described as "wearing a black, close-fitting tunic; she was rather short and had a band round her chestnut-coloured hair. She was pale, and had the largest eyes that have ever been seen in any human head" (66). While I earlier examined several plausible interpretations of this scene, Horsford's rather implausible interpretation was this: "Gudrid's namesake—the pale-faced, yellow-haired, large-eyed visitor, in dark woven-cloth petticoat, who spoke Icelandic, and visited Thorfinn's wife at the site of Gerry's Landing—was here in 1009" (*The Discovery of the Ancient City of Norumbega* 42). In Horsford's view, she was part of an earlier and continuing Norse colony pursuing "the vigorous prosecution of the industry of *māsur wood*" (42). Thus, concluded Horsford, "it is certain from the foregoing that Northmen, to say nothing of the mixed race, were here . . . from 999 to 1347,—that is, from the Landfall of Leif to the departure of the last timber-ship from Nova Scotia or Cape Breton" (42).

"Māsur wood," according to Horsford the economic engine of the colony, also refers to a line in *The Greenlanders' Saga*. After leaving Vinland, Karlsefni and Gudrid sailed first to Greenland and then to Norway, where Karlsefni "sold his cargo" (70). Before setting out to return to Iceland, Karlsefni was approached by "a man from Bremen, in Saxony," who offered him a good price for a "carved gable-head" (70–71). While the saga never really makes clear just what this is, it does state that "Karlsefni did not know what kind of wood it was made from: it was *mosuri*, and had come from Vinland" (71). Most often translated as "maple," the word probably applied to a variety of tree species, especially those species harvested in Labrador and Vinland and then shipped to Greenland and Iceland (and elsewhere). These species may have been particularly prized in the shipbuilding trades. Thus Horsford was not misguided in assuming that the harvesting of lumber for export *could* have supported an ongoing colonial enterprise. But there is no archaeological evidence that it did. And the sagas indicate that hostility from the large populations of Native peoples soon became too threatening for the fledgling Norse colony to withstand.

Since Horsford read the sagas eclectically and selectively, however, this seems to have made no impression on him. Instead, in *"the ancient Boston Back Bay,"* Horsford conjured docks and wharves where "the māsur blocks that had floated down the Charles" were arrested by a dam and "taken out and piled to dry and await their turn to be shipped" (Horsford's emphasis, *The Discovery of the Ancient City of Norumbega*, 38–39). Then, "at the present Watertown," they were "conveigh[ed] . . . into the Ocean through the Charles River" (39). But his newly discovered seaport of Norumbega was much more than a mere shipping station: "Here, besides the conveniences for piling under cover the māser [sic] blocks, there were storehouses for dried salmon, for the peltry purchased in its season, and not impossibly for the Indian corn grown on the plains of Newton, Danvers, Millis, and Holliston. On the shores above and below were . . . shops for barter, and dwellings for all classes, and necessarily, with the culture of the Northmen, provision for amusement, for public worship, and for the wants of government,—the Althing, to which these early (perhaps earliest) self-governing people were accustomed" (39). Indeed, when a stretch of land in southwestern Cambridge looked to Horsford like a natural amphitheater where the Althing, or general assembly, might have met, "he purchased this site and enclosed it with a series of square cut granite posts linked together by a heavy chain" (Falnes 237). This both preserved the site for future excavations and also stood as another memorial to what Horsford believed might once have been there.

More startling than all this, though, was Horsford's manipulation of what he thought he knew about Indians. Misreading certain statements composed by sixteenth- and seventeenth-century explorers and missionaries to North America—particularly their lack of comment on Indians' having a darker skin color—Horsford assumed that they had seen Natives with white ancestry along the coast.[17] This gave rise to his conviction that there had been "mixed race" inhabitants in Norumbega (*The Discovery of the Ancient City of Norumbega* 42). In another chain of errors, he asserted that he had himself seen and photographed "along the banks of the Charles" stone sinkers that must have been used by Thorvald Eiriksson and his men when they "subsisted through their first winter on the salmon of the Charles." In Horsford's view, these were among the "implements which we know from the Sagas were in use here by the Northmen" (44). Horsford persisted in identifying these as evidence of Norse presence despite the fact that he knew them to be "similar to . . . the salmon sinkers used by the Indians" (44). The implication, of course, was that the fishing sinkers, as well as several other known indigenous implements, had been introduced among the Indians by the Norse.

Even more wrongheaded than this imputation of technology transfer were Horsford's notions about Native languages. His knowledge of Native speech, we recall, was based on his childhood acquaintance with his father's missionary work in western upstate New York. But those were Iroquoian-speaking peoples, a cultural and linguistic group completely different from the Algonquian-speaking peoples of New England. Nonetheless, with his ignorance no barrier to certitude, Horsford insisted that several place names along the coast were "of palpable Norse derivation" when, in fact, they derived from early French and English corruptions of local Algonquian places names (*The Discovery of the Ancient City of Norumbega* 14). "We have other names of Norse derivation in Massachusetts," he added in a footnote, "as for example, Nauset, Naumkeag, Naumbeak, Namskaket, and Amoskeag" (14n1). In truth, each of these is composed of clearly identifiable (and easily translatable) Algonquian stem and root combinations, with no hint of any linguistic inflections from Old Norse, the other key language that Horsford did not know. Had he simply consulted the readily available *The Composition of Indian Geographical Names Illustrated from the Algon-*

kin Languages (1870), written by James Hammond Trumbull, a professor at Yale, Horsford could have avoided this error. As Trumbull's work made clear, all the place names listed in Horsford's footnote referred to water sites where specific kinds of fish might be caught (see Trumbull 28–32).[18]

But without this kind of knowledge, Horsford's entire claim to having rediscovered Norumbega continued to rest on a base of quirky and entirely erroneous philology. First, in an effort to revive the old idea that "Norumbega" was somehow related to the Old Norse name for Norway, he asserted that "the Indians of the tribes of the Algonquin family, which prevailed throughout New England . . . could not utter the sound of *b* without prefixing to it the sound of *m*" (*The Discovery of the Ancient City of Norumbega* 19). Then he asserted, "Many hundred years ago the country we call Norway was called Norbegia and Norobega, which are the same philologically . . . as Noruega, or Norvega, or Norwega; the b is the equivalent of *u*, or *v*, or *w*" (19). Finally, he connected his misunderstanding of Algonquian pronunciation patterns to his equally imperfect knowledge of the medieval (Latin and Old Norse) names for Norway to arrive at the following: "Vinland belonged to Norway,—that is, Norbega. But the Indians among whom the Norwegians came . . . could not readily say *Norbega*, but said, because it was easier of utterance, *Nor'mbega*. This was the name later given by the natives" to various explorers along the coast when asked the name of their country, and it was subsequently entered on some of the old maps (19). "This name," concluded Horsford, "seems to have been used in the sense of 'belonging to Norway'" (19). And because "Portuguese, Spanish, Italian, French, Dutch, and English navigators coming to our shores spelled the name *Nor'mbega* variously," it appeared differently spelled and with several variations on different maps (19–20). As a result of both his archaeological observations and his philological investigations, for Horsford the case was now proven beyond doubt. Vinland was the name for the larger Norse territory that stretched from Rhode Island to the Saint Lawrence and included Massachusetts. Norumbega was its Indian name as well as the name for Vinland's main seaport and urban center. Thus, according to Horsford, "Vinland and Norumbega are one" (17).[19]

Horsford's enormous wealth, combined with his munificent gifts to several institutions, including the American Geographical Society, helped earn him both influence and a hearing. The father of five daughters and a strong advocate for women's education, Horsford had also made substantial gifts over the years to Wellesley College. Not surprisingly, therefore, in 1886 the college named its newest residential building Norumbega Hall, according to Horsford, "in honor of the discovery which was communicated to the public at about the time the corner-stone of the Hall was laid" (*The Discovery of the Ancient City of Norumbega* 6). Aware that most New Englanders would "doubtless connect their first conception of Norumbega with the well-known poem of Whittier," Horsford had sent a letter about his discoveries to Whittier and, with the president of Wellesley, importuned the poet to compose a poem for the official opening of the hall (9). Whittier happily acceded to the request, noting that at the hall's opening ceremonies in 1886, his "sonnet . . . was read by President Alice E. Freeman, to whom it was addressed" (*The Complete Poetical Works* 239).[20]

In the sonnet, titled "Norumbega Hall," Whittier acknowledged that while "the spires / Of the sought City" did not rise "on Penobscot's wooded bank" nor elsewhere, now "at last its mystery is made known— / Its only dwellers maidens fair and young." The hall's opening meant that "Norumbega is a myth no more" (239–40). Whittier also sent a letter to Horsford that read, in part, "I had supposed that the famed city of Norumbega was on the Penobscot, when I wrote my poem some years ago; but I am glad to think of it as on the Charles, in our own Massachusetts" (qtd. in Horsford, *The Discovery of the Ancient City of Norumbega* 9–10). Both the letter and the original poem, still spelled "Norembega," were reprinted in *The Discovery of the Ancient City of Norumbega*. And because he believed in the power of poetry to persuade, in addition to reprinting the Whittier poem, Horsford also commissioned for that volume a lengthy pseudo-epic by the Boston journalist and sometime poet Edward Henry Clement (1843–1920).[21] Titled simply "Vinland," Clement's rhymed couplets retold the Vinland episodes from the sagas, but not before repeating the now-familiar charge that Columbus had traveled to Iceland for the purpose of learning what the "sagas taught / Of ancient trips to Western seas" (qtd. in Horsford, *The Discovery of the Ancient City of Norumbega* 58).

Horsford's persistence and his ability to use his wealth to good advantage were not the only factors that brought him adherents. In the Boston-Cambridge area, his so-called discoveries played both to regional and to racial pride. As Clement put it in "Vinland," "Gothic pith is in our bones," and New Englanders were the direct descendants of "sturdiest stocks of old Caucasian, — / Liberty, self-rule, their passion" (qtd. in Horsford, *The Discovery of the Ancient City of Norumbega* 58–59). From the Norse to "our own Mayflower" and "from folk-mote to the Commonwealth" of Massachusetts was "one straight march" (59). As a

240 Chapter Five

result, present-day New Englanders, especially those in Massachusetts and Rhode Island, were (58)

> the kindred race
> Dwelling in the very place
> Where the Norsemen moored their ships
> And left their names on savage lips.

In an address in 1889 to the American Geographical Society, which Horsford reprinted near the beginning of *The Discovery of the Ancient City of Norumbega*, the president of that Society, Judge Charles Patrick Daly, sounded the same theme.[22] "We have hitherto but inadequately appreciated the Northmen as a race," said Daly, pointing to "their adventurous spirit, their capacity, and the degree of civilization to which they had attained in an age when Europe was but emerging from the darkness that had enveloped it for many centuries" (7). Daly then paraphrased a "learned Assyrian scholar" who had recently declared "that the primitive home of the Aryans . . . that great civilizing race . . . was some place in the southeastern part of Scandinavia; which would make the Northmen the progenitors of the Greeks, the Romans, and, with the exception of one or two races, of all the nations of modern Europe; which, [if true,] . . . would make them the greatest race in the history of mankind" (7). Accepting the premise that "America was discovered by the Northmen five centuries before the arrival of Columbus, and that for a considerable period thereafter they maintained a settlement," Daly found Horsford's discoveries "especially interesting at this period, when we are preparing to celebrate the four hundredth anniversary of the discovery of this continent by Columbus" (7–8). Consequently, in 1889, Daly said he was eager to see Horsford's "facts . . . brought to light" (7).[23]

But warm endorsements from an honored poet like Whittier, from various Scandinavian American societies, or even from the president of the American Geographical Society did not mean that Horsford's ideas were widely accepted. They were not. Horsford's former colleagues at Harvard who studied Scandinavian languages and literatures generally remained dubious about most of his archaeological finds. Even so, those same scholars shared with Horsford a desire to link New England, and particularly Massachusetts, with the Norse. In September 1911, when Christiania University (now the University of Oslo) in Norway celebrated the one-hundredth anniversary of its founding, Harvard sent Professor F. Herman Gade as its delegate to the festivities.[24] Gade bore congratulatory greetings from the Harvard faculty that read, in part, "The same shores of New England, where the Pilgrims and Puritans planted their first institutions of learning were, we believe, more than six centuries earlier discovered and as 'Vinland the good,' enjoyed by the great Norse seafarers, Leif Erikson, Thorvald, and Thorfinn." Equally important, stressed the Harvard letter, was a shared affinity for seeking freedom. The Norse who came to America, the letter continued, "were descendants of pilgrims who to escape oppression in Norway had in their Viking ships emigrated to Iceland as the English Mayflower Pilgrims later came to Plymouth" (qtd. in Falnes 242). In this way, the Harvard professors, no less than Horsford, were also fabricating their region's link to a grand and ancient past. Horsford had earlier tried to make that link tangible by "discovering" what he believed were physical remains. Harvard's letter to Christiania University reforged the link by once again installing the Norse as precursor pilgrims in what was then the nation's dominant myth of origins.

The Passionate Feminist Partisan: Marie A. Brown

Memorializing the Norse discoverers with statues in public places or with plaques at newly identified archaeological sites was not enough for Marie Adelaide Brown Shipley (1843–1900). She wanted Americans to read "the old Norse sagas," to "shake off this palsying superstition" of Christianity, and to take as their national models "the Icelandic republicans of the olden time" (Shipley, *The Icelandic Discoverers of America* 172). The way to begin, she argued throughout her book, *The Icelandic Discoverers of America; or, Honor to Whom Honor Is Due* (1887), was with "the recognition of the claims of the Norse discoverers" (177). If all this could be accomplished, she promised, then "the people of this Republic . . . would retrieve at a single stroke all the blunders of the past and inaugurate a new era" of human freedom and happiness (177).

Born Marie Adelaide Brown in New York City in 1843, she spent some of her childhood years in Albany, where her father served for a time as librarian of the State Library. Her mother came from the well-connected Roe family of upstate New York. Because her father, Robert Brown, was the son of Scots immigrants, Brown attributed her own "peculiarly strong sympathy for everything from the northern lands" to that genetic inheritance (Brown, "Marie A. Brown: A Brief Autobiography" 1). When she was in her mid-forties, Brown married John B. Shipley, an Englishman who both shared her views and also had his own reasons for pressing the case for Norse discovery. Following their marriage and their move to England, Brown published under her married name and even republished some of her earlier works under the name of Mrs. John B. Shipley or Marie A. Shipley, or sometimes Marie Adelaide Brown Shipley. In order not to confuse her writings and ideas with those of her husband, I will refer to her as "Brown" in this discussion and to him as "Shipley."

By the time she was in her twenties, Brown had become an ardent feminist, publishing articles protesting a woman's lack of rights in marriage. In an article published in 1869 in *Boston Traveler* which was reprinted in *The Revolution*, the journal founded by Elizabeth Cady Stanton and Susan B. Anthony, Brown condemned the fact that, under the law as it then stood, the wife "owns nothing—all is his; she controls nothing, for the reins of power are held by another, and she is driven with the rest of the chattels; she can change nothing, for a word of protest endangers the threadbare support she endures" (Brown, "The Pecuniary Independence of Wives" 355). Albeit in more generalized terms, the theme of women's rights was one to which she would return even in her writings about the Norse. As with Matilda Joslyn Gage, it may have been Brown's feminism that first induced her to question Christianity, a step that eventually led her to attack Roman Catholicism for what she viewed as its conspiracy against both women and the Norse.

Through the 1870s, most of Brown's publications were mainly translations into English of contemporary Swedish poetry and novels. But by the end of the 1870s, she was already beginning to publish newspaper and magazine articles, and especially lengthy review essays, all focused on "the ancient Norsemen, whose heroic lives ... [are] linked with our own early destiny. They are in fact our Pilgrim Fathers, having effected the first landing on the coast of Massachusetts" (Brown, "A New History" 837–38). By the 1880s, she had become an indefatigable proponent of replacing Columbus with Leif Eiriksson as the true discovery hero. One of her most influential articles—influential because she circulated it widely, sending copies to members of the American Philosophical Society and to key members of Congress, among others—was "The Viking Exhibition," published in the *Independent* in February 1888. This was the article in which she first laid out her proposal for a grand "Viking Exhibition" to accompany the "celebration of the founding of our Constitution," a celebration originally planned for the following year in Washington (Brown, "The Viking Exhibition" 5). In that article, she made her position abundantly clear. "It does not lie at all in my plan," she wrote, "to have the honor of the discovery of America shared between Leif Erikson and Columbus, or to have a joint celebration in any sense of the word. The man who simply followed Leif Erikson and imitated his achievement, 500 years afterward, is in no wise to be regarded as the equal of the original discoverer, as little as Spain, the country that was his patron, monarchical, benighted, priest-ridden land that it was then, and is still, was the equal of the republican Iceland of the tenth century" (6). A month after the *Independent* article appeared, on 16 March 1888, Brown addressed the Select Committee of the U.S. Senate on the Centennial of the Constitution and the Discovery of America, and there she made her case in person.

When speaking before the Senate committee, Brown insisted that committee members were not hearing her voice alone but, rather, "the united voice of the nations of the Scandinavian North; . . . the united voice of the Scandinavians of the United States, who, were this fact [of Norse discovery] recognised by the nation they have adopted, would at once be transformed from aliens into compatriots, sharing our pride in a common ancestry."[25] Brown also said she spoke for many others, including "Great Britain, Germany, France," and "all the learned societies of Europe" (Shipley and Shipley 31). She then quoted from a variety of sources, all suggesting Columbus's prior knowledge of the Norse discoveries and, based on these sources, she argued that various ecclesiastical centers scattered across Europe and Iceland—and particularly "buried records in Rome"—held documents that substantiated both the Norse discovery and also Columbus's awareness of it (36–37).

On behalf of the U.S., Brown proposed to travel to every relevant archive, including those in Iceland and Rome, in order to search out, transcribe, and prepare "for publication by the Government" all the documents that proved the case (Shipley and Shipley 38). "It is not right," she asserted, "that this nation should lack the evidence, the full accounts, of the events in its own early history" (37). Additionally, while on her search for documents, Brown proposed to collect Norse-related "relics and antiquities . . . from the various museums of Europe," to be exhibited, along with the newly published documents, in the Viking Exhibition that she and others wanted erected as part of the centennial celebration of the Constitution.

To help support her in these efforts, Brown formally petitioned Congress to grant her "an appropriation adequate to the accomplishment of this grand object," and to include in that appropriation money for "an English friend of mine, Mr. John B. Shipley, of London" (Shipley and Shipley 37).[26] Shipley, she assured Congress, would provide invaluable assistance and was "a gentleman admirably qualified for the work, and as well versed in the subject as I am" (37–38). As events unfolded, Congress never appropriated the funding for a celebration of the Constitution, and so no Viking exhibit was ever mounted in Washington in 1889. As the introduction to the book that Brown (now Mrs. John B. Shipley) and Shipley coauthored in 1890 noted, "nothing came of" her appearance before the Senate committee, and "no appropriation was made" to enable her research (xiii).

The book that the two coauthored was *The English Rediscovery and Colonization of America*, with John B. and Marie A. Shipley printed on the title page as authors. The book is really an assemblage of separate pieces, each written either by Brown or by Shipley, rather than a cowritten text. Although signed by "The Authors," the introduction is dominated by Shipley's particular interest in the Norse discovery question, an interest that was decidedly political. In Shipley's historical schema, "The American civilization of the present day is the direct consequence of the Cabot voyages, and of the English colonization which arose out of the [land] claims of England . . . based upon those voyages" (Shipley and Shipley vi–vii). In turn, he continued, the Cabots' voyages "were directly inspired by the knowledge, derived through the English trade with Iceland in the fifteenth century, of the earlier Scandinavian voyages and explorations" (vii). Thus, Columbus and Spain really had no legitimate claim to American recognition. Instead, "the paramount claim" was England's, the country that "bestowed upon [Americans] language, laws, and free institutions, all of which are largely founded on the same Scandinavian civilization under which [the Americans'] country was originally discovered" (xv). With that crucial historical link established, Shipley bewailed the fact that the U.S. and England "were severed more than a hundred years ago by the exactions, interference, and greed of an English monarch," and he suggested that, based on their shared history, the two now "ought to be reunited" (vii). In other words, the U.S. was to become again "a portion of Greater Britain," like Canada, Australia, and South Africa (vii).

His appeal was unapologetically and breathtakingly imperialistic in scope: "With a common language, common ideas, common aims, and their forces united to secure the peace and progress of mankind, the two great powers [i.e., the U.S. and Great Britain] would form a governing force for the world, leading it on to higher progress, and repressing acts of injustice, wherever perpetrated" (Shipley and Shipley vii). Like many other Englishmen of his class and generation, for Shipley, imperialism wore the benign face of "the white man's burden," and the

Civil War had briefly aroused renewed hopes of England's again embracing at least part of the U.S. within the British fold.

But the American Revolution was not so easily undone, and, anyway, the U.S. had imperial designs of its own. In addition to expanding across the Pacific, the U.S. was seeking to cultivate a regional sphere of influence in Central and South America. And this is precisely what most vexed Shipley. As he complained in that same introduction, "At present the political ambition of the United States is . . . devoted to the task of dominating the entire New World, and shutting out for ever European influence of every description, whether commercial or political" (Shipley and Shipley vii). As a result, instead of using 1889 to celebrate the Constitution and recognize Leif Eiriksson's discovery, the U.S. had invited "all the governments of North and South America, except Canada, to send delegates to a Pan-American Conference to be held in Washington" that year (viii). In Shipley's view, this was all part of a grand "scheme for drawing South American trade away from Europe, to the advantage of the United States" (ix). And it proved to him "how little genuine concern for historic truth can be expected from [the U.S.] when the truth happens to conflict with their political or commercial interests" (xv).

Over the next decade, in books, pamphlets, and articles, Shipley continued to espouse his vision of a U.S. reunited with England. But his efforts had no more effect than had Brown's petition to Congress for an appropriation to support her research on the Norse discovery. Neither one, however, seems to have been daunted by these setbacks. For her part, according to the introduction, Brown "obtain[ed] the widest possible circulation of her views through the newspaper press, thus getting the subject discussed from Maine to California" (Shipley and Shipley xiv). She embarked on "a very extensive lecture tour" that took her, among other places, "to Winnipeg in Manitoba, where she received a far more hearty welcome than anywhere in the States." Unlike many Americans, apparently, "the Canadians felt pride and joy in believing that a part of Canada, certainly Labrador and Nova Scotia, were in the Vinland that Leif Erikson discovered" (xiv). Still, despite the lukewarm reception she received in some—but hardly all—American venues, Brown continued to lecture widely and to publish articles and book reviews about the Norse. And in New England, she could almost always depend on a warm reception. As the *Boston Daily Globe* reported, her lecture in October 1887 in the Tremont Temple attracted "an immense audience" ("America's Discovery" 2).

In 1889, Brown attempted to establish "a new journal to be published weekly at Chicago," titled *Leif Erikson*, its editorial content dedicated "to prov[ing] . . . that the Norsemen discovered America, and that Columbus was an imposter" ("Notes and News" 141). Probably due to a lack of finances, only four issues were ever published. More important, through 1891, Brown continued to update and reissue her most comprehensive work, *The Icelandic Discoverers of America; or, Honor to Whom Honor Is Due*, which had first been published in London in 1887. As indicated in her text, Brown's decision to put her ideas into book form in 1887 had been precipitated by the fact that Americans were then looking ahead to celebrating the one-hundredth anniversary of constitutional government in 1889 and, beyond that, in 1892, to celebrating the four-hundredth anniversary of Columbus's first landfall in the Bahamas.[27]

In the opening chapter of *The Icelandic Discoverers of America*, Brown made clear that she was intent on wholly rewriting the accepted discovery story:

> For Christopher Columbus substitute the Norsemen; for Spain substitute the Scandinavian North; for the date 1492 substitute the dates 982–85; for San Salvador and San Domingo substitute Greenland, Labrador, Nova Scotia, Rhode Island, and Massachusetts; . . . for a discoverer who stole his information, thus buying himself name and repute at the Spanish court, and who went to America in search of gold and slaves, also to appropriate new territory for the preaching of the Gospel, substitute the genuine discoverers, who were adepts in the art of navigation, . . . and who being above the incentives of lucre and Papal patronage, devoted themselves to industry, commerce between the newly discovered continent, Greenland, Iceland, and Scandinavia, and such a thorough and intelligent exploration of it as to rouse the cupidity of southern Europe, five hundred years after their discovery. (Shipley 9–10)

"The duty of Americans," therefore, insisted Brown, was the immediate "acknowledgement of the truth" (56).

In order to acknowledge that "truth," Brown asserted that Americans would also have to confront "the continued encroachments of the Roman Catholic power in the United States" (Shipley 54). "The efforts of Rome," she continued, were aimed at "stifl[ing] liberty for ever by putting all nations . . . under the perpetual rule of the Church." To this end, the Church had maintained "their long-continued policy of at once concealing the discovery of the Norsemen and substituting that of Columbus for it" (54, 56). In fact, she averred, "the wish expressed for a general celebration [in 1892–93] of the discovery of America by

Columbus, is the first wary move of the Roman Catholic Church to uproot freedom from American soil" (57). What was to become the Chicago World's Fair was thus, for Brown, merely a cog in the inexorably turning wheels of a Roman plot.

Given the fact of Brown's earlier feminist essays, it is hardly surprising that at least some of her quarrel with the Catholic Church had a decidedly feminist tone. She quoted contemporary Scandinavian writers who had stated, "In paganism . . . woman seems almost to have been man's equal" (Shipley 81). She contrasted her own wholly romanticized view of pagan Norse sexual relations with those of the Church: "The Norsemen's belief in love between the sexes and deep reverence for it, [was] a belief that the Christian religion immediately expunged from its ethics" (80). And she embedded her feminism within the period's racist distinctions between so-called northern and southern peoples. "Among the Northern race," wrote Brown, "romance, constancy, devoted love, and chivalrous attachment to the [female] sex so highly honoured, were the atmosphere of their lives . . . while in the South, women were either shut up in the convents, debauched, or turned into zeros by the thraldom of the medieval marriage, in which women were only to bear children and bless God" (81).

In Brown's larger political taxonomy, the Church, as an avatar of the southern races, had long been at odds with "the Northern race." The Church, which she claimed had forced itself on the Scandinavian nations, represented repression. The Scandinavians represented freedom. Originally, "the pagan Norsemen and the Roman Catholics had the same visible aim," explained Brown, "the conquest of the world. . . . One desired to obtain dominion to the end of freedom, the other to the end of slavery." Where the Norse succeeded, "they established free institutions, good laws, physical and mental well-being." Where the Church succeeded, "they founded cathedrals and monasteries, destroying all law but that of the Church" (Shipley 82). Now, according to Brown, "the Church of Rome" was seeking "to slip the yoke of spiritual subjection over [the] necks [of] . . . the American people, the descendants of the Vikings" (99). After all, she reasoned, "the Church that has fought the Scandinavians for ages in Europe, is not likely to fraternize or coalesce with American institutions that are the natural outgrowth of the Scandinavian spirit" (98).

By inducing Americans "to do homage" to a Catholic discoverer, Brown suggested, the Church was simultaneously seducing them into paying homage to the Church for which he sailed. Thus Columbus, with "his southern heart," also had to become a major villain in the piece

(Shipley 99). Brown portrayed Columbus, like his Church, as secretive and deceitful, a slaver who lusted after wealth, and she devoted an entire chapter to his visit to Iceland and his supposed prior knowledge of the Norse voyages. Moreover, "thoroughly in unison with" the bigoted spirit of Spain and the Church, Brown's imagined Columbus "attend[ed] *autos-de-fé*" where "he probably saw his share of Lutherans burned, ladies included" (149–50). Since Martin Luther did not post his famous ninety-five theses on the church door until 1517, and since organized congregations of those who identified themselves as Lutherans did not emerge until much later, it is impossible for Columbus to "have beguiled the tedium of . . . waiting" for his ships to be outfitted by watching Lutherans burned at the stake for heresy in 1492 (149). But, again, historical accuracy was sacrificed as Brown attempted to position Lutheranism, the established church of the Scandinavian nations, as inherently northern in spirit and thus a threat to the Church of Rome.

Throughout her book, Brown quoted from almost every historian, scholar, and antiquarian who had published on the discovery question before her, American and European alike. Without distinguishing between credible and entirely bogus sources, and without noting how many of her sources were merely parroting the work of earlier writers, Brown created the illusion of a dense and well-researched text. Unlike Anderson, with whom she had a difficult and sometimes contentious professional rivalry, she was relatively scrupulous about identifying her sources, quoting from them at length, and including the quotation marks. This, too, added to the impression that *The Icelandic Discoverers of America* was a trustworthy text and helped garner Brown a number of favorable reviews. In reality, of course, the book demonstrated only that Brown was an adept researcher, able to amass every statement and conjecture that helped her case, as well as to massage even the slightest hints into so-called evidence, and organize it all into a coherent (if often repetitive) whole. The only area in which she was at all original was in the ninth chapter, where she argued for "the beneficial results to the present age and posterity of attributing this momentous discovery to the true persons" (Shipley 165).

The crux of her argument was that the U.S. stood at a turning point, engaged in a battle that the nation did not yet even recognize. Continuing her screed against Catholicism, which she now extended to include Protestantism, Brown repeated her view that "it is the unceasing effort of the Romish Church, even through the channels of Protestantism, to regain its lost dominion, to bring back the Middle Ages upon the earth" (Shipley 176). Since its inception, she continued, the Church had battled all forms of what it considered "apostasy," including "paganism, the Reformation, science, rationalism, [and] republicanism." Now that same "apostasy has reached its worst stage in . . . the United States, which, in the framing of their Constitution, have given . . . a mortal affront to the Church" (176). In other words, in framing a republic that separated church and state, its structures derived from the rationalism of the eighteenth-century Enlightenment, the U.S. by definition, claimed Brown, challenged Catholicism's long-sought hegemonic tyranny. And so, she declared, it was necessarily in the U.S. that "the battle must be fought out. It is not to be supposed for an instant that Americans will repudiate science, rationalism, and republicanism; . . . the only mistake has been that they have not yet realized the discrepancy between loyalty to the Constitution and loyalty to the Christian religion" (176). "The battle [that] must be fought out" thereby took on the grandeur of a patriotic struggle for the preservation of some of the nation's most cherished institutions.

For Brown, the battlegrounds were the upcoming centennial celebrations of the Constitution and the Columbus Quadricentennial. These offered "the immediate occasion for discussion [of] . . . the relative claims of Columbus and the Norse discoverers to American recognition" (Shipley 176). Whether Columbus or the Norse were chosen for recognition at these celebrations had consequences not just for the U.S. but for the entire world, she claimed. Indeed, she elaborated, the use made by the Church "of the two discoveries of America, and its treatment of the discoverers" constituted "the pivot upon which all history has turned" (180). To recognize Columbus, she wrote, was to condone the "robbery, spoliation, plunder, marauding, and depredations of every kind" that followed upon the activities of Spain and the Church in the Americas (181). "Every sending-out of missionaries to the heathen is a marauding expedition," she added for emphasis (181). Thus, she concluded, "in insisting on the recognition of Columbus' claims, the Church demands from the United States, and from the world, *public* sanction of these crimes and permission to continue them" (Brown's emphasis, 181).

By contrast, if Americans would only acknowledge their Nordic heritage through the recognition of the Norse discovery, they would attain both "national integrity" and also "the ideal of the ancient Scandinavians . . . : the majesty of self-relying humanity" (Shipley 177, 180). For Brown, of course, that self-reliance went hand-in-hand with "tear-[ing] down Christianity" (192). Freed from the cant, superstition, and machinations of the "Romish Church" and its Protestant adherents, and with the U.S. leading the way, Brown posited that the entire world could be filled with "republic[s], carried on under rationalistic principles" (192). As her ideal, she projected a romanticized version of a pre-Christian ancient Icelandic republic, and she believed that, in place of the tenets of Christianity, the Iceland of old "will serve as a model for the reconstruction of modern commonwealths" (192). In this way, not only the U.S., but all the world, would "inaugurate a new era" (177).

Beyond securing a secular republic governed by reason rather than by religious dogma, Brown also promised that if Americans would "endeavour to emulate the glorious example of their [Nordic] ancestors," they could reawaken within themselves "the moral force contained in the Sagas" and thereby "do away with . . . the life-long misery of nine-tenths of those born to the earth" (Shipley 194, 166, 172). For Brown, ancient Iceland represented "in many respects an ideal civilization," a place where women were honored and enjoyed real power, and a republic peopled by "a race mentally and physically sound, whose thoughts, words and acts were strong and vigorous" (165). As descendants of that race, this was what Americans could yet become and thereby experience "a life diametrically opposite from that of which we are now cognisant" (167). In effect, Brown was offering an escape from modern malaise. However illogical her train of reasoning, her promises certainly had their appeal, especially for those urban dwellers who were finding the cities increasingly confining and their workplaces stultifyingly sedentary and routinized. These were the comfortably middle-class readers suffering from the period's "nervous diseases," readers eager for a sense of authenticity, personal meaning, vigorous challenge, and, as Brown phrased it, the chance to become "human and natural again" (172). All they had to do, she declared, was give up "the pious tradition that Columbus discovered America, in 1492" (194).[28]

The Legacy of the Passionate Partisans

All their efforts notwithstanding, neither these passionate partisans nor the many other advocates for the Norse discovery story succeeded in wholly displacing Columbus. In 1893, Anne Whitney's statue of Leif Eiriksson in Boston was joined by a statue of Columbus set on the grounds of the city's Cathedral of the Holy Cross and later moved to Revere, a town seven miles outside of Boston.[29] That same year, despite the excitement that attended the arrival of the *Viking* from Norway, images of Columbus dominated the Chicago World's Fair. There was the massive Columbian fountain, said to be based on a symbolic design sketched by Columbus himself. There was a grand triumphal arch topped by a statue of Columbus standing in a chariot drawn by four horses that were led by two female figures. And there was a large statue of Columbus facing a rising sun, suited in armor, and claiming possession of the New World for Spain. On behalf of the intensely commercial interests of the fair, Columbus was offered to the public as a symbol of America's material progress, advances in science, and ongoing achievement. To cement these associations, in 1893 the U.S. issued its first commemorative postage stamps, a set of sixteen, each engraved with a depiction of a different event from Columbus's career.

This is not to say that those who argued for Leif Eiriksson as the true discoverer had had no impact. They certainly had. Many schoolbooks and most popular histories made at least some reference to the Viking hero. Some even devoted entire opening chapters to the Norse voyages. At the same time, several folklorists were busily interviewing members of the New England Indian communities in an effort to find evidence of Norse influence in traditional Indian lore.[30] The folklorists' working thesis was that the New England Natives had known the Norse colonizers and even incorporated elements from pagan Norse mythology into their own stories and legends.

That said, perhaps the most significant impact of the Leif Eiriksson supporters was their ability to spread misgivings about Columbus the man. In the run-up to the Chicago World's Fair, a number of serious historians took another look at the Columbian legacy. Prominent among these was Justin Winsor, then director of the Boston Public Library and later the librarian of Harvard College, who, in 1891, published *Christopher Columbus and How He Received and Imparted the Spirit of Discovery*. Without taking any position on whether Columbus knew about the earlier voyages of the Norse, Winsor nonetheless substantiated many of the other critical judgments made by the Leif Eiriksson advocates. Correcting Irving's efforts to "create a hero," Winsor portrayed Columbus as a man deeply flawed and lacking in moral vision: "His discovery was a blunder; his blunder was a new world; the New World is his monument! Its discoverer might have been its father; he proved to be its despoiler.... He left it a legacy of devastation and crime" (60, 512). Thus, just as he had been for Anderson and Brown, for Winsor too, Columbus was a slaver who "proved a rabid seeker for gold and a viceroyalty" (512). That damning assessment aside, Winsor's work circulated in educated and scholarly circles only, while popular celebrations of Columbus and the Quadricentennial continued to be planned in all the major cities, not just Chicago. Indeed, as of 1892, a year before the World's Fair opened in May 1893, there were twenty-nine statues or monuments to Columbus scattered all across the U.S., each in its own way reproducing and reinforcing a particular construction of a shared national history.

One of the most imposing of these statues, unveiled in New York City in October 1892, demonstrated the growing influence of the city's immigrant Italian community but also elicited some of the same anti-immigrant bias that had informed the writings of several of the Leif Eiriksson supporters. As part of New York's Quadricentennial celebration, the unveiling of the statue was marked by addresses from a host of dignitaries. These included President Benjamin Harrison and government officials from Italy. The statue was then blessed by the Catholic archbishop of New York, Michael Augustine Corrigan. A gift to the city, paid for by donations from Italians and Italian Americans, the statue had been created in Italy by the Italian sculptor Gaitano Russo and then brought by ship to New York. With the statue itself set on a high column, Russo's monument to Columbus stands eighty-four feet high, the largest of the Columbian monuments then erected in any U.S. city (except for those at the fair). It was prominently placed at Eighth Avenue and Fifty-ninth Street, near the entrance to Central Park, in what quickly became known as Columbus Circle. Yet for all the pomp and circumstance that had attended its unveiling, only a month later, on 28 November 1892, the *New York Times* reported that the monument had become "a sort of mecca" for "troops" of the "swarthy sons of the Sunny South [who] wander about the bit of marble, looking it over with deepest interest" ("New Shrine for Italians" 2). No anti-immigrant spokesperson could have phrased it more snidely.

What is interesting in this regard is that, while issues of race, ethnicity, and religion certainly hovered in both the background and the foreground, none of the three most passionate partisans of the Norse discovery was ever overtly anti-immigration in their writings. For Horsford, focused exclusively on finding Norse remains in and around his beloved Cambridge, immigrants and immigration simply weren't germane. For Anderson and Brown, one the son of immigrants, the other the granddaughter of immigrants—albeit the *right kind* of immigrant stock—to have been anti-immigration would have been both hypocritical and impolitic. What they sought, instead, was to valorize the nineteenth-century immigration from Scandinavia by linking American democracy to a distant Nordic past. In so doing, Anderson and Brown helped to "bolster the authority" of a Brahmin elite that was itself striving to forge "a direct and unbroken link between the present, the intermediary past of the founding fathers, and a medieval past in which Teutonic tribes had planted the original seeds of contemporary democracy" (Mancini 873). This strategy of aligning themselves with a Brahmin agenda had two salient effects.

First, it served to distinguish the Scandinavians from other immigrant groups. This was important because, although the bulk of the anti-immigrant propaganda was directed at the Jews from eastern Europe, the Italians from the "Sunny South," and the Irish, some anti-immigrant nativist groups lumped all immigrants together as a threat to American civilization. The charge was made that, together, all these groups were mongrelizing and degrading the native stock. But if the Norse (or, more generally, the Scandinavians) could be seen as ancestors and progenitors of that allegedly superior racial stock, then by definition they were already proto-Americans. As the cultural historian JoAnne Marie Mancini has pointed out, Anderson's *America Not Discovered by Columbus*, in particular, emphasized "the freedom-loving racial characteristics of the Norwegians" in order "to suggest to Americans that their own racialist ideology implied that race, rather than ethnicity or national origin, should be the primary category for judging immigrants." Thus "Scandinavians' racial heritage would make them good Americans without [the need for] abusive programs of assimilation" (882). Moreover, according to Mancini, by insisting upon the Norse as first discoverers, Anderson's text "insinuat[ed] the Norsemen into the heart of American national history" (883). No longer would old stock Americans from the Northeast view the new Scandinavian immigrants pouring into the Midwest as merely crude or alien backwoods farmers.

The second salient effect of aligning their arguments with the racialist historical agenda of Brahmin New England was that Anderson and Brown helped make the immigrants themselves feel like rightful Americans. After all, they said, Leif Eiriksson's first discovery had made possible all subsequent discoveries, whether by Columbus or the Cabots. Thus, both by race and by history, these new Scandinavian immigrants who followed in Leif Eiriksson's path were *entitled* to become Americans. In part, this is what Brown was asserting when she pled with the Senate subcommittee to recognize the Norse discovery so that "the Scandinavians of the United States" could thereby "be transformed from aliens into compatriots, sharing our pride in a common ancestry" (Shipley and Shipley, *The English Rediscovery and Colonization* of America* 31). Additionally, by stressing the physical vigor and spirit of independence of the ancient Norse, and ascribing these characteristics to their descendants, both Anderson and Brown tacitly suggested to their Scandinavian American readers that they themselves represented a surety against the danger of America's racial stock becoming degraded and effete. In short, as opposed to the immigrants from Ireland and from eastern and southern Europe, the immigrants from Scandinavia could now see themselves as the bulwark protecting the nation from committing race suicide.[31] It was an argument few other groups (with the exception of the English and Germans) could claim.

One unanticipated consequence of this kind of thinking came to the fore with the outbreak of the First World War in 1914. Although President Woodrow Wilson did not move the U.S. into that war until the spring of 1917, a great deal of anti-German propaganda flooded the American media, especially after a German submarine torpedoed and sank the British liner *Lusitania* in early 1915. The *Lusitania* was, in fact, functioning as a wartime cargo transport, secretly carrying arms and munitions from the U.S. to England, but this information was not released at the time. Consequently, the loss of 1,198 lives, including 124 Americans, was characterized in the press as a slaughter of innocents by inhuman "Huns" and scheming "Junkers." In the face of this new and growing anti-German hysteria, the notion that old stock Americans were descendants of ancient freedom-loving Germanic/Gothic/Teutonic tribes required some readjustment. Accordingly, as the historian Higham has pointed out, "The leading race-thinkers strove . . . to bring their theories into harmony with the spirit of the hour" (218).

Since "the spirit of the hour" was decidedly anti-German, the strategy employed was to prove that modern Germans weren't really Germanic after all. In several books and many more popular magazine articles, published both during and right after the war, a number of the "race-thinkers" argued that "most present-day inhabitants of Germany are Alpines rather than Nordics," that is, descendants of peoples from central rather than northern Europe (Higham 218).[32] Supposedly, "90 per cent of the German Nordics had been killed off in the wars of the previous three hundred years" (218). An admiring report on the views of one of these race theorists that appeared in the Hearst newspapers in 1918 even suggested that "the modern German population was actually descended from Asiatic barbarians" (218).

What was happening is clear: America's Nordic strain was being disentangled from its previous associations with northern Germanic tribes and modern Germanic peoples and undergoing, as it were, a kind of purification. References to early American colonists as descendants of Germanic or Teutonic peoples were excised from books about U.S. history, and American bloodlines were now characterized as Nordic, a term with longtime Viking associations. As Clinton Stoddard Burr, one of the major race theorists, put it in his book *America's Race Heritage* (1922), "Americanism is actually the racial thought of the Nordic race, evolved after a thousand years of experience" (208). In Burr's estimation, as "offshoots of England," the American colonies "were founded and settled by the purest Nordics from Northwest Europe, by intensely liberty-loving, capable folk" (208). Of course, this is precisely what the passionate (and even the dispassionate) partisans of the Leif Eiriksson discovery story had been arguing all along. It had always been their contention that America owed its democratic institutions to its historic heritage from the Northmen, and that this could best be recognized by honoring Leif Eiriksson as the true discoverer. But, ironically, in the upsurge of racialist thinking that followed the First World War, both Vinland and Leif Eiriksson were pushed aside. Neither is mentioned in *America's Race Heritage* nor in most books of its ilk. Instead, newly aided and abetted by the supposed science of eugenics, the issue became a call for "a cessation of immigration to save America for Nordic humanity" (231).[33] Thus, the racialist and ethnocentric paradigms that had always nestled at the core of the romance were now displacing the adventure of first discovery and attempted colonization, which once figured so prominently in America's romance with a Viking past.

6

"We could not discerne any token or signe, that ever any Christian had been before":

THE PHANTOM OF FIRST CONTACT

A people who called themselves *Etchemins*, meaning "real people" as opposed to animals, monsters, and other people [once occupied a] homeland stretch[ing] from the Kennebec to the Saint John River. . . . West of them lived a people the French called *Armouchiquois*, from the Etchemin word meaning "dog people." Included among them were the Abenakis ("dawn land people"), whose homeland extended from the Kennebec to the Merrimack River, and west to Lake Champlain. Their name for themselves was *Alnambak*, meaning "real people"; the name Abenaki is what Indians living in Quebec called them.

North and east of the Etchemins lived people the French called *Souriquois*, known today as Mi'kmaqs (meaning "kin friends"). Their original name for themselves was *L'nu'k* meaning . . . "humans" or "people."

All these people spoke closely related languages, and had long traded with one another. . . . This peaceful exchange was upset in the sixteenth century with the arrival of the French in Mi'kmaq country. Redirecting their trade to these newcomers . . . the Mi'kmaqs gained access to guns and sailing vessels, allowing them to raid their neighbors along the coast for the things they had earlier obtained through trade. Allied with them in this raiding were the Etchemins living east of Schoodic, who are known today as Passamaquoddys ("people of the pollack plenty place") and Maliseets ("funny talkers"). Collectively, these people were called *Tarrentines* ("traders") by the English.

To defend themselves against these raiders from downeast, the western Etchemins entered into an alliance with those Abenakis living between the Kennebec and Cape Neddick. Known as the *Mawooshen* Confederacy, the name means "band of people walking or acting together." . . .

Disaster befell the Mawooshen Confederacy in 1615, when Mi'kmaq raiders managed to kill [the grand chief of the Confederacy].

On top of this came "the great dieing," an epidemic that killed off up to 90 percent of coastal populations. To replenish their numbers, the local Etchemins encouraged their surviving Abenaki allies, who were under pressure from the growth of English colonies to the south, to join their communities. It is these descendants of the old Mawooshen Confederacy who became known as Penobscots....

By 1700, in the face of continued pressures from the English, the Penobscots joined with other Abenakis as well as their former adversaries downeast to form the Wabanaki ("dawn land") Confederacy. On a grander scale, it represented a revival of the old Mawooshen idea. Still today, these people of northern New England and Canada's Atlantic Provinces are collectively known as Wabanakis.

—WILLIAM A. HAVILAND, "Who Was Here First?" (2008)

After having seen two or three Indians do the same thing, it is at once reported to be a custom of the whole *Tribe*.... Add to this that there are many tribes in these countries who agree in a number of things, and differ in many others; so that, when it is said that certain practices are common to the Indians, it may be true of one tribe and not true of another.

—From FATHER PAUL LE JEUNE (1633),
in Reuben Gold Thwaites, *The Jesuit Relations* (1896–1901)

First Peoples in the Dawnland

If, from the colonial period through the nineteenth century, many influential Euro-Americans had persuaded themselves that burial mounds and massive ceremonial centers could only have been produced by some archaic non-Indian "higher" civilization, early twentieth-century anthropologists proved no more adept at accepting Native Americans' longtime tenure in the land. In part, this may be because advanced scientific tools for accurately dating many artifacts did not really become available until later in the century. Thus the highly regarded physical anthropologist at the Smithsonian Institution's National Museum of Natural History, Dr. Aleš Hrdlička, insisted that "not a scrap of bone or implement . . . can generally and with full confidence be accepted as geologically ancient." In an article in *Scientific American* in July 1926, he concluded unequivocally, "As to the antiquity of the Indian himself, that cannot be very great" (qtd. in Thomas, *Skull Wars* 148). But their own origin stories as well as "linguistic distributions in the Northeast" suggest that the Algonquian-speaking peoples whom English, French, and Dutch colonists would eventually dispossess had, in fact, "been a very long time in place" (Haviland and Power 66).[1] The archaeological remains of a Native campsite in Highgate, Vermont, for example, date back at least 9,000 years.

According to the archaeologists William A. Haviland and Marjory W. Power, both linguistic and archaeological evidence support the view that, after successive population influxes—most from the Southwest—by at least six thousand years ago (and likely even before), "speakers of Proto-Algonquian dialects probably lived in a belt stretching from the Great Lakes across New York and New England into the Atlantic Provinces of Canada to southern Labrador" (67; see also 201–2).[2] By the sixteenth century and the beginning of major European contacts, peoples speaking languages related to the Eastern Algonquian family ranged at least as far south as present-day North Carolina (see Simmons 11).

At some point in this long history, Iroquoian-speaking peoples from a homeland in the Appalachian uplands also began moving toward the Northeast. As Haviland and Power explain, "Prior to 2500 b.c., New York and New England were probably occupied exclusively by people speaking Proto-Algonquian dialects. At that point, speakers of an early Iroquoian dialect expanded into south central New York; later expansion by Iroquoian speakers caused a separation between speakers of Central and Eastern Algonquian" (68).[3] The permanent settlement of Iroquoian speakers within what had once been the exclusive territory of Algonquian speakers introduced not only a wedge separating previously contiguous peoples but also a new source of cultural influence. This led to competition for trade and game, to periods of warfare, and, as well, to trade and to exchanges of technology and the transference of such things as clay pottery styles.

Perhaps because of this confrontation with cultural difference or, more simply, because of their longtime contiguity and trade relationships, well before the European assaults of the sixteenth century, the ancestors of those who are currently known as the Wabanaki peoples had developed a variety of cooperative alliances and, together, demonstrated "considerable linguistic and cultural unity when compared to their neighbors, the Iroquois-speaking Mohawks to the west, the Central Algonquian-speaking Cree-Montagnais-Naskapi north of the St. Lawrence, and the various Algonquian-speaking peoples of the Hudson Valley and southern New England" (Haviland and Power 156–57). Originally dependent solely on hunting, fishing, and gathering, about two thousand years ago, where climate and soil conditions permitted, some of these peoples began growing "hard flint corn, kidney beans, and squash, as well as tobacco" in extensive village gardens (Prins, "Children of Gluskap" 104).[4] Scholars estimate that by exploiting the advantages of field rotation, a village of four hundred people might easily have utilized between 330 and 580 acres for planting over a fifty-year period (see Prins, "Children of Gluskap" 104). A salubrious growing season could produce crops sufficient for the needs of the village *and* surplus for barter. At a major trading site at Naskeag in Maine, there is considerable archaeological evidence that farm produce was exchanged for animal hides and for Mi´kmaq copper sourced to the Minas Basin off Nova Scotia. One aspect of this extensive trade "all too often overlooked," write Haviland and Power, is that, "traditionally, peoples in the Northeast did not trade with one another solely, or even primarily, to procure consumable commodities, no matter how useful these might have been. Rather, it was the act of trade itself that was important, for it provided a means of maintaining contact and communication between different communities that might otherwise be hostile to one another. Through trade, information was exchanged, conflicts resolved, and friendly relations maintained" (214).

To recover the full complexity of this world, in the words of one early English arrival, "as it was when the *Indians* solely possess it," however, is now almost impossible (Josselyn 105). Prior to the European onslaught that began in the sixteenth century, not only were there many more Native inhabitants living in Quebec, the Canadian Maritimes, and New England than those who survived the successive plagues and later warfare between European colonizers, but there were also many more distinctive groups and a wider array of cultural distinctions between groups. Even among the Eastern Algonquian-speaking Wabanaki ancestors, language and dialect boundaries reflected subtle differences in social organization, belief systems, ritual and ceremony, material culture, and a variety of other cultural features. Moreover, linguistic groupings did not necessarily signify homogeneous or identical cultural practices across communities. That is why, in 1633, the Jesuit missionary Father Paul Le Jeune repeatedly cautioned other missionaries against making facile assumptions about pan-tribal commonalities. What "may be true of one tribe," he noted, might "not [be] true of another" (qtd. in Thwaites 6:27). But in the face of almost two centuries of conflict—as Native peoples attempted to rein in European claims on their lands and then took sides as allies with the French or English in their wars for territory—whole villages died out or remnants of one group joined another. In that process, not only entire communities, but also many unique cultural practices, were lost forever.

In 1676, following the bitter and bloody conflict that the New England colonists called King Philip's War, for example, "some of the defeated Indians escaped northward to take refuge among the Abenaki in northern New England and New France" (A. Taylor 202). Three thousand Indians had died in the conflict, "a quarter of their population in southern New England" (202). At the beginning of the eighteenth century, the English tried to lure back Wabanaki peoples who had earlier fled to New France. In 1713, conferring with delegates from the Penobscot and Kennebec River areas, the English asked them, "Draw your remaining Indians from Canada into their Own places upon English Grounds" (qtd. in Dickason 117). Many responded to the appeal of regaining their traditional lands and did return, bringing with them family members, stories, and cultural practices adopted while in Canada. Still, the movements of peoples and cultural practices back and forth across borders and between communities was far from over. It would be repeated when the group now known as the St. Francis Abenaki of Odanak, Quebec, fled from Maine to Canada during the period that U.S. history texts label as the French and Indian Wars (roughly 1689 through the fall of Quebec and Montreal in 1759–60). And it would be repeated yet again as Algonquian communities sometimes took different sides, or even attempted neutrality, during the American Revolution.

Even before these dislocations, however, from the Canadian Maritimes throughout New England, the fur trade drastically altered the Indians' world. Eager to obtain the trade goods that pelts, especially beaver, could secure, bands and tribes extended their hunting territories and killed more animals. "The northern Algonquian peoples began to hunt throughout the year. A Montagnais explained, 'The Beaver does everything well, it makes kettles, hatchets, swords, knives, bread, in short, it makes everything'" (A. Taylor 98). With the men away for longer periods in increasingly remote regions, the women gradually assumed more responsibilities for managing village activities. And with the men now concentrating on hunting animals for the fur trade, rather than for food, the women compensated by stepping up their gathering and horticulture. Ironically, this made women and children even more dependent on the metal hoes obtained through the fur trade because metal hoes greatly eased the labor of tilling the soil for the planting of corn, beans, and squash. The old pattern of activities and encampments regulated by the four seasons was severely disrupted, and, in the end, beaver populations in the Canadian Maritimes and the northeastern U.S. were almost wholly depleted. Beyond all this, though, the Indians found themselves engulfed by warfare unlike any they had known before, warfare from which they often tried to run.

That said, what Native peoples could not outrun—and what no relocation could protect them from—were the devastating diseases introduced by Europeans. As Haviland and Power put it, by the turn of the sixteenth century, "boatloads of French and Portuguese fisherman were making regular trips to the Grand Banks, coming ashore to cure their catches and trade with the inhabitants. Although Newfoundland was the scene of most of these early contacts, they soon spread to the shores of the Maritimes. Between 1504 and 1534 there was frequent contact between Basque, Breton, British, Norman, and Portuguese fishermen and Micmacs, who in turn were in regular contact with their Abenaki neighbors to the south and west" (209). Through these contacts, diseases like cholera, diphtheria, influenza, measles, chicken pox, smallpox, bubonic plague, typhoid, and typhus were introduced by the Europeans into populations that had no immunity to them. And epidemics began to follow the Native peoples' own age-old cross-ethnic contacts with one another, whether summer gatherings or meetings for trade.

The nature of the trade changed, too. Rather than allow Europeans to control the trade (and reap all its profits), sea-hardy Mi'kmaq mariners stole or traded for French and Basque shallops and, by the 1580s, were serving as "middlemen who facilitated trade between French ships in the Gulf of St. Lawrence" and Algonquian-speaking fur hunters "as far south as Massachusetts" (Axtell, "The Exploration of Norumbega" 158; see also Bourque and Whitehead 142). When Bartholomew Gosnold led the first English exploration of the New England coast in 1602, one member of his crew reported meeting with just such a party of Native middlemen near what is now Cape Neddick, Maine. There were "six Indians in a baske [i.e., Basque] shallop with a mast and saile, an iron grapple, a waistcoat and breeches of black serge, made after our sea fashion, hose and shoes on his feet" (qtd. in Bourque and Whitehead 132). As with the Indians in the Basque shallop encountered by Gosnold's company, Native traders described by subsequent Europeans had also adopted elements of European dress and spoke a language that included French, English, and Basque vocabularies. They had quickly become dominant traders and easily mastered even the largest European sailing vessels. A seventeenth-century Jesuit missionary commented that the Mi'kmaq handled these ships "as skillfully as our most courageous and active sailors in France" (qtd. in Bourque and Whitehead 140). But the sad irony of this success was that the Native sailors had now also become lethal disease carriers, from the shores of Nova Scotia to the Saint Lawrence and the entire Gulf of Maine.

The earliest epidemics went unreported, and, for a time, Europeans continued to note only the handsomeness and health of the Native peoples. Indeed, a protein-rich diet and the regular use of sweat baths had once made the Wabanaki strong and healthy. And without domesticated livestock—with which European peasants often lived in close proximity—Native peoples were not exposed to the pathogens carried by these animals and the disease vectors they represented. In Maine, the would-be English colonist John Josselyn described the local Indians as "tall and handsome timber'd people" who "live long, even to an hundred years of age" (89, 93).

Even so, Europeans were not entirely blind to what was happening. One French missionary commented that the Mi´kmaq and other eastern Wabanaki peoples "are astonished and often complain that since the French mingle with and carry on trade with them, they are dying fast and the population is thinning out" (qtd. in Bourque and Whitehead 144). Similarly, the charter of 1620 that formed the Council and authorized "the planting, ruling, ordering, and governing of New-England, in America" explicitly noted, "Within these late Yeares there hath by God's Visitation reigned a wonderfull Plague . . . amongst the Sauages." For the Pilgrims, "the utter Destruction, Deuastacion, and Depopulacion of that whole Territorye" represented a sign of God's special favor to his chosen people: "Almighty God in his great Goodness and Bountie toward Us and our People, hath thought fitt and determined, that those large and goodly Territoryes, deserted as it were by their naturall Inhabitants, should be possessed and enjoyed by . . . our Subjects and People" ("The Charter of New England" 69, 70). For the "naturall Inhabitants," that is, the Native peoples, by contrast, 1616 marked the height of the period called by both Indians and Europeans "the Great Dieing."[5]

The Illusion of Firstness

It has now become almost axiomatic among non-Natives who write about the history of North America that "the Indians who first beheld the white strangers from another world" left that event unrecorded (Axtell, *The Invasion Within* 7). In the opening chapter of *The Invasion Within* (1985), for example, James Axtell repeated the notion that Native peoples could not record their "first encounters" with Europeans because "they were unable to write down their impressions close to the event" (7). But aside from the question of what may or may not have been recorded, do we really even know what constituted a *first encounter*?

In 1605, at the behest of a group of Catholic investors in England, Captain George Waymouth explored the islands and coastal waterways of Maine in search of a suitable location to plant a colony. James Rosier, a member of the exploratory expedition (who may have been a Catholic priest), recorded a dated running narrative of the voyage which was published that same year in London. According to Rosier, Waymouth's company saw no "token or signe, that ever any Christian had been before" (139). This conclusion, Rosier explained, was based on the fact that the crew had spotted no indication of "cutting [of] wood, digging for water, or setting up Crosses (a thing never omitted by any Christian travellers)," and a task that the Waymouth group repeatedly and successfully accomplished.[6] Yet Rosier's descriptions of their many encounters with Native peoples make clear that they could not have been the first Europeans to visit the area. The Natives seemed at once sophisticated in the ways of trade with the Europeans and, at the same time, suspicious of them.[7] The Natives made clear that "they had Furres and Tabacco to traffique with us," but would not board Waymouth's vessel, insisting instead that the English come on land to trade (126).

Statements like these should make us at least skeptical of those many sixteenth- and seventeenth-century visitors to New England and New France who regularly reported that they were the first Europeans ever seen by the Natives and, as such, a source of wonder to them. The Europeans' motives for such assertions may have been political. Navigators sailing under patents from the French and English were generally instructed—as was Cabot in 1497—to "occupy and possess" *only* those lands "unknown to all Christians" (qtd. in Robert A. Williams 121). Similarly, Queen Elizabeth's patent to Walter Raleigh in 1584 enjoined him to explore and claim lands "not actually possessed of any Christian prince, nor inhabited by Christian people" (qtd. in Kornwolf 2:527). One way to claim *firstness*, and thus assert possession, was to report that the Natives greeted these ships as previously unknown wonders. Moreover, the emphasis on Native *wonder*, implying both naïveté and primitive development, helped persuade financial backers in Europe that these lands would prove relatively easy to "occupy and possess" because any local resistance could be handily overcome.

In reality, claims to *first* contact are almost impossible to verify. In addition to what we know to have been Norse contacts with indigenous peoples, there were many other contacts from Europe, and some of these much earlier than is generally recognized. As the historians Richard D'Abate and Victor A. Konrad point out, while "our understanding of the early explorations of the Northeast remains imperfect, . . . it is fairly certain that . . . the offshore banks of Labrador, Newfoundland, and Cape Breton were fished heavily starting in the early fifteenth century" (xxii). According to the archaeologist Alice Beck Kehoe, "there is [even] tenuous evidence" of Basque fishing vessels in the Canadian Maritimes "go[ing] back to the late fourteenth century" and "kept secret by Basque entrepreneurs" (198). If the evidence cited by Kehoe proves accurate, then these Basque vessels would have followed upon the last recorded Norse ship to carry a cargo of timber from Labrador (in 1347) by less than fifty years, and the Basque would have predated Columbus by a hundred years. What remains uncertain, however, is to what degree (beyond gathering fresh water and perhaps some hunting) these early fishing parties ventured onshore or encountered the local inhabitants.

All we know with certainty is that European fishing fleets had been skirting the coasts of North America at least since the second half of the fifteenth century, mostly in search of cod. According to the archaeologist Brian Fagan, "In the eighth century, the Catholic Church created a huge market for salted cod and herring by allowing the devout to consume fish on Fridays, the day of Christ's crucifixion, during the forty days of Lent and on major feast days" (69). Since fish spoils, however, and there was no means of refrigeration, "dried salt cod and salted herring quickly" became the fish of choice, both because they kept better than other fish and because they were easily transported in bulk (69). Of these, cod was preferred for its even greater durability. But after centuries of aggressive fishing by Basques, Bretons, and the English, the known cod stocks were becoming depleted. Eager for the riches that cod brought to national fisheries and enabled by improvements in ship design, "the more enterprising Basque and English skippers sought new fishing grounds farther out in the Atlantic" (76).

By 1450, the Basque were regularly fishing off Greenland and then probably dropped southward along the Labrador coast to Newfoundland "not soon afterward" (Fagan 77). "There," says Fagan, "they found not only whales but cod in abundance" (77). In 1480, British merchants also sent ships far to the west in search of cod (see Fagan 77). By 1497, when John Cabot sailed down the coast of Newfoundland, he encountered "a sea teeming with cod, where Basque fishing vessels abounded" (77). Maps of the period seem also to indicate that "the Portuguese were increasingly familiar with the Newfoundland coast and the Grand Banks in the early sixteenth century, and they may have engaged in some incidental trading with the Indians" (Snow, *Archaeology* 44). For some decades before the turn of the sixteenth century, therefore, Algonquian peoples who had long hunted in Newfoundland and Labrador and fished and followed the whales in the same waters, had observed—and perhaps even begun trading with—the steady seasonal stream of European fishing vessels that arrived each summer and then sailed with the fall westerlies. These fishing vessels may sometimes have cured their catches onshore.[8] The fact that we have no accounts of these early fishing expeditions written by the fishermen themselves is not surprising. The crews were rarely literate; even the captains probably had only minimal literacy. Most important, in the stiff competition for the cod trade, no vessel wanted to reveal the whereabouts of its fishing grounds. Still, they were seen by others, by explorers like Cabot and most likely by the local inhabitants.

Preserving Indigenous Memory

If, with regard to the Atlantic coast of North America, a moment of *first* contact with Europe is, at best, a slippery concept, then is the contention that Native peoples never recorded these so-called first encounters any more reliable? In other words, is Axtell's assertion that nonliterate Native peoples "were unable to write down their impressions close to the event" entirely accurate (*The Invasion Within* 7)? Setting aside the assumption that alphabetic literacy is the only means of recording an event, we can look to petroglyph evidence in Maine for at least a partial answer to that question.

In southern Somerset County in Maine, just downstream from treacherous rapids, "a ledge of metamorphosed shale juts out into the Kennebec [River], forming a natural dock for canoes and, as it happens, a relatively smooth surface for petroglyphs" (Snow, "The Solon Petroglyphs" 282). Because the ledge is located about a quarter mile below the Solon-Embden bridge, on the west (or Embden Township) side of the river across from the town of Solon, the rock images are variously referred to as the Solon Petroglyphs, the Embden Petroglyphs, or the Embden-Solon Petroglyphs. Most local residents say the glyphs are closer to Embden, so I will refer to them as the Embden Petroglyphs.

The anthropologist Dean R. Snow has studied the Embden site

intensively and reports that "there are about ninety distinct petroglyphs in a band eight meters long and two wide. Several more are too faint to be traced accurately, and the original number may have approached two-hundred" ("The Solon Petroglyphs" 282). The archaeologist Mark Hedden, who has studied all the known petroglyph sites in Maine, observes that at some sites, like Embden, "later designs may overlay earlier designs" ("3,500 Years" 10). This "indicate[s] repeated visits by more than one native practitioner, probably over periods of time ranging from a generation or two... to many centuries (Embden) to millennia (Machias Bay)" (8). Hedden has "concluded that recorded Maine petroglyphs constitute a culturally homogenous sample, with time depth of at least 3,000 years." They thus offer "a palimpsest" of Algonquian cultural expression from precontact through the postcontact period (7). Snow concurs and also places the Embden Petroglyphs "within the general distribution of Algonquian languages" and peoples ("The Solon Petroglyphs" 282).

One particular glyph at Embden is clearly from the "historic" period and seems to illustrate Hedden's contention that "the imagery and subjects in the petroglyphs changed after European contact" ("Contact Period" 11). While some have tried to identify the glyph as a Native dwelling or as the building in which "the local chief and his councilors met," most observers—both Native and non-Native—say it is definitely not an Indian structure (Ray 18). Apparently carved at a later period from the other glyphs at Embden, the center of this glyph shows, according to Hedden, a European-style "post and beam structure with parallel arcs into the gable roof" ("Contact Period" 10). Hedden identifies the structure as "represent[ing] a chapel built at Old Point in Norridgewock for the Jesuit Father Rasles in 1722" (10). The "parallel arcs into the gable roof" he identifies as symbolizing "the path to the sky," or heaven, an adaptation of an old Algonquian "lattice" figure.[9] (See figure 9.) Hedden's speculation derives from the fact that "the petroglyph ledge... is not far upstream from Father Rasles Jesuit mission at Old Point. In a 1722 letter... Father Rasles expressed his pride in his last chapel, a fine building constructed by a carpenter... hired from the New England colonies by the Norridgewocks," an Abenaki/Wabanaki people (10, 18, n. 2).

Hedden may well be correct in this identification, although the absence of any cross on the glyph—a cross that would surely have been prominently affixed to Rasles's chapel—leaves open another possibility. The first building like this that was seen by local Algonquian peoples was the large storehouse with a north gable end constructed

The Phantom of First Contact   267

9. Detail from Embden Petroglyphs in Maine,
showing a European-style structure which appears to
have a gable roof and what may be the outline of a fence or
palisade and some kind of fowl within that enclosure.
Photograph copyright Mark Hedden.

in 1607 as part of the short-lived Popham Colony located at the tip of Sabino Head near the mouth of the Kennebec River.[10] (The colonists named their settlement Fort St. George, but it has come to be known by the name of its first elected leader, Captain George Popham.) The colony was built as a fort, with a palisaded fence enclosing the storehouse and several cabins. Thus the curved parallel lines joined by spaced bars, which appear to emerge from the left of the pitched roof, and identified by Hedden as the "path to the sky," may more probably represent a surrounding fence or palisade. There also appear to be fowl of some kind—ducks, geese, or chickens—just below that enclosure. Because the colony was relatively well funded and well supplied, we may presume that the colonists brought with them breeding fowl from Europe.[11] The storehouse itself was the largest building within the enclosure and was of medieval-style "earthfast" construction, which often resembles post-and-beam construction. But earthfast structures were quicker to put up because they required less preparation of the beams and no foundation.

Reports composed by several of the colonists suggest that the local Native peoples were at first suspicious of the newcomers. Just two years earlier, the English captain George Waymouth had treated the Indians treacherously and kidnapped five young men. Possibly because two of those captives had been repatriated and now spoke some English, there was a period of trade and accommodation between the Indians and the colonists before relations altogether soured. The Popham colonists had brought with them several cannons. From their brief sojourn in England, the two repatriated Natives surely knew the damage a cannon might do. Moreover, the continuous exploratory expeditions sent out by the colony may well have suggested to the local bands that still more English colonists would follow and establish additional permanent settlements.[12] Relations between the Indians and the English became increasingly tense. As a consequence, feeling themselves threatened, after little more than a year, the one hundred or so (all male) colonists returned to England in the fall of 1608. But the Natives' memory of this first English colony in their midst may remain preserved in the rocks at Embden, perhaps intended as a kind of warning against future such settlements. In short, whether we take the Embden petroglyph to represent Father Rasles's chapel or the earlier Popham Colony storehouse, it is clear evidence that Algonquian peoples employed petroglyphs to record not just ritual or shamanic experiences but also this-world historical events, including what the Natives perceived as important early contacts with Europeans.

If any further evidence is required, that evidence is provided by Hedden in his review of "Contact Period Petroglyphs in Machias Bay, Maine." There Hedden discusses "three pecked . . . representations of seventeenth century sailing vessels" at different locations around the bay (1). "The architecture of the three single-masted ships," he writes, "matches the known features of small vessels used by French, English, and Dutch mariners of the first third of the seventeenth century . . . based on an analysis of visible features of hull and rigging" (1, 3). Their location in the Machias Bay area places them "in the approximate center of the historic range of Passamaquoddy/Malecite groups" (2). Their subject matter leaves no doubt that "the making of petroglyphs by Native Americans in Machias Bay continued through the Contact period and into the historic period" (17). Moreover, according to Hedden, "the ship images are directly associated with traditional Native American imagery and show the same manner of execution" (1). Thus, despite their new and different subject matter, these petroglyphs of seventeenth-century sailing vessels reveal both verifiable historical data *and* considerable cultural continuity.

Clearly, the petroglyph carvers at Machias Bay went to considerable lengths to incise telling details. The shapes of the three vessels are, variously, "good matches for the superstructure in English, Dutch and Flemish galleons constructed between 1585 and 1590" and the Dutch Cromster of 1600 (Hedden, "Contact Period" 6). And even though all three of the Machias Bay ship glyphs display a single main mast, they also show rather different configurations for their multiple sails and rigging, consistent with the different kinds of ships being depicted. None of this should surprise since the carvers at Machias Bay were themselves members of groups who depended on the rivers and the ocean for much of their food supply. They were expert mariners in their own right, and they would have been acute observers of other peoples' ship technology.

Of course, as Hedden and most other archaeologists and anthropologists agree, "by tradition the petroglyphs were made by Native American religious leaders we call shamans" ("Contact Period" 1). Even so, this does not exclude the depiction of this-world historical events that the shaman needed to manipulate and the group needed to remember and pass on. The glyph images discussed here, after all, represented portentous events that surely required communication with and, possibly, interventions from the *manitous* (i.e., kin beings) or "grandfathers."[13]

At Machias Bay, a shaman carver may have been both recording real events and, at the same time, importuning the "grandfathers" to help him appropriate the powers of the strange vessels for his own purposes. Through the intercession of the manitous, the shaman symbolically converted the strangers' vessel into his own. Indeed, the very act of recording these unique vessels by pecking them into the rock face was also a (symbolic) form of capturing and taking possession of them. The images were thus reservoirs of potency that could be called upon again and again. The ships thereby became the shaman's, for rituals and for his own spirit-journeys. And the ships forever also became his peoples'—as a reminder of any stories associated with them. Moreover, at the time of their carving (and presumably for a long time afterward), these "pictorial-iconic representations could be read and interpreted by many people other than their creator" (Boone 22). They thus permitted intelligibility across family, band, and even ethnic divisions; they also permitted intelligibility across dialect barriers. In that way, the ongoing recording of images on rocks once ensured a dynamic continuity of historical and cultural memory among the Wabanaki. My point, then, is simply this: as evidenced by the petroglyphs at Embden and at Machias Bay—and contrary to received assumptions—Native peoples did indeed attempt to record at least their early *significant* (if not their *first*) experiences of "behold[ing] the white strangers from another land" (Axtell, *The Invasion Within* 7).

Yet however useful, rock engravings had their limitations. Weathering could gradually erode the images. The ledges at important sites could become so filled up and layered over that new images were difficult to add, and old ones became difficult to read. Even more important, restricted as they were to certain "power places," rock engravings were not portable. Their communicative potential required the physical presence of those who could make sense of them. Over time, then, as the authority of the shamans was gradually eroded under the influence of the missionaries, as some groups were removed from their homelands, and as the appropriate sites for carving petroglyphs became less accessible under pressure from European settlement, the *stories* recorded in the glyphs became ever more dependent on oral transmission. What must be understood, therefore, is that the petroglyphs had never been graphic images that stood in isolation. They had always functioned as cues that reminded some "reader" or storyteller of the events associated with the image. Thus Hedden likens the glyphs to "beads on a rosary string" ("3,500 Years" 8). The petroglyphs were the skeleton that cued an elder, a shaman, or a storyteller to go beyond those details captured in the rock images and *flesh out* the entire story.

One of the most vivid impressions made upon Europeans who met them for the first time was that "the Indians were very fond . . . of hearing stories" (Denys 418). Even when those same Europeans understood neither the meaning nor the import of the stories to which the Indians "all listened in deep silence," they did at least recognize that Native stories were serious business, albeit often attended "with intervals for laughing" (419). As the Frenchman Nicolas Denys observed among the Mi'kmaq of Acadia in the 1650s and 1660s, every story "was always as heard from a grandfather" and frequently referred to "matters . . . ancient" (418–19). Some stories (really story cycles) even "required all the day and evening" for their telling (419).[14] The orderly transmission of tradition—and storytelling in particular—was short-circuited, however, by the staggering death tolls from imported diseases and ongoing warfare. Most vulnerable to disease were the very old, the keepers of the community's knowledge, and the very young, those to whom, under ordinary circumstances, that knowledge would have been transmitted.

During the colonial period, most Eastern Algonquian-speaking communities in Canada and northern New England allied themselves with the French, while the Iroquois allied with the English, and a few southern New England Algonquian-speakers, especially in the Cape Cod area, also allied with the English. Later, these groups became even more divided in their competing loyalties to the British and the "Americans" during the Revolutionary War. As a consequence, Wabanaki nations in particular and Eastern Algonquian-speakers in general sometimes fought on different sides and shed one another's blood. More often, though, in order to survive white incursions, Wabanaki peoples took in refugees across ethnic lines, intermarried, and formed a confederation for the future protection of their lands and people. But as whole villages died out and remnants of one group joined another, over time, certain stories and legends particular to one group were altogether lost or became conflated with similar or analogous stories and legends from another group. Additionally, under the influence of missionaries and a "civilizing" education imposed by a surrounding non-Indian populace, Wabanaki peoples (as they had always done) revised their stories in order to adapt to yet another experiential reality. Yet however altered or adjusted, stories and storytelling persisted as Wabanaki peoples determinedly attempted to hold on to at least some of their traditional cultural practices and belief systems.

Thus, despite the challenges of imported diseases, warfare, dispossession, population losses, forced acculturation, and coerced religious conversions, Wabanaki peoples preserved many stories, even if in truncated or piecemeal fashion, and storytelling remained a vital part of Native culture. Because of that, from the 1840s through the 1880s, the Baptist missionary Silas Tertius Rand was able to collect a wealth of Mi'kmaq and Maliseet stories in Nova Scotia. At about the same period, Charles Godfrey Leland collected stories from Algonquian-speaking peoples in New England for *The Algonquin Legends of New England* (1884). And one of Leland's many assistants, Abby Langdon Alger, recalled that "in the summer of 1882 and 1883, . . . whenever I found myself in the company of Indians[, t]he supply of legends and tales seem[ed] to be endless" (vii).

Similarly, through the 1940s, the folklorist Fanny Hardy Eckstorm continued to collect and publish the stories told her by her (mostly Penobscot and Passamaquoddy) Maine neighbors. And from about 1904 until his death in 1950, the anthropologist Frank G. Speck repeatedly lived among and produced major ethnographic studies of Iroquoian- and Algonquian-speaking groups in Canada, Maine, Connecticut, Virginia, and elsewhere. Perhaps because his family was of mixed Dutch and Mahican heritage, and he himself had spent his grammar school years in the care of a Mohegan family friend who was one of the last Native speakers of the Algonquian languages of southern New England, Speck not only learned Native languages readily but also routinely included stories in most of his published studies.[15] Following in their teacher's footsteps, Speck's students Wilson D. Wallis and Ruth Sawtell Wallis studied the Mi'kmaq first in 1911–12 and then again in 1953. In 1955 they produced an ethnographic comparison of the Mi'kmaq in the two different time periods, and they included in their book *The Micmac Indians of Eastern Canada* almost two hundred pages of stories and story fragments.[16]

That said, there are hints in the writings of all these collectors that they sensed how perishable were the oral cultures they so assiduously recorded. Despite an often unspoken acknowledgment shared with their sources that many of these stories could be lost when the storyteller died, the collectors also picked up their informants' conflicted responses to sharing the stories with outsiders. As Alger put it in her preface to *In Indian Tents* (1897), "Only the very old men and women remember these stories now; and though they know that their legends will soon be buried with them, and forgotten, it is no easy task to induce them to repeat them" (viii). Her mentor, Leland, stated, "The old Indians all declare that most of their lore has perished" (*The Algonquin Legends of New England* 7). After almost forty years of weekends spent collecting stories across the Maritime Provinces of Canada, Rand noted, "I have never found more than five or six Indians who could relate these queer stories; and most, if not all, of these are now gone" (qtd. in Webster vi). In 1911, the Wallises discovered that "with few exceptions, only the older men, and indeed only a few of these, knew many tales" (Wallis and Wallis 319). Repeatedly, like Alger, Leland, Rand, and the Wallises, these non-Native collectors seem to have anticipated the 1997 warning of the poet, novelist, and essayist N. Scott Momaday (Kiowa) that the "ancient chain of language we call the oral tradition" is "always but one generation removed from extinction" (10). Yet insofar as the old stories remained alive, they too represented one means of recording what Denys referred to as "matters . . . ancient," including memories of early encounters with Europeans.

Following a Will-o'-the-Wisp

In June 2000, Wayne Newell, a Passamaquoddy elder, educational leader, and a teacher at the Pleasant Point School in Indian Township, Maine, agreed to talk with me, even though he had communicated in advance that he didn't think he could be of much help. On a drizzly overcast afternoon, we chatted on a screened-in porch at the back of his home on the Passamaquoddy reservation near Peter Dana Point. On the other side of the lake on which his house was perched, he pointed out, was an archaeological dig site estimated to be 5,500 years old. His people and their ancestors had been in Maine for a very long time.

Newell seemed both amused and bemused by my project. "We're the descendants of people who were converted from their original beliefs," he reflected, "and alienating you from your traditions is part of the conversion process." This reminded him of an old story in which a young Passamaquoddy is knocked out somehow and awakes to find himself in the realm of the *Mikumwess*, the "little people" or "rock people." Over time, the young man comes to enjoy living with the Mikumwess—until, that is, he learns that the price for staying with them is the surrender of his own religion. The message of the story, of course, is that the price of admission to the world and culture of some Other is the abandonment of an essential part of who you were before. Surely once a cautionary tale for those who encountered the proselytizing missionaries of old, it is a story that may not survive much longer. As Newell explained, what still remained of the oral tradition among the Passamaquoddy had been further eroded during the 1960s by the introduction of television, which replaced many of the rituals of family storytelling; by the increased availability of telephones, which reduced the frequency of visits between friends and relatives (and, hence, other storytelling opportunities); by the spreading out of the community into areas beyond the reservation, and, with that, the loss of fluency in the language. Even the larger houses which accompanied increased prosperity had had an impact: larger houses with many rooms provided private space within the family and thus less contact between family members, especially cross-generational contact.

That loss of formal and frequent storytelling notwithstanding, Newell shared some of his own curiosities and conjectures. He recalled, for example, that in the stories he had heard as a child, the Wabanaki culture hero Gluskap was described as "fair-skinned." And he said he'd always wondered why the Beothuk (an Algonquian group that occupied Newfoundland in the precontact era but died out in the nineteenth century) had supposedly moved inland from their coastal villages in ancient times and been described in early documents as notably "fearful" of Europeans. Could they have been driven inland by some hostile encounter with Vikings, he wondered?[17] And had Beothuk memory of that contact persisted over time to influence their reaction to later contacts with Europeans?

Newell was familiar with the two Vinland sagas, he said, and certain elements within them rang familiar. The noisemakers brandished by the Skraelings to scare off the Norse reminded him of homemade flutes or whistles whirled on the end of a string, a noisemaker he too had made as a child. Wabanaki peoples had once regularly employed such devices to frighten enemies by convincing them that their "numbers were larger than they actually were." The red cloth that the Norse offered in trade for pelts would have been valued by his people because "red was a spiritual color" for the Passamaquoddy. But when all was said and done, Newell could recall hearing no stories that clearly related to any arrival of the Norse.

In his view, such stories would initially have been treated as "local news," interesting but not necessarily resonant with wider meaning. Over time, the "local news" might have been forgotten altogether, or, if there had been repeated or memorable contacts, that news might have been turned into "old" stories passed from one generation to another. But as the Indians found themselves overwhelmed by new invaders who could neither be ignored nor defeated, and as their populations dwindled from disease and constant warfare, the older stories of strangers arriving from the east by sea got eclipsed by the new catastrophe, or the old stories were remade to fit the new situation. Still, he thought, some fragments might survive somewhere.

The author and storyteller Joseph Bruchac (Western Abenaki) is convinced that there are survivals. After decades of collecting the lore and legends of Eastern Woodlands peoples, both Iroquoian and Algonquian, he firmly believes that "traditional stories have real historical memories within them." When we chatted at his home in Greenfield Center, New York, in March 2003, he said, "We have stories among the Abenakis that go back to ten thousand years ago." So survivals in stories of events that went back only a thousand years struck him as very likely. Although he knew of no old stories that explicitly identified their protagonists as Norse (or Viking), he was aware of several with tantalizing clues. Wabanaki peoples, in particular, had long told of ancient encounters with "hard-skinned dangerous people who came from the north." Arrows were said to bounce off their skins, and these strangers were described as having "no human sympathies." Obviously, it is tempting to speculate that stories of "hard-skinned dangerous people who came from the north" might suggest parties of Norse exploring southward from L'Anse aux Meadows, wearing chain mail tunics to protect themselves in potentially hostile territory. Arrows would appear to bounce off their skins. But heavy chain mail tunics would have been extremely uncomfortable attire for an exploratory expedition. Moreover, Eskimoan peoples from the Arctic were also venturing southward during this period, and they are known to have worn a kind of armor made from stringing together the split bones of animals (see LeBlanc 23). Arrows would have appeared to bounce off their bodies, too.

Bruchac also recalled that Willie Dunn (Mi'kmaq métis) had once told him a Mi'kmaq story said to come down from precontact times. In this story, a group of Mi'kmaq in a canoe were lost in a dense fog, when they met up with an unfamiliar kind of boat with a number of strange people in it. The strangers were described in the story as "liver-colored, or pink." The two groups "helped one another get their bearings" and then parted. For Bruchac, stories like these contain memories of the earliest contacts with Europeans, perhaps Norse, and invite further investigation.

Mi'kmaq mothers and grandmothers on traditional lands along the Miramichi Bay in New Brunswick, Canada, still sometimes tell their children that their people have blue eyes because they are the descendants of Vikings. Some Mi'kmaq claim Viking ancestry on the basis of the fact that early explorers described Indians in their area as light-skinned with green or even blue eyes. Yet, as many historians point out, from the second half of the fifteenth century onward, any number of European fishing fleets hauling cod off the Labrador coast could easily have explored southward into the Gulf of Saint Lawrence and the large inviting bay of the Miramichi or into other Mi'kmaq territories along the Saint Lawrence River. Moreover, in 1525 the Portuguese founded a short-lived colony somewhere on the north side of Cape Breton Island, on the edge of Mi'kmaq territory. That same year, a fifty-ton Spanish caravel landed at Cape Breton, returning to Spain filled with male and female captives for slaves. The anthropologist Harald E. L. Prins speculates that if the captives were Mi'kmaq, then the Mi'kmaq code of revenge "would have spelled disaster for Cape Breton's fledgling [Portuguese] colony," and he notes a French pilot's log from 1559 that reported the Natives having "put an end" to the little settlement (*The Mi'kmaq* 45). If there were any European survivors, Prins further speculates, then perhaps "some women and children" were allowed to live and may have been adopted (45). So even if the claims about the earliness of these traits are accurate, light-colored eyes and brown or blond hair might have derived from several sources. In short, while traditions about contacts with peoples from elsewhere, long before the sixteenth century, permeate the stories of Native groups along the Atlantic seaboard, we can never really be certain to what they may refer. Still, as Bruchac has written, "Long before Columbus, some of our stories tell us, men came from the direction of the sunrise and stayed for a time" (*Our Stories* 46–47).

But in the twenty-first century, to recover among Native peoples any reliable trace memory of a contact that occurred a thousand years in the past is like following a will-o'-the-wisp, that faint elusive light that sometimes plays at night over marshy grounds. At best, there are hints, tantalizing clues, and conjectures. Even what appears at first as hard evidence turns out to be subject to conflicting interpretations. Yet stories about *some* first contacts—or even first sightings—have endured.

Sitting in his office on Indian Island one afternoon in June 2005, James G. Sappier, then-chief of the Penobscot Nation, shared a story his mother had told to him and his siblings when they were children. His mother, Mary Madeline Polchies Sappier (also Penobscot)—called Madeline by her friends and family—had indicated that it was a very old story, passed down through the grandmothers. The story, as Chief Sappier remembered it, was as follows:[18]

> Long ago, our people were observing a large canoe coming up the river. The men were poling the canoe up through the river, as it was shallow and the tide was out. They were steadily moving up the river to a place where they finally tied it up. There were no women on this canoe. Where they tied up their canoe, today this place is called Winterport.
>
> They were strange looking men, very whitish, pale skinned and a lot of hair on their faces. They left the canoe and waded to shore and staying on the shore, they took red clay and mud from the river banks and placed it all over their bodies. Native women in seeing this thought they were trying to look like our Tribal members.
>
> In observing this the members [of the Penobscot group watching the strangers] thought that they were covering themselves with mud and red clay to look like us and also protect themselves from black-fly and mosquito bites. After they finished covering themselves, they then went inland and gathered food and water. They were not here long as within a couple of days they untied their canoe and rode the tide down the river in their large strange-looking canoe with strange-looking men. We followed them until they went out on the big water [i.e., the Atlantic Ocean].

> This canoe was much larger than our war canoe and held a lot more men. Our people did not know these people nor where they came from. No one in the Tribe approached them as they did not act right and were unknown strangers[,] some being very loud.

When he finished telling the story, Jim (as he invited me to call him), reiterated that, for her part, his mother knew only that this event had happened "a very long, long time ago, long before white people began arriving more frequently in greater numbers."

Unfortunately, despite the story's emphasis on the earliness of the event it describes, there is no way to know precisely when this sighting took place. We know only that it is thought to predate the more significant European arrivals of the seventeenth century and that it occurred near present-day Winterport, located a few miles above the southern end of the Penobscot River where it empties into Penobscot Bay and the Atlantic Ocean. Winterport is where the river turns from salt to fresh water. Both the men and their craft are unknown to the Native observers, and nothing in the story offers any definitive clue as to the identity of the "strange looking men." In order to be poled through the water at low tide, however, this "large strange-looking canoe" must have been a vessel with a relatively shallow draft. This feature was characteristic of the sixteenth-century Basque and French shallops as well as the Norse knarrs used by the Vinland colonists. Some of the later European vessels, like the small pinnaces, also had a relatively shallow draft, and the use of long oars to help "pole" a vessel through shallow waters was common practice among both the Norse and the later European arrivals. Moreover, most of the Europeans who came to America, whether as fishermen, explorers, or would-be colonists, were bearded, and many of these came onshore to gather food and water. As a result, a plausible case could be made that this story contains trace memories of a sighting of Norse, or a sighting of crew members from Champlain's exploratory expedition up the Penobscot River in 1604, or a sighting of any one of several other early European visitors to Maine. Or perhaps, as Wayne Newell might suggest, the story conflates traces of more than one early expedition that anchored for a time near Winterport before heading back "out on the big water."

All those possibilities aside, there is another aspect of Madeline Sappier's story that compels attention. Given the story's strong implication that it describes a *first* sighting of previously unknown men, the story is remarkably free of any suggestion of surprise, fear, awe, or wonder on the part of the Native observers. Instead, the story expresses a matter-of-fact curiosity about the reasons for the strangers' odd actions (covering themselves with red clay from the river bank) and a mild reproof of their "loud" behavior. To be sure, these Penobscot ancestors were wary and, all unseen, prudently watched the strangers and followed their craft until it entered the Atlantic. The Penobscots could also feel relatively secure because they knew themselves to be numerically superior, even though the strangers arrived in a canoe "much larger than a war canoe and held a lot more men." Still, the story tells us that the strangers "did not act right and were unknown," so why does their arrival raise no obvious alarm?

In an article published in 1994 titled "The Exploration of Norumbega," the historian James Axtell may have provided at least part of the answer. After surveying a wealth of fifteenth-, sixteenth-, and seventeenth-century documents written by Europeans who encountered Native peoples, Axtell concluded that "no matter how early a European ship is known to have touched on New England's shores, Indian reactions or possessions suggest that it had been preceded by others" (154). By way of example, Axtell cited the Portuguese navigator Gaspar Corte-Real. When Corte-Real kidnapped fifty-seven Indians in 1501, probably along the Maine coast, he was certain that other Europeans had been there before him. One Native possessed "a piece of broken gilt sword," which the Venetian ambassador in Lisbon identified as "certainly . . . made in Italy"; a Native boy was wearing in his ears "two silver rings," identified as made in Venice (qtd. in Axtell, "Exploration" 154). Very possibly, these had been barter items exchanged by John Cabot, an Italian from Genoa, who had sailed the North American coast in 1497 under a patent from Henry VII of England. But whatever the source of these items, one fact is certain: because in Native North America, communities knew what was going on in other communities within about a three-hundred-mile radius, by the turn of the sixteenth century, the arrival of strangers in the lands of the Wabanaki was already old news. That news had traveled the old traditional trading routes and been told and retold at the summer gatherings.

But there may be another, less obvious explanation for the apparent lack of alarm in Madeline Sappier's story. Among the Passamaquoddy of Maine, Leland found two very different versions of the coming of Gluskap, the shared Wabanaki culture-hero and culture-bringer. In *The Algonquin Legends of New England*, Leland included the following: "It is told in traditions of the old time that Glooskap was born in the land of the Wabanaki, which is nearest to the sunrise; but another story says that he came over the sea in a great stone canoe, and that this canoe was an island of granite covered with trees" (28–29). The second story does not appear in Rand, so there is no way to determine how widespread it may have been. Also, at the remove of well over a century since the story was collected, there is no way now to determine whether the story contains the kernel of some barely remembered ancient migration or some other ancient notable arrival from across the Atlantic.[19] At most, it suggests that the advent of a being (or beings) from some foreign land in a different kind of vessel—for both of which the stone canoe presumably serves as a synecdoche or symbolic correlative—was not such an exceptional idea after all, at least among some Wabanaki groups. To put it another way, sightings of strangers in strange vessels from "over the sea" did not necessarily imply *firstness*, nor did they always have to bode impending disaster.

7

Contact and Conflict Again

WHAT NATIVE STORIES TELL US

> The Great Spirit saw that the [white] man he had made wanted the whole world, therefore he sent him to chase the sun; when he comes to the great waters he shall make large vessels, so he can chase the sun across the great waters, because he wants all the world; he shall slay his brother because he wants all things; he shall know no one because he wants the power over all the earth. . . . The white man will feel it as a duty to his children to seek new lands for them, and . . . he will not rest until he finds the land the Great Spirit gave unto you. He shall not pass away without first having put his foot upon all the lands that have been made; therefore look for him always.
> —KLOSE-KUR-BEH'S [i.e., Gluskap's] prophecy in Joseph Nicolar, *The Life and Traditions of the Red Man* (1893)

> Even while struggling to maintain themselves within colonial relationships that sought to dispossess and then "disappear" them, Indian peoples forged their own modernity and destiny. Nowhere is Indian resistance and survival more remarkable than in their still incompletely successful efforts to persuade non-Indians to officially recognize their survival as Indian peoples.
> —JEAN M. O'BRIEN (White Earth Ojibwe), *Firsting and Lasting: Writing Indians out of Existence in New England* (2010)

The Dream of the Floating Island: A Mi'kmaq Tale

In part prompted by the research agendas of John Wesley Powell and the field research reports of people like Garrick Mallery at the Smithsonian Institution's Bureau of Ethnology (later the Bureau of American Ethnology), the 1880s saw what several scholars have called "an efflorescence" in the collection of Wabanaki artifacts and folklore (Day, "The Western Abenaki Transformer" 75). For folklorists, Wabanakis in both Canada and the U.S. were of special interest because, unlike so many of the western tribes, the Mi'kmaq, Maliseet, Passamaquoddy,

Penobscot, and Abenaki peoples still inhabited at least small portions of their former homelands, still knew many stories associated with those long-familiar landscapes, and still spoke their Native languages. Not since Schoolcraft's pioneering *Algic Researches* (1839) had Algonquian peoples been the subject of this kind of scholarship.

Unquestionably the most important contributor to the collection of Mi'kmaq (and some Maliseet) lore was Silas Tertius Rand (1810–99), born in Cornwallis, Nova Scotia. Ordained a Baptist minister in 1834, in the 1840s Rand became a preacher in Charlottetown, Prince Edward Island, and thereafter devoted the remainder of his life to mission activity among the Mi'kmaq. Largely self-taught, but with a gift for languages, Rand learned several Native dialects and began translating Protestant religious materials for the purpose of bringing the Indians into the Protestant fold.

His task, as he saw it, was to wrest the Indians from the "traditions of barbarism" and help them "to become like white men" (qtd. in Webster xviii). As he put it in 1850, this meant saving the Mi'kmaq from the "darkness, superstition, and bigotry of Romanism" (to which the Mi'kmaq had been converted by the Catholic French) and bringing them to Protestant enlightenment (*A Short Statement* 11). Intent on the "civilizing, educating and Christianizing [of] the semi-savage Indians of the maritime provinces," Rand poured most of his prodigious energies into running his mission in Hantsport, Nova Scotia, and into translating the Bible, hymns, and various religious tracts into the Mi'kmaq, Maliseet, and Mohawk languages (qtd. in Webster xvii). Thus, when a friend suggested that Rand undertake a more systematic collection of "Glooskcap Legends," the missionary replied that "he was unable to undertake so great a task—his work was Evangelization!" (qtd. in Whitehead, *Stories* 218). Even so, fascinated by the stories he was hearing, he managed to amass some nine hundred handwritten quarto pages between 1847 and 1889, most of it gathered from Native storytellers in Nova Scotia and Prince Edward Island. Rand's commitment to recording "the traditionary romances of the Micmacs" derived from his conviction that these stories helped to demonstrate "the intellectual capacity of the Indians" and thereby "the possibility of elevating them in the scale of humanity" (qtd. in Webster xlii–xliii).

As Rand described his method of collecting, the stories were related to him, "in all cases, in Micmac." He took notes in English (sometimes using Pitman shorthand) and then would later "write out the story in English from memory, aided by the brief notes [he] had made": "But this was not all; I always read over the story in English to the one who related it, and made all necessary corrections" (qtd. in Webster v). Once Rand was satisfied that he had an acceptable transcript of the story in English, he destroyed his original notes. As his editor and compiler stated in her preface to *Legends of the Micmacs*, "the translations only have been preserved, in no case the narration in the original language" (Webster v).

Eager to disseminate his evidence of the Mi'kmaqs' considerable intellectual capacities as well as to participate in the larger community of ethnologists and folklorists, Rand began to share some of his collected stories and his research on the Mi'kmaq language with others, including Schoolcraft and Mallery. He was particularly generous to the prominent folklore collector Charles Godfrey Leland, to whom he sent "a manuscript of eighty-four Micmac tales" in February 1884 (Leland, *The Algonquin Legends of New England* 7). When Leland mined Rand's as yet unpublished manuscripts for his own *Algonquin Legends of New England*, published later in 1884, he focused almost exclusively on the stories of "Glooskap, who is by far the grandest and most Aryan-like character ever evolved from a savage mind" (2). For Leland, this suggested a pre-Columbian Nordic influence, and he read into almost every Wabanaki tale in his collection evidence of that influence. "Its resemblance to the Norse is striking," he repeated throughout the volume (132–33). In this, Rand and Leland had much in common. Like Leland, Rand also "was convinced he found linguistic and folkloric evidence to tie Native North Americans to ancient civilizations of the Old World" (Abler, "Glooscap Encounters" 134–35).

Intrigued by Leland's repeated notice in Rand's manuscripts of "some curious coincidences between the Norse myths and those of the Wabanaki or Northeastern Algonquins [sic], to which branch the Micmacs belong," Eben Norton Horsford purchased Rand's manuscripts "soon after the death of Dr. Rand, in 1889" (Webster vi). Horsford then made a gift of Rand's papers to the Library of American Linguistics at Wellesley College "and placed [them] in the charge of the Department of Comparative Philology for publication" (vi). Subsequently, Horsford funded the publication of Rand's collection, *Legends of the Micmacs*, which finally appeared in 1894, five years after Rand's death. As Horsford knew, Leland had suggested that the "resemblances" he noted between Norse and Algonquian "myths" were "to be explained by the theory of direct transmission," that is, direct contact (vi).[1] Swept up by the nineteenth century's Viking craze, and convinced that Leif Eiriksson's Vinland had been situated near Cambridge along the Charles River, Horsford fervently hoped "that traces of the Northmen might be found in [Rand's] Indian tales, and that the language of the Micmacs might, upon closer study, reveal the impress of the early Norse invaders" (vii). So he saw to it "that [Rand's] works should be published, and thus placed within the reach of investigators" (vii).

In fact, there is no clear "impress of the early Norse invaders" in any of the Mi'kmaq stories collected by Rand, including his Gluskap stories. Even so, the story of a young girl's dream presages the fulfillment of Gluskap's prophecy about the coming of the white man, and it shares with many stories of Gluskap's farewell a sense of dire foreboding. The story was published twice, both times posthumously. Prepared for publication by Rand before his death, under the title, "The Coming of the White Man Revealed. Dream of the White Robe and Floating Island," the story appeared first in May 1890 in the *American Antiquarian*. Helen L. Webster, the faculty member in the Department of Comparative Philology at Wellesley College who oversaw the publication of Rand's full collection, *Legends of the Micmacs*, and wrote both the book's preface and its introduction, then published the story in 1894 under the title "The Dream of the White Robe and the Floating Island" in the *Legends* volume. Because the story is not widely known and has not previously been the subject of literary or textual analysis, I quote it here in full in the version from *Legends of the Micmacs* (225–27). This version includes two footnotes provided by Rand. In those few instances where the version published in the *American Antiquarian* is different, those differences are inserted in boldface within brackets.

[The Coming of the White Man Revealed.]
THE DREAM OF THE WHITE ROBE AND THE
FLOATING ISLAND.

[This account of the coming of the white man, revealed
to a young woman in a dream, was related to me by
Josiah Jeremy, Sept. 26, 1869.]

WHEN there were no people in this country but Indians, and before any others were known **[before they knew of any others]**, a young woman had a singular dream. She dreamed that a small island came floating in towards the land, with tall trees on it, and living beings,—among whom was a man dressed **[and amongst others a young man dressed]** in rabbit-skin garments. The next day she related her dream, and sought for an interpretation. It was the custom in those days, when any one had a remarkable dream, to consult the wise men, and especially the magicians and soothsayers.* These pondered over the girl's dream, but could make nothing of it. The next day an event occurred that explained it all. Getting up in the morning, what should they see but a singular little island, as they supposed, which had drifted near to the land and become stationary there! There were trees on it, and branches to the trees, on which a number of bears, as they supposed, were crawling about.† They all seized their bows, arrows, and spears, and rushed down to the shore, intending to shoot the bears; what was their surprise to find that these supposed bears were men, and that some of them were lowering down into the water a very singularly constructed canoe, into which several of them jumped and paddled ashore. Among them was a man dressed in white,—a priest with his white stole on,—who came towards them making signs of friendship, raising his hand towards heaven, and addressing them in an earnest manner, but in a language which they could not understand.

The girl was now questioned respecting her dream. Was it such an island as this that she had seen? Was this the man? She affirmed that they were indeed the same. Some of them, especially the necromancers, were displeased; they did not like it that the coming of these foreigners should have been intimated to this young girl, and not to them. Had an enemy of the Indian tribes with whom they were at war been about to make a descent upon them, they could have foreseen and foretold it by the power of their magic; but of the coming of this teacher of a new religion they could know nothing.

The new teacher was gradually received into favor, though the magicians opposed him. The people received his instructions, and submitted to the rites of baptism; the priest learned their tongue, and gave them the Prayer Book written in what they call *abootŭlooeëgäsĭk'* (ornamental mark-writing); a mark standing for a word, and rendering it so difficult to learn that it may be said to be impossible.

[No new paragraph; no break.] This **[And this]** was manifestly done to keep the Indians **[done for the purpose of keeping the Indians]** in ignorance. Had their language been reduced to writing in the ordinary way, the Indians would have learned the use of writing and reading, and would have advanced in knowledge so as to be able to cope with their more enlightened invaders; and it would have been a more difficult matter for the latter to cheat them out of their lands **[lands, etc.]** and other rightful possessions.

Such was Josiah's story. The priests who gave them this pictorial writing, whatever their motives may have been, certainly perpetrated one of the grossest possible literary blunders. It is bad enough for the Chinese, whose language is said to be monosyllabic and unchanged by grammatical inflection; but Micmac is polysyllabic, endless [**partly syllabic, "endless,"**] in its compounds and grammatical changes, and utterly incapable of being represented by signs.

* Like the Egyptians, Chaldees, and other nations.
† It is needless to say that it was a vessel with masts and yards, and sailors upon them moving about.

Like so many of the older Mi'kmaq narratives, this story is multilayered and complex. To begin with, the revelation of the strangers' imminent arrival comes as "a singular dream" dreamt by a "young woman" (later called a "young girl") rather than as a dream that came to any of "the wise men," "magicians," or "soothsayers." And when the young woman related her dream to them "for an interpretation," none of these could make anything of it. In general, among most of the Northeastern Woodlands tribes, "belief in knowledge gained through dreams" was ubiquitous and unquestioned (Phillips 62). Dreams could reveal "future events and the efficacy of courses of action" and dreams came to everyone (62). As the French missionary priest Chrétien LeClercq complained of the Mi'kmaq in 1691, "Our Gaspesians are still so credulous about dreams that they yield easily to everything which their imagination or the devil puts into their heads when sleeping and this is so much the case among them that dreams will make them come to conclusions upon a given subject quite contrary to those which they had earlier formed" (*New Relation* 227).

When any individual demonstrated a special capacity for frequent and powerful dreams, that person became a kind of formalized dream practitioner for the group. Among the Penobscot of Maine, such dreamers were "known as *ki'ugwa'sowi'no* 'man who searches about in dreams'" (Speck, "Penobscot Shamanism" 268). In the first decades of the twentieth century, Speck studied the Penobscot and reported he was told that, in earlier times, the duty of these dream practitioners "was to warn of danger so that those who received the warning could employ means to ward the trouble off or to avoid it. The power of the dreamer was employed not only for individuals but also for the benefit of the community. Before undertaking a hunting trip, parties would induce a dreamer to lie down, go to sleep, and 'look around.'" The hunting party would then proceed in accordance with "the dreamer's revelation. Dreamers, moreover, were often induced to accompany hunting or war parties in order to serve with their gifts of vision" (269). Such "dream functionaries," as Speck termed them, had also been active among "neighboring tribes (Micmac, Malecite, Passamaquoddy, Abenaki)," and there may even have been different kinds of practitioners (273, 272). While some "dream functionaries" seem simply to have slept in order to gain their visions, another class of dream practitioners employed "spirit" helpers or medicine bundles or drummed and sang in order to put themselves into a trance-like state (see Phillips 63).[2]

What appears to have rendered the young woman's dream "singular" was that it contained an order of information for which none of the recognized "dream functionaries"—that is, the "wise men, and especially the magicians and soothsayers"—were prepared. For those who could dream and predict all else in the Indians' precontact world, *this* dream was out of their ken. Had an Indian enemy "been about to make a descent upon them, they could have foreseen and foretold it by the power of their magic." But this was different. This dream had no precedent. And the fact that this dream could have no precedent was emphasized by the story's opening: this all took place "when there were no people in this country but Indians, and before any others were known."

What further underscores the unprecedented nature of the dream is the identity of the dreamer. She is a "young woman" whose youthfulness then gets emphasized when she is later called a "young girl." While everyone was expected to have dreams—boys and girls as well as adults of both sexes—and while females did sometimes become "dream functionaries," the point here is that the girl is *not* one of these. She cannot interpret her dream. But she is able to receive the dream precisely because she is so young. Because of her youth, her conceptual patterns are not yet fully formed. In other words, not yet fully trained or socialized into all her people's belief structures, she is able to see what they cannot. She still has the capacity to serve as a conduit for visions that go beyond what is already known or anticipated by her people, even if she cannot understand the meaning of what she envisions.

When the dream becomes manifest "the next day," there are subtle alterations between what was dreamt and what actually appeared. The young woman had reported seeing in her dream, on the floating island, "living beings,—among whom was a man dressed in rabbit-skin garments." But when the "singular little island . . . drifted near to the land and become stationary there," what the Indians saw were "a number of bears" who were subsequently identified as "men." And the man whom the girl dreamed was "dressed in rabbit-skin garments" now appeared, instead, as "a man dressed in white, — a priest with his white stole on." The girl affirms that what has materialized as "the coming of these foreigners" *is* what she saw in her dream. But the altered descriptors and the symbolic iconology of the story suggest much more.

In Mi'kmaq lore, the rabbit is a trickster figure, a figure whose actions bring disruption either by word or by deed (or by both together). In many stories, Rabbit (as a character whose name is capitalized in the story) is also usually a thief. Thus, the appearance of a rabbit figure — here "a man dressed in rabbit-skin garments" — is a warning of some imminent moment of chaos or disorder.

Additionally, the Mi'kmaq word for "bear" also carries the double meaning of "no one" or "not quite human."[3] In one recorded Mi'kmaq story, for example, two young girls get stuck in a tree and appeal to a passing bear, "Take us down — even if you are only a sort of man" (see Wallis and Wallis 425). And while bear meat was a delicacy among the Mi'kmaq, bears were also known to be dangerous. Bears are thus highly ambiguous figures in Mi'kmaq lore, at once sources of food, sometimes very human in their movements and actions, and yet capable of easily crushing the unwary hunter with their enormous bulk and strength (see Wallis and Wallis 35–36). That may explain why the Indians in the story "all seized their bows, arrows, and spears, and rushed down to the shore, intending to shoot the bears" — either as food or as harbingers of danger (or both).

Also symbolically significant is the transformation of "a man dressed in rabbit-skin garments" into the similarly phrased "a man dressed in white." White is one of the four colors of the traditional Mi'kmaq "medicine wheel" (also sometimes called "the wheel of life"). Among their other meanings, each of the four colors is associated with a direction, and white refers to the East (that is, the realm of the rising sun).[4] The "man dressed in white" is thereby associated with origins "to the east." Even more important, "the man dressed in white" is then further identified as "a priest with his white stole on." This connected train of association and transfiguration necessarily attaches a potentially ominous meaning to the priest, whose original incarnation was as a "man dressed in rabbit-skin garments." Taken together, the appearance of a trickster rabbit figure in the girl's dream, the *no one* (or "only a sort of man") bear-beings who turn out to be human, and the final emergence of "a man dressed in white" portray more than just the arrival of previously unknown foreigners from the East. These are all also warning signals of some impending disruption.

As his full title for the version in *The American Antiquarian* ("The

Coming of the White Man Revealed") as well as his bracketed prefatory note above suggest, Rand accepted this as a narrative about the *first* "coming of the white man," whom he appears to have assumed were the French. But the French probably were not the first Europeans encountered by the Mi´kmaq as, aside from the even earlier Norse, the other early exploratory ships were probably Basque or Portuguese fishing vessels. That history aside, what seems most to have interested the Baptist missionary is that the story provided both him and the storyteller an occasion to criticize the Catholic missionaries sent by the French. In fact, in the paragraph that precedes the break and in the two closing paragraphs, it may be difficult to know just where the storyteller Josiah Jeremy's voice breaks off and where Rand's begins. Did Jeremy actually state that the Mi´kmaq "*submitted* to the rights of baptism," thereby hinting at resistance, or was this Rand's (perhaps unconscious) editorializing? Moreover, given the historical records that seem to indicate the Mi´kmaq took readily to the hieroglyphic scripts designed for them by various Catholic priests, is it plausible that Jeremy characterized these scripts as "so difficult to learn that it may be said to be impossible"? After all, those hieroglyphic scripts had a long history among the Mi´kmaq, and even in Jeremy's day, they were still in use.

Regrettably, much of what is known today about precontact Algonquian scripts on birch bark begins with the very missionaries who so assiduously attempted to replace the indigenous images with their own. The *Relation of Father Gabriel Druillettes* (1651–52) describes students in his catechism classes "using a bit of charcoal for a pen, and a piece of bark instead of paper" to take down their lessons. Ministering to the Natives of Maine, Druillettes had never instructed his pupils in writing and did not recognize the "characters" they employed (qtd. in Schmidt and Marshall 4). Sebastien Rasle, a French Jesuit missionary who began to work among the Indians of the Kennebec River area toward the end of the seventeenth century, described how one of the locals "took the bark of a tree upon which with coal he drew." Rasle commented that "This is all the writing the Indians have, and they communicate among themselves by these sorts of drawings as understandingly as we do by our letters" (267). Persuaded that he was dealing with a preliterate culture, Rasle never pursued the potential implications of his analogy between the Natives peoples' "drawings" and European "letters." But his contemporary, the Recollect missionary LeClercq, recognized that the Indians' habit of "writing" on birch bark might be something he could exploit for the purposes of conversion.

Based on the Indians' marks and "drawings," what LeClercq developed was something approaching a pictographic (or hieroglyphic) alphabet. Then, on sheets of birch bark, he produced a series of hieroglyphic billets (or leaflets) filled with prayers and Bible passages that he distributed to his pupils as study aids.[5]

A series of missionaries who followed LeClercq then adopted (or sometimes adapted and refined) his writing system. The last of these, Abbé Antoine Simon-Pierre Maillard, a member of the Spiritan order who settled at the Malagawatch mission on Cape Breton Island in 1736, anticipated that the French would not long hold out against British claims to Canada and so took the added step of organizing "a cadre of hieroglyphic-literate [Indian] specialists . . . to serve as lay catechists under the leadership of prayer chiefs" (Schmidt and Marshall 10). In this way, not only did Maillard further disseminate the script among the Mi´kmaq in Canada but, as well, he ensured the continuity of Catholic practices even if the Anglican British eventually took the French colony (as they did) and ousted the priests. Still, there is a certain irony in the fact that none of the missionaries from any of the orders (Franciscan, Jesuit, Recollect, or Spiritan) ever chose to teach the Indians *alphabetic* literacy—*despite the Indians' entreaties*. But teaching the Indians European letters and thereby giving them direct access to Christian and secular texts alike could prove dangerous. As Maillard himself wrote, "I believe that if they would read and write our language, they would be able to induce a lot of troubles among the nation both at the religious and political levels" (qtd. in Schmidt and Marshall 11). Thus Jeremy had good reason to reject the priests' scripts and approve the story's identification of the priest with a trickster rabbit figure.

However, without some knowledge of this history, one might suspect that, in the two closing paragraphs following the break, Rand was putting his own words in Jeremy's mouth. Yet Rand was careful to insert the sentence "Such was Josiah's story" *following* what appears above as the first of these paragraphs, thereby seeming to indicate that everything preceding that sentence actually came from Josiah Jeremy and not from Rand. The source of confusion, therefore, lies in the fact that in the version of the story earlier published in the *American Antiquarian*, what appears above as the penultimate paragraph was not indented as a new paragraph but was integrated into what still appeared to be Jeremy's narrative.[6]

So who is really speaking in these last two paragraphs? Was it Rand or Jeremy who protested the priests' refusal to teach the Mi´kmaq alphabetic literacy and viewed this as an intentional ploy "to keep the Indians in ignorance"? Was it Rand or Jeremy who characterized the Europeans as "invaders"? And was it Rand or Jeremy who accused the Europeans of cheating the Indians "out of their lands and other rightful possessions"? Historical context, textual clues, and the earlier version of the story published in the *American Antiquarian* suggest that we really are hearing Jeremy's voice here, albeit a voice filtered through a Protestant missionary's own anti-Catholic biases.[7] After all, Rand at least partly endorsed many of Jeremy's assertions (and wrote them down) because they laid the blame for the Indians' current poverty and lack of education directly at the feet of the priests who wouldn't transliterate the Indians' language "to writing in the ordinary way"—the very task to which Rand had dedicated himself as he translated hymns and Bible passages into Mi´kmaq by using twenty-two characters from the English alphabet.[8]

We probably hear Rand's voice directly only in the story's final paragraph above. In this closing note, with the phrase "whatever their motives may have been," Rand briefly gave the benefit of the doubt to the Catholic missionaries who had preceded him. But as a scholar of languages—their grammars and their vocabularies—he could not forgive the priests for the *linguistic* blunder of attempting to reduce a language as grammatically complex as Mi´kmaq to "pictorial writing." And he could not forgive them for having "perpetrated one of the grossest possible *literary* blunders" when they attempted to translate the exalted language of holy scripture into "pictorial writing" for an Indian language that itself was "utterly incapable of being represented by signs" (my emphasis). As both linguist and missionary, Rand wanted the story-loving Indians of the Maritimes to know the stories from the scriptures in all their "literary" glory and complexity—and in the Indians' own highly nuanced grammar.

But for all his attentiveness to the details of vocabulary and grammar, Rand did not always grasp the symbolic meanings of the stories he was hearing in Mi´kmaq. When he discussed the story of *Koolpejot* in an *American Antiquarian* article published in January 1890, for example, Rand admitted that, at first, he understood Koolpejot only as "a great medicine man; he has no bones, always lies out in the open air, and is rolled over from one side to the other twice a year, during spring and fall." Rand later learned what the story was really about when "An intelligent Indian . . . suggested to me that this was a figurative representation of the revolution of the seasons" ("The Legends" 8). Similarly, Rand probably did not grasp all the "figurative" meanings embedded in "The Dream of the White Robe and the Floating Island." And nothing in Rand's extant papers hints that Jeremy tried to enlighten him.

Nonetheless, we can still hear the encoded expressions of resistance in Jeremy's narrative. The dream and the arrival of the foreigners took place in some distant past. But their meaning is *his* present. As Jeremy well understood, the symbolic prefigurations in the girl's prophetic dream eventually took on their real historical meaning: "This teacher of a new religion," like the trickster rabbit, tricked the Indians out of learning to read and write "in the ordinary way" and thereby facilitated the Indians' being cheated "out of their lands and other rightful possessions." The not-quite-human bears proved to be only "more enlightened invaders"—human, but in the Indians' eyes, dangerous, powerful, and in their guile and deception "only a sort of man."

While we have no way of knowing how attuned Rand was to these symbolizations, his scrupulous methods for recording these stories suggest that he did not intentionally or substantially alter any of the nuances of Jeremy's narrative. To know that with any certainty, of course, we would have to examine Rand's early notes taken in English or shorthand. But it is precisely such intermediate jottings that Rand destroyed. And today, one cannot even check the manuscripts from which Webster compiled the *Legends* volume because almost the entire Rand collection purchased by Horsford was destroyed in a 1914 fire that consumed Wellesley's College Hall. As a result, there is no way to establish anything even close to what literary scholars would consider an authoritative text.[9]

But then the notion of a fixed authoritative text would have seemed preposterous to the storyteller Josiah Jeremy. Mi'kmaq storytelling has always been about maintaining cultural continuity rather than establishing fixed or unalterable narratives. In traditional Mi'kmaq practice, "each retelling of a story, even by the same person, might be different" (Whitehead, *Stories* 2). According to Ruth Holmes Whitehead, an expert on Mi'kmaq history and culture in Canada, "The structure was fluid, accommodating itself to the teller's will" (2). Thus, even today, "individual story-tellers often transfer elements from one [story] cycle to another" according to their "intent or whim" (2). The object is always to adapt the story to the needs or context of the current moment.

According to Jeremy's narrative, the story's precipitating event took place "when there were no people in this country but Indians, *and before any others were known*" (my emphasis). Since European vessels and their crews were probably being sighted repeatedly by at least some

Native groups from about 1450 on, this sentence—combined with the "singular" nature of the girl's dream—seems to point to an even earlier time, a time before the Mi´kmaq had any knowledge of the European strangers. To date, the only *authenticated* earlier first arrival of non-Natives was the arrival of the Norse around the year 1000. But the Norse only imperfectly fit the physical descriptions of the men in the girl's dream.

Typically, on the cold seas, Norse seamen wore heavy woolen or leather trousers, a sleeveless leather jerkin, a warm wool cape, or a hip-length fur-lined woolen coat and fur hat. Although the Norse were known to hunt Arctic hare, only rarely were hare or rabbit skins used as coat linings; if used at all, the soft rabbit fur lined leather boots and wool mittens. Thus, only the perfidious actions of the Norse, rather than their actual clothing, could have suggested the Indians' associations of the Norse with Rabbit the Trickster. Alternatively, like the berserkers of legend, with their bearskin capes, Norse seafarers also wore long hooded capes of animal skins (with the fur side turned inward) which were oiled to make them waterproof. From a distance, the long dark fur capes with hoods could conceivably make men look like bears. And upon closer inspection, these tall, burly, bearded Greenlanders may have appeared to the Native peoples as *mu'in*, bear-like and not quite men. The association of these men with bears may even have been accentuated by pre-Christian Viking warriors' occasional habit of wearing a bear tooth pendant around the neck. The pendant both denoted and was intended to ensure the warrior's physical strength. Although the Vinland voyagers mainly planned to exploit natural resources and perhaps to colonize as farmers, we can safely surmise that many of these adventurers had at one time also been warriors, because the sagas repeatedly report that the men had shields and swords. We also know that, like the later European vessels, the Norse knarr carried smaller by-boats (tow-boats or dinghies), which were routinely "paddled ashore" so that crew members could scout the country and gather fresh water.

However tantalizing this reading, though, it is also the case that from a distance, Norse seafarers and the later Basque fishermen and French explorers appeared to dress pretty much alike. They all wore heavy linen or wool shirts and pants, leather jerkins (or leather aprons in the case of the Basque), wool capes, or capes with various animal skin linings, and most were bearded. And it is not unthinkable that fur resembling that of a white rabbit was observed by Natives in at least some of their garments. Moreover, a foreigner "who came towards them making signs of friendship, raising his hand towards heaven, and addressing them in an earnest manner, but in a language which they could not understand" might refer to any number of early arrival moments, with or without priests (Rand, *Legends* 226).

We also know that many of the early European fishing and exploratory vessels had priests aboard to say mass. But it was not any of these *first* priestly arrivals who "learned [the Mi'kmaq] tongue, and gave them the Prayer Book written in ... (ornamental mark-writing)." That began with LeClercq in 1678. Thus Jeremy's story was hardly about the arrival of one specific priest. Instead, his story conflated into a single unified narrative a series of events that occurred in different places over many years and involved several different personages.[10] In traditional Mi'kmaq fashion, the purpose of the story was not to chronicle each and every specific event—in the way Euro-Americans write history—but rather to distill the connections between and the shared meanings of these events.

This is true, too, of the physical descriptors in the story, which were intended to convey not just the appearance but also the *nature* of these strangers. Significantly, it was the nature of the strangers that linked the first arrival with those that followed. "A man dressed in rabbit-skin garments," men who look like bears, and "a man dressed in white"—all these particular details have been selected so as to identify the strangers with tricksters, bringers of discord, thieves, potential brutality, and, with the white garment, origins in the East. To be sure, all this reflects events related in the sagas: cheating the Natives in trade in *Eirik the Red's Saga* and, in *The Greenlanders' Saga*, an unprovoked act of murderous violence. But murderous violence, cheating the Natives in trade, and sowing discord and disruption were also the hallmarks of the later European invasions. Therefore, in a sense, Jeremy's story of a supposedly *first* arrival both *fore*told and also *told* all the ensuing European arrival moments to follow. It was all the *same* story, over and over again.

Which raises this question: What purpose did it serve to tell such a story and keep it alive? The obvious answer is that some kernel of the story was first preserved as a fragment of historical memory which served as a warning. If they appeared again, these foreigners were to be recognized for what they were. They were to be regarded with suspicion. They could be dangerous. And the Mi'kmaq should not be as unprepared as they were the first time, "when there were no people in this country but Indians, and before any others were known."

But over time the story grew and changed, preserving several phases in the process by which seriatim Mi'kmaq storytellers systematically reinterpreted and restructured the meaning of contact so as to rationalize, after the fact, their people's current experiential reality. The concept of a discrete and identifiable first contact was thereby blurred within a symbolically paradigmatic narrative that came to encompass the events of at least three centuries. And by Jeremy's day, the story performed yet another kind of cultural work. It confirmed that there was wisdom in the old ways and that dreams needed to be attended to. They were not delusions that "the devil [put] into their heads," as the priests had preached, but powerful communications that dared not be dismissed. What the young girl's dream portended symbolically did eventually play out in reality. The story thereby confirmed the power of the old ways as an important conceptual weapon in the ongoing struggle between Mi'kmaq belief systems and invasive European worldviews.

Although probably popularized by the various nineteenth-century Native revitalization movements, these first contact prophecy (or foretelling) tales are not easily dated, nor do we even know when they were most widely circulated. But it is not difficult to understand *why* they were told and retold. Functionally, these stories effectively integrated a broken and fractured present into a culturally cohesive continuum, and they thereby helped make sense of the present moment. To put it another way, prophecy tales are not merely the representations of cultural continuity; they are themselves the carriers of that continuity. As this Mi'kmaq story about a girl's dream makes clear, the present is at once the sad fulfillment of her prophetic dream and simultaneously the proof of cultural perdurability. The story thereby maintains a kind of narrative congruence between a traditional past and a postcontact present. And for Jeremy, prophecy not only allowed the present to remain faithful to the past; prophecy also promised that the future, too, would remain faithful to the past.

In traditional Mi'kmaq storytelling, as performed by Jeremy, stories were rarely told in isolation. Instead, the teller spun out several stories (or an entire story cycle), and Mi'kmaq listeners understood that the stories were meant to be comprehended *intertextually*. That is, they were meant to relate to, elaborate upon, and/or comment on one another. And so that same day, Jeremy told Rand another story. This was the story of "Glooscap . . . leav[ing] the Indians," carried on the back of a huge whale "across the water, to a distant land in the west" (Rand, *Legends* 228). Pointedly, however, Jeremy made sure to include in this story a reference to Gluskap's promised return by ending the story with the following: "The Micmacs expect his return in due time, and look for an end of their oppressions and troubles when he comes back" (229).

Understood intertextually, the story about the young girl's prophetic dream and the story about Gluskap's farewell—with its embedded promise of return—combined into a narrative not solely of loss but of continuity. This, then, was the subtext that Jeremy was trying to convey: *The prophesied depredations of the white man notwithstanding, the story of the Mi´kmaq people has not yet played itself out in full. There is still more and better to come, an end to current "oppressions and troubles." That, too, has been foretold. And as the girl's prophetic dream demonstrated, that which has been foretold does come to pass.* Given the fact that, in the 1860s, the provincial governments of Canada continued their policies of forced assimilation even as the populations of Native peoples continued to dwindle, it was imperative that all these stories be retold and kept alive. For traditionally inclined tribal members like Josiah Jeremy, it was these stories that projected the Mi´kmaqs' survival. All by themselves, these prophecy tales proclaimed the Indians' authority over their own history, past, present, and future.

The Many Arrivals of the White Man: Joseph Nicolar's *The Life and Traditions of the Red Man* (1893)

> Because of our geographic location in the Northeast, our Dawn Land ancestors were among the first Indians to discover Europeans on our shores. Long before Columbus, some of our stories tell us, men came from the direction of the sunrise and stayed for a time.
>
> —JOSEPH BRUCHAC
> (Western Abenaki), *Our Stories Remember* (2003)

When Joseph Nicolar (1837–94) was growing up, there was as yet no school on the Penobscot Nation's Indian Island reservation near Old Town, Maine. Not until 1878 did nuns from the Catholic order the Sisters of Mercy establish an elementary school, but by then, Nicolar was already in his fifties. Nonetheless, because as a young boy he had shown an eager aptitude for learning, at a time when few Penobscots received any schooling whatever, Nicolar "was allowed to attend his first school" at about age twelve and, altogether, "attended schools in Rockland, Warren, Brewer, and Old Town" (Eckstorm, *Indian Place*

Names 238, 237). According to the Maine folklorist Fanny Hardy Eckstorm (who knew the family), Nicolar had "perhaps the best education of all the Indians of his time"—even though that education extended only through "grammar school" (237, 238). Still, limited though it was, this education taught Nicolar how to write in English and turned him into a lifelong avid reader. But Nicolar's education was hardly confined to what he learned in school or from his readings. On both sides of his family, he inhabited a world rich with tradition and story.

His father, Tomer (i.e., Thomas) Nicola, was a direct descendant of "Half-Arm" Nicola, who lost part of his right forearm (hence his name) in 1724, when the colonial Massachusetts militia attacked and burned the Norridgewock Indian village on the upper Kennebec River (see Eckstorm, *Old John Neptune* 31–32, 175n). As young Joseph had heard more than once, Half-Arm Nicola was among the 150 Norridgewock survivors, most of whom managed to reach safety in Quebec. But instead of fleeing to Quebec, the wounded Nicola rescued the Norridgewock church's iron cross and brought it to Indian Island. Nicolar's mother, Mary Malt (i.e., Martha) Neptune, came from an equally impressive lineage. The daughter of John Neptune, a famous hereditary Penobscot subchief, hunter, and *meteoulin* (or shaman), Mary Neptune Nicola was a powerful woman and a prodigious storyteller in her own right. And because Nicolar's father died when the boy was only nine, he and his siblings were mostly raised within the large extended Neptune family of his mother. There, from his mother, from other Neptune family members, and from John Neptune himself, he learned hunting skills, crafts, tribal history, and a wealth of traditional stories.

Putting together the stories told by family members with all the stories he had gathered from other Penobscots over a lifetime, Nicolar spent his last years composing in English a written narrative that traced his peoples' past from the first moments of the world's creation by the Great Spirit to the first explorations and eventual permanent settlement of the white man in "the Red-man's world."[11] In 1893, just a year before his death at age sixty-seven, Nicolar self-published his narrative under the title *The Life and Traditions of the Red Man*. Even though the advent of Europeans comprised a relatively small part of that book, it was not a story Nicolar could entirely omit. The coming of the white man was a significant facet of Northeastern Algonquian prophecy lore. That the white man "will not rest until he finds the land the Great Spirit gave unto you" (i.e., the Indians) had been foretold both by the Great Spirit and by Klose-kur-beh, Nicolar's spelling for the legendary culture hero and culture-bringer of the Wabanaki peoples.[12] In Nicolar's version, Klose-kur-beh (also spelled Gluscap, Gluskabe, Klooscap, etc. by other writers) is the first man created by the Great Spirit, witnesses the initial creation, and is subsequently instructed by the Great Spirit in both spiritual and practical knowledge. Klose-kur-beh is then to act as teacher and ethical guide to his people. Klose-kur-beh and *his* people, however, are not the only human beings created by the Great Spirit.[13]

As Klose-kur-beh explains, "This I learned from the Great Spirit,— that he made another man like me" and then another (Nicolar 110–11). "These men shall be one white and one black. And further," Klose-kur-beh continues, the Great Spirit decreed "three seasons, a season for each man" (111). "The growing season shall be the Red man's season. The gathering season shall be the Black man's season, and the cold season shall be the White man's season" (111). The season associated with the Indian, "this growing season[,] shall be pleasant to mankind, because it will bring forth many beautiful colors, pleasing to the eye" (111). The "Black man" and his season receive little elaboration and promptly disappear from the text. But winter, the white man's season, is "a season that . . . shall destroy everything" (111).[14]

Ominous foreshadowings of the white man's prophesied arrival are scattered throughout the first two chapters of Nicolar's text, along with Klose-kur-beh's prediction "The first sign of his coming shall appear to you in the form of a swan towards the rising of the sun" (Nicolar 115). But no further mention is made of these arrivals until the headnote to chapter 4: "The winter and the seven years famine.—The discovery of the first white man's track" (142). That headnote notwithstanding, there is no such "discovery" in chapter 4, a chapter largely given over to the onset of a major climatic shift "which will bring much suffering, because there shall come snow and hail which will cover all the land in great depths" (157). In fact, not until chapter 5 is "the first white man's track" actually spotted.

Despite all the prior warnings, the first appearance of Europeans does not immediately prove destructive. It does not coincide with Klose-kur-beh's prediction that "the first sign of his coming shall appear to you in the form of a swan towards the rising sun" (Nicolar 115). Nor does it identify the Europeans with the arrival of "the cold season." On the contrary, Nicolar emphasizes that the first sign of Europeans occurs with the *waning* of the long and intense "coming of the ice on the earth" detailed in chapter 4 (158). In chapter 5, when the strangers actually arrive, the temperatures are now moderating, winters are less harsh, and the people rejoice at finding that "the large game . . . animals [are] surviving the destructive period *then passing*" (159, my emphasis). Indeed, as May-May the woodpecker, Klose-kur-beh's sometime helper and emissary, announces to the people, no more will winter come "in a fury" and bring on years of "famine" (158). And as the snow melts "all away," this is when the "strange tracks" are first *discovered* (162–63). Significantly, Nicolar uses the vocabulary of discovery only when referring to the Indians' discovery of the several European arrivals. Yet as the old man accompanying the hunting party makes clear, it is not discovery in the sense of encountering something unforeseen but, rather, coming upon the sign of what had already been foretold.

"Young [Indian] men . . . out on a hunt," who, "according to custom had taken one old man with them, . . . come out to the seashore in a little cove where a small brook came out to the sea" and there "discovered a man's track" (Nicolar 162). What the hunters ascertain from the track is "that some one had been carrying water from the brook to the salt water shore, but no canoe of any kind could be seen" (162). When "this news was brought to the old man," the whole group goes to investigate the tracks and, together, confirms that they are not Indian tracks (162–63). At this, the old man—probably an elder or a medicine practitioner brought along to help ensure the hunting party's success—begins to cry and reveals why: "Upon seeing the strange tracks, all the warnings which have been given us, how that a time is coming when we must look for the coming of the white man from the direction of the rising sun . . . came upon me so fresh I could not withhold the tears." The old man now fears "that a great change must follow . . . because his coming will put a bar to our happiness, and our destiny will be at the mercy of the events" (163). Yet consistent with May-May's promise of a warmer climate, the people gather "a good crop of corn" and are said to enjoy their "old happiness" "for many times seventy summers and winters" (164).[15] In effect, the sighting of the strange tracks proves wholly uneventful.

Only after the people enjoy many more annual "good crop[s]" and many years of happiness does Klose-kur-beh's prophecy finally come into play. In a series of episodes that appears to collapse elements from earthquakes, passing comets, plumes of volcanic ash covering the sun and spreading out over land and sea, as well as a meteor strike just off the coast, Nicolar links the arrival of Europeans with portentous natural phenomena. To begin with, "a very dense fog came over the whole country and remained seven moons, and during that time no fish could be found . . . therefore the supply of food became scant," including "other game food" (Nicolar 164). The "spiritual men" (or shamans) labor in vain "to search and find out the cause" (164). All they can divine are "voices of men on the sea in the direction where the sun rises" (164). Following the instructions in Klose-kur-beh's prophecy, "the old men" (or band leaders) decide "to send to north land [that is, Klose-kur-beh's abode] for help," after which a "loon was heard coming through the air from the north land" (164–65).[16] Loons were often helpers or emissaries for Klose-kur-beh. Upon landing, however, "instead of being a loon it was an aged woman," and with her comes "a gentle breeze of wind . . . which continued until all the fog had been blown away" (165). The loon's transformation into human form permits communication in the language of the people as opposed to that of the animals, and her transformation into "an *aged* woman" establishes her as a person of wisdom, who must be respected and attended to.

The old woman immediately uncovers the source of the mysterious famine-inducing fog. She points to the people "who are floating there, . . . toward the mid-ocean," and identifies them as the cause of it all: "The[se] people," she explains, "have brought upon you this trouble and hunger, you cannot find the animals because the days have been so dark, you cannot find fish because there is a covering over all the fish which the power of these people have placed there, it is the spiritual power that is in them" (Nicolar 165). And she adds, "If the power that is in you has not the force to overcome it, woe unto you" (165). The coming contest between peoples is thus constructed as something that transcends martial battles or confrontations of brute strength. Instead, this will be an opposition of *spiritual powers*, that is, moral and metaphysical forces inherent in human beings that can be called upon for good or for harm. Understood this way, the fog is portentous on two levels simultaneously. At the most obvious level, it disrupts the natural order of things, initiating a famine. But at the more ominous level, it manifests the arrival of those who *can and do* disrupt the natural order of the world by exercising their considerable powers badly.

The old woman then explains that it is her "duty now either to capture these persons or make them flee": "If we succeed in capturing them, their mission in bringing misery and suffering among you will virtually be at an end. But if they succeed in making their escape, look for them again some day in the same direction" (Nicolar 166). Using various ritual implements, the old woman says she will attempt to spear and draw to shore what the text, for the first time, identifies as "the 'K'chi-wump-toqueh'—white swan" of Klose-kur-beh's original prophecy (166).[17]

This very old Native locution for European vessels held both descriptive and symbolic value. From a distance, at full sail, the multimasted European ships with their billowing canvas or linen sails bleached white by sun and salt spray did, in fact, resemble a white swan gliding on water with its wings extended upward. And like the migratory swans, in the fifteenth, sixteenth, and seventeenth centuries, European ships also came and went according to the seasons. This permitted the ships to take advantage of seasonally prevailing wind patterns and ocean currents. Moreover, because of the linguistic linkage between the words for "white," "light," and "dawn," for many Northeastern Algonquian groups, the color white denoted origins in the East.

The men inside the white swan, says the old woman, "are white, the same color like the bird" (Nicolar 167). But the old woman is not overly confident that they can be captured. If they escape, the people will have succeeded "only [in] draw[ing] in a dead swan" (167). In that event, the loon woman predicts that the strangers will surely return, only this time they "shall depend upon the power they have gathered in their learning" (166). The white men's moral capacities for causing harm, in other words, will in future be enhanced by the power of their "learning" (or technology). And, to be sure, despite the loon woman's efforts, when the swan "was drawn ashore," it "was found dead. Nothing could be seen on the bird excepting one large hole in its back. And upon looking into this hole only three vacant seats could be seen" (168). The boat is empty, the white men have escaped, and once again something covers the water and hides the fish.

The loon woman proposes to fly back "to the north land," but promises, "Before the sun goes down I will return and shall then break up all the covering which have been hiding the fish" (Nicolar 168). This time her appearance is even more dramatic. "The same white loon [came] from the north very swiftly, and when it reached the place opposite where the dead swan lay, it made its usual circles, there it stood very high and very still for a few moments, then it turned itself into a great ball of fire, and fell swiftly down to the water; and when it struck the water, the earth shook and the roar of it was great. So great was the roar, all the land shook and stood trembling for a long time" (168). The roiling water brings fish back to the surface, but "this great shock also brought back the fog. The return of the fog, however, was but a short duration, it only remained seven days and when it cleared away and the sun shone there was much happiness, because the people were already catching as many fishes as was needed" (168).

Once more we have elements that suggest earthquake, volcanic ash, a comet, or even a meteorite strike off the coast.[18] But the geological and cosmological details are of no real interest to Nicolar.[19] For him, what is important in this event is that, while the loon woman did not succeed in capturing the white men, she did effectively dispel the harm for which she says they are responsible.

Some years after "all these different events"—the text doesn't say how many years after—"the white man" is again sighted, this time "sailing in his strange craft along the coast" (Nicolar 169). Nicolar never says whether the men in this ship are the same strangers as those whose track had been found or whether they are those who had previously come in the white swan. This ambiguity contributes to an impression of separate and multiple early arrivals and explorations. What the text does tell us unambiguously is that "these people were considered very strange because they were not white as the snow, and not so white as the people expected them to be, but were brown and hairy people" (169). It is possible, of course, that this was Nicolar's way of slyly commenting on the arbitrariness of racial categories. After all, as Nicolar well knew, "red man" was a commonly accepted pan-Indian identifier rather than an accurate color descriptor.[20] That said, it is far more probable that one or another of Nicolar's sources, "the old traditional story tellers," used precisely such language in order to convey Native peoples' memories of the several different—and differently complected—European ethnic groups who arrived over time as fishermen and as first explorers (96).

"This long looked for event"—that is, the arrival of those "not white as the snow"—leads the people to select "some good spiritual men . . . [to go] along the coast to watch the strange people's movements . . . until [their] true description and habits had been learned" (Nicolar 169). Some time later—after a prolonged period of intertribal hostilities—"those that were sent to follow and watch the movements of the strange people . . . returned and gave an accurate account of their discoveries, the description of those people, the size of their large canoe which was propelled by a brown colored cloth spread in the wind, and had smaller canoes lashed on the side of the large one" (173). "The hairy men would lower [the smaller canoes] to the water, get into them and move around in them every time the big canoe finds a quiet and safe harbor in which it can lay while the men be out examining the shores, islands, and rivers" (173). Ever faithful to their charge, the Native watchmen "followed the [strange] people up into a large river which was so wide at its mouth that they [i.e., the Indians] did not cross its waters, because their canoes were so small they considered it a danger-

302 Chapter Seven

ous thing to undertake and were obliged to keep near the land on the south side of the river. But the strange people went up it so far [that] the river became much narrower and their [i.e., the Indians'] small canoe could cross it without much difficulty" (174).[21] Additionally, we learn that the strangers fish "every calm morning," hauling "very large fishes up over the side of their big canoe." On land, they carry away "only some water" (174). They "talk in a language [the Indians] could not understand," though no direct contact is made, and the strangers' speech is merely overheard (174). When last seen, "the big canoe" was out at sea, "heading . . . in the southern direction" (173).

Everything the watchmen recount "established the fact that [the] white man had come to the red man's world. This discovery was not looked upon as anything strange, since it had been foretold by the old prophets" (Nicolar 174). The Native elders consult among themselves and with the people. "And after the subject had been fully discussed by all the people throughout the country, it was thought best, and was so decided, that when the strange people came, to receive them as friends, and if possible make brothers of them" (174).

But Nicolar does not immediately pursue any of this. Repeating what is by now a familiar strategy, again he has the white man disappear from the narrative and turns his attention to renewed intertribal hostilities. As a result, despite the paragraphs about the European arrivals, chapter 5 is almost wholly occupied with Indian–Indian relations. Not until the headnote to the final chapter, chapter 6, does Nicolar signal that he will once again take up the story of Europeans: "The winding up the war with the May-Quays [i.e., the Mohawks].—The grand council [of peace] established.—The arrival and settlement of the white man" (184).[22]

As chapter 6 unfolds, warfare between allied Algonquian peoples and the Mohawks, an Iroquoian-speaking people, is briefly punctuated by "an exciting news . . . brought from the extreme north to the effect, that the white man's big canoe had come again, and had landed its people who are still remaining on the land on the north shore of the 'Ma-quozz-bem-to-cook, Lake River,' and have planted some heavy blocks of wood in the form of a cross" (Nicolar 184–85).[23] The river referred to here is probably the Saint Lawrence, the river to the Great Lakes. Nicolar describes the newcomers in some detail, and they seem not to be "the brown and hairy" people of the previous chapter: "These people are white and the lower part of the faces of the elder ones are covered with hair, and the hair is in different colors, and the eyes are not alike, some have dark while others have light colored eyes, some have eyes the color of the blue sky" (185). Although the identity of all the prior arrivals was consistently unspecified, it is clear from this and subsequent passages that Nicolar intends us to understand that this latest group of strangers is French. Beginning in the seventeenth century, the French established permanent trading posts and Catholic missions at various sites along the northern banks of the Saint Lawrence and "are still remaining."[24] By the end of the seventeenth century, in addition to France's missionary villages along the Saint Lawrence, at least six priests were living in various Native villages in Maine.[25] These were the Europeans whose priests assiduously learned the local Native dialects and successfully proselytized all across what they called New France. As Nicolar noted, "The most striking character of his [i.e., the priests'] works was in his endeavors in converting the people to become believers in his spiritual teachings" (186).

What is noteworthy about this latest news of European arrivals is that it occasions "no excitement." Reinforcing his text's implied suggestion of multiple prior appearances of Europeans—even if most of these have not been explicitly delineated—Nicolar simply reports that the Native people view *this* landing as "an old affair" (185). Therefore, the issue for them is neither the uniqueness of the arrival nor the singularity of contact but, rather, "what kind of treatment [the whites] will extend to the red people" (185). Despite all the warnings from Klose-kur-beh in previous chapters, the news from "the extreme north" seems promising. The whites "have shown nothing only friendship" (185). The white man gives "his hand as a brother"—with "brother" signifying equal status to the Algonquians—and so "the red man of the north never had any trouble with the white man" (185). Given the long history of warfare between indigenous populations and European settler groups in North America, this statement may seem disingenuous—that is, until we remind ourselves that Nicolar was referring to the generally amicable relations between the Algonquian-speaking peoples of Maine and New France and the French, their partners in trade and their allies in battles against the Iroquois League.[26]

Returning once more to the stories of *his* people, Nicolar again takes up the ongoing warfare between the Algonquians and the Iroquoians. In so doing, he eliminates any allusions to the ways Native peoples became caught up in Dutch, French, and English competition for dominance in the fur trade and, subsequently, in English and French contests for New World empire. Steadfastly, he represents all the warfare as *Indian* warfare fought on *Indian* lands, for exclusively *Indian* military and political ends. Thus, not until the closing paragraphs of chapter 6,

304 Chapter Seven

following the conclusion of "all the wars among the red people," does the white man reappear (Nicolar 194):

> This ended all the wars among the red people. Next follows the coming of the white man, as has been stated, the strange people had already planted blocks of wood in the form of a cross, and also how kind and brotherly he was, had such a weight in the heart of the red man the people waited with much interest to see him come again. The conquest of the northerners [i.e., the Wabanaki Confederacy] over the May-Quays [Mohawks] was so pleasing to all the people they were ready to accept anything offered them by almost anyone in the form of peace, so when the white man came and lived among them they were ready to receive and believe his doctrine. The reason of this ready belief was because the teaching was similar to the one the spiritual men of the people had been teaching, so when the white man's missionaries came they had an easy task in converting to its folds many and all that could be reached.
>
> At about this period another white man came in his big canoe and landed on the shore of the eastern coast almost in the midst of the northern country, on a high island very near the spot where Klose-kur-beh and the dog killed the first moose. Here the white man planted his cross, and here he lingered until after many other white men came. Here the red man received the religion of the white man. The red man was now ready to be converted and resigned himself to wait for the future fate that may come. (194)

In both of these two paragraphs describing successive French arrivals, Nicolar is not interested in the specifics of the arrivals but, rather, on their lasting impact on Native peoples. In both paragraphs, that impact is the fact of religious conversion. That said, Nicolar maintains the "red people" as his central agents and actors. In the penultimate paragraph, the Native people embrace the white man's religious doctrine only "because the teaching was similar to the one the spiritual men [i.e., the shamans or dream diviners] of the people had been teaching." Indigenous belief systems are not wholly extinguished, says Nicolar, but simply adapted and carried on in a different form. Similarly, in the last paragraph, "the red man received the religion of the white man," but while the invading settler population plants its crosses and *lingers*, it does not displace Native priority. By locating *this* arrival "very near the spot where Klose-kur-beh and the dog killed the first moose," Nicolar alludes to a well-known traditional story and thereby gives referential primacy to the space as first and foremost an *Indian place*. This tactic at once reminds readers of the precontact traditional roots of Native culture and also quietly installs the white man in a landscape that, long before his coming, was already rich with history and symbolic significance.[27]

A brief final reference to the white man appears in a closing section about traditional (precontact) Penobscot lifeways that Nicolar labeled simply "Conclusion." Here, in the book's last paragraph, Nicolar mentions "a natural medicinal water," that is, a bubbling mineral spring, "which was found to contain very powerful healing powers" (199). It had been "considered very valuable, and the spot was visited by all the people from all parts of the country, and they continued their visits until after the white man came. The people did not wish to . . . go without enjoying the great benefit of the medicine waters, and kept going there until the white man took possession of it" (199). In other words, with the introduction of European notions of private property, the spring was no longer available to all and, in Nicolar's day, it was in "the hands of an individual, a white man, of the town of Deering, Maine" (200).

On the one hand, Nicolar was quietly contrasting the Euro-American ethic of private ownership—even of natural resources—with the Indian ethic of shared communal use. On the other hand, he was also using this anecdote to remind readers of Klose-kur-beh's prophetic warning about the white man's greed and selfishness: he will "grasp all things for his comfort," and "he shall want all the land" (113, 115). With this anecdote, the essential truth of Klose-kur-beh's initial prophecy is confirmed, and Nicolar's references to the white man come to an end. Yet, for Nicolar, precisely because of its implications in the present, Klose-kur-beh's prophecy remained vital and enduring, "very significant and important" (95). At least in part, that prophecy also predicted his people's survival.

By the closing decades of the nineteenth century, the Penobscots had lost most of their land base and were desperately poor. Their precious Penobscot River, upon which they still depended for food and water, was fast being polluted by the paper mills and tanneries along its banks, and the paper mills belched noxious fumes into the air. The forests in which the Penobscots still hunted wild game were being decimated by the lumber industry, and Mother Earth was being dug up for stone and granite quarries. Just as Klose-kur-beh had foreseen, the white man drew "things for his own convenience from the water, from the air, and from deep down in the earth" (Nicolar 113). And "because the substance of the water, air and earth have been drawn out, and used for comfort sake, . . . all things have been left like the empty hornet's nest," depleted and uninhabitable (113).

Following decades of out-migration from their Indian Island reservation and a series of devastating cholera epidemics, the Penobscots—once the most populous and powerful organized Native group in Maine—numbered only four hundred in the census of 1890. Even "the old traditional story tellers have all gone to the happy hunting ground," Nicolar observed (96). Clearly, the Penobscots' world and their future as a distinctive culture were imperiled. It was thus urgent that the people be reminded of what Klose-kur-beh had also promised: that the white man "shall live fast, and pass away quickly," while the Indians "shall live slow, and shall linger a long while beyond your [white] brother" (114). This was the culture hero's prophecy of the Penobscots' ultimate survival, a warrant of continuity urgently needed during a period when Klose-kur-beh's other, more dire prophecies were so manifestly coming true. In short, Klose-kur-beh's pronouncements preserved a meaningful past, explained an unhappy present, and also predicted for the Indians a future that would outlast the white man's. Nicolar's overarching design, therefore, offered itself as a salvific prophecy text that refused the white man's trope of the Vanishing Indian.

Despite the apparent wealth of detail in each of the arrival moments described in *The Life and Traditions of the Red Man*, we really do not learn anything substantive about the specific ethnic or national identities of these seriatim arriving white men—until, that is, the arrival of the French. But even those passages effectively conflate a series of arrivals, from Champlain onward through the subsequent arrivals of several missionary priests. That these last arrivals *are* the French is clearly coded in their location along the Saint Lawrence, in the statements of friendship and alliance, in the emphasis on their proselytizing and mission activity, and in the fact that they "are still remaining" (Nicolar 186). By contrast, the identities of the other arrivals are far more ambiguous. For that, we have to tease out what we can from clues in the text.

But this is not easy because, for the modern reader accustomed to dates and clear chronologies, Nicolar's text is sometimes difficult to follow.[28] He was attempting to recover a world without calendars and without the means of (or need for) chronicling events year by year. As all the old stories made clear, for the precontact Penobscot, the marking of time had become ritualized, with combinations of the spiritual number seven denoting longer or shorter passages of cyclical time. As a consequence, no meaningful specific date for any event in his text can be calculated from Nicolar's many references to combinations of the number seven. The other traditional Penobscot device for locating an event in time was to note any unusual natural phenomenon that had roughly coincided with that event. Thus, specific or noteworthy human occurrences were often remembered in stories as associated with seasonal changes, with dramatic climatic shifts, or with cosmological happenings. But again, using these references to calculate specific dates is tricky, at best, although not entirely impossible.[29] When their oral culture was still intact, the Penobscot would have found these devices wholly sufficient for the passing on of significant history and traditions.

But by the end of the nineteenth century, when Nicolar was writing, much of the oral culture had been lost. Moreover, by the time Nicolar was growing up, the Penobscot had long included "a large number of the offspring of neighboring Wabanaki peoples and [even some] Europeans" (Speck, *Penobscot Man* 15). And just as the Penobscot Nation was itself now "blended with other Wabanaki communities," so too were its stories and customs a blend of multiple traditions and remnant memories from many different groups (16). Among other things, this means that we cannot be absolutely certain of the precise provenance of any story (or story segment), nor can we be certain of the territory—and, hence, the geographical locations—referenced in the stories Nicolar retells. All we can state with reasonable assurance is that Nicolar's stories ultimately derived from one or another of the culturally related northern Eastern Algonquian-speaking peoples who once inhabited parts of the present-day Canadian Maritime Provinces, the Saint Lawrence River Valley, Maine, and perhaps areas in Vermont, New Hampshire, and Massachusetts, as well.

These caveats notwithstanding, and even if apocryphal, that is, constructed with the knowledge and experience of hindsight, Klose-kur-beh's predictions about the coming of the white man are generally historically and climatologically accurate. Europeans did come to North America from the East, the direction of "the rising of the sun" (Nicolar 111). And as Klose-kur-beh also predicted, not until the white man "brings his women and children . . . will [he] come to stay, and he shall want all the land" (115). No less prescient was Klose-kur-beh's prediction that "the cold season shall be the White man's season" (111). Between 1600 and 1700—the era of increasing permanent colonization—New England experienced extremely cold temperatures and brutal winters, resulting in repeated crop failures, famine, and the spread of disease. The years 1670 through 1710 were the worst of this period, known as the Little Ice Age.[30] For the indigenous populations, on many levels, "the White man's season" was indeed, in Klose-kurbeh's words, "the season that . . . shall destroy everything" (111).

Significantly, however, "the discovery of the first white man's track" *follows after*—and is not coincident with—a period of colder climate (Nicolar 142). On the contrary, that track is discovered during a period of moderating temperatures when the snow "was fast melting away and . . . summer came, bringing with it the birds, leaves, plants, and flowers" (163). "A good crop" of corn is harvested, "which brought back the old happiness which the people enjoyed for many times seventy summers and winters" (164). In other words, this initial sign of European presence—the "strange tracks" discovered by the hunting party—occurred at the beginning of a lengthy period of warmer temperatures and successful horticulture (163, 162).

That climatic information does not describe the much colder seventeenth century, the century of both multiple arrivals and settlement, but, rather, a much earlier span of time known as the Medieval Maximum or the Medieval Warming Period. In New England, the warming appears to have taken effect by about A.D. 900 and lasted until the gradual onset of the Little Ice Age, around 1350. Consistent with Nicolar's narrative, indigenous peoples took advantage of the warmer climate (and longer growing season) to expand their horticulture, including the introduction of corn (or maize) into parts of Maine.[31] The only Europeans definitely known to have been exploring North America at this period were the Norse. As the archaeologist Brian Fagan explains, it was these "unusually mild conditions [that] allowed the Greenlanders to voyage to North America" (14).[32] What Nicolar's text may be describing, therefore, is simply a brief first sighting without consequences. The old man who accompanies the hunting party identifies the strange tracks as evidence of "the coming of the white man" and cries bitterly at what this portends. But according to Nicolar's text, nothing happens. The people are happy, gather good crops, and continue unchanged "for many times seventy summers and winters" (Nicolar 164).

In addition to the information about warming climate, there is another clue in Nicolar's text that may suggest at least some residual memory of a Norse visit. This is the later description of "the strange people['s]" ship—their "big canoe"—that the watchmen are sent to observe (173). When the watchmen "returned and gave an accurate account of their discoveries," they described a "large canoe which was propelled by a brown colored cloth spread in the wind, and had smaller canoes lashed on the side of the large one" (173). Clearly, this is not the "white swan" of the episode involving the loon woman and the "very dense fog" (164). Rather, it sounds like the large single-masted seagoing cargo ships, called knarrs, used by the medieval Norse from the ninth through the fourteenth and early fifteenth centuries. The knarr was "the ideal ship for voyages of exploration" both because it could carry heavy loads for long voyages and because "it [could] sail both in deep waters and in shallow ones" (Vinner 108). The knarr hoisted a single woven woolen sail, the sail taking on the color of the wool from which it had been loomed. Most such sails were shades of gray, brown, or even black.[33] Moreover, as in Nicolar's text, the larger knarrs carried smaller boats lashed to the interior sides. These allowed the crew to split up and explore independently. In Nicolar, the strangers use the smaller boats to "examin[e] the shores, islands, coves and rivers" (173).

No less important, the "large canoe . . . propelled by a brown colored cloth" not only seems to *look* like a knarr but, as Nicolar retells the watchmen's journey, the "large craft" also *performs* like a knarr (173). It navigates with ease both the river's wide mouth and its narrower channels, as well as the open ocean (see Nicolar 174). When last seen, "the big canoe had sailed far out in the ocean," heading "in the southern direction" (173). As Max Vinner of the Roskilde Ship Museum in Denmark explains, because of its shallow draft, a medieval knarr could "penetrate deep into all the bays and far up all the rivers" (108). Additionally, these ships were "specially designed for sailing in the open seas" (96). All this appears to be what the Native watchmen observed.

Yet however intriguing this interpretation, it is the case that fifteenth- and sixteenth-century Basque, Portuguese, and French shallops, too, had a shallow draft, and many of the earlier shallops carried only a single sail. Like the Norse knarrs, these sails were of natural-colored wool, although they could sometimes be linen. Some of these ships were almost as agile as the Norse knarrs in their ability to navigate both rivers and the ocean. Even more important in undermining a Norse identity for this arrival, though, is the physical description of the strange men and the description of their main activity. Compared to other European men, Scandinavian males generally have less body hair, and even if their skin had been darkened by sun exposure, the medieval Norse would hardly have appeared to the Natives as "brown and hairy people" (Nicolar 169). Additionally, the Norse would not have spent "every calm morning . . . [hauling] very large fishes up over the side of their big canoe" (174). They were intent on gathering grapes and finding sources for timber. So it is far more probable that this particular arrival episode refers to some later, post-Norse fishing vessel that, for whatever reasons, used its smaller boats to "examine the shores, islands, and rivers" (173).[34]

Finally, though, we have to remember that Nicolar was not writing history. Instead, he saw his task as preserving "traditions which have been handed down" through oral transmission (96). To that end, he wove together strands of many different related stories compiled from many different local indigenous sources. Determined as he was to preserve "*all* the pure traditions which have been handed down," Nicolar wove into his narrative whatever remained of these variant stories, perhaps incorporating similar events from several stories into one, but keeping as much as he could of what he had heard (95, my emphasis). To put it another way, several different encounter events probably contributed to each of Nicolar's episodes of sightings and contact.

If this is the case, then we can better understand why his narrative is constructed as it is. Nicolar simply placed the individual episodes in the order in which they best served one of his organizing narrative themes, and that theme was the increasing realization by Native peoples that the white man had, indeed, "come to the red man's world"—and would keep coming (174). Thus, the first episode is merely the discovery of a stranger's track. The second episode confirms Klose-kur-beh's prophecies about the white man's arrival in a white swan from the East and, ominously, the white man's destructive potential. The third episode shows the Europeans actually exploring "the shores, islands, coves and rivers" (173). Thereafter, all the subsequent arrivals are associated with the planting of crosses and permanent settlement. As a result, within a narrative that covers long expanses of time, no consequential signal moment of *firstness* emerges. Instead, Nicolar offers an escalating pattern wholly consistent with what many Wabanaki peoples probably experienced.

On 14 June 1893, as Nicolar's book rolled off the presses of a small-job printer in Bangor, Maine, newspapers across the U.S. reported that a replica of a medieval Viking ship from Bergen, Norway, had now sailed into the harbor at New London, Connecticut. A single-masted vessel with a single sail, the *Viking* "carried the Norwegian flag at the stern, an American flag in the bow, and a red standard with a golden lion at the masthead."[35] As reported by the *New York Times* and other papers, during the ocean crossing, the ship also carried "the flag of the old-time Norwegian Vikings, a red square with a black raven" ("Voyage of the Viking Ship" 8). From New London, the ship voyaged to Newport, Rhode Island, New York City, "and then by way of the Hudson River and Erie Canal to the lakes," making several brief stops before reaching its main destination, the World's Columbian Exposition in Chicago, in July 1893 (8).

Nicolar surely knew about this much-heralded event, not only because the New England newspapers covered the story, but also because many on Indian Island were eagerly following all the news of the World's Fair. Several of their Penobscot neighbors were then participating in the "living exhibits" of traditional tribal villages erected next to the fair's Anthropology Building. (See figure 10.) Every day these Penobscot participants gave regularly scheduled demonstrations of crafts like basket weaving and canoe construction. When they were off duty, they may even have visited some of the fair's other exhibits. Still, no one seems to have identified the arrival of the replica vessel propelled by a single sail with any story in Nicolar's text. And nothing in Nicolar's writings—which included his book and local newspaper articles about Native language and material culture—suggests that he ever connected any incident in *The Life and Traditions of the Red Man* with the arrival of the Norse. As he boasted in his preface, he had quoted from "no historical works of the white man" and used indigenous sources only (95). It was, after all, his *people's* memories and traditions that he sought to preserve, not the white man's.

Despite the eagerness of folklore collectors like Leland and Rand to find evidence of Norse influence in the Native tales they collected, none is really there. Even less is there any significant trace of some remembered "first encounter" with those who might be identified as Norse. The many details in Josiah Jeremy's story about a young girl's dream of a floating island seem more intentionally symbolic—and thereby prophetic—than representational of a particular identifiable historic event. Joseph Nicolar's narrative offers a virtual palimpsest of multiple arrival moments but only one slender climatological clue that one of these—significantly, the first sighting of a strange footprint—might be Norse. In sum, in the extant stories told by Eastern Algonquian-speaking peoples from the Canadian Maritime Provinces and Quebec through northern New England, there is nothing about first encounters with Europeans that specifically mirrors or corresponds to the detailed interactions between the Norse and the Skraelings as described in the two Vinland sagas.[36]

10. Penobscot Village at the World's Columbian Exposition in Chicago in 1893, with the fair's internal elevated railway in the background. Four Penobscot families lived in the three birch bark wigwams and one birch bark longhouse. Photographer unknown. Photograph provided by James Eric Francis, Penobscot Nation tribal historian.

This should not surprise us. Cultures that predominantly depend upon oral transmission must be economical about choosing what is to be remembered and passed on. If any pictographic images related to the Norse were ever pecked into petroglyphs, these were probably long ago eroded or have not yet been discovered.[37] And if any pictographic writings on birch bark ever recorded the coming of the Norse, these have long disintegrated and disappeared. What remains, then, is an oral tradition repeatedly compromised by multiple catastrophic cultural upheavals. In the face of those upheavals, any stories about the Norse that might once have existed either were lost altogether or, as Wayne Newell surmised, were folded into stories about later and more consequential encounters with Europeans. For Native peoples, after all, the coming of the Norse really wasn't of much consequence. At most, the Norse represented a relatively minor and short-lived intrusion into an indigenous world that remained intact during the foreigners' sojourn in North America and continued so after their departure.

In other words, the entire Vinland venture never represented for Native peoples, as it did for the Icelanders, a major punctuation point in an ongoing national historic epic of heroic adventuring and expansive exploration. The only real impact of the Norse, if any, was as a residual memory that functioned as an imperfect portent of the later and more devastating contacts to follow. Even so, the incontrovertible fact of the Vinland venture, combined with the very paucity of Native information about it, opens an interesting imaginative opportunity for a modern-day Native storyteller to probe the entire concept of *first contact*. Amid the many protests that attended the Quincentenary of Columbus's so-called discovery in 1992, Joseph Bruchac (Western Abenaki) pulled together hints and fragments from indigenous lore and did precisely that.

"The Ice-Hearts": Joseph Bruchac's Parable of First Contact

The poet, novelist, composer of short stories, nonfiction writer, and storyteller Joseph Bruchac was born in 1942 of mixed Euro-American and Native American heritage. As a boy growing up in the Adirondack foothills of Greenfield Center, New York (where he still resides), Bruchac listened with fascination to the nature lore and stories recited by his Abenaki grandfather.[38] The Abenaki (also sometimes referred to as the Western Abenaki) are the Eastern Algonquian-speaking peoples who once occupied territories in western Maine, New Hampshire, and Vermont. In the seventeenth and eighteenth centuries, most of their villages were decimated by imported diseases and, during the colonial wars, repeatedly attacked by the English allied with the Iroquois League. Entire villages scattered, with many survivors seeking shelter in the French settlements along the Saint Lawrence.[39] Thus, like their Algonquian cousins along the Atlantic coast—who now collectively refer to themselves as Wabanaki and call their coastal homelands Wôbanakik, or the Dawnland—these Western Abenaki tribes also suffered catastrophic losses of both populations and territories once European settlement began in earnest. Even so, remnants of ancient traditions and old stories seem to have survived, and Bruchac has spent most of his adult life listening to and collecting the stories of Northeastern Woodlands peoples, both Algonquian and Iroquoian. As might be expected from the author of a book called *Our Stories Re-*

member, Bruchac believes that "traditional stories have real memories within them."[40] When I visited him in his upstate New York home in March 2003, he told me he had become persuaded that "we have stories among the Abenakis that go back ten thousand years ago."[41]

Bruchac's short story "The Ice-Hearts" goes back only a little over one thousand years. And although Bruchac notes that "it draws on traditional materials," he also quite clearly stated to me that it is "a work of fiction."[42] In composing this story, Bruchac pieced together fragments from many different tribal stories about ancient encounters with hairy cannibal giants, blue-eyed stone-coated giants, liver-colored (that is, pink) people, ice-hearted strangers with no human sympathies, hard-skinned strangers impervious to arrows, and so on. Clearly knowledgeable about descriptions of encounters between the Norse and the indigenous peoples they called Skraelings, Bruchac teases out of the two Vinland sagas potential clues to the latent meanings in the extant Native fragments he has collected. His purpose, however, is neither to validate the historicity of the sagas nor to make claims about Native memories of Norse contact. Instead, following the storytelling practices of his Abenaki forebears, Bruchac aims to weave from his sources a narrative about ancient events that, by analogy, speaks a lesson for the present. He therefore calls this tale "a parable."[43]

First published in 1992 in a collection of Bruchac's stories titled *Turtle Meat and Other Stories*, "The Ice-Hearts" begins in winter when strangers with "sky-colored eyes" invade the unidentified Indians' unnamed "peaceful village" (3). The absence of identifying names notwithstanding, the text contains suggestive clues about the places and peoples intended. The marauding strangers make their way to the Indians' village by coming "down *the long river*," a translation of *Kwani Tewk*, the old Abenaki name for the Connecticut River (3, my emphasis). The strangers carry with them smaller knives, long knives, axes, and big shields "cold to the touch as stone," and they wear a metallic clothing—or body armor, possibly chain mail—"grey and hard, the color of flint" (5, 3). When two of the murderous marauders are captured, the Indians see that one has "hair the color of fire" and the other hair "the color of autumn grass" (7). We also learn that one of the captured strangers is named "Eric" (8). The Indian narrator of the tale describes them as "tall . . . men who looked like no people we had ever seen before" (4).

Lest there be any doubt about the strangers' identity, Bruchac has his Indian narrator report that the two captives "at first . . . called [the Indians] 'Sgah-lay-leens,'" a reference to the word "Skraelings" in the sagas (7). But since the "r" sound doesn't exist in the Abenaki language, the Native narrator transliterates "Skraelings" to "Sgah-lay-leens." In yet another allusion to the sagas, the Indians manage to wound two of the intruders with arrows. For the most part, the narrator tells us, the armor worn by the strangers is so hard that the "arrows broke when they struck" (3). But in one instance, "whether by luck or good aim," an arrow "went into one of the few places which was not armored on [the stranger's] body" and struck him "in the eye" (5). Another of the intruders falls when a spear "pierc[es] his neck" (5). Similarly, in *The Greenlanders' Saga*, Eirik's youngest son, Thorvald (the younger brother of Leif Eiriksson), is wounded by a Skraeling's arrow while exploring Vinland—and dies there.

While the physical descriptions of the strangers, the name Eric, and the allusions to details from the sagas make clear that the marauding Ice-Hearts are meant to be the Norse, the identity of the Indians in the story is less certain. If the Native village is located along the Connecticut River, as the story hints, then the village is probably in western New Hampshire or eastern Vermont, the homelands of the Western Abenaki when Europeans arrived in the sixteenth and seventeenth centuries. In the story, these Indians have cornfields, as did the Abenaki—but so, too, did several Iroquoian communities.[44] The village also has a longhouse, more usually a feature of Iroquoian, rather than Algonquian, villages—though, again, there are exceptions.[45] The leaders of the village are "the Old Men Who Wear the Horns of Office," a seeming reference to the headdress with antlers most often associated with Iroquoian chiefs and clan elders. (Wabanaki and Abenaki chiefs and subchiefs were usually described as wearing circular headdresses of feathers sewn into woven bands.) Additionally, the Old Men Who Wear the Horns of Office are said to speak on behalf of the village and deliberate with other village leaders "at the meetings of the Great League" (7). This too seems to be a reference to the alliance of Iroquoian tribes later called the League of the Iroquois (or the Iroquois Confederacy). What confuses matters even further is that the narrator states that he and others from his village "once... went to raid against the People Who Live Where The Dawn Begins" (5). The peoples of the Dawnland, of course, were the coastal Algonquians, and this is probably a reference to the ancestors of the Penobscot, Passamaquoddy, and Maliseet of Maine. When the French first arrived at the beginning of the seventeenth century, these coastal Maine peoples had long been suffering raids both from the Mi'kmaq, another closely related Eastern Algonquian-speaking group, as well as from Iroquoians, especially the Mohawk.[46]

So who *are* the Indians in the village attacked by the Ice-Hearts? Are they Algonquian peoples? Or are they some tribe of Iroquoians? As Bruchac is aware, archaeological evidence suggests that the Norse explored at least as far south as the Saint Lawrence. And there is good evidence that, prior to 1600, some Iroquoian and Algonquian groups lived in relative proximity to one another, especially in the Saint Lawrence River Valley. Thus the sudden appearance of non-Native strangers in the area would surely have been incorporated into the stories of *both* peoples.[47] As Bruchac explained to me, because he was drawing on so many different traditional Northeastern Woodlands sources, both Iroquoian and Algonquian, he "deliberately blurred the names of specific places and the identities of specific peoples."[48] From Bruchac's point of view, this "deliberate vagueness about where and who" served his larger thematic purposes.[49] It underscored the fact that he was "not writing cultural history" but, rather, creating a generic "parable about the meeting of Native peoples and Europeans."[50] Interestingly, in constructing that parable, Bruchac utilized the first American literary genre to also offer notions about "the meeting of Native peoples and Europeans."

Following the phenomenal success of the first published captivity narrative, Mary White Rowlandson's *A True History of the Captivity and Restoration of Mrs. Mary Rowlandson, a Minister's Wife in New-England* (1682), the genre that became known as the *Indian captivity narrative* emerged as one of the most popular literary forms in North America.[51] The only literary form that truly originated in America, such narratives remained popular well into the twentieth century. Whether an authentic account of actual events, like Rowlandson's, or a sensationalized account of wholly fictional events, these narratives generally told the same basic story. A white man or woman, sometimes along with other family members, is captured by Indians at some frontier outpost and is forced to live with the Indians and adapt to Indian lifeways for an extended period of time. Rowlandson spent "eleven weeks and five days" among the Narragansetts (29). In most of these narratives, life with the Indians is experienced as brutal and brutalizing, and the captive is grateful to be rescued or ransomed at the end. Trekking with the Narragansetts up and down the Connecticut River Valley through most of the winter of 1675, Rowlandson characterized her captors as a "company of hell-hounds" and experienced her captivity as a testing of her Puritan faith (3). The ransom that secured her freedom symbolically became for her a sign of her eventual spiritual redemption.

In other narratives, by contrast, the captive reports being relatively well treated by his or her captors, and after a while even accepts adoption into the tribe. In John Filson's *The Discovery, Settlement And present State of Kentucke . . . To which is added, . . . The Adventures of Col. Daniel Boon, one of the first Settlers*, originally published in 1784, Daniel Boone describes two separate captivity episodes, both relatively benign. Boone's putatively first-person narrative, supposedly taken down by Filson from Boone's dictation (though probably largely an invention of Filson's pen), boasts that the Indians' "affection for me was . . . great." Boone goes on to say, "I was adopted, accordin [sic] to their custom, into a family where I became a son, and had a great share in the affection of my new parents, brother, sisters, and friends" (Filson 64–65).

In Mary Jemison's bestselling narrative of 1824, Jemison is captured by a raiding party of French and Indians on the Pennsylvania frontier in 1758.[52] She was then about twelve years of age. At the time her narrative appeared, Jemison was already in her eighties, living with her children in upstate New York on land that had been deeded to her just after the American Revolution by her former Seneca captors. Because Jemison could neither read nor write (although she spoke "English plainly and distinctly"), her words were taken down by a local schoolteacher named James Everett Seaver (xi). Seaver's *A Narrative of the Life of Mrs. Mary Jemison* is filled with dramatic details of Indian warfare practices and rich with details about Seneca daily life, in large part because Jemison was adopted into the tribe and eventually married two Indian husbands (with whom she had several children). Claiming absolute fidelity to Jemison's words and sentiments, Seaver devoted several pages to Mary's description of the adoption process. She was given new clothes and a new name and was ritually adopted by two sisters by whom "[she] was ever considered and treated . . . as a real sister, the same as though [she] had been born of their mother" (39). With what appears to be genuine nostalgia, Jemison describes a wholly satisfying life with these "kind good natured women; peaceable and mild in their dispositions; temperate and decent in their habits, and very tender and gentle towards me" (40).

Whether these were accounts of enforced captivity or eventual adoption, Indian captivity narratives provided an eager reading public with otherwise unavailable glimpses into the cultures and daily lives of peoples whom most Euro-Americans regarded as Other: foreign, mysterious, barbaric, and even exotic. This was surely one main source of their popularity. But there was something else, too. With few exceptions, even those narratives that painted relatively sympathetic pictures of Native cultures—like Boone's and Jemison's—nonetheless left no doubt as to which culture was civilized and which was yet in need of a civilizing transformation. Even Jemison, who, as Seaver noted in his introduction, "seemed to take pride in extoling [the Indians'] virtues," was still quoted by him as providing graphic details about "the barbarities which were perpetrated upon" white prisoners by those same Indians (xiii, 149). Of course, the unacknowledged subtext behind these narratives was precisely the construction of contact as a confrontation between the barbarous and the civilized. And for those many Euro-Americans who considered only their own culture to be civilized, this both explained and justified their conquest of the *un*civilized.

"The Ice-Hearts" at once acknowledges and also echoes these literary precursors. In the first published Indian captivity narrative, Rowlandson described being forced by her Narragansett captors to travel with them up and down the Connecticut River Valley. Bruchac locates his Indians' "peaceful village" in that same valley. Both texts open in the winter season. And both texts open with a violent intrusion followed by scenes of carnage. But while Bruchac repeatedly nods in the direction of these literary models, he also turns the model on its head. Instead of Indians breaking in upon a colonial frontier fort, in "The Ice-Hearts" those with "the coldness of ice in their sky-colored eyes" break in upon a Native "peaceful village" (3). And instead of the captive telling the story, in "The Ice-Hearts" the storyteller is the captor. These reversals effectively dismantle the standard captivity narrative's easy assumptions about who is civilized and who is barbaric.

Bruchac's narrator is an Indian named Fox Looking Around. At the time he is telling the tale, he is "a very old man," passing on to a younger generation a story of events from his past (8). Fox Looking Around begins by remembering the night during "the Moon of Long Nights" (i.e., December) when those the Indians come to call the Ice-Hearts invaded the sleeping village (3). "Ice was frozen to their faces, frozen in the hair that covered their faces. . . . And their hearts, it seemed, were made of ice, too, for they came down on our peaceful village and killed. . . . They killed and stole food and then vanished back into the storm which seemed to have given them birth" (3). Thus, all unprovoked, the Ice-Hearts kill two Indians: an old man barely roused from sleep and "a brave man. . . . [who] had a reputation as a healer" (4). The old man is stabbed through the stomach; the healer's "head [is] almost cut from his body" (4).

So strange are these invaders and their weaponry that the Indians cannot be sure whether they are "men or spirits" (4). Whatever the strangers may be, recalls Fox Looking Around, the Indians "had to drive them out": "We let fly with our weapons" (4). The Indians' weapons prove inadequate, however: "Most of our arrows and spears bounced off their hard bodies" (5). But the Indians are determined to protect the women and children in the longhouse, and so Fox Looking Around and his fellows "stayed back [out of the range of the knives and axes brandished by the Ice-Hearts], picking up our arrows as they bounced off and firing again" (5). In the mêlée, two of the Ice-Hearts are wounded—one by an arrow "in the eye," the other by "a spear piercing his neck" (5). Both are "carried off by the others" as the Ice-Hearts retreat from the longhouse, retracing their steps "in the deep soft snow" outside (5).

At first, the Indians are reluctant to pursue the retreating invaders. But Fox Looking Around signals three friends to put on their snow shoes, and, together, the four young braves go "over the hill" with the intention of "cut[ting] off some of the Ice-Hearts from the others. And so it happened" (5). The four return to the longhouse with several of "the weapons of the Ice-Hearts" and with two captives in tow (5). At this juncture, the captivity story proper actually begins, although Bruchac has already embedded in Fox Looking Around's narration clues that this is going to be a very different kind of captivity story. Unlike so many of the Indian captivity narratives composed by Euro-Americans, Fox Looking Around never reduces the Other to the merely barbaric.

To begin with, he acknowledges with some respect that "they were hard fighters" (3). Even more important, he allows these strange invaders the humanity of shared laughter. As he and his fellows move in on the two Ice-Hearts they are about to capture, one of the Ice-Hearts "raised his axe up quickly, as if he meant to throw it" (3). To avoid the blow, one of the Indians throws "himself to the ground," and "as he hit the ground he farted" (3). According to Fox Looking Around, "[This] was so funny that we all laughed"—the Indians and Ice-Hearts alike (3). And he continues: "Just as we laughed, they laughed, a laughter which took away the grimness and anger from their eyes. That was when we saw how young they were" (3–4). Then, again departing from the standard captivity narratives in which the Indians' attack is presented as unmotivated by anything other than blood-lust, Bruchac has his narrator tell us that during the Ice-Hearts' invasion of the longhouse, their leader "was grabbing . . . at the pieces of meat drying above the fire" (4). And when the Indians remove the body armor and the "heavy coats" from the two captive Ice-Hearts, they see that "the men were still big, but they were thin. Their ribs showed and the bones of their shoulders stuck out" (6). The motive behind the raid then becomes apparent: "They attacked us . . . for food because they were starving" (6). The initial cruelty of the invaders is thus instantly mitigated by the desperation of their plight.

Yet the Indians remain puzzled. "But there is plenty of game around here," says one woman (6). Fox Looking Around suggests, "Maybe they only know how to fight and not how to hunt" (6). After all, "the weapons the Ice-Hearts carried were not for hunting game animals" (6). Finally, the Indians conclude that the Ice-Hearts must have come from some place "strange indeed if it bred men who knew only how to kill other human beings and not how to hunt to keep themselves and their families alive" (6). Of course, the Norse in Vinland *did* hunt wild game, according to the sagas. So, while this statement is not entirely accurate and better fits the later European arrivals, here it is used to emphasize the cultural differences between the two peoples.[53]

Speculations about the motivations and the origins of the Ice-Hearts aside, the Indians understand that "something had happened which never had happened before" (6). Men unlike any they had previously encountered have now made their way to the Indians' world. The immediate challenge is what to do with the two who have been captured. Because "two women no longer had husbands and there were children without a father now," there is considerable sentiment to kill the captives right away (6). But after a full day of deliberation—"The sun was going down when everyone had spoken"—the decision is made to adopt the captives (7). One is adopted by the widow of the old man who had been stabbed in the stomach, and this captive is renamed "Woodpecker." The other is adopted by the family of the healer whose "head [was] almost cut from his body" and is renamed Bear Chest (4). As in Jemison's narrative of her life among the Seneca, here too the captives are given new names, taught the Indian language, and become fully integrated into the lifeways of the tribe. As Fox Looking Around tells it, "They grew fat from our food and married good women who gave us many children" (7).

The adoption of Bear Chest proves particularly serendipitous. Because he "was hairy all over his body and especially on his chest," not only is he renamed "Bear Chest" but he is also adopted by the Bear Clan (7). "That was appropriate in more ways than we knew," recalls Fox Looking Around (7). "The Bear Clan . . . has always been known for its healers," and "it turned out that Bear Chest knew how to set broken limbs and knew other ways of healing which helped many" (7). The uncle of the healer killed by the Ice-Hearts teaches Bear Chest "other things about medicine and the fame of Bear Chest as a doctor spread among [the] people as the years passed" (7). Thus, in the sharing of medical knowledge across the two cultures, the Indians gain valuable new healing practices, and Bear Chest effectively takes the place of the healer decapitated by his fellow Ice-Hearts. In *this* captivity narrative, there is valuable knowledge to be gained from *both* cultures.

Although the Indians in this story have some expectation that the Ice-Hearts will one day return to their village, in fact they never do. Instead, "stories came to [the Indians] over the years" of strange arrivals to the east, along the coast (8). "The People of the Dawn passed on tales of big men like our Ice-Hearts. They came in canoes larger than a lodge and fought the way our Ice-Hearts fought. But all of them were wiped out and no more boats came" (8). From the point of view of the Indians, says Fox Looking Around, these invaders "were like the storms which blow in sometimes from the big salt water . . . storms [that] are strong at first, but they falter and die" (8). Yet as Fox Looking Around is warned by the captive renamed Woodpecker—a man to whom he has become almost a brother over the years—"It has not ended. . . . Others like my people will come someday" (8). The story thus closes on an ominously prophetic note as Bruchac has his characters predict the history we know all too well.

Woodpecker explains to Fox Looking Around that he and his fellow Ice-Hearts "came to this place to take land," and he continues: "We came from a place where there was not land enough for our people" (8).[54] He is convinced that someday, "others like my people will come" again, only this time "more people will die" (8). In order to keep their land, the Indians "will have to fight and keep on fighting for a long time," urges Woodpecker (8). But he promises, "If you stay close to this land, if you do not give it up, it will win again. Tell that to our children" (8–9). And this is precisely what Fox Looking Around is doing as he tells his story. "Woodpecker and Bear Chest have been dead for many seasons," he tells his listeners, "and some of you are their children. Your skins are pale, perhaps, and some of you have eyes the color of the sky. But you are real human beings, just as your fathers became real human beings after we adopted them" (8). Based on what Woodpecker has told him, however, what Fox Looking Around most wants his audience to understand is that "the story of the Ice-Hearts is [not] over": "One day more of those people of the storm, those people who know how to kill other human beings but do not know how to grow crops or hunt, will come to this place where we live. There may be more of them then and they may have strange ideas of keeping the land for themselves" (8). He then repeats Woodpecker's predictions and Woodpecker's admonition not to give up the land. Having done that, Fox Looking Around closes with a version of the conventional Algonquian tag for an oral narration: "This is where my story ends" (9).

On the surface, the story is deceptively simple. But like most Native American stories, it contains layers of meaning and depths of nuance. At the center of the story is a verbal pun that raises complicated questions about how we recognize one another's common humanity across the divides of cultural difference. Or, to put it in the terms articulated within "The Ice-Hearts," how does the frightening Other become a "*real* human being" (8, my emphasis)?

Clearly, the Indians recognize the invaders as human. But they are "*strange* men who looked like no people we had ever seen before," and they speak "no language we had heard before" (4, my emphasis). There are initial conjectures that "these strange men were from the world of spirits" (4). During the deliberations over what to do with the two captives, one speaker says the Ice-Hearts "are like the monsters in the old stories" (6). The real crux of the matter, however, is that the Indians do not view the Ice-Hearts as civilized. Their speech sounds to the Indians like "growling" (4). Their weapons "were not for hunting game animals" (6). As a result, these strangers are starving despite an abundance of available game. The only explanation the Indians can come up with is that "the place they came from must have been strange indeed" (6). What transforms the two captives into the recognizably civilized is their acculturation to Native ways. Gradually, the two captives "learned [Indian] words, [and] the past and their old way of talking fell away from them" (7). "Real human speech opened from their mouths" (8). They marry, have children, and become valued members of the community. As Fox Looking Around explains to those listening to his story, "Your fathers became real human beings after we adopted them" (8). In short, they became "*real* human beings" because they embraced what the Indians recognized as culture.

Although Bruchac never explicitly calls attention to it, most Native American readers will immediately understand the story's implicit pun on "real human beings." It is a loose translation of the name that many Native groups across the continent employ for themselves. In other words, while many Native groups identify themselves as people from a certain place or locale (like the Wôbanakikiiak, the People of the Dawnland), embedded in that identification is the designation of themselves as something like "the people" (the suffix *-iak* meaning "the *human* beings" as opposed to other kinds of beings), or "the *real* human beings" (as opposed to human beings from different tribes or cultures). The only requirement for qualifying as one of "the people" or as "a real human being" was participation in the group's shared culture. That is why Native groups so easily adopted outsiders—whether members of other tribes or, postcontact, Euro-Americans and Africans. As Fox Looking Around reminds the others in the longhouse when the fate of the captives is being debated, "Many people here have relatives who were adopted in the past. Now they are part of us" (6–7). In a different way, he makes the same point to those listening to his story, some of whom are the children of the two adopted Ice-Hearts: "Your skins are pale, perhaps, and some of you have eyes the color of the sky. But you are real human beings, just as your fathers became real human beings after we adopted them" (8). For the Indians, neither appearance nor origins are any bar to full membership in the group. The only qualification for status as a real human being is culture.

This would suggest, however, that Bruchac's parable illustrates only one ominous outcome when different cultures collide: the total annihilation of one by the other, either through conquest or assimilation. But in fact the story suggests another possible outcome, too, albeit an outcome difficult to achieve. What if seemingly incompatible cultures could somehow learn to exchange and adapt? The Indians in the story benefit from Bear Chest's knowledge of "how to set broken bones," while Bear Chest becomes a famous healer because he also learns from the Indians "other things about medicine" (7). Another Indian confiscates an axe from the captive Ice-Hearts, but instead of using it as a weapon, as they did, he adapts it for his own purposes, "us[ing] the axe for many years clearing space for cornfields and cutting poles for lodges" (5). These brief suggestive moments of cross-cultural accommodation notwithstanding, Woodpecker's predictions for the future suggest a far more formidable challenge ahead.

According to Woodpecker, when "others like my people will come someday," what will be at issue in the confrontation is the land (8). As Woodpecker had explained to Fox Looking Around before he died, the Ice-Hearts "came to this place to take land" (8). In that statement, the radically different relationship to land within the two cultures is positioned front and center. For the Europeans, land is inert, something to be possessed, there for the taking. Sharing what Woodpecker has told him, Fox Looking Around attempts to prepare his young listeners for these unfamiliar concepts when he tells them that the invaders who come in the future "may have strange ideas of keeping the land for themselves the way you might keep a favorite ball or a pair of moccasins" (8). But this is not how the Indians relate to the land. Having become a real human being, even Woodpecker had come to understand the land as part of the Indians' living community. He understood that the land has its own being-ness and its own powers. "This land of yours is strong," Woodpecker told Fox Looking Around. "It is strong and . . . if you stay close to this land, if you do not give it up, it will win again" (8–9). None of this will be easy though. "You will have to fight," predicted Woodpecker, "and keep on fighting for a long time" (8).

It is surely no accident that Bruchac published "The Ice-Hearts" in 1992, just as the nation debated the meaning of Columbus's so-called discovery some five hundred years earlier. For Native peoples, of course, that fateful landfall was nothing short of a catastrophe, initiating waves of invasion, genocide, and the ongoing colonialist occupation of traditional homelands and sacred sites. For African Americans, Europe's claims to possession of a new continent set in motion a chain of events that brought on the horrors of the Middle Passage and, in Bruchac's words, "the experience of . . . being taken right out of their culture, being denied every aspect of their culture, being dropped onto a completely foreign land, segregated by race and treated as animals, bought and sold as property" (qtd. in Ricker 176). In contradistinction to the celebration of the World's Columbian Exposition in Chicago a hundred years earlier, in 1992 most Europeans and Euro-Americans understood that marking the five-hundredth anniversary of Columbus's arrival was a much more complicated undertaking. Retiring the old vocabularies of discovery, celebration, and commemoration, public events committees, scholarly conferences, and museum exhibits opted instead for more neutral terms like "encounter," "convergence," and "crossroads of cultures." But these strategies often functioned more as a band-aid than as a cure for long-simmering feelings of anger, rage, resentment, guilt, and even remorse.

Into this volatile reassessment of five hundred years of history, Bruchac introduced a contact story that differently addressed the traumas of historical memory. The Indians in "The Ice-Hearts" are invaded, but they successfully fend off the invaders. With only arrows as their weapons, the Indians prove their valor against the iron and steel weaponry of the Europeans. More important still, in "The Ice-Hearts," the Indians—not the Europeans—are the agents of civilization. And they are agents who can express toward their attackers both empathy ("they attacked us ... because they were starving") and sympathy (the strangers came from a place that "bred men who knew only how to kill other human beings and not how to hunt to keep themselves and their families alive"). Empathy, sympathy, respect, and even compassion toward the two captive Ice-Hearts are markers of their culture. The Indians thus become the exemplars of what constitutes a truly *humane* culture.

By the same token, the barbarians in the story—that is, the Europeans—demonstrate their capacity to grow and change. As Bruchac explained in an interview in the journal, *MELUS*, in 1996, "I don't believe that people are limited by race. Their limitations are by culture, not blood. If you are so deeply embedded in one culture that you cannot see another, then you'll never understand certain things" (qtd. in Ricker 174). But, of course, the two captive Ice-Hearts come to see and truly understand the culture into which they have been adopted. That's why Bear Chest can become a famous healer. And that's why Woodpecker is so concerned to preserve the Indians' special relationship to their land, especially in the face of the future invasions that he foresees.

In the Western tradition, a parable is a short, relatively simple story that points to a moral. Ideally, it is also a story whose details parallel or correlate to the particular situation which calls it forth; it thus functions by analogy. In the Native American tradition, according to Bruchac, "when stories are told ... they always serve a double purpose. Stories entertain and they instruct. They delight and they teach" (introduction to *I Become Part of It* 2). Additionally, as with the Western parable, "the larger structuring elements of the story are unchangeable," but the Native storyteller adjusts the details and the emphases "dependent upon the atmosphere of the audience and the reason for telling the story" (qtd. in Ricker 172). In this instance, the atmosphere that called forth Bruchac's parable of contact was the acrimony on all sides that attended the Columbian Quincentenary. The reason for creating the story was to teach a lesson that is potentially both hopeful and healing. After all, just as Euro-Americans have exploited tales of a Viking past as a means of validating their right to a presence on this continent, so too Native storytellers keep alive their own stories of contact as one means of validating their peoples' rightful historical priority in an ancient homeland. Here, intended solely as a parable, "The Ice-Hearts" is neither a historical reconstruction nor, really, a story about the Norse. It simply uses a known historical fact—the venturing of the Norse to North America—and joins that fact to Native traditions about long-ago confrontations with hairy strangers in order to illustrate the possibility that, by means other than invasion and conquest, we human beings have the capacity to enter into worlds not our own. We can learn from difference, and we can adopt and adapt. In short, we need not always fear or attempt to destroy the Other.

Epilogue

HISTORY LESSONS

> But what is the true American past? How far back does the past go in a "nation of immigrants"? One group of "Americans" has roots as deep as the rocks. They go back, at the very least, thirty thousand years.
>
> —JOSEPH BRUCHAC (Western Abenaki),
> preface to *Survival This Way* (1987)

Lesson One: The Kensington Stone and Invincible Beliefs

In the course of the twentieth century, the disciplines of archaeology, anthropology, and ethnology became far more sophisticated, with more and better tools of scientific analysis at their disposal. With those advances, the many imputed nineteenth-century Norse "finds" in the U.S. were reexamined and deemed to be altogether bogus or something else entirely. When examined by hydrologists and geologists, for example, the Norse Pond in eastern Maine—often used to lure summer visitors to the Lubec area—turned out to be a natural feature and not a product of Norse engineering.[1] The infamous crumbling stone tower in Newport, Rhode Island, was excavated from 1948 through 1949 and then again studied and surveyed in 1991 and 1993. "Among the thousands of fragments found [in and around the tower], none were older than the colonial period" (Hertz 376). Today, archaeologists who have "studied the evidence" say that "it is now possible almost with certainty to exclude a pre-Columbian dating of the tower" (376).

Despite these scientifically based debunkings, there has always been a cadre of enthusiasts who hold to their belief in a New England Vinland and Norse presence within the territorial United States. The substance of that belief, however, no longer centers on Dighton Rock, on the Newport tower, or on several other so-called finds but, rather, on the famous Kensington Stone. In November 1898, a Swedish immigrant farmer named Olof Ohman dug up a 202-pound engraved stone slab while "grubbing out" tree stumps on his farm near Kensington, Minnesota (Wallace and Fitzhugh 381). The runic inscription on the stone dated it to 1362. The translation of the inscription provided by the archaeologists Birgitta Linderoth Wallace and William W. Fitzhugh in their article "Stumbles and Pitfalls in the Search for Viking America" reads as follows:

> 8 Goths [i.e., Gotlanders or Swedes] and 22 Norwegians on an exploration journey from Vinland to the west. We had camp by 2 skerries [or, possibly, sheds] one day's journey north from this stone. We were [out] to fish. One day after we came home [we] found 10 men red of blood and dead. AVM [i.e., Ave Virgen Maria] Save [us] from evil. [We] have 10 men by the sea to look after our ships 14 day's travel from this island [In the year] 1362. (381)

That a group of eight Swedes and twenty-two Norwegians made their way so far into the interior of the U.S. at this date seems highly improbable. There is no evidence of any surviving Vinland colony at this period nor, indeed, evidence of any Norse colony in North America that would have had sufficient manpower to launch such an expedition. Were the voyagers originally from Iceland, some word of their journey would surely have shown up in the voluminous Icelandic records. And because manpower was scarce in underpopulated Greenland at this period, it is hardly credible that "the Greenlanders would ... have sent their small North American working parties far into the interior, away from the safety of shore and ships" (Seaver, *The Last Vikings* 209). After all, as the Greenlanders knew well, Karlsefni's company had abandoned their Vinland venture because they found the new land populated by potentially hostile Natives.

Those facts notwithstanding, and with America's Viking romance still in full flower, when first unearthed, the engraved stone "created a sensation." What happened next is best summarized in Wallace and Fitzhugh's discussion of it:

> It was exhibited at a local bank in Alexandria, and newspaper articles publishing translations of the text appeared in local newspapers. A transcription said to have been made by Ohman was sent to Professor Olaus Breda at the Department of Scandinavian Languages at the University of Minnesota. Breda concluded that it was modern, because it contained numbers that were not proper runic numbers. Arrangements were then made to have the actual stone inspected for authentication at the Germanic Department of Northwestern University. The Chicago *Daily Inter Ocean* noted that "if authentic [the inscription] is destined to revolutionize previous researches of archaeologists" (21 February 1899), and the *Chicago Tribune* reported that it could be "the oldest record of American history" (20 February 1899). (381)

But that enthusiastic prediction did not pan out. A respected professor at Northwestern, along with leading runologists and philologists from Sweden, Norway, and Denmark, all "declared both the text and the runes modern" (381). The runes did not correspond to known fourteenth-century runes found in Scandinavia. The stone slab was then returned to Ohman, who, having been a stonemason in his native Sweden, was suspected of having perpetrated the forgery. Until his death, Ohman denied having carved the inscription, but he never denied that he knew runic writing and that he had an intense interest in history.

Over the ensuing years, and still today, the Kensington Stone, as it is generally known, has continued to be the subject of often bitter controversy.[2] Although most archaeologists now view it as a fraud, books and articles still regularly appear that argue for the stone's authenticity and offer new theories about who carved the stone and what the inscription *really* means.[3] Today the stone resides in the private Runestone Museum in Alexandria, Minnesota. According to Wallace and Fitzhugh, when inquiries about the stone are directed to the National Museum of Natural History, the Smithsonian Institution's Department of Anthropology unambiguously replies with a statement "saying that scholarly opinion has judged the Kensington Stone to be a nineteenth-century creation" (383).

The most recent research appears to confirm this view as well as the fact that the farmer Ohman probably did, in fact, know the runic writing that appeared on the stone. When the Kensington Stone was exhibited in Sweden in 2004, some of its more eccentric runes were identified as consistent with a newly discovered runic alphabet used in the nineteenth century by itinerant journeymen tailors. The two Swedish provinces in which this unusual runic system was utilized were both adjacent to Ohman's home province of Hälsingland (see Sköld). The assumption, therefore, is that whoever carved the Kensington Stone was "familiar" with that particular "runic system" (Powell, "The Kensington Code" 70).

When it was first discovered, though, "the Kensington Stone prompted a rash of Scandinavian finds in Minnesota and nearby regions of the Upper Midwest" (Wallace and Fitzhugh 384). It was like antebellum New England all over again, with Viking "finds" everywhere, but with even more fantastical stories about how and why they got there. With nothing in the sagas or in the written Icelandic records to explain the mystery, whole new narratives had to be invented. As the cultural historian Mancini has remarked, "the 'normal' geography

330 Epilogue

of American discovery" had to be rewritten yet again, and Americans now had to "create a new mental map of the American past. All in all, it was too much to ask" (892). In the end, the doubt and suspicion surrounding the Kensington Stone only served to reawaken all the previous questions and doubts associated with the many "finds" in New England. As a result, except for those with an invincible belief in the stone's medieval origins, confidence in the reliability of *any* evidence for a Vinland on U.S. soil was forever undermined.

Lesson Two: Origin Stories and National Identity

Happily, Americans no longer—out of jealousy or insecurity—actively compete with Europe to claim a romantic and storied ancient past. There is no longer a perceived need to anchor our history in any invented notion of "antiquities in our Western World, which prove it to be quite as old as the European" (Simms, "The Discoveries of the Northmen" 418). The antiquity of the continent and the long presence of its many First Peoples is already well established. And archaeologists are every day uncovering evidence of earlier and earlier human habitation in the Americas.

Moreover, in the twenty-first century, valorizing either Leif Eiriksson or Christopher Columbus no longer impinges on questions of national identity or immigration policy. Although debates over immigration continue to dominate our politics, and although many of these debates are tinged with racial anxieties and identity politics not unlike those of the nineteenth century, none of these debates any longer invokes the sagas or a Norse discovery as either relevant or evidentiary. The nation is now unequivocally multiethnic, multicultural, and interracial, with those groups once labeled minorities moving rapidly into a new majority. As a result, we can no longer insist upon any single defining origin story that begins in Europe. Our citizens, including our Native American citizens, now trace their ancestry to every continent.

To be sure, many nonprofessional as well as professional archaeologists and historians remain on the lookout for hard evidence of Norse presence within the borders of the United States. But with the Ingstads' discoveries in Newfoundland, the story does seem to have shifted to Canada. Happily, it is no longer a pressing matter of regional pride or national destiny that Vinland be located on U.S. soil rather than somewhere across our northern border. Today, a Vinland find anywhere in the U.S. would prove a genuine source of pleasure to those of Scandinavian descent and a potential boon to local tourism, and it would require yet another revision of our history books. Yet it would not alter our always problematic construction of a shared national identity. For that, the sagas—along with the Columbus discovery story and Plymouth Rock—are of no use whatever. Each, in its own way, is too parochial. In order to construct a viable national identity, as Paula Gunn Allen (Laguna Pueblo) understood in 1974, "above all, America needs a tradition that is relevant to this continent and the life upon it; America needs a sense of history, a sense of America's place in eternal time, a way to use history as renewal, not as denial. To do this," Allen urged, "America must absolve herself of the historic guilt toward her [indigenous] predecessors and heal the split in her soul" (33).

Lesson Three: The Sagas as Prophecy Texts

Nowadays, *The Greenlanders' Saga* and *Eirik the Red's Saga* have taken their place within a larger body of transoceanic texts that we call "contact narratives." The sagas remain important and unique in their *firstness*, but otherwise—like so many contact narratives—they recount one party's experience of meeting a previously unknown people on a landscape which, for one of the groups, is also strange and unfamiliar. As such, the sagas repeat the central theme of all contact narratives, whether composed in Mexico by the conquistadors or in New England by a Native storyteller: the bewilderment of encountering radical *otherness* and the need somehow to incorporate that new experience into the group's already existing conceptual patterns and worldview.

But the Vinland sagas are unique in more than just their chronological firstness. They are also unique in that, unlike the European contact texts of a later period, the sagas do not shade over into narratives of conquest and colonialism. Because the Norse and the indigenous peoples met as autonomous groups with roughly equivalent technologies, and because the Norse were so few in number, the Norse could never even attempt to achieve political, military, or cultural sway over the Skraelings. And they certainly never attempted to exert sovereignty over Vinland or its inhabitants. However much Thorfinn Karlsefni and the other Vinland voyagers might have wished for a different outcome, in fact their venture resulted only in seriatim journeys to this good new land. Thus the sagas reveal a colonialist project that is never realized but only ever-incipient.

This perhaps explains why the two Vinland sagas overwhelmingly strike the modern reader as prescient with the tragedy that would begin to unfold some five hundred years later: the steady annihilation of the Native peoples and indigenous cultures of America. For even though amicable trade with the Skraelings clearly brought the Norse great profits, nonetheless the Natives represented to the Norse, above all else, an obstacle both to colonization and to the unfettered exploitation of Vinland's abundant resources. And since neither Iceland nor Greenland in the eleventh century had populations large enough to immigrate in massive numbers and by force overcome the Natives of Vinland, the plan to colonize Vinland had to be abandoned. But beginning in the seventeenth century, aided by firearms and bringing with them epidemic diseases against which the Native populations had no immunity, Europeans in ever-increasing numbers again explored, exploited, and settled the same lands that the Norse had called Vinland. Once again, the Europeans began to see the Natives not as "our brethren of the same land," Thomas Jefferson's fine phrase, but as obstacles to expanding colonization (307). And once again, as in the sagas, trade turned to treachery as the Europeans substituted cheap rum and brandy for the metal trade goods sought by the Indians; cross-cultural contact morphed into a collision of cultures, as European nations appropriated Native homelands in the competition for dominance in the New World; and Europe's enterprising expansionism turned violent. Little wonder that, in contrast to the celebratory effusions of the nineteenth century, most Americans today read the sagas as the tacit preamble to a tragic and very American tale.

This is the insight embedded in William T. Vollmann's *The Ice-Shirt* (1990). In that novel, an all-too-credulous and repeatedly pedantic narrator attempts to pinpoint the Vinlanders' landfalls: "From the astronomical observations that they took, we know that they must have landed near New Jersey. But other scholars, some of even greater repute than I, say that the Greenlanders stayed at Cape Cod, in Maine, in Newfoundland, in North Carolina" (216). Then, in a dream-like narrative based on the sagas, Vollman's text sings an elegy both for "the new country [that] offered so much of freshness and greenness" and for the Indians "growing deeper and deeper into death" (219, 310). In other words, wherever the real Vinland may have been located geographically, its symbolic meaning is *here*.

Lesson Four: The Vikings Are Still with Us

For the most part, twentieth and twenty-first century Americans have encountered Vikings in the *kitsch* of popular culture. Images of Vikings are everywhere: in the movies, in the logo of football's Minnesota Vikings, in popular comic strips, in both adult and juvenile fiction, television documentaries, animated feature films for children, and video games for young and old alike.[4] Through it all, however, the most enduring image of the Norsemen, and one that still inspires, is as explorers and adventurers. We hear an echo of that remnant of the nineteenth-century romance in the decision of the National Air and Space Administration (NASA) to name its project of summer 1976 the Viking Mission to Mars. This was the mission that initiated the search for evidence of life on Mars, and the choice of its name tacitly acknowledged that the next great First Contact moment would be with previously unknown life forms beyond our home planet.

Coverage of the Viking Mission circulated worldwide. And with it circulated also a particularly American subtext: the magnificent accomplishment of the Norse voyages to North America in the tenth and eleventh centuries was now matched and symbolically continued with the U.S. mission to discover for the first time evidence of life on another planet. This was the twentieth century's grand adventure, and Americans were the bold new Vikings. Displacing the old paradigm of race with a prideful image of national technological supremacy, the romance of space exploration now permitted Americans to embrace a wholly new and very different Viking heritage.

Notes

Prologue

1. See Daniel Peters, *The Luck of Huemac* (1981); *Tikal* (1983); and *The Incas* (1991).

2. Subsequent "AMS radiocarbon dates on twigs and small branches" preserved at the site "date the Norse occupation to somewhere right before or after A.D. 1000" (Wallace, "L'Anse aux Meadows, Leif Eriksson's Home in Vinland" 121).

3. As a Mi´kmaq elder explained to the seventeenth-century French missionary Abbé Maillard, "In olden times, instead of the birchbark we use now, our ancestors used moose skins, from which they had plucked the hair, and which they had scraped and rubbed so thoroughly that they were like your finest skins. They soaked them several times in oil and then they placed them on the canoe frame, just as we do with birchbark today, fitted them, stretched them and fixed them by sewing them, sometimes with animal tendons, sometimes with spruce roots" (qtd. in Whitehead, *The Old Man Told Us* 20).

4. Petroglyphs in Norway clearly indicate that although skin boats were "a legacy . . . of the early Stone Age," that legacy "maintain[ed] itself well into the Bronze Age" (Brøgger and Shetelig 28). Pre-Christian Norse mythology retained scattered references to such craft.

5. Originally reported in the *Denver Post*, 12 Oct. 1991.

6. When I visited the area in June 2000, a number of local people still believed the Spirit Pond runestones to be authentic and even arranged for me to visit with Elliott's widow at her home. My husband, my research assistant, and I were all graciously received. A retired schoolteacher, Elliott's widow was happy to share old newspaper clippings and odd "finds" brought home by her late husband over the years. But she declined to say whether she believed any of his discoveries to be authentic. "I just don't know" was her only answer.

1. The Politics of American Prehistory

1. D'Arcy McNickle (Cree/Salish) earlier entered this same debate in *They Came Here First: The Epic of the American Indian* (1949).

2. Pagden's translated quotation is from Bartolomé de las Casas, *Historia de las Indias*, ed. Augustín Millares Carlo, 3 vols. (Mexico, 1951), 1:149.

3. This statement is translated from Alexander Von Humboldt, *Vues des Cordillères et Monumens des peuples indigènes de l'Amérique* (Paris, 1810), 1–3.

4. This statement typifies Schoolcraft's tendency to sometimes flatten *all* Indian peoples into a single homogeneous whole, too often ignoring specificities of language, belief structures, artistic and technological development, and social organization.

5. Despite amassing a wealth of linguistic and archaeological evidence to dispel continuing claims that Greeks or Celts had once inhabited (or at least visited) North America—thus accounting for discoveries of antiquities alleged to be beyond the capacities of Indian manufacture—Schoolcraft never wholly dismissed the possibility that perhaps some "works are due to a people of higher civilization than the ancestors of the existing aboriginal race." Thus Schoolcraft detected among some North American Indians the influence of "transferred Indian civilization" from (in his view) the "superior" arts of "the Toltec, the Aztec, the Peruvian." Still, he never entirely rejected the notion of an earlier non-Indian pre-Columbian "intrusive civilization in the Ohio valley" (*Historical and Statistical Information* 4:132).

6. Hopewell culture (named for the landowner of one of its principal sites in the Ohio Valley) spread among the rivers of the Midwest and East, establishing extensive trade routes, large ceremonial centers, and proliferating Indian farming villages. Elaborately constructed earthen mounds served as ceremonial sites; other mounds were for burials. The Hopewell culture thrived until about A.D. 500 and then, for reasons still not known, went into decline.

7. The statement is from Jedediah Morse, *A Report to the Secretary of War, of the United States, on Indian Affairs* (1822; reprint, New York: Augustus M. Kelley, 1970), 357–59.

8. "Americus" refers to Amerigo Vespucci (1454–1512), an Italian who sailed under the Spanish flag and claimed to have reached the North American mainland on 16 June 1497, eight days before John Cabot.

9. The "learned Swede" was Peter Kalm (1716–79), a Swedish-Finnish botanist, naturalist, and agricultural economist, and a friend and student of the renowned naturalist Carl Linnaeus. Seeking seeds that might prove useful for Swedish agriculture and industry, Kalm traveled through parts of North America, arriving in Philadelphia in September 1748, where he was befriended by both Franklin and John Bartram. Franklin held to his view regarding Norse discovery throughout his life and expanded on it in a letter written in 1781 to Court de Gébelin: "If any Phenicians arriv'd in America, I should rather think it was not by the Accident of a Storm, but in the Course of their long and adventurous Voyages; and that they coasted from Denmark and Norway over to Greenland, and down Southward by Newfoundland, Nova Scotia, &c. to New England, as the Danes themselves certainly did some Ages before Columbus" (35:35–36).

10. In the 1820s, the U.S. government began removing the Cherokee, Creek, Seminole, Choctaw, and Chickasaw peoples to lands west of the Mississippi River. Timothy Dwight served as the president of Yale College from 1795 to 1817.

11. In 1767, Charles Townshend, the chancellor of the exchequer, pushed through Parliament a series of acts that levied duties on goods that had previously been untaxed. These new taxes were mainly intended to defray the costs of British troops stationed in the American colonies. But the taxes were unpopular because the revenues would also be used to pay the salaries of royal officials in the colonies, thus depriving colonial assemblies of their power to withhold salaries from uncooperative or overly meddlesome royal officials. When Americans demonstrated against the new taxes and boycotted the newly taxed goods, Parliament reluctantly backed down in 1770, repealing all the duties except the one on tea. Then in 1773, Parliament passed the Tea Act, granting to the British East India Company exclusive rights to sell its teas to the Americans and thus depriving American importing merchants of any share in the lucrative trade.

12. Mather's reticence on the subject of possible cultural and racial mixing was to be expected. For while the (mostly male) French settlers in New France and Acadia often mixed and intermarried with the local Native peoples, forming a distinctive métis population in Canada, the English in New England (who came as family groups) rarely did. The symbolically powerful and politically pragmatic marriage of (Anglican) John Rolfe of Virginia to Pocahontas in 1614 represented a union that ministers in Boston would never have encouraged (not even with Indian converts like Pocahontas).

13. John Eliot (1604–90) was the first to preach to the Indians in their Native tongue, thus earning the sobriquet "Apostle to the Indians." Outside of Boston in 1651, he established the first of his fourteen villages of Praying Indians; and in the 1660s, he translated both the Old and New Testaments into a local Indian language. This translation was the first complete Bible printed in the English colonies. Roger Williams (1603–83) protested the expropriation of Indian rights and lands under the terms of the Bay Colony's royal charter; upon founding a settlement at Providence, Rhode Island, in 1636, he began immediately to live with and minister to the Indians. His knowledge of Indian languages led to the publication of his *A Key into the Languages of America* (1643).

14. From Andrew Jackson, "Message from the President of the United States to the Two Houses of Congress . . . December 7, 1830," U.S. 21st Cong. 2nd House Doc. No. 2 (1830), 19–22. Jackson's description of "monuments and fortresses . . . spread over the extensive regions of the west" refers to the Mississippian culture (which appeared later than the Hopewellian mound-builder culture of Ohio). Mississippian sites were found throughout Alabama, Arkansas, Florida, Georgia, Illinois, Kentucky, Oklahoma, Tennessee, and, of course, Mississippi. About a millennium ago, Mississippian peoples began living in large towns dominated by mounds that supported residential and ceremonial buildings; some towns had more than a hundred mounds. Among other artifacts left behind by these peoples were beautiful carvings on stone, shell, and copper.

15. In fact, the great city-states of the Mississippian culture, with their monumental public plazas and ceremonial platforms, were thriving communities until initial contact with Europeans in the sixteenth century. Hernando de Soto landed in Tampa Bay, Florida, in May 1539 with a private army of six hundred soldiers, two hundred horses, and three hundred pigs. Seeking fabled cities of gold, for four years he marched through "what is now Florida, Georgia, North and South Carolina, Tennessee, Alabama, Arkansas, and Texas," bringing both warfare and disease to the peoples he encountered. Even more lethal, perhaps, were "the pigs, which multiplied rapidly and were able to transmit their diseases to wildlife in the surrounding forest," according to Charles C. Mann (44–45). The result was cascading human and other species destruction. Mann writes, "No Europeans visited this part of the Mississippi Valley for more than a century." When they did, Europeans saw only depleted populations in small, widely scattered villages. Some anthropologists and epidemiologists estimate a population "drop of nearly 96 percent" in some areas, reports Mann (44–45).

16. MacLean speculated that the surviving Mound Builder people, after being driven out of the Ohio Valley, eventually "immigrate[d] into Mexico," where they later became either the Aztecs or the Toltecs (*The Mound Builders* 148).

17. As Powell explained in his introduction to the volume, Mallery's interest in Native American petroglyphs and other forms of picture-writing "commenced in the field" when, as a colonel stationed "at Fort Rice, on the upper Missouri river, in the autumn of 1876," Mallery had studied—and published articles about—a pictographic Dakota calendar. Soon after, Powell continued, "upon the organization of the Bureau of Ethnology, in 1879, Col. Mallery was appointed ethnologist, and has . . . continued in that duty without intermission, supplementing field explorations by study of all accessible anthropologic literature and by correspondence" ("Report of the Director," *Tenth Annual Report* xxvii). Mallery's report included not only his own extensive firsthand research but also lengthy quotations from the work of many others. In "Picture-Writing," Mallery noted, "An essay entitled 'Pictographs of the North American Indians: A Preliminary Paper,' appeared in the Fourth Annual Report of the Bureau of Ethnology. The present work is not a second edition of that essay, but is a continuation and elaboration of the same subject" (25). The earlier essay was also Mallery's.

18. Mallery did not entirely dismiss the possibility of pre-Columbian contacts, however. For example, he speculated that "if as many Japanese and Chinese vessels were driven upon the west American coast in prehistoric times as are known by historic statistics to have been so driven, the involuntary immigrants skilled in drawing and painting might readily have impressed their styles upon the Americans near their landing place to be thence indefinitely defused." In other words, Mallery did not altogether discount the possibility of limited contacts and even some cultural influence emanating from such contacts. But as he explicitly emphasized, his specu-

lation about wayward Japanese or Chinese vessels and "involuntary immigrants" in ancient times was only a hypothesis, and "this hypothesis would not involve migration" ("Picture-Writing" 772).

19. In "Report of the Director," *Twelfth Annual Report of the Bureau of Ethnology, 1890–91*, Powell attributed the origin of the lost superior races theory to Benjamin Smith Barton (xlii). But Barton was himself more ambiguous in his *New Views of the Origin of the Tribes and Nations of America* (1798). In discussing "the large earthen fortifications or walls, the mounds, and other similar works, which have been discovered in America," Barton concluded that these were "so many proofs of the higher degree of population" in certain parts of ancient North America (xcv). That said, a "higher degree of population" did not necessarily also imply a higher degree of civilization, even though many readers easily leaped to that interpretation.

20. The Huns were a nomadic people who originated in north-central Asia. They rode small fast horses and were organized into effective military units for invasion and conquest. Part of the Great Wall was built to help keep them out of China, following successful incursions in the third century B.C. Their best-known leader was Attila, who died in 453 as his armies attacked Italy.

21. This statement comes from Representative Richard Wilde, *Register of Debates*, 6:1093 (Washington: *Congressional Record*).

22. The Dawes Act was finally repealed in 1934.

2. Contact and Conflict

1. Other explanations for the etymological derivation of *viking* have also been put forward. For a brief summary, see Ferguson 3–5.

2. In "Old Icelandic Prose," the saga scholar Sverrir Tómasson summarizes the general style of the sagas as follows: "The vocabulary used in the sagas is usually concerned with actions, describing everyday objects, such as tools and clothing. Paragraphs are generally short, with main clauses and paratactic clauses predominant. Long sentences with subordinate clauses are rare as little in the way of logical analysis occurs. Present tense and past tense often appear in the same sentence, and indirect speech changes into direct speech without any markers. . . . Wording is often formulaic, which is indicative of both an oral storytelling tradition and a literary tradition. . . . The narrator very seldom makes himself present in the narrative" (129).

3. Vellum was a fine parchment made from the processed skin of a sheep or calf. It absorbed color well, so that medieval vellum manuscripts were often lavishly decorated and illustrated.

4. I have preferred this particular translation because the footnotes provide variant readings and offer useful additional information about events in the text. A more recent excellent translation, with a different opening chapter, is by Kunz (636–52).

5. Never mentioned in either of the two Vinland sagas is the fact that, in

978, "when the western districts of Iceland were fully settled," there was a disastrous attempt to colonize Greenland that predated Eirik the Red's exploration (see Magnusson and Pálsson 16–17).

6. Most scholars generally agree that the eleventh-century Norse had difficulty reckoning longitude but "could hold course accurately on a latitude, by observing the sun and stars" (Magnusson and Pálsson 12). Here, the sun and stars are obscured both by storm clouds and by the dense fog.

7. Tyrkir may originally have been a slave, taken during a Viking raid in Germany by Eirik the Red or his father, but a slave who, over time, became a trusted servant or retainer; or he may have been a servant from the very first. The Vikings were known to take captives from the countries they raided, and these captives subsequently played different roles, from warriors to slaves to household servants. Some became freemen and attained genuine status within Viking society.

8. For example, in June 1963 a Maliseet elder in New Brunswick, Canada, recalled a friend who "always took his two sons into the woods" where "all winter they would trap in the woods": "I remember him, one time when they came back in the spring. . . . They came in a canoe they had made in the woods, using moosehide" (Teeter 175).

9. Because most Indian canoes are curved at the top, when overturned on dry land they do not sit flat on the ground. In *The Bark Canoes and Skin Boats of North America*, Adney and Chapelle explain that when used in this manner, "the tops of the ends and one gunwale rested on the ground. If the ends were high enough, as in the old Malecite type, one gunwale was raised off the ground far enough to permit a man to crawl under. If, as in the Micmac canoes, the ends were too low to allow this, they were raised off the ground by short forked sticks resting against the end thwarts and the upper gunwale and the heels stuck into the earth" (71–72). With the canoe somewhat raised in this manner, it could serve both as a shelter for sleeping or as a concealing blind for those on a hunt. Not until the contact period did Native canoes begin to have seats; until then, Indians sat in their canoes on bended knees. This left more room in the canoe to carry cargo or people.

10. The name Thorstein the Black most probably refers to his hair color (as Eirik the Red referred to hair color). However, there is also the possibility that this sobriquet refers to Thorstein the Black's personality or demeanor. After all, he warns Thorstein Eiriksson that he is "very unsociable" and lives alone with his wife, Grimhild (62).

11. The Englishman John Josselyn, who first visited Maine in 1638–39 and then again from 1663 through 1671, described the Native peoples as "tall and handsome timber'd people, . . . pale and lean . . . black eyed which is accounted the strongest for sight, and generally black hair'd" (89). In his important essay "From White Man to Redskin: Changing Anglo-American Perceptions of the American Indian," the historian Alden T. Vaughan notes that "throughout the colonial period and beyond," most "Anglo-Americans be-

lieved that American Indians were approximately as light-skinned as Europeans" (919).

12. The Norse used a variety of different kinds of axes, each differently shaped for its particular purpose. There were axes for felling trees, axes for working wood, and the larger and lethal battle axes.

13. For a succinct discussion of goading episodes in the Icelandic sagas, see Byock, *Feud in the Icelandic Saga* 256–57.

14. See *The Greenlanders' Saga* 69 n. 1.

15. The Icelandic word that Magnusson and Pálsson choose to translate as "maple" also has another meaning: "burl" or "burly wood" (see Kunz 651n). In fact, "a butternut burl that had been cut with a metal tool" was discovered at the L'Anse aux Meadows site (Wallace, "The Viking Settlement" 213).

16. The other saga often cited for this "unusual" emphasis is *Laxdaela Saga*, whose main character "is above all a leader, a queen" (see Tómasson 135).

17. As her name implies, Aud the Deep-Minded is a woman of wisdom and deep intelligence. She is the courageous wife of a courageous Viking warrior-king. She is shrewd and resourceful, with the foresight to have "a ship built secretly in a forest" so that she can make her escape from the British Isles after the deaths of her husband and son (*Eirik the Red's Saga* 75). She honors the responsibilities and rituals of family and, before going to Iceland, sails first to Orkney, where "she gave away in marriage" her granddaughter, the daughter of her now-deceased son (75). She recognizes a person's worth, whatever his or her status, and she is generous and magnanimous. Upon arriving in Iceland, she "gave land to members of her crew," frees Vifil, and gives him land, too (76). Above all else, Aud the Deep-Minded is "a devout Christian" (75). All these are attributes that Gudrid, too, will exhibit. Foreshadowing, a frequent device in the sagas, thus allows us to anticipate Gudrid's qualities even before they actually unfold in the narrative.

18. See *Eirik the Red's Saga* 85 n. 1; Kunz 660n.

19. *Eirik the Red's Saga* further explains Thorstein Eiriksson's concerns in a later paragraph. According to the saga, "It had been the custom in Greenland since Christianity came there to bury people in unconsecrated ground near the farms where they died; a stake was driven into the ground above the dead person's breast and later, when the priests arrived, the stake would be pulled out and holy water poured down the hole and funeral rites performed, however long after the burial it might then be" (90).

20. According to the archaeologist Niels Lynnerup, "It must be borne in mind that the notion of the Vikings as especially tall and powerful is . . . somewhat unfounded. Actually, the people of the Viking Age were smaller than later medieval populations" (288).

21. Such confusions are explained by "the general Norse concept of the world." As Seaver describes it in *The Last Vikings*, this "was no different from that of their contemporaries elsewhere in Europe, with a spherical world taken for granted and Asia, Africa and Europe envisaged as interconnected

and accounting for the world's entire land mass" (211). This may explain why, in some sources, Vinland was assumed to be connected to Africa.

22. Returning from Vinland and attempting to reach Greenland, Bjarni's ship is blown off course, and "they found themselves in waters infested with maggots" [or ship-worms] (*Eirik the Red's Saga* 103). The ship is soon "riddled with them and had begun to sink" (103). But they had only "one ship's-boat which had been treated with tar made from seal-blubber," impermeable by the maggots, and that "boat would not hold more than half of them" (103). In the end, Bjarni bravely gives up his place in the boat to another and returns to the sinking ship. The saga reports, "It is said that Bjarni and all those who were on the ship with him perished there in the maggot sea. Those in the ship's-boat sailed away and reached land, where they recounted this story" (104).

23. In "Vinland Revisited," Pálsson also attributes the term *Hvítramannaland* and the stories of a White Man's Land to legendary "Irish romance" (29).

24. In *The Medieval Icelandic Saga*, which Sigurðsson published in 2004, he again asserted his conviction that the Vinlanders had sailed "the coastal regions stretching from northern Labrador south to the Hudson River and the site of modern-day New York" (301).

25. For a full and persuasive discussion, see Edmund Carpenter's *Norse Penny*.

26. Author's conversation with Passamaquoddy elder and educator, Wayne Newell, 21 June 2000, at Newell's home in Indian Township, Maine. Archaeological evidence suggests that the ancient Beothuk wintered at Red Indian Lake at the head of the Exploits River in Newfoundland. In summers, the Exploits River provided easy access to Notre Dame Bay, also in Newfoundland, where the Beothuk took birds, seals, and salmon and other fish. The ethnologist Ingeborg Marshall writes that these Beothuk "settlements on the coast suggest marine orientation with a limited back-up system for hunting terrestrial animals" like the caribou (263). The reasons for and the timing of the Beothuk's move inland remain uncertain. As Marshall comments, "Whether the extensive interception of migrating caribou herds along the Exploits River and at Red Indian Lake that resulted in the more interior-oriented subsistence economy of some Beothuk bands was a prehistoric [i.e., predating sixteenth-century European contacts] phenomenon or developed in the historic period [i.e., after sixteenth-century European contacts] has not been established" (263). Oral lore among surviving Algonquian tribes describes the Beothuk as notoriously fearful of Europeans, perhaps due to a prior encounter with Norse, and attributes their move inland to this possibility, thereby dating the move to what Marshall calls the "prehistoric" period. As a result of a long history of brutal treatment by Europeans and hostilities with the Mi´kmaqs, the Beothuk died out as a people and a culture in the first two decades of the nineteenth century.

27. In an article published in 2009, Wallace presented evidence gleaned from the sagas to argue that the goal of Karlsefni's expedition was never immediate colonization but, rather, "exploration for resources and their subsequent exploitation.... Colonization may have been considered a future possibility" ("L'Anse aux Meadows, Leif Eriksson's Home in Vinland" 116).

3. Anglo-America's Viking Heritage

1. In *Memory's Nation: The Place of Plymouth Rock*, the scholar John Seelye makes no claims one way or another as to "whether or not the Pilgrims actually came ashore on the Rock" (640). In his magisterial study of Plymouth Rock's iconic significance over time, Seelye examines the Rock's political uses rather than its historical authenticity.

2. For a discussion of Simms's Revolutionary War romances, see Kolodny, *The Lay of the Land* 115–32.

3. In Mott's *Golden Multitudes: The Story of Best Sellers in the United States*, Cooper's *The Spy* appears as a bestseller in 1821, and the first of Cooper's Leatherstocking novels, *The Pioneers*, appears on the list for 1823 (305). Cooper's *The Last of the Mohicans* was a bestseller in 1826, and *The Pathfinder* appears on Mott's list for 1840 (306). Simms's *The Yemassee*, the first of the Revolutionary War romances, is listed by Mott as a "better seller" for 1835 (318).

4. In *Golden Multitudes*, Mott notes that "historical works had long been the favorite fare of many American readers and a few of them had become long-time best sellers," with the popular historical romances of the period "stimulat[ing] the public taste" (95).

5. See Mott, *Golden Multitudes* 305, for the bestselling titles between 1811 and 1821.

6. Rafn and his Danish colleagues sought sponsorship and members for the Royal Society of Northern Antiquaries from across Europe and the U.S. So many prominent Americans joined the society that a separate American membership section was organized. Included among the many political, artistic, educational, and cultural leaders of the day enrolled as society members were Jared Sparks, Henry Wadsworth Longfellow, Noah Webster, and Benjamin Silliman of Yale. Edward Everett, who served briefly as the editor of the *North American Review* and later became governor of Massachusetts (1836–39), and his older brother, the writer and diplomat Alexander Hill Everett, were also enrolled members of the society; both wrote lengthy and generally laudatory reviews of *Antiquitates Americanæ* when it appeared.

7. Few copies of the original "Abstract" have survived. Happily, the entire "Abstract" was published as the prefatory opening to Schoolcraft's "The Ante-Columbian History of America," 430–34, and it is from this reprinting that I quote here.

8. Especially eager for acceptance in educated and professional circles,

Rafn emphasized particular aspects of his sources that coincided with the discipline (or disciplines) of the journal for which he was writing. In an article composed in 1859 for the *Journal of the American Geographical and Statistical Society*, for example, Rafn emphasized both geography and statistics. "It is the total result of the nautical, geographical and astronomical evidences in the original documents," he wrote, "which places the situation of the countries discovered beyond all doubt" ("Northmen in America" 178). His nautical and geographical evidence, based on the sagas, was that "the number of days' sail between the several newly-found lands, the striking description of the coasts, especially the white sand-banks of Nova Scotia and the long beaches and downs of a peculiar appearance on Cape Cod (the Kjalarnes and Furdustrandir of the Northmen) are not to be mistaken" (179). His statistical geographic evidence was "the astronomical remark [in *The Greenlanders' Saga*] that the shortest day in Vineland was 9 hours long, which fixes the latitude of 41° 24' 10", or just that of the promontories which limit the entrances to Mount Hope Bay, where Leif's booths were built, and in the district around which the old Northmen had their head establishment, which was named by them Hop" (179). What kind of peer review this two-page article received is impossible to determine. The headnote simply reads "Communicated by Prof. Ch. C. Rafn, and founded on his work 'Antiquitates Americanæ'" (178).

9. Davis's lecture was first published in 1838–39 and, according to Falnes, "it had reached a twentieth edition by 1848" (227 n. 67).

10. Despite Rafn's efforts to protect his scholarship from misrepresentation in the hands of others, few writers could refrain from conjectures and speculations of their own. One example appears in John Warner Barber's *The History and Antiquities of New England* (1842), according to its title page "collected and compiled from authentic sources." After a summary of the Vinland voyages based on Rafn's *Antiquitataes Americanae*, Barber wrote the following: "In 1121, Vinland was visited by bishop Eric, and as there is no account of his return, it seems probable that he spent his days there" (11). What Barber fails to mention is that the *Icelandic Annals* give no account of the bishop ever having reached Vinland or what the purpose of his journey might have been. As a result, comments like Barber's helped fuel further speculations that the Vinland colony had survived into the twelfth century and that the bishop was ministering to the Norse, the Native inhabitants, or both.

11. Like Bryant, Sydney Howard Gay (1814–88) was also a native New Englander. From 1872 to 1874, Gay was a member of the editorial staff of the *New York Evening Post* under Bryant. In 1874, Bryant, then eighty years old, was asked to undertake a popular history of the U.S. He agreed, but only with the understanding that Gay would serve both as collaborator and as the major author. Bryant's only substantive contribution was a preface, and he died before the entire work was completed.

Notes to Pages 113–122   345

12. Established by the New Sweden Company, the colony included immigrants from both Sweden and Holland and was located on the Delaware River in parts of present-day Pennsylvania, New Jersey, and Delaware. In 1655, a Dutch force led by Peter Stuyvesant captured the colony's main fort and compelled New Sweden's surrender. The Swedish colonists were allowed to keep their lands and possessions and continue their national customs. As a result, Swedes continued to immigrate to the colony even though it was now under Dutch rule.

13. Paul Henri Mallett's *Monumens de la Mythologie et de la Poésie des Celtes et Particulièrement des Anciens Scandinaves* was originally published in Copenhagen in 1755–56.

14. In *The Promise of America*, Odd S. Lovoll writes, "Norwegian emigration [to the U.S.] in the nineteenth century began dramatically on July 4, 1825, with the sailing of the sloop *Restauration* from Stavanger on the southwestern coast of Norway. On board were fifty-two persons, crew and passengers, who all intended to emigrate. The *Restauration* reached the port of New York on October 9, after . . . fourteen weeks across the Atlantic. During this time a child was born, so that on arrival there was an additional passenger" (9).

15. In the appendix, "Voyages of the Scandinavians" (sometimes also titled "Scandinavian Discoveries"), Irving wrote, "As far as the author of the present work has had experience in tracing these stories of early discoveries of portions of the New World, he has generally found them very confidant deductions, drawn from very vague and questionable facts." Irving then went on to admit, however, that "there is no great improbability . . . that such enterprizing and roving voyageurs as the Scandinavians, may have wandered to the northern shores of America, about the coast of Labrador, or the shores of Newfoundland; and if the Icelandic manuscripts said to be of the thirteenth century, can be relied upon as genuine, free from modern interpolation, and correctly quoted, they would appear to prove the fact. But granting the truth of the alleged discoveries," said Irving, "they led to no [significant] result" (256).

16. Falnes states that "the book was a distinct success; in 1844 it was issued in a French translation" with some new materials added (215).

17. Henry Rowe Schoolcraft (1793–1864) began a nineteen-year career in the federal Indian service in 1822 when he was appointed the first Indian agent at Sault Ste. Marie, Michigan. Thereafter he worked mostly with various Ojibwa bands—all Central Algonquian-speakers—in Michigan and Wisconsin. He married in Michigan, and his mother-in-law was a Native-speaking Ojibwa from Michigan. He embarked on pioneering studies of Ojibwa language and oral culture, published several articles on Ojibwa ethnology, and in 1839—the same year as his article in the *American Biblical Repository* appeared—he published his first collection of Indian myths and legends in a popular two-volume work titled *Algic Researches*.

18. In "The Ante-Columbian History of America," Schoolcraft explained,

"By the term Algic we comprehend that generic race of men, who, (say) in 1600, were found scattered, in various independent bands, along the Atlantic border, between the Floridian peninsula and the gulf of St. Lawrence.... This race lined the whole United States border of the Atlantic, and extended westward to the lakes, etc." (445). Today we term these peoples collectively as Algonquians, meaning that they speak related Algonquian languages and share many cultural practices and affinities.

19. For a general discussion of the several so-called Norse artifacts discovered in America, including Dighton Rock and the Newport tower, see Wallace and Fitzhugh 374–84. For a discussion of the Newport tower, including references to several recent studies and excavations, see Hertz 376.

20. In the British Isles, Cambrensis was a common nineteenth-century term for the people of Wales. Throughout the 1830s and 1840s, crop failures and increasing poverty in Ireland drove many Irish to emigrate to other parts of the British Isles. Because the Irish brought with them their Catholic religion, this migration stirred fears of invading "popery" in largely Protestant Great Britain. Anti-Irish sentiment thus joined with anti-Catholic prejudices in both religious and political life all across Great Britain, and at times became particularly virulent in Wales. See Paul O'Leary's "When Was Anti-Catholicism? The Case of Nineteenth- and Twentieth-Century Wales" for an excellent review of the subject.

21. In *The History of South Carolina*, Simms referred to "the slave-trade, which alone could supply an agricultural people, in a tropical region, with its adequate proportion of physical labor" (424). In his many novels, Simms portrayed several characters who were clearly slaves, but he presented them as child-like and happy. The more vicious aspects of slavery never entered his writings.

22. The Seminole were one of what were then known as the Five Civilized Tribes, which also included the Choctaw, Cherokee, Creek, and Chickasaw. In the eighteenth century, the Seminole had separated from the Creek Nation and, to escape encroaching white settlement, fled to Florida. There they absorbed remnants of the Apalachee tribe and runaway slaves. They first fought against Andrew Jackson in 1817–18. Led by Chief Osceola, they again battled U.S. forces in the Second Seminole War of 1835–42, after which most were removed to Oklahoma. President John Tyler's proclamation ended hostilities in Florida as of 10 May 1842. By that time, the U.S. had become weary of both the expense and the atrocities of the Seminole Wars. Having been inaccessible to U.S. troops during the wars by hiding in the swamps, many Seminole remained in Florida even after the removal of 1842. As a result, the Seminole were never completely driven from their Florida land base.

23. See L. B., "Antiquitates Americanæ," *The Western Messenger Devoted to Religion, Life, and Literature* 5.4 (1838), 1–14; L. B., "Inscription Rocks: Found in the States of Massachusetts and Rhode Island," *Western Messenger* 6.2

(1838), 81–87. *The Western Messenger* (1835–41) was a monthly magazine that carried articles about literature and religious matters, edited by William Henry Channing and James Freeman Clarke, both of whom served as clergymen in the Unitarian Church and were actively involved in the Transcendentalist movement centered around Ralph Waldo Emerson, Henry David Thoreau, and others in New England.

24. See "America First Discovered by the Scandinavians," *Catholic Telegraph* 7.34 (1838), 265.

25. George Perkins Marsh (1801–82) ran for Congress as a Whig and was elected in 1843, serving until 1849. He opposed the admission of Texas as a slave state and argued against U.S. involvement in the Mexican War. He was also instrumental in helping to establish the Smithsonian Institution. Two of his later publications provided a firm foundation for the environmental movement of the twentieth century: *Man and Nature* (1864), later revised as *The Earth as Modified by Human Action* (1874).

26. Acknowledging the impact of Rafn's work, Marsh also made explicit that Scandinavians were one component of that Gothic blood. A brief anecdote referred to "the true Gothic spirit of that noble Dane" (39). The Dane referred to here was probably the Danish philosopher and religious theorist Søren Kierkegaard (1813–55).

27. Today the term "Anglo-Saxon" refers to any member of the Germanic peoples who inhabited and ruled England from the fifth century A.D. to the time of the Norman Conquest in 1066. The Anglo-Saxons are believed to be descendants of four different Germanic peoples—the Angles, Saxons, Jutes, and Friesians—who originally migrated from northern Germany to England in the fifth century. Archaeological evidence suggests that small groups of first arrivals antedated the Roman withdrawal from England ca. 410. The various Anglo-Saxon kingdoms spoke dialects of what is now known as Old English. Ethnically, the so-called Anglo-Saxons actually comprised an admixture of Germanic peoples with England's preexisting Celtic inhabitants and subsequent Danish and Norwegian Viking invaders.

28. Motley's three major historical works were *The Rise of the Dutch Republic* (1855), *History of the United Netherlands* (1861–68), and *The Life and Death of John Barneveld* (1874).

29. This propensity for erasing Indians from nineteenth-century New England historical narratives written by non-Indians is brilliantly and thoroughly examined by Jean M. O'Brien (White Earth Ojibwe) in *Firsting and Lasting*, a study of how these writers "implicitly [made] arguments about what counts as legitimate history, and who counts as legitimate peoples" (xviii).

30. During the Great Potato Famine in Ireland (1847–54), nearly a million Irish died of starvation and disease; 1,600,000 immigrated to the U.S. between 1847 and 1854. A period of renewed cultural nationalism and political activism in mid-nineteenth-century Italy was known as the "Risorgimento."

Its main political objective was the reunification of Italy, which was finally effected in 1870. But those forces in favor of reunification experienced major military defeats in 1848 and 1849, and, as a result, many Italians—especially those who had favored reunifying Italy as a democratic republic—fled to the U.S. as political refugees. Other Italians came during this period—and afterward—because of the economic problems that accompanied and followed the political unrest. German immigrants included both Catholics and Protestants as well as liberals who were largely secular. Often called "the German Forty-Eighters," these refugees from revolution brought with them Marxist and radical ideas. The U.S. xenophobia of the 1850s was due, in part, to anxiety over the perceived threat of immigrant radicals importing unorthodox ideas. These ideas included labor organizing and improved wages for the working poor, ideas seen by some Americans as a threat to American institutions.

31. On the other side of the Atlantic, in 1855 the French Count Joseph Arthur de Gobineau predicted the decline of Anglo-Saxon America because the country was now being overwhelmed by "the most degenerate races of olden day Europe. They are the human flotsam of all ages," and first among these "degenerate races" were the Irish (161). In both its original French and in English translation, Gobineau's *The Inequality of the Human Races*, considered one of the earliest examples of scientific racism, soon had wide currency in the U.S.

32. It was Catholicism, as a massive institution ruled from Rome, that was suspect. And two central dogmas of Catholicism—the virgin birth and transubstantiation—were regarded by most Protestants as superstitions arising from the uneducated credulity of the Dark Ages.

33. At this point, too, many American poets, like (James) Bayard Taylor (1825–78), continued to celebrate heroic Norse themes and sing the praises of "manly" Germanic ancestors. Taylor's "The Norseman's Ride" (1846), for instance, written ten years before he first visited Scandinavia in the summer of 1856, depicts an ancient "Norseman, as armed for battle," called forth from his grave to enter "Walhalla" (*The Poetical Works* 17). Again invoking images of manly heroism, in his poem, "Steyermark" (1848), Taylor praised the men of the Austrian federal state of Steiermark (also known as Styria) along the Danube: "These men are framed in the manly mould / Of their stalwart sires, of the times of old" (14). Taylor later became a recognized expert in German literature, and he continued to write about northern Europe.

34. The first permanent European settlement in North America was founded by the Spanish in 1565 near present-day St. Augustine, Florida.

4. New England Poets of Viking America

1. According to the archaeologist William A. Haviland in "The Case of the Deer Isle Giant," "by the time the first European explorers arrived in the northeast, Mi'kmaq Indians had long been mining copper in the Minas

Basin of Nova Scotia, which they traded to people living far to the south and west of them" (4). In that same article, Haviland also discusses the propensity of those untrained in modern forensics to overestimate the stature of individuals based solely on skeletal remains (3–4).

2. Norway was ruled by Danish governors until 1814, when Denmark ceded it to Sweden. In 1905 the union with Sweden was dissolved, and Norway became an independent constitutional monarchy.

3. Longfellow's letter to Rafn of December 1835 also reveals that Longfellow was one of the many Americans from whom Rafn sought information "concerning the Indians of Massachusetts, Rhode Island and Connecticut." Longfellow replied that he could provide only "vague and unsatisfactory information, it being a subject to which I have never given any particular attention," and, instead, he gave Rafn the names of others in the U.S. who might prove more helpful (*Letters* 1:531–32).

4. This and all subsequent quotations from Longfellow's journals come from the unpublished manuscripts in the Longfellow Papers (MS Am 1340) in Houghton Library at Harvard University. These journal entries are referenced only by date.

5. Either as a headnote or as a note at the end of the volume, Longfellow published this note with most subsequent reprintings of "The Skeleton in Armour" (the shorter title he employed for the poem in book publication). In his note, he recalled that "a skeleton had been dug up at Fall River, clad in broken and corroded armor; and the idea occurred to me of connecting it with the Round Tower at Newport, generally known hitherto as the Old Windmill." He then quoted from a report by Rafn, published in 1838–39, which asserted, in capital letters, "THIS BUILDING WAS ERECTED AT A PERIOD DECIDEDLY NOT LATER THAN THE TWELFTH CENTURY." For his part, however, Longfellow stated, "I will not enter into a discussion of the point. It is sufficiently well established for the purpose of a ballad" ("The Skeleton in Armour" 29–30, 31).

6. As this letter to his father indicates, Longfellow understood himself to have written a ballad rather than a saga. He called the poem a saga solely for the purpose of giving it "a Northern air." As Longfellow knew from his studies of medieval Icelandic sagas, "The Skeleton in Armour" was in no formal sense a saga. Like the two Vinland sagas, the original Icelandic sagas were prose (not poetry) narratives and were rarely told by a single identified speaking voice, like the skeleton's. Even so, there are elements in the poem that can be found in traditional sagas, including the protagonist's adventures at sea, feuds and battle scenes, and even the abduction of a bride.

7. In order to avoid this unhappy possibility, Longfellow told his father he would make "a modest request" of his readers. He would ask that if they had "not leisure to study it through *ten times*, then do not read it once" (*Letters* 2:269). Of course, the comment was meant as humorous, but it nevertheless reveals at least some level of apprehension as the poem went to press.

8. On 26 December 1841, Longfellow wrote this to his father: "My Bal-

lads &c are at length published. . . . The first edition was small; only about 400, and went off immediately. The second, of 500, came out yesterday. . . . A large-paper edition will be in readiness soon; it being already printed and in the binder's hands" (*Letters* 2:364). Longfellow's *Ballads and Other Poems* was a critical success, and in this letter, he makes clear that it was also an immediate commercial success, having gone through three printings in the course of a few short months.

9. Coleridge's "Rime of the Ancient Mariner" first appeared in 1798 as the lead-off poem for *Lyrical Ballads*, the joint poetry venture that resulted from the collaboration of Coleridge and William Wordsworth. At this point, the poem had no marginal gloss, a device that Coleridge added later. Coleridge continued to revise the poem over the years, adding and deleting stanzas and restoring the archaisms and antique diction previously edited out by Wordsworth. Editions of Coleridge's poems published in 1828, 1829, and 1834—all prepared by Coleridge himself—show these ongoing alterations. Longfellow was probably familiar with the version of the "Rime" in the *Poetical Works* volume (published in 1834, the year of Coleridge's death), which contained all the restored archaisms and the marginal gloss. In addition to Coleridge, other influences have been suggested. In *Henry Wadsworth Longfellow*, Wagenknecht offers a summary (236 n. 8).

Elements of the love story in "The Skeleton in Armour" are clearly borrowed from *Frithiof's Saga* (1825) by Esaias Tegnér, the great Swedish poet whom Longfellow much admired. Some infrequent similarities in wording and imagery in the two poems also indicate influence. Longfellow later included an English translation of "Frithiof's Saga" in his massive *The Poets and Poetry of Europe* (1845), 146–63. For a useful review of the verbal similarities and the similarities in thought between the two poems, see Edward Thorstenberg's "The Skeleton in Armour and the Frithiof Saga" (1910).

10. With the exception of a few minor spelling differences, there are no variant versions or textual difficulties associated with this poem. Therefore, all my quotations from the poem follow the version first published in the *Knickerbocker* (1841). Because most readers will find the poem in many other sources, I have identified all my quotations simply by stanza number.

11. Also called a "berserker"; the word may be of Icelandic origin, derived from the Old Icelandic words for a bearskin cape or bearskin covering of some kind.

12. "The first bold viking" could easily have referred to Bjarni Herjolfsson or Leif Eiriksson, although it is also quite possible that, even at this early stage, Longfellow was considering a wholly invented story line. The "storm-spirits and devil-machinery underwater" suggest that Longfellow may have been reading Coleridge's last collection, *Poetical Works* (1834), with the final revised version of the "Rime of the Ancient Mariner." This version contained the marginal gloss, as well as sometimes lurid evocations of the spectral and the supernatural at sea.

13. Although not usually thought of as a political writer, Longfellow was not above embedding political messages in his poetry. For example, in *The Song of Hiawatha* (1855), he incorporated a quiet allegory about the need for political union in the first part of the poem, "The Peace Pipe." Here the Gitche Manito expresses his impatience with the ongoing "wrangling" among the various tribes:

> All your strength is in your union,
> All your danger is in discord;
> Therefore be at peace hence forward,
> And as brothers live together.

Written six years before the outbreak of civil war, these lines obviously had political relevance, urging compromise to avoid disunion.

14. According to a friend of Mary's who had accompanied the Longfellows on this journey, as Mary lay dying, "Henry was able to command his feelings" so as not to agitate Mary with his own grief. But once she had passed and "there was no longer cause for restraint he gave vent to his grief and wept bitterly till sleep came to his relief" (Crowninshield 184–85).

15. About seven months after Mary's death, while still in Europe, Longfellow met young Fanny (Frances Elizabeth) Appleton and her family. The Appletons were from Boston. After a long courtship, Henry and Fanny were married in Boston in July 1843. Following eighteen happy years together (and the birth of five children), Fanny died tragically in July 1861 when the light summer dress she was wearing accidentally caught fire from a near-by candle.

16. Because this language sounds so much like Hawthorne's, I have always suspected that this review may have been written by him. Longfellow and Hawthorne were classmates at Bowdoin College in Maine, and Hawthorne admired Longfellow's poetry. In 1839–41, Hawthorne was employed at the Boston Custom House, and, for additional income, he was taking on a variety of writing and editing assignments. It is not out of the question that he agreed to review a book by an old college friend whose poetry he thought well of.

17. According to this reviewer's summary of the poem, when Old Hildebrand opposes the match, "the lady . . . (as ladies usually do) differed in opinion from her sire, and availing herself of a dark night, and a ladder of rope, committed her person to the protection" of her suitor ("Longfellow's Ballads and Poems," *United States Magazine and Democratic Review* 186). Of course, none of these details exists in the poem itself. Longfellow's lines read simply, in the skeleton's voice, "Should not the dove so white / Follow the sea-mew's flight, / Why did they leave that night / Her nest unguarded?" The marginal gloss is even more straightforward: "Is discarded by Hildebrand, but steals the maiden away at night."

18. As the reviewer for *Arcturus* had hoped, this planted legend did indeed

"take root" ("Longfellow's Ballads and Poems" 215). It became intertwined with the actual discovery of a European in full armor, unearthed in the last years of the nineteenth century in the mouth of Greenlaw Cove, on Campbell's Island, in Maine. The burial also contained the body of a Native companion, and both had been carefully laid to rest in the local Indian manner. "With the European was the iron blade of a halberd, an iron hatchet marked with a Maltese Cross, . . . and the muzzle of a blunderbuss" (Haviland, *At the Place of the Lobsters and Crabs* 7). Archaeologists have since determined that the European was not an eleventh-century Viking but "most likely" someone associated with the seventeenth-century French outpost located near present-day Castine, where the French had "had a presence as early as 1615" (10; see also Spiess).

19. While this was the prevailing opinion, not all reviewers shared it, or shared it completely. The reviewer for the *New York Review* stated that Longfellow "does not belong to any of the particular schools of poetry, but seems determined . . . to mark out his own poetical path. . . . He swears neither by Pope, nor Wordsworth, neither by Byron, nor Southey" ("Longfellow's Poems" 240). The reviewer for *Graham's Lady's and Gentleman's Magazine* castigated Longfellow for being too "didactic" in his poetry, "a habit deduced from German study" ("Review of New Books" 190).

20. Taylor's poem was published first in the *United States Magazine, and Democratic Review* 19.101 (1846), 368. Whittier's essay commending the poem appeared in the *National Era* 1.33 (1847), 1.

21. Page references here are to the original publication of the poem in the *Knickerbocker*. Whittier made some minor spelling changes but no substantive textual changes when he included "The Norsemen" in his various editions of his collected poems.

22. For some readers, these lines seem to hint at what nowadays might be taken as an almost homoerotic fascination with the "stalwart crew." Given the historical context in which these lines were composed, however, they are best understood not solely as homoerotic, but also as emphasizing the hypermasculinity of these *manly* New England precursors. For the sober New England intellectuals who wrote about the Northmen, that hypermasculinity was part of their appeal (even while those same writers often deplored the Northmen's wild excesses).

23. *Culdee* is an Irish word that literally means "servant of god."

24. Griswold's anthologies included both literary selections and biographical sketches. Whittier was well represented in the first two: *Poets and Poetry of America* (1841) and *Prose Writers of America* (1847).

25. "His most dangerous brush came in 1838 when the newly dedicated Pennsylvania Hall, erected [in Philadelphia] under Abolitionist auspices, was destroyed and burned by a surging mob of fifteen thousand. Disguised in a wig and long white overcoat, Whittier mingled with the crowd and managed to save some personal possessions while his office [in the building] was being sacked" (Pickard 25).

26. If he suspected that his physical maladies were some sort of test or punishment from god, he never said so, and, anyway, this would have been incompatible with the loving and beneficent god of the Quakers.

27. Throughout the 1840s and 1850s, Whittier's writings continued to champion the cause of abolition. But now he also found time—and inspiration—for poetry that was more personal, more self-reflective, and poetry that championed also the natural beauty as well as the stories and legends of his beloved New England. After the *Atlantic Monthly* was founded in Boston in 1857 by a group of leading New England literary figures, Whittier "found it increasingly more advantageous to his pocket and popularity" to contribute as often as possible to this decidedly prestigious venue (Kribbs xix). There, until his death, he joined the ranks of Emerson, Longfellow, Motley, Lowell, Oliver Wendell Holmes, Harriet Beecher Stowe, and other prominent authors.

28. "Norembega" was first published in June 1869 in the *Atlantic Monthly*, 662–65. Whittier subsequently included it in his next poetry collection, *Miriam, and Other Poems*, published in Boston in 1871.

29. Johann Georg Kohl (1808–78), a native of Bremen, Germany, studied the history of American coastal geography as part of his interest in historical cartography. He traveled widely in both the U.S. and Canada, became a corresponding member of the Massachusetts Historical Society, and lectured at the Smithsonian Institution in Washington. He sought out and associated with many prominent American writers, including Longfellow. He published extensively in both English and German. In all, he produced twenty-five volumes on Europe, North America, and the Atlantic Ocean. He continues to be credited with having made a significant scientific contribution to the history of the study of American coastal geography.

30. One explanation for the origin of the word "Norumbega" appears in Kirsten Seaver's "Norumbega and 'Harmonia Mundi.'" Seaver reviews the history of the word's appearance on early maps in *The Last Vikings* (215–17).

31. See, for example, A. C. Hamlin's "Supposed Runic Inscriptions" (1857) and Joseph Williamson's "The Northmen in Maine" (1869).

32. Samuel de Champlain (1567–1635) founded Port Royal in Nova Scotia in 1605, and in 1608 he brought his colonists to Quebec. These settlements were centers for the lucrative fur trade with the local Natives, providing a new source of wealth for France.

33. Whittier's essay appeared as the introduction to Stanley Pumphrey's book, also titled *Indian Civilization*, published in 1877 in Philadelphia by the Bible and Tract Distributing Society.

34. Whittier was unable to attend the Boston meeting and deliver the talk himself. It was read in his absence by another attendee. When published, "The Indian Question" carried the following headnote: "Read at the meeting in Boston, May, 1883, for the consideration of the condition of the Indians in the United States" (238).

35. "A Moosehead Journal" first appeared in November 1853 in *Putnam's Magazine*.

354 Notes to Pages 191–197

36. In a letter of 8 December 1868 to James B. Thayer, who had reviewed *Under the Willows, and Other Poems* for the *Daily Advertiser*, Lowell wrote candidly about his writing. *Under the Willows* mostly reprinted his earlier poems, and so Lowell looked back to the 1850s in this letter and explained that many works of that period had been thwarted or left unfinished because "something broke my life in two," an obvious reference to the death of his first wife in 1853. Lowell also acknowledged to Thayer that many of the reprinted early poems in the collection "are moody" (*Letters* 2:10–11). These remarks may shed some light on the composition of "The Growth of the Legend," although it is not one of the poems Lowell mentions in his letter to Thayer.

37. *Poems, Second Series* appeared early in 1848, followed by *Fable for Critics*, a verse satire with often shrewd estimations of his literary contemporaries, including himself; *The Biglow Papers, First Series*; and just in time for Christmas, *The Vision of Sir Launfal*, a verse parable derived from legends of the Holy Grail in Sir Thomas Malory's *Le Morte d'Arthur* and influenced also by Alfred, Lord Tennyson's publication of "Sir Galahad" in 1844.

38. Maria's death overwhelmed Lowell with grief, and he set about preparing a memorial volume of her poems in an edition of fifty copies, intended for circulation only among friends and family members. Titled simply *Poems*, the little volume appeared in 1855.

39. Charles Frederick Briggs (1804–77) edited the *Broadway Journal*, *Putnam's Magazine*, and the *New York Times*. He published two novels dealing with his own early life: *The Adventures of Harry Franco* (1839) and *Working a Passage* (1844). The autobiographical fiction, *The Trippings of Tom Pepper*, appeared in two volumes, 1847–50.

40. All the quotes from "Hakon's Lay" are from its publication in *Graham's American Monthly Magazine* in January 1855.

41. Satisfying neither side of the debate, the Compromise of 1850 admitted California to the Union as a free state, while the New Mexico and Utah territories were formed and allowed to make their own decisions about slavery.

42. The Kansas-Nebraska Act of 1854 repealed the Missouri Compromise of 1820 and allowed all new territories to decide for themselves whether to permit or prohibit slavery.

43. Lowell objected to "any general confiscation of Rebel property," but, as he wrote in his essay "Reconstruction," first published in the *North American Review* in 1865, he wanted to ensure that the former slaveholders were henceforward rendered "powerless for mischief" (*The Writings* 5:226, 225). For Lowell, the ultimate goal of Reconstruction was "not to punish, but to repair; . . . emancipating the master from the slave, as well as the slave from the master" (5:222–23).

44. Lowell liked the poem so much in its new rewritten version that he seriously considered naming the volume in which it was to appear "The Voy-

age to Vinland, and Other Poems." But his publisher "would not hear of it," and so, as Lowell told Norton in that same letter, "I hit upon 'Under the Willows,' and that it is to be" (*Letters* 2:2).

45. See, for example, Thurin 82. Lowell was not the only writer to adapt Norse mythology to American themes. Inevitably, the ongoing project of reconceiving the Norse as acceptable proto-Americans resulted in a rewriting of their pagan mythology in Christian terms. Several writers took on the challenge, most prominent among them Julia Clinton Jones, who began her writing career in 1878 with the publication of a long epic poem entitled *Valhalla, the Myths of Norseland: A Saga in Twelve Parts*. As Lowell had done ten years before in "The Voyage to Vinland," Jones also used the myth of the world conflagration for her own purposes. She turned the new Earth that arises after the conflagration into a kind of New Jerusalem and identified the new god as the "High and Mighty One" and "the Judge Supreme," intentional echoes of the Judeo-Christian godhead (131, 145). Jones understood herself to be participating in the larger contemporary project of reenvisioning the Norse in order to link Americans more firmly to their Norse ancestry. "It is much to be deplored," she complained in her preface, "that so slight a knowledge of Scandinavian Mythology prevails, popularly, with those who boast descent [through England], . . . and whose pride it is that in their veins flows the blood that long ago thrilled through the bold hearts of the Vikings, descendants of the old Norse Gods" (7).

46. For the knowledgeable nineteenth-century reader, Lowell's poem glaringly distorted the history preserved in the two Vinland sagas and contained at least one obvious anachronism. As for the history, Bjarni Herjolfsson never intentionally sailed a ship to Vinland nor explored its "wooded shores." That was Leif Eiriksson's achievement. Gudrid never sailed with Bjarni. She was part of a later colonizing expedition to Vinland led by her husband, Thorfinn Karlsefni. The anachronism in the poem, which had also been apparent in the original "Hakon's Lay," was the blurring of the distinction between Fate, Luck, and Opportunity. Medieval Icelandic literature spoke of the Fates (that is, demigoddesses called the *Norns*) and Luck, an inherent quality that was also sometimes an aspect of Fate. The Norns ruled over the destinies of mortals (and sometimes even over the destinies of the gods), and no one can change what they have decided. When the skald Hakon sings of "Opportunity, / Seeking the hardy soul that seeks for her," he is hardly reflecting this more static concept of Fate. Rather, he is really appealing to a mid-nineteenth-century American self-image of dynamic enterprise and limitless personal possibilities. Of course, Lowell never intended to write a poem that reproduced the life and thought of the medieval Norse. In fact, he expressed only contempt for what he called the literary "effort to raise a defunct past" (*Letters* 2:85). He roundly criticized that strain in Romanticism, castigating some of his contemporaries for creating "modern antiques" (1:357).

47. See Duberman for the context in which Lowell referred to the Belknaps, the Goulds, and Boss Tweed as "swindlers" (274).

48. For an overview of Lowell's social and political ideas during his later years, see Duberman 352–63.

49. Each of these men also employed Scandinavian themes, subject matter, or references in at least some of their later writings, although none of these specifically related to the Norse in the U.S. For example, upon learning of Tegnér's death in 1846, Longfellow composed a skaldic homage to the Swedish poet called "Tegnér's Drapa" (or praise-song). In Longfellow's *Tales of a Wayside Inn* (1886), a series of narrative poems modeled on Chaucer's *Canterbury Tales*, the musician's tale is called "The Saga of King Olaf" and recounts the story of the tenth-century Norwegian king who first championed Christianity. In 1868, Whittier wrote "The Dole of Jarl [i.e., earl] Thorkell," a poem which pits pagan ritual sacrifice against an act of Christian charity during a time of famine in ancient Norway. Lowell's writings subsequent to "The Voyage to Vinland" do not display any continuing Viking or Scandinavian focus but are, nonetheless, marked by occasional references and allusions to both.

50. The phrase is from Lincoln's brief remarks, often called the Gettysburg Address, delivered on 19 November 1863, at the dedication of the new national cemetery at Gettysburg, Pennsylvania.

51. The most notable among the novels for young adults was a trilogy written by a Swedish American, Ottilie A. Liljencrantz, published between 1902 and 1906. In all three novels, Liljencrantz took her readers to a Vinland clearly set in New England. In her "Note of Acknowledgment" in the first of these works, *The Thrall of Leif the Lucky: A Story of Viking Days* (1902), she indicated that she was "indebted to the studies of such Norse antiquarians as Rafn, . . . Mallet, . . . Anderson, . . . Tegner, [and] . . . Eben Norton Horsford," among many others (n.p.). In each novel, Liljencrantz introduced a cast of invented characters alongside the personages found in the sagas. There are quotations from Longfellow, Whittier, and others throughout the series as well as barely disguised allusions to familiar features of Vinland lore like the Newport tower and Longfellow's "Skeleton in Armour."

52. In fact, by the 1870s, "in the heightened patriotic atmosphere after the conclusion of the Civil War, . . . the study of American writers was beginning to enter the classroom" for the first time (Giles 131). It was now generally agreed that the U.S. had produced a unique literature of its own, a view initially propounded in 1878 when Moses Coit Tyler published the first *History of American Literature*.

53. Gage lived most of her life in and around Syracuse, New York. As a child during the 1830s, she had circulated antislavery petitions. When a women's rights convention was held in Syracuse in 1852, Gage spoke there and formally entered the movement. During the 1870s, she wrote a series of articles protesting the brutal and unjust treatment of American Indians. She knew

these issues firsthand because she was adopted into the Wolf Clan of the Mohawk Nation and wrote about what she believed to be the more democratic and egalitarian form of government practiced by the Six Nations Iroquois Confederacy.

54. For a balanced scholarly overview of the status of women throughout medieval Scandinavia, see Birgit Sawyer and Peter Sawyer, *Medieval Scandinavia* 188–213.

55. An accompanying "silver and ivory toilette set" for the table was ornamented with "small silver walrus faces," thereby "continu[ing] the allusion to the Arctic realm of Viking seafarers" (Wheary, "Vanity of Vanities" 103).

56. These Viking Revival items were placed in Sallie Dooley's bedroom on the second floor of the Dooleys' sprawling mansion—on the estate they named Maymont—in Richmond, Virginia, where they may still be viewed today. The Maymont mansion was built in 1893. Through a generous bequest from the Dooleys, in 1926 Maymont became a museum and park open to the public.

5. The Challenge to Columbus

1. In 1888, Gustav Storm (1845–1903), a professor of medieval Norwegian history and literature at the University of Christiania (now the University of Oslo), published, in Norwegian, *Studier over Vinlandsreiserne, Vinlands geografi og ethnografi*. A year later, in 1889, probably with the help of his brother Johan Storm, a scholar of French and English languages and literatures, he published an English translation under the title *Studies on the Vinland Voyages*.

2. John Patterson MacLean (1848–1939) lived most of his life in Ohio. He studied at Normal University and Saint Lawrence Seminary and became a Universalist minister, preaching mostly in Ohio. An antiquarian with a particular interest in the archaeological remains in the Mississippi and Ohio Valleys, he was also the author of *The Mound Builders: Being an Account of a Remarkable People that Once Inhabited the Valleys of the Ohio and Mississippi* (1879).

3. In 1844, Samuel Laing (1780–1868) published the first English translation of the *Heimskringla*, the thirteenth-century Icelandic history of the medieval Scandinavian kings, generally attributed to Snorri Sturluson. A native of Kirkwall in the Orkneys, Laing had studied at the University of Edinburgh and spent most of his later years in that city. A second edition of Laing's translation of the *Heimskringla* was issued in 1889, edited by the Norwegian American professor Rasmus B. Anderson.

4. Benjamin Franklin DeCosta (1831–1904) was the scion of a family that had come to Boston in 1699. In 1856 he graduated from the Biblical Institute of Concord, New Hampshire, and entered the Episcopal ministry in 1857. He served as chaplain of Massachusetts troops during the Civil War, and after

leaving the army, he settled in New York and for a period served as editor of the *Christian Times* (1854–66). In 1881 DeCosta became rector of the Church of St. John the Evangelist in New York City and was known to be a supporter of various labor movements. In October 1899, he withdrew from the Episcopal ministry and became a member of the Roman Catholic Church. Following the death of his wife in 1901, he prepared for the priesthood, and in November 1903 he was ordained by the bishop of Fiesole.

5. DeCosta hoped that future history books would also give due credit to "the Cabots, who saw the American Continent before Columbus could possibly have done so" (*The Pre-Columbian Discovery of America by the Northmen* 58).

6. Charles Sprague Smith (1853–1910) was born in Andover, Massachusetts, and attended Amherst College. He went abroad in 1875 and spent five years in the study of languages and literatures, first at the University of Berlin, subsequently at the Sorbonne, and later at various institutions in Italy and Spain, finally ending up at Oxford University, where he received a certificate honoring his academic accomplishments. He returned to the U.S. in 1880, taught at Columbia University, and in 1895 he organized the Comparative Literature Society in an effort to promote and integrate the different ethnic and national cultures of the diverse immigrants to the U.S. In later years, he became involved in the education of the working classes.

7. The larger oceangoing knarrs used for voyages to North America probably had somewhat higher sides than the Gokstad ship, a second deck, and extra trusses that could withstand heavy seas and could also provide some shelter for cargo, animals, and crew. These larger vessels had a cargo capacity of two hundred tons.

8. According to the *New York Times* story published on 1 November 1893, "The Norwegian Committee offered to give the ship to the Smithsonian Institution but the donation was declined because there was no money to pay for transportation and the erection of the house. So the ship will be placed alongside the only remaining original one on the grounds of Christiania," now Oslo ("The Viking Ship Sails Away" 8).

9. In this, McGee was following the highly regarded Catholic historian John Gilmary Shea, who turned the Viking discoverers into good Catholics. Shea's scholarly *History of the Catholic Missions among the Indian Tribes of the United States, 1529–1854* (1855) opened with a chapter titled "Norwegian Missions in New England." There he insisted upon the Catholic faith of the Vikings and argued that the Catholic Church had thus been the first organized European institution in the New World generally and in the U.S. particularly.

10. Anderson was born in Albion in Dane County, Wisconsin, and was a professor at the University of Wisconsin at Madison from 1867 to 1883. There he was the founding head of the Department of Scandinavian Studies, the oldest such department in any U.S. university. He established a publish-

ing house that focused on translations of texts mostly from Scandinavia and northern Europe. From 1885 to 1889, Anderson served as the U.S. ambassador to Denmark. Upon his return to the U.S. in 1889, he became the editor of the Norwegian-language weekly *Amerika* and served in that position until 1922.

11. In *The Life of the Admiral Christopher Columbus by His Son Ferdinand*, the following statement appears: "In a memorial or note that he [Columbus] wrote ... he says, 'In the month of February, 1477, I sailed one hundred leagues beyond the isle of Tile [i.e., Thule or Iceland], whose southern part is in latitude 73 degrees N, and not 63 degrees as some affirm; nor does it lie upon the meridian where Ptolemy says the West begins, but much farther west. And to this island, which is as big as England, the English come with their wares, especially from Bristol'" (Columbus 11). Columbus says nothing of his activities in Iceland, nor does he say why he journeyed there. Unfortunately, Fernando Colón's original Spanish manuscript for this biography of his father, along with its accompanying documents, long ago disappeared. What remains is a (sometimes questionable) Italian translation from 1571 of the biography only. There is no way to authenticate any of the letters quoted.

12. Much of Anderson's discussion of Gudrid's visit to Rome is lifted almost word for word from an unidentified English translation of a passage from Gabriel Gravier's *Découverte de l'Amérique par les Normands au Xe Siècle*, 106–7. Anderson provides neither quotation marks nor attribution. This is a good example of his practice throughout the book.

13. There is no explanation in the *Annals* of the purpose of the bishop's voyage, nor any further record of him. We cannot even know if he ever reached Vinland.

14. Interestingly, this reviewer never challenged Anderson's basic premise that the Norse had preceded Columbus and landed in New England. If the reviewer was in fact Lodge, then that apparent omission is explained by Lodge's well-known general acceptance of the Norse discovery story and by his personal eagerness to contemplate New Englanders' lineal descent from Norse ancestors. What Lodge objected to were the overblown exaggerations that tended to make these ideas seem preposterous.

15. For more information on the fate of Dighton Rock, see Falnes 230–31.

16. Skepticism regarding the Newport tower and Dighton Rock as physical evidence of Norse landfalls in New England had been expressed for some years by several prestigious New England historical societies. In 1877, for example, the Prince Society of Boston published *Voyages of the Northmen to America* with an introduction by "the Rev. Edmund F. Slafter, A.M." Slafter made clear that "whatever confidence may at first have been felt or expressed in this opinion [about the tower and the rock as 'the work of the Scandinavian voyagers'], the forty years that have since elapsed have left no trace of such a belief ... in the minds of distinguished antiquaries and historians of the present day. The ground has been carefully surveyed, and the conclusion

has been reached that no remains are to be found on the coasts of America, that can be traced to the visits of the Northmen in the tenth century" (11). While Slafter did not challenge the idea that the Northmen had visited *somewhere* in North America, he nonetheless insisted that "the opinion of Professor Rafn, as to the identity of the places visited [is]. . . . open to revision on all points" (12).

17. A typical comment on the Indians' skin color was published by Father Gabriel Sagard, a member of the Recollect order, in 1632 in *The Long Journey to the Country of the Hurons*: "All the American nations and tribes that we saw on our travels are of a tawny colour all over . . . ; not that they are so at birth, for they are of the same nature as ourselves, but, since they are naked, from the heat of the sun beating on their naked backs, and because they grease and anoint the body very frequently with oil or grease, as well as with paint of different colours" (136). In other words, to this French missionary, the Indians appeared to be "of the same nature" as the Europeans, that is, white, and it was only due to the sun and the application of various skin oils and paints (usually dark berry juices) that their skin seemed to darken to "tawny."

18. For example, in *The Composition of Indian Geographical Names*, Trumbull identified *Amoskeag* as meaning "the place of small fish" (31). *Naumkeag*, according to Trumbull, generally meant "the fishing place" and, more specifically, the place where eels were in abundance (28, 31).

19. Lavishly illustrated with reproductions of "maps, ancient and modern, charts, sketches, photographs, drawings, manuscripts, [and] original plans and surveys," Horsford's privately funded publication in 1889 of *The Discovery of the Ancient City of Norumbega* represented the culmination of over a decade of work. In fact, the book is really a report of that work, a report first delivered orally at a special session of the American Geographical Society held in Watertown on 21 September 1889.

20. Whenever it was published, "Norumbega Hall" was always accompanied by Whittier's headnote explaining the circumstances of its composition: "Norumbega Hall at Wellesley College, named in honor of Eben Norton Horsford, who was one of the most munificent patrons of that noble institution, and who had just published an essay claiming the discovery of the site of the somewhat mythical city of Norumbega, was opened with appropriate ceremonies, in April 1886. The following sonnet was written for the occasion, and was read by President Alice E. Freeman, to whom it was addressed" (*The Complete Poetical Works* 239).

21. Clement was a son of Massachusetts and an active advocate for the education of former slaves after the Civil War. In 1865 he took up residence in Savannah, Georgia, to aid in that effort. When ex-Confederates resumed power in the South in 1867, Clement lost his journalism post in Savannah and returned to Boston. After holding several journalistic posts in New York and Newark and Elizabeth, New Jersey, Clement again returned to Boston

as associate editor of the *Transcript*, becoming editor in chief in 1881. He dabbled in poetry throughout his career, with Tennyson as his model.

22. Charles Patrick Daly (1816–99), born in New York City, was elected to the New York State Assembly in 1843 and appointed to the New York Court of Common Pleas in May 1844; he eventually became chief justice. He lectured on law at Columbia University Law School and was elected as a member of the American Geographical Society in 1855. He was elected to the Governing Board in 1858, and he assumed the presidency of the Society in 1864, a position he held until his death.

23. In 1893, shortly after Horsford's death that year, his friend Elizabeth G. Shepard published *A Guide-Book to Norumbega and Vineland*. In it, she briefly retold the saga stories of Vinland as she detailed the walks and streetcar lines that would take a visitor to all the "wonderful archaeological discoveries made along the Charles River" (7). If one did not tarry too long at any one site, she assured readers, "all . . . may be accomplished in a day" (47). Shepard dedicated the little volume to "the memory of Eben Norton Horsford" and warmly recommended his five major books. "They will bear most careful and thorough study," she promised (48). The titles recommended by Shepard were *The Discovery of the Ancient City of Norumbega*; *The Landfall of Leif Erikson, A.D. 1000 and the Site of His Houses in Vineland*; *The Defences of Norumbega and a Review of the Reconnaissances of T. W. Higginson, Henry W. Haynes, etc.*; *The Problem of the Northmen*; and a posthumous volume, *Leif's House in Vineland* (1893).

24. Gade's attendance at the festivities, along with that of several other delegates from U.S. universities, was reported in "The University Centenary" 7.

25. "By the Scandinavian North," explained Brown in *The Icelandic Discoverers of America*, "is meant . . . Sweden, Norway, Denmark, and Iceland" (Shipley 195). She did not include Finland, probably because Finland had been annexed by Russia in 1809 and did not proclaim its independence until 1917. A republic was established in 1919.

26. That same year, 1888, Brown also petitioned both the National Museum (now the Smithsonian Institution) and the American Philosophical Society for funding. Neither was forthcoming.

27. In 1876 the nation had celebrated its one-hundredth birthday with a Centennial Exposition in Philadelphia. The fair was a great success, attracting money and visitors from all over the U.S. and from around the world. As Brown was aware, the success of this fair prompted calls for the U.S. to host future world's fairs, with the centenary of the Constitution in 1889 and the Quadricentennial of Columbus's landing in 1892 put forward as appropriate occasions.

28. Brown also had a secondary agenda, but it was never a central focus in *The Icelandic Discoverers of America*. She hoped that recognition of the Norse discovery would be accompanied by a greater appreciation of the peoples

and accomplishments of "the Scandinavian North" so that the region would finally "resume its true rank, and stand forth as the acknowledged intellectual and moral leader of the civilized world, as attested by every page of its history!" (Shipley 208).

29. For a brief summary of the controversy surrounding the Columbus statue, see Headley 53.

30. In 1884, for example, "in the legends of the Wabanaki Indians," the folklorist Charles Godfrey Leland claimed to have found "not only incidents but verbal passages almost identical with some in the [Norse] Elder Edda" ("The Edda among the Algonquin Indians" 222, 225).

31. Between 1880 and 1889, immigration from Scandinavia totaled 761,783 persons, or 12.7 percent of all arriving immigrants. From 1890 to 1899, that number dropped to 390,729, or 10.5 percent of the total. The percentages represented by Scandinavians dropped again between 1900 and 1909 (5.9) and between 1910 and 1919 (3.8). By comparison, immigration from the German Empire between 1880 and 1889 totaled almost 1.5 million persons, or 27.5 percent of all arriving immigrants. That rate dropped off considerably between 1890 and 1899, but even then well over a half million Germans immigrated to the U.S., constituting 15.7 percent of the total. Russian immigration picked up significantly between 1890 and 1899, when Russians (mostly Jews escaping the pogroms and enforced conscription into the czar's army) totaled 450,101 persons, or 12.7 percent of incoming immigrants. Between 1900 and 1909, that number jumped to over 1.5 million Russian immigrants, or 18.3 percent of the total (United States, Bureau of the Census 324–25).

32. According to one prominent race theorist, "The Alpine race is found throughout Central Europe, with ramifications into Asia. . . . When we come to the Slavs, we find that the Alpine type is predominant" (Burr 134–35).

33. Burr and others like him successfully argued for eugenics screening at Ellis Island. "Our incoming immigrants," wrote Burr, "will be minutely examined by a corps of eugenics experts, who will make certain beyond the shadow of a doubt that we shall 'carry on' the heritage left to us by our pioneer Nordic forefathers" (232).

6. The Phantom of First Contact

1. See Day, "Oral Tradition as Complement."

2. Archaeologists and anthropologists distinguish between Paleo-Indians, Vergennes, and Archaic periods preceding the Wabanaki peoples of the historic period. As Haviland and Power acknowledge, however, "There is presently widespread acceptance of the view that cultural and ethnic continuity have characterized the regions . . . for the last 2,000 years at least" (201). The Wabanaki peoples talk of "the Oldest Ones," "ancient ones," "ancestors," and "grandfathers," postulating an unbroken continuity that goes back even earlier. Because the archaeological record does, in fact, support the claim to ethnic, cultural, and linguistic continuity in some areas dating back to "some

6,000 or so years ago," I have chosen to follow the Indian model of connection and continuity over time and have preferred not to introduce technical material culture distinctions like "Archaic," "Vergennes," or "early Woodland" (see Haviland and Power 201–2).

3. According to contemporary European observers, in the seventeenth century Lake Champlain "marked the divide between Iroquoian peoples on the west and Abenakis on the east" (Haviland and Power 154).

4. Discussing "the earliest corn and beans in northern New England," Haviland and Power write, "Recent evidence in the region strongly suggests that the adoption of horticulture occurred almost simultaneously in interior riverine and coastal settings by A.D. 1100 at the latest" (140). Although there is as yet no archaeological or biological evidence to support their view, the Indians themselves place the date much earlier. There is evidence for the cultivation of tobacco in Vermont about 2,300 years ago.

5. The English, French, and Dutch kept few records of local population numbers, so the timing and impact of seriatim diseases is difficult to reconstruct. But recorded epidemics "swept the St. Lawrence (in 1535) and affected populations in New England (between 1564 and 1570, and again in 1586)" (Haviland and Power 209). More epidemics followed, and "the infamous 1617–18 epidemic in the Gulf of Maine" proved "catastrophic" (Bourque and Whitehead 144). Even before that, however, "the Micmacs are known to have suffered a major population decline" (Haviland and Power 209). In the 1660s, Josselyn recorded that "the *Mattachusetts*," once "very populous, . . . by the plague were brought from 30000 to 300" (89). While Josselyn's numbers may not be entirely trustworthy, they do nonetheless capture his impression of the magnitude of the devastation. Due to a lack of reliable data, it is almost impossible to calculate the death rates caused by these early epidemics. But Haviland and Power note that "in Mexico, where the Spanish kept much better records than did the Dutch, French, and British farther north, we know that European diseases caused a 90 percent reduction in native populations within 100 years of first contact. As the native Mexicans were biologically the same as all the other native peoples of eastern North America, the same thing must have happened all along the eastern seaboard, including New England. The records at our disposal, imperfect though they are, support this contention" (208). In this regard, we must also remember that those who survived the onslaught of European diseases were often left sterile or infertile. As a result, Native population numbers were slow to recover, even after an epidemic had passed through.

6. "We carried with us a Crosse, to erect . . . [and] set it up in the manner of the former" (Rosier 139).

7. One prior event that helps to explain the Maine Natives' suspicion of Waymouth is that, in 1580, the Englishman James Walker came ashore on the west side of Penobscot Bay and stole three hundred moose hides from a Native wigwam.

8. According to Snow, "Codfishing was the primary enterprise, and the

Portuguese, Spanish, and French all had plenty of cheap salt in which to pack their fish for the voyage home. They rarely established drying stations on land, and, unless they ran low on provisions, they had no good reason to land at all." By the last quarter of the seventeenth century, however, because "the English and other northern Europeans did not have easy access to cheap salt, . . . consequently they established land stations for the purpose of drying their catches before returning home" (Snow, *Archaeology* 44).

9. Rajnovich reproduces figures that look similar to these parallel arcs which she terms "lattice" figures and identifies as "either the sign of the midewiwin or a shaking tent of the jiissakid" (also a medicine practitioner) (34–35). These interpretations are based largely on what is known about Ojibway (a Central Algonquian-speaking people) medicine practices. If Wabanaki groups also once utilized this lattice figure, then the carver at Embden may have purposefully conflated it with his representation of the chapel, thus adding another level of indigenous spiritual significance to his carving of a Christian religious structure.

10. Although highly unlikely, we must also consider the possibility that this structure refers to a brief French settlement of 1604 on Neutral Island in the Saint Croix River between Maine and New Brunswick. Or it may represent any number of later seventeenth-century trading structures built by the English in and around the Kennebec. We can never really know because no technology yet exists that allows researchers scientifically to date a petroglyph precisely. At best, inferences are drawn from known historical information, from deductions about style and cultural contexts, and from weathering and patination of the rock surface.

11. These English colonists landed at Sabino Head, a half mile from the mouth of the Kennebec River, on 18 August 1607. In the spring, a resupply ship arrived and reported "all things in good forwardness" (qtd. in Tabor 1). Live fowl and farm animals were not unusual cargo for resupply ships of this period, so it is very possible that these were transported to the fledgling colony either in an initial voyage or in the resupply ship. In 1994, under the direction of the archaeologist Jeffrey P. Brain, serious excavations of the site commenced. Those excavations have so far revealed a large trenched fortification within which the colonists erected a chapel, several dwelling houses, and a large storehouse, the largest structure within Fort St. George. The roof of the storehouse was thatched. Inside the floor surface of the storehouse, "Brain found ceramics, glass trade beads, case bottle fragments, a clay pipe, many nails, lead munitions, armor, and iron hardware" (Tabor 5). In the southeastern corner of what had once been the storehouse, Brain also found "a caulking iron, used in shipbuilding"—and surely used in the construction of the pinnace that eventually conveyed many of the colonists back to England in 1608 (5). According to Brain, all these finds are "consistent with an early 17th century English military trading establishment" (qtd. in Tabor 5).

12. At the same time that the colonists were building their fort, they also

built a small pinnace suitable for cruising the coast and exploring the rivers. Both in search of a suitable place to locate the colony and, once that place had been chosen, in efforts to explore the surrounding country, these first English colonists in Maine engaged in frequent expeditions along the coast and up the Penobscot and Kennebec Rivers. At least some of the colonists' eagerness to explore nearby waterways may have derived from their belief that they were close to the fabled northwest passage to Asia. In 1607, George Popham, elected president of the colony, sent a report to King James I claiming that local Native peoples had indicated that "just seven days away lies 'none other than the Southern Ocean, stretching towards the land of China'" (qtd. in Tabor 3). More likely, the Indians were pointing to one or more of the Great Lakes.

13. Insofar as petroglyphs are known to record shamanic "spirit" journeys or other kinds of shamanic communications with the manitous (or powerful kin-beings), they regularly appear at places that serve as thresholds or provide a passage between different realms of the shared landscape. Whirlpools, rapids, deep lakes, rock faces with deep crevices—all these allow the people and their manitous "to enter each other's worlds and talk to each other directly" (Rajnovich 14). Additionally, insofar as petroglyphs record important events, teachings, or stories, they also appear at places that would be visited frequently, especially important portage points on seasonal hunting routes, as at both Embden and Machias Bay.

14. Denys's *The Description and Natural History of the Coasts of North America (Acadia)* was first published in France in 1672 and composed from memory. His original choice of a title was apparently *Coasts of North America from New England to the River Saint Lawrence*, but he changed that title just before publication. In fact, when Denys wrote, New France (later called Acadia) included Nova Scotia, New Brunswick, Prince Edward Island, parts of present-day Quebec, and all of present-day Maine; these are the areas—and the Native peoples of those areas—described by Denys.

15. Lest there be any confusion because of the apparent similarity in the names, the reader should be aware that the Mahicans and the Mohegans are quite separate and distinct Native groups. The Mahicans, an Eastern Algonquian-speaking people, at the time of contact occupied territories from Lake Champlain southward into the western part of Dutchess County, New York, and from the valley of the Schoharie Creek in the west to south-central Vermont in the east. The Mohegans (closely allied with the Pequots), also an Eastern Algonquian-speaking group, were mostly located in eastern Connecticut during the early contact period.

16. Story collections put together by non-Natives must always be approached with caution. On the one hand, as Alger understood, Native peoples are often reluctant to share their traditions with outsiders, and when they do, there may be elements of self-censorship. Certain kinds of stories will not be told at all; others may be told with deletions or some other

mode of modification. And even when a story is shared, the teller may withhold vital information about its symbolic contents or its multiple layers of meaning. In 1911, the Wallises found "the old men, with whom rested the final sanction [as to what might be shared with outsiders], ... suspicious of the whites and their ways" (5). Similarly, the archaeologist James L. Swauger, who has studied petroglyphs and pictoglyphs in the upper Ohio Valley for over forty years, wryly remembers "the knowing look on the face of John Reese, Shawnee, who said [referring to a particular petroglyph], 'Do you think we'd tell you the real name and power of a design? Sure, we'll tell you something to keep you happy, but we'd never tell you the truth. Power lies in the true knowing and revealing the truth would kill the power'" (6). The same is also sometimes said of the "designs" in stories.

17. For the most authoritative ethnographic study of the Beothuk, with information relating to Wayne Newell's speculations, see Marshall, especially 258–63, 272, 529 n. 26; also see Sutherland 239.

18. With his permission, I tape-recorded Chief Sappier as he told the story, and I also took notes. I then sent him a transcription of what he had said, and he shared that transcription with his siblings to see if their memories of the story coincided with his. For the most part, they did. Published here is the version of my transcription as corrected and amended by Chief Sappier and his siblings. I have not changed or corrected their punctuation or sentence structure, but, to ensure clarity, I have interpolated one comma and some additional words and phrases in square brackets.

19. There are also stories among the Wabanaki of Gluskap traveling in a stone canoe from America to Europe and even first discovering Europe (or at least England and France). According to one version collected by Leland, "This [journey] was before the white people had ever heard of America" (*The Algonquin Legends of New England* 128). Another version of this story appears in Rand. With regard to the story of Gluskap's arrival from "over the sea" in a stone canoe in the land of the Wabanaki, it must be read and interpreted with caution. Leland is known to have pieced together different story fragments according to his own preconceived ideas about Norse (and other) early European arrivals. That said, if accurately recorded, this story appears to contain a suggestion of migration. Although largely discounted by many archaeologists and anthropologists, some recent archaeological studies have postulated an ancient migration across the Atlantic from Europe to North America as part of the earliest peopling of the continent; see Stanford and Bradley 54–55; Kehoe 18–19. For the counterargument, see Straus.

7. Contact and Conflict Again

1. Nowadays, most scholars of folklore incline to the view that analogous narrative structures, or parallel myths, may derive from some form of shared cultural ancestry in the ancient past. Or, just as easily, they may de-

velop among far-flung cultures wholly independently of one another, generated by common human experiences and without the need for Leland's assumption of "direct transmission." Indeed, many modern scholars look upon statements like Leland's as a species of cultural chauvinism. The Indians are too "savage" to have come up with such clever or "Aryan"-like stories on their own, and so we must postulate European—in this case, Norse—influence.

2. In 1637, a Montagnais (Innu) "shaman" told a missionary, "I believe in my dreams,—I interpret them, and also the dreams of others; I sing and beat my Drum, in order to be lucky in the chase and to cure sickness" (qtd. in Phillips 63–64). Clearly, these were once powerful and influential individuals. And just as clearly, they were seen as a threat to the Christianizing imperatives of the early missionaries. Again among the Mi´kmaq in 1691, LeClercq complained, "They imagine . . . that their jugglers can know from their Devil . . . the best places for hunting, and that all the dreams of these imposters are just so many revelations and prophecies" (*New Relation* 210). "Some of these jugglers also meddle with predictions of future affairs," he added (223). Almost two hundred years later, echoing LeClercq in his history of the Abenaki of Quebec, published in 1866, Abbé Joseph Pierre Anselme Maurault reported, "They had jugglers who could foretell good or bad fortune by messages from the spirits" (125). Although such practices were dying out under the influence of Christianity, nonetheless Maurault noted, "The shamans had a way of predicting . . . good and bad weather, good or bad fortune in hunting, the mishaps which will happen on a journey, the result of a [war] campaign and a thousand other things" (29).

3. *A Dictionary of the Micmac Language* (1902), compiled by Jeremiah S. Clark "from [Rand's] Phonographic [i.e., phonetically marked] Word-Lists," lists *moo* as meaning "not," a prefix "used only with other words"; *mooin* is translated simply as "a bear" (Rand 101). Unfortunately, neither of Rand's dictionaries—from English to Mi´kmaq (1888) or from Mi´kmaq to English (posthumously published in 1902)—indicates whether he *heard* the double meaning of "a bear, Mooin" (*Dictionary of the Language of the Micmac Indians* 32). Clearly, Rand understood the grammar of negation in Mi´kmaq and listed the prefix *moo* as meaning "not" (181). Yet the earlier English-to-Mi´kmaq dictionary, prepared by Rand himself, translates "bear" as *mooin* (without any alternative dialect spellings such as *muin*, *moo'in*, *mou'een*, or *mu-win*). And it translates "No one" as *mowwĕn*, again without alternative spellings and with no indication that the two words—*mooin* and *mowwĕn*—might be interchangeable or, to the ear, almost indistinguishable in some dialects (32, 180). In short, there is no way to check whether Rand was aware of the story's pun. Even after forty years of collecting stories and studying the language, Rand knew that he had not entirely mastered Mi´kmaq. Among the papers in the Silas Tertius Rand Collection held by Acadia University in Wolfville, Nova Scotia, are many (often undated) miscellaneous

notes in Rand's handwriting, reminding himself to follow up on questions of language that he did not yet understand (see Deposit No. D1900.06: 3/17). In that same collection, a notebook in Rand's handwriting dated "Hantsport, August 1885" includes the following: "This is a scribbling book in which questions are inserted in the Mi'kmaq language and words for examination, before they are entered in the dictionary" (see Deposit No. D1900.06: 3/18).

4. The other colors on the Mi'kmaq medicine wheel, with their directional association, are yellow, to the south; red, to the west; and black, to the north. In Mi'kmaq, the word for "daylight" or "dawn," *wŏbŭn*, has the same root as the word for "white," *wobāe* or *wŏbăāk* (see Rand, *Dictionary of the Language of the Micmac Indians* 76, 280).

5. LeClercq celebrated the enormous success of his experiment, noting that his pupils demonstrated "so much readiness in understanding this kind of writing" that they learned their lessons "in a single day" and even taught the script to their friends and family members (qtd. in Schmidt and Marshall 6). Use of LeClercq's script spread from one band to another, and—as two Canadian scholars put it—"receiving hieroglyphic leaflets from the ... priest ... became a matter of great significance to the Mi'kmaq" (Schmidt and Marshall 7).

6. In the version of the story from the *Legends* volume printed here, both the line break and the paragraph break following the word "impossible" were probably introduced by Webster, Rand's editor.

7. For a discussion of Rand's attitude toward and relationships with Catholic priests who continued to minister to the Mi'kmaq, see Virginia P. Miller's "Silas T. Rand, Nineteenth Century Anthropologist among the Micmac," especially 240–45; see also Abler, "Protestant Missionaries."

8. Rand determined that certain consonants, such as "x," had no corresponding sound in Mi'kmaq and so simply omitted them when translating religious texts into the Mi'kmaq language. For these translations, Rand utilized the phonetic spelling system originated and popularized by Sir Isaac Pitman, the English educator who also invented a phonetic shorthand system.

9. Compounding that textual problem is the fact that Webster, Rand's editor at Wellesley, says that "in preparing this work for publication," she made "some changes ... deemed necessary for the sake of greater clearness ... [and] to remove ... grammatical inaccuracies." Webster also regularized "the spelling of some of the Indian proper names" (viii).

10. By 1600, the French were actively engaged in the fur trade along the Saint Lawrence, but it was not until 1604 that Membertou, a Mi'kmaq band chief, persuaded them to establish the first permanent European trading post in Canada at Port Royal, at the mouth of the Annapolis River along the shores of the Bay of Fundy (the large bay separating New Brunswick from the peninsula of Nova Scotia). The first missionary in Canada was the secular priest Jessé Fleché, who survived less than a year at Port Royal, in 1610.

There Fleché baptized twenty-one Mi´kmaq, including Membertou and his family. The priest died soon after. He was followed by the arrival in 1611 of the first two Jesuit missionaries to work in Canada, Pierre Biard (1567–1622) and Enemond Massé (1575–1646).

11. Nicolar, *The Life and Traditions of the Red Man*, edited, annotated, and with a history of the Penobscot Nation and an introduction by Annette Kolodny, 106. All quotations are from this latest edition.

12. The different Wabanaki ethnic groups have their own unique Gluskap story cycles, but many stories—in slightly altered versions—are shared in common. According to the anthropologist Frank Speck, Gluskap "is the legendary hero and transformer personage of the Wabanaki tribes" and "is responsible for a number of important innovations in the lives of men and animals" ("Penobscot Tales" 6–7). To him, or to his mother, Woodchuck, are attributed the invention of such things as snowshoes and the moose-call (for hunting), technologies vital to survival. It was also Gluskap who introduced tobacco and taught its uses. And just as he functioned as a culture bringer, so too he transformed the world to make it habitable. According to the Penobscots, "the Penobscot river itself is his own creation after killing a monster frog that caused a world drought, the released waters finally flowing away to form the river" (7). Gluskap stories are believed to carry a quasi-historical core of remembered cultural change over time.

13. For background on and an interpretive reading of Nicolar's entire text, see Kolodny, "Introduction to Joseph Nicolar's 1893 *The Life and Traditions of the Red Man*," 35–88. For a discussion of how Nicolar's text contributed to the Penobscot Nation's efforts to protect their fragile riverine ecosystem in the nineteenth century, see Kolodny, "Rethinking the 'Ecological Indian.'"

14. By specifically mentioning only the black man, the red man, and the white man, Nicolar eliminates by silence any reference to then-current theories about the possible Asian antecedents of Native peoples.

15. Multiples of seven, the number sacred to many Eastern Algonquian groups, here signify not literal years but significant passages of cyclical time. Use of the number seven is thus almost always ritualized and/or symbolic.

16. The loon was one of those fowl (along with ducks and geese) that served in the old stories as Klose-kur-beh's scouts, bringing messages of warning or danger. The plaintive cry of the loon was often associated with lamentation or mourning. And there is an old Penobscot hunters' belief that "when loons cry at night the wind will blow next day" (Speck, "Penobscot Tales" 33).

17. In an e-mail dated 15 August 2005, the linguistics expert Conor McDonough Quinn notes that the current Penobscot form of Nicolar's *k'chi-wump-toqueh* has come to refer to the Canada goose and literally translates as "great, venerable Canada goose." Quinn speculates that the element in the word connoting "white" may refer "to the white patch on the Canada goose's neck." I would add that Nicolar's term (or close variants) may once

370 Notes to Pages 301–302

have had several referents, but that after the indigenous North American swan species were hunted almost to extinction in the nineteenth century, the word came more and more to refer to the large bird that did still exist, the Canada goose.

18. The suggestion of a meteorite seems particularly prominent: the apparent pause before the meteorite burns up as it plunges into the Earth's atmosphere, "a great ball of fire"; the tremendous force, or "great shock," of impact; the roar and aftershocks following impact, perhaps even setting off some seismic (or earthquake) activity; and the vaporization and particulate matter of the meteorite's breakup that would darken the atmosphere for a time and bring "back the fog."

19. Like Nicolar's text, David Cusick's (Tuscarora Iroquois) *Sketches of Ancient History of the Six Nations* (1826) cannot be read as literal history in the common meaning of that term. It is rather a highly idiosyncratic assemblage of various Iroquoian traditions (and perhaps inventions) and may not be entirely reliable. That said, it does depict the fall of a fiery object from the sky into a nearby body of water (11). Several Algonquian groups, including the Ojibwa of the upper Great Lakes region and the Menomini, also of the Great Lakes region, have similar stories about fiery stars falling to Earth, scorching the land and melting the rocks. In some stories, these celestial bodies are said also to have had fiery tails, suggesting comets. In all the stories with which I am familiar, however, there is no mention of the object's falling into or near a body of water, which renders the Nicolar and Cusick versions unique.

20. By Nicolar's day, "red man" functioned as a pan-Indian identifier, used by the Indians as well as by Euro-Americans. For a history of Native use of the phrase, see Shoemaker.

21. Nicolar's statement that the Native canoes "were so small" that the Indians considered it dangerous to cross the wide mouth of the river is puzzling (174). From the very earliest records, Europeans were consistently impressed with the handcrafted birch bark canoes used by Northeastern Algonquian peoples. These included seagoing canoes used for hunting seals and porpoises, as well as canoes suited for travel from the white waters of rushing rivers to the expanses of the Great Lakes. As Sebastian Rasles, the Jesuit missionary to the Norridgewock village on the Kennebec River in Maine, observed in 1732, in their birch bark canoes, the Indians were able to "cross the arms of the sea, and sail [sic] on the most dangerous rivers, and on lakes from four to five hundred leagues in circumference" (Thwaites 67:139). One plausible explanation for Nicolar's statement is that, as he indicates in his text, the Indians were then engaged in intertribal warfare, and the larger canoes—which could carry up to ten men—were being used to transport war parties. The watchmen sent to follow the newcomers were provided only smaller canoes, which may, in fact, have obliged them "to keep near the land" (Nicolar 174).

22. While chapter 6 is the last numbered chapter, it is followed by a section called "Conclusion," which concentrates mostly on traditional material culture (194–200).

23. Early explorers and colonizers erected crosses as signs of European possession and as signs that they were intent on missions of conversion. In 1497, for example, John Cabot erected a cross on the Newfoundland coast. In 1534, Jacques Cartier and his crew erected a thirty-five-foot cross in Mi´kmaq territory, at Gaspé Harbor at the mouth of the Saint Lawrence. In May 1536, on his second voyage, Cartier erected yet another large cross at the mouth of the Saint Charles River at Quebec. Indeed, wherever they traveled in Canada and New England, early explorers and adventurers (Catholic and Protestant alike) reported leaving crosses to signify their presence or claim possession, or simply as a guidepost for future travelers. In the autumn of 1846, Henry David Thoreau explored the backwoods of Maine. He and his companions encountered a large wooden cross of significant age. One of Thoreau's companions who was familiar with the Maine woods commented, "Large wooden crosses, made of oak, still sound, were sometimes found standing in this wilderness, which were set up by the first Catholic missionaries who came through to the Kennebec" (*The Maine Woods* 60).

24. Under the sponsorship of Pierre du Gua, Sieur de Monts—who funded and accompanied this expedition—the French navigator Samuel de Champlain led a group of (male) settlers to Acadia in New France in 1604. The previous year, Champlain had visited the Saint Lawrence. In 1604, he first led the prospective settlers to Dorchet Island (also called Île Sainte-Croix) in the Saint Croix River, on the current boundary between the U.S. and Canada. But the island quickly proved unsuitable, and in 1605 the colony was moved to Port Royal (now Annapolis Royal) in Nova Scotia. This was the first permanent European settlement in North America north of Florida. From Acadia in 1606 and 1607, Champlain explored the coasts to the south and west. When de Monts found it impossible to monopolize the fur trade from Port Royal, he and Champlain moved on to the Saint Lawrence in 1608, and there Champlain established another colony and fur-trading post at what is now Quebec. Champlain headed this new expedition, leaving France in 1608 with thirty-two (male) colonists. More colonists arrived the following June, and Champlain is credited with the founding of Quebec. When Champlain died in 1635, the Quebec colony extended along both shores of the Saint Lawrence. Nicolar's text appears to have trace memories of all these events, albeit conflated and out of order.

25. The list of early French missions and missionaries is long. In 1615, Catholic priests from the Recollect order (Franciscans) began establishing missions in Quebec, followed in 1625 by Jesuits. The conversions in Maine began even earlier, in 1611, when Pierre Biard and Enemond Massé, Catholic missionaries from France, first attempted a settlement named Saint Saveur on Mount Desert Island. This mission was destroyed by an English raiding

372 Notes to Pages 303–307

party from Virginia in 1613. But more French missions followed. According to the historian James Axtell, in Maine "Catholic missionaries were ensconced in [Algonquian] villages long before the English realized the strategic need for native allies, and had converted most of native Maine to the Roman faith. The process had been well begun in the interior by Father Druillettes in the late 1640s and by Capuchins at the mouth of the Penobscot in the early 1650s. In 1687," continues Axtell, "Abbé Pierre Thury, a graduate of the Quebec Seminary, established a mission on the Penobscot, followed seven years later by Vincent Bigot and Sébastien Râle [also Rasle or Rasles], who founded the Jesuit mission at Norridgewock on the upper Kennebec. By 1699 at least six Jesuits were living with and administering the sacraments to villagers on the Saco, Androscoggin, and Kennebec rivers" (*Invasion* 248).

26. Because in Nicolar's lifetime, the white population of Maine consisted of the descendants of the English as well as the French—and many other ethnic groups, as well—it is also possible that he took the politic route, constructing a benign and generic "white man" without specific national or ethnic identity.

27. For a more extensive reading of this passage, see Kolodny, "Introduction" (67).

28. Nicolar never intended to write history in the commonly understood meaning of the word. In fact, there is evidence that "at the time of his death," having already published *The Life and Traditions of the Red Man*, Nicolar "was engaged in writing a history of the Penobscot Tribe" (Hunt, *Report of the Agent of the Penobscot Tribe . . . for the Year 1894* 10). This statement in the 1894 report of the Indian agent who knew Nicolar well strongly suggests both that Nicolar knew how to compose a more conventional history text—and was in the process of doing so—and also, more important, that Nicolar understood *The Life and Traditions of the Red Man* as something other than history. Regrettably, the unfinished history manuscript has not survived. During my years of working with many members of the Penobscot Nation to reprint the Nicolar text, I asked everyone, including direct descendants and other family members, about any surviving handwritten manuscripts. Nicolar's grandson, Charles Norman Shay, has never found or even heard of any history manuscript, nor have any other family members. In fact, *no* handwritten manuscripts by Nicolar appear to have survived.

29. The transformation of the loon woman into a kind of fireball has one possible known historical referent: the appearance of a particularly bright comet in December 1664. The Englishman John Josselyn reported, "In the year 1664, a Star or Comet appeared in *New-England* in *December* in the *South-East*, rising constantly about one of the clock in the morning, carrying the tail lower and lower till it came into the *West*. . . . A fortnight after[,] it appeared again" (37). In 1807, a giant fireball exploded over Connecticut, an explosion visible for miles and from which several smaller meteors rained down. Stories about this event still circulated when Nicolar was a boy and

may have prompted retellings of even more ancient stories about earlier such events. Therefore, we must at least consider the possibility that Nicolar simply conflated (or confused?) the features of a meteor strike with the similar features of a comet or other natural events associated in stories with the early arrival of Europeans. The other details of this episode's association between a European arrival and a catastrophic natural event seem to point to the beginning of the seventeenth century, particularly the year 1600, when the Mount Huanyaputina volcano in southern Peru underwent a massive eruption, setting off waves of seismic activity and discharging "at least 19.2 cubic kilometers of fine sediment into the upper atmosphere" (Fagan 104). As with Nicolar's "dense fog" and the covering over the water and fish, the discharge from Mount Huanyaputina "darkened the sun and moon for months and fell to earth as far away as Greenland" (104). (The eruption in 1883 of the Krakatoa volcano in Indonesia may have revived stories and memories of this earlier volcanic event. Krakatoa also spread debris worldwide, darkening the skies and altering the climate.) Moreover, as in Klose-kur-beh's prophecy that the white man's would be the "cold season," the "Huanyaputina ash played havoc with global climate," making the "summer of 1601 the coldest since 1400 throughout the northern hemisphere" (104). Nicolar's additional emphasis on the repeated "trembling" of the earth and ocean also suggests that he may have been combining stories about the seismic activity set off by Huanyaputina with stories about several other like events. A strong earthquake in the Saint Lawrence Valley region near Trois Rivières, Quebec, was recorded on 11 June 1638 and felt throughout the French settlements in Canada as well as the English settlements in New England. Another earthquake hit the same area in 1658. And an even more powerful event, with aftershocks continuing for six months, began on 5 February 1663 and "was widely felt over much of northeastern America, from Montreal to Boston" (Kovach 170). Many early European colonists recorded their surprise at the frequency and ferocity of earthquakes in New France and New England. In Maine, Josselyn reported "a terrible earthquake" in April 1667, and "before that a very great one in 1638, and another in 58 and in 1662–63. . . . Earthquakes are frequent in the Countrie" (42). All these events—the eruption of Huanyaputina in 1600, the major quakes of 1638, 1658, and 1663, as well as the appearance of the comet in 1664—certainly punctuated the period during which Europeans increasingly explored and established themselves along the Saint Lawrence and across both New France and New England. In one way or another, all these events would have been incorporated into stories related to white swans and European arrivals.

30. See MacDougall 56; Fagan x.

31. "One recently obtained date from a site in western Maine suggests that maize was cultivated there by 1000 B.P.," that is, A.D. 950 (Bourque 87).

32. "For two or more centuries," continues Fagan, "Greenland ships took passage to North America by sailing north and west and letting southerly

ocean currents carry them to their destination. Then they sailed directly home on the prevailing southwesterly winds" (14).

33. See Jesch 160–66.

34. According to the *Encyclopedia of Ships and Seafaring*, as the Hanseatic League gradually gained control of the merchant trade along the Baltic and North Sea coasts, expanding exponentially during the fourteenth century and early fifteenth, it "encouraged the building of larger and better boats." The design that became standard was known as the Hansa cog, a trading vessel particularly adapted to the Baltic and "to the rough waters of the North Sea." "All cogs had a single central mast with a square sail," the sails "tanned with a dressing made from bark to inhibit rot." But while "the average trading cog built to cross the North Sea" could drive through those waters, the cog also had some severe limitations, and its "lack of sailing qualities" made it an unlikely vessel for Atlantic crossings (32). By the fourteenth century, the cog was already beginning to be replaced by two- and three-masted ships with multiple sails of heavy canvas. These were the carracks and caravels that finally made possible "the great voyages of exploration in the 15th century" (34). The caravel, "originally designed for fishing," went through several modifications of the rigging on its three masts and quickly "began to be used for ocean voyages" (34). On his first voyage across the Atlantic in 1492, Columbus sailed in the largest of his three caravels. And when John Cabot sailed across the North Atlantic to Newfoundland in 1497, he too sailed in a three-masted caravel.

35. The *Viking* started out with a single mast and sail, a "mainsail, which was the only one originally carried," according to a report on 14 June 1893 in the *New York Times* ("The Viking Ship Is Here" 1). But after encountering a severe storm at sea, the ship's captain added a second sail. Again, as reported by the *New York Times*, "A reefed foresail, corresponding to a staysail, had been added later to make the vessel more manageable and to endeavor to make better headway" (1). Although briefly useful, the second sail was an ahistorical addition. While in the U.S., the *Viking* adhered to the design of the original medieval ship of which it was a replica, displaying a single mainmast and sail.

36. One possible exception to this statement may be a story told in 1961 by eighty-seven-year-old Gabriel Sylliboy, then the Mi'kmaq grand chief in Canada. The story is about his people's first encounter with Europeans but clearly shows the influence of Canadian school books because it tells of "the time that Christopher arrived" and assumed he had landed in "the part of the world called India" (3, 5). Sylliboy's narrative appears to conflate into the character of "Christopher" several different early arrival episodes, though none suggest the Norse.

37. At a petroglyph site near Peterborough, Ontario, a relatively large image of a very unusual boat has "led visitors to the site to remark upon the 'Viking' character of the . . . boat and to wonder whether the site itself might

have been influenced by the Vikings" (Vastokas and Vastokas 126). The archaeologists who first conducted a major study of the site, however, as well as most other petroglyph experts, reject such an interpretation in favor of a reading that embeds the image solely within precontact Algonquian shamanic practices. For a full discussion, see Vastokas and Vastokas 121–28.

38. Bruchac and his wife still live in the same house in Greenfield Center, New York, where Bruchac was raised by his grandparents. In an interview with Meredith Ricker in 1996 for the journal *MELUS*, Bruchac recalled that although his grandfather told stories, he "would not talk about his Native ancestry" (Ricker 162).

39. Today, the peoples who call themselves Abenaki are mainly located in two large communities in the Canadian province of Quebec. The Saint Francis Abenaki occupy lands on the eastern bank of the Saint Francis River, about six miles from where it joins the Saint Lawrence. Their village is called Odanak. A second group resides at Becanour near Trois Rivières (see Hallowell 6). Although not yet federally recognized, other communities of Abenaki still live near Swanton, Vermont, and elsewhere in both Vermont and New Hampshire. Because the early French settlers and missionaries tended to name indigenous peoples generically according to observed commonalities in culture and language (as opposed to the English, who named Indian groups according to the names of their separate villages), the French referred to most of the Eastern Algonquian-speaking peoples with whom they came in contact as *Abenaki*. The term is probably a corruption of *Wabanaki*, which the French had difficulty pronouncing correctly. Many anthropologists and ethnologists still follow the French model and refer to all these peoples as Abenaki (sometimes distinguished as Eastern or Western Abenaki, according to the location of their original homelands).

40. Private conversation with the author at Bruchac's home, 21 March 2003. Quoted by permission.

41. Ibid.

42. Ibid.

43. Ibid.

44. Many anthropologists and ethnohistorians cite evidence that corn was first introduced to Northeastern Algonquian peoples through trade with Iroquoians to the south and west.

45. Bruchac believes that his Abenaki ancestors also had a version of the longhouse in their villages, and he has constructed a replica of a traditional Abenaki longhouse on his property in upstate New York. The Iroquois call themselves Ho-de-no-sau-nee, which literally translates as "people of the longhouse."

46. By the middle of the seventeenth century, the French had successfully forged an alliance with the Eastern Algonquian-speaking peoples of New Hampshire, Vermont, Maine, Acadia, and New France, including the Mi´kmaq. Thus, after 1653, notes the archaeologist and ethnohistorian

Bruce Bourque, "French sources rarely mention hostilities among Algonquian groups, probably because they and their neighbors were forced to close ranks in the face of a new threat: increasing Iroquois aggression from the West" (127).

47. The French navigator Jacques Cartier led three voyages of exploration to the Saint Lawrence region, in 1534, 1535–36, and 1541–42. On each of these voyages, Cartier interacted with both Algonquian and Iroquoian peoples, most prominently with Iroquoians from the Saint Lawrence Valley. Yet in 1603 Samuel de Champlain noted that the Iroquois had disappeared from the Saint Lawrence, presumably under pressure from the Algonquian groups who also claimed the territory. Most archaeologists and ethnohistorians now concur that, antedating this "disappearance of Iroquoian-speaking populations from the Saint Lawrence Valley sometime just prior to 1600," Algonquians and Iroquoians had lived in relative proximity to one another, at times engaging in trade and at other times in warfare (Bourque 127).

48. Private conversation with the author at Bruchac's home, 21 March 2003. Quoted by permission.

49. Ibid.

50. Ibid.

51. No copy exists of the first New England edition, printed under the title *The Soveraignty and Goodness of God, Together with the Faithfulness of His promises displayed: Being a narrative of the Captivity and Restauration of Mrs. Mary Rowlandson*. A second edition utilizing this same title appeared in 1682 (Cambridge, Mass.: Samuel Green), but extant copies are damaged and incomplete. Most subsequent American editions were reprinted from the English edition (London: Joseph Poole, 1682), and so the work has come to be known under the title of the English edition, *A True History of the Captivity and Restoration of Mrs. Mary Rowlandson, A Minister's Wife in New-England*. Although Rowlandson was not the first New Englander to be captured by Indians, she was the first to commit her experiences to writing and have that writing published. All quotations here are from the London 1682 edition.

52. For a full discussion of *A Narrative of the Life of Mrs. Mary Jemison*, see Kolodny, *The Land before Her*, 68–81.

53. The Norse on Greenland were primarily livestock farmers, but they were also big game hunters, utilizing spears, the bow and arrow, and, to some extent, axes. They extensively hunted caribou, walrus, and polar bears. They also hunted seals, which they clubbed.

54. If the Ice-Hearts are meant to be Norse, this statement can refer only to Norway or Iceland, because there was no paucity of arable land on Greenland, only too few people to work all the land that was available.

Epilogue

1. I am indebted to Harold W. Borns Jr., professor of geological sciences at the University of Maine at Orono, for sharing this information with me during my research visit to Maine in June 2000.

2. For a useful summary of the stone's history and the controversy surrounding it, see Wallace's and Fitzhugh's "Stumbles and Pitfalls in the Search for Viking America," especially 380–84.

3. See, for example, Reiersgord's *The Kensington Stone: Its Place in History* (2001) and Nielsen and Wolter's *The Kensington Rune Stone: Compelling New Evidence* (2006).

4. In 1958, the movie *The Vikings* proved an enormous box office hit, while the poster advertising the movie, over the years, became almost an icon in itself. In the poster, a blond, square-jawed Kirk Douglas, dressed in a nail-studded leather shirt, one arm raised with fist closed, stands as an emblem of stalwart defiance, with the prow of his Viking warship just behind him. In 1961, when the National Football League granted a franchise to Minnesota, the new team was nicknamed "The Vikings." Their chosen logo was a blond-haired Viking warrior wearing a horned helmet, the helmet itself a product of popular invention and not something any medieval Scandinavian would have recognized or worn. Accommodating the continuing desire of many Minnesotans to believe in the authenticity of the Kensington Stone, the official fan website explains the team's name as follows: "The Vikings are named after Norsemen, the Scandinavian warriors that settled modern-day Minnesota."

Works Consulted

Abbott, John S. C. *The History of Maine, from the Earliest Discovery of the Region by the Northmen until the Present Time.* Boston: B. B. Russell, 1875.

Abler, Thomas S. "Glooscap Encounters Silas T. Rand: A Baptist Missionary on the Folklore Fringe." *Earth, Water, Air and Fire: Studies in Canadian Ethnohistory.* Ed. David T. McNab. Waterloo, Ontario: Wilfrid Laurier University Press, 1998. 127–41.

———. "Protestant Missionaries and Native Culture: Parallel Careers of Asher Wright and Silas T. Rand." *American Indian Quarterly* 16.1 (1992), 25–37.

"An account of the discovery of Vinland, or America, by the Icelanders, in the eleventh century, taken from Mallett's Northern Antiquities, volume I." *American Museum, or Universal Magazine* 6.2 (1789), 159–62.

"An account of the discovery of Vinland, or America, by the Icelanders, in the eleventh century, taken from Mallett's Northern Antiquities. Concluded from Vol. VI. page 162." *American Museum, or Universal Magazine* 7.6 (1790), 340–44.

Adam of Bremen. *History of the Archbishops of Hamburg-Bremen by Adam of Bremen.* 1075. Trans. F. J. Tschan. New York: Columbia University Press, 1959.

Adams, Henry. *History of the United States of America during the Second Administration of James Madison.* 9 vols. Vol. 3. 1891. New York: Antiquarian Press, 1962.

Adney, Edwin Tappan, and Howard I. Chapelle. *The Bark Canoes and Skin Boats of North America.* Washington: Smithsonian Institution Press, 1983.

Alexander, Floyce. "Emerson and the Cherokee Removal." *ESQ: A Journal of the American Renaissance* 29.3 (1983), 127–37.

Alger, Abby Langdon. *In Indian Tents: Stories Told by Penobscot, Passamaquoddy and Micmac Indians.* Boston: Roberts Brothers, 1897.

Allen, Chadwick. *Blood Narrative: Indigenous Identity in American Indian and Maori Literary and Activist Texts.* Durham: Duke University Press, 2002.

Allen, Paula Gunn. "The Savages in the Mirror: Phantoms and Fantasies in America." 1974. *Off the Reservation: Reflections on Boundary-Busting, Border-Crossing, Loose Canons.* Boston: Beacon, 1998. 22–35.

"America Discovered and Christianized in the Tenth and Eleventh Centuries." *American Catholic Quarterly Review* 13.50 (1888), 211–37.

"America Not Discovered by Columbus." *Literary World: A Monthly Review of Current Literature* 5.6 (1874), 86–87.

Works Consulted

"America's Discovery: Credit Due to Leif Rather Than to Columbus." *Boston Daily Globe*, 30 Oct. 1887, 2.

Anderson, Rasmus Bjorn. *America Not Discovered by Columbus: An Historical Sketch of the Discovery of America by the Norsemen, in the Tenth Century.* 1874. Chicago: S. C. Griggs, 1877.

Appleton, Thomas Gold. *A Sheaf of Papers.* Boston: Roberts Brothers, 1874.

Arneborg, Jette. "Greenland and Europe." *Vikings: The North American Saga.* Ed. William W. Fitzhugh and Elisabeth I. Ward. Washington and New York: Smithsonian Institution Press in association with the National Museum of Natural History, 2000. 304–17.

Atwater, Caleb. "Description of the Antiquities Discovered in the State of Ohio and Other Western States." *Transactions and Collections of the American Antiquarian Society.* Worcester, Mass., 1820. 1:105–267.

Axtell, James. "The Exploration of Norumbega: Native Perspectives." *American Beginnings: Exploration, Culture, and Cartography in the Land of Norumbega.* Ed. Emerson W. Baker et al. Lincoln: University of Nebraska Press, 1994. 149–65.

———. *The Invasion Within: The Contest of Cultures in Colonial North America.* New York: Oxford University Press, 1985.

Baker, Emerson W., et al., eds. *American Beginnings: Exploration, Culture, and Cartography in the Land of Norumbega.* Lincoln: University of Nebraska Press, 1994.

Bancroft, George. *History of the United States, from the Discovery of the American Continent, to the War of Independence.* 1834. Edinburgh: A. Fullarton, 1843.

Barber, John Warner. *The History and Antiquities of New England, New York, New Jersey, and Pennsylvania.* Hartford, Conn.: H. S. Parsons, 1842.

Barton, Benjamin Smith. *New Views of the Origin of the Tribes and Nations of America.* Philadelphia: John Bioren, 1798.

"Bayard Taylor's Posthumous Books." *New Englander* 4.158 (1881), 40–48.

Beamish, North Ludlow. *The Discovery of America by the Northmen, in the Tenth Century, with Notices of the Early Settlements of the Irish in the Western Hemisphere.* London: T. and W. Boone, 1841.

Bederman, Gail. *Manliness and Civilization: A Cultural History of Gender and Race in the United States, 1880–1917.* Chicago: University of Chicago Press, 1995.

Bell, Michael J. "'The Only True Folk Songs We Have in English': James Russell Lowell and the Politics of the Nation." *Journal of American Folklore* 108.428 (1995), 131–55.

Benton-Benai, Edward. *The Mishomis Book: The Voice of the Ojibway.* Hayward, Wisc.: Indian Country Communications, 1988.

Bercovitch, Sacvan. *The Rites of Assent: Transformations in the Symbolic Construction of America.* New York: Routledge, 1993.

Berry, Henry N., IV. "Earthquakes in Maine." Maine Geological Survey.

Maine Department of Conservation. 10 Jan. 2005. Available at state website.
Blight, David W. *Race and Reunion: The Civil War in American Memory*. Cambridge: Belknap Press of Harvard University Press, 2001.
Boone, Elizabeth Hill. "Introduction: Writing and Recording Knowledge." *Writing without Words: Alternative Literacies in Mesoamerica and the Andes.* Ed. Elizabeth Hill Boone and Walter D. Mignolo. Durham: Duke University Press, 1994. 3–26.
Boone, Elizabeth Hill, and Walter D. Mignolo, eds. *Writing without Words: Alternative Literacies in Mesoamerica and the Andes.* Durham: Duke University Press, 1994.
Bourque, Bruce J. *Twelve Thousand Years: American Indians in Maine.* Lincoln: University of Nebraska Press, 2001.
Bourque, Bruce J., and Ruth H. Whitehead. "Trade and Alliances in the Contact Period." *American Beginnings: Exploration, Culture, and Cartography in the Land of Norumbega.* Ed. Emerson W. Baker et al. Lincoln: University of Nebraska Press, 1994. 131–47.
Bradford, William. *Of Plymouth Plantation: The Pilgrims in America.* 1856. Ed. Harvey Wish. New York: Capricorn, 1962.
Brøgger, A. W., and Haakon Shetelig. *The Viking Ships: Their Ancestry and Evolution.* 1951. London: C. Hurst, 1971.
Brown, Marie Adelaide. "Marie A. Brown: A Brief Autobiography." *Leif Erikson* 1.1 (1889), 1.
———. "A New History of the United States." *Galaxy: A Magazine of Entertaining Reading* 21.6 (1876), 836–42.
———. "The Pecuniary Independence of Wives." *Revolution* 3.23 (1869), 355.
———. "The Viking Exhibition." *Independent, Devoted to the Consideration of Politics, Social and Economic Issues* 40.2046 (1888), 5–6.
Bruchac, Joseph. "The Ice-Hearts." *Turtle Meat and Other Stories.* Duluth, Minn.: Holy Cow! Press, 1992. 3–9.
———. Introduction to *I Become Part of It: Sacred Dimensions in Native American Life.* Ed. D. M. Dooling and Paul Jordan-Smith. New York: Parabola Books, 1989. 1–8.
———. *Our Stories Remember: American Indian History, Culture, and Values through Storytelling.* Golden, Colo.: Fulcrum, 2003.
———. Preface to *Survival This Way: Interviews with American Indian Poets.* Tucson: Sun Tracks and University of Arizona Press, 1987. ix–xiii.
———. *Return of the Sun: Native American Tales from the Northeast Woodlands.* Freedom, Calif.: Crossing Press, 1989.
———. *The Wind Eagle and Other Abenaki Stories.* Greenfield Center, N.Y.: Bowman Books, 1985.
Bryant, William Cullen. *Prose Writings of William Cullen Bryant: Travels, Addresses, and Comments.* 2 vols. 1884. Ed. Parke Godwin. Vol. 2. New York: Russell and Russell, 1964.

Bryant, William Cullen, and Sydney Howard Gay. *A Popular History of the United States*. London: Sampson Low, Marston, Searle, and Rivington, 1876.

Burr, Clinton Stoddard. *America's Race Heritage*. New York: National Historical Society, 1922.

Bushman, Claudia L. *America Discovers Columbus: How an Italian Explorer Became an American Hero*. Hanover, N.H.: University Press of New England, 1992.

Byock, Jesse L. *Feud in the Icelandic Saga*. Berkeley: University of California Press, 1982.

———. *Medieval Iceland: Society, Sagas, and Power*. Berkeley: University of California Press, 1988.

———. *Viking Age Iceland*. London: Penguin, 2001.

"Carl Christian Rafn and the Ante-Columbian Era." *Round Table: A Saturday Review of Politics, Finance, Literature, Society* 3.27 (1866), 145–47.

Carlson, Suzanne. "The Spirit Pond Inscription Stone: Rhyme and Reason. Part I—Rhyme." *NEARA Journal* 28.1–2 (1993), 1–7.

———. "The Spirit Pond Inscription Stone: Rhyme and Reason. Part II—Reason." *NEARA Journal* 28.3–4 (1994), 74–82.

Carpenter, Charles H., Jr. *Tiffany Silver*. New York: Dodd, Mead, 1978.

Carpenter, Edmund. *Norse Penny*. New York: Rock Foundation, 2003.

Catlin, George. *Letters and Notes on the Manners, Customs, and Conditions of the North American Indians*. 2 vols. 1841. Ed. Marjorie Halpin. New York: Dover, 1973.

Chaillu, Paul Belloni du. *The Viking Age: The Early History, Manners, and Customs of the Ancestors of the English-Speaking Nations*. 2 vols. New York: Scribner's, 1889.

Champlain, Samuel de. "Discovery of the Coast of the *Almouchiquois* as far as the Forty-Second Degree of Latitude, and Details of this Voyage." 1605. *Sailors Narratives of Voyages along the New England Coast 1524–1624*. Ed. George Parker Winship. 1905. New York: Burt Franklin, 1968. 65–97.

Channing, William Ellery. *The Collected Poems of William Ellery Channing the Younger, 1817–1901*. Facsimile ed. Ed. Walter Harding. Gainesville, Fla.: Scholars' Facsimiles and Reprints, 1967.

———. *The Wanderer: A Colloquial Poem*. Boston: James R. Osgood, 1871.

Chapin, Alonzo Bowen. "Ante-Columbian History of America. Dighton Rock,—Language of Skrællings, etc." *American Biblical Repository*. Second series 2.3–4 (1839), 191–96.

Chapin, Howard M. Introduction to Roger Williams, *A Key into the Language of America*. London: Gregory Dexter, 1643. Reprinted Providence: Rhode Island and Providence Plantations Tercentenary Committee, 1936. Republished Ann Arbor: Gryphon Books, 1971. n.p.

"The Charter of New England, November 3, 1620." *America's Founding Charters: Primary Documents of Colonial and Revolutionary Era Governance*.

3 vols. Vol. 1. Ed. Jon L. Wakelyn. Westport, Conn.: Greenwood Press, 2006. 68–78.
Choate, Rufus. *Addresses and Orations of Rufus Choate*. Boston: Little, Brown, 1878.
Christiansen, Peter. "William T. Vollmann's *The Ice-Shirt*: Updating Icelandic Traditions." *Critique: Studies in Contemporary Fiction* 38.1 (1996), 52–67.
Churchill, Edwin A., and Emerson W. Baker. "Introduction to Part III." *American Beginnings: Exploration, Culture, and Cartography in the Land of Norumbega*. Ed. Emerson W. Baker et al. Lincoln: University of Nebraska Press, 1994. 169–71.
Clark, Harry Hayden. "Lowell's Criticism of Romantic Literature." *PMLA* 41.1 (1926), 209–28.
Clinton, DeWitt. *Discourse Delivered before the New-York Historical Society, at Their Anniversary Meeting, 6th December, 1811*. New York: James Eastburn, 1812.
Clover, Carol J. *The Medieval Saga*. Ithaca: Cornell University Press, 1982.
———. "Regardless of Sex." *Speculum* 68 (1993), 363–87.
Cole, Thomas. "Essay on American Scenery." 1835. *American Monthly Magazine*. New Series 1 (Jan. 1836), 1–12. Reprinted in *American Art 1700–1900: Sources and Documents*. Ed. John W. McCoubrey. Englewood Cliffs, N.J.: Prentice Hall, 1965. 100–110.
Columbus, Ferdinand [Fernando Colón]. *The Life of the Admiral Christopher Columbus by His Son Ferdinand*. Trans. and ed. Benjamin Keen. 1959. New Brunswick, N.J.: Rutgers University Press, 1992.
"The Columbus Celebration in New York." *Christian Union* 46.17 (1892), 726–28.
Cooper, James Fenimore. *The Pioneers; or, The Sources of the Susquehanna: A Descriptive Tale*. 1823. *The Works of James Fenimore Cooper*. Vol. 4. New York: G. P. Putnam's Sons, 1893.
Cox, Steven L. "A Norse Penny from Maine." *Vikings: The North Atlantic Saga*. Ed. William W. Fitzhugh and Elisabeth I. Ward. Washington and New York: Smithsonian Institution Press in association with the National Museum of Natural History, 2000. 206–7.
Crowninshield, Clara. *The Diary of Clara Crowninshield: A European Tour with Longfellow, 1835–1836*. Ed. Andrew Hilen. Seattle: University of Washington Press, 1956.
Cusick, David. *David Cusick's Sketches of Ancient History of the Six Nations*. 1826. 3rd ed. Lockport, New York: Turner and McCollum, 1848.
D'Abate, Richard. "On the Meaning of a Name: 'Norumbega' and the Representation of North America." *American Beginnings: Exploration, Culture, and Cartography in the Land of Norumbega*. Ed. Emerson W. Baker et al. Lincoln: University of Nebraska Press, 1994. 61–88.
D'Abate, Richard, and Victor A. Konrad. General introduction to *American Beginnings: Exploration, Culture, and Cartography in the Land of Norumbega*.

Ed. Emerson W. Baker et al. Lincoln: University of Nebraska Press, 1994. xix–xxxvii.

Day, Gordon M. "Oral Tradition as Complement." *In Search of New England's Native Past*. Ed. Michael K. Foster and William Cowan. Amherst: University of Massachusetts Press, 1998. 127–35.

———."The Western Abenaki Transformer." *Journal of the Folklore Institute* 13.1 (1976), 75–89.

Debo, Angie. *A History of the Indians of the United States*. Norman: University of Oklahoma Press, 1970.

DeCosta, Benjamin Franklin. *The Northmen in Maine: A Critical Examination*. Albany, New York: Joel Munsell's Sons, 1870.

———. *The Pre-Columbian Discovery of America, by the Northmen, with Translations from the Icelandic Sagas*. 1868. 2nd ed. Albany, New York: Joel Munsell's Sons, 1890.

Deloria, Vine, Jr. Foreword to David Hurst Thomas, *Skull Wars: Kennewick Man, Archaeology, and the Battle for Native American Identity*. New York: Basic Books, 2000. xv–xviii.

———. "Indians, Archaeologists, and the Future." *American Antiquity* 57.4 (1992), 595–98.

Denys, Nicolas. *The Description and Natural History of the Coasts of North America (Acadia)*. 1672. Ed. and trans. William F. Ganong. Toronto: Champlain Society, 1908.

Diamond, Jared. *Collapse: How Societies Choose to Fail or Succeed*. New York: Penguin, 2006.

Dickason, Olive Patricia. *Canada's First Nations: A History of Founding Peoples from Earliest Times*. Norman: University of Oklahoma Press, 1992.

Dillehay, Thomas D. *The Settlement of the Americas: A New Prehistory*. New York: Basic Books, 2000.

"Discovery of America by the Norsemen." *Massachusetts Quarterly Review* 6 (Mar. 1849), 189–214.

"Discovery of America by the Northmen." *Christian Advocate and Journal* 27.52 (1852), 208–10.

Dowe, William. "The Ericssons: An Old Story and a New One." *Graham's American Monthly Magazine of Literature, Art, and Fashion* 42.4 (1853), 385–90.

Duberman, Martin. *James Russell Lowell*. Boston: Houghton Mifflin, 1966.

Dwight, Timothy. *Travels in New England and New York, 1821–22*. 4 vols. Ed. Barbara Miller Solomon. Cambridge: Belknap Press of Harvard University Press, 1969.

Ebenesersdóttir, Sigríður Sunna, et al. "A New Subclade of mtDNA Haplogroup C1 Found in Icelanders: Evidence of Pre-Columbian Contact?" *American Journal of Physical Anthropology* 144.1 (Jan. 2011), 92–99.

Eckstorm, Fanny Hardy. *Indian Place Names of the Penobscot Valley and the Maine Coast*. Orono: University of Maine Studies 2nd ser. no. 55, 1941.

———. *Old John Neptune and Other Maine Indian Shamans*. Portland, Maine: Southworth-Anthoensen Press, 1945.

"Editors' Table." *Godey's Magazine and Lady's Book* 33.1 (1846), 44–46.

Einarsson, Stefán. *A History of Icelandic Literature*. New York: Johns Hopkins University Press for The American-Scandinavian Foundation, 1957.

Eirik the Red's Saga. Trans. Magnus Magnusson and Hermann Pálsson. *The Vinland Sagas: The Norse Discovery of America*. Ed. Magnus Magnusson and Hermann Pálsson. London: Penguin Books, 1965. 75–105.

Eliot, John. *John Eliot's Indian Dialogues: A Study in Cultural Interaction*. Ed. Henry W. Bowden and James P. Ronda. Westport, Conn.: Greenwood Press, 1981.

Emerson, Ralph Waldo. "Cherokee Letter: Letter to Martin Van Buren, President of the United States." Concord, Mass., 23 April 1838. *Ralph Waldo Emerson: Selected Essays, Lectures, and Poems*. Ed. Robert D. Richardson Jr. New York: Bantam, 1990. 101–5.

———. *English Traits*. 1850. *The Collected Works of Ralph Waldo Emerson*. Vol. 5. Ed. Philip Nicoloff, Robert E. Burkholder, and Douglas Emory Wilson. Cambridge: Harvard University Press, 1994.

———. Journal CO. *The Journals and Miscellaneous Notebooks of Ralph Waldo Emerson*. Ed. A. W. Plumstead and William H. Gilman. Cambridge: Belknap Press of Harvard University Press, 1975. 11:366–452.

Encyclopedia of Ships and Seafaring. Ed. Peter Kemp. London: Stanford Maritime, 1980.

Everett, Alexander Hill. "The Discovery of America by the Northmen." [Article 1.] *United States Magazine and Democratic Review* 2.5 (1838), 85–96.

———. "The Discovery of America by the Northmen." [Article 2.] *United States Magazine and Democratic Review* 2.6 (1838), 143–58.

Everett, Edward. *The Discovery and Colonization of America and Immigration to the United States*. Boston: Little, Brown, 1853.

———. "The Discovery of America by the Northmen." *North American Review* 46.98 (1838), 161–203.

Fagan, Brian. *The Little Ice Age: How Climate Made History, 1300–1850*. New York: Basic Books, 2000.

Falnes, Oscar J. "New England Interest in Scandinavian Culture and the Norsemen." *New England Quarterly* 10.1 (1937), 211–42.

Felton, C. C. "*Lays of My Home, and Other Poems*." Review. *North American Review* 57.121 (1843), 509–10.

Fenton, William N., and Elisabeth Tooker. "Mohawk." *Handbook of North American Indians: Northeast*. Ed. Bruce G. Trigger et al. Washington: Smithsonian Institution, 1978. 15:466–80.

Ferguson, Robert. *The Vikings: A History*. New York: Viking/Penguin, 2009.

Filson, John. *The Discovery, Settlement And present State of Kentucke: And An Essay towards the Topography, and Natural History of that important Country: To which is added, An Appendix, Containing, The Adventures of Col.

Daniel Boon, one of the first Settlers, comprehending every important Occurrence in the political History of that Province. Wilmington, Del.: James Adams, 1784.

"The First Discoverers of America." *Putnam's Monthly Magazine of American Literature, Science, and Art* 4.23 (1854), 1–13.

Fitzhugh, William W. "Puffins, Ringed Pins, and Runestones: The Viking Passage to America." *Vikings: The North Atlantic Saga*. Ed. William W. Fitzhugh and Elisabeth I. Ward. Washington and New York: Smithsonian Institution Press in association with the National Museum of Natural History, 2000. 11–25.

Fløttum, Sivert. "The Norse in America: Saga versus Reality." Unpublished paper made available to the author and quoted by permission.

Folsom, George. "Discovery of America by the Northmen." *New York Review* 2.4 (1838), 352–71.

Forbes, Jack D. *The American Discovery of Europe*. Urbana: University of Illinois Press, 2007.

Franchot, Jenny. *Roads to Rome: The Antebellum Protestant Encounter with Catholicism*. Berkeley: University of California Press, 1994.

Franklin, Benjamin. *The Papers of Benjamin Franklin*. 39 vols. Ed. Leonard W. Labaree et al. New Haven: Yale University Press, 1959– .

Friedrich, Horst. "Sectarianism versus Comprehensiveness." *NEARA Journal* 28.1–2 (1993), 12–14.

Frydendahl, Knud. "The Summer Climate in the North Atlantic about the Year 1000." *Viking Voyages to North America*. Ed. Birthe L. Clausen. Trans. Gillian Fellows Jensen. Roskilde, Denmark: Viking Ship Museum, 1993. 90–94.

Gage, Matilda Joslyn. *Woman, Church and State: A Historical Account of the Status of Woman through the Christian Ages*. Chicago: Charles H. Kerr, 1893.

Gardiner, Robert, ed. *The Earliest Ships: The Evolution of Boats into Ships*. Annapolis: Naval Institute Press, 1996.

Gathorne-Hardy, Geoffrey M. *The Norse Discoverers of America, the Wineland Sagas*. Oxford: Clarendon Press, 1921.

Giles, Paul. "Medieval American Literature: Emerson, Longfellow, and the Longue Durée." *REAL: The Yearbook of Research in English and American Literature* 23 (2007): 113–32.

Gobineau, Joseph Arthur, Comte de. *The Inequality of the Human Races*. 1855. *Selected Political Writings of Arthur Comte de Gobineau*. Ed. Michael Bedliss. New York: Harper and Row, 1970. 60–175.

Gräslund, Anne-Sofie. "Religion, Art, and Runes." *Vikings: The North Atlantic Saga*. Ed. William W. Fitzhugh and Elisabeth I. Ward. Washington and New York: Smithsonian Institution Press in association with the National Museum of Natural History, 2000. 55–69.

Gravier, Gabriel. *Découverte de l'Amérique par les Normands au Xe Siècle*. Paris: Maisonnueve, 1874.

The Greenlanders' Saga. Trans. Magnus Magnusson and Hermann Pálsson. *The Vinland Sagas: The Norse Discovery of America.* Ed. Magnus Magnusson and Hermann Pálsson. London: Penguin Books, 1965. 47–72.

Greenwald, Emily. *Reconfiguring the Reservation: The Nez Perces, Jicarilla Apaches, and the Dawes Act.* Albuquerque: University of New Mexico Press, 2002.

Grinde, Donald A. Introduction to *The Unheard Voices: American Indian Responses to the Columbian Quincentenary 1492–1992.* Ed. Carole M. Gentry and Donald A. Grinde. Los Angeles: University of California American Indian Studies Center, 1994. iii–xii.

Groseclose, Barbara S. *Emanuel Leutze, 1816–1868: Freedom Is the Only King.* Washington: Smithsonian Institution Press, 1975.

Grund, Francis J. Preface to Charles Henry Hormes. "The Discovery of America. By the Icelanders." Trans. Francis J. Grund. *Graham's American Monthly Magazine of Literature, Art, and Fashion* 42.5 (1853), 545.

Hallowell, Irving A. Foreword to Henry Lorne Masta. *Abenaki Indian Legends, Grammar and Place Names.* Victoriaville, Quebec: La Voix de Bois-Francs, 1932. 6–12.

Hamell, George R. "Strawberries, Floating Islands, and Rabbit Captains: Mythical Realities and European Contact in the Northeast during the Sixteenth and Seventeenth Centuries." *Journal of Canadian Studies* 21.4 (1986–87), 72–94.

Hamlin, A. C. "Supposed Runic Inscriptions." *Proceedings of the American Association for the Advancement of Science.* 10th meeting, August 1856. New York: G. P. Putnam, 1857. Part 2: 214–16.

Handbook of North American Indians. 20 vols. Gen. ed. William C. Sturtevant. Washington: Smithsonian Institution Press, 1970–78.

Haviland, William A. *At the Place of the Lobsters and Crabs: Indian People and Deer Isle, Maine, 1605–2005.* Solon, Maine: Polar Bear, 2009.

———. "The Case of the Deer Isle Giant: An Archaeological Mystery Solved?" *Maine Archaeological Society Bulletin* 49.1 (2009), 3–5.

———. "Who Was Here First?" Guest column. *Island Advantages,* 17 Apr. 2008, 4.

Haviland, William A., and Marjory W. Power. *The Original Vermonters: Native Inhabitants, Past and Present.* Revised ed. Hanover, N.H.: University Press of New England, 1994.

Hawthorne, Nathaniel. "Preface to *The Marble Faun: or The Romance of Montebeni.*" 1859. *The Complete Novels and Selected Tales of Nathaniel Hawthorne.* Ed. Norman Holmes Pearson. New York: Random House, 1937. 589–91.

Headley, Janet A. "Anne Whitney's 'Leif Eriksson': A Brahmin Response to Christopher Columbus." *American Art* 17.2 (2003), 41–59.

Hedden, Mark. "Contact Period Petroglyphs in Machias Bay, Maine." *Archaeology of Eastern North America Journal* 30 (2002), 1–20.

———. "3,500 Years of Shamanism in Maine Rock Art." *Rock Art of the East-*

ern Woodlands. Ed. Charles H. Faulkner. American Rock Art Research Association, Occasional Paper 2, San Miguel, Calif., 1996. 7–24.

Hermannsson, Halldór. *Icelandic Manuscripts*. Ithaca: Cornell University Library, 1929.

Hertz, Johannes. "The Newport Tower." *Vikings: The North Atlantic Saga*. Ed. William W. Fitzhugh and Elisabeth I. Ward. Washington and New York: Smithsonian Institution Press in association with the National Museum of Natural History, 2000. 376.

Higham, John. *Strangers in the Land: Patterns of American Nativism, 1860–1925*. New Brunswick, N.J.: Rutgers University Press, 1955.

"A Historical Sketch of the Discovery of America by the Norsemen in the Tenth Century." Review. *North American Review* 120.246 (1875), 194–6.

Holand, Hjalmar R. *Explorations in America before Columbus*. New York: Twayne, 1956.

———. *Norse Discoveries and Explorations in America 982–1362: Leif Erickson to the Kensington Stone*. 1940. New York: Dover, 1969.

Horsford, Eben Norton. *The Defences of Norumbega and a Review of the Reconnaissances of Col. T. W. Higginson, Professor Henry W. Haynes, Dr. Justin Winsor, Dr. Francis Parkman, and Rev. Dr. Edmund F. Slafter: [Followed by] A Letter to Judge Daly*. Boston: Houghton Mifflin, 1891.

———. *Discovery of America by Northmen: Address at the Unveiling of the Statue of Leif Erikson, October 29, 1887*. Boston: Houghton Mifflin, 1888.

———. *The Discovery of the Ancient City of Norumbega: A Communication to the President and Council of the American Geographical Society at their Special Session in Watertown, November 21, 1889*. 1889. Boston: Houghton Mifflin, 1890.

———. *The Landfall of Leif Erikson, A.D. 1000, and the Site of his Houses in Vineland*. Boston: Damrell and Upham, 1892.

———. *Leif's House in Vineland*. Boston: Damrell and Upham, 1893.

Howard, Leon. *Victorian Knight-Errant: A Study of the Early Literary Career of James Russell Lowell*. Berkeley: University of California Press, 1952.

Hunt, George H. *Report of the Agent of the Penobscot Tribe of Indians for the Year 1894*. Augusta, Maine: Burleigh and Flint, 1894.

"The Icelandic Discovery of America." Review of *The Finding of Wineland the Good: The History of the Icelandic Discovery of America*. Ed. Arthur Middleton Reeves. *Nation* 52.1333 (1891), 54–56.

"An Indian Mound Opened." *Louisville Advertiser*. Reprinted in *Boston Courier*, 30 Apr. 1842, n.p.

Ingstad, Anne Stine. *The Discovery of a Norse Settlement in America: Excavations at L'Anse aux Meadows, Newfoundland 1961–1968*. Trans. Elizabeth Seeberg. New York: Columbia University Press, 1977.

Ingstad, Helge. *The Apache Indians: In Search of the Missing Tribe*. Trans. Jeanine K. Stenehjem. Lincoln: University of Nebraska Press, 2004.

———. *Westward to Vinland: The Discovery of Pre-Columbian Norse House-*

sites in North America. Trans. Erik J. Friis. New York: St. Martin's Press, 1969.

Irmscher, Christoph. *Longfellow Redux.* Urbana: University of Illinois Press, 2006.

Irving, Washington. *The Life and Voyages of Christopher Columbus.* 1828. Ed. John Harmon McElroy. Boston: Twayne, 1981.

——. "Voyages of the Scandinavians." *Voyages and Discoveries of the Companions of Columbus.* Ed. James W. Tuttleton. Boston: Twayne, 1986. 255–60.

Islandske Annaler indtil 1578. Ed. Gustav Storm. Det Norske Historiske Kilderskriftfonds Skrifter 21. Christiania, Norway: A. W. Brøgger, 1888.

Jacobson, Matthew Frye. *Whiteness of a Different Color: European Immigrants and the Alchemy of Race.* Cambridge: Harvard University Press, 1998.

Jarves, James Jackson. *The Art Idea.* 1864. Ed. Benjamin Rowland Jr. Cambridge: Belknap Press of Harvard University Press, 1960.

Jefferson, Thomas. "To Brother Handsome Lake." 3 Nov. 1802, Washington, D.C. *The Portable Thomas Jefferson.* Ed. Merrill D. Peterson. New York: Viking, 1975. 305–7.

Jesch, Judith. *Ships and Men in the Late Viking Age: The Vocabulary of Runic Inscriptions and Skaldic Verse.* Woodbridge, U.K.: Boydell / Boydell and Brewer, 2001.

Jewett, Sarah Orne. *The Normans.* 1886. New York: G. P. Putnam's Sons, 1905.

——. "A War Debt." *Harper's New Monthly Magazine* 90.2 (1895), 227–37.

Jochens, Jenny. "Consent in Marriage: Old Norse Law, Life, and Literature." *Scandinavian Studies* 58 (1986), 142–76.

——. "Old Norse Magic and Gender." *Scandinavian Studies* 63 (1991), 305–17.

Joe, Rita. "Mi´kmaq Hieroglyphics." *Song of Eskasoni: More Poems of Rita Joe.* Charlottetown, Prince Edward Island: Ragweed Press, 1988. 35.

Jones, Julia Clinton. *Valhalla, the Myths of Norseland: A Saga in Twelve Parts.* San Francisco: Edward Bosqui, 1878. Reprinted New York: R. Worthington, 1880.

Josselyn, John. *John Josselyn, Colonial Traveler: A Critical Edition of "Two Voyages to New-England."* 1674. Ed. Paul J. Lindholdt. Hanover, N.H.: University Press of New England, 1988.

Kadir, Djelal. *Columbus and the Ends of the Earth: Europe's Prophetic Rhetoric as Conquering Ideology.* Berkeley: University of California Press, 1992.

Kaland, Sigrid H. H., and Irmelin Martens. "Farming and Daily Life." *Vikings: The North Atlantic Saga.* Ed. William W. Fitzhugh and Elisabeth I. Ward. Washington and New York: Smithsonian Institution Press in association with the National Museum of Natural History, 2000. 42–54.

Kammen, Michael. *Mystic Chords of Memory: The Transformation of Tradition in American Culture.* 1991. New York: Vintage / Random House, 1993.

Kehoe, Alice Beck. *America before the European Invasions.* London: Longman, 2002.

Kellogg, Robert. Introduction to *The Sagas of Icelanders: A Selection*. New York: Viking Penguin, 2000. xv–liv.

Kidd, Kenneth. "A Radiocarbon Date on a Midewiwin Scroll from Burntside Lake, Ontario." *Ontario Archaeology* 35 (1981), 41–43.

Kohl, Johann Georg. *A History of the Discovery of the East Coast of North America, Particularly the Coast of Maine; from the Northmen in 990, to the Charter of Gilbert in 1578.* Vol. 1. *Documentary History of the State of Maine.* Ed. William Willis. Portland: Bailey and Noyes, 1869.

Kolodny, Annette. "Fictions of American Prehistory: Indians, Archaeology, and National Origin Myths." *American Literature* 75.4 (2003), 693–721.

———. "Introduction to Joseph Nicolar's 1893 *The Life and Traditions of the Red Man*." Joseph Nicolar. *The Life and Traditions of the Red Man*. Edited, annotated, and with a history of the Penobscot Nation and an introduction by Annette Kolodny. Durham: Duke University Press, 2007. 35–88.

———. *The Land before Her: Fantasy and Experience of the American Frontiers, 1630–1860*. Chapel Hill: University of North Carolina Press, 1984.

———. *The Lay of the Land: Metaphor as Experience and History in American Life and Letters*. Chapel Hill: University of North Carolina Press, 1975.

———. "Letting Go Our Grand Obsessions: Notes toward a New Literary History of the American Frontiers." *American Literature* 64.1 (1992), 1–18.

———. "Rethinking the 'Ecological Indian': A Penobscot Precursor." *ISLE: Interdisciplinary Studies in Literature and Environment* 14.1 (2007), 1–23.

———. "A Summary History of the Penobscot Nation." Joseph Nicolar. *The Life and Traditions of the Red Man*. 1893. Edited, annotated, and with a history of the Penobscot Nation and an introduction by Annette Kolodny. Durham: Duke University Press, 2007. 1–34.

Kornwolf, James D. *Architecture and Town Planning in Colonial North America*. 3 vols. Baltimore: Johns Hopkins University Press, 2002.

Kovach, Robert L. *Early Earthquakes of the Americas*. New York: Cambridge University Press, 2004.

Kribbs, Jayne K. Introduction to *Critical Essays on John Greenleaf Whittier*. Boston: G. K. Hall, 1980. xiii–xl.

Kunz, Keneva. "The Vinland Sagas." *The Sagas of Icelanders: A Selection*. Trans. Keneva Kunz. New York: Viking Penguin, 2000. 626–74.

Lalemant, Jerome. "The Earthquake." Trans. Susan Castillo. *The Literatures of Colonial America: An Anthology*. Ed. Susan Castillo and Ivy Schweitzer. Oxford and Malden, Mass.: Blackwell, 2001. 179–81.

Lears, T. J. Jackson. *No Place of Grace: Antimodernism and the Transformation of American Culture, 1880–1920*. New York: Pantheon, 1981.

———. *Rebirth of a Nation: The Making of Modern America, 1877–1920*. New York: Harper, 2009.

LeBlanc, Steven A. "Prehistory of Warfare." *Archaeology* 56.3 (2003), 19–25.

LeClercq, Chrètien. *New Relation of Gaspesia, with the Customs and Religion of the Gaspesian Indians*. Trans. and ed. William F. Ganong. Toronto: Champlain Society, 1910.

———. "You Tell Us That France Is an Earthly Paradise." Trans. Patricia Clark Smith. *Western Literature in a World Context*. 2 vols. Ed. Paul Davis, Gary Harrison, David M. Johnson, Patricia Clark Smith, and John F. Crawford. New York: St. Martin's Press, 1995. 2:503–5.

Leland, Charles Godfrey. *The Algonquin Legends of New England, or, Myths and Folk Lore of the Micmac, Passamaquoddy, and Penobscot Tribes*. Boston: Houghton Mifflin, 1884.

———. "The Edda among the Algonquin Indians." *Atlantic Monthly* 54.322 (1884), 222–34.

Lescarbot, Marc. *The History of New France*. 3rd ed. 1618. Ed. and trans. W. L. Grant. 3 vols. Toronto: Champlain Society, 1907–14.

Levett, Christopher. *My Discouery of Diverse Riuers and Harbours, with their Names, and Which Are Fit for Plantations, and Which Not*. 1628. *Sailors Narratives of Voyages along the New England Coast 1524–1624*. Ed. George Parker Winship. 1905. Reprinted New York: Burt Franklin, 1968. 98–151.

Levin, David. *History as Romantic Art: Bancroft, Prescott, Motley, and Parkman*. Stanford: Stanford University Press, 1959.

Liljencrantz, Ottilie A. *Randvar the Songsmith: A Romance of Norumbega*. New York: Harper, 1906.

———. *The Thrall of Leif the Lucky: A Story of Viking Days*. Chicago: A. C. McClurg, 1902.

———. *The Vinland Champions*. New York: Appleton, 1904.

Lillo, George. *The Christian Hero: A Tragedy. As it is acted at the Theatre Royal in Drury-Lane, By His Majesty's Servants, By Mr. Lillo*. London: John Gray, 1735.

Litwicki, Ellen M. *America's Public Holidays, 1865–1920*. Washington: Smithsonian Institution Press, 2000.

Longfellow, Henry Wadsworth. *The Complete Poetical Works of Henry Wadsworth Longfellow*. Household ed. Boston: Houghton Mifflin, 1894.

———. "Footsteps of Angels." *The Complete Poetical Works of Henry Wadsworth Longfellow*. Household ed. Boston: Houghton Mifflin, 1894. 4.

———. *The Letters of Henry Wadsworth Longfellow*. 6 vols. Ed. Andrew Hilen. Cambridge: Belknap Press of Harvard University Press, 1966–82.

———. "Mezzo Cammin." *The Complete Poetical Works of Henry Wadsworth Longfellow*. Household ed. Boston: Houghton Mifflin, 1894. 40.

———. *The Poets and Poetry of Europe with Introductions and Biographical Notices by Henry Wadsworth Longfellow*. 1845. New, revised and enlarged ed. Philadelphia: Porter and Coates, 1871.

———. "Saga of the Skeleton in Armour." *Knickerbocker, New-York Monthly Magazine* 17.1 (1841), 52–54.

———. "The Skeleton in Armour." *Ballads and Other Poems*. Cambridge, Mass.: John Owen, 1842. 29–41.

———. *Tales of a Wayside Inn*. Boston: Ticknor and Fields, 1863.

"Longfellow's Ballads and Other Poems." Review. *North American Review* 60.116 (1842), 114–16.

"Longfellow's Ballads and Poems." Review. *Arcturus: A Journal of Books and Opinion* 3.15 (1842), 214–20.

"Longfellow's Ballads and Poems." Review. *United States Magazine and Democratic Review*, ns 10.44 (1842), 182–93.

"Longfellow's Poems." Review. *New York Review* 10.19 (1842), 240–45.

Loring, John. *Magnificent Tiffany Silver*. New York: Harry N. Abrams, 2001.

Lovoll, Odd S. *The Promise of America: A History of the Norwegian-American People*. Minneapolis: University of Minnesota Press, 1984.

Lowell, James Russell. *The Biglow Papers*. 1848. Ed. Thomas Wortham. DeKalb: Northern Illinois University Press, 1977.

———. "Cambridge Thirty Years Ago." 1854. *The Writings of James Russell Lowell*. Cambridge ed. Vol. 1. Boston: Houghton Mifflin; and Cambridge: Riverside Press, 1893. 43–99.

———. "Columbus." 1848. *The Writings of James Russell Lowell*. Vol. 7. Boston: Houghton Mifflin; and Cambridge: Riverside Press, 1895. 148–57.

———. *The Complete Poetical Works of James Russell Lowell*. Cambridge ed. Boston: Houghton Mifflin, 1897.

———. "Democracy." 1884. *Literary and Political Addresses*. Vol. 6 of *The Writings of James Russell Lowell*. 10 vols. 1890–96. Riverside ed. Boston: Houghton Mifflin; and Cambridge: Riverside Press, 1894. 7–37.

———. "The Growth of the Legend: A Fragment." 1848. *The Writings of James Russell Lowell*. Riverside ed. Vol. 7. Boston: Houghton Mifflin; and Cambridge: Riverside Press, 1895. 198–201.

———. "Hakon's Lay." *Graham's American Monthly Magazine of Literature, Art, and Fashion* 46.1 (1855), 72.

———. *Letters of James Russell Lowell*. 2 vols. Ed. Charles Eliot Norton. New York: Harper and Brothers, 1894.

———. "A Moosehead Journal." 1853. *The Writings of James Russell Lowell*. Riverside ed. Boston: Houghton Mifflin; and Cambridge: Riverside Press, 1892. 1:1–42.

———. "No. V. Speech of Honourable Preserved Doe in Secret Caucus." "Biglow Papers. Second Series." 1862. *The Writings of James Russell Lowell*. Vol. 8. Riverside ed. Boston: Houghton Mifflin; and Cambridge: Riverside Press, 1896. 311–28.

———. "No. VII. A Letter from a Candidate for the Presidency in Answer to Suttin Questions Proposed by Mr. Hosea Biglow." "The Biglow Papers. First Series." 1848. *The Writings of James Russell Lowell*. Vol. 8. Boston: Houghton Mifflin; and Cambridge: Riverside Press, 1896. 106–15.

———. "The Place of the Independent in Politics." 1888. *Literary and Political Addresses*. Vol. 6 of *The Writings of James Russell Lowell*. 10 vols. 1890–96. Riverside ed. Boston: Houghton Mifflin, 1894. 190–221.

———. "Reconstruction." *North American Review* 100.2 (1865), 540–59.

———. "Reconstruction." 1865. *Political Essays*. Boston: Houghton Mifflin, 1892. 210–38.

———. "The Voyage to Vinland." 1869. *The Writings of James Russell Lowell*. Riverside ed. Vol. 9. Boston: Houghton Mifflin; and Cambridge: Riverside Press, 1896. 220–30.

———. *The Writings of James Russell Lowell*. 10 vols. Riverside ed. Boston: Houghton Mifflin; and Cambridge: Riverside Press, 1890–96.

Lutz, John Sutton, ed. *Myth and Memory: Stories of Indigenous-European Contact*. Vancouver: UBC Press, 2007.

Lynnerup, Niels. "Life and Death in Norse Greenland." *Vikings: The North Atlantic Saga*. Ed. William W. Fitzhugh and Elisabeth I. Ward. Washington and New York: Smithsonian Institution Press in association with the National Museum of Natural History, 2000. 285–94.

MacDougall, Pauleena. *The Penobscot Dance of Resistance: Tradition in the History of a People*. Hanover, N.H.: University Press of New England, 2004.

MacLean, John Patterson. *A Critical Examination of the Evidences Adduced to Establish the Theory of the Norse Discovery of America*. Chicago: American Antiquarian Office, 1892.

———. *The Mound Builders: Being an Account of a Remarkable People that Once Inhabited the Valleys of the Ohio and Mississippi, Together with an Investigation into the Archæology of Butler County*. Cincinnati: Robert Clarke, 1879.

———. "Pre-Columbian Discovery of America. III.—The Sagas and America." *American Antiquarian and Oriental Journal* 16.3 (1892), 139–54.

———. "Pre-Columbian Discovery of America. IV.—Norse Remains in America." *American Antiquarian and Oriental Journal* 14.4 (1892), 189–99.

Maddox, Lucy. *Removals: Nineteenth-century American Literature and the Politics of Indian Affairs*. New York: Oxford University Press, 1991.

Magnusson, Magnus, and Hermann Pálsson. Introduction to *The Vinland Sagas: The Norse Discovery of America*. New York: Penguin Books, 1965. 7–43.

Maillard, Antoine Simon-Pierre. *An Account of the Customs and Manners of the Micmakis and Maricheets Savage Nations, Now Dependent on the Government of Cape-Breton. From an Original Manuscript-Letter, Never Published*. London: Hooper and Morley, 1758.

Mallery, Arlington, and Mary Roberts Harrison. *The Rediscovery of Lost America*. 1951. New York: E. P. Dutton, 1979.

Mallery, Garrick. "Pictographs of the North American Indians: A Preliminary Paper." *Fourth Annual Report of the Bureau of Ethnology, 1882-'83*. Washington: Government Printing Office, 1886. 13–256.

———. "Picture-Writing of the American Indians." *Tenth Annual Report of the Bureau of Ethnology, 1888-'89*. Washington: Government Printing Office, 1893. 6–822.

Mallett, Paul Henri. *Northern Antiquities: or, A Description of the Manners, Customs, Religion, and Laws, of the Ancient Danes*. Trans. Thomas Percy. London: Carnan, 1770.

Mancini, JoAnne Marie. "Discovering Viking America." *Critical Inquiry* 28.4 (2002), 868–907.

Mann, Charles C. "1491." *Atlantic Monthly* 289 (Mar. 2002), 41–53.

Marcus, G. J. "The Navigation of the Norsemen." *Mariner's Mirror* 39.2 (1953), 112–31.

Marsh, George Perkins. *The Goths in New-England: A Discourse Delivered at the Anniversary of the Philomathesian Society of Middlebury College, August 15, 1843.* Middlebury, Vt.: J. Cobb Jr., 1843.

Marshall, Ingeborg. *A History and Ethnography of the Beothuk.* Montreal: McGill–Queen's University Press, 1996.

Marx, Robert F. *In Quest of the Great White Gods: Contact between the Old and New World from the Dawn of History.* New York: Crown, 1992.

Masta, Henry Lorne. *Abenaki Indian Legends, Grammar and Place Names.* Victoriaville, Quebec: La Voix des Bois-Francs, 1932.

Mather, Samuel. *An Attempt to Shew, That America Must Be Known to the Ancients; Made at the Request, and to Gratify the Curiosity, of an Inquisitive Gentleman: To which Is Added an Appendix, Concerning the American Colonies, and Some Modern Management Against Them. By an American Englishman.* Boston: Kneeland, 1773.

Maurault, Joseph Pierre Anselme. *Histoire des Abenakis: Depuis 1605 Jusqu'à Nos Jours.* Sorel, Quebec: Imprimé à l'atelier typographique de la "Gazette de Sorel," 1866.

McCance, M. "Stole." *New Catholic Encyclopedia.* Ed. Editorial staff at Catholic University of America. New York: McGraw-Hill, 1967. 13:722.

McGee, Thomas D'Arcy. *The Catholic history of North America. Five discourses. To which are added two discourses on the relations of Ireland and America.* Boston: P. Donahoe, 1855.

McGlinchee, Claire. *James Russell Lowell.* New York: Twayne, 1967.

McNickle, D'Arcy. *They Came Here First: The Epic of the American Indian.* New York: Farrar, Straus and Giroux, 1949. Reprinted New York: Octagon / Farrar, Straus and Giroux, 1975.

McSweeny, Z. F. "The Character of Our Immigration, Past and Present." *National Geographic Magazine* 16.1 (1905), 1–16.

Melville, Herman. *Moby-Dick.* 1851. Norton critical ed. 2nd ed. Ed. Hershel Parker and Harrison Hayford. New York: Norton, 2009.

Micmac Texts. Compiled and translated by Albert D. DeBlois. Hull, Quebec: Canadian Museum of Civilization, 1990.

Miller, Virginia P. "Silas T. Rand, Nineteenth Century Anthropologist among the Micmac." *Anthropologica* 22.2 (1980), 235–49.

Mitchill, Dr. "On the Population of America." *New-York Weekly Museum* 5.4 (1816), 53–55.

Momaday, N. Scott. *The Man Made of Words: Essays, Stories, Passages.* New York: St. Martin's Press, 1997.

Moody, John. Preface to Joseph Bruchac. *The Wind Eagle and Other Abenaki Stories.* Greenfield Center, N.Y.: Bowman Books, 1985. i–iii.

Morrison, Kenneth M. "Mapping Otherness: Myth and the Study of Cultural Encounter." *American Beginnings: Exploration, Culture, and Cartography in the Land of Norumbega*. Ed. Emerson W. Baker et al. Lincoln: University of Nebraska Press, 1994. 119–29.

Motley, John Lothrop. "From *Historic Progress and American Democracy*." 1843. *Representative Selections*. Ed. Chester Penn Higby and B. T. Schantz. New York: American Book, 1939. 87–118.

Mott, Frank Luther. *Golden Multitudes: The Story of Best Sellers in the United States*. New York: Macmillan, 1947.

Mott, Wesley. "Thoreau and Lowell on 'Vacation': *The Maine Woods* and 'A Moosehead Journal.'" *Thoreau Journal Quarterly* 10.3 (1978), 14–24.

"The National Centennial." *Washington Post*, 15 Feb. 1889, 4.

Neijmann, Daisy, ed. *A History of Icelandic Literature*. Lincoln: University of Nebraska Press, 2006.

"The New Biglow Papers." Review. *Nation* 3.72 (1866), 386–88.

"Newport Fast Waking Up." *New York Times*, 11 June 1893, 3.

"New Shrine for Italians." *New York Times*, 28 Nov. 1892, 2.

Nicolar, Joseph. *The Life and Traditions of the Red Man*. 1893. Edited, annotated, and with a history of the Penobscot Nation and an introduction by Annette Kolodny. Durham: Duke University Press, 2007.

Nicoloff, Philip L. *Emerson on Race and History: An Examination of "English Traits."* New York: Columbia University Press, 1961.

Nielsen, Richard, and Scott F. Wolter. *The Kensington Rune Stone: Compelling New Evidence*. Minneapolis: Lake Superior Agate, 2006.

Noble, Louis L. *The Course of Empire, Voyage of Life and Other Pictures of Thomas Cole*. New York: Cornish, Lamport, 1853.

Noonan, James Charles. *The Church Visible: The Ceremonial Life and Protocol of the Roman Catholic Church*. New York: Viking Penguin, 1996.

"Not to See the Viking Ship." *New York Times*, 25 Sept. 1892, 6.

"Notes and News." *Science* 13.316 (1889), 141.

Obama, Barack. *Leif Erikson Day, 2009: A Proclamation by the President of the United States*. White House website, 7 Oct. 2009.

O'Brien, Jean M. *Firsting and Lasting: Writing Indians Out of Existence in New England*. Minneapolis: University of Minnesota Press, 2010.

Odess, Daniel, Stephen Loring, and William W. Fitzhugh. "*Skraeling*: First Peoples of Helluland, Markland, and Vinland." *Vikings: The North Atlantic Saga*. Ed. William W. Fitzhugh and Elisabeth I. Ward. Washington and New York: Smithsonian Institution Press in association with the National Museum of Natural History, 2000. 193–205.

Oestreicher, David M. "Unmasking the *Walam Olum*: A 19th-Century Hoax." *Bulletin of the Archaeological Society of New Jersey* 49 (1994), 1–44.

O'Leary, Paul. "When Was Anti-Catholicism? The Case of Nineteenth- and Twentieth-Century Wales." *Journal of Ecclesiastical History* 56.2 (2005), 308–25.

O'Malley, John W. *The First Jesuits*. Cambridge: Harvard University Press, 1993.

Pagden, Anthony. *European Encounters with the New World: From Renaissance to Romanticism*. New Haven: Yale University Press, 1993.

Palfrey, John Gorham. *History of New England during the Stuart Dynasty*. Vol. 1. 1858. Boston: Little, Brown, 1865.

Pálsson, Hermann. "Vinland Revisited." *Northern Studies: The Journal of the Scottish Society for Northern Studies* 35 (2000), 11–38.

Peters, Daniel. *The Incas*. New York: Random House, 1991.

———. *The Luck of Huemac*. New York: Random House, 1981.

———. *Tikal*. New York: Random House, 1983.

Phillips, Ruth B. "Like a Star I Shine: Northern Woodlands Artistic Traditions." *The Spirit Sings: Artistic Traditions of Canada's First Peoples*. Toronto: Glenbow-Alberta Institute/McLelland and Stewart, 1987. 51–92.

Pickard, John B. *John Greenleaf Whittier: An Introduction and Interpretation*. New York: Holt, Rinehart and Winston, 1961.

"The Planet Earth Today: Meteorite vs. Meteor, Meteoroid and Micrometeoroid." *Space Today Online*, 21 Mar. 2005.

Pope, Peter E. *The Many Landfalls of John Cabot*. Toronto: University of Toronto Press, 1997.

Powell, Eric A. "The Kensington Code." *Archaeology* 63.3 (2010), 20, 62–70.

Powell, John Wesley. "Report of the Director." *Tenth Annual Report of the Bureau of Ethnology, 1888–'89*. Washington: Government Printing Office, 1893. ix–xxx.

———. "Report of the Director." *Twelfth Annual Report of the Bureau of Ethnology, 1890–91*. Washington: Government Printing Office, 1894. ix–lxv.

Prince, John Dyneley. *Passamaquoddy Texts*. New York: G. E. Stechert, 1921.

Prins, Harald E. L. *Asticou's Island Domain: Wabanaki People at Mount Desert Island, 1600–2000*. Boston: National Park Service, 2007.

———. "Children of Gluskap: Wabanaki Indians on the Eve of the European Invasion." *American Beginnings: Exploration, Culture, and Cartography in the Land of Norumbega*. Ed. Emerson W. Baker et al. Lincoln: University of Nebraska Press, 1994. 95–117.

———. *The Mi´kmaq: Resistance, Accommodation, and Cultural Survival*. Ft. Worth, Texas: Harcourt Brace College Publishers, 1996.

Pritchard, Evan T. *No Word for Time: The Way of the Algonquin People*. Tulsa, Okla.: Council Bluff Books, 1997.

Purtell, Joseph. *The Tiffany Touch*. New York: Random House, 1971.

Rafn, Carl Christian. *America Discovered in the Tenth Century*. New York: William Jackson, 1838.

———. "Discovery of America by the Northmen." *Christian Advocate and Journal* 27.52 (1852), 208.

———. "Northmen in America." *Journal of the American Geographical and Statistical Society* 1.6 (1859), 178–79.

Rafn, Carl Christian, ed. and comp. *Antiquitates Americanæ, sive Scriptores Septentrionales Rerum Ante-Columbianarum, in America.* Copenhagen: Royal Society of Northern Antiquaries, 1837.

Rafn, Carl Christian, Thomas H. Webb, and John M'Caul. *Supplement to the Antiquitates Americanæ.* Copenhagen: Secretary's Office of the Royal Society of Northern Antiquaries, 1841.

Rajnovich, Grace. *Reading Rock Art: Interpreting the Indian Rock Paintings of the Canadian Shield.* Toronto: Natural Heritage / Natural History, 1994.

Rand, Silas Tertius. "The Coming of the White Man Revealed: Dream of the White Robe and Floating Island." *American Antiquarian* 12.3 (1890), 155–56.

———. *Dictionary of the Language of the Micmac Indians, Who Reside in Nova Scotia, New Brunswick, Prince Edward Island, Cape Breton and Newfoundland.* Halifax: Nova Scotia Printing, 1888. Reprinted Ottawa: Laurier, 1994.

———. *A Dictionary of the Micmac Language.* Transcribed and alphabetically arranged by Jeremiah S. Clark. Charlottetown, Prince Edward Island: Patriot Publishing, 1902.

———. *Legends of the Micmacs.* New York: Longmans, Green, 1894.

———. "The Legends of the Micmacs." *American Antiquarian* 12.1 (1890), 3–14.

———. *A Short Statement of Facts Relating to the History, Manners, Customs, Language, and Literature of the Micmac Tribe of Indians in Nova Scotia.* Halifax, Nova Scotia: James Bowes and Sons, 1850.

Rasle, Sebastien. "Letter from Norridgewock." 12 Oct. 1723. *Collections and Proceedings of the Maine Historical Society* 4 (1893), 267.

Ray, Roger B. "The Embden, Maine Petroglyphs." *Maine Historical Society Quarterly* 27.1 (1987), 14–23.

"Recent Literature." *Atlantic Monthly* 39.231 (1877), 114.

Reed, Christopher Robert. *"All the World Is Here!" The Black Presence at White City.* Bloomington: Indiana University Press, 2000.

Reeves, Arthur Middleton. *The Finding of Wineland the Good: History of the Icelandic Discovery of America.* London: H. Frowde, 1890.

Reid, John G. "Political Definitions: Creating Maine and Acadia." *American Beginnings: Exploration, Culture, and Cartography in the Land of Norumbega.* Ed. Emerson W. Baker et al. Lincoln: University of Nebraska Press, 1994. 173–90.

Reiersgord, Thomas E. *The Kensington Rune Stone: Its Place in History.* St. Paul: Pogo Press, 2001.

"The Relation of a Voyage unto New England. Began from the *Lizard*, the first of June 1607, by Captain Popham in the ship the Gift, and Captain Gilbert in the Mary and John." *Sailors Narratives of Voyages along the New England Coast 1524–1624.* Ed. George Parker Winship. 1905. Reprinted New York: Burt Franklin, 1968. 154–75.

"Review of New Books: *Ballads and Other Poems.* By Henry Wadsworth Longfellow." *Graham's Lady's and Gentleman's Magazine* 20.3 (1842), 189–90.

Richter, Daniel K. *Facing East from Indian Country: A Narrative History of Early America*. Cambridge: Harvard University Press, 2001.

Ricker, Meredith. "A *MELUS* Interview: Joseph Bruchac." *MELUS* 21.3 (1996), 159–78.

Rodríguez, J. Javier. "The U.S.-Mexican War in James Russell Lowell's *The Biglow Papers*." *Arizona Quarterly* 63.3 (2007), 1–32.

Rogin, Michael Paul. *Fathers and Children: Andrew Jackson and the Subjugation of the American Indian*. New York: Knopf, 1975. Reprinted with a new introduction by the author, New Brunswick, N.J.: Transaction, 1991.

Rosier, James. "A True Relation of Captaine George Waymouth his Voyage, made this present yeere 1605; in the Discoverie of the North part of Virginia." 1605. *Sailors Narratives of Voyages along the New England Coast 1524–1624*. Ed. George Parker Winship. 1905. Reprinted New York: Burt Franklin, 1968. 98–151.

Ross, Margaret Clunies. "The Development of Old Norse Textual Worlds: Genealogical Structure as a Principle of Literary Organisation in Early Iceland." *Journal of English and Germanic Philology* 92 (1993), 372–85.

Rowlandson, Mary White. *A True History of the Captivity and Restoration of Mrs. Mary Rowlandson, a Minister's Wife in New-England*. London: Joseph Poole, 1682.

Running Wolf, Michael, and Patricia Clark Smith. *On the Trail of Elder Brother: Glous'gap Stories of the Micmac Indians*. New York: Persea, 2000.

Sagard, Father Gabriel. *The Long Journey to the Country of the Hurons*. 1632. Trans. H. H. Langton. Ed. George M. Wrong. Toronto: Champlain Society, 1939.

Sanger, David. "Semi-Subterranean Houses in the Ceramic Period along the Coast of Maine." *Maine Archaeological Society Bulletin* 50.2 (2010), 23–46.

Sawyer, Birgit, and Peter Sawyer. *Medieval Scandinavia: From Conversion to Reformation, circa 800–1500*. Minneapolis: University of Minnesota Press, 1993.

Sayre, Gordon M. "The Mound Builders and the Imagination of American Antiquity in Jefferson, Bartram, and Chateaubriand." *Early American Literature* 33.3 (1998), 225–49.

Schmidt, David L., and Murdena Marshall, eds. and translators. *Mi´kmaq Hieroglyphic Prayers: Readings in North America's First Indigenous Script*. Halifax, Nova Scotia: Nimbus, 1995.

Schoolcraft, Henry Rowe. *Algic Researches*. New York: Harper and Row, 1839.

———. "The Ante-Columbian History of America." *American Biblical Repository* 1.2 (1839), 430–49.

———. *Historical and Statistical Information, Respecting the History, Condition and Prospects of the Indian Tribes of the United States*. 5 vols. Published by Authority of Congress. Philadelphia: Lippincott, Grambo, 1851.

Scudder, Horace Elisha. *James Russell Lowell: A Biography*. 2 vols. Boston: Houghton Mifflin, 1901.

Seaver, James Everett. *A Narrative of the Life of Mrs. Mary Jemison, Who was taken by the Indians, in the year 1755, when only about twelve years of age, and has continued to reside amongst them to the present time*. Canandaigua, N.Y.: J. D. Bemis, 1824.

Seaver, Kirsten A. *The Last Vikings: The Epic Story of the Great Norse Voyages*. London: I. B. Tauris, 2010.

———. "Norumbega and 'Harmonia Mundi' in Sixteenth-Century Cartography." *Imago Mundi* 50 (1998), 34–58.

———. "Unanswered Questions." *Vikings: The North American Saga*. Ed. William W. Fitzhugh and Elisabeth I. Ward. Washington and New York: Smithsonian Institution Press in association with the National Museum of Natural History, 2000. 270–79.

Seelye, John. *Memory's Nation: The Place of Plymouth Rock*. Chapel Hill: University of North Carolina Press, 1998.

"Settlement Effected in Vineland, by Thorfinn." *Family Magazine; or, Monthly Abstract of General Knowledge* 5.1 (May 1838), 328.

Shay, Florence Nicola. *History of the Penobscot Tribe of Indians*. 1941. Reprinted Indian Island, Maine: Penobscot Nation Museum, 1998.

Shea, John Gilmary. *History of the Catholic Missions among the Indian Tribes of the United States, 1529–1854*. 1855. New York: AMS Press, 1973.

Shepard, Elizabeth G. *A Guide-Book to Norumbega and Vineland; or, The Archaeological Treasures Along Charles River*. Boston: Damrell and Upham, 1893.

Sherwin, Reider T. *The Viking and the Red Man: The Old Norse Origin of the Algonquin Language*. New York: Funk and Wagnalls, 1940.

Shipley, John B., and Marie A Shipley. *The English Rediscovery and Colonization of America*. London: Elliot Stock, 1890.

Shipley, Mrs. John B. [Marie A. Brown]. *The Icelandic Discoverers of America; or, Honor to Whom Honor Is Due*. New York: John B. Alden, 1891.

Shoemaker, Nancy. "How Indians Got to Be Red." *American Historical Review* 102.3 (1997), 625–44.

Sigurðsson, Gísli. "An Introduction to the *Vinland Sagas*." *Vikings: The North Atlantic Saga*. Ed. William W. Fitzhugh and Elisabeth I. Ward. Washington and New York: Smithsonian Institution Press in association with the National Museum of Natural History, 2000. 218–19.

———. *The Medieval Icelandic Saga and Oral Tradition: A Discourse on Method*. Trans. Nicholas Jones. Cambridge: Harvard University Press, 2004.

———. "The Quest for Vinland in Saga Scholarship." *Vikings: The North Atlantic Saga*. Ed. William W. Fitzhugh and Elisabeth I. Ward. Washington and New York: Smithsonian Institution Press in association with the National Museum of Natural History, 2000. 232–37.

Silliman, Stephen W. "Culture Contact or Colonialism? Challenges in the Archaeology of Native North America." *American Antiquity* 70.1 (2005), 55–74.

Silverberg, Robert. *Moundbuilders of Ancient America: The Archaeology of a Myth*. Greenwich, Conn.: New York Graphic Society, 1968.

Simmons, William S. *Spirit of the New England Tribes: Indian History and Folklore, 1620–1984*. Hanover, N.H.: University Press of New England, 1986.

Simms, William Gilmore. "The Discoveries of the Northmen." *Magnolia; or Southern Monthly* 3.9 (1841), 417–21.

———. *The History of South Carolina from its First European Discovery to its Erection into a Republic*. 1845. New and revised ed. New York: Redfield, 1860.

"The Skeleton in Armor." Review. *New-York Tribune*, 3 Nov. 1876, 6.

Skelton, R. A. "The Geography of the Vinland Map in Relation to Its Sources." *The Vinland Map and the Tartar Relation*. Ed. R. A. Skelton, Thomas E. Marston, and George D. Painter. New ed. New Haven: Yale University Press, 1995. 144–239.

Sköld, Tryggve. "Edward Larssons alfabet och Kensingtonstenens." *DAUM-Katta* 13 (Winter 2003), 5–11.

———. "Kensingtonstenens Språk." *DAUM-Katta* 15 (June 2005), 5–12.

Slafter, Edmund F. Introduction to *Voyages of the Northmen to America*. Boston: Prince Society, 1877. 1–24.

Sloane, William M. "History and Democracy." *American Historical Review* 1.1 (1895–96), 1–30.

Smith, Charles Sprague. "The Vinland Voyages." *Journal of the American Geographical Society of New York* 24.1 (1892), 510–35.

Smith, John. "A Description of New England." 1616. *Sailors Narratives of Voyages along the New England Coast 1524–1624*. Ed. George Parker Winship. 1905. Reprinted New York: Burt Franklin, 1968. 210–48.

Smith, Joshua Toulmin. *The Northmen in New England, or America in the Tenth Century*. Boston: Hilliard, Gray, 1839.

Smithsonian Institution, National Museum of Natural History. "Global Volcanism Program: Worldwide Holocene Volcano and Eruption Information." 9 Dec. 2004. Online at http://www.volcano.si.edu.

Snow, Dean R. *The Archaeology of New England*. New York: Academic Press/Harcourt Brace Jovanovich, 1980.

———. "Eastern Abenaki." *Handbook of North American Indians: Northeast*. Ed. Bruce G. Trigger et al. Washington: Smithsonian Institution Press, 1978. 15:137–47.

———. "The Solon Petroglyphs and Eastern Abenaki Shamanism." *Papers of the Seventh Algonquian Conference, 1975*. Ed. William Cowan. Ottawa: Carleton University, 1976. 281–88.

Spack, Ruth. *America's Second Tongue: American Indian Education and the Ownership of English, 1860–1900*. Lincoln: University of Nebraska Press, 2002.

Sparks, Jared. "Antiquities of North America." *American Monthly Magazine*, ns 1 (Jan. 1836), 67–71.

Speck, Frank G. *Beothuk and Micmac*. New York: Museum of the American Indian / Heye Foundation, 1922.

———. "The Eastern Algonkian Wabanaki Confederacy." *American Anthropologist* 17.3 (1915), 492–508.

———. *Penobscot Man: The Life History of a Forest Tribe in Maine*. Philadelphia: University of Pennsylvania Press, 1940.

———. "Penobscot Shamanism." *Memoirs of the American Anthropological Association* 6.4 (1919), 237–88.

———. "Penobscot Tales and Religious Beliefs." *Journal of American Folk-Lore* 48.187 (1935), 1–107.

Spiess, Arthur E. "A Skeleton in Armor: An Unknown Chapter in Maine Archaeology." *Maine Archaeological Society Bulletin* 23.2 (1982), 31–34.

Stanford, Dennis, and Bruce Bradley. "The Solutrean Solution." *Discovering Archaeology* 2.1 (2000), 54–55.

Stengel, Marc K. "The Diffusionists Have Landed." *Atlantic Monthly* 285.1 (2000), 35–48.

Storm, Gustav. *Studies on the Vineland Voyages*. 1888. Copenhagen: Thiele, 1889.

Straus, Lawrence Guy. "Solutrean Settlement of North America? A Review of Reality." *American Antiquity* 65.2 (2000), 219–26.

Sturluson, Snorri. *The Heimskringla; or, The Sagas of the Norse Kings from the Icelandic of Snorre Sturlason*. 4 vols. Trans. Samuel Laing. 1844. Ed. Rasmus B. Anderson. London: J. C. Nimms, 1889.

Sutherland, Patricia D. "The Norse and Native North Americans." *Vikings: The North Atlantic Saga*. Ed. William W. Fitzhugh and Elisabeth I. Ward. Washington and New York: Smithsonian Institution Press in association with the National Museum of Natural History, 2000. 238–47.

Swann, Brian, ed. *Algonquian Spirit: Contemporary Translations of the Algonquian Literatures of North America*. Lincoln: University of Nebraska Press, 2005.

Swauger, James L. "Petroglyphs, Pictographs, and the Last Thirty-Five Years." *Rock Art of the Eastern Woodlands*. Ed. Charles H. Faulkner. American Rock Art Research Association, Occasional Paper 2, San Miguel, Calif., 1996. 3–6.

Sylliboy, Gabriel. "Nestuwita: Sultimk — Remembering." *Micmac Texts*. Comp. and trans. by Albert D. DeBlois. Hull, Quebec: Canadian Museum of Civilization, 1990. 3–41.

Tabor, William H. "Maine's Popham Colony." *Athena Review: Journal of Archaeology, History, and Exploration* 3.2 (2002). Online at http://www.athenapub.com.

Taylor, Alan. *American Colonies*. New York: Viking, 2001.

Taylor, [James] Bayard. "The Norseman's Ride." *United States Magazine, and Democratic Review* 19.101 (1846), 368.

———. *The Poetical Works of Bayard Taylor*. Household ed. 1880. Boston: Houghton Mifflin, 1907.

Teeter, Karl V. *Tales from Maliseet Country: The Maliseet Texts of Karl V. Teeter*. Trans. and ed. Philip S. LeSourd. Lincoln: University of Nebraska Press, 2007.

Thirslund, Søren. "Navigation by the Vikings on the Open Sea." *Viking Voyages to North America*. Ed. Birthe L. Clausen. Roskilde, Denmark: Viking Ship Museum, 1993. 109–17.

Thomas, Cyrus. "Report of the Mound Explorations of the Bureau of Ethnology." *Twelfth Annual Report of the Bureau of Ethnology, 1890–'91*. Washington: Government Printing Office, 1894. 1–730.

Thomas, David Hurst. *Skull Wars: Kennewick Man, Archaeology, and the Battle for Native Identity*. New York: Basic Books, 2000.

Thoreau, Henry David. *Cape Cod*. 1865. Ed. Joseph J. Moldenhauer. Princeton: Princeton University Press, 1988.

———. *The Maine Woods*. 1864. Intro. Edward Hoagland. New York: Penguin, 1988.

Thorstenberg, Edward. "The Skeleton in Armour and the Frithiof Saga." *Modern Language Notes* 25.6 (1910), 189–92.

Thurin, Erik Ingvar. *The American Discovery of the Norse: An Episode in Nineteenth-Century American Literature*. Lewisburg, Pa.: Bucknell University Press, 1999.

Thwaites, Reuben Gold, ed. *The Jesuit Relations and Allied Documents*. 73 vols. Cleveland: Burrows Bros., 1896–1901.

Tómasson, Sverrir. "Old Icelandic Prose." *A History of Icelandic Literature*. Ed. Daisy Neijmann. Lincoln: University of Nebraska Press, 2006. 63–173.

Trautmann, Frederic, trans. and ed. "A German in Minnesota Territory." *Minnesota History* 49.4 (1984), 126–39.

Trillin, Calvin. *Runestruck*. Boston: Little, Brown, 1977.

———. "U.S. Journal: Maine. Runes." *New Yorker*, 5 Feb. 1972, 70–74.

Trumbull, James Hammond. *The Composition of Indian Geographical Names Illustrated from the Algonkin Languages*. Hartford, Conn.: Case, Lockwood and Brainard, 1870.

"Under the Willows and Other Poems." Review. *Atlantic Monthly* 23.136 (1869), 262–64.

United States. Bureau of the Census. *Decennial Immigration to the United States, 1880–1919*. Monograph No. 7. Washington: Government Printing Office, 1927.

"The University Centenary." *American Scandinavian* 4.11 (1911), 7.

Vastokas, Joan M. "History without Writing: Pictorial Narratives in Native North America." *Gin Das Winan: Documenting Aboriginal History in Ontario*. Ed. Dale Standen and David McNab. Champlain Society, Occasional Paper No. 2, Toronto, 1996. 48–64.

———. "Interpreting Birch Bark Scrolls." *Papers of the Fifteenth Algonquian Conference*. Ed. William Cowan. Ottawa: Carleton University Press, 1984. 425–44.

---. "Native Art as Art History: Meaning and Time from Unwritten Sources." *Journal of Canadian Studies* 21.4 (1986–87), 7–36.

---. "The Peterborough Petroglyphs: Native or Norse?" *The Rock Art of Eastern North America*. Ed. Carol Diaz-Granados and James R. Duncan. Birmingham: University of Alabama Press, 2004. 277–89.

Vastokas, Joan M., and Romas K. Vastokas. *Sacred Art of the Algonkians: A Study of the Peterborough Petroglyphs*. Peterborough, Ontario: Mansard, 1973.

Vaughan, Alden T. "From White Man to Redskin: Changing Anglo-American Perceptions of the American Indian." *American Historical Review* 87.4 (1982), 917–53.

"The Viking Ship at Chicago." *New York Times*, 13 July 1893, 8.

"The Viking Ship Is Here." *New York Times*, 14 June 1893, 1.

"The Viking Ship Is Here." *New York Times*, 18 June 1893, 1.

"The Viking Ship Sails." *New York Times*, 2 May 1893, 11.

"The Viking Ship Sails Away." *New York Times*, 1 Nov. 1893, 8.

"Viking Starts to Chicago." *New York Times*, 27 June 1893, 1.

Vilhjálmsson, Thorsteinn. "Navigation and Vinland." *Approaches to Vínland*. Ed. Andrew Wawn and Thórunn Sigurdardóttir. Reykjavik: Sigurdur Nordal Institute, 2001. 107–21.

The Vinland Sagas: The Norse Discovery of America. Trans. and intro. Magnus Magnusson and Hermann Pálsson. London: Penguin, 1965.

Vinner, Max. "*Unnasigling*—The Seaworthiness of the Merchant Vessel." *Viking Voyages to North America*. Ed. Birthe L. Clausen. Trans. Gillian Fellows Jensen. Roskilde, Denmark: Viking Ship Museum, 1993. 95–108.

Vollmann, William T. *The Ice-Shirt*. New York: Viking Penguin, 1990.

"Voyage of the Viking Ship." *New York Times*, 15 Mar. 1893, 8.

Wagenknecht, Edward. *Henry Wadsworth Longfellow: His Poetry and Prose*. New York: Ungar, 1986.

---. *John Greenleaf Whittier: A Portrait in Paradox*. New York: Oxford University Press, 1967.

Wahlgren, Erik. *The Vikings and America*. New York: Thames and Hudson, 1986.

Wallace, Birgitta Linderoth. "An Archaeologist's Interpretation of the *Vinland Sagas*." *Vikings: The North Atlantic Saga*. Ed. William W. Fitzhugh and Elisabeth I. Ward. Washington and New York: Smithsonian Institution Press in association with the National Museum of Natural History, 2000. 225–31.

---. "L'Anse aux Meadows, Leif Eriksson's Home in Vinland." *Journal of the North Atlantic*. Special volume 2 (2009), 114–25.

---. "L'Anse aux Meadows, the Western Outpost." *Viking Voyages to North America*. Ed. Birthe L. Clausen. Roskilde, Denmark: Viking Ship Museum, 1993. 30–42.

---. "The Viking Settlement at L'Anse Aux Meadows." *Vikings: The North*

Atlantic Saga. Ed. William W. Fitzhugh and Elisabeth I. Ward. Washington and New York: Smithsonian Institution Press in association with the National Museum of Natural History, 2000. 208–16.

Wallace, Birgitta Linderoth, and William W. Fitzhugh. "Stumbles and Pitfalls in the Search for Viking America." *Vikings: The North Atlantic Saga*. Ed. William W. Fitzhugh and Elisabeth I. Ward. Washington and New York: Smithsonian Institution Press in association with the National Museum of Natural History, 2000. 374–84.

Wallis, Wilson D., and Ruth Sawtell Wallis. *The Micmac Indians of Eastern Canada*. Minneapolis: University of Minnesota Press, 1955.

Ward, Elisabeth I. "Reflections on an Icon: Vikings in American Culture." *Vikings: The North Atlantic Saga*. Ed. William W. Fitzhugh and Elisabeth I. Ward. Washington and New York: Smithsonian Institution Press in association with the National Museum of Natural History, 2000. 365–73.

Ward, Samuel. "Days with Longfellow." *North American Review* 134.306 (1882), 456–66.

Wawn, Andrew. "Victorian Vinland." *Approaches to Vinland*. Ed. Andrew Wawn and Thorunn Sigurdardottir. Reykjavik: Sigurdar Nordal Institute, 2001. 191–206.

Webster, Helen L. Preface and introduction to Silas Tertius Rand, *Legends of the Micmacs*. New York: Longmans, Green, 1894. v–xlvi.

Wells, Ida B., Frederick Douglass, Irvine Garland Penn, and Ferdinand L. Barnett. *The Reason Why the Colored American Is Not in the World's Columbian Exposition*. 1893. Ed. Robert W. Rydell. Urbana: University of Illinois Press, 1999.

Wheary, Dale Cyrus. "A Tiffany and Company Tour de Force at Maymont." *Maymont Notes* 3 (2003–4), 18–21.

———. "Vanity of Vanities: A Tiffany and Company Rediscovery." *Antiques* 173.4 (2008), 102–3.

Wheaton, Henry. *History of the Northmen, or Danes and Normans, from the Earliest Times to the Conquest of England by William of Normandy*. London: John Murray, 1831.

Wherry, James D. Introduction to Joseph Nicolar, *The Life and Traditions of the Red Man*. 1893. Reprinted Fredericton, New Brunswick: Saint Anne's Point Press, 1979. ix–xvi.

Whitehead, Ruth Holmes. "A New Micmac Petroglyph Site." *Occasional: An Occasional Journal for Nova Scotian Museums* 13.1 (1992), 7–12.

———. *The Old Man Told Us: Excerpts from Micmac History, 1500–1950*. Halifax, Nova Scotia: Nimbus, 1991.

———. *Stories from the Six Worlds: Micmac Legends*. Halifax, Nova Scotia: Nimbus, 1988.

Whitehead, Ruth Holmes, and Harold McGee. *The Micmac: How Their Ancestors Lived Five Hundred Years Ago*. Halifax, Nova Scotia: Nimbus, 1983.

Whittier, John Greenleaf. "The Better Land." 1844. *The Prose Works of John Greenleaf Whittier*. 3 vols. Boston: Houghton Mifflin, 1904. 3:280–83.

———. *The Complete Poetical Works of John Greenleaf Whittier*. Ed. Horace E. Scudder. Cambridge ed. Boston: Houghton Mifflin, 1894.

———. "Indian Civilization." Introduction to Stanley Pumphrey. *Indian Civilization: A Lecture by Stanley Pumphrey of England. With an Introduction by John Greenleaf Whittier*. Philadelphia: Bible and Tract Distributing Society, 1877. 5–7.

———. "Indian Civilization." 1877. *The Prose Works of John Greenleaf Whittier*. 3 vols. Boston: Houghton Mifflin, 1904. 3:232–35.

———. "The Indian Question." 1883. *The Prose Works of John Greenleaf Whittier*. 3 vols. Boston: Houghton Mifflin, 1904. 3:238–39.

———. *Legends of New-England*. Hartford, Conn.: Hanmer and Phelps, 1831. Facsimile ed., with an introduction by John B. Pickard. Gainesville, Fla.: Scholars' Facsimiles and Reprints, 1965.

———. *The Letters of John Greenleaf Whittier*. 3 vols. Vol. 1. *1828–1845*. Ed. John B. Pickard. Cambridge: Belknap Press of Harvard University Press, 1975.

———. "Norembega." *Atlantic Monthly* 23.140 (1869), 662–65.

———. "Norumbega Hall." 1886. *The Complete Poetical Works of John Greenleaf Whittier*. Ed. Horace E. Scudder. Cambridge ed. Boston: Houghton Mifflin, 1894. 239–40.

———. "The Norsemen." *Knickerbocker, New-York Monthly Magazine* 17.1 (1841), 16–18.

———. "The Poetry of the North." *National Era* 1.33 (1847), 1.

———. "The Poetry of the North." 1847. *The Prose Works of John Greenleaf Whittier*. 3 vols. Boston: Houghton Mifflin, 1904. 3:396–400.

———. *The Prose Works of John Greenleaf Whittier*. 3 vols. Vol. 3. Boston: Houghton Mifflin, 1904.

Williams, Robert A., Jr. *The American Indian in Western Legal Thought: The Discourses of Conquest*. New York: Oxford University Press, 1990.

Williams, Roger. *A Key into the Language of America*. London: Gregory Dexter, 1643. Reprinted with an introduction by Howard M. Chapin. Providence: Rhode Island and Providence Plantations Tercentenary Committee, 1936. Republished Ann Arbor: Gryphon Books, 1971.

Williamson, Joseph. "The Northmen in Maine." *Historical Magazine and Notes and Queries Concerning the Antiquities*, 2nd ser. 5.1 (1869), 30–31.

Willis, William. Editor's preface to *Documentary History of the State of Maine*. Vol. 1. Ed. William Willis. Portland: Bailey and Noyes, 1869. i–viii.

Winsor, Justin. *Christopher Columbus and How He Received and Imparted the Spirit of Discovery*. Boston: Houghton Mifflin, 1891.

———. *Native American Antiquities and Linguistics*. Ed. Anne Paolucci and Henry Paolucci. New York: Council on National Literatures, Griffon House, 1995. Originally published as Justin Winsor, *Aboriginal America: Narrative and Critical History of America*, vol. 1. Boston: Houghton Mifflin, 1889.

Wiseman, Frederick Matthew. *The Voice of the Dawn: An Autohistory of the Abenaki Nation*. Hanover, N.H.: University Press of New England, 2001.

Wood, William. *New England's Prospect*. 1634. Ed. Alden T. Vaughan. Amherst: University of Massachusetts Press, 1977.

Zamora, Margarita. *Reading Columbus*. Berkeley: University of California Press, 1993.

Zinn, Howard. *A People's History of the United States, 1492–Present*. 1980. New York: Harper Collins, 2001.

Þorláksson, Helgi. "The Vinland Sagas in a Contemporary Light." *Approaches to Vinland*. Ed. Andrew Wawn and Þórunn Sigurðardóttir. Reykjavik: Sigurður Nordal Institute Studies 4, 2001. 63–77.

Index

Note: page numbers in italics refer to illustrations.

Abbott, John S. C., 117–21, 131
Abenaki, 4, 256–57, 261, 281, 286, 367n2, 375n39, 375n45. *See also* Western Abenaki
Abler, Thomas S., 282
"Account of the Discovery of Vinland, An" (*American Museum*), 113
Adam of Bremen, 228
Adams, Henry, 148
Adney, Edwin Tappan, 58, 340n9
African Americans, 324
Alger, Abby Langdon, 271, 272, 365n16
Algic Researches (Schoolcraft), 281, 345n17
Algonquian peoples. *See* Native Americans
Algonquin Legends of New England, The (Leland), 271, 272, 278, 282, 366n19
Allen, Chadwick, 16
Allen, Paula Gunn, 151, 331
Alnambak, 256
Althing (national assembly, Iceland), 46–47, 73, 236
"America Discovered and Christianized" (*American Catholic Quarterly Review*), 213–14
America Discovered in the Tenth Century (Rafn), 106, 109–11
American Antiquarian, 283, 287–88, 289–90
American Catholic Quarterly Review, 214
American Geographical Society, 220, 238, 240, 360n19
American Indian Movement (AIM), 11
American literature, supposed Scandinavian roots of, 208

American Museum, 113
American national imagination: Columbus and, 11–12; immigrant vs. non-immigrant, 13–14; Leif Eiriksson vs. Columbus in, 12; manliness and, 206–8, 352n22; origin stories and national identity, 330–31; Rafn and, 119–21. *See also* New England poets of Viking America; prehistory politics of contact vs. isolation; racial narratives
American Nervousness (Beard), 206
America Not Discovered by Columbus (Anderson), 225–31, 253
American Romantic narratives (19th-century): colonial and pre-Columbian frontiers in, 153; Icelanders and, 46; *Landing of the Norsemen* (Leutze), *118*; Longfellow and, 162–63, 166–67, 204; New England as birthplace, 146–50; Norse in, 131–32; racial ancestry and nationalism in, 132–46; Rafn and, 105–12; Rafn's influence and, 112–21; Romantic Movement in America, 103–5; Schoolcraft and Palfrey vs. Rafn, 121–25; Simms and Beamish, 105, 125–31; Viking Revival and, 209–12, *211*; Vinland colony and, 101–2. *See also* New England poets of Viking America; racial narratives; Rafn, Carl Christian
"America's Discovery" (*Boston Daily Globe*), 245
America's Race Heritage (Burr), 255
Anderson, Magnus, 222
Anderson, Rasmus B., 225–31, 252–54, 356n51, 357n3, 358n10, 359n12

Anglo-Saxons, 347n27
"Ante-Columbian History of America, The" (Schoolcraft), 108–9, 122–23, 343n7, 345n18
Anthony, Susan B., 209, 242
Antiquitates Americanæ (Rafn), 23–24, 105–12, 124, 125–27, 131–32, 135, 153, 154, 173, 179, 343n6
"Appendix, An" (Mather), 28–30
Appleton, Fanny (Frances Elizabeth), 351n15
Appleton, Thomas Gold, 206
"Archaeologist's Interpretation, An" (Wallace), 74, 91, 95–97
Archaeology (Snow), 364n8
Archaic period, 362n2
Arcturus, 166, 351n18
Ari Thorgilsson (Ari the Learned), 49, 58
Arnold, Benedict, 122
Atlantic Monthly, 166, 183, 186–87, 193, 353n27
Attempt to Shew, That America Must Be Known to the Ancients, An (Mather), 26–31
At the Place of the Lobsters and Crabs (Haviland), 352n18
Attila the Hun, 339n20
Atwater, Caleb, 24
Aud the Deep-Minded, 75, 77, 341n17
Avaldamon, 91
axes, Norse, 341n12
Axtell, James, 261, 262–63, 265, 270, 278, 372n25

Ballads and Other Poems (Longfellow), 155–56, 164, 350n8
Bancroft, Herbert, 34, 117, 138, 139–40, 145
banishments, 71
Barber, John Warner, 124, 344n10
Bark Canoes and Skin Boats of North America, The (Adney and Chapelle), 340n9
Barlow, Joel, 12
Barton, Benjamin Smith, 339n19
Bartram, John, 336n9
Basque fishermen, 261, 264–65, 292

Beamish, North Ludlow, 125–29, 135, 153
Beard, George M., 206
bear figures (*mu'in*), 287, 292, 367n3
Bederman, Gail, 206
Bell, Michael J., 144
Beothuk, 98–99, 342n26
Bering land bridge, 21
berserkers, 160, 162, 167, 204, 292, 350n11
Berulfsen, Bjarne, 1
Betrothed, The (Manzoni), 103
"Better Land, The" (Whittier), 178, 183
Biard, Pierre, 371n25
Biglow Papers, The (Lowell), 186–88, 190–91, 193, 354n37
Bigot, Vincent, 372n25
Bjarni Herjolfsson: in *Eirik the Red's Saga*, 80, 82–85, 89, 92, 341n22; in *The Greenlanders' Saga*, 51–53, 55; references to, 12, 109, 188, 191, 197, 198, 214, 355n46
Bjorn (son of Gudrid and Thorfinn Karlsefni), 73
Boone, Daniel, 317
Boone, Elizabeth Hill, 269
Borns, Harold W., Jr., 377n1
Bourque, Bruce J., 261–62, 363n5, 373n31, 376n46
Brahmin elite of New England, 162, 203, 229, 253
Brain, Jeffrey P., 364n11
Brattahlid, Greenland, 97
Breda, Olaus, 328–29
Briggs, Charles F., 194, 354n39
Brøgger, A. W., 6
Brown, Marie Adelaide (later Shipley): *The English Rediscovery and Colonization of America* (Shipley and Shipley), 244–45, 253–54; *The Icelandic Discoverers of America*, 241, 246–50, 361n25, 361n28; on immigration and racism, 252–54; life and career of, 241–42; "Marie A. Brown: A Brief Autobiography," 241; "A New History," 242; "The Pecuniary Inde-

pendence of Wives," 242; Senate committee address (1888), 243–44; "The Viking Exhibition," 213, 242–43
Brown, Robert, 241
Bruchac, Joseph, 274–75, 276, 295, 313–16, 318–26, 327, 375n38
Bryant, William Cullen, 19, 112–13, 149, 207, 344n11
Bull, Ole, 230, 234
Bureau of (American) Ethnology, Smithsonian Institution, 35–40, 42, 338n17
burial practices, Norse, 81–82, 341n19
Burr, Clinton Stoddard, 255, 362nn32–33
Butternut trees, 98
Byock, Jesse L., 46, 72–73, 341n13

Cabot, John, 244, 264–65, 278, 336n8, 371n23, 374n34
"Cambridge Thirty Years Ago" (Lowell), 194
Canadian Arctic sites, 99
canoes, birch bark, 58, 370n21
canoes, moose-hide. *See* skin-boats
Cape Breton Island colony, Portuguese, 275
Cape Cod, 97
Cape Cod (Thoreau), 147
captives, of Norse, 90–91, 340n7
captivity narratives, 316–18
caravels, 222, 275, 374n34
Carlson, Suzanne, 15
Cartier, Jacques, 371n23, 376n47
"Case of the Deer Isle Grant, The" (Haviland), 348n1
Catholic History of North America, The (McGee), 224
Catholicism. *See* religion
Catlin, George, 25, 36
Central Algonquian-speakers, 122, 123, 258, 345n17, 364n9
Champlain, Samuel de, 180–83, 277, 306, 353n32, 371n24, 376n47
Channing, William Ellery, 146–47, 347n23
Chapelle, Howard I., 58, 340n9

Chapin, Alonzo Bowen, 123–24
Charter of New England (1620), 262
Chaucer, 208, 356n49
Cherokee, removal of, 128–29
"Cherokee Letter" (Emerson), 129
"Children of Gluskap" (Prins), 258–59
Choate, Rufus, 104, 105
Christiania University (now University of Oslo), 240–41
Christianity. *See* religion
Christiansen, Reidar Th., 1
Christopher Columbus (Winsor), 251–52
Civil War, 195–96, 200
Clarke, James Freeman, 347n23
Clement, Edward Henry, 239–40, 360n21
Cleveland, Grover, 194
Clinton, DeWitt, 32, 33–34, 40
cod fishing fleets, 264–65, 363n8
coin (Norse) found in Maine, 97–98
Cole, Thomas, 103, 105
Coleridge, Samuel Taylor: *Lyrical Ballads* (Coleridge and Wordsworth), 350n9; *Poetical Works*, 350n9, 350n12; "Rime of the Ancient Mariner," 156, 157–58, 159, 161, 350n9, 350n12
Colón, Fernando, 359n11
color symbolism, 287
Columbiad, The (Barlow), 12
"Columbus" (Lowell), 191–93, 201, 206
Columbus, challenges to: *America Not Discovered by Columbus* (Anderson), 225–31; antebellum, 145–46; anti-Catholic, 29, 224; Brown and Shipley, 241–50; Catholic responses to, 224–25; Chicago World's Fair and competing narratives, 215–20, 251; DeCosta, 218–19; *Discovery of the Ancient City of Norumbega* (Horsford), 231–40; earlier voyages and, 108, 111, 191, 228–29, 243, 248; Harvard letter to Christiania University, 240–41; Quadricen-

Columbus, challenges to (*cont.*)
  tennial and, 213–15; racial anti-immigrant, 218, 252–55; Smith and, 219–20; Viking Ship and, 220–24; Winsor and, 251–52
Columbus, Christopher: Catholicism and, 224; image of, 225; *Life and Voyages of Christopher Columbus* (Irving) and, 114, 192, 345n15; as "man of science," 224; national imagination and, 11–12; Native American lore and, 374n36; route of, 9; son's biography of, 227, 359n11; statues, monuments, and images of, 250–51, 252; as villain or flawed character, 247–48, 251–52
"Columbus Celebration in New York, The" (*Christian Union*), 225
Columbus Day, 11, 13, 223–25
Columbus Quadricentennial (1892), 213–15, 225, 249, 252, 361n27
Columbus Quincentenary (1992), 11, 19, 313, 324–25
comets, 298, 301, 370n19, 372n29
"Coming of the White Man Revealed" (Rand), 283–85, 287–88
Composition of Indian Geographical Names, The (Trumbull), 237–38, 360n18
Compromise of 1850, 195, 354n41
Constitution Centennial, 213–15, 242–43, 249, 361n27
contact, "first." *See* "first" contacts, issue of
"Contact Period Petroglyphs in Machias Bay" (Hedden), 266, 268–69
contact vs. isolation. *See* prehistory politics of contact vs. isolation
Cooper, James Fenimore, 104–5, 134, 153, 343n3
copper working by Algonquians, 152, 348n1
Corrigan, Michael Augustine, 252
Corte-Real, Gaspar, 278
Critical Examination of the Evidences, A (MacLean), 218
Crowninshield, Clara, 351n14
Cusick, David, 370n19

D'Abate, Richard, 264
Daly, Charles Patrick, 240, 361n22
Davis, Asahel, 111, 344n9
Dawes Act (General Allotment Act of 1887), 41, 42, 339n22
Day, Gordon M., 280
DeCosta, Benjamin Franklin, 121, 218–19, 224–25, 357n4–358n5
Découverte de l'Amerique par les Normandes (Gravier), 359n12
Deerslayer, The (Cooper), 153
Defences of Norumbega (Horsford), 234
Deloria, Vine, Jr., 19–20, 22, 42–43
Demarest, Arthur, 20, 21
"Democracy" (Lowell), 203
democracy and "republic" idea, 46, 138–39, 214, 227
Den Norske Maalsag (Anderson), 226
Denys, Nicolas, 270, 272, 365n14
Description and Natural History of the Coasts of North America, The (Denys), 365n14
de Soto, Hernando, 338n15
Dickason, Olive Patricia, 260
Dictionary of the Micmac Language, A (Clark), 367n3
Dighton Rock, 124; Anderson on, 226; in *Biglow Papers* (Lowell), 187–88; Chapin on, 123–24; historical societies on, 359n16; Mather on, 26, 37; Rafn on, 106; relocation of, 231; Schoolcraft and Palfrey on, 122–23; Sparks on, 152–53
Dillehay, Thomas D., 21
"Discoveries of the Northmen, The" (Simms), 125–28, 330
Discovery, Settlement and present State of Kentucky (Filson), 317
Discovery and Colonization of America, The (Everett), 144–46, 224
"Discovery of America, The" (Everett), 101, 108, 132–34
"Discovery of America by the Norsemen" (*Massachusetts Quarterly*), 135
Discovery of America by the North-

men, The (Beamish), 125–26, 135, 153
"Discovery of America by the Northmen, The" (Everett), 115–17
Discovery of a Norse Settlement in America, The (Ingstad), 5
Discovery of the Ancient City of Norumbega (Horsford), 233–40, 360n19
"Dole of Jarl Thorkell, The" (Whittier), 356n49
Dooley, James Henry, 210
Dooley, Sallie, 210, 357n55
Dorset people, 92, 99
Douglas, Kirk, 377n4
"Dream of the White Robe and the Floating Island": color symbolism in, 287–88; dreams and dreamers in, 285–86; intertextuality of, 294–95; Norse influence and, 291–93; purpose of, 293–94; Rabbit and bear figures in, 286–87, 292; text of, 283–85; voice and textual issues in, 288–91
dreams in Native traditions, 285–86, 367n2
Druillettes, Father, 288, 372n25
Duberman, Martin, 196, 202–3
du Gua, Pierre, Sieur de Monts, 371n24
Dunlap, Frances, 193
Dunn, Willie, 275
Dwight, Timothy, 27–28, 29, 336n10

earthquakes, 298, 300
Eastern Algonquians and ancestors. *See* Native Americans
Ebeneserdóttir, S. S., 91
Eckstorm, Fanny Hardy, 271, 295–96
"Edda among the Algonquin Indians, The" (Leland), 362n30
Eirik Gnupsson, Bishop, 100, 101, 227, 228, 235, 344n10
Eirik the Red: in *Eirik the Red's Saga*, 75–82; in *The Greenlanders' Saga*, 49–53, 56, 60, 63, 71; Karlsefni and Gudrid and, 73; references to, 109; religion and, 47

Eirik the Red's Saga: Aud the Deep-Minded (chapters 1 and 3), 75, 77, 341n17; Bjarni Grimolfsson, (chapter 13), 92, 342n22; as contact narrative, 331; contradictions in, 89–90; Eirik and Thorbjorn Vifilsson (chapter 2), 75–76; *The Greenlanders' Saga* and, 49, 93; Gudrid and Karlsefni (chapter 14), 92–93; Gudrid's destiny (chapter 4), 77–78; Gudrid's lineage (chapter 3), 76–77; as history and literature, 10; Leif Eiriksson and (chapter 5), 78–81; Magnusson's and Pálsson's version of, 48–49; as prophecy text, 331–32; retellings of, 107, 188; *Saga of Olaf Tryggvason* and, 214; Skraelings (chapters 10–12), 85–92; style of, 48; Thorfinn Karlsefni and Gudrid (chapter 7), 82; Thorfinn Karlsefni in Vinland (chapters 8–9), 82–85; Thorstein Eiriksson (chapter 6), 81–82; Wallace in, 95; writing, compilation, adaptation of, 48–49
Eliot, Charles W., 203
Eliot, John, 31, 337n13
Elliott, Walter, 14, 335n6
Embden-Solon petroglyphs, 265–68, 267, 364n9
Emerson, Ralph Waldo, 103, 129, 140–42, 208, 347n23
Encyclopedia of Ships and Seafaring (Kemp), 374n34
English as "kindred" of Vikings, 121
English Rediscovery and Colonization of America, The (Shipley and Shipley), 244–45, 253–54
English Traits (Emerson), 140–42, 208
epidemics among Native Americans, 261–62, 270, 363n5
Eskimoan archeological sites, 99
Etchemins, 256
Everett, Alexander Hill, 115–17, 132–34, 343n6
Everett, Edward, 101, 108, 116, 144–46, 224, 343n6

Exploits River, 342n26
"Exploration of Norumbega, The" (Axtell), 261, 278
"extermination," mythic narrative of, 33–35
Eyrbyggia Saga, 79, 127

Fable for Critics (Lowell), 354n37
Fagan, Brian, 264–65, 308, 373n32
fake Norse artifacts: Kensington Stone, 327–30, 377n4; in local Maine museum, 16–17; motivations for, 17; Spirit Pond runestones, 14–15, *15*, 335n6
Fall River (Mass.) skeleton, 106–7, 151–55, *152*, 161. *See also* "Skeleton in Armor"
Falnes, Oscar J., 111, 136, 235, 237, 344n9, 345n16
Farnham, Paulding, *211*, 212
Felton, C. C., 173, 178
Feud in the Icelandic Saga (Byock), 72–73, 341n13
Filson, John, 317
Finding of Wineland the Good, The (Reeves), 216, 218
Finnbogi, 69–70, 109
"first" contacts, issue of: conflict and disease, 259–62; fishing expeditions, 264–65; illusion of firstness, 263–64; length of Native American land tenure prior to, 257–59; Native storytelling and, 270–79, 294, 310, 311–13; petroglyphic evidence, 265–70, *267*; recordkeeping and, 262–63, 265. *See also* American Romantic narratives; Columbus, challenges to
"First Discoverers of America, The" (*Putnam's Monthly Magazine*), 146
Firsting and Lasting (O'Brien), 280, 347n29
fishing fleets, European, 264–65, 363n8
Fitzhugh, William W., 44–45, 97, 98
Flateyjarbók, 49, 100
Fleché, Jessé, 368n10
Fløttum, Sivert, 97
folklore and pre-Christian practices, Norse: doppelgänger apparitions in, 66–67; prayers for food in, 84–85; prophecies from deceased bodies in, 62–63, 81; supernatural beings and mysterious sleeps, 59; sybil foretelling of Gudrid's destiny, 77–78; Unipeds in, 74, 90
Folsom, George, 112, 132
Forbes, Jack D., 21
Fort St. George, 267–68, 364nn11–12
Franchot, Jenny, 143, 144
Franklin, Benjamin, 27, 28, 32, 43, 336n9
French and Indian Wars, 260
Freydis Eiriksdottir: in *Eirik the Red's Saga*, 79, 83, 87–88; in *The Greenlanders' Saga*, 52, 69–72; references to, 109
Friedrich, Horst, 15
Frithiof's Saga (Tegnér), 350n9
"From White Man to Redskin" (Vaughan), 340n11
"frontier," 1, 153
Fugitive Slave Act, 195
Furdustrands (Wonder Beaches), 84, 85, 110, 344n8
fur trade, 260, 303, 368n10

Gade, F. Herman, 240–41, 361n24
Gadsden Purchase, 195
Gage, Matilda Joslyn, 209, 356n53
Gardiner, Robert, 6
Garrison, William Lloyd, 174
Gay, Sydney Howard, 19, 112–13, 207, 344n11
genealogies: of Eirik the Red, 50; of Gudrid Thorbjornsdottir, 63, 76–77; Hauk Erlendsson's insertion of, 74; of Herjolf Bardarsson, 51–52; Iceland bishops and, 93; Levin's racist "genealogical relationship," 140; manliness and, 206; in sagas, 72–73; Thoreau and, 147. *See also* racial narratives
General Allotment Act of 1887 (Dawes Act), 41, 42, 339n22
genetic studies, 91

Gesta Hammaburgensis Ecclesiae Pontificum (Adam of Bremen), 228
Giles, Paul, 356n52
"Glooscap Encounters" (Abler), 282
Gluskap (Klose-Kur-Beh) stories: fulfillment story, 17–18; Leland's collection of, 282; prophecy, 1, 280, 296–310; Rand's collection of, 281–83; Speck on, 369n12; stone canoe voyage, 278–79, 366n19; versions of coming of Gluskap, 278–79; about whale, 294–95
goading speech, 70, 87–88
Gobineau, Joseph Arthur de, 348n31
Godkin, Edwin Lawrence, 216
Gokstad (ship), 222–23
Golden Multitudes (Mott), 343nn3–5
Gosnold, Bartholomew, 261
Goths in New-England, The (Marsh), 136–37
Grant, Ulysses S., 195–96, 202
Gravier, Gabriel, 359n12
"Great Ireland," 126–27
Green, Samuel, 376n51
Greenland: abandonment of, 101; activities on, 376n53; attempted colonization of (A.D. 978), 340n5; Christianity in, 47, 60, 61, 78, 79, 214–15; Eirik's discovery of, 50; famine in, 77; projectile points in, 97; settlement of, 46–47, 50–51, 61
Greenlanders' Saga, The: Bjarni Herjolfsson's voyage (chapters 2–3), 51–53; Bruchac's "Ice Hearts" and, 315; as contact narrative, 331; Eirik the Red (chapter 1), 49–53; *Eirik the Red's Saga* and, 49, 74; as family saga, 51; Freydis's voyage and murders (chapters 8–9), 69–72; Herjolf Bardarsson genealogy (chapter 2), 51–52; as history and literature, 10, 73–74; Leif Eiriksson's voyage (chapters 3–4), 53–56; Magnusson's and Pálsson's version of, 48–49; old texts and manuscripts of, 49, 74; as prophecy text, 331–32; references to, 227–28, 235–36, 344n8; retellings of, 107, 113, 115; structure and style of, 48–49; Thorfinn Karlsefni and Gudrid in Iceland (chapter 9), 72–73; Thorfinn Karlsefni's and Gudrid's colonization attempt (chapter 7), 63–69; Thorstein's voyage (chapter 6), 60–63; Thorvald's voyage, 56–60; Wallace in, 95; writing, compilation, adaptation of, 48–49
Greenwald, Emily, 41, 42
Grimhild, 61–62, 340n10
Grimm, Jacob, 103
Grimm, Wilhelm, 103
Griswold, Rufus, 173, 352n24
"Growth of the Legend, The" (Lowell), 188–91, 192–93, 201
Gudrid Thorbjornsdottir: destiny of, foretold by sybil, 77–78; in *Eirik the Red's Saga*, 74–78, 88–93, 341n17; in *The Greenlanders' Saga*, 56, 61–67, 72–73; in Leutze painting, 118; prophecy of, in "Voyage to Vinland" (Lowell), 199–201; references to, 106, 179, 197, 355n46; Rome pilgrimage and, 227–28, 359n12; strange woman and, 65–67, 235–36
Guide-Book to Norumbega and Vineland, A (Shepard), 361n23

"Hakon's Lay" (Lowell), 194–95, 355n46
Hale, Edward Everett, 230
Hansa cogs, 374n34
Harald Bluetooth, 47
Harrison, Benjamin, 252
Harvard College, 194, 196, 240–41
Hauk Erlendsson the Lawman, 74, 93
Hauksbók, 74, 92, 93
Havemeyer, Henry Osborne, 209
Haviland, William A., 257–58, 261, 348n1, 352n18, 363n4
Hawthorne, Nathaniel, 105, 165, 351n16
Hay, John, 207

Hayes, Rutherford B., 193, 202
Hedden, Mark, 266–70
Heimskringla (Sturluson), 208, 357n3
Helgi, 69–70, 109
Helluland ("Stone Slab-Land"), 53, 83, 110, 226
Henry Wadsworth Longfellow (Wagenknecht), 163, 350n9
Herder, Johann Gottfried von, 138
Herjolf Bardarsson, 51, 52
Hertz, Johannes, 327
Higham, John, 144, 145, 254
Historical and Statistical Information (Schoolcraft), 23–24, 33
"Historical Sketch of the Discovery of America" (*North American Review*), 229–30
"Historic Progress and American Democracy" (Motley), 139–40
History and Antiquities of New England, The (Barber), 124, 344n10
History as Romantic Art (Levin), 140
History of American Literature (Tyler), 356n52
History of Maine, The (Abbott), 117–21, 131
History of New England during the Stuart Dynasty (Palfrey), 122
History of South Carolina, The (Simms), 130–31, 346n21
History of the Catholic Missions among the Indian Tribes (Shea), 358n9
History of the Conquest of Mexico (Prescott), 144
History of the Discovery of the East Coast (Kohl), 179
History of the Northmen (Wheaton), 114–15
History of the United States (Adams), 148
History of the United States (Bancroft), 117, 139–40, 145
Ho-de-no-sau-nee. *See* Iroquois
Holmes, Oliver Wendell, 203, 230
Hóp (Hope, or "tidal lagoon"), 86–89, 95–96, 110, 344n8
Hope Leslie (Sedgwick), 104–5

Hopewell culture, 24–25, 127, 336n6
Horsford, Eben Norton, 230–40, 282, 356n51, 360n19
Horsford, Jedidiah, 234
Howe, Julia Ward, 154–55
Hrdlička, Aleš, 257
Huanyapuntina, Mount, 373n29
Humboldt, Alexander von, 22, 108
Huns, 40, 339n20
Hunt, George H., 372n28
Hvítramannaland ("White Men's Land"), 92, 110, 126–27, 342n23

I Become Part of It (Bruchac), 325
"Ice Hearts" (Bruchac), 314–16, 318–26
Iceland: Aud the Deep-Minded in, 75; conversion of, 47; Eirik banished from, 50; Greenland and, 46–47, 50–51; Irish influence on, 93–94; Karlsefni and Gudrid in, 72–73; Native American genetic material in, 91; romanticization of, as "republic," 46, 214, 227, 241, 250; saga tradition and, 44–49; settlements in, 45–46;
Icelandic Annals, 99, 100, 111, 117, 228, 235, 344n10, 359n13
Icelandic Discoverers of America, The (Shipley), 241, 246–50, 361n25, 361n28
"Icelandic Discovery of America, The" (Godkin), 216
Ice-Shirt, The (Vollmann), 332
immigrants and anti-immigration bias: belonging and, 13–14; eugenics screening and, 362n33; racism and anti-Catholicism and, 143–44, 252–55, 348n30; statistics of, 362n31
"Importance of Illustrating New-England History" (Choate), 104
Independent, 213, 242–43
Indian captivity narratives, 316–18
Indian Civilization (Pumphrey), 353n33
"Indian Civilization" (Whittier), 184–85

"Indian Mound Opened, An" (*Louisville Advertiser*), 25
"Indian Question, The" (Whittier), 185–86, 353n34
Indian Removal Acts, 128–29
Indians, American. *See* Native Americans
"Indians, Archaeologists" (Deloria), 19–20, 22, 42–43
Inequality of the Human Races, The (Gobineau), 348n31
Ingstad, Anne Stine, 5, 8
Ingstad, Helge, 5–6, 8–9, 93, 95, 213
In Indian Tents (Alger), 272
Innu (Montagnais and Naskapi), 4, 8, 91, 96, 97, 258, 367n2
Invasion Within, The (Axtell), 262–63, 265, 270, 372n25
Ireland and the Irish, 125–27, 143, 346n20, 347n30, 348n31
Irish travel tales, 93–94
Irmscher, Christoph, 167
Iroquois (Ho-de-no-sau-nee), 32, 98, 235, 237, 258, 271, 274, 302–3, 313–16, 357n53, 363n3, 370n19, 375–76nn44–47
Irving, Washington, 114, 192, 227, 251, 345n15
Islendinga sögur (Sagas of the Icelanders), 47–49. *See also* sagas
isolation hypotheses, 21, 22–23, 41
Italy, 347n30

Jackson, Andrew, 34, 128–29, 133, 337n14, 346n22
Jacobson, Matthew Frye, 143–44
Jarves, James Jackson, 104
Jefferson, Thomas, 332
Jemison, Mary, 317–18
Jeremy, Josiah, 283–85, 288–91, 293–95, 311
Jesuit Relations, The (Thwaites), 257
Jewett, Sarah Orne, 121, 142, 205
John Greenleaf Whittier (Pickard), 173–74
Johnson, Andrew, 187, 196
Johnson, Lyndon B., 231

Jones, Julia Clinton, 207, 355n45
Josselyn, John, 259, 262, 340n11, 363n5, 372n29
jugglers, 367n2

Kaland, Sigrid H. H., 55
Kalm, Peter, 336n9
Kansas-Nebraska Act (1854), 195, 354n42
k'chi-wump-toqueh' (white swan or Canada goose), 299–300, 369n17
Kehoe, Alice Beck, 264
Kellogg, Robert, 47
"Kensington Code, The" (Powell), 329
Kensington Stone, 327–30, 377n4
Kierkegaard, Søren, 347n26
King Philip's War, 260
Kjalarness (Keel Point), 57, 83, 85, 344n8
Klose-Kur-Beh. *See* Gluskap (Klose-Kur-Beh) stories
knarrs, 222, 309, 358n7
Knickerbocker, 153, 168, 173, 177, 350n10, 352n21
Kohl, Johann Georg, 179–80, 353n29
Konrad, Victor A., 264
Koolpejot, 290
Krakatoa, 373n29
Krossaness ("Cross Place"), 60
Kross Hills, Iceland, 75
Kunz, Keneva, 49, 339n4

Labrador, 53, 91
Laing, Samuel, 218, 357n3
Land before Her, The (Kolodny), 2
Landing of the Norsemen (Leutze), 118
Landnámabók (*The Book of Settlement*), 49–51
language: alphabetic literacy, 289; *Dictionary of the Micmac Language* (Clark), 367n3; Horsford on, 237–38; mimicry and, 66; Native, 258; Old Norse (Old West Norse, or Old Icelandic), 48; pictographic script, 36–37, 312; Proto-Algonquian dialects, 258; translation of religious texts, 368n8

"L'Anse aux Meadows, Leif Eriksson's Home in Vinland" (Wallace), 91, 96, 98, 342n26
L'Anse aux Meadows, Newfoundland, 5–6, 8–10, 18, 43, 95–98, 213, 335n2, 341n15
"L'Anse aux Meadows, the Western Outpost" (Wallace), 95
las Casas, Bartolomé de, 22, 335n2
Last Vikings, The (Seaver), 58, 99, 101, 180, 328, 341n21, 353n30
Laxdaela Saga, 341n16
Lay of the Land, The (Kolodny), 2
Lays of My Home, and Other Poems (Whittier), 173, 178
Lears, Jackson, 183, 203, 205–7
LeBlanc, Steven A., 275
LeClercq, Chrétien, 285, 288–89, 293, 367n2, 368n5
Lecture on the Discovery of America by Northmen, A (Davis), 111, 344n9
Legends of New-England (Whittier), 173
Legends of the Micmacs (Rand), 282, 291, 293, 368n6
Leif Eiriksson: Columbus vs., in national imagination, 12; in *Eirik the Red's Saga*, 74, 76, 78–80, 83–84; in *The Greenlanders' Saga*, 52–57, 59, 61, 63, 69, 73; as "Leif the Lucky," 56, 80; monuments to, 219, 229–30, 232, 250; references to, 107, 109, 114, 121, 191, 194–95, 197, 226–27, 241, 355n46; on *Vinland Map*, 12
Leif Eiriksson Day, 231
Leif Erikson (journal), 246
Leif's houses (Leifsbudir), Vinland: Anderson on, 226; in *Eirik the Red's Saga*, 85; in *The Greenlanders' Saga*, 56–57, 60, 63, 69, 95–96; Ingstad on, 213; Rafn on, 110
Le Jeune, Paul, 257, 259
Leland, Charles Godfrey, 272, 278, 282, 362n30, 366n19, 367n1
Letters and Notes on the Manners, Customs, and Conditions of North American Indians (Catlin), 25
"Letting Go Our Grand Obsessions" (Kolodny), 3–4
Leutze, Emanuel Gottlieb, *118*
Levin, David, 140
Lewey, Moses, 16–17
Life and Traditions of the Red Man (Nicolar), 1, 17–18, 280, 295–311, 369n11, 372n28
Life and Voyages of Christopher Columbus (Irving), 114, 192, 345n15
Life of the Admiral Christopher Columbus by His Son Ferdinand (Colón), 359n11
Liljencrantz, Ottilie A., 207, 356n51
Lillo, George, 28
Lincoln, Abraham, 187, 195–96, 206, 356n50
L'nu'k, 256
Lodge, Henry Cabot, 229, 359n14
Longfellow, Fanny Appleton, 351n15
Longfellow, Henry Wadsworth: *Ballads and Other Poems*, 155–56, 164, 350n8; *The Complete Poetical Works*, 161; Fall River and, 154–55, 161; "Footsteps of Angels," 163–64; Hawthorne and, 165, 351n16; Kohl and, 353n29; *Letters*, 154–56, 162, 164, 349n3, 349nn7–8; Liljencrantz and, 356n51; Lowell and, 196; marriages of, 163–64, 351n15; "Mezzo Cammin," 163; *The Poets and Poetry of Europe*, 350n9; Rafn and, 153–54, 343n6, 349n3; Scandinavian Memorial Association and, 230; *The Song of Hiawatha*, 351n13; *Tales of a Wayside Inn*, 356n49; "Tegnér's Drapa," 356n49. *See also* "Skeleton in Armor"
Longfellow, Mary Storer Potter, 163–64, 351n14
"Longfellow's Ballads and Poems" (*United States Magazine and Democratic Review*), 156, 164–65, 351n17
"Longfellow's Poems" (*New York Review*), 167, 352n19
loons, 299, 300, 369n16

Loring, John, 212
Loring, Stephen, 97, 98
Lovoll, Odd S., 345n14
Lowell, Frances Dunlap, 193
Lowell, James Russell: *The Biglow Papers*, 186–88, 190–91, 193, 354n37; "Cambridge Thirty Years Ago," 194; "Columbus," 191–93, 201, 206; *Complete Poetical Works*, 186; "Democracy," 203; *Fable for Critics*, 354n37; "The Growth of the Legend," 188–91, 192–93, 201; "Hakon's Lay," 194–95, 355n46; *Letters*, 196–97, 199, 354n36, 355n46; life, career, and politics of, 186–87, 193–94, 202–4; "Moosehead Journal," 188–89, 353n35; "The Place of the Independent in Politics," 203–4; *Poems*, 354n38; *Poems, Second Series*, 188, 354n37; "Reconstruction," 354n43; Scandinavian Memorial Association and, 230; *The Vision of Sir Launfal*, 354n37; "The Voyage to Vinland," 195, 196–202, 204, 206, 355n46; *Under the Willows, and Other Poems*, 197, 354n36, 355n44; *The Writings*, 187–88, 196, 208, 354n43
Lowell, Maria White, 193, 354n38
Luther, Martin, 248
"Lycidas" (Milton), 40
Lynnerup, Niels, 341n20
Lyrical Ballads (Coleridge and Wordsworth), 350n9

Machias Bay petroglyphs, 268–69
MacLean, John Patterson, 35, 216–18, 338n16, 357n2
Maddox, Lucy, 22, 23, 25, 33
Magnusson, Magnus, 48–49, 51, 74, 80, 90, 93, 341n15
Mahicans, 271, 365n15
Maillard, Abbé Antoine Simon-Pierre, 289, 335n3
Maine Historical Society, 179–80
Maine Woods, The (Thoreau), 371n23
Maliseets, 4, 58, 98, 256, 268, 271, 280–81, 286, 315, 340n8

Mallery, Garrick, 36–37, 41, 282, 338nn17–18
Mallett, Paul Henri, 113–14, 345n13, 356n51
Malory, Thomas, 354n37
Mancini, JoAnne Marie, 253, 329–30
manliness, American, 206–8, 352n22
Mann, Charles C., 338n15
Manzoni, Alessandro, 103
"Marie A. Brown: A Brief Autobiography" (Brown), 241
Marion, Francis, 105
Markland ("Forest-Land"), 53, 83, 90–92, 96, 110, 226, 235
Marsh, George Perkins, 136–37, 149–50, 347nn25–26
Marshall, Ingeborg, 342n26
Marshall, John, 129
Marshall, Murdena, 289, 368n5
Martens, Irmelin, 55
Massachusetts Historical Society, 231–33
Massachusetts Quarterly Review, 135
Massé, Enemond, 371n25
Mather, Cotton, 26, 106
Mather, Samuel, 26–31, 42
Maurault, Joseph Pierre Anselme, 367n2
Mawooshen Confederacy, 256–57
McGee, D'Arcy, 224, 358n9
McGlinchee, Claire, 193
McNickle, D'Arcy, 335n1
Medieval Iceland (Byock), 46
Medieval Icelandic Saga (Sigurðsson), 342n24
Medieval Warming, 9, 50–51, 308
Melville, Herman, 210
Membertou, 368n10
"Memoir of the European Colonization, A" (Zestermann), 34
Menomini, 370n19
meteorites, 301, 370n18
Mexicans, 145
Mexican War, 186–87, 192
"Mezzo Cammin" (Longfellow), 163

Micmac Indians of Eastern Canada, The (Wallis and Wallis), 272

Miˊkmaq: ancestors of, 96; Beothuk and, 342n26; copper working by, 348n1; culture and geography of, 280–81; dreams and, 285–86; epidemics and, 261, 262; French alliance with, 375n46; fur trade and, 368n10; hieroglyphic scripts and language of, 288–90, 293, 367n3; "medicine wheel" color symbolism of, 287, 368n4; names for, 256; population decline of, 363n5; prophets of, 367n2; raids by, 315; Rand's translations for, 368n8; skin-boats and, 6, 58, 335n3, 340n9; storytelling among, 270, 275, 281–83, 291, 294–95; trade and, 259, 261–62; Vinland location and, 6–7; Wabanaki Confederacy and, 4; Wallis and Wallis studies of, 272. *See also* "Dream of the White Robe and the Floating Island"; Gluskap (Klose-Kur-Beh) stories

Miˊkmaq, The (Prins), 275

Miller, Virginia P., 368n7

Milton, John, 40

missionaries, 31, 214–15, 288–89, 303, 337n13, 368n10, 371n25. *See also* religion

Mississippian culture, 127, 337n14, 338n15

Mitchill, Samuel Latham, 31–33

Moby-Dick, 210

Mohawks, 258, 281, 302, 304, 315, 357n53

Mohegans, 272, 365n15

Momaday, N. Scott, 272

Montagnais and Naskapi (Innu), 4, 8, 91, 96, 97, 258, 367n2

"Moosehead Journal, A" (Lowell), 188–89, 353n35

moosehide canoes. *See* skin-boats

Motley, John Lothrop, 137–40, 347n28

Mott, Frank Luther, 343nn3–5

Mound Builder hypotheses, 24–25, 33–35, 37–38, 338n16. *See also* Hopewell culture; Mississippian culture

Mound Builders, The (MacLean), 35, 357n2

Narragansetts, 316, 318

Narrative of the Life of Mrs. Mary Jemison, A (Seaver), 317–18

Naskapi and Montagnais (Innu), 4, 8, 91, 96, 97, 258, 367n2

Naskeag (Maine) trading site, 259

Nation, 216

National Anti-Slavery Standard, 186, 193

"National Centennial, The" (*Washington Post*), 215

nationalism, American. *See* American national imagination; American Romantic narratives; prehistory politics of contact vs. isolation; racial narratives

Native Americans (Indians; Eastern Algonquians; Abenaki; Wabanaki): abduction of, by Norse, 90–91; belonging and, 14; conflict and disease of, 259–62, 363n5; continuity of, 362n2; as discoverers of America, 11; erasure of, in history, 138, 347n29; Gage and, 356n53; Horsford on, 237–38; length of land tenure of, 257–59; missions to and conversion of, 31, 184–85, 337n13; oral tradition and, 270–79; perceived skin color of, 66–67, 340n11, 360n17; pictographic script of, 36–37, 312; Plains Indians and reservations, 184; removal and assimilation policy for, 22, 23, 27, 33, 34, 128–29, 133, 336n10; treaties with, 185. *See also* "first" contacts, issue of; petroglyphs; *Skraelings*; storytelling and oral tradition, Native; "superior races" predating Indians, hypothesis of

nativism, 143–44, 223–24, 253. *See also* racial narratives

Neptune, John, 296

Neptune, Mary Malt, 296

Newell, Wayne, 272–74, 277, 312, 342n26
New England, glorification of, 112–13, 146–50
New England poets of Viking America: Longfellow's "Skeleton in Armor," 151–67; Lowell's *Biglow Papers*, 186–88, 190–91, 193; Lowell's "Columbus," 191–93, 201; Lowell's "The Growth of the Legend," 188–91; Lowell's "Hakon's Lay," 194–95; Lowell's "The Voyage to Vinland," 195–202, 204; Norse images and, 204–5; Whittier's "Indian Civilization" and "The Indian Question," 184–86, 353n34; Whittier's "Norembega," 178–83; Whittier's "Poetry of the North," 167–68, 181, 183–84; Whittier's "The Norsemen," 168–73, 177–78. *See also* American Romantic narratives; *specific poets*
New France, 371n24
"New History, A" (Brown), 242
Newport (Rhode Island) stone tower, 106–7, 122–23, 153, 160, 165–66, 327, 349n5
New Relation (LeClercq), 285
"New Shrine for Italians" (*New York Times*), 252
New Sweden colony, 113, 345n12
New Views of the Origin of the Tribes and Nations of America (Barton), 339n19
New-York Historical Society, 33–34
New York Review, 167, 352n19
New York Times, 215, 220–23, 221, 252, 310–11, 358n8, 374n35
New-York Weekly Museum, 31–32
Nicola, Tomer ("Half-Arm"), 296
Nicolar, Joseph, 1, 17–18, 280, 295–311, 372–73nn26–29
Njal's Saga, 197
No Place of Grace (Lears), 183, 203, 206
Nordland, Odd, 1
"Norembega" (Whittier), 178–83, 204, 208, 353n28

Normans, The (Jewett), 121, 142
Norse. *See specific topics and persons*
"Norse and Native North Americans, The" (Sutherland), 44
"Norseman's Ride, The" (Taylor), 167, 348n33
"Norsemen, The" (Whittier), 153, 168–73, 177–78, 204, 352nn21–23
Norse Pond (Maine), 327
"Norse Remains in America" (MacLean), 217
Norse sagas. *See Eirik the Red's Saga*; *Greenlanders' Saga, The*; sagas
North American Review, 22, 101, 111, 116, 164–65, 173, 178, 193, 229
Northern Antiquities (Mallett), 113–14
"Northmen in America" (Rafn), 344n8
Northmen in New England, The (Smith), 112
Norton, Charles Eliot, 196–97, 199–201, 203, 355n44
Norumbega, 101, 178–83, 233–40, 361n23
"Norumbega and 'Harmonia Mundi'" (Seaver), 353n30
"Norumbega Hall" (Whittier), 239, 360n20
Norway, conversion of, 47

Obama, Barack, 231
O'Brien, Jean M., 280, 347n29
Odess, Daniel, 97, 98
Ohman, Olof, 327–29
Ojibwe, 280, 345n17, 347n29, 364n9, 370n19
Olaf the White, 75, 77
Olaf Tryggvason, 47, 79–80, 214
Old Icelandic Free State, 46
"Old Icelandic Prose" (Tómasson), 339n2
Old John Neptune (Eckstorm), 296
Old Norse (Old West Norse, or Old Icelandic), 48
Osceola, Chief, 346n22
Our Stories Remember (Bruchac), 276, 313–14
Ovaegir, 91

pagan rituals. *See* folklore and pre-Christian practices, Norse
Pagden, Anthony, 22, 335n2
Paleo-Indians, 362n2
Palfrey, John Gorham, 122–25
Pálsson, Hermann, 48–49, 51, 74, 80, 90, 93–94, 341n15, 342n23
Passamaquoddy, 4, 7, 16, 36, 58, 256, 268, 271–74, 278, 280–81, 286, 315, 342n26
Pathfinder, The (Cooper), 153, 343n3
"Pecuniary Independence of Wives, The" (Brown), 242
pemmican, 89
Penobscot Man (Speck), 307
Penobscot Nation, 4, 7, 17, 36, 58, 257, 276–81, 285, 295, 305–7, 315, 369nn11–13, 372n25, 372n28
"Penobscot Shamanism" (Speck), 285–86
"Penobscot Tales" (Speck), 369n12, 369n16
Penobscot Village, Chicago World's Fair, 311, 312
Percy, Thomas, 113–14
Peters, Daniel, 2, 16
petroglyphs: Catlin on, 25; contacts, evidence of, 265–70; of Embden-Solon, 265–68, 267, 364n9; fake, 14–17; limitations of, on rock, 270, 312; locations of, 365n13; of Machias Bay, 268–69; at Peterborough site (Ontario), 374n37; "Picture-Writing of the American Indians" (Mallery), 36–37; Schoolcraft on, 24; skin-boats in, 335n4. *See also* Dighton Rock
Phillips, Ruth B., 285, 286, 367n2
Phoenicians, 26, 152–53
Pickard, John B., 173–74, 178
pictographic script on birch-bark, 36–37, 312
"Picture-Writing of the American Indians" (Mallery), 36–37, 41
Pioneers, The (Cooper), 104–5, 343n3
"Place of the Independent in Politics, The" (Lowell), 203–4
Plymouth Rock, 104, 105, 343n1

Pocahontas, 337n12
Poems (Lowell), 354n38
Poems, Second Series (Lowell), 188, 354n37
"Poetry of the North, The" (Whittier), 167–68, 181, 183–84
Poets and Poetry of Europe, The (Longfellow), 350n9
Popham, George, 267, 365n12
Popham Colony, 267–68, 364nn11–12
Popular History of the United States, A (Bryant and Gay), 112–13
Portuguese colony on Cape Breton Island, 275
Potter, Mary Storer, 163–64, 351n14
Powell, Eric A., 329
Powell, John Wesley, 35–36, 38–40, 41, 338n17, 339n19
Power, Marjory W., 257–58, 261, 363n4
"Pre-Columbian Discovery of America" (MacLean), 217
Pre-Columbian Discovery of America, by the Northmen (DeCosta), 121, 218–19, 224–25, 358n5
prehistory politics of contact vs. isolation: Bering land bridge, 21; in Bureau of Ethnology reports, 35–40; Catlin on rock drawings and, 25; Chinese and Japanese vessels, 338n18; consequences and implications of, 40–43; Deloria on Indians "outside historical time," 19–20, 22, 42–43; of Eastern Algonquian speakers, 10; Europe, hypothesis of first contacts in, 21–22; frontier wars and "superior races" as predating Indians, 20; isolation hypothesis, 21, 22–23, 41; Mather's providential history, 26–31; Mitchill's lecture on racial origins, 31–33; Mound Builder hypotheses, 24–25, 33–35, 338n16; multiple migrations, 10, 20–21, 26–27; Schoolcraft report to Congress, 22–24, 42. *See also* Ameri-

can Romantic narratives; *specific writers*
Prescott, William, 144
Prins, Harald, E. L., 258–59, 275
prophecy: of Gudrid's destiny, 77–78; of Klose-Kur-Beh, 1, 280, 283, 296–310; in Mi´kmaq lore, 294–95; Thorstein Eiriksson and, 62–63, 81; in "Voyage to Vinland" (Lowell), 199–201
Prose Works, The (Whittier), 184–85
Pumphrey, Stanley, 353n33
Puritans, 31, 133, 136, 137, 150, 241
Purtell, Joseph, 209

Quakers, 167, 171, 176–77, 184
"Quest for Vinland, The" (Sigurðsson), 49, 96
Quinn, Conor McDonough, 369n17

Rabbit the Trickster, 286–87, 292
racial mixing in French vs. English colonies, 337n12
racial narratives: anti-Catholicism and, 137, 139, 142–46, 348nn30–32; anti-German, 254–55; anti-immigrant, 253–54, 362n33; blood ties and, 134–36; Brown and, 247; after Civil War, 205; Columbus and, 218, 252–55; "Discovery of America" (Everett), 132–34, 144–46; *English Traits* (Emerson), 140–42; First World War and, 254–55; *Goths in New-England* (Marsh), 136–37; Motley and Bancroft on, 137–40; *Roads to Rome* (Franchot), 143, 144; Spanish-American War and, 207; "superior races" and, 20, 24–25, 33–35, 37–38, 127; *Whiteness of a Different Color* (Jacobson), 143–44
Rafn, Carl Christian: "Abstract," 108–9, 111, 121–22; *America Discovered in the Tenth Century*, 106, 109–11; *Antiquitates Americanæ*, 23–24, 105–12, 124, 125–27, 131–32, 135, 153, 154, 173, 179, 204, 343n6; arguments against, 121–25, 216, 360n16; death of, 119; followers of, 112–21, 125–32, 147–48, 179, 226, 344n10, 356n51; impact of, 111–12, 343–44nn6–8; Longfellow and, 153–54, 343n6, 349n3; Lowell on, 188; "Northmen in America," 344n8; *Supplement to the Antiquities Americanæ*, 106–7, 121, 153
Rajnovich, Grace, 364n9, 365n13
Raleigh, Walter, 263
Rand, Silas Tertius, 271, 272, 279, 281–83, 288–95, 366n19, 367n3, 368n8
Randvar the Songsmith (Liljencrantz), 207
Rasles (Rasle, Râle), Father Sebastien, 266, 288, 370n21, 372n25
Ray, Roger B., 266
Rebirth of a Nation (Lears), 205, 207
Reconstruction, 196, 202–3
"Reconstruction" (Lowell), 354n43
Red Indian Lake, 342n26
"red man," 301, 370n20
Reese, John, 366n16
Reeves, Arthur Middleton, 216, 218
Relation of Father Gabriel Druillettes, 288
religion: anti-Catholicism, 213, 246–50; Brown on, 242, 246–50; Catholic pro-Norse arguments, 213–15; Catholics and Columbus, 224; Christianity in America, 214–15, 226–27, 358n9; conversion of Scandinavia, 47, 60, 61, 78, 79, 214; crosses and, 60, 75, 263, 371; French missionary villages, 303; Indian conversion, 31, 184–85, 303, 337n13, 368n10; Lutheranism, 248; Mather on biblical past, 29–31; Norse burial practices and, 81–82, 341n19; Old Norse religion and Christianity, 47, 78; Protestant vs. Catholic, 29, 215, 224–25, 281, 288; Quakers, 167, 171, 176–77, 184; racial anti-Catholicism, 137, 139, 142–46, 348n32; sagas and Christianity, 48–49; Whittier and, 167, 171, 175–78, 183–85. *See also* folklore and pre-Christian practices, Norse

Report of the Agent of the Penobscot Tribe (Hunt), 372n28
"Report of the Mound Explorations" (Thomas), 37–38
republic, Iceland romanticized as, 46, 214, 227, 241, 250
Restauration (sloop), 114, 231, 345n14
"Rethinking the 'Ecological Indian'" (Kolodny), 369n13
Revolution, American: Mather and, 28–30
Rice, Alexander H., 230
Ricker, Meredith, 324, 325, 375n38
"Rime of the Ancient Mariner" (Coleridge), 156, 157–58, 159, 161, 350n9, 350n12
Roads to Rome (Franchot), 143
Rogin, Michael Paul, 41
Rolfe, John, 337n12
Roman Catholic Church. *See* religion
Romantic Movement, 103–5. *See also* American Romantic narratives
Rosier, James, 263, 363n6
Round Table, 119
Rowlandson, Mary White, 316, 318, 376n51
Royal Society of Northern Antiquaries, 105–8, 153, 154, 188, 343n6
Runestruck (Trillin), 14
Russo, Gaitano, 252

Saga of Olaf Tryggvason, 214
"Saga of the Skeleton in Armour, The" (Longfellow). *See* "Skeleton in Armor"
Saga of Thorfinn Karlselfni, The. *See Eirik the Red's Saga*
Sagard, Gabriel, 360n16
sagas: challenges to evidentiary value of, 216–17; clerical writers of, 48–49; as contact narratives and prophecy texts, 331–32; discrepancies in, 93; *Eyrbyggia Saga*, 79; family, 51; *Frithiof's Saga*, 350n9; genealogies in, 72–73; goading speech in, 70, 87–88; Iceland and tradition of, 44–49; imprecision of, on Native groups, 94; *Islendinga sögur*, 47–49; *Laxdaela Saga*, 341n16; *Njal's Saga*, 197; recitation of, 73; retellings of, 107, 109; as secular literature, 73; style of, 339n2. *See also Eirik the Red's Saga*; *Greenlanders' Saga, The*
"Sagas and America, The" (MacLean), 217
Sappier, James G., 276–77, 366n18
Sappier, Mary Madeline Polchies, 276–78
"Savages in the Mirror, The" (Allen), 151
Sawyer, Birgit, 357n54
Sawyer, Peter, 357n54
Sayre, Gordon, 35
Scandinavian Memorial Association, 230
Schmidt, David L., 289, 368n5
Schoolcraft, Henry Rowe, 22–24, 26, 33, 37, 42, 108–9, 121–24, 281, 282, 336nn4–5, 343n7, 345nn17–18
Scott, Walter, 39, 103, 105, 134
Seaver, James Everett, 317–18
Seaver, Kirsten A., 58, 99–101, 180, 328, 341n21, 353n30
Sedgwick, Catharine Maria, 104–5
Seelye, John, 148, 204
Seminole Wars, 127, 346n22
Senate select committee on the Centennial of the Constitution (1888), 243
Seneca, 317
"Settlement Effected in Vineland" (*Family Magazine*), 112
Seyersted, Brita Lindberg, 7
Seyersted, Per, 7–8
shallops, 261, 277, 309
shamanism, 269, 285–86, 365n13
Shawnee, 235
Shay, Charles Norman, 372n28
Shea, John Gilmary, 358n9
Shepard, Elizabeth G., 361n23
Shetelig, Haakon, 6
Shipley, John B., 244–45, 253–54

Shipley, Marie Adelaide Brown. *See* Brown, Marie Adelaide
Short Statement, A (Rand), 281
Sigrid, 81
Sigurðsson, Gísli, 49, 96, 342n24
Silverberg, Robert, 34
Simmons, William S., 258
Simms, William Gilmore, 105, 125–31, 330, 346n21
size of people in Viking Age, 341n20
Skálholtsbók, 74, 93
"Skeleton in Armor" (Longfellow): "Ancient Mariner" (Coleridge) vs., 156, 157–58, 159, 161; as ballad vs. saga, 349n6; critical reception of, 164–67; Fall River and, 154–55, 161; letters and journal entries on, 155–56, 161–62; Leutze and, 118; Longfellow's Scandinavian studies and travels, 153–54; marginal glosses in, 156–57; passion in, 163–64, 208; publication of, 156; Romantic self-expression and, 162–63, 166–67, 204; text of, 157–59; timing and context of, 153; unromanticized love story of, 159–61
Skelton, R. A., 12–13, 100
Sketches of Ancient History of the Six Nations (Cusick), 370n19
skin-boats (moose-hide canoes): construction of, 335n3; Maliseet elder on, 340n8; Norse references to, 5, 96; in petroglyphs, 335n4; in sagas, 57–58, 86; as shelter, 340n9
Skraelings (Indians as mentioned in Norse sagas): descriptions of, 66–67, 86; in *Eirik the Red's Saga*, 85–89; in *The Greenlanders' Saga*, 57–58, 64–68; in "Ice Hearts" (Bruchac), 314–15; imprecision of identities of, 94; interpretations of, 113–14; term, 3, 58
Skull Wars (Thomas), 257
Slafter, Edmund F., 359n16
slavery, American, 13, 173–75, 186, 195, 352n25
Smith, Charles Sprague, 219–20, 358n6

Smith, Joshua Toulmin, 112
Smith, Patricia Clark, 6–7
Snorri (son of Gudrid and Thorfinn Karlsefni): in *Eirik the Red's Saga*, 88, 92; in *The Greenlanders' Saga*, 65, 67, 72–73; references to, 106
Snorri Sturluson, 357n3
Snorri Thorbrandsson, 82–90
Snow, Dean R., 265–66, 363n8
Snow-Bound (Whittier), 178
social Darwinism, 36, 41–42. *See also* racial narratives
"Solon Petroglyphs, The" (Snow), 265–66
Song of Hiawatha, The (Longfellow), 351n13
Spanish-American War, 207
Spanish settlement in North America, 348n34
Sparks, Jared, 151–53, 343n6
Speck, Frank G., 271–72, 285–86, 307, 369n12, 369n16
"Spirit Pond Inscription Stone, The" (Carlson), 15
Spirit Pond runestones, 14–15, *15*, 335n6
Stanton, Elizabeth Cady, 209, 242
statues and monuments: of Columbus, 250–52; of Leif Eiriksson, 219, 229–31, 232, 250
Stengel, Mark K., 20, 21
"Steyermark" (Taylor), 348n33
Stories from the Six Worlds (Whitehead), 291
Storm, Gustav, 216, 357n1
Storm, Johan, 357n1
storytelling and oral tradition, Native: contact-narrative, 272–76; "Dream of the White Robe and the Floating Island," 283–95; folklorists and, 280–81; "Ice Hearts" (Bruchac) and, 314–16, 318–26; intertextuality comprehension and, 294–95; *Life and Traditions of the Red Man* (Nicolar) and, 295–311; loss of, 270–71, 273; Madeline Sappier's story, 276–78; non-Native collections of, 271–72, 281–83, 365n16; Norse influence

424   Index

storytelling (cont.)
    and, 283, 320; role of, 270; symbolic meanings, 290–91. See also Gluskap (Klose-Kur-Beh) stories
Straumfjord ("Stream Fjord"), 84, 85, 89, 95–96, 110
Straum Island ("Stream Island"), 84
Studies on the Vinland Voyages (Storm), 216, 357n1
"Stumbles and Pitfalls in the Search for Viking America" (Wallace and Fitzhugh), 328–29
"superior races" predating Indians, hypothesis of: frontier wars and, 20; Mallery on, 37; Mound Builder hypotheses, 24–25, 33–35, 37–38; Powell on, 38–40; Simms on, 127, 130–31
Survival This Way (Bruchac), 327
Sutherland, Patricia, 44, 99
Swauger, James L., 366n16
sybils (prophetesses), 77–78
Sylliboy, Gabriel, 374n36

Tabor, William H., 364n11, 365n12
Tales of a Wayside Inn (Longfellow), 356n49
taxation in British colonies, 28, 337n11
Taylor, Alan, 260
Taylor, James Bayard, 167, 348n33
Tea Act (1733), 28, 337n11
Tegnér, Esaias, 350n9, 356n49, 356n51
"Tegnér's Drapa" (Longfellow), 356n49
Tennyson, Alfred, 354n37, 361n21
Tent on the Beach (Whittier), 178
Thayer, James B., 354n36
things (public assemblies), 46
Thjodhild, 47, 50, 79, 80
Thomas, Cyrus, 37–38, 41
Thomas, David Hurst, 34, 257
Thorbjorn Vifilsson, 75–78, 80
Thoreau, Henry David, 103, 146–47, 188, 347n23, 371n23
Thorfinn Karlsefni: Brattahlid site and, 97; in *Eirik the Red's Saga*, 74, 82–93, 101; in *The Greenlanders' Saga*, 63–69, 71–73; references to, 106–10, 123, 179, 226, 236, 355n46
Thorgunna, 79
Thorhall Gamlason, 82–83
Thorhall the Hunter, 83–85
Thorir (Thor-er), 56, 61, 76, 147
Thorstein (husband of Sigrid), 81
Thorstein Eiriksson: in *Eirik the Red's Saga*, 78–82; in *The Greenlanders' Saga*, 52, 60–63, 340n10; references to, 109, 194
Thorstein the Black, 61–63, 340n10
Thorvald Eiriksson: in *Eirik the Red's Saga*, 74, 79, 83, 86, 90; in *The Greenlanders' Saga*, 49–50, 52, 56–60; references to, 109, 110, 226, 241
Thorvard, 52, 70, 83
Thrall of Leif the Lucky, The (Liljencrantz), 356n51
Thule people, 99
Thury, Pierre, 372n25
Thwaites, Reuben Gold, 257, 259
Tidal Lake (or tidal lagoon). See Hóp
Tiffany, Lewis Comfort, 209
Tiffany and Company, 209–12, *211*
"Tiffany Company Tour de Force" (Wheary), 210
time, ritual marking of, 306–7
Tómasson, Sverrir, 339n2
Townshend, Charles, 337n11
Townshend Acts (1767), 28, 337n11
trade, 64–65, 86–87, 259, 260–62, 303, 332, 368n10
Travels in New England and New York (Dwight), 27
Trillin, Calvin, 14
True History of the Captivity and Restoration, The (Rowlandson), 316
Trumbull, James Hammond, 238, 360n18
Turtle Meat and Other Stories (Bruchac), 314
Tyler, John, 346n22
Tyler, Moses Coit, 356n52
Tyrkir, 55, 340n7

"Unanswered Questions" (Seaver), 100, 101
Under the Willows, and Other Poems (Lowell), 197, 354n36, 355n44
Unipeds, 74, 90, 179
United States Magazine and Democratic Review, 156, 164–65, 351n17

Vaetild, 91
Valdidida, 91
Valhalla, The Myths of Norseland (Jones), 355n45
Van Buren, Martin, 129
"Vanity of Vanities" (Wheary), 357n55
Vastokas, Joan M., 375n37
Vastokas, Romas K., 375n37
Vaughan, Alden T., 340n11
vellum, 339n3
Vergennes period, 362n2
Vespucci, Amerigo, 30, 336n8
Vifil, 75, 77
Viking (ship), 220–24, *221*, 310–11, 374n35
Viking Age, 44–45, 341n20
"Viking" as term, 44
"Viking Exhibition, The" (Brown), 213, 242–43
Viking Revival in crafts and design, 209–12, *211*
Vikings, Minnesota (football team), 377n4
Vikings, The (movie), 377n4
"Viking Settlement, The" (Wallace), 98, 341n15
Vinland: impermanent settlement of, 101; place names in, 53, 83–84; as "Vinland the good," 241; as "wild place," 71. See also Leif's houses (Leifsbudir), Vinland; sagas
"Vinland" (Clement), 239–40
Vinland, explorations of. See *Eirik the Red's Saga*; *Greenlanders' Saga, The*
Vinland, location of: Abbott on, 117; Beamish on Ireland and, 125–29; Fløttum on, 97; Horsford on Norumbega and, 233–34, 238; imprecision of, in sagas, 94; L'Anse aux Meadows hypothesis, 5–6, 8–10, 18, 43, 95–98, 213, 335n2, 341n15; Massachusetts Historical Society on, 233; Rafn on, 107, 110; Sigurðsson on, 96; Simms on South and, 126–31; skin-boats and Mi'kmaq at, 6; Wallace on, 95–96; Wheaton on, 115
Vinland Map and the Tartar Relation, The (Skelton et al.), 12–13
Vinland sagas. See *Eirik the Red's Saga*; *Greenlanders' Saga, The*; sagas
"Vinland Voyages, The" (Smith), 220
Vinner, Max, 309
Vision of Sir Launfal (Lowell), 354n37
volcanoes, 298, 300–301, 373n29
Vollmann, William T., 332
Voluspá, 200
Voyages of the Northmen (Prince Society of Boston), 359n16
"Voyage to Vinland, The" (Lowell), 195, 196–202, 204, 206, 355n46

Wabanaki Confederacy, 4, 257, 304
Wabanakis and ancestors. See Native Americans; Skraelings
Wagenknecht, Edward, 163, 350n9
Walker, James, 363n7
Wallace, Birgitta Linderoth, 9, 74, 91, 92, 95–98, 328–29, 335n2, 341n15, 342n27
Wallis, Ruth Sawtell, 272, 292, 366n16
Wallis, Wilson D., 272, 292, 366n16
"Wanderer, The" (Channing), 147
Ward, Julia, 154–55
Ward, Samuel, 155, 162, 167
"War Debt, A" (Jewett), 205
Waymouth, George, 263, 268, 363n7
weapons, 64–65, 67–68, 341n12
Webster, Helen H., 272, 281–83, 291, 368n6, 368n9
wedding of Gudrid and Karlsefni, 82

Wellesley College, 238–39, 282, 360n20
Western Abenaki, 4, 274, 280, 295, 313–15, 327, 375n39. *See also* Abenaki
"Western Abenaki Transformer, The" (Day), 280
Westward to Vinland (Ingstad), 5, 93, 213
Wheary, Dale Cyrus, 210, 357n55
Wheaton, Henry, 114–15
Whitehead, Ruth Holmes, 10, 261–62, 281, 363n5
Whiteness of a Different Color (Jacobson), 143–44
Whitney, Anne, 231, 232, 250
Whittier, John Greenleaf: "The Better Land," 178, 183; *The Complete Poetical Works*, 175, 181–82, 239, 360n20; "The Dole of Jarl Thorkell," 356n49; "Indian Civilization," 184–85; "The Indian Question," 185–86, 353n34; *Lays of My Home, and Other Poems*, 173, 178; *Legends of New-England*, 173; *Letters*, 173–77; life and career of, 173–78, 352n25–353n27; Liljencrantz and, 356n51; "Norembega," 178–83, 204, 208, 353n28; "The Norsemen," 153, 168–73, 177–78, 204, 352nn21–23; "Norumbega Hall," 239, 360n20; "The Poetry of the North," 167–68, 181, 183–84; *The Prose Works*, 184–85; religion and, 167, 171, 175–78, 183–85; Scandinavian Memorial Association and, 230; *Snow-Bound*, 178; *The Tent on the Beach*, 178
Williams, Robert A., 263
Williams, Roger, 31, 337n13
Willis, William, 178–79
Winsor, Justin, 251–52
Woman, Church and State (Gage), 209
women: in Indian societies, 260; in Norse society, 74, 75, 82, 357n54; rights of, in America, 195, 209, 242
Wordsworth, William, 350n9
World's Columbian Exposition (Chicago, 1893), 211, 212, 215, 220–23, 251, 311, 312
World War I and anti-German propaganda, 254–55

xenophobia. *See* racial narratives

Yale University, 12–13, 238

Zestermann, C. A. A., 34
Zinn, Howard, 207

ANNETTE KOLODNY is College of Humanities Professor Emerita of American Literature and Culture at the University of Arizona. She is the author of *Failing the Future: A Dean Looks at Higher Education in the Twenty-first Century* (Duke, 1998); *The Land before Her: Fantasy and Experience of the American Frontiers* (1984); and *The Lay of the Land: Metaphor as Experience and History in American Life and Letters* (1975); and the editor of *The Life and Traditions of the Red Man* by Joseph Nicolar (Duke, 2007) and (with William L. Andrews et al.) *Journeys in New Worlds: Early American Women's Narratives* (1990).

Library of Congress Cataloging-in-Publication Data
Kolodny, Annette
In search of first contact : the Vikings of Vinland,
the peoples of the dawnland, and the Anglo-American anxiety
of discovery / Annette Kolodny.
p. cm.
Includes bibliographical references and index.
ISBN 978-0-8223-5282-2 (cloth : alk. paper)
ISBN 978-0-8223-5286-0 (pbk. : alk. paper)
1. America—Discovery and exploration—Norse.
2. America—Literatures—History and criticism.
3. Sagas—History and criticism. I. Title.
PN843.K65 2012
809'.897—dc23   2012011578